LAND REGISTRATION

Kenneth G C Reid
Professor of Scots Law in the University of Edinburgh

and

George L Gretton
Lord President Reid Professor of Law Emeritus in the University of Edinburgh

Avizandum Publishing Ltd
Edinburgh
2017

Published by
Avizandum Publishing Ltd
25 Candlemaker Row
Edinburgh EH1 2QG

First published 2017

© Kenneth G C Reid and George L Gretton 2017

The right of Kenneth G C Reid and George L Gretton to be identified as authors of this Work has been asserted by them in accordance with sections 77 and 78 of the Copyright, Designs and Patents Act 1988.

ISBN 978-1-904968-70-2

British Library Cataloguing in Publication Data
A catalogue entry for this book is available from the British Library

All rights reserved. No part of this publication may be reproduced, stored in a retrieval system, or transmitted in any form or by any means, electronic, mechanical, photocopying, recording or otherwise, without the written permission of the copyright holder. Application for the copyright owner's permission to reproduce any part of this publication should be addressed to the publisher.

Typeset by Waverley Typesetters, Warham, Norfolk
Printed and bound by Martins the Printers, Berwick-upon-Tweed

Contents

Preface — v
Glossary — vii
Table of Statutes — xi
Table of Orders, Rules and Regulations — xxiii
Table of Cases — xxvii
Abbreviations — xxix

1	Historical Introduction	1
2	The 1979 Act and its Reform	23
3	The Land Register and the Keeper	44
4	The Land Register: Structure and Contents	55
5	Plans and the Cadastral Map	75
6	Registrable Deeds	91
7	Completing the Land Register	103
8	Applications for Registration	122
9	Acceptance, Rejection, Registration	153
10	Advance Notices	170
11	Inaccuracies and their Rectification	195
12	The Guarantee of Title (1): Realignment of Rights	217
13	The Guarantee of Title (2): The Keeper's Warranty	239
14	Liabilities of the Keeper	263
15	Liabilities of those using the Land Registration System	276
16	Examination of Title	284
17	Positive Prescription and *a non domino* Dispositions	305
18	Caveats	323
19	Electronic Conveyancing	329
20	Leases	339

Appendix I: Land Registration etc (Scotland) Act 2012 — 347
Appendix II: Land Register Rules etc (Scotland) Regulations 2014 — 417

Index — 439

Preface

The system of land registration in Scotland was substantially recast by the Land Registration etc (Scotland) Act 2012, which came into force on 8 December 2014; and the 2012 Act, in turn, was based on the comprehensive review of land registration law conducted by the Scottish Law Commission between 2003 and 2010. The authors of this book were, successively, the Law Commissioners in charge of the project.

The purpose of the book is to explore the 2012 Act in the light of the policy choices which underlie it, and to make from provisions which may sometimes seem disparate or unyielding a coherent account of the law of land registration. This should not, however, be seen as an 'official' account. The text of the Act departs in innumerable respects from the draft legislation submitted with the Scottish Law Commission's final report. But, in any event, we have approached this legislation in the same way as we would approach any other, as a series of provisions which require to be understood and explained, both by themselves and in relation to one another.

In one important respect our task has been made easier. A key aim of the 2012 Act was to reintegrate the law of land registration with the ordinary law of property. Unlike the predecessor legislation of 1979, therefore, there is no need to seek in the 2012 Act the answers to all questions concerning the creation and extinction of real rights in land. By and large, these questions are governed once more by the familiar principles which have evolved in Scots law over many centuries, and indeed have Roman roots. The concern of the 2012 Act is primarily with matters of registration rather than with matters of substantive property law.

This is a book about the law of land registration. Yet the law is so closely intertwined with its practice that it is hardly possible to write intelligibly about the former without saying a great deal about the latter. In the first half of the book, in particular, there is much material about matters of practice. In preparing this material we have made extensive use of the website of Registers of Scotland, and in particular of the indispensable series of *General Guidance* which covers a broad range of topics. We have also been fortunate that the staff at Registers of Scotland have been so willing to answer our questions and, in some cases, even to read complete chapters of the book. Here we would particularly mention Martin Corbett, Sarah Duncan, John King, Sarah Meanley, and Kevin Ramsay. To them, and to others at Registers of Scotland who have helped us in various ways, we are extremely grateful. They should not be taken as endorsing everything that we say. The responsibility for the contents of the book is ours alone.

We have attempted to state the law and practice as at 18 July 2016, although it has sometimes been possible to take account of later developments.

Kenneth G C Reid
George L Gretton
November 2016

Glossary

Actual inaccuracy A Land Register entry that is false. See para 2.8. Compare *bijural inaccuracy*.

Advance notice A notice that enters the Land Register, if so authorised by the prospective granter of a deed. It gives to the prospective grantee a 35-day protected period. Provided that the deed itself is registered in this period, the deed has priority over other entries in the Land Register or Register of Inhibitions from the same period. See chapter 10.

A non domino By a non-owner.

Application record The record of pending registration applications – in effect the *Keeper's* in-tray. See para 4.32.

APR Automatic plot registration ('APR') is the process by which title to an unregistered *plot of land* is registered in the *Land Register* as a mandatory by-product of the registration of certain types of deed in relation to the land (most notably *long leases* or assignations of *long leases*). See para 7.9. APR is thus a form of *first registration*.

Archive record The record of documentation supporting a registration, such as copies of dispositions. See para 4.31.

ARTL Automated registration of title to land ('ARTL') is the system of electronic conveyancing and registration which can be used as an alternative to the traditional, paper-based system. See chapter 19.

Base map The map used by the *Keeper* as an underlayer for the *cadastral map*. Currently, this is the Ordnance Survey map. See para 5.3.

Bijuralism The simultaneous application of two different systems of law: in the case of Scottish land registration these are (i) the special rules of registration of title, and (ii) the ordinary rules of the law of property. Bijuralism was a feature of the 1979 Act but is avoided by the 2012 Act.

Bijural inaccuracy An entry in, or omission from, the Land Register which is inaccurate according to the ordinary law of property but not according to the rules of registration of title. See para 2.8. Compare *actual inaccuracy*. Bijural inaccuracies were a feature of the 1979 Act but are not found in the 2012 Act other than in transitional provisions.

Cadastral map A map of Scotland, based on the *base map*, which shows title boundaries. See paras 5.6 and 5.7.

Cadastral unit The *cadastral map* is divided into cadastral units, corresponding to individual *plots of land*. See para 5.8.

Caveat An entry on a *title sheet* warning of an action in court that might affect the title to the property. See chapter 18.

Curtain principle The principle that it should be possible to take a register of title, such as the *Land Register*, at face value, so that there is no need to look at the deeds that lie behind it. A 'curtain' is thus drawn between the register and the underlying deeds.

Deferred indefeasibility A system of land registration in which a title is unchallengeable by reason of *Register error* but not by reason of *transactional error*. Compare *immediate indefeasibility*. The 2012 Act is, with qualifications, a system of deferred indefeasibility.

Designated day 8 December 2014 – the day on which the 2012 Act came fully into force, replacing the 1979 Act.

Encumbrance A right encumbering (ie burdening) land that is held by a person who is not the owner of that land. As well as *subordinate real rights* this includes some public-law rights such as public rights of way. Encumbrances appear in the C (securities) section and the D (burdens) section of a *title sheet*.

First registration The registration of a property for the first time in the *Land Register*.

Guarantee of title Title in the *Land Register* is normally guaranteed against invalidity. The guarantee takes one or other of two forms. Either (i) the invalidity is denied effect (in which case the registered title cannot be changed, and whoever suffers thereby is compensated), or (ii) the invalidity is accorded effect (in which case the registered title is changed, and whoever suffers thereby is compensated). In the 2012 Act scheme, the former is called *realignment* of rights so as to conform with the terms of the Register, and the latter comes under the heading of the *Keeper's warranty*. See para 12.2.

Immediate indefeasibility A system of land registration in which a title is unchallengeable on the grounds of either *Register error* or *transactional error*. The 1979 Act embodied a certain type of immediate indefeasibility although with important qualifications. Compare *deferred indefeasibility*.

Keeper The Keeper of the Registers of Scotland, in whose name all acts and decisions are made. The Keeper heads the Registers of Scotland, and is responsible for numerous registers, two of which are the *Land Register* and the *Register of Sasines*. See paras 3.15–3.21.

Keeper's warranty The guarantee of title conferred by the *Keeper* on registration of a deed in the *Land Register*. See chapter 13.

KIR Keeper-induced registration ('KIR') is the *first registration* of a *plot of land* on the Keeper's own initiative and expense, and without the participation or consent of the owner. See paras 7.19–7.24.

Land Register The Land Register of Scotland was established by the 1979 Act to replace, on a phased basis, the *Register of Sasines*. See paras 2.1–2.5. As a result of the 2012 Act, it consists of four parts: (i) the *cadastral map*, (ii) the *title sheet record*; (iii) the *application record*; and (iv) the *archive record*.

Long lease A lease of over 20 years.

Midas touch The principle, under the 1979 Act, that everything that the Keeper registered became valid even if the deed on which the entry in the Register was based was itself invalid. See paras 2.7 and 2.13. The Midas touch is discarded by the 2012 Act.

Money or mud Where two persons claim the same property, the solution of the 2012 Act (as, previously, of the 1979 Act) is usually to award one person the ownership of the property (the 'mud') and the other person an entitlement to compensation from the *Keeper* for the property's value (the 'money'). See para 12.2.

Off-register right An *encumbrance* which is constituted without registration, such as a public right of way or a short lease (ie a lease for 20 years or less). See paras 4.26–4.28.

Pertinent A right attached to a *plot of land* which can be either corporeal (eg a right in common to a recreational area) or incorporeal (eg the right to enforce a servitude or real burden).

Plot of land An area of land owned by one person, or one set of persons. Separate tenements such as salmon fishing rights and mineral rights are deemed to be plots of land, as are flats in tenement buildings. See paras 4.2–4.4.

Real right A direct right in land (or moveable property). Real rights divide into (i) the right of ownership, and (ii) the subordinate real rights, which are a type of *encumbrance*.

Realignment In certain cases where there is a discrepancy between what the Register says and the actual rights of the parties, the latter may, under the 2012 Act, be changed ('realigned') so as to conform to the former. Those who suffer as a result are compensated. Realignment protects those acquiring property in good faith. See chapter 12.

Register error An inaccuracy which already affected the *title sheet* at the time of a transaction. See para 12.4. Compare *transactional error*.

Register of Sasines Established by the Registration Act 1617, the Register of Sasines is a register of deeds. See paras 1.1–1.12. It is being replaced by the *Land Register*, which is a register of title.

Registration of deeds A property registration system in which deeds are registered but there is no official statement as to the effect the deeds have. The *Register of Sasines* is a register of deeds. See para 1.13. Compare *registration of title*.

Registration of title A property registration system in which there is an official statement, in relation to each property, as to what its boundaries are, who the owner is, and who has other rights (eg security rights) in the property. The *Land Register* is a title registration system. See para 1.13. Compare *registration of deeds*.

Subordinate real right See *real right*.

Title sheet A document in the *Land Register* which sets out the title to a *plot of land*. It is divided into four sections: the A section identifies the property and any *pertinents*; the B section identifies the owner; the C section sets out any heritable securities; and the D section sets out any other *encumbrances*. See paras 4.5 ff.

Title sheet record The set of all *title sheets* in the *Land Register*.

Torrens system A system of registration of title developed in the 1850s in South Australia by Robert Torrens. See para 1.14. Systems based on the Torrens system (of which there are many round the world) are themselves often called Torrens or Torrens-type systems.

Table of Statutes

Abolition of Feudal Tenure etc (Scotland)
  Act 2000 345
  s 1 8
  s 2 25
  s 4 . . . . 7, 94
    (2) 94
  s 5 12
  ss 17–19 66
  ss 17, 18 148
  s 46 66
  s 58 120
  s 65 97
  s 65A 342
  s 67 339
  s 76(1) 24
  sch 12 24
Act of 1469 (APS ii 95 c 3, RPS
  1469/17) 1
Act of 1504 (APS ii 253 c 35, RPS
  A1504/3/135) 1
Act of 1540 (APS ii 360 c 14, RPS
  A1540/12/21) 1, 3
Act of 1555 (APS ii 497 c 21, RPS
  A1555/6/22) 1, 2, 3
Act of 1587 (APS iii 455 c 50, RPS
  A1587/7/60) 1, 2, 3
Act of 1599 (APS iv 184) 2, 3
Act of 1600 (APS iv 237 c 36, RPS
  1600/11/49) 2, 3, 6, 8
Act of 1609 (APS iv 407) 2
Act of 1669 (APS vii 556 c 4, RPS
  1669/10/15) 5
Act of 1672 (APS viii 80 c 40, RPS
  1672/6/50) 8
  s 32 8
  s 36 12
Act of 1686 (APS viii 600 c 33, RPS
  1686/4/49) 5, 8, 12
Act of 1696 (APS x 60 c 18, RPS
  1696/9/136 . . . . 4, 5, 8
Ancient Monuments and Archaeological
  Areas Act 1979
  s 1(10) 92
Arbitration (Scotland) Act 2010
  s 2(1), (3) 324
  sch 1 r 49(c) 324

Bankruptcy (Scotland) Act 2016
  s 26 . . . . 191, 192

Bankruptcy (Scotland) Act 2016 (*cont*)
  s 78 192
  s 98 244
  sch 4 para 3 192
Bankruptcy and Diligence etc
  (Scotland) Act 2007 175
  s 83(1) 166
  s 159 . . . . 166, 295
    (4)(b) 295
  s 161 166
  s 169 324
Burgage Registers Act 1681 (APS viii
  248 c 13, RPS 1681/7/35) 14
Burgh Registers (Scotland) Act 1926
  s 1 15
  sch 1 14

Civil Partnership Act 2004
  s 106(1A) 295
Community Empowerment (Scotland)
  Act 2016
  s 74 . . . . 46, 164
Companies Act 1929 44
Companies Act 2006
  pt 21A (ss 790A–790ZG) 45
  s 859A 158
  s 859E(1) 186
Conveyancing (Scotland) Act 1874
  (37 & 38 Vict c 94)
  s 4(2) 8
  s 25 14
Conveyancing (Scotland) Act 1924
  s 4 . . . . 96, 109
  s 4A 96, 108, 109, 114, 115
  s 4B 108
  s 44 166
  s 46(1) 129
  s 46A 98, 231, 323
    (1) 129, 198
  schs B, BA 96
Conveyancing and Feudal Reform
  (Scotland) Act 1970 . . . . 92, 123
  s 9(2) 342
  s 10(4) 246
  s 13(4) 100
  s 24 314
Crofters (Scotland) Act 1993
  s 19D(6) 167

xi

Crofting Reform (Scotland) Act 2010
  s 3 46

Electronic Communications Act 2000
  s 7(2)(a)...................... 333
  s 8 330

Health and Social Services and Social Security Adjudication Act 1983
  s 23 189
Housing (Scotland) Act 2006
  pt 2 (ss 71–97) 331

Infeftment Act 1845 (8 & 9 Vict c 35)
  s 1 7
Interpretation and Legislative Reform (Scotland) Act 2010
  sch 1 75

Land and Buildings Transaction Tax (Scotland) Act 2013
  s 1(1) 142
  s 3 142
  s 4(2)(a)...................... 142
  s 5(1) 142
  s 29 142
  s 30 338
    (1), (2)(a).................. 142
  s 40(2), (4)................... 143
  s 43(1) 129, 143, 338
  sch 1 para 1 142
Land Reform (Scotland) Act 2003
  pt 3A (ss 97B–97Z)............. 164
  s 1 .... 291, 294
  s 22 .... 65, 71, 197, 232, 242, 294
  s 36 46
  s 37(5)(e)..................... 164
  s 40(1) 129, 164
  s 97F 46
  s 97N.......................... 164
Land Reform (Scotland) Act 2016
  pt 5 (ss 45–73)................ 164
  ss 39–42....................... 45
  s 41 45
  s 43 .... 45, 144
  ss 52, 53...................... 46
  s 61 164
Land Registers (Scotland) Act 1868 (31 & 32 Vict c 64) ....
  s 6 9
  s 7 11
  s 8 .... 9, 52
  s 14........................... 184
  s 25 125
Land Registration Act 1925
  s 20 30

Land Registration Act 2002
  s 3(3)......................... 341
Land Registration (Scotland) Act 1979 .... 5, 22, 23, 44, 97, 330
  s 1 23
    (1) 24
  s 2 .... 27, 93
    (1)(a)............ 28, 94, 107, 341
      (i) 105
      (ii), (iii).............. 28, 103
      (v).................... 103, 105
    (b)........................ 104
    (2) 28
    (3) 28, 109
    (4)(a)....................... 94
    (c) 93, 343
    (5) 104, 105
  s 3(1) 30, 343, 344
    (a) 5, 27, 30, 32, 166,
                  215, 234, 235, 261, 266,
                  289, 290, 293, 294, 297,
                  300, 301–04
    (3) 24, 103, 341, 342
    (6) 96
  s 4(1) 29, 54, 127
    (a) 131
    (2) 29, 127
    (a) 79
    (b) 95
    (c) 315
    (3) 29, 168
  s 5(1) 25, 29
    (a)(i) 27
    (2)–(5) 29
    (2C)......................... 331
  s 6 .... 55, 133
    (1) 27
    (a) 26, 61, 75, 79
    (c) 295
    (2) 60, 64
    (4) 24, 27, 64, 65, 71, 197, 294
    (5) 49, 50
  s 8(4)......................... 107
  s 9 .... 27, 31, 39, 201, 202
    (1) 31, 34, 54, 261, 293
    (3) 31, 32, 33, 202
    (a) 214, 215, 219, 260,
                  265, 291, 293, 300
      (i), (ii) 291, 300, 303
      (iii)......... 34, 227, 235, 291,
                    300, 303, 305, 314
      (iv)........ 35, 214, 228, 288,
                   291, 300, 303
  s 10 .... 35, 306, 313, 305, 306
  s 11 47
  s 12 .... 31, 229

Land Registration (Scotland) Act 1979 (cont)	Land Registration etc (Scotland) Act 2012 (cont)
s 12(1) 33, 34, 35, 235	s 5 45
(a) 260, 267	(1), (2) 58
(b) 31, 209, 215, 260,	s 6 . . . .
263, 266, 267	(1)(a)(i) 61, 79, 141
(c), (d) 269, 270	(ii), (iii) 61
(2) . . 29, 35, 203, 209, 248, 261, 266	(b) 61, 146, 147, 269, 291
(3) 35, 240, 261, 266	(c), (d) 62
(d) 241	(e) 61
(f) 241, 296	(f) 62, 291
(n) 35, 136, 254, 262, 265, 279	(2) 62, 64
s 13(1) 36, 257, 264	s 7(1)(a) 63, 128, 137
(2) 36, 253	(b) 58, 63, 141
(3) 36, 253	(2) 63, 64
(4) 35, 254, 261, 262, 265, 266	s 8 . . . . 132, 293
s 14 317	(1) 64, 128, 137
s 15(3) 95	(2) 64
(4) 44, 92	s 9 . . . . 132, 147, 293
s 16 . . . . 44, 92	(1) 242
(1) 246	(a) 64, 65, 71, 197, 269, 294
s 19 89	(iii) 128, 137
s 25(1) 53, 210	(b) 65, 232, 294
s 28(1) 5, 24, 70	(c) 301
s 29 . . . . 23, 44, 168, 340	(d) 65, 71, 132, 197, 294
(2), (3) 65, 92, 340	(e) 65, 71, 197, 294
s 30(2) 47	(f) 65, 132, 242
sch 3 . . . . 44, 65, 92, 340	s 10(2)(a), (b) 66
para 5(a)–(c), (d) 340	(c) 66, 127, 295
Land Registration etc (Scotland) Act	(d) 66, 325
2012 . . . . 36, 42, 44	(e) 59, 61, 84
pt 1 (ss 1–20) 128, 130, 145	(3) 60, 64, 84, 119
pt 4 (ss 56–64) 42, 170	(4) 59, 197
pt 6 (ss 62–72) 323	(5) 60, 73
pt 7 (ss 73–79) 35, 209, 218	s 11(1) 78
pt 9 (ss 86–95) 344	(a) 59, 72, 84
s 1(1) 44	(3) 85
(2) 13, 51, 271	(6) 75, 241
(3), (4) 46	(7) 77
(5) 47, 271	(8) 59
ss 2–15 41	s 12(1) 56, 57, 78, 213
s 2 . . . . 25, 45, 55, 72, 93, 196	(2) 67, 79, 80, 89, 206, 212, 213
(c) 306, 309	(3) 67, 69
ss 3–13 196	(4) 78
s 3 78	(5) 56, 78
(1) 25, 56, 133, 200	s 13(1) 82
(a) 70	(2)–(4) 57
(2) 56, 112, 133, 200, 294, 301	(2) 81
(3) 103	s 14 306
(4) 55, 81, 291	(1) 73
(5) 55, 291	(a) 288
(7) 67, 69	(2) 73
s 4(1) 133	(3)(b) 73
(1)(a) 56	(4) 60, 73, 227, 255
(b) 57	s 15 . . . . 74, 208
(2) 56, 133	(b) 74
	s 16(1) 56, 69

Land Registration etc (Scotland) Act
  2012 (*cont*)
  s 16(2)(b). 63
    (3), (4), (5), (8) 69
  ss 17–19 292
  s 17(2) 67, 140
    (3) 67
    (4), (5) 68
  s 18 . . . . 62, 64
    (1)(a) 67, 130
      (b) 68
    (2)(a) 67
      (b), (c), (d) 68
    (3)(a) 68
      (b) 64, 68
    (4), (5) 68
  s 19 89
  s 20 68
  ss 21–23 133
  ss 21–26 41
  ss 21–28 271
  s 21 . . . . 86, 159, 110, 157
    (1) 24, 123, 128
    (2) 54, 124, 127, 133, 157,
                  159, 161, 186, 212, 322
    (3) 29, 54, 127, 133, 150,
             157, 158, 160, 163, 186, 249
  s 22 . . . . 116, 127, 338
    (1)(a) 110, 116, 127, 130,
                  131, 132, 138, 145, 146
      (b) 95, 128
      (c), (d), (e). 129
    (2) 95, 124
  s 23 . . . . 116, 127, 131
    (1)(a) 123, 124
      (b) 128, 186, 249, 280
      (c) 85, 87, 131, 179, 307
      (d) 65, 85, 132, 146
      (e) 132
    (2) 88, 131
      (b)(ii) 130
    (3) 131
    (4) 65, 132
  s 24 . . . . 110, 113, 114
    (2) 112, 296
    (3) 112, 342
    (4) 112
    (5) 115
    (6) 114, 115
    (7) 114, 342
  s 25 . . . . 110, 127, 131, 133
    (1)(a) 128, 131, 186, 249, 280
      (b) 85, 87, 131, 307
      (c) 65, 85, 132
  s 25(1)(d) 132
    (2) 88, 131
    (3) 131

Land Registration etc (Scotland) Act
  2012 (*cont*)
  s 25(4) 65, 132
    (5) 111, 131
      (a) 112
  s 26 . . . . 113, 114, 127, 133, 138
    (1) 130
      (a) 128, 130, 186, 249, 280
      (b) 130
      (c) 86, 130, 179, 307
      (d) 86, 87, 130
    (2) 130
    (3) 88, 130
    (4) 131, 132
    (5) 131
  ss 27–29 41
  s 27 . . . . 123, 56, 116
    (1) 322
    (2) 114, 116, 123, 322
    (3) 127, 133
      (a) 116
        (i) 116
      (b) 114, 116
    (4) 127, 133, 150
    (6)–(8) 114, 116
  s 28 . . . . 116, 117, 127, 131, 133
    (1) 86
      (a) 117, 131
      (b) 65, 117, 132
    (2) 88, 131
    (3) 131
    (4) 65, 117, 132
  s 29 . . . . 118, 135
    (2) 92
  s 30 . . . . 110, 133, 307
    (1) 165
    (2) 243
      (a) 112, 114, 115, 165, 308
      (b) 165
      (c) 112, 114, 115, 165
      (d) 165
      (e) 73, 165
    (4) 165
    (5) 63, 110, 119, 165, 230, 250
  s 31 . . . . 133, 307
    (1) 164
    (2)(a) 164, 186, 308
      (b), (c) 165
      (d) 73, 165
    (4) 165
  s 32 295
    (1) 66
      (b) 165, 166
  s 32(2) 66, 166
    (3) 166
  s 33(1) 74, 153
    (2) 153

Land Registration etc (Scotland) Act
2012 (cont)
- s 33(3) 74, 154
- s 34 .... 160, 319
  - (1) 251
    - (a) 156, 163
    - (b) 249
- s 35(1) 156
  - (2) 156, 278
  - (3) 156, 273
- s 36 .... 63, 74, 124, 153, 154, 157, 159, 168, 170, 228, 254, 278
- s 37 170
  - (1) 63, 74, 124, 135, 154, 159, 168, 228, 254, 278
  - (2) 154, 169
  - (3), (4) 169
- s 38 169
- s 39(1), (2) 154
  - (4), (5), (6) 155
  - (7) 156
  - (8) 155, 156
- s 40 215
  - (1) 162, 163
    - (a), (b) 162
    - (c) 164
    - (d) 146, 162
  - (2)(a) 163
  - (3), (4), (6) 163
- s 41 .... 111, 118
  - (1) 162, 163
  - (2) 162
    - (a), (b) 162, 163
  - (6) 163
- s 42 164
  - (2) 164
- ss 43–45 41
- s 43 .... 94, 157, 160, 315
  - (1)–(4) 311, 321
  - (1) 129, 157, 315, 316, 320, 322
  - (2) 157
  - (3) 316
  - (4) 316, 317, 319, 321
  - (5) 129, 321, 322
  - (6)(a) 320
    - (b) 320, 322
- s 44 309
  - (1) 250, 269, 320, 321
  - (2) 250, 320
  - (3) 320
- s 45 317
  - (1)–(3) 164
  - (1)–(5), (6) 319
- s 46 .... 122, 123
- s 47(1) 124
  - (2) 125
- s 48 .... 28, 41, 108, 110

Land Registration etc (Scotland) Act
2012 (cont)
- s 48(1)(a) 94, 97, 108, 143
  - (b) 111, 296, 341, 342
  - (c) 112, 342
  - (d) 104, 107, 342, 343
  - (2) 113, 303, 342
  - (3)–(5) 96
  - (3) 113, 114, 115
  - (4) 91, 115
  - (6) 108, 143
  - (7) 114, 116
  - (9) 115
- s 48A 45, 144
  - (2) 144
- s 48B 45, 144
  - (2) 144
- s 49 174
  - (1) 91, 94, 128, 183
    - (a)–(c) 91
    - (a), (b) 97
  - (2) 91, 167, 168
    - (b) 167
    - (d) 168
  - (3) 91, 167
  - (4) 98, 167, 198, 285, 290, 296, 320
- s 50 .... 7, 74, 94, 168
  - (1)–(3) 94
  - (2) 63, 74, 167, 198, 211, 285, 290, 296, 307
  - (4)(a), (b), (5) 94
- s 51 .... 65, 97, 168
  - (1)(b) 97
  - (2), (3), (4) 97
- s 52 .... 92, 97, 298
  - (2) 235, 342, 343, 344
  - (3) 48, 340, 342
- s 53 96
  - (3) 115
- s 54 98
- s 55 99
- s 56 .... 173, 174
  - (1)(a) 174
    - (b) 178
    - (d) 179
      - (i), (ii), (iii) 179
    - (e) 183
  - (2) 88, 180
  - (3) 180
  - (4) 183
- s 57 173
  - (1) 172, 174, 176, 183
- s 57(2) 176
  - (3) 178
  - (4)(a)(i) 172, 173, 180
    - (ii) 180

Land Registration etc (Scotland) Act
  2012 (cont)
  s 57(4)(b) 183
  s 58(1), (2) 184
    (3) 173, 184
    (6), (7) 184
  s 59 . . . . 186, 187
    (1)(b)(ii) 190
    (2) 155, 186, 187, 188, 190, 193
    (3)(a), (b). 186
  s 60 . . . . 186, 187
    (2) 186, 190
    (3)(a), (b). 186
  s 61(1) 173, 191
    (a) 196
    (b) 191
    (2) 188
    (3), (4) 189
  s 62(1) 74, 173
    (a) 181
    (b) 73, 181
    (2) 181
  s 63 . . . . 181, 184
    (1) 181
    (3)(a), (b). 181
    (4) 74
      (a) 173, 181
      (ii) 73
    (5) 182
  s 65 . . . . 60, 120, 196, 271
    (1)(a) 98, 197
    (b) 196
    (c) 197
    (2)(b). 196
    (3) 76, 198, 241
    (4) 98, 198
      (a) 231
  s 66 83
    (3) 83
  s 67 . . . . 100, 230, 295
    (1) 323
    (2) 100
    (3), (4), (5) 324
  s 68 230
    (1) 326
    (2) 327
    (3) 326
  s 69 . . . . 230, 327
    (2), (3), (5) 327
  s 70 . . . . 230, 327
  s 71 327
    (2) 230, 327
  s 72 326
  ss 73–79. . . . . 260, 271
  s 73 . . . . 111, 136, 218, 239,
                241, 246, 267, 288, 296
    (1) 143, 239, 251, 252, 256, 293

Land Registration etc (Scotland) Act
  2012 (cont)
  s 73(1)(a) 240, 280
    (b) 232, 242, 294
    (2) 229, 251
    (a)–(c)   65, 232, 242, 271, 294
    (c) 242, 269
    (d) 241, 293
    (e)–(g) 271
    (e) 241, 293
    (f) 228, 251, 296
    (g) 241
    (h) 229, 241
      (i) 262
    (ha) 120
    (i) 83, 241
    (3) 246, 252
    (4) 240
    (5) 229, 239, 320
  s 74. . . . . 111, 116, 121, 239, 267
    (1) 239, 246, 252
      (a) 240
      (b) 232, 242
    (2), (3). 241
    (3)(a). 120
  s 75 35
    (1) 158, 229, 251
      (a) 160, 241, 251, 296
      (b) 229, 249
    (2) 249, 295, 325
    (3) 66, 229, 250, 251
    (4) 250, 320
      (b) 66
  s 76 . . . . 251, 296
    (3) 252
    (4) 295, 325
    (5) 251
      (a) 66
  s 77(1) 256, 259
    (2) 252, 258
    (3) 253, 259
    (4), (5). 217, 246, 253
  s 78 . . . . 229, 241, 255
    (a) 241, 269
    (b) 227, 228, 253, 254, 258,
                262, 284, 296, 297, 304
      (ii) 255
    (c) 257, 262, 279, 284, 296, 297
      (i). 255
      (ii) 136
    (d)–(f). 264
  s 78(d) 258, 259
    (e) 257
    (f) 258
  s 79 264
    (1) 258
      (a) 257, 259

Land Registration etc (Scotland) Act
2012 (cont)
s 79(1)(b)(i), (ii) 257
 (2), (3). 258
s 80 . . . . 54, 60, 98, 120, 162, 195,
         201, 229, 346
 (1) 66, 71, 121, 148, 196,
      215, 229, 253, 259, 261,
         271, 290, 320
 (2) 66, 71, 121, 206, 208,
      213, 215, 253, 261, 271
 (3) 213
 (4) 206
  (a) 73, 208
  (b) 146, 186, 208
 (5) 208
 (6) 209
s 81 . . . . 206, 309–10, 321
 (1), (2), (3) 309
 (3)(a)(i) 320, 321
s 82 . . . . 207, 210, 267, 324
 (2) 210
  (c) 54
s 83 . . . . 54, 210, 323
s 84 . . . . 121, 209, 271
 (1) 268
  (a) 208, 268, 273
  (b) 268, 269
 (2)–(4) 269
 (5), (6), (7) 269
s 85 . . . . 209, 271
 (a), (b), (c). 269
 (d), (e), (f), (g) 268
ss 86–90. 305
ss 86–92. . . . . 121, 202, 209
ss 86–93. . . . . 162, 195, 246,
         247, 252, 263
s 86 . . . . 40, 136, 167, 200, 212,
      213, 219, 222–28, 230, 231,
      232, 234, 236, 237, 246,
      263, 265, 278, 279, 285–88,
      290, 291, 292, 295, 297, 299,
        302, 304, 307, 320
 (1) 224
  (a) 224
  (b) 285, 286
 (2) 222, 225, 228
 (3) 225, 228, 285
  (a) 38, 200, 224, 225, 286
   (i) 224
   (ii) 225, 226, 229, 287
  (b) 220, 225, 229
  (c) 227, 254, 310
  (d) 222, 228, 237
  (e) 225
   (i) 230, 295, 326
   (ii). 234

Land Registration etc (Scotland) Act
2012 (cont)
s 86(3)(b). 228, 230, 305
 (4)(b)   168, 200, 225, 228, 232, 287
 (5)(b). 224, 226
 (6) 225, 228, 287
s 87 . . . . . 200, 219, 222, 223, 227, 285
 (1) 223
 (2) 225, 227, 287
s 88 . . . . 200, 219, 234, 263, 265,
        297, 298, 299, 300
 (1) 234
  (b). 299
 (2) 234
 (3) 234, 299
  (a), (b) 200
  (c) 254, 310
  (d). 234, 298
  (f) 326
  (g). 305
 (4)(b) 200, 299
s 89 . . . . 200, 219
 (2) 300
s 90 . . . . 220, 230, 236, 237, 241,
       263, 265, 301, 302
 (1) 236, 237
  (b). 302
 (3) 302
  (a). 236
  (b). 237
  (c) 236, 237, 254, 310
  (d). 237, 326
  (e). 237, 305
 (4)(b), (6) 236, 302
s 91 . . . . . 149, 200, 219, 222, 230–34,
       242, 247, 294, 295
 (1) 232, 233
  (b). 200, 231
 (2) 228
  (a). 232
  (b). 230, 232, 295, 326
 (3) 232
 (4) 232, 242
  (a)–(c) 232
  (d). 294
  (e). 232, 242
s 92 . . . . 200, 219, 234, 235, 301
 (1) 234
  (b). 200
 (2) 234
  (b). 326
s 92(4) 234
s 93 . . . . 222, 233, 234, 294
s 94 . . . . 149, 162, 200, 209, 215,
     216, 218, 231, 233, 235, 236,
     260, 263, 271, 279, 313
 (1), (2). 264

Land Registration etc (Scotland) Act 2012 (*cont*)
- s 94(2)(b). 263
  - (3)–(6) 266
  - (3), (4), (5) 264
  - (6). 257
    - (a), (b), (c) 265
- s 95 . . . . 257, 260, 266, 271
  - (1)(a) 259, 266
  - (b). 264
    - (i) 264
  - (2)–(4) 266
  - (2) 264
  - (3)(a) 264
  - (4) 264
- s 99 330
  - (1) 329
- s 100 . . . . 128, 332
- s 101. 95, 140
- s 102 61
- s 103 . . . . 161, 209, 324
  - (1) 53, 210
  - (2) 54
  - (3) 161
- s 104 . . . . 72, 73, 164
  - (1) 49, 230, 269
    - (c). 173, 288
  - (2) 50, 270
    - (a) 173
  - (3) 49, 50
  - (4) 50, 51, 230
  - (5)(a), (b), (7) 50
- s 105 50
- s 106 . . . . 50, 164, 269
  - (1)(b), (c). 270
  - (2) 270
- s 107 49
- s 108 . . . . 52, 275
- s 109 52
- s 110. 125
  - (3)(b). 118
- s 111. . . . . 71, 124, 136, 139, 144,
  149, 158, 253, 256, 262,
  264, 276–79, 281
  - (1) 278
  - (2)(a) 279
  - (3) 278
  - (4)(a) 279
  - (5) 279
  - (6) 279
    - (a). 279
- s 112 . . . . 71, 281–83
  - (1)(a) 181, 282
  - (b). 282
  - (2) 282
  - (3) 283
  - (4) 282, 283

Land Registration etc (Scotland) Act 2012 (*cont*)
- s 112(5), (6)–(8) 283
  - (7), (8), (9) 283
- s 113(1) 48, 63, 64, 65, 82,
  91, 111, 116, 128, 137, 174,
  178, 181, 225, 236, 286
  - (2) 128, 165, 249
    - (a). 280
  - (3)(b). 63
- s 114(2) 308
- s 115(1)(d) 169
- s 119. . . . . 23, 288
- s 120(1) 288, 313, 314
- s 121 282
- s 123(2) 108, 111, 112
- sch 1 68
  - paras 6–10 64
  - para 8(b) 64
- sch 2 . . . . 92, 97, 340
  - para 2. 342
    - (d) 48
  - para 16. 342
  - paras 17, 22 340
- sch 3 65
  - paras 5, 7, 13 332
- sch 4
  - para 1. 58
  - para 2. . . . . 58, 71, 128
  - para 3. . . . . 58, 128
  - paras 4, 5 58
  - para 6. 80
  - paras 7 ff 58, 80
  - para 9. . . . . 58, 80
  - para 10. 58
  - para 11B 113
  - para 12. 73,
  - para 14. 210
  - para 15. . . . . 260, 267
  - paras 17–24 202
  - para 17. . . . . 32, 201, 202, 204,
    216, 223, 260, 261, 265,
    291, 293, 300, 302, 314
    - (b). 201, 202
  - para 18. . . . . 205, 216, 288, 291,
    293, 300, 303
  - paras 19–21 . . . . 201, 265
  - para 19. 261
  - para 20(a), (b) 261, 262
    - (c) 262
- sch 4
  - paras 22–24 216
  - para 22. . . . . 201, 202, 204, 210,
    212, 214, 260, 265, 291,
    293, 300, 303, 314
  - paras 23, 24 . . . . 201, 266
  - para 25. 70

Land Registration etc (Scotland) Act
  2012 (cont)
  sch 5
    para 5 125
    paras 17–25 92
    para 17(7) 100
    para 18(2) 305, 306, 313
      (4) 321
      (5) 312
      (6) 269, 270, 279
      (7) 264, 270
        (b) 253
    para 19 23
      (9) 92
        (b) 340
    para 39(2) 94
      (4) 66
      (6) 97
    para 43(4) 66
Land Registry Act 1862 (25 & 26 Vict
  c 53) 17, 18, 103
Land Tenure Reform (Scotland) Act
  1974
  s 18 340
  sch 6 para 1 340
Land Transfer Act 1897 (38 & 39
  Vict c 87) 18, 103
Law Reform (Miscellaneous Provisions)
  (Scotland) Act 1985 . . . . 323, 328
  s 8 . . . . 99, 198, 203
    (3), (3A), (4) 99
    (7), (8A) 323
  s 8A 99, 198
Leases Act 1449 (APS ii 36, RPS
  1450/1/16–17) 341
Legal Writings (Counterparts and
  Delivery)(Scotland) Act 2015
  s 4 129
Long Leases (Scotland) Act 2012 93,
    100, 148
  part 4 (ss 45–61) 344
  ss 1–4 344
  ss 1–7 294
  s 1(3), (4) 339
  s 4 113
    (1)(b) 344
  s 5(1) 345
  s 6(2), (3), (4) 345
  s 7 345
  ss 14–28 345
  s 14 345
  s 23 345
  ss 29, 30, 31, 32 345
  ss 63, 64 339
Lord Clerk Register (Scotland) Act 1879
  (42 & 43 Vict c 44)
  ss 6, 8 12

Matrimonial Homes (Family Protection)
  (Scotland) Act 1981
  s 6(1A) 295

National Trust for Scotland Confirmation
  Act 1938
  s 7 64

Prescription Act 1617 (APS iv 543
  c 12, RPS 1617/5/26) 2
Prescription and Limitation (Scotland)
  Act 1973
  s 1 . . . . 199, 267, 298, 305, 310,
      312, 313, 320
    (1) 214, 288, 289, 305, 311, 312, 313
      (a) 306, 312
      (b) 121, 306, 310, 311, 313
    (2) 289, 310
      (a) 311
      (b) 199, 310, 311
  s 4 . . . . 225, 309
  s 5(1A) 267, 289, 312, 321
  s 6 . . . . 269, 270, 279
  s 7 . . . . 253, 260, 264
    (1) 253
  s 8 . . . . 200, 293
  s 11(1) 253, 264, 279
    (4) 253, 264
  sch 1
    para 1(ac) 279
      (ad) 269
      (d) 260, 270
      (e) 253, 260
    para 2(e) 253, 264
  sch 3 para (a) 120, 268
    (i) 208
Proceeds of Crime Act 2002
  pt 7 (ss 327 – 340) 282
Public Finance and Accountability
  (Scotland) Act 2000
  s 9 . . . . 13, 52
Public Registers and Records (Scotland)
  Act 1948
  s 1 13
    (1) 52
  s 2 8
Public Registers and Records (Scotland)
  Act 1950
  s 1 12
Real Rights Act 1693 (APS ix 271 c 22,
  RPS 1693/4/63) 6, 273
Register of Sasines Act 1829 (10 Geo
  IV c 19) 14
Register of Sasines (Scotland) Act
  1987 11

Registration Act 1617 (APS iv 545
 c 16, RPS 1617/5/30) 1, 2–8, 12,
  14, 46, 340
Registration of Leases (Scotland) Act
 1857 (20 & 21 Vict c 26). 92, 97,
  339–40
 s 1 . . . . 57, 111, 296, 340, 341
  (1) 342
  (2) 48, 342
 s 2 343
 s 3 . . . . 301, 340, 342, 343
 s 12 340
 s 13, 14. 343
 s 16 340
 s 17. 341
 s 20A 343
  (2)(a). 343
 s 20B 344
  (1)(a) 235
  (2) 298, 342
  (3) 296, 298, 344
 s 20C 341
 s 20D 342
 s 22B(1)(a). 301
 schs ZA, ZG 340, 343
 schs A, G 343
Requirements of Writing (Scotland) Act
 1995. . . . . 330, 339–40
 pt 3 (ss 9A–9G) 331, 332
 s 1(2) 333
 s 1A 329
 s 2B 331
 s 3(1)(b) 129
  (c) 332
 s 6 . . . . 96, 129
  (3)(a), (b). 129
 s 9B(1), (2) 332
  (2)(a). 333
  (b) 332
 s 9C 129, 332
  (1)(b). 332
 s 9F 337
 s 9G 96, 128, 129
  (1), (2). 334
  (3). 332
  (6)(a). 129, 334
  (b) 129
 s 12(1) 91, 333
  (3) 333, 335
  (4) 333
 sch 2 129
Sale of Goods Act 1979
 s 25 . . . . 40, 223
Salmon and Freshwater Fisheries
 (Consolidation)(Scotland) Act
 2003
 s 66 342
Scotland Act 1998
 s 90B 82
 s 126(8) 13, 52, 271
Scotland Act 2016
 s 36 82
Secretary of State for Scotland Act 1885
 (48 & 49 Vict c 61)
 s 5 12
Sheriff Courts (Scotland) Act 1907
 sch 1 324
 r 51.2 324
 r 51.2(3)(a), (b), (c) 327
 r 51.3 324
  (1), (2), (3) 327
 form 51.3-A. 324, 327
 forms 51.3-B, 51.3-C 327
Small Business, Enterprise and
 Employment Act 2015
 sch 3 45
Succession (Scotland) Act 1964
 s 15 224
  (2) 108
Tenements (Scotland) Act 2004
 s 3 . . . . 69, 291
 s 12 65
  (3) . . . .
 189
 s 13 65
 s 26(1) 69
Territorial Sea Act 1987
 s 1(1) 48, 82
Title Conditions (Scotland) Act
 2003. 92
 s 1(3) 62
 ss 2–4. 65
 s 2 241
 s 3 . . . . 198, 241
 s 4(1) 167, 168, 292
  (5) 108, 124, 126, 143,
   167, 292
 s 9(2)(a) 298, 301
 s 10 65
 s 10(2A) 189
 s 10A 65
 ss 16, 17, 18 . . . . 200, 293
 s 44 48
 ss 49–57. 66
 s 49(2) 148
 s 50 148
 s 51 66
 ss 52, 53, 56 148
 s 58 66
 s 69 123
 s 75 236
  (1) 108, 124, 126, 143,
   242, 243, 292

Table of Statutes

Title Conditions (Scotland) Act 2003 (*cont*)
- s 75(3)(b)............. 131, 243, 292
- s 76 241
- s 120 .... 124, 126, 143
- s 122(1) 64, 148
- (2), (3) 148

Titles to Land (Scotland) Act 1858 (20 & 21 Vict c 76) 3
- s 1 7
- s 19 9

Titles to Land Consolidation (Scotland) Act 1868 (31 & 32 Vict c 101)..........
- s 15 .... 7, 123
- s 142............. 6, 12, 124, 156

Titles to Land Consolidation (Scotland) Act 1868 (31 & 32 Vict c 101) (*cont*)
- s 148........................ 11
- s 159(1), (2)................. 323
- s 159A 166

Town and Country Planning (Scotland) Act 1997
- s 75 .... 65, 92, 132
- s 161(2) 65

Tribunals (Scotland) Act 2014
- s 20 54
- ss 27–29..................... 54
- ss 46–50..................... 54

Trusts (Scotland) Act 1921
- s 21 108

Table of Orders, Rules and Regulations

Act of Sederunt (Amendment of Fees in the Department of the Registers of Scotland) 1977, SI 1977/1623 12
Act of Sederunt (Register of Sasines Procedure Amendment) 1977, SI 1977/70 12
Act of Sederunt (Rules of the Court of Session 1994) 1994, SI 1994/1443 324
    r 105.2(3)(a), (b), (c) 327
    r 105.3 324
        (1), (2), (3) 327
    r 105.5 98
    r 105.6 99
    form 105.3-A 324, 327
    forms 105.3-B, 105.3-C 327
    form 105.5 98
    form 105.6 99
Act of Sederunt (Rules of the Court of Session and Sheriff Court Rules Amendment No 2) (Miscellaneous) 2014, SSI 2014/291 .... 43, 324
    para 3(3) 98, 99
Automated Registration of Title to Land (Electronic Communications) (Scotland) Order 2006, SSI 2006/491 .... 330, 331

Electronic Documents (Scotland) Regulations 2014, SSI 2014/83 43
    reg 1 332
        (2) 334
    reg 2 332
    reg 3(b) 333
    reg 5 .... 333, 335
    reg 6 .... 332, 334
        (b), (c) 334
Electronic Signatures Regulations 2002, SI 2002/318 333
    reg 2 333

Fees in the Registers of Scotland (Consequential Provisions) (Amendment) Order 2013, SSI 2013/15 43

Land Register Rules etc (Scotland) Regulations 2014, SSI 2014/150 295
    r 2(b) 181
    r 3(1) 177, 181, 337
        (a) 177
        (b) 178
        (2) 178
        (3) 177
            (a) 177
            (b) 178
    r 4(1), (2), (3) 183
    r 5 180
    r 6 .... 181, 251
    r 7 .... 62, 96, 123, 135, 248
    r 8 82
    r 9 .... 146, 316
        (3) 333
    r 10(1), (2) 153

Land Register Rules etc (Scotland) Regulations 2014, SSI 2014/150 (*cont*)
 r 10(3)–(5) 154
 r 11(1) 153
 r 12 196
  (1) 61, 62
   (b) 295
   (d) 296
  (3) 63
 r 13 249
 r 15(a) 325
  (b), (c), (e) 327
 r 17 199
 r 18(1) 318
  (2) 317
 sch 1
  pt 1 .... 179, 180
  pt 2 179
  pt 3 181
  pt 4 .... 62, 96, 123, 135, 248
  pt 5 .... 325, 327
  pt 6 251
 sch 2 317
Land Register of Scotland (Automated Registration) etc Regulations 2014,
 SSI 2014/347 .... 43, 172, 331
 reg 1(2) 336
 reg 2 331
 regs 3–6 336
 reg 3 336
  (1) 336
 reg 4(1)–(3) 336
  (3), (4) 337
  (5), (6) 336
 regs 5, 6 336
 reg 8 .... 123, 135
 reg 9(3) 332, 334, 335
 sch 2 .... 337, 338
Land Register of Scotland (Rate of Interest on Compensation) Regulations 2014,
 SSI 2014/194 .... 43, 258, 264, 266, 269
Land Registration (Scotland) Act 1979 (Commencement No 1) Order 1980,
 SI 1980/1412 27
Land Registration (Scotland) Act 1979 (Commencement No 16) Order 2002,
 SSI 2002/432 28
Land Registration (Scotland) Rules 1980, SI 1980/1412 23
 r 4(2) 79
 r 23 78
Land Registration (Scotland) Rules 2006, SSI 2006/485 317
 rr 3–7 24
 r 4(1)(b) 61
  (2) 26, 78
 r 5(j) 295
 r 6(2) 64
 r 8 .... 57, 81
 r 9 29
  (1), (2) 123
  (3) 124
 rr 12, 13, 15, 16 29

Table of Orders, Rules and Regulations xxv

Land Registration (Scotland) Rules 2006, SSI 2006/485 (*cont*)
   r 17(1) 34, 208
      (2) 323, 324
   r 18(1) 162
   r 20 78
   r 23 25
   sch 1 29
Land Registration etc (Scotland) Act 2012 (Amendment and Transitional) Order
   2014, SSI 2014/346 43
Land Registration etc (Scotland) Act 2012 (Commencement No 1) Order 2012,
   SSI 2012/265 43
Land Registration etc (Scotland) Act 2012 (Commencement No 2 and Transitional
   Provisions) Order 2014, SSI 2014/41 43
   art 3 331
Land Registration etc (Scotland) Act 2012 (Designated Day) Order 2014,
   SI 2014/127 43
Land Registration etc (Scotland) Act 2012 (Incidental, Consequential and
   Transitional) Order 2014, SSI 2014/190 43
   art 7 .... 177, 183, 184
   sch 177, 183, 184
Lands Tribunal for Scotland Rules 1971, SI 1971/218
   sch 2 210
Lands Tribunal for Scotland Amendment (Fees) Rules 2014, SSI 2014/24 210
Lands Tribunal for Scotland Amendment (Fees) Rules 2015, SSI 2015/199 .... 43, 324

Ordinary Cause Rules 1993
   r 51.2 324
   r 51.2(3)(a), (b), (c) 327
   r 51.3 324
      (1), (2), (3) 327
   form 51.3-A 324, 327
   forms 51.3-B, 51.3-C 327

Register of Sasines (Application Procedure) Rules 2004, SSI 2004/318 12
   r 2(b) 177, 183
      (c) 184
   sch pt 2 .... 177, 183
   sch pt 3 184
Register of Sasines (Application Procedure) Amendment Rules 2006, SSI 2006/568 12
Register of Sasines (Methods of Operation) (Scotland) Regulations 2006,
   SSI 2006/164 11
Register of Sasines (Microcopies) (Scotland) Regulations 1989, SI 1989/909 11
Register of Sasines (Registers Direct) (Scotland) Regulations 1998, SI 1998/3099 11
Register of Scotland Executive Agency Trading Fund Order 1996, SI 1996/1004 .... 13, 52
Register of Scotland (Fees) Order 2014, SSI 2014/188 .... 43, 125
   sch 1 pts 1, 3 338
   sch 1
      para 1(1) 125
         (b) 125
        (2) 125, 126
         (b) 117, 125
        (3) 125
         (b) 117
        (7) 49, 50
        (8), (10) 126
        (11) 114
      para 3(1)(a) 150, 159
         (b) 156

Registers of Scotland (Fees) Order 2014, SSI 2014/188 (*cont*)
  sch 1 para 3(2) 126
               (b) 181
            (3)(a)(i) 325
                  (ii), (iii), (iv) 327
               (b) 327
            (4) 251
  paras 9, 10 126
  para 13 161
Registers of Scotland (Information and Access) Order 2014, SSI 2014/189 43
  art 2 50
  art 3 .... 49, 50
  art 4 73
    (1) 49
Registers of Scotland (Voluntary Registration, Amendment of Fees etc) Order 2015, SSI 2015/265 43
  art 2 .... 114, 116
  art 3 113
  art 4 125
    (2) 117
    (5) 114
    (7) 117

Scottish Adjacent Waters Boundaries Order 1999, SI 1999/1126 48

Table of Cases

Balfour v Keeper of the Registers of Scotland 2015 SLT (Lands Tr) 185 .... 53, 206
Balfour v Kinsey 1987 SLT 144 242
Braes v Keeper of the Registers of Scotland [2009] CSOH 176, 2010 SLT 689 271
Brookfield Developments Ltd v Keeper of the Registers of Scotland 1989 SLT
 (Lands Tr) 105 .... 54, 134
Burnett's Tr v Grainger [2004] UKHL 8, 2004 SC (HL) 19 .... 7, 42, 94
Burr v Keeper of the Registers of Scotland, 12 Nov 2010, Lands Tr 204, 205
Burton v Keeper of the Registers of Scotland 2014 SLT (Lands Tr) 69 .... 26, 37, 53,
205, 215

Campbell-Gray v Keeper of the Registers of Scotland 2015 SLT (Lands Tr) 147 205
Caparo Industries plc v Dickman [1990] 2 AC 605 272
Chalmers v Chalmers [2015] CSIH 75, 2015 SLT 793 30
Chief Land Registrar v Caffrey & Co [2016] EWHC (Ch) 161, [2016] PNLR 23 277
Cobham v Minter 1986 SLT 336 246
Crawford v Campbell 1937 SC 596 343

Davidson v Mackenzie (1856) 19 D 226 273
Dougbar Properties Ltd v Keeper of the Registers of Scotland 1999 SC 513 .. 35, 227, 254

Foster v Keeper of the Registers of Scotland 2006 SLT 513 54

Gray v Keeper of the Registers of Scotland 2014 SLT (Lands Tr) 117 .... 26, 33, 37,
204, 205, 215
Griffiths v Keeper of the Registers of Scotland, 20 Dec 2002, Lands Tr 34, 293
Gyle Shopping Centre General Partners Ltd v Marks and Spencer plc [2016]
 CSIH 19, 2016 GWD 10-205 68

Hunter v Hanley 1955 SC 200 277

Jones v Wood 2005 SLT 655 99

Kaur v Singh 1999 SC 180 .... 32, 33, 34, 37, 202, 205
Keeper of the Registers of Scotland v MRS Hamilton Ltd 2000 SC 271 201

Love-Lee v Cameron of Lochiel 1991 SCLR 61 .... 308, 314
Lundin Homes Ltd v Keeper of the Registers of Scotland 2013 SLT
 (Lands Tr) 73 .... 26, 79, 141, 292

McCoach v Keeper of the Registers of Scotland, 19 Dec 2008, Lands Tr 34, 279
McKenna v Keeper of the Registers of Scotland, 21 Aug 2015, Lands Tr 205
Mactaggart (J A) & Co v Harrower (1906) 8 F 1101 148
Mathers v Keeper of the Registers of Scotland 2015 GWD 3-68 .... 37, 204, 205, 215
Miller Homes Ltd v Keeper of the Registers of Scotland 2014 SLT
 (Lands Tr) 79 .... 141, 292
MRS Hamilton Ltd v Keeper of the Registers of Scotland 2000 SC 271 .... 266, 270

Neale (F G) (Glasgow) Ltd v Vickery 1973 SLT (Sh Ct) 88 63
Nicol v Keeper of the Registers of Scotland 2013 SLT (Lands Tr) 56 .... 26, 37, 204, 215

Orkney Housing Association Ltd v Atkinson 2011 GWD 30-652 .... 34, 293

Palmer v Beck 1993 SLT 485 258

Palmer's Trs v Brown 1989 SLT 128 342
Playfair Investments Ltd v McElvogue [2012] CSOH 148, 2013 SLT 225 175
PMP Plus Ltd v Keeper of the Registers of Scotland 2009 SLT (Lands Tr) 2 .... 26, 53,
54, 79, 134, 141, 142, 292
Pye (J A) (Oxford) Ltd v United Kingdom (2006) 43 EHRR 3; (2008)
46 EHRR 45 313

Rivendale v Clark [2015] CSIH 27, 2015 SC 558..202, 205
Rivendale v Keeper of the Registers of Scotland, 30 Oct 2013, Lands Tr 204, 205
Rodger v Crawford (1867) 6 M 24.. 343
Rodger (Builders) Ltd v Fawdry 1950 SC 483 193

Safeway Stores plc v Tesco Stores Ltd 2004 SC 29 .... 37, 204, 205, 213
Santander UK plc v Keeper of the Registers of Scotland [2013] CSOH 24,
2013 SLT 362... 27, 30, 203, 233, 272
Schubert Murphy v The Law Society [2014] EWHC 4561 (QB), [2015] PNLR 15.... 272
Scottish Parliamentary Corporate Body v The Sovereign Indigenous Peoples of
Scotland [2016] CSOH 65, 2016 SLT 761 50
Sebry v Companies House [2015] EWHC 115 (QB), [2015] 4 All ER 681 272
Shanks v Gray 1977 SLT (Notes) 26 257
Sharp v Thomson 1997 SC (HL) 66; revsg 1995 SC 455 .... 7, 42, 94, 233
Shetland Salmon Farmers Association v Crown Estate Commissioners 1991
SLT 166... 48
Short's Tr v Keeper of the Registers of Scotland 1996 SC (HL) 14 54
Stamfield's Creditors v Scot (1696) 4 Brown's Supp 344... 125
Stevenson-Hamilton's Exrs v McStay 1999 SLT 1175 201
Stevenson-Hamilton's Exrs v McStay (No 2) 2001 SLT 694.. 34
Stuart v Stuart, 27 July 2009, Stonehaven Sh Ct.. 85

Tesco Stores Ltd v Keeper of the Registers of Scotland 2001 SLT (Lands Tr) 23 204
Trade Development Bank v Warriner and Mason (Scotland) Ltd 1980 SC 74................ 74

Van Eck v Keeper of the Registers of Scotland 2014 SLT (Lands Tr) 117......... 26, 37, 215

Wallace v University of St Andrews (1904) 6 F 1093... 308
Wight v Keeper of the Registers of Scotland 2015 SLT (Lands Tr) 195....................... 210
Willemse v French [2011] CSOH 51, 2011 SC 576 85
Wilson v Keeper of the Registers of Scotland 2000 SLT 267 255

Yaxley v Glen [2007] CSOH 90, 2007 SLT 756... 34, 292
Young v Leith (1847) 9 D 932; affd (1848) 2 Ross LC 103 .... 7, 30

Abbreviations

1979 Act	Land Registration (Scotland) Act 1979
2012 Act	Land Registration etc (Scotland) Act 2012
ALJ	*Australian Law Journal*
APS	Thomas Thomson et al, *The Acts of the Parliaments of Scotland*, 11 vols (1814–72)
Bankton	Andrew McDouall, Lord Bankton, *An Institute of the Laws of Scotland in Civil Rights* (1751–53; reprinted, Stair Society vols 41–43, 1993–95)
Bell, *Commentaries*	George Joseph Bell, *Commentaries on the Law of Scotland and on the Principles of Mercantile Jurisprudence* (7th edn, by J McLaren, 1870)
Bell, *Principles*	George Joseph Bell, *Principles of the Law of Scotland* (4th edn, 1839; reprinted, Edinburgh Legal Education Trust, 2010)
CLJ	*Cambridge Law Journal*
Craig, *Jus Feudale*	Thomas Craig of Riccarton, *Jus Feudale* (3rd edn, 1732, transl Lord Clyde, 1934)
Dunedin Report	*Reports by the Royal Commission on Registration of Title in Scotland* (1910, Cd 5316)
Erskine	John Erskine, *An Institute of the Law of Scotland* (1st edn, 1773; reprinted, Edinburgh Legal Education Trust, 2014)
General Guidance	A series of publications by Registers of Scotland, available at www.ros.gov.uk/about-us/2012-act/general-guidance, which provides guidance on a wide range of matters concerning registration practice
Henry Report	*Scheme for the Introduction and Operation of Registration of Title to Land in Scotland: Report by a Committee appointed by the Secretary of State for Scotland* (Cmnd 4137, 1969).
Hume, *Lectures*	*Baron David Hume's Lectures* (ed G C H Paton; Stair Society vols 5, 13, 15, 17–19; 1939–58)
JLSS	*Journal of the Law Society of Scotland*
JR	*Juridical Review*

Low Report	*Report of the Committee Appointed on 31st January 1896 by the Right Honourable Lord Balfour of Burleigh, Her Majesty's Secretary for Scotland, to enquire into the present system of land registration in Scotland* (C 8727, 1898)
LRR 2014	Land Register Rules etc (Scotland) Regulations 2014, SSI 2014/150
LR(S)A 1979	Land Registration (Scotland) Act 1979
LR(S)A 2012	Land Registration etc (Scotland) Act 2012
Macmillan Report	Scottish Home Department, *First Report of the Committee on Land Registration in Scotland* (Cmd 7451, 1948)
Morton/Bannatyne Report	*Report of the Commissioners appointed to inquire as to the State of the Registers of Land Rights in the Counties and Burghs of Scotland* (1863)
Passage of the Land Registration etc (Scotland) Bill 2011	Scottish Parliament, *Passage of the Land Registration etc (Scotland) Bill 2011* (2013, SPPB 174, ISBN 978-1-78307-085-5) (available at www.scottish.parliament.uk/parliamentarybusiness/Bills/44469.aspx)
Registration Manual	Registers of Scotland, *Registration Manual* (https://rosdev.atlassian.net/wiki/display/2ARM/Home)
Reid Report	*Registration of Title to Land in Scotland: Report by a Committee appointed by the Secretary of State for Scotland* (Cmnd 2032, 1963)
RoS	Registers of Scotland
RPS	*Records of the Parliaments of Scotland to 1707* (www.rps.ac.uk)
SLC DP 125	Scottish Law Commission, *Discussion Paper No 125 on Land Registration: Void and Voidable Titles* (2004: www.scotlawcom.gov.uk)
SLC DP 128	Scottish Law Commission, *Discussion Paper No 128 on Land Registration: Registration, Rectification and Indemnity* (2005: www.scotlawcom.gov.uk)
SLC DP 130	Scottish Law Commission, *Discussion Paper No 130 on Land Registration: Miscellaneous Issues* (2005: www.scotlawcom.gov.uk)
SLC Report 222	Scottish Law Commission, *Report No 222 on Land Registration* (2010: www.scotlawcom.gov.uk)
SLG	*Scottish Law Gazette*
SLT	*Scots Law Times*
Stair	James Dalrymple, Viscount Stair, *The Institutions of the Law of Scotland* (6th edn, by D M Walker, 1981)

Chapter 1

Historical Introduction

REGISTRATION OF DEEDS

1.1 Beginnings

The origins of land registration in Scotland lie in a series of statutes from the sixteenth century. These provided for the registration of instruments of sasine, the notarial deed recording the ceremony of sasine by symbolical delivery which was needed for the transfer of land. Statutes were passed in 1504, 1540, 1555 and 1587,[1] and these in turn owed something to an earlier Act of 1469 concerning the registration of reversions.[2] The first Acts were restricted to the sasines of those who held directly of the Crown, and may have had as their object the more reliable collection of Crown dues;[3] it was only with the Act of 1555 that subaltern holdings came to be included. Registration was in the sheriff court books, and the scheme required the recording of only the briefest particulars of the deed in question. Initially, this was little more than the date on which sasine was given,[4] but later, from 1555 onwards, the required information was 'the day and moneth of the geving of the said sesing, the name of the landis contenit in the samin, the name of the notar and witnes contenit thairintill'.[5] The legislation appears to have been widely ignored, not least because no sanction was imposed for a failure to register.[6] Thomas Craig (1538?–1608), who was presumably in position to know, reported that the 1555 Act fell into neglect 'as a result of popular dislike'.[7] Its subsequent ratification by the Act of 1587, with the exhortation that it 'be put to dew executioun in all pointis', appears to have done little to revive its fortunes.

---

1 Acts of 1504 (APS ii 253 c 35, RPS A1504/3/135), 1540 (APS ii 360 c 14, RPS 1540/12/21), 1555 (APS ii 497 c 21, RPS A1555/6/22), and 1587 (APS iii 455 c 50, RPS 1587/7/60). In an early indication of concern about fees, the 1555 Act provided that the sheriff's clerk was to take no more than 2s for his labours. As we will see, this was to be a recurring issue.
2 Act of 1469 (APS ii 95 c 3, RPS 1469/17).
3 That was the view of W Ross, *Lectures on the History and Practice of the Law of Scotland relative to Conveyancing and Legal Diligence* (2nd edn, 1822) vol II, 204. Ross's overall assessment was: 'Thus a kind of register was instituted for Crown infeftments only, and, of consequence, of no general use'.
4 More precisely, sheriffs and others giving sasine were required to record 'the day and yeir that thai gaif the sesing' (1504 Act) or subsequently, under the 1540 Act, 'the day, the moneth of the gevin of the said sesing and the name of the landis contenit in the samin'.
5 Act of 1555 (APS ii 497 c 21, RPS A1555/6/22). An obvious omission was the name of the parties.
6 For this and other developments prior to the Registration Act 1617, see J M Thomson, *The Public Records of Scotland* (1922) 104–06; L Ockrent, *Land Rights: An Enquiry into the History of Registration for Publication in Scotland* (1942) 67–72; C D Farran, *The Principles of Scots and English Land Law* (1958) 207–08; C F Kolbert and N A M Mackay, *History of Scots and English Land Law* (1977) 279–82.
7 Craig, *Jus Feudale* II.7.23.

More ambitious provision for registration made at the end of the century was scarcely more successful. A register under the control of the Secretary of State was established by an Act of 1599,[8] and all instruments of sasine, reversions, and various other deeds were enjoined to be registered there on pain of absolute nullity. The measure seems to have attracted the opposition of notaries public, perhaps because it threatened the traditional (if indifferently executed)[9] practice of recording deeds in their protocol books.[10] Inefficiency or even corruption on the part of local registrars may also have contributed to the failure of the 'Secretary's Register',[11] as did the fact that neither the 1599 Act nor a confirming Act of 1600[12] was put into print.[13] At any rate, after a brief few years of operation, the register was abolished by an Act of the Convention of Estates. The preamble to this Act, passed in 1609,[14] was vigorous in its condemnation of an 'unnecessair register' which occasioned 'neidles extraordinaire and most unnecessair trouble tormoyle fascherie and expens' to the lieges and whose only purpose was 'to acquire gayne and commoditie to the clerksis keiparis thairof'. The history of land registration in the sixteenth century, therefore, was largely a history of failure.

1.2 Registration Act 1617

This, then, was the unpromising background to the Act of 1617,[15] which is still in force[16] and which established a register, the Register of Sasines, that has endured to the present day. Why a new register should be set up so soon after the failure of the old is unclear. In his account of the Act, Ockrent mentions only general factors, such as the need for reliable records following the upheaval in land rights produced by the Reformation of 1560,[17] as well as the overall suitability of the Scottish system of transfer, with its insistence on writs, rather than mere possession, for the introduction of registration.[18] But if the timing is hard to explain, the policy motivations are manifest from the Act itself. Two aims predominated: publicity and the protection of

---

8 APS iv 184. This was an Act of the Convention of the Estates of July 1599, later converted into an Act of Parliament in November 1600 (APS iv 237 c 36, RPS 1600/11/49).
9 For the many deficiencies in notarial practice, see Ockrent (n 6) 56–65. Erskine II.3.39 thought that the protocol books were of little assistance, partly because they were not lodged in any public office until an Act of 1587 and partly because 'notaries at this day, even when they keep protocols, seldom insert in them any instruments which are not thought of more than ordinary importance'.
10 For the failure of the Act, see Ockrent (n 6) 69–72.
11 This despite the firm injunction in the Act of 1600 that the 'deputtis' be 'of gude fame, literature and conversatioun', a formula that (see para 1.7 below) was to be repeated in the Registration Act 1617.
12 RPS 1600/11/49.
13 Ross (n 3) 205: 'These acts were not printed, and consequently little attended to.'
14 APS iv 407.
15 APS iv 545 c 16, RPS 1617/5/30. For commentary on the 1617 Act, see Sir George Mackenzie, *Observations on the Acts of Parliament* (1687) 352–54; Lord Kames, *Elucidations respecting the Common and Statute Law of Scotland* (2nd edn, 1800) 291–97.
16 Though naturally it has been amended from time to time.
17 In this respect the Registration Act 1617 is closely linked with the Prescription Act of the same year (APS iv 543 c 12, RPS 1617/5/26).
18 Ockrent (n 6) 45–53.

acquirers.[19] Conversely, the need to make land available for secured lending, often a motivation in other countries at least in a later period,[20] does not seem to have been a major consideration.

1.3 '… ane publick register …'

Publicity was a central aim of the 1617 Act, as it had been of some of the earlier statutes. There was to be a fully public register – 'ane publick register' – which was 'patent to all oure soverane lordis liegis', an expression broader than that typically found in the legislation of the previous century where the need for interest was prescribed ('all utheris haifand interes may haif recours tharto').[21] Furthermore, in place of the meagre details which were all that the earlier legislation had required,[22] the clerks were required 'to engrose the haill bodie of the write in the register'. As instruments of sasine repeated the terms of the (unregistered) conveyance on which the transfer was founded,[23] there was full disclosure of the transfer. The effect was for ownership of land, and the encumbrances and conditions to which it was subject, to become a matter of public knowledge. In that way, George Joseph Bell explained, 'the credit of landed men in Scotland may be estimated with great correctness',[24] thus assisting not only those proposing to lend money, but anyone intending to enter into relations with anyone else. As Sir George Mackenzie pointed out, that might even include those wishing to marry off their daughters:[25]

> When men are to bestow their Daughters, they are by our Registers, informed, and assured of the condition of those with whom they deal, and by their means, men are kept from giving their Daughters and their Fortunes, or a considerable share thereof, to Bankerupts, and Cheats.

The benefits of publicity, it seemed, were limitless.

---

19 Bell, *Principles* § 772: 'The laws establishing the record of sasines had two objects in view: the first was to guard against forgery, by making conveyances known; the next (suggested as an improvement on the system) was to give information to all persons interested in knowing the state of the property.' Even in modern times, these aims have remained of central importance: see Scottish Home Department, *First Report of the Committee on Land Registration in Scotland* (Cmd 7451, 1948) ('Macmillan Report') para 9; *Registration of Title to Land in Scotland: Report by a Committee appointed by the Secretary of State for Scotland* (Cmnd 2032, 1963) ('Reid Report') para 11.
20 See eg Ockrent (n 6) 14.
21 The phrase is taken from the Act of 1555. Similar wording can be found in the Acts of 1540 and 1587.
22 Ross (n 3) 205: 'Such abbreviations of sasine as were entered in terms of the preceding act, were too short to answer the purpose of information to third parties. The infeftment might be qualified and clogged with burdens and conditions, of which these short notes could give no information.' The requirement in the 1617 Act to engross the instrument of sasine was anticipated in the Acts of 1599 and 1600 which set up the failed Secretary's Register.
23 That conveyance was either a grant in feu (feu charter, feu contract, or feu disposition) or a grant by 'substitution' (disposition). Provision for the registration of conveyances themselves had to await the Titles to Land (Scotland) Act 1858 (21 & 22 Vict c 76).
24 Bell, *Commentaries* I, 717. Compare the position in England in the same period where, from a Scottish perspective, there was 'an invincible repugnance to a system which allows all a man's financial and other transactions to become public property': see J W Brodie-Innes, 'Some outstanding differences between English and Scots Law' (1915) 27 JR 28, 43.
25 G Mackenzie, 'An Answer to some Reasons printed in England, against the overture of bringing into that Kingdom, such Registers as are used in Scotland', in *Pleadings in some remarkable Cases before the Supreme Courts of Scotland since the year 1661, To which, the Decisions are subjoyn'd* (1673) 221, 225. Mackenzie's example seems trivial only to modern eyes. Nonetheless, it is the only example known to the authors in which land registration is justified by reference to the marriage market.

1.4 '… mak no faithe in judgment .. in prejudice of a third pairtie …'

Apart from publicity, the other main objective of the 1617 Act was to suppress fraud and protect third parties.[26] Whether fraud was more prevalent in Scotland than elsewhere in Europe can reasonably be doubted.[27] Yet in Mackenzie's estimation sellers of land were intrinsically untrustworthy,[28] for in the limited market of the seventeenth century no honest man had reason to sell his estate but only 'prodigals, who are too vitious, or distrest persons, who are ordinarily under too many necessities to be believed'. Certainly the opening words of the Act present a dismal picture:

> Oure soverane lord, considering the gryit hurt sustened by his majesties liegis by the fraudulent dealing of pairties who, having annaliet thair landis and ressavit gryit soumes of money thairfore, yit, be thair unjust concealing of sum privat right formarlie made by thame, rendereth subsequent alienatioun done for gryit soumes of money altogidder unproffitable, whiche can not be avoyded unles the saidis privat rightis be maid publict and patent to his hienes liegis …[29]

No acquirer, it seems, could be sure that the land was free from latent real rights or even that the person selling it was still the owner.[30] It was the purpose of registration to end this uncertainty, so that 'purchasers and creditors might know with whom they might safely contract',[31] and that land values might rise accordingly.[32] 'Privat rightis' would 'be maid publict' by registration of the deed by which they were constituted. If this requirement were neglected, the right would 'mak no faithe in judgment by way off actioun or exceptioun in prejudice of a third pairtie'. Third parties, in other words, took the land free from unregistered deeds. And for those deeds that made it to the Register, the proper informing of third parties was, as a later Act put it, 'the great use and designe of their registration'.[33]

---

26 This is sometimes characterised as 'security of title', by which is meant the security of a person seeking to acquire (as opposed to the security of the current owner): see para 1.15 below.
27 Ockrent (n 6) 12–13, who points out that contemporary legislation for land registration in France and Denmark also gave the elimination of fraud as a motivation.
28 Mackenzie (n 25) 224: 'what frail securities have such as are forced to rest upon the ingenuity of sellers, who of all people are least to be trusted?'
29 The RPS translation is: 'Our sovereign lord, considering the great hurt sustained by his majesty's lieges by the fraudulent dealing of parties who, having alienated their lands and received great sums of money for that, yet, by their unjust concealing of some private right formerly made by them, renders subsequent alienation done for great sums of money altogether unprofitable, which cannot be avoided unless the said private rights be made public and patent to his highness's lieges …'
30 Erskine II.3.39: 'This latency … of sasines, rendered all conveyances of heritable rights most insecure; for purchasers could not know by any research, whether the lands for which they were to give their money, had not been formerly sold, or charged with debts.'
31 These words come from the preamble to the Act of 1693 (APS ix 271 c 23, RPS 1693/4/64).
32 Mackenzie (n 25) 225: 'By these, the price and value of Land is much raised, for by how much more the purchase is certain, by so much more it is worth.'
33 Act of 1696 (APS x 60 c 18, RPS 1696/9/136). Equally, the recording of such deeds was a protection against 'fire, loss and accidents, to which they are exposed whilest they are kept in privat hands: Whereas, after registration, nothing can destroy them, but what ruines the whole Kingdom': see Mackenzie (n 25) 226.

Yet, at least with hindsight, the protection conferred by the Act had obvious limitations.[34] As 60 days[35] were allowed for registration, there was a significant period during which a deed might be fully effective even though unregistered and undiscoverable.[36] Further, as Lord Kames was later to lament, some important deeds were not eligible for registration at all,[37] although matters were improved by subsequent legislation, and the original list of registrable deeds – essentially reversions and associated deeds, instruments of sasine, and renunciations of wadsets[38] – was gradually augmented, starting in 1669 with instruments of resignation *ad remanentiam*.[39] Even so, some real rights would continue to be constituted off-register and acquirers remained vulnerable to what, very much later, the Land Registration (Scotland) Act 1979 was to call 'overriding interests'.[40] Finally, the protection conferred by the 1617 Act was entirely negative in nature. Acquirers had the assurance that most relevant deeds were on the Register, but there was no positive guarantee that such deeds were valid. Registration did not make a bad deed good, so that whether a deed was bad or good was a matter for the assessment of the acquirer.

Whatever the shortcomings, however, the 1617 Act was a radical step in the direction of protecting acquirers of land. By this 'excellent statute', wrote Viscount Stair, 'purchasers in Scotland, may know better the condition of those with whom they contract about infeftments, and be more secure of lurking rights, than anywhere (so far as I can learn) in the world'.[41] This protection from 'lurking rights' was indeed one of the key achievements of the Act.

1.5 Effect on property law

A matter of controversy in modern times has been the effect of registration statutes on the ordinary law of property.[42] As originally understood, however,

---

34 Bell, *Commentaries* I, 717. Apart from those mentioned in the text, there was the serious, if temporary, difficulty caused by the Act of 1686 (APS viii 600 c 33, RPS 1686/4/49), by which a deed marked by the clerk as registered was deemed to be registered even if, as appears to have been common, it had not actually been entered on the Register. Such deeds were thus invisible to acquirers. This accommodating rule was removed a decade later by the Act of 1696 (APS x 60 c 18, RPS 1696/9/136).
35 '... thriescore dayes efter the date of the seasing ...'
36 Under the Act an unregistered deed was fully effective for its first 60 days, but thereafter could not be pled against third parties. Thus a person acquiring within the 60-day period was initially subject to the unregistered deed, but then ceased to be so subject if the deed was not registered within the period.
37 Kames (n 15) 296–97. Characteristically, Kames' preferred solution was for the Court of Session to extend the list of registrable deeds, on the basis that 'it was undoubtedly the purpose of the legislature, to facilitate the commerce of land, by securing *bona fide* purchasers, for a valuable consideration, against such latent rights as are real, and consequently are effectual against purchasers'. It might be observed that the 1617 Act makes no requirement of either good faith or valuable consideration.
38 The full list was 'reversiounes, regresses, bandis and writtis for making of reversiounes or regresses, assignatiounes thairto, dischargis of the same, renunciatiounes of wodsettis and grantis off redemptioun, and siclyik all instrumentis of seasing'. Deeds for land held on burgage tenure were exempt on the basis that many burghs had registers of their own: see para 1.11 below.
39 Act of 1669 (APS vii 556 c 4, RPS 1669/10/15). See Stair II.11.4, who speculates as to whether their omission from the 1617 Act was 'by inadvertency or of purpose'.
40 Defined in s 28(1) of the Land Registration (Scotland) Act 1979. By s 3(1)(a), the acquirer's registration was subject to overriding interests. The current law remains the same, although the term has been abandoned.
41 Stair II.11.4. The accolade of 'excellent statute' also appears in Stair II.3.20.
42 See para 2.7 below.

the effect of the 1617 Act was probably rather modest. Prior to 1617, the transfer of land involved three distinct stages.[43] First, a conveyance was drawn up and executed by the transferor. Next, legal possession or 'sasine' was given to the transferee by delivery of an appropriate symbol such as earth and stone. This ceremony had to take place on the land itself and was in practice conducted by agents ('baillies') on behalf of the parties accompanied by witnesses and overseen by a notary public. Finally, the whole transaction – conveyance followed by sasine – was written up by the notary public in the form of an instrument of sasine. It was this notarial instrument which, under the Act of 1617, was to be registered and which gave the new register its name. In cases where the transaction proceeded by substitution rather than subinfeudation (ie so that the transferee replaced the transferor in the feudal chain, holding of transferor's superior rather than of the transferor), the further step of entry with the superior was required.

On how registration might fit into this three- (or four-) stage system, the 1617 Act was fatally unclear.[44] Registration was needed, and within 60 days, if the instrument of sasine was to affect third parties, for an unregistered deed made 'no faithe in judgment by way off actioun or exceptioun in prejudice of a third pairtie who hathe acquyred ane perfyit and lauchfull right to the saidis landis and heretages'. But – and in (presumably deliberate) contrast to the statute which had established the Secretary's Register[45] – this consequence was declared to be without prejudice to a right 'to use the saidis writtis aganis the pairtye maker thairof, his heiris and successoures'. When, then, was ownership of the land to pass? Did it pass with the drawing up of the instrument of sasine, as before, albeit on the basis that the ownership so conferred was defeasible in a question with third parties? Or had the Act added a new and mandatory step, so that registration was now constitutive of ownership?

Either view produces a workable enough system of land transfer represented, in modern law, by the systems found in France and Germany respectively.[46] What was less workable was a failure to choose between them. Yet for more than two centuries after the Act of 1617, the law hesitated to make the choice;[47] and if

---

43 The procedure described in the text encompasses the later innovation of conveyances *a me vel de me*. Where this device was not used, the transferor resigned the fee to the superior, and it was the superior who made the grant to the transferee. For further details, see eg Scottish Law Commission, *Report No 168 on Abolition of the Feudal System* (1999) paras 7.1–7.3; K G C Reid, *The Law of Property in Scotland* (1996) paras 87–93 (G L Gretton).
44 A later Act, the Real Rights Act 1693 (APS ix 271 c 22, RPS 1693/4/63), provided that real rights on which sasine was taken were to 'be preferable and preferred according to the date and priority of the registrations of the sasines', but this was intended less as a statement of general principle than as a means of bringing to an end what had become an anomalous distinction between the respective priorities of public and base infeftments. For background, see Scottish Law Commission, *Discussion Paper No 128 on Land Registration: Registration, Rectification and Indemnity* (2005) paras 5.55–5.57. A statement that registered deeds 'shall in competition be preferable according to the date of registration' appears in s 142 of the Titles to Land Consolidation (Scotland) Act 1868 (32 & 32 Vict c 101).
45 Act of 1600 (APS iv 237 c 36, RPS 1600/11/49). There the sanction for non-registration was simply that the deed was 'utherwayes to be null and to mak na fayth in judgement nor outwith and the said nullitie to be ressavit be way of exceptioun'.
46 And in the countries in the French and German traditions. In French law, an unregistered deed of transfer is not opposable to a good-faith acquirer; in German law, ownership is not acquired until the deed is registered.
47 Ockrent (n 6) 89–96; Farran (n 6) 210–12; Kolbert and Mackay (n 6) 284–86.

Kames was firm in his view that an unregistered instrument of sasine was 'no better than if the solemnity of delivering earth and stone were omitted', or in other words null,[48] his contemporary, Walter Ross, thought that such a sasine was 'at least a real right'.[49] That the issue was not seen as pressing is indicated by the failure to deal with it in one of the regular Acts on the subject of registration which were passed during the seventeenth century. In the end, it was left to the Court of Session, in the landmark case of *Young v Leith* (1847),[50] to decide by a majority that registration was constitutive of ownership, and that an unregistered instrument of sasine left the property rights undisturbed.

The tale has an unexpected coda. Right at the end of the twentieth century the argument was renewed that ownership of land might pass without registration, and following the decision in *Sharp v Thomson*[51] it seemed, for a time, as if that view had been accepted by the House of Lords. It was only with the later decision of the House of Lords in *Burnett's Tr v Grainger*[52] that it was possible to reassert the orthodoxy established by *Young v Leith*. Today it is beyond dispute that ownership passes only with registration. Indeed the matter is now the subject of express statutory provision.[53] But the previous and enduring uncertainty on a point so fundamental to the law of property is hardly to the credit either of the 1617 Act or of the Scottish system of land transfer itself.

1.6 Simplification of land transfers

If registration was to confer ownership, and in a public manner, then the way might have seemed open to simplify the rather cumbersome system of land transfer. Yet, for the first two centuries after the creation of the Register of Sasines, the law clung tenaciously to the old forms. Change, however, when it eventually came, came quickly.[54] In 1845 the ceremony of symbolical delivery ceased to be necessary,[55] and in 1858 instruments of sasine too were abandoned, with conveyances becoming directly registrable in their place.[56] Thereafter ownership was transferred merely by registration of the conveyance, a rule which still survives today. Until the feudal system was laid to

---

48 Kames (n 15) 295.
49 Ross (n 3) 210. Erskine's views (II.3.40) appear to have been similar: 'The not registration, therefore, does not avoid the seisin; it is only a ground for postponing it in a question with third parties, who may claim the same subject under a title which has no dependence upon that seisin.' Insofar as Stair II.11.11 is to contrary effect, Erskine thought that he had been misled by Craig, *Jus Feudale* III.3.25.
50 (1847) 9 D 932. The opinions on both sides display great learning and insight. The decision of the Court of Session was upheld by the House of Lords: see (1848) 2 Ross LC 103.
51 1997 SC (HL) 66, reversing the decision of the First Division reported at 1995 SC 455.
52 [2004] UKHL 8, 2004 SC (HL) 19. For a review of the debate, see Scottish Law Commission, *Discussion Paper No 114 on* Sharp v Thomson (2001) and *Report No 208 on* Sharp v Thomson (2007). The large amount of periodical literature which was generated is listed on pp 44–47 of the Report.
53 Land Registration etc (Scotland) Act 2012 s 50, replacing s 4 of the Abolition of Feudal Tenure etc (Scotland) Act 2000.
54 See eg Ockrent (n 6) 112–21.
55 Infeftment Act 1845 (8 & 9 Vict c 35) s 1.
56 Titles to Land (Scotland) Act 1858 s 1, later re-enacted as s 15 of the Titles to Lands (Consolidation) (Scotland) Act 1868. In partial replacement for the instrument of sasine, a warrant of registration was endorsed on the conveyance requesting the registration of the deed: see para 1.8 below.

rest in 2004,[57] registration was declared to be the equivalent both of the giving of sasine and of entry with the superior.[58]

1.7 Mechanics of registration

Unlike the failed register which it replaced, the Register of Sasines was set up under the direction of the Lord Clerk Register and not the Secretary of State.[59] Like that register there were, in addition to a central register in Edinburgh, seventeen local or 'particular' registers, with an open choice between the particular or the central register.[60] In an expression familiar from earlier legislation,[61] the particular registers were to be run by deputes 'of guid fame, literature and conversatioun'. Their fee was capped at 26 shillings and 8 pence for each leaf used in transcribing the deed; if less than a full leaf were needed, the cost was to be reduced *pro rata*.

The method of registration was straightforward. Each deed was copied into the Register[62] and then returned to the ingiver marked with a certificate showing the date of registration and the page number in the relevant volume. But the time allowed for this, a mere 48 hours, often proved insufficient, meaning either that registration was late or, in a growing abuse, that the deed was certified and returned without ever having been entered in the Register.[63] Matters were made easier with the introduction of minute books in the closing decades of the seventeenth century,[64] and in practice it seems to have been accepted as sufficient compliance with the Act if the (much briefer) entry there was made within the required 48 hours even if transcription on to the Register came later.[65] A further advantage of minute books was to record the date and time on which deeds were presented and so to ensure that deeds were registered in the right

---

57 Abolition of Feudal Tenure etc (Scotland) Act 2000 s 1, which came into force on 28 November 2004.
58 In addition to the statutes mentioned in the previous footnotes, see Conveyancing (Scotland) Act 1874 (37 & 38 Vict c 94) s 4(2).
59 This was provided for by the 1617 Act.
60 The 1617 Act listed their locations: Kirkwall, Inverness, Elgin, Aberdeen, Dundee, Perth, Stirling, Cupar, Edinburgh, Lauder, Selkirk, Hamilton, Glasgow, Dunbarton, Ayr, Wigtown, and Dumfries. For later changes, see Ockrent (n 6) 79.
61 Act of 1600 (RPS 1600/11/49).
62 In the words of the 1617 Act, the deputes were required 'to engross the haill bodie of the write in the register under the payne of deprivatioun of the clerk of his place and service and of the office of notarie in all tyme thairefter'.
63 The abuse was facilitated by the Act of 1686 (APS viii 600 c 33, RPS 1686/4/49) which provided that certification of a deed 'shall make the samen sufficient and valide for the security of the pairty, albeit by the omission or negligence of the keeper of the register or his deputs they should not be found booked or insert in the register'. This ill-judged provision was repealed after only a decade by the Act of 1696 (APS x 60 c 18, RPS 1696/9/136).
64 The first legislative attempt to establish minute books was the Act of 1672 (APS viii 80 c 40, RPS 1672/6/50). The relevant part of this lengthy Act, which is mainly about courts, appears in s 32 of the RPS transcription. This followed on from an Act of Sederunt of 6 June 1663. Its lack of success may be judged by the fresh provision made by the Act of 1693 (APS ix 271 c 23, RPS 1693/4/64).
65 For minute books generally, see Ockrent (n 6) 97–108. The requirement that the ingiver (or, when after 1868 postal presentation was allowed, a clerk) sign the entry in the minute book survived until 1948: see Public Registers and Records (Scotland) Act 1948 s 2, implementing a recommendation in para 28 of the Macmillan Report (n 19).

order, something which could not previously be taken for granted.[66] Indeed it was not long before the date in the minute book came to be regarded as the date of registration itself.[67]

That keepers of the local registers often fell short of acceptable standards is clear from the constant stream of litigation on matters such as inaccurate transcription of deeds and irregularities in the minute books.[68] Nonetheless, by the close of the seventeenth century a reasonably efficient system of registration seems to have been in operation, and the legislative framework too had largely been established. Although there were to be later changes, mentioned below, it is striking how much of the current system was already in place. The Register was public. It was constitutive of rights. Deeds were minuted on receipt, copied rather than kept, and returned with a certificate of registration. The roots even of the post-2012 Act Land Register lie firmly in the seventeenth century.

1.8 Later developments

The flow of legislation which had been such a feature of the seventeenth century came to a sudden end with the disbandment of the Scottish Parliament at the start of the eighteenth.[69] Significant further legislation had to wait until the middle of the nineteenth century. By the Registration of Leases (Scotland) Act 1857, the class of registrable deeds was extended to include leases of more than 31 (now 20) years; and, following a thorough review of registration practice by a government commission in 1863,[70] an entire Act was devoted to the organisation of the registers. The most important feature of the Land Registers (Scotland) Act 1868 was the abolition, with almost immediate effect, of the particular registers.[71] A reliable postal service meant that local registers,[72] and the personal presentment of deeds,[73] were no longer a necessity, while to continue with a local as well as a general register put potential acquirers to the trouble and expense of a

---

66 The mischief which the Act of 1693 (APS ix 271 c 23, RPS 1693/4/64) was designed to solve was stated in the preamble to be that previous Acts 'have been much frustrated by the keepers of the registers not inserting the same in the registers at the time and in the order they were presented to them, whereby none could know by inspection of the registers what writes appointed to be registrate were in the hands of the keepers of the registers, and thereby could not securely bargain'. Accordingly, the Act directed that in future 'the writes shall be registrate exactly conform to the order of the said minute book'.
67 This, however, was not formalised by legislation until s 19 of the Titles to Land (Scotland) Act 1858.
68 Ockrent (n 6) 80–83, 102–07. Earlier (at 74), Ockrent describes the litigation under the Act as 'prolific'. Bell, *Commentaries* I, 719 thought that some of these problems could have been avoided if the deed had been retained in the Register and a copy returned.
69 This seems unlikely to have been a coincidence: see Anonymous, 'Registers of Sasines' (1832–36) 2 Edinburgh Law Journal 73, 76.
70 This resulted in the impressive and informative *Report of the Commissioners appointed to inquire as to the State of the Registers of Land Rights in the Counties and Burghs of Scotland* (1863) ('Morton/Bannatyne Report'). The Commissioners were Charles Morton and W Bannatyne.
71 Land Registers (Scotland) Act 1868 (31 & 32 Vict c 64) s 8. See Morton/Bannatyne Report (n 70) 14–16 and 23–26. The last register closed at the end of 1871. As compensation for the loss of office, the keepers received two-thirds of their net profits for the previous five years: see J Burns, 'Reforms in registration' (1898) 10 JR 35, 45.
72 The burgh registers, however, remained in place until well into the following century: see para 1.11 below.
73 Section 6 of the 1868 Act made provision for presentation by post; on receipt of the deed a clerk at the Register was to be treated as the ingiver.

search in both.[74] Despite the expected gains in efficiency, however, the abolition was controversial, and right up to the end the particular registers were used more heavily that the general register in Edinburgh.[75] With the resulting increase in business it became necessary to organise the general register into 'counties', of which today there are 33.[76]

The registration process too was beginning to assume its modern form.[77] After some false starts, the minute books, containing 'minutes' of each deed,[78] came to be indexed both by person and by property, a matter of urgent necessity in view of the large numbers of deeds now found in the registers; they were also printed.[79] And from 1871 onwards, this 'key'[80] to the registers was supplemented by search sheets, a sort of ledger for each property on which were entered brief details of any deed registered in relation to that property.[81] By these means it became possible to conduct rapid and reliable searches of a Register which was itself going through a period of rapid growth. Whether two such 'keys' to the Register, one (the minute book) much more detailed and initially much more reliable than the other, were needed was for decades a matter of

---

74 Anonymous (n 69) 85: 'It has long been felt a grievance, that a safe bargain cannot be made about even an acre of ground, without a search in *two* distinct registers of sasines. The expense, where the estate is large, may be tolerated, but in the case of small properties, where it is so much more frequently incurred, it is out of all proportion to the importance of the transaction.' In the interests of ready searching, the author's solution was the opposite of what was actually done, namely to abolish the general register and to divide the particular registers into registers for individual parishes.
75 Ockrent (n 6) 138–41.
76 This had been recommended in the *Third Report of Her Majesty's Law Commissioners, Scotland: Conveyancing* (Parliamentary Papers 1837–8 (C 114) xxix, 1) xxxix. The 33 counties are Aberdeen, Angus, Argyll, Ayr, Banff, Berwick, Bute, Caithness, Clackmannan, Dumfries, Dunbarton, East Lothian, Fife, the Barony and Regality of Glasgow, Inverness, Kincardine, Kinross, the Stewartry of Kirkcudbright, Lanark, Midlothian, Moray, Nairn, Orkney and Shetland, Ross and Cromarty, Roxburgh, Selkirk, Stirling, Sutherland, West Lothian, and Wigtown. For previous divisions, see Ockrent (n 6) 142–43.
77 For an account of the registration process as it was in the early 1960s, see Reid Report (n 19) paras 14–24.
78 For details, see *Report of the Committee Appointed on 31st January 1896 by the Right Honourable Lord Balfour of Burleigh, Her Majesty's Secretary for Scotland, to enquire into the present system of land registration in Scotland* (C 8727, 1898) ('Low Report') paras 48 and 49. The minute of a writ 'is an analysis and abridgement of its contents, specifying the nature and date of the Writ, the names of the parties, the lands affected, and the character of the transaction, whether sale, loan, discharge, or the like'. Its preparation 'is the most important step in the process of registration. On its accuracy, completeness, and clearness, the whole system of searching and the preparation of the Search Sheet depend.' Some of the difficulties of preparing such minutes were considered in the Morton/Bannatyne Report (n 70) 9–10.
79 Morton/Bannatyne Report (n 70) 10–11, 17–18; Ockrent (n 6) 109–12. See Anonymous (n 69) 76–85 for background and for the extreme difficulty of conducting searches in the registers as late as the 1830s. Printed (and so unsigned) copies of the minute books were known as 'abridgements'. The development of indexes owed much to Thomas Thomson, advocate, who held the (part-time) position of Deputy Clerk Register from 1806 to 1841. For a brief account of Thomson's remarkable career, see T Clarke, 'Thomson, Thomas (1768–1852)', *Oxford Dictionary of National Biography* vol 54, 554 (2004).
80 The word comes from the Low Report (n 78): see eg para 152.
81 Ockrent (n 6) 146–59; Low Report (n 78) paras 75–181. Search sheets were introduced without legislative sanction; although the idea was already current, having been developed in the Morton/Bannatyne Report (n 70) 27–32, 52–53, they were not included in the 1868 Act, perhaps due to opposition at the Register (which certainly existed) or because they were seen as less important than the other changes. A government Bill of 1893 (the Land Registers (Scotland) Bill: HC Bill 447) would have provided a legislative basis but, for reasons which are unclear, did not proceed to the statute book.

controversy.[82] In the 1920s a committee chaired by Lord Fleming recommended that minute books be dispensed with,[83] and a provision to that effect was included in a government Bill in 1948.[84] In the face of strong opposition, however, the government set up a committee under Lord Macmillan and accepted its unanimous recommendation that both minute books and search sheets should be retained.[85] Finally, the practice developed of logging newly-arrived deeds in a receipt book known as the presentment book.[86] This gave the date of presentment, the name of the deed, and the parties. Its existence was recognised by a provision in the 1868 Act to the effect that no error there contained was to 'affect injuriously' the registration of any deed in the Register.[87]

In one way or another, therefore, deeds were – and are – captured three times (in the presentment book, the minute book, and the relevant search sheet) in addition to the formal process of registration itself.[88] For registration the deed must be transcribed in full into a record volume, and until modern times this was done by hand,[89] the suggestion of using printing having been examined and then rejected.[90] In 1934, however, photocopying replaced manual transcription (by that time often done by typewriter).[91] This in turn gave way to microcopying on to microfiche in 1990,[92] and then, from 2006 onwards, to copying in electronic form.[93] Meanwhile, beginning in 1993, steps were taken to digitise key parts of the existing Register, and remote computer consultation by the public (through 'Registers Direct') became possible in 1999.[94]

82 In the evidence presented to the Low Committee and reproduced in the Appendix, search sheets were criticised as being incomplete and as diverting resources at the Register which could be better spent making the registration process faster.
83 *Report of a Committee on the Registration of Writs* (1928, with a supplementary report in 1932).
84 This was in the Public Registers and Records (Scotland) Bill, which passed into law (although without the provision) in the same year.
85 Macmillan Report (n 19) paras 17–27. All of the evidence heard by the committee, over three days in Edinburgh's Signet Library, was to the effect that search sheets were too brief and informal to take the place of minute books: see Lord Macmillan, *A Man of Law's Tale* (1952) 224.
86 Ockrent (n 6) 143.
87 Land Registers (Scotland) Act 1868 s 7.
88 The process is described in the Low Report (n 78) paras 47–52, and examples of entries in the minute book and search sheets are given on pp 94–95 of the Appendix. In describing the registration process, s 148 of the Titles to Land Consolidation (Scotland) Act 1868 mentions only the minute books and the 'register books'.
89 A cumbersome process undertaken by dedicated 'engrossing clerks'. After a deed was engrossed into the Register it was checked against the original by being read out loud twice.
90 Morton/Bannatyne Report (n 70) 36–37; Low Report (n 78) paras 182–99. A provision for printing was nonetheless included in the Land Registers (Scotland) Bill 1893 (HC Bill: 447) cl 5, but in the event the Bill did not pass into law.
91 In the early years of the century at least two government Bills were introduced to allow 'photo-zincography' or 'photo-lithography' but neither passed into law. See Land Registers (Scotland) Bill 1900 (HC Bill 322) and Registration of Land Writs in Scotland Bill (*Hansard* HL Deb vol 119 cols 74–77 (9 March 1903)). Clause 4 of the 1900 Bill empowered the Treasury to pay compensation for loss of employment to any engrossing clerk who had served for seven years or more.
92 Register of Sasines (Microcopies) (Scotland) Regulations 1989, SI 1989/909. This is the first of three statutory instruments made under the Register of Sasines (Scotland) Act 1987.
93 Register of Sasines (Methods of Operation) (Scotland) Regulations 2006, SSI 2006/164. 'Electronic form' is defined by reg 1(2) as 'a digital image, or series of such images, which is capable of being stored in a computer or other similar device'.
94 Register of Sasines (Registers Direct) (Scotland) Regulations 1998, SI 1998/3099. Since the mid-1990s both the presentment book and the minute book have been generated by an IT system although paper copies are also kept. New entries on the search sheet were made electronically from the late 1990s onwards, and digital images were made of the existing paper search sheets, thus allowing electronic searching.

Since 1868 it has been possible to apply for registration at any time during the grantee's life rather than within the 60 days stipulated by the 1617 Act;[95] for no further incentive to register was needed once it became clear that only registration could carry ownership and other real rights.[96] Conveyances, directly registrable after 1858, required at first to contain a warrant requesting registration, but in recent years the warrant has been replaced with an application form.[97] The requirement that the certificate of registration endorsed on the original deed before its return be signed by the Keeper or a clerk was removed in 1950.[98]

1.9 Administration and governance

Under the 1617 Act the Register of Sasines was to 'appertene and belang to the present clerk of register and his deputtis', and by the end of the century, if not before, those deputies who were in charge of the local (or 'particular') registers had come to be known as 'keepers'.[99] As the Lord Clerk Register[100] was an officer of the Court of Session, that Court maintained a supervisory role in relation to the Register of Sasines[101] and from time to time passed Acts of Sederunt on matters concerning registration.[102] Indeed the last such Act of Sederunt dates from as recently as 1977.[103] In 1879 the office of Lord Clerk Register was reduced to a ceremonial role, and governance of the Register passed to the Deputy Clerk Register, but power to make appointments was reserved to the Treasury and then, after that office was established in 1885, to the Secretary of Scotland.[104] The current office of Keeper of the Registers of Scotland dates from 1948, and carries administrative responsibility for various registers including the Register of

---

95 Titles to Land Consolidation (Scotland) Act 1868 s 142.
96 See para 1.5 above.
97 Abolition of Feudal Tenure etc (Scotland) Act 2000 s 5. For background, see Scottish Law Commission, *Report No 168 on Abolition of the Feudal System* (1999) paras 7.34–7.36. Warrants of registration ceased to be necessary on 28 November 2004. The replacement application form is set out in the Register of Sasines (Application Procedure) Rules 2004, SSI 2004/318, as amended by the Register of Sasines (Application Procedure) Amendment Rules 2006, SSI 2006/568. A non-statutory application form had been in existence since 1992 in order to facilitate the computerisation of the presentment book.
98 Public Registers and Records (Scotland) Act 1950 s 1. This followed a recommendation of the Macmillan Report (n 19) para 28.
99 The word appears in the Act of 1693 (APS ix 271 c 23, RPS 1693/4/64) and in the Act of 1686 (APS viii 600 c 33, RPS 1686/4/49).
100 For the office of Lord Clerk Register, see Morton/Bannatyne Report (n 70) 7–8.
101 A direct legislative basis lay in the exhortation, in s 36 of the Act of 1672 (APS viii 80 c 40, RPS 1672/6/50), after laying a series of duties on the keepers of the registers in respect of minute books, 'that the care of seeing the premissis done and performed, aftir the expireing of this commission, is committed to the lords of session'. A government Bill introduced in 1848, the Registers of Sasines (Scotland) Bill (HC Bill 589), sought to improve matters, the preamble narrating that 'whereas the Court of Session have, in virtue of various Acts of the Scottish and of the British Parliaments, been in use to regulate by Acts of Sederunt the keeping of said Registers, and the Minute-books of the same, but doubts have arisen as to the authority of the said Court to regulate such rates or dues ..'. In the event, the Bill did not pass into law.
102 For a full account of the position of the Court of Session and its gradual decline, see Low Report (n 78) paras 7–46. Some examples of Acts of Sederunt are listed in para 19.
103 Act of Sederunt (Register of Sasines Procedure Amendment) 1977, SI 1977/70; Act of Sederunt (Amendment of Fees in the Department of the Registers of Scotland) 1977, SI 1977/1623.
104 Lord Clerk Register (Scotland) Act 1879 (42 & 43 Vict c 44) ss 6 and 8; Secretary for Scotland Act 1885 (48 & 49 Vict c 61) s 5. The Treasury retained the power to fix salaries and emoluments. The position of Deputy Clerk Register had existed since 1806, the first holder being the celebrated Thomas Thomson: see n 79 above.

Sasines and, since 1979, the Land Register of Scotland.[105] Administrative support is provided by what was once a department of the Scottish Office but, since 1990, has been a non-ministerial department[106] known as Registers of Scotland.[107] And, far from being an officer of the Court of Session, as would once have been the case, the Keeper is now the holder of a non-ministerial office of the (devolved) Scottish Government.[108] More is said about the Keeper in chapter 3.

1.10 Premises

At one time the General Register of Sasines was held, along with other public records, in unsuitable accommodation in the basement of Parliament House in Edinburgh. But on 27 June 1774 the foundation stone was laid for purpose-built premises at the north end of North Bridge, itself only recently completed.[109] James Boswell was there, as might be expected, and was disappointed by what he saw:[110]

> I was very angry that there was no procession, no show or solemnity of any kind upon such an occasion. There was a fine sight both of well-dressed people and mob, so that there was spirit enough in the country to relish a show; and such things do good. It should have been laid either privately in the morning, or with some dignity. But cards were sent to all the judges as private men, and they accordingly dropped in, one by one, without their gowns and several of them with bob-wigs. The Lord Provost too was there as a private citizen. To appear so at noon before a crowd of spectators was very poor.

After this unimpressive start, building work proceeded slowly and in fits and starts, and the building was not ready for occupation until well into the 1780s.[111] Designed by Robert Adam and paid for out of funds confiscated from Jacobite estates, it was to provide a magnificent home for the Register of Sasines and other public records.[112] 'The character of Register House', it has been said, 'is that of the dignified civil servant, fastidiously dressed'.[113] Today, however, while the historical records remain in Register House, Registers of Scotland are based in Meadowbank House, an undistinguished if functional modern building on the east side of the city.[114]

---

105 Public Registers and Records (Scotland) Act 1948 s 1; Land Registration etc (Scotland) Act 2012 s 1(2). The first of these provisions split the office of Keeper of the Registers and Records of Scotland into (i) the Keeper of the Registers of Scotland, and (ii) the Keeper of the Records of Scotland. Lending its support to this division, the Macmillan Report (n 19) para 6 noted that, whereas the latter role required an expert in history, the former needed 'an intimate knowledge of the technicalities of Scottish conveyancing. It is obvious that the combination in one person of qualifications so diverse can very rarely occur.'
106 Formerly an executive agency.
107 Since 1 April 1996, Registers of Scotland has operated as a trading fund: see Registers of Scotland Executive Agency Trading Fund Order 1996, SI 1996/1004. It is currently regulated by the Public Finance and Accountability (Scotland) Act 2000 s 9.
108 Scotland Act 1998 s 126(8).
109 A new building had first been proposed in 1722, and for a time the plan was for it to be built on the grounds of Heriot's Hospital.
110 W K Wimsatt Jr and F A Pottle (eds), *Boswell for the Defence, 1769–1774* (1960) 227.
111 Even so, there was much work still needing to be done. For details, see A J Youngson, *The Making of Classical Edinburgh, 1750–1840* (1966) 65–68 (with photographs).
112 Morton/Bannatyne Report (n 70) 25: 'every possible provision has been made in it for the safe custody of the Registers', including fire-proofing. The lack of suitable buildings was one of the concerns about the local registers.
113 J Gifford, C McWilliam and D Walker, *The Buildings of Scotland: Edinburgh* (1984) 286.
114 The move was made in 1976: see 'Good-bye Register House' (1976) 21 JLSS 62.

1.11 Burgh registers[115]

Land lying within the royal burghs and held on burgage tenure[116] was excluded from the 1617 Act[117] on the basis that 'books', albeit often rudimentary in nature, were already maintained by the town clerks.[118] Registration there was not mandatory, however, until an Act of 1681, itself modelled on the 1617 Act, required that instruments of sasine and certain other deeds 'shall be insert in the toun-clerk's books' within 60 days on pain of nullity against third parties.[119] Even after 1681 the burgh registers remained distinct from and independent of the other local land register, the particular Registers of Sasines, and when the latter were abolished, in 1868, burgh registers were given a temporary reprieve.[120] This was partly because their variable standard made them hard to assimilate into a national system.[121] But it was also partly because of their relative insignificance. With the rapid urbanisation of the nineteenth century, only a small part of towns and cities lay within the boundaries of the historic royal burgh (for example, only 140 out of 6,216 acres in Edinburgh and 1,700 out of 11,861 acres in Glasgow).[122] The number of deeds presented for registration was correspondingly small: in the year 1895 there were 19 burgh registers in which fewer than 20 deeds were recorded and a further 31 with fewer than 100; only 12 registers managed more than 100, with Glasgow the highest with 759 deeds.[123]

Burgage tenure ceased to be a distinct tenure in 1874 and was assimilated to ordinary feudal tenure.[124] Thereafter the closure of the burgh registers seemed only a matter of time. In 1898 a committee chaired by Lord Low concluded that abolition was the proper course of action.[125] The town clerks,

---

115 This topic can only be dealt with briefly here. For detailed treatments, see Ockrent (n 6) 163 ff; Morton/Bannatyne Report (n 70) 32–36; Low Report (n 78) paras 248–94.
116 This was a privileged form of feudal tenure found in most but not quite all of the royal burghs. Although there was some controversy on the point, it seems that the land was held directly of the Crown without an intermediate subject superior. No feuduty or feudal casualties were payable.
117 'It is always declared that this present act sall nowayis be extendit to instrumentis of seasing and reversiounes thairin contened gevin be provestis and bailyeis of frie burghis royall of landis lyand within thair libertyes and friedomes haldin be the saidis burghis in frie burgage of his majestie, nor to na uther heretable writtis thairoff, nor yit to reversiounes incorporat in the bodye of the infeftmentis maid to the persounes aganis quhome the saidis reversiounes ar useit.'
118 In fact, only 65 of the 72 royal burghs maintained a register. The exceptions were Anstruther-Easter, Campbeltown, Dornoch, Inveraray, Kilrenny, Peterhead, and Wick: see Low Report (n 78) para 248. The Burgh Registers (Scotland) Act 1926 sch 1 lists each burgh which, at that time, maintained a register.
119 Burgage Registers Act 1681 (APS viii 248 c 13, RPS 1681/7/35).
120 Morton/Bannatyne Report (n 70) 32–33.
121 The lack of an index and poor descriptions of the properties were common shortcomings: see Low Report (n 78) Appendix 108. An Act of Parliament had been needed in 1829 – the Register of Sasines Act (10 Geo IV c 19) – in order to give retrospective validation to entries which failed to transcribe the notarial docquets from instruments of sasine. The verdict of Burns (n 71) 43 was that 'the present system (if the word is not a misnomer) is discredited, if only on the ground that it is thoroughly unbusinesslike'.
122 Low Report (n 78) para 282.
123 Low Report (n 78) Appendix 109.
124 Conveyancing (Scotland) Act 1874 s 25. This was part of the extensive mid-Victorian reforms of land law and conveyancing. The main reason for the assimilation was persistent doubts as to the true nature of burgage tenure, and in particular whether it was competent for the burgh magistrates (who held directly of the Crown) to sub-feu (as they often did in practice).
125 Low Report (n 78) paras 261–85.

mindful perhaps of the income which registration provided, offered strenuous resistance.[126] Burgh registers, they argued, had worked well for centuries. Their accessibility made them popular with local people and local law agents. As compared with the General Register of Sasines in Edinburgh, their workings were 'economical, efficient, and expeditious'.[127] Far from being abolished, they should be extended so as to cover the whole of the towns and cities in question.[128]

Such views may have delayed abolition but they were not able to prevent it. Nonetheless, when legislation to dismantle the registers was finally passed, in 1926, after earlier Bills had failed,[129] it sought to avoid confrontation by providing that a register could not be discontinued for as long as its current keeper remained in office.[130] The reprieve turned out to be more generous than had perhaps been intended. While the registers in Glasgow and Edinburgh closed in 1927 with Aberdeen following in 1931, a number of burghs hung on until after the War, with the last register of all, for the Burgh of Dingwall, remaining in operation until 30 June 1963. It was only then, some 350 years after the Register of Sasines was first established, that all deeds relating to land in Scotland came to be registrable in a single register. As it happens, this state of affairs was to last for less than 20 years.[131]

1.12 Reputation and evaluation

There is much that is impressive in the development of Scottish land registration. If the Register of Sasines is not quite 'the oldest land register in the world' – in the patriotic claim of Registers of Scotland[132] – it is certainly amongst the earliest. It is true that in Cologne, Hamburg, Magdeburg and some other Germanic cities a rudimentary system of registration can be traced to the later Middle Ages,[133] but this seems to have been comparable to Scotland's burgh registers and was correspondingly limited in scope. The novelty of the Register of Sasines was its comprehensive and its national character.[134] That this was something of which to

---

126 Low Report (n 78) Appendix 105–12.
127 Low Report (n 78) Appendix 106.
128 Low Report (n 78) Appendix 105–06, 111–12.
129 Land Registers (Scotland) Bill 1893 (HC Bill 447) cl 15; Land Registers (Scotland) Bill (HC Bill 322) cl 12. Both were government Bills, and both provided for an immediate, rather than a phased, abolition.
130 Burgh Registers (Scotland) Act 1926 s 1.
131 Until 1981, when the first county (Renfrew) became operational for the Land Register of Scotland.
132 www.ros.gov.uk/services/registration/sasine-register.
133 For an account in English, see C P Cooper, *Notes respecting Registration and the Extrinsic Formalities of Conveyances* (1831). The publication of this work reflected the growing interest in land registration in England coupled with an awareness of the need to consult the law of other European jurisdictions (but not, apparently, Scotland) where systems of land registration were long-established. In his preface, the author refers to the subject of land registration as being one 'that now engages the public attention' (iii), and substantial parts of the book, on land registration in Austria, Prussia and Bavaria (pp 63 ff), were originally written at the request of the (English) Real Property Commissioners. For a survey at the end of the century, see R Burnett Morris, *A Summary of the Law of Land and Mortgage Registration in the British Empire and Foreign Countries* (1895).
134 Ockrent (n 6) 13: 'Apart from Scotland, and evidently Denmark, ... it would appear no other country in Europe could boast of having complete national registers in the seventeenth century.'

be proud was not lost on Scottish commentators.[135] Sir George Mackenzie, towards the end of the seventeenth century, made play of Scottish exceptionalism:[136]

> [A]s some Sciences, Trades and Inventions flourish more, because more cultivat in one Nation then another, humane nature allowing no universal excellency, and God designing thus to gratifie every Countrey that he hath created; So Scotland hath above all other Nations, by a serious and long experience, obviated most happily all frauds, by their publick Registers.

A century later, Scotland's claim to the admiration of others seemed no less strong, Walter Ross ending his account of the development of land registration in a spirit of evident self-satisfaction:[137]

> Thus was the system of registration in land rights brought to perfection; and the kingdom continued to enjoy the good effects resulting from it at home, and the honour of the invention abroad.

That this happy result contrasted with England's failure to develop any kind of national system of registration[138] could only be a matter for further celebration.[139]

This view survived well into the nineteenth century. As late as 1863 the Commissioners appointed to review the state of the registers in Scotland felt able to characterise what they found as 'the most complete and practically useful system which has yet been devised in any country'.[140] Yet within a generation the Scottish lead was to look distinctly less secure.[141] No doubt the Register of Sasines was, in its way, an admirable institution which, with appropriate modernisation,[142] could withstand the substantial increase in business brought by the late-Victorian age.[143] But it could not be overlooked that an entirely new type of land registration

---

135 See eg Anonymous (n 69) 73: 'Certain parts of the law of Scotland, and some of her institutions, enjoy a high reputation for the enlightened principles on which they are founded, and the practical benefits resulting from their establishment. Our poor laws – our parish schools – our sheriff courts – our system of banking – and our public registers, have met not only with general approval at home, but have each, in their turn, been the subject of eulogy in the sister country.'
136 Mackenzie (n 25) 222. As the context was a rejoinder to an English pamphlet which had opposed the idea of registration, it may be that Mackenzie allowed himself a degree of exaggeration.
137 Ross (n 3) 214. Earlier (207) he had written of 'the celebrated statute we are now analysing, which forms one of the most celebrated areas in our law'.
138 For the history of land registration in England, see S Anderson, 'Property', in *The Oxford History of the Laws of England* vol XII (2010) 213–31; E Cooke, *The New Law of Land Registration* (2003) 15–34. Briefer coverage can also be found in other works such as A W B Simpson, *A History of the Land Law* (2nd edn, 1986) 280–83, and T B F Ruoff et al, *Ruoff and Roper on the Law and Practice of Registered Conveyancing* (looseleaf) ch 1.
139 England indeed was supposed to be casting a furtive eye over the border in order to copy the Scottish system: see eg Anonymous, 'A few remarks on English and Scots law' (1832–36) 2 Edinburgh Law Journal 381. The whole purpose of Mackenzie (n 25) was to explain the benefits of (Scottish) land registration to a sceptical English public.
140 Morton/Bannatyne Report (n 70) 13.
141 J Burns, 'Registration of title to land – Royal Commission's Reports' (1910–11) 22 JR 284.
142 Some of which was described at para 1.8 above.
143 The Law Commissioners who were appointed in the 1830s to consider a variety of subjects, including 'the expediency of making any alteration in the present system of Registration of Deeds relating to Landed Property, particularly in regard to the local Registers for Counties', professed themselves satisfied with the current arrangements: 'The records, indeed, at present, are under very intelligent and skilful superintendence, which has carried reform into every branch of the establishment, providing for the preservation of records that were perishing, insuring the proper formation of those that are in progress, and rendering the whole accessible and available to the public in a degree, and ultimately at a rate, which will make the great registers of the country,

system, originating in the Hanseatic cities of north Germany, was now coming into vogue and seemed likely to be adopted in England itself.[144] That system was registration of title.

REGISTRATION OF TITLE

1.13 Registration of deeds and registration of title

'Apparently every system of registration in the Empire can be classed as deeds registration or title registration': so wrote James Hogg at the start of his magisterial survey of *Registration of Title to Land throughout the Empire* published in 1920.[145] A deeds register is one which holds copies or summaries of all significant deeds affecting land; a title register commits itself as to the deeds' legal effect, and guarantees the result. The former registers deeds; the latter registers the property rights for which the deeds vouch. So if a person applies to register a disposition of land, a deeds register will disclose the disposition and a title register the fact that the person is now owner.[146]

The Register of Sasines, of course, was a register of deeds. The question came to be whether Scotland should abandon such a register and adopt instead a register of title.

1.14 Origins and development

From modest beginnings in a few cities of northern Germany,[147] registration of title spread to many of the German states in the nineteenth century as well as to the territories of the Habsburg Empire.[148] On the other side of the world, meanwhile, registration of title was introduced to South Australia in 1858, partly at the instigation of Robert Torrens, a member of the legislative assembly and

---

not in name, but in reality, a publication to the lieges': see *Third Report of Her Majesty's Law Commissioners* (n 76) xxxviii. By mid-century, however, the rapid increase of business had made reform seem necessary. In the period 1863–1928 the existing system of registration was subject to four separate committees of inquiry (conveniently listed in Appendix B to the Macmillan Report (n 19)), namely (a) the Morton/Bannatyne Report (n 70) (1863); (b) the report by Lords Gifford and Curriehill (1875); (c) the Low Report (n 78) (1897); and (d) the report chaired by Lord Fleming on the Registration of Writs (1928, with a supplementary report in 1932): available at National Records of Scotland HH41/2672. For a review of the Low Report, see Burns (n 71).

144 As recommended by the *Report of the Commissioners appointed to consider the Subject of Registration of Title with reference to the Sale and Transfer of Land* (1857, C 2215) and implemented, in the first place, by the Land Registry Act 1862 (25 & 26 Vict c 53).
145 J E Hogg, *Registration of Title to Land throughout the Empire: a treatise on the law relating to warranty of title to land by registration and transactions with registered land in Australia, New Zealand, Canada, England, Ireland, West Indies, Malaya, &c* (1920) 1.
146 For a full account of registration of title, see *Reports by the Royal Commission on Registration of Title in Scotland* (1910, Cd 5316) ('Dunedin Report') 28. Note, however, that it supposes what is not necessarily the case, namely that entries on the register 'shall have absolute validity, and shall be on all occasions and for all purposes complete legal proof of the rights and liabilities recorded in it.'
147 Morris (n 133) 103; M Raff, *Private Property and Environmental Responsibility: A Comparative Study of German Real Property Law* (2003) ch 3.
148 The position at the end of the century was the subject of a report to Parliament by C Fortescue-Brickdale, the Assistant Registrar of the English Land Registry: see *Registration of Title to Land: General and Detailed Reports of the Assistant Registrar of the Land Registry on the Systems of Registration of Title now in operation in Germany and Austria-Hungary* (1896, C 8139). A summary can be found at pp 7–8.

later registrar-general for deeds,[149] and within a few decades this 'Torrens system' could be found throughout Australia, in New Zealand, in the prairie provinces and territories of Canada, and in parts of the United States of America. The developments in the two hemispheres were linked for, notwithstanding Torrens' claim that his system was modelled on the registration of ships, it is now clear that it was influenced by a Hamburg lawyer resident in Adelaide, Ulrich Hübbe, although the extent of this influence remains contested.[150]

When England, after long deliberation, took some first tentative steps towards a national system of land registration, it was natural that registration of title should be favoured over what by now seemed the distinctly old-fashioned system of registration of deeds.[151] The initial legislation, in 1862 and 1875,[152] was a failure, largely because the scheme was voluntary, but an Act of 1897,[153] over strong opposition from the legal profession, made registration compulsory, although initially only for the county of London.[154] The previous year the Assistant Registrar of the Land Registry had visited Germany and Austria-Hungary and produced a detailed report on their systems of registration of title.[155]

For as long as the English system was unsuccessful, Scottish lawyers could regard it with equanimity, even condescension. But by the start of the new century there was a growing view that Scotland too should introduce, or at least consider introducing, a system of registration of title. A pamphlet issued by Glasgow Corporation, itself a prolific user of the Register of Sasines, set out the case for change,[156] and in 1906 the new Liberal Government established a Royal Commission, under the chairmanship of the Lord President, Lord Dunedin, to 'inquire into the expediency of instituting in Scotland a system of Registration of Title'.[157] A pilot scheme ran for a few months in Fife.[158] As in England, the legal profession turned out to be largely opposed to any move from the current

---

149 See R R Torrens, *The South Australian System of Conveyancing by Registration of Title, with Instructions for the Guidance of Parties dealing, illustrated by Copies of the Books and Forms in use in the Lands Titles Office* (1859).
150 Raff (n 147) ch 1; A Esposito, 'A Comparison of the Australian (Torrens) System of Land Registration of 1858 and the Law of Hamburg in the 1850s' (2003) 7 Australian Journal of Legal History 193; A Esposito, 'Ulrich Hübbe's Role in the Creation of the Torrens System of Land Registration in South Australia' (2003) 24 Adelaide LR 263; H K Lucke, 'Ulrich Hübbe or Robert R Torrens – The Germans in Early South Australia' (2005) 26 Adelaide LR 211; G Taylor, 'Is the Torrens System German?' (2008) 29 Journal of Legal History 253; G Taylor, 'The Torrens System – Definitely not German' (2009) 30 Adelaide LR 195; H K Lucke, 'Ulrich Hübbe and the Torrens System: Hübbe's German Background, His Life in Australia and His Contribution to the Creation of the Torrens System' (2009) 30 Adelaide LR 213.
151 The supposed shortcomings of a system of registration of deeds (or 'assurances') were set out at p 10 of the *Report of the Commissioners* (n 144). In particular, such a system would do nothing to eliminate the need for repeated examination of title, or facilitate the transfer of land. The *Report* makes no attempt to draw on the experience of registration of deeds in Scotland.
152 Land Registry Act 1862 (25 & 26 Vict c 53); Land Transfer Act 1875 (38 & 39 Vict c 87).
153 Land Transfer Act 1897 (60 & 61 Vict c 65).
154 Anderson (n 138) 190–222.
155 *Registration of Title to Land* (n 148). It raised some interest in Scotland: see J Burns, 'Land transfer in Germany and Austria' (1897) 9 JR 155.
156 Noted in Anonymous, 'Land Transfer reform in Scotland' (1904) 16 JR 316.
157 The Royal Commission reported in 1910: see Dunedin Report (n 146). Voluminous *Minutes of Evidence* were published at the same time, as Cd 5357, and record ten days of oral evidence.
158 The results are described by John Maclagan, the Chief Assistant Keeper, in *Minutes of Evidence* (n 157) 198–201.

system,[159] but those whose writing guided the profession on conveyancing matters were divided, with James Sturrock sceptical of the benefits of registration of title[160] but Professor J P Wood of Edinburgh University[161] and John Burns[162] strongly in favour.

1.15 For and against

The main argument in favour of registration of title was its potential to reduce what today would be called transaction costs (and especially information costs).[163] The Register of Sasines, it was accepted, already achieved publicity and also security of title in the sense of protecting acquirers from fraud caused by latent deeds.[164] In neither respect was it found seriously wanting.[165] But what the Register of Sasines could not do was to remove 'the necessity for the constant re-examination of Title-Deeds whenever any transaction in connection with the property takes place',[166] a cost which bore particularly heavily on the low-value transactions which constituted a majority of all transactions.[167] This cost would be avoided by a system of registration of title, at least once a title had completed the hazardous journey to the register. As the Glasgow Corporation pamphlet put it, a title register was like 'a balance sheet bringing out the net result' rather than, as with the Register of Sasines, 'a system of books with no balance sheet struck, no columns added up, and containing only part of the entries necessary to arrive at the balance'.[168] Who could not prefer the former to the latter? And might such a system not be so simple that laymen could do their own conveyancing and save the expense of employing a lawyer?[169]

But even if the superiority of registration of title were conceded, it did not follow that it should be introduced in Scotland. To move from one system of registration to another would be complicated and expensive. Whether it could be justified would depend on an assessment of that complexity and

---

159 Dunedin Report (n 146) 13. This was mainly on the ground that the existing system already achieved most of the objectives of registration of title.
160 J S Sturrock, 'Registration of title and Scottish Conveyancing' (1908–09) 20 JR 1. Sturrock was the editor of *Conveyancing according to the law of Scotland: being the lectures of the late Allen Menzies* (1900).
161 J P Wood, *Lectures on Conveyancing* (1903) chs 5 and 6. In the book's preface, Wood wrote that: 'I suppose that nowhere is there to be found a better system of land titles by registration of deeds. But I am clear that the time has now come when this system should give place to the more excellent plan of registration of title.'
162 J Burns, 'Registration of title to land – Royal Commission's Reports' (1910–11) 22 JR 237 and 284. Burns (at 285) even sought to connect registration of title to feudal conveyancing by comparing its 'new and clean grant' to the renewal of investiture by charters of resignation.
163 Anonymous (n 156) 317–18. The thinking in England had been on similar lines: see *Report of the Commissioners* (n 144) 10.
164 See paras 1.2–1.4 above.
165 That was thought to be so even in respect of security of title: see Dunedin Report (n 146) 8; Sturrock (n 160) 14.
166 Sturrock (n 160) 14.
167 Dunedin Report (n 146) 14 ('the comparatively large cost of small transactions').
168 Anonymous (n 156) 318.
169 The question of whether laymen might indeed be able to do so was the subject of different views in the Dunedin Report (n 146). While one of the four constituent reports thought that 'this was not at all unlikely to happen in a considerable number of cases, especially with large landowners who employ factors' (40), Lord Dunedin's view (12) was much more sceptical and, in the event, has turned out to be correct.

expense as well as of the likely benefits of the new system.[170] In this calculation an important factor was the merits of the current system, including the fact that search sheets already met some of the functions of the title ledgers or sheets found under systems of registration of title, thus allowing the Register of Sasines to be presented, with some plausibility, as being 'half way between' a deeds and a title register.[171] This insight, however, cut both ways. It might suggest that the transition from deeds to title register would not be hard, for at least one crucial 'stepping stone' was already in place.[172] But equally it might suggest that further development of the existing system would be easier and wiser than its abandonment in favour of something which, in the Scottish context, had not been tried and tested.[173]

In the debates in and around the Royal Commission both approaches were to be found. After four years of deliberation, and unable to agree a common line, the members of the Commission ended up issuing four separate reports.[174] Three were broadly supportive of the introduction of registration of title.[175] The fourth, by the chairman, Lord Dunedin, and two of his colleagues,[176] enlarged at some length on the difficulties of introduction, questioned the advantages that registration of title would bring, and concluded 'that it is not expedient, and would, indeed, be impracticable, *de plano*, to introduce a system of registration of title for the whole of Scotland instead of the existing system'.[177] So firm a conclusion from so authoritative a source was enough for the idea to be abandoned for a generation.

England, meanwhile, was enduring a Royal Commission of its own.[178] The 1897 Act, although an improvement on its predecessors, had resulted mainly in the registration of 'possessory' titles rather than the 'absolute' titles which alone could take full benefit from registration of title.[179] New legislation was needed to fix this and other problems and, after a delay during the years of the War, was finally passed in 1925.[180] As things turned out, the (English) Land Registration Act of 1925 was to be of much greater significance for Scotland than the four competing reports of the Scottish Royal Commission.

---

170 Dunedin Report (n 146) 42; Sturrock (n 160) 2.
171 This was the conclusion of Fortescue-Brickdale in his 1897 report: see *Registration of Title to Land* (n 148) para 300, n. See also Burns (n 71) 39: 'The search-sheet is not a register of title, but it is the only approach to it that we have, and therein lies its value.'
172 Burns (n 162) 285.
173 Sturrock (n 160) 13–15.
174 For a highly critical assessment, see Burns (n 162).
175 Dunedin Report (n 146): reports by (i) J Smith Clark and Samuel Chisholm (19–25); (ii) C Fortescue-Brickdale and R Munro Ferguson (27–44); and (iii) Sheriff N J D Kennedy (45–46). The last of these was more equivocal than the others, but thought that, if registration of title were to be introduced, it should be modelled on systems which already exist as this would 'more quickly and effectively prepare the way for codification of the land law of the United Kingdom' (46).
176 Dunedin Report (n 146): report by Lord Dunedin, W J Dundas, and John Prosser (5–15).
177 Dunedin Report (n 146) 15.
178 The Royal Commission on the Land Transfer Acts issued two reports, in 1909 (Cd 4509, with evidence in Cd 4510) and in 1911 (Cd 5483).
179 Lord Dunedin and his colleagues commented that the predominance of possessory titles 'deprives registration of title of one of its chief advantages, and that it would only be a system of registration of absolute title which would have any attraction in Scotland': see Dunedin Report (n 146) 5.
180 Anderson (n 138) 221–31.

1.16 Reid Committee

The evident success of the English legislation of 1925 led, in time, to renewed interest in registration of title in Scotland. A fresh review, instituted in 1948, lapsed due to the ill-health of its chairman, Lord Macmillan.[181] After further delay, a second committee was appointed in 1959 under the chairmanship of another of the Scottish judges in the House of Lords, Lord Reid. It finally reported in 1963,[182] having sat for sixteen days, of which six were given up to oral evidence.[183]

While the issues were much the same as those which had exercised Lord Dunedin's Royal Commission half a century earlier, the arguments in favour of change were, or were made to seem, much stronger. The present arrangements, the Reid Committee conceded, had 'great merits' and were 'a practical system which works well'.[184] The legal profession, as before, was opposed to change.[185] But in the light of public demand that 'the cost of transactions in heritable property shall be as low as possible', the current system was too cumbersome and expensive.[186] Not only were solicitors' fees a third higher in Scotland than in England, but the complexity of the work was putting undue pressure on the legal profession itself, particularly in view of 'disturbing evidence' that a large rise in conveyancing business had not been accompanied by a commensurate rise in the number of solicitors. On the contrary, there had been more practising solicitors in 1910 than in 1960.[187] Matters could not be allowed to continue as they were.

Nonetheless, the Committee was not unanimous as to what should be done. Two of the members[188] wished to limit intervention to further reform of the Register of Sasines, in particular by introducing certification of titles by the Keeper supported by a (limited) state guarantee.[189] The remaining seven, sceptical as to whether mere reform could achieve a sufficient reduction in transaction costs, supported the introduction of registration of title.[190] Crucially, and by contrast to the Royal Commission of 1910, this recommendation had the support of the chairman.

In reaching this view, and in setting out the key features of the proposed new system,[191] the Reid Committee relied almost entirely on the English Act of 1925. Whereas the 1910 Royal Commission had considered the Torrens system and the systems of registration of title found in Germany and Austria-Hungary, the Reid Committee was only concerned to see whether the English system could be made to work in Scotland. As for systems elsewhere, 'conditions there are so different',

---

181 Macmillan (n 85) 222–25. For contemporary comment, see T B Smith, 'Registration of title to land' 1948 SLT (News) 67. Before Lord Macmillan's resignation, the committee managed to produce a report on the question of whether minute books should be discontinued in the Register of Sasines: see para 1.8 above. This was described on the title page as the 'first report' of the committee, but there was not to be a second.
182 Reid Report (n 19). Typical for its time, its consideration of topics is often exasperatingly brief.
183 Reid Report (n 19) para 2. Appendix A lists the organisations and individuals who gave evidence, whether written or oral.
184 Reid Report (n 19) para 57. See also S R Simpson, *Land Law and Registration* (1976): 'Scotland has indeed a very good deeds system' (104).
185 Reid Report (n 19) para 159(d).
186 Reid Report (n 19) paras 60–63.
187 3,412 as against 3,259: see para 63.
188 H J Carlton and Sir Charles Connell.
189 Reid Report (n 19) paras 129–46, 155–63.
190 Reid Report (n 19) paras 148–54.
191 As to which see paras 89–123.

the Committee explained, that they were not worthy of investigation.[192] The policy choices implicit in the English system, such as the protection for proprietors in possession,[193] were taken by the Reid Committee on trust, without discussion. The implications of the new system for property law were largely ignored. With hindsight it is easy to criticise. And if the parochialism of the Committee's approach, and the lack of deep reflection or even of curiosity, were perhaps typical for their time, the consequences for the eventual legislation were, unfortunately, to be rather serious.

1.17 The road to the 1979 Act

As the Reid Committee itself had suggested,[194] the delivery of its report was followed by the setting up of an expert committee to tease out the details of how the proposed new system might work. A pilot scheme was also set up centred on the parish of Renfrew.[195] Under the chairmanship of the Professor of Conveyancing at Edinburgh University, G L F Henry, the expert committee met on an astonishing 101 occasions over a period of four years.[196] The resulting report included a 70-clause Bill as well as model land registration rules, draft forms, and an explanatory commentary.[197] After almost a decade of further delay a Land Registration (Scotland) Bill was introduced to the House of Lords on 23 November 1978.

In preparing draft legislation, the Henry Committee had felt it necessary to say that it had 'no intention of usurping the function of the Parliamentary draftsman'.[198] It need not have worried. The Land Registration Bill bore little resemblance to the Henry Committee's draft in respect of form, and less than might have been expected in respect of substance. The Bill was short and gave the impression of having been put together in a hurry. Its Parliamentary passage was disrupted by the Government's defeat on a no-confidence motion on 28 March 1979, meaning that the final stages had to be compressed into the few days left before the dissolution.[199] Royal Assent was given on 4 April. From start to finish – from Lord Dunedin's Royal Commission to the Act's Royal Assent – it had taken 70 years.

---

192 Reid Report (n 19) para 66. Later, the Henry Committee was to do a little better, looking at a range of Torrens systems. Even so, the Germanic systems, which might have been especially useful in view of Scotland's generally civilian system of property law, were dismissed with the thought that 'in determining to what extent we should investigate any current system we were governed by the fact that our task was to devise a system suitable to the law and practice of conveyancing in Scotland': see *Scheme for the Introduction and Operation of Registration of Title to Land in Scotland: Report by a Committee appointed by the Secretary of State for Scotland* (Cmnd 4137, 1969) ('Henry Report') para 6.
193 Reid Report (n 19) para 115: 'In England we understand that only very exceptionally is the Register rectified in the face of possession; whether or not he has a valid title, the person in possession is normally allowed to remain, and compensation is paid to the other claimant. We take the view that the same rule should apply in Scotland.'
194 Reid Report (n 19) paras 67 and 90.
195 Henry Report (n 192) paras 10–15.
196 Henry Report (n 192) para 2.
197 The Bill, Rules, and forms comprise, respectively, parts I–III of the Committee's scheme of registration of title (pp 13–135). The provisions of the Bill are to be referred to as 'paragraphs' and the provisions of the Rules as 'rules' (para 19). The scheme 'in general follows the outlines of Chapters VII and VIII of the Reid Committee Report' (para 16).
198 Henry Report (n 192) para 19.
199 Parliament was dissolved on 7 April 1979. For further discussion of the preparation and passing of the Bill, see K G C Reid, 'Beneficial Ownership and the Land Register', in A J M Steven, R G Anderson and J MacLeod (eds), *Essays in Honour of Professor George Gretton* (forthcoming, 2017).

Chapter 2

The 1979 Act and its Reform

THE 1979 ACT

2.1 Introduction

Given the fundamental nature of the change involved, the legislative basis of registration of title, in its first incarnation, was surprisingly slender. No more than 20 sections of the Land Registration (Scotland) Act 1979 were given up to the topic, and this was supplemented by delegated legislation in the form of Land Registration Rules, themselves rather short. Over time amendments were made to the Act, and the original Land Registration Rules of 1980[1] were replaced by the Rules of 2006.[2] Nonetheless the provisions on registration of title remained disconcertingly brief until they were replaced, on 8 December 2012, by the 124 sections and five schedules of the Land Registration etc (Scotland) Act 2012.[3]

Now that the relevant provisions of the 1979 Act have been repealed, they can properly be referred to in the past tense. But as many of those holding title to land today acquired their title under the 1979 Act, the rules in that Act will remain of importance for years to come. In this chapter we seek to give an overview account of the 1979 Act; more detailed analysis of particular points can be found elsewhere.[4]

2.2 The Land Register of Scotland

The 1979 Act established a new register, the Land Register of Scotland.[5] Like the Register of Sasines, it was public and under the management of the Keeper of the Registers of Scotland. Unlike that register, it was conceived, not as a

---

1 Land Registration (Scotland) Rules 1980, SI 1980/1413, as amended by SI 1982/974, SI 1988/1143, SI 1995/248, SI 1998/3100, and SSI 2004/476.
2 Land Registration (Scotland) Rules 2006, SSI 2006/485.
3 The relevant provisions of the 1979 Act were repealed by the Land Registration etc (Scotland) Act 2012 s 119, sch 5 para 19. The only significant survivor is the 'translation' provision, s 29. This provides that, subject to the exceptions listed in sch 3, 'any reference, however expressed, in any enactment passed before, or during the same Session as, this Act or in any instrument made before the passing of this Act under any enactment to the Register of Sasines or to the recording of a deed therein shall be construed as a reference to the register or, as the case may be, to registration'. We do not know why the 'translation' provision was left in the 1979 Act.
4 See the following texts, with references: G L Gretton and A J M Steven, *Property, Trusts and Succession* (1st edn, 2009) ch 6; G L Gretton and K G C Reid, *Conveyancing* (4th edn, 2011) ch 8; *Professor McDonald's Conveyancing Manual* (7th edn by D A Brand, A J M Steven and S Wortley, 2004) paras 11.20 ff. For accounts which focus on the practical aspects of the Act, see I Davis and A Rennie (eds), *Registration of Title Practice Book* (2nd edn, 2000); A J McDonald, *Registration of Title Manual* (1986).
5 Land Registration (Scotland) Act 1979 s 1.

23

register of deeds, but of 'interests in land',[6] by which was meant, more or less, real rights in land.[7] The general idea was that, for any given property, the Land Register would list the real rights, and the names of those who held them. Deeds themselves were not to be registered, only rights; but as applications for registration were based on deeds or other documents, and as copies were retained as before, it remained normal, if not strictly accurate, to refer to the deeds too as having been registered.[8]

With the exception of the right of long lease, which now had to be registered,[9] the Act did not alter the fact that certain subordinate real rights, such as servitudes and short leases, could be acquired without registration. Such rights, however, were given the new name, taken from English legislation, of 'overriding interests'.[10] Some overriding interests could be 'noted' on the Register, although not registered as such;[11] their (general) absence from the Register was an unavoidable limitation on what was sometimes called the 'mirror principle',[12] ie the objective of presenting a complete account of the rights affecting any given plot of land.

The mechanism for presenting this information was (and continues to be under the 2012 Act) a 'title sheet', held nowadays in electronic form and divided into four sections: (A) the property section; (B) the proprietorship section; (C) the charges section; and (D) the burdens section.[13] The Register, in effect, comprised a collection of title sheets. The names of the sections give a good idea of their content. The property section identifies the property; the proprietorship section gives the name and designation of the current owner (but not of previous owners); the charges section (now renamed the securities section, in conformity with Scots terminology) lists any heritable securities; and the burdens section gives the details

---

6 LR(S)A 1979 s 1(1). Once much in vogue, the term 'interest in land' has now been largely removed from private-law legislation, especially by the Abolition of Feudal Tenure etc (Scotland) Act 2000 s 76(1), sch 12; see also Scottish Law Commission, *Report No 168 on Abolition of the Feudal System* (1999) para 9.5. Draft amendments to remove the term from the 1979 Act itself were prepared by the Scottish Law Commission but not proceeded with, partly because of the evident complexity which they would produce and partly in anticipation of the replacement of the 1979 Act by new legislation. The term does not appear in the 2012 Act.
7 The definition in LR(S)A 1979 s 28(1) was 'any right in or over land, including any heritable security or servitude but excluding any lease which is not a real right'.
8 The registration of deeds is restored by the Land Registration etc (Scotland) Act 2012 s 21(1).
9 LR(S)A 1979 s 3(3). The provision also applied to ownership rights under udal tenure. A long lease as a contract was effective without registration, but registration was necessary for the lease to have real effect.
10 'Overriding interest' is subject to a lengthy definition in LR(S)A 1979 s 28(1). The term and indeed the concept are dispensed with by the 2012 Act, although off-register rights remain, as before: see Scottish Law Commission, *Report No 222 on Land Registration* (2010) ('SLC Report 222') paras 7.1–7.15, and paras 4.26–4.28 below.
11 LR(S)A 1979 s 6(4). Such interests could not simply be 'registered' because registration under the Act had specific legal consequences: see para 2.7 below.
12 This term is widely used in the international literature on registration of title. It seems to have been coined by Theodore Ruoff, the Chief Land Registrar in England and Wales: see T Ruoff, 'An Englishman looks at the Torrens system' (1952) 26 Australian LJ 118, 162, 194 and 228 at 118 (reprinted, with other papers on land registration, in T Ruoff, *An Englishman Looks at the Torrens System: Being some Provocative Essays on the Operation of the System after One Hundred Years* (1957)). The concept is, however, not free from difficulty. The term could be taken as suggesting that the rights in the property exist independently of the register and that the task of the register is to record them with mirror-like accuracy. That is true for some types of right. But for the most part a title-registration system means that registration is a necessary condition for the right in question to be constituted, transferred or extinguished.
13 Further details can be found in the Land Registration (Scotland) Rules 2006 rr 3–7.

of real burdens, of such servitudes as have been constituted by registration, and of other encumbrances. Each title sheet has its own number, which includes an abbreviated version of the name of the county,[14] and the property could (and can) be described in conveyancing deeds simply by reference to the number.[15]

Title sheets represented interests in land rather than (as now under the 2012 Act)[16] physical plots. Following the pattern long since established for search sheets in the Register of Sasines,[17] a separate title sheet was created for every ownership (or 'property') interest[18] and for every long lease or long sub-lease. These were what were sometimes called the 'primary' interests in land,[19] and for every physical plot[20] there might be two or more such interests (and hence title sheets): ownership, long lease, long sub-lease, and so on. Other real rights were merely 'secondary' interests in land and, not commanding title sheets of their own, were entered on the title sheets of the primary interest to which they were most closely related.[21] So real burdens were entered in the burdens section of the ownership title sheet of the land that they burdened; a standard security over a lease was entered in the charges section of the leasehold interest.

In practice, the title sheets were supplemented by an application record (listing pending applications for registration), an archive record (containing copies of all documents presented for registration), and a digital mapping system (a geospatial database which included an index map).[22] None of these, however, was recognised by the legislation or, therefore, was formally part of the Land Register, an omission which has been put right by the 2012 Act.[23]

2.3 Description by OS map

In deeds recorded in the Register of Sasines, the manner in which property was described varied from the precise to the impressionistic, and from the brief to the verbose.[24] In the twentieth century there was an increasing tendency to use

---

14 Eg REN12345: see para 3.9 below.
15 Land Registration (Scotland) Rules 2006 r 23. The idea of a dedicated number or symbol goes back to the *Report of the Commissioners appointed to inquire as to the State of the Registers of Land Rights in the Counties and Burghs of Scotland* (1863) ('Morton/Bannatyne Report') 39–40, when it was rejected by the Keeper as 'unworkable in practice, and attended with much danger'.
16 Land Registration etc (Scotland) Act 2012 s 3(1): see further paras 4.3 and 4.6 below.
17 For search sheets, see para 1.8 above.
18 Under feudal law, ownership (*dominium*) was itself divided into the right of *dominium utile* and one or more rights of superiority (*dominium directum*). Each had its own title sheet. The potential complexity was so great that it was sometimes used as an argument against introducing registration of title at all: see eg *Reports by the Royal Commission on Registration of Title in Scotland* (1910, Cd 5316) ('Dunedin Report') 9–10. On the abolition of the feudal system on 28 November 2014, all superiority rights were extinguished (and their title sheets deleted), and the right of *dominium utile* was upgraded to a right of full ownership: see Abolition of Feudal Tenure etc (Scotland) Act 2000 s 2. Landownership ceased to be feudal and became allodial.
19 Although the term does not appear in the legislation.
20 Or for every separate tenement carved out of a plot, eg minerals or the right of salmon fishings.
21 LR(S)A 1979 s 5(1).
22 SLC Report 222 paras 4.1–4.14.
23 LR(S)A 2012 s 2. See further para 4.1 below.
24 An instructive account of the types of description then commonly encountered was given in the Morton/Bannatyne Report (n 15) 37. For example, rural properties were 'sometimes distinguished by a reference to the amount in Scots money at which they stood valued in the national census or valuation of lands in Scotland made in the fifteenth century, as a "twenty pound land", or "thirty-shilling land", or "ten merk land", and so on. Then there often follows a long string of descriptive words – castles, towers, fortalices, manor places,

plans, at least for deeds splitting off plots of land for the first time. Even so, many descriptions were of a low standard, making it difficult or impossible to know the precise location of the boundaries.

As long ago as 1863, the Commission appointed to examine the state of the land registers had 'considered whether the elaborate Survey of Scotland by the Ordnance Department, now far advanced towards completion, might not be rendered available to supersede the rude and cumbrous style of description of property usual in our deeds'[25] before concluding that the task was too hard to be contemplated as part of a reform of land registration.[26] Half a century later, and based on the experience of the Torrens and other systems of registration of title, the Royal Commission chaired by Lord Dunedin thought that 'without identification by map ... there cannot be any system of registration of title properly so called, because mapping is the only method whereby it is possible to have an office identification of units of land, without which the register cannot be conclusive'.[27] Conscious of the difficulty of translating poor Sasine descriptions on to an OS map, the Reid Committee was to be more cautious, concluding that, while maps should be used 'in the great majority of cases', it would sometimes be necessary to supplement or even replace a map with a written description drawn verbatim from the titles.[28]

In the event, the 1979 Act required that all descriptions of land in the property section of title sheets must 'consist of or include a description of it based on the Ordnance Map'.[29] But the fears of the Reid Committee have since proved to be well-founded, and the accurate plotting of Sasine descriptions is a persistent source of difficulty and concern, and of claims against the Keeper.[30]

A difficulty of a different kind was the limitations of scale imposed by the OS map itself. On the Land Register, the title plan used (and uses still) the largest OS scale available for the area in question. This is one of 1:1250, 1:2500 or 1:10,000 depending on whether the area is, respectively, urban, rural or moorland.[31] Even on the largest of these (1:1250), however, 1 millimetre on the title plan is the equivalent of 1.25 metres on the ground, so that there is an inbuilt degree of

---

houses, biggings, yards, orchards, parks, mosses, muirs, meadows, outfield and infield, milns, miln lands, multures, sucken and sequels, woods, fishings, coal, coalheughs, tenants, tenandries and services of free tenants, *annexis, connexis*, parts, pendicles, and pertinents whatsoever.' Another type of description relied on 'the ancient names of a great number of small farms and fields'.

25 Morton/Bannatyne Report (n 15) 37.
26 Morton/Bannatyne Report (n 15) 37–40.
27 Dunedin Report (n 18) 7. The Report added that maps would allow an 'unprofessional man ... to see for himself whether or not the proposing seller really is proprietor of what he proposes to sell'.
28 *Registration of Title to Land in Scotland: Report by a Committee appointed by the Secretary of State for Scotland* (Cmnd 2032, 1963) ('Reid Report') para 102. This was faithfully followed by para 36 of Part I of the scheme devised by the Henry Committee: see *Scheme for the Introduction and Operation of Registration of Title to Land in Scotland: Report by a Committee appointed by the Secretary of State for Scotland* (Cmnd 4137, 1969) ('Henry Report').
29 LR(S)A 1979 s 6(1)(a). See also Land Registration (Scotland) Rules 2006 r 4(2). The description on the Register, furthermore, must be self-contained and not dependent on extrinsic evidence: *PMP Plus Ltd v Keeper of the Registers of Scotland* 2009 SLT (Lands Tr) 2, para 60; *Lundin Homes Ltd v Keeper of the Registers of Scotland* 2013 SLT (Lands Tr) 73, paras 60–62.
30 See eg *Nicol v Keeper of the Registers of Scotland* 2013 SLT (Lands Tr) 56; *Burton v Keeper of the Registers of Scotland* 2014 SLT (Lands Tr) 69; *Gray v Keeper of the Registers of Scotland* 2014 SLT (Lands Tr) 117; *Van Eck v Keeper of the Registers of Scotland* 2014 SLT (Lands Tr) 117.
31 *Registration of Title Practice Book* (n 4) para 4.22.

imprecision.[32] In cases where a plan accompanying the deed was drawn to a more generous scale, registration made matters less clear not more.[33]

2.4 Entering the Register

Entry to the Register of Sasines was possible in only one way: by registration (or 'recording') of a deed. By contrast, the 1979 Act provided four points of entry to the Land Register.[34] As before, registration was the way in which deeds – or, more accurately, interests in land based on deeds – gained access to the Register.[35] A conveyancing transaction, therefore, led to registration. But there could also be 'noting', in the case of overriding interests,[36] and 'rectification', where an error on the Register needed to be corrected.[37] Finally, when a property switched from the Register of Sasines to the Land Register, and the new title sheet had to be populated from the existing Sasine deeds by, for example, listing existing heritable securities and real burdens,[38] this information was 'entered' rather than registered.

Importantly, of the four methods of adding to or altering the Register, only two – registration and rectification – had distinct (though different)[39] legal effects. Noting, as its name implied, was simply a means of giving information. And the entering of existing rights on a new title sheet had no effect on the validity or otherwise of those rights, for they had already been constituted (or, as the case may be, not constituted) by registration of a deed in the Register of Sasines. If, however, they were omitted (whether deliberately or by accident), this had legal consequences, for most encumbrances were extinguished by the mere fact of not being included in the title sheet.[40]

2.5 Operational areas

It was taken for granted that the new Register could not be extended to the whole country at the same time but would have to be introduced in phases, county by county.[41] Renfrewshire, part of which had acted as a pilot for the Henry Committee,[42] was chosen as the first county, and became an 'operational area' for the purposes of the 1979 Act on 6 April 1981.[43] Thereafter the intention was for matters to proceed fairly rapidly, with the whole country to be operational by 1989.[44] Not only would

---

32 *Registration of Title Practice Book* (n 4) para 4.26.
33 Scottish Law Commission, *Discussion Paper No 130 on Land Registration: Miscellaneous Issues* (2005) ('SLC DP 130') paras 2.14–2.23. For mapping more generally, see ch 5 below.
34 With the ending of the noting of overriding interests, these have been reduced by the 2012 Act to three.
35 LR(S)A 1979 s 2: see para 2.6 below.
36 LR(S)A 1979 s 6(4): see para 2.2 above.
37 LR(S)A 1979 s 9: see para 2.9 below.
38 LR(S)A 1979 ss 5(1)(a)(i) and 6(1).
39 Further, while registration almost always had a legal effect, rectification had a legal effect only in respect of bijural inaccuracies: see, respectively, paras 2.7 and 2.9 below.
40 LR(S)A 1979 s 3(1)(a): see para 2.7 below. This, however, was subject to the possibility of reinstatement by rectification: see eg *Santander UK plc v Keeper of the Registers of Scotland* [2013] CSOH 24, 2013 SLT 362.
41 That had been the recommendation of both the Reid Committee and the Henry Committee: see Reid Report (n 28) paras 92 and 93; Henry Report (n 28) paras 20–22.
42 Paragraph 1.17 above.
43 Land Registration (Scotland) Act 1979 (Commencement No 1) Order 1980, SI 1980/1412.
44 *Registration of Title Practice Book* (1st edn, 1981) para A.102.

this reduce the period during which two registration systems were in use for the same type of transaction, but it would also ensure that the benefits of registration of title were made available as widely and as quickly as possible.[45] In the event, the processing of titles proved more difficult and slower than originally anticipated, thus giving some succour to those who, for decades past, had argued that the cost of change of registration system would exceed any benefit that could arise from it.[46]

After the admission of Glasgow to the new Register in 1985, the timetable fell into serious arrears and it was to be seven years before a further county – Clackmannanshire, the smallest in Scotland – could be added. The larger population centres outside the Glasgow area had to wait: Aberdeen until 1996 and Midlothian (which includes Edinburgh) until 2001. The final counties became operational only in 2003.[47] A complete list of the 33 counties and the dates on which they became operational can be found in chapter 3.

Even when a county became operational, deeds in some types of case continued to be recorded in the Register of Sasines.[48] The reasons for this were practical. Before registration was possible in the Land Register, a title sheet had to be made up; and as title sheets were only allowed for primary interests in land (ie for ownership and long lease), it followed that, in the first instance, only deeds concerning such interests – typically dispositions or the grant or assignation of a long lease – could (and must) be registered in the Land Register.[49] For the time being, standard securities and other secondary interests in land continued to be registered in the Register of Sasines, and this would change only when and if the primary interest to which they related had made the switch to the new Register.[50] There was also another constraint. As 'first registration' (ie the first time on which a primary interest was registered in the Land Register) involved significant work and expense, it was felt that donations (which do not normally involve an examination of title) should be exempt.[51] So a disposition (or assignation of a lease) by way of gift did not trigger first registration,[52] with the result that land which was handed down the family rather than sold would remain in the Register of Sasines for the foreseeable future.

Where a transaction triggered first registration, a new title sheet was (and is) made up by the Keeper's officials on the basis of the Sasine titles and the name of the applicant was entered in the proprietorship section. The switch, once made, was irreversible. A property, having entered the Land Register, would not revert to the Register of Sasines; and all future deeds in relation to that property, whether concerning primary or secondary interests, required likewise to be registered in the Land Register.

---

45 Both points were made by the Henry Report (n 28) paras 21 and 22.
46 Paragraphs 1.15 and 1.16 above.
47 Land Registration (Scotland) Act 1979 (Commencement No 16) Order 2002, SSI 2002/432.
48 To some extent this continues to be true. But the Land Registration etc (Scotland) Act 2012 s 48 provides for the phased closure of the Register of Sasines, and the stage is approaching when no deeds can be recorded there. See ch 7.
49 LR(S)A 1979 s 2(1)(a).
50 LR(S)A 1979 s 2(2), (3).
51 Reid Report (n 28) para 91.
52 LR(S)A 1979 s 2(1)(a)(ii) required 'valuable consideration'. Transfer in consideration of marriage was treated as valuable consideration: see s 2(1)(a)(iii).

Nonetheless many properties remained on the Register of Sasines. By the end of 2014, when the 2012 Act replaced the Act of 1979, the move from Sasine to Land Register was little more than half-way complete as measured by number of titles and around a quarter complete as measured by land mass. Some 1.5 million titles, representing about 58% of all property titles and 26% of Scotland's land mass, were held on the Land Register and were being added to at a rate of around 45,000 per year.[53] One of the objects of the 2012 Act was to speed this process up; and since the Act was passed the ambitious – some would say unattainable – target has been announced of completing the Register by 2024.[54]

2.6 Registration: mechanics[55]

Applications for registration were made on the basis of a deed or other document. An application form required to be completed,[56] and the Keeper had a broad general discretion to accept the application or refuse it, although there were a small number of circumstances (such as where the property was insufficiently described to be identified on the OS map) where applications had to be refused.[57] As part of this process the Keeper's staff examined the deed and, in cases of first registration, the Sasine title which lay behind it.[58] If the validity of the title was in doubt, the Keeper was more likely to exclude indemnity than to refuse the application altogether.[59] Assuming the application was accepted, the date of registration was the date on which it was received, and this date was preserved even where the application was deficient and required to be corrected or supplemented by further documentation.[60]

Registration was (and is) completed by entering the applicant's name in the appropriate section of the title sheet – in the proprietorship section in the case of a disposition, for example, and in the charges section in the case of a standard security. For first registrations it was necessary to make up a new title sheet on the basis of the Sasine writs which accompanied the application.[61] On completion of registration the deed was returned to the applicant accompanied, in the case of a primary interest in land, by an official copy of the title sheet known as a land certificate, and in the case of a standard security by a charge certificate.[62] The land

---

53 Registers of Scotland, *Completion of the Land Register: Public Consultation* (2014) paras 4, 16 and 17. For more on completion of the Register, see para 2.14 below.
54 See para 7.4 below.
55 For fuller details of the procedure, see Scottish Law Commission, *Discussion Paper No 128 on Land Registration: Registration, Rectification and Indemnity* (2005) ('SLC DP 128') part 4.
56 Land Registration (Scotland) Rules 2006 r 9. The forms were set out in sch 1. Unlike the current system, a different form was used depending on whether the application was for first registration (form 1), a dealing in registered land (form 2), or a transfer of part (form 3).
57 LR(S)A 1979 s 4(1), (2).
58 Under the current system the examination of the title has largely been abandoned, Registers of Scotland relying instead on the certification of the applicant's solicitor: see paras 8.11 and 8.15 below.
59 LR(S)A 1979 s 12(2). For indemnity see para 2.10 below. Latterly, however, the Keeper's practice was often to refuse applications made on the basis of *a non domino* dispositions: see *Registration of Title Practice Book* (n 4) para 6.4.
60 LR(S)A 1979 s 4(3); Land Registration (Scotland) Rules 2006 rr 12 and 13. This system too has been abandoned under the 2012 Act; instead, under the 'one-shot' rule a defective application will be rejected: see Land Registration etc (Scotland) Act 2012 s 21(3), and para 9.10 below.
61 LR(S)A 1979 s 5(1).
62 LR(S)A 1979 s 5(2)–(5); Land Registration (Scotland) Rules 2006 rr 15 and 16.

certificate, of which there could only be one, was seen as the 'title deed' for the property and (until the requirement was dropped in 2006) had to be submitted to the Keeper whenever an application for registration was made. The land certificate could be updated and the idea was that it would exist for decades, growing dog-eared as it passed from owner to owner.

2.7 Registration: legal effect

Little attention was given at first to the legal effect of registration, and the relevant provision in the Act was mystifying in its opaqueness.[63] In time, however, it came to be accepted that registration had two broad effects, one positive and the other negative.[64] The positive effect was to give legal force to the change made to the Register as a result of the application. So when, in respect of a disposition, the Keeper changed the name in the proprietorship section from A (the granter of the disposition) to B (the grantee and applicant for registration), the result was for B to become owner in place of A. And when, in respect of a discharge of a standard security, the Keeper removed the security from the charges section, the result was to extinguish the security. Of course, in the normal case the applicant's deed would be valid, in which case there was no difference in outcome[65] between registration in the Land Register and in the Register of Sasines. But even if the deed was not valid, the result in respect of the Land Register was unchanged: the act of registration took effect anyway.[66]

The negative effect was confined to applications in respect of primary interests. On being registered as proprietor of a primary interest (ie as owner of land or tenant under a long lease), an applicant took the property subject only to those heritable securities, real burdens and other encumbrances which were listed on the title sheet.[67] If, in error – typically made on first registration – an encumbrance had been missed out, that encumbrance would be extinguished at the moment of registration of the applicant's title. Only overriding interests were exempt: an encumbrance constituted off-register (such as a short lease or prescriptive servitude) would continue to affect the property despite not being mentioned on the title sheet.

Neither effect was novel in the context of systems of registration of title. Both could be found in the English legislation of 1925 on which the 1979 Act was based,[68] and under the Torrens systems of Australia and elsewhere. But the positive effect, in particular, rewrote the rules of transfer in Scotland. For hundreds of years, ownership of land had been transferred by a consensual juridical act signified by a written deed or deeds and, until 1845, by symbolical delivery performed on the land itself. Registration, when introduced in 1617, supplemented rather than replaced this consensual act; indeed until *Young v Leith* in 1847[69] it was not settled

---

63 LR(S)A 1979 s 3(1). For an analysis of the difficulties, see SLC DP 128 paras 5.1–5.7
64 Scottish Law Commission, *Discussion Paper No 125 on Land Registration: Void and Voidable Titles* (2004) ('SLC DP 125') paras 5.1–5.6; SLC DP 128 paras 5.8–5.15.
65 There was still, however, a difference in legal effect, because in the Land Register the result derived from the alteration in the Register and not from the deed which led to that alteration.
66 See eg *Santander UK plc v Keeper of the Registers of Scotland* [2013] CSOH 24, 2013 SLT 362 (forged discharge); *Chalmers v Chalmers* [2015] CSIH 75, 2015 SLT 793 (forged disposition).
67 LR(S)A 1979 s 3(1)(a).
68 Land Registration Act 1925 s 20.
69 (1847) 9 D 932.

that it was needed to obtain a real right.[70] The 1979 Act turned this process on its head. Admittedly, in the future as in the past, dispositions would continue to be granted and delivered. But now it was registration, and registration alone, which brought about the transfer. For registration of title, under the 1979 Act, embraced a system of 'title by registration'[71] – of title flowing from the Register itself rather than from the underlying disposition. The juridical act which mattered was that of the Keeper and not that of the parties. From the perspective of property law the result was startling and unsettling.[72] Worse, the scheme turned out to have conceptual and practical difficulties which led, in time, to calls for its replacement.[73]

2.8 'Actual' inaccuracy and 'bijural' inaccuracy

The Register could sometimes be wrong. In the language of the 1979 Act there might be an 'inaccuracy';[74] and 'inaccuracy' in turn was the key to both 'rectification' and 'indemnity'.[75] In principle, the Keeper was able to rectify inaccuracies, but had then to indemnify anyone suffering loss as a result.[76] In the event that rectification was not possible, as for various reasons was often the case,[77] any person suffering loss as a result of *non*-rectification – or in other words, due to the continuation of the inaccuracy – was, equally, entitled to indemnity.[78] 'Inaccuracy' was thus one of the core ideas of the Act. On it depended the prospects for both rectification and indemnity. The term, however, was left undefined in the Act, and it was to take a number of years before litigation came to determine its meaning.

At its simplest an inaccuracy might be no more than a typographical error – an obvious mis-transcription of a word or name at the time of registration. It could also come about by supervening events – by the dissolution (in the case of a body corporate) of the owner, for example, or the extinction of a right by prescription – so that an entry which was correct when first made might become incorrect later on. All these are examples of where the Register failed to represent the actual legal and factual position. In the terminology later employed by the Scottish Law Commission, they were 'actual' inaccuracies.[79]

But there could also be a different kind of mistake. On registration the Keeper might attribute rights to the wrong person, or remove a right which ought still to exist. Thus suppose that Betty drew up a disposition of land in her own favour, forged the signature of Alan, the owner, and presented the disposition for

---

70 Paragraph 1.6 above.
71 A term often used to describe the result of the English system of registration of title, and of the many Torrens systems which employ 'immediate indefeasibility': see eg A Goymour, 'Mistaken registrations of land: exploding the myth of "title by registration"' (2013) 72 CLJ 617. For an early example of the usage, by the pioneering scholar of registration of title, see J E Hogg, 'The progress of registration of title' (1915) 27 JR 195, 201.
72 See eg K G C Reid, *The Law of Property in Scotland* (1996) paras 673 and 685. Not least of the innovations was the displacement of the rule *nemo plus juris ad alienum transferre potest quam ipse haberet*.
73 See paras 2.11–2.16 below.
74 LR(S)A 1979 s 9(1).
75 LR(S)A 1979 ss 9 (rectification) and 12 (indemnity).
76 LR(S)A 1979 s 12(1)(a).
77 LR(S)A 1979 s 9(3), discussed at para 2.9 below.
78 LR(S)A 1979 s 12(1)(b).
79 SLC Report 222 paras 17.6, 17.10 and 17.11.

registration. The Keeper, knowing nothing of the forgery, would substitute Betty's name for Alan's as the owner of the property. That there was then a mistake in registration was evident enough. But what was less clear was whether the Register was 'inaccurate' in the sense of the Act. The effect of registration, after all, was to confer ownership on Betty (and so take it away from Alan), for under the 1979 Act title flowed from the Register and not from the underlying forged deed.[80] Far from being wrong in showing Betty as owner, therefore, the Register was absolutely correct. How then could it be 'inaccurate'? Yet this line of argument led to unacceptable results. If the Register was accurate, there was nothing to rectify, meaning that Alan could neither seek the return of his property nor claim indemnity in its stead. In effect, his property would have been expropriated by the state, and reassigned to a fraudster (Betty), without compensation. In place of his real right Alan would have only a delictual claim against Betty for fraud, the value of which would depend on Betty's traceability and solvency.

Behind examples like this lay a broader point. Title by registration was in its nature indiscriminate, conferring rights on the undeserving as well as the deserving, and so removing rights from the unwilling (or unknowing) as well as from the willing.[81] Some method was needed to repair the injury this sometimes caused, and under the scheme of the 1979 Act this could only be done through the idea of 'inaccuracy'. A second type of inaccuracy was therefore needed to supplement the first. In showing Betty as owner, the Register was certainly accurate according to the actual law, as laid down by the rules of land registration. But, equally plainly, it was inaccurate under 'ordinary' property law because, under that law, no rights could be carried by a forged – and therefore void – deed. In this discrepancy lay the promise of a solution, and one moreover of which traces could be found in the report of the Reid Committee.[82] If the position as shown on the Register was different from the result which would have been achieved by ordinary property law, then the Register should be treated as 'inaccurate' to that extent. It could then be rectified or, failing rectification, indemnity would be payable to any person suffering loss.[83] There was of course some cost in terms of complexity. The system must work, bijurally, with two different types of property law – with property law according to the Act and with 'ordinary' property law as well. But without the idea of 'bijural' inaccuracy[84] – inaccuracy by reference to ordinary property law – the system could hardly work at all.

2.9 Rectification

To correct an 'actual' inaccuracy was to make a change at the level of information rather than of right. This neither conferred rights nor did it take them away. There was no reason, therefore, to limit its occurrence: an error, once uncovered, could simply be corrected, and no one would be worse off as a result.[85]

---

80 LR(S)A 1979 s 3(1)(a).
81 It was for this reason that the Scottish Law Commission referred to the automatically curative qualities of registration as 'the Midas touch': see para 2.13 below.
82 Reid Report (n 28) para 114.
83 See eg *Kaur v Singh* 1999 SC 180 (forged disposition).
84 For this terminology, see SLC Report 222 paras 17.6 – 17.9. The term 'bijural' is used once in the LR(S)A 2012, in the heading to para 17 of sch 4.
85 Under the Act rectification was restricted only where it was to the prejudice of a proprietor in possession: see s 9(3)(a). The correction of an actual inaccuracy did not cause prejudice.

'Bijural' inaccuracies were a different matter. To rectify the actual legal position (as measured by the 1979 Act) by reference to what *ought* to have been the legal position (as measured by ordinary property law) was to take rights away from one person and give them to another.[86] If this were to be allowed without restriction, there would be little difference as to title between the Register of Sasines and the Land Register, and many of the advantages conferred by registration of title would be lost. But equally, if it were not to be allowed at all, unworthy acquirers would sometimes be favoured over innocent former owners. Some compromise between these positions needed to be struck. If an acquirer was fraudulent or otherwise at fault (as in the example considered earlier), then it was easy enough to say that the former owner should be preferred. All systems of registration of title, indeed, achieve that result. But if both acquirer and former owner were innocent, then choosing between them was much harder.

A standard example was (and is) identity fraud.[87] Colin owns land. Duncan steals his identity and grants a disposition, in Colin's name, to Eilidh, an innocent purchaser. The signature on the disposition is forged. Eilidh, unaware of the forgery, presents the disposition for registration and is registered as owner. Under the 1979 Act the Register was bijurally inaccurate: Eilidh was, but should not have been, the owner. But should Colin, the 'true' or 'should-be' owner,[88] be able to get the property back? Should, in other words, the Register be rectified so as to remove Eilidh as proprietor and restore the position of Colin? Or alternatively should rectification be refused so that Eilidh kept, and Colin lost, the property? Whoever lost the property was entitled under the Act to compensation ('indemnity') from the Keeper.[89] That meant that if the 'mud' (ie the property) was not forthcoming, there was at least the consolation of the 'money'.[90] But as most people preferred the mud to the money, there remained the problem of how it should be allocated.

In the interests of lowering transaction costs and facilitating acquisitions – two leading aims of registration of title – it might be expected that acquirers would be preferred to the 'true' owners. That, on the whole, is the approach taken by Torrens systems.[91] The 1979 Act, however, following the legislation of 1925 in England,[92] did not go quite so far. In general acquirers would indeed be preferred, but only where they were in possession of the land.[93] A person who was not using land had no special claim on its retention; and so if or to the extent that an acquirer did not possess, the 'true' owner could recover by rectification.[94] This protection for 'proprietors in possession' had certain qualifications, of which the most important was where the inaccuracy had been caused by the proprietor's own fraud or

---

86 This is because, although the Act did not say so, rectification of bijural inaccuracies reallocated rights: see SLC DP 128 paras 6.6–6.9.
87 *Kaur v Singh* 1999 SC 180, 188 per Lord President Rodger.
88 The first use of the term 'true' owner may be in the Reid Report (n 28) para 115.
89 LR(S)A 1979 s 12(1).
90 The terminology is taken from T W Mapp, *Torrens' Elusive Title: Basic Legal Principles of an Efficient Torrens' System* (1978) para 4.24.
91 See eg P O'Connor, 'Registration of title in England and Australia: a theoretical and comparative analysis', in E Cooke (ed), *Modern Studies in Property Law* vol 2 (2003) 81, 84–89; P O'Connor, 'Registration of invalid dispositions: who gets the property?', in E Cooke (eds), *Modern Studies in Property Law* vol 3 (2005) 45.
92 Reid Report (n 28) para 115.
93 LR(S)A 1979 s 9(3).
94 See eg *Gray v Keeper of the Registers of Scotland* 2014 SLT (Lands Tr) 117.

carelessness (as with Betty in the example given earlier).[95] But as most acquirers/proprietors took up possession, and as the qualifications to the protection rarely applied, the overall effect was that acquirers were usually protected. Under the 1979 Act, therefore, the mud generally went to the acquirer and the money to the 'true' owner.

The actual provisions in the Act gave rise to a certain amount of difficulty. Beginning, rather misleadingly, with the proposition that the Keeper could rectify any inaccuracy on the Register, s 9 then proceeded to rule out rectification to the prejudice of a 'proprietor in possession' except in limited circumstances such as fraud.[96] Neither 'proprietor' nor 'possession' was defined, and it took litigation and reflection before it was settled that a 'proprietor' was a person entered on the Register as holder of a primary (but not a secondary) interest in land,[97] and that 'possession' included civil possession such as possession through a tenant.[98] Acquirers of secondary interests, such as standard securities, were not protected, and would lose their rights (but be paid indemnity).[99] Although the Keeper could rectify on his own initiative, most rectifications in practice came about either by court order or as a result of a formal application by the 'true' owner.[100]

2.10 Indemnity

Bijural inaccuracies led, potentially, to an indemnity payment from the Keeper.[101] If the inaccuracy came to be rectified, payment was due to the (now former) holder of the right (Eilidh in the example given above);[102] if rectification was refused, usually because the current holder was in possession, payment was due to the person who should have held the right (Colin).[103] From the point of view of the latter, this was compensation for loss of a right. From the point of view of the former, it was the operation of a public guarantee of title or, to put it another way, of a form of (compulsory) title insurance for which a part of the fee payable on registration was the premium. Such public insurance is a characteristic, though not an essential, feature of registration of title. Although apparently unknown in the systems of Continental Europe, it is a prominent part of both the Torrens

---

95 LR(S)A 1979 s 9(3)(a)(iii). See eg *Stevenson-Hamilton's Exrs v McStay (No 2)* 2001 SLT 694; *McCoach v Keeper of the Registers of Scotland*, 19 Dec 2008, Lands Tr (unreported), on which see K G C Reid and G L Gretton, *Conveyancing 2008* (2009) 121–33. For the example involving Betty, see para 2.8 above.
96 SLC DP 128 paras 6.12 and 6.13.
97 For the difference between primary and secondary interests, see para 2.3 above.
98 *Kaur v Singh* 1999 SC 180; SLC DP 125 para 4.12.
99 The position of servitudes, however, was never conclusively determined: see *Griffiths v Keeper of the Registers of Scotland*, 20 Dec 2002, Lands Tribunal (unreported); *Yaxley v Glen* [2007] CSOH 90, 2007 SLT 756; *Orkney Housing Association Ltd v Atkinson* 2011 GWD 30-652. The doubt arose because, although a servitude was a secondary right, it could only be held in association with a primary right (ie ownership). See K G C Reid and G L Gretton, *Conveyancing 2007* (2008) 124–26, and *Conveyancing 2011* (2012) 98–102.
100 The Keeper was bound to rectify where ordered to do so by a court: see LR(S)A 1979 s 9(1). Applications for rectification were made on form 9: see Land Registration (Scotland) Rules 2006 r 17(1).
101 By contrast, no loss resulted from the rectification of actual inaccuracies.
102 See para 2.9 above.
103 LR(S)A 1979 s 12(1). Indemnity was also due under this provision for the loss or destruction of any document while lodged with the Keeper, and for an error or omission in any land or charge certificate or in any information given by the Keeper in writing.

and the English systems, and there was never any doubt that it would be adopted in Scotland too.[104] It is retained by the 2012 Act, although reconceptualised, in relation to acquirers, as a warranty of title by the Keeper.[105]

Indemnity was payable regardless of whether the Keeper had been at fault. As with any form of insurance, however, there were a large and growing number of exclusions.[106] Many were narrow and targeted; some were puzzling or even inexplicable.[107] The most important was the exclusion for fraud and carelessness, so that a person who was author of his own misfortune had no claim to be compensated by the Keeper.[108] An equivalent exclusion was in place in respect of the protection against rectification for proprietors in possession.[109] If, therefore, a title was bad due to the fraud or carelessness of the acquirer (or of the acquirer's solicitor), the Register could be rectified and no indemnity was payable to the acquirer.

In addition to the standard exclusions, it was open to the Keeper, at the time of registration, to exclude indemnity from a title in whole or in part, though the legislation gave no guidance as to when this should happen.[110] Indemnity was rarely excluded in practice except where registering an *a non domino* disposition – something the Keeper became increasingly reluctant to do – or where a boundary overlap had been detected. Exclusion of indemnity allowed positive prescription to run, which was not otherwise possible for Land Register titles.[111] At the same time, it deprived the applicant of the protection against rectification normally accorded to proprietors in possession.[112]

Where indemnity was payable, the Act was laconic as to how it should be quantified, saying merely that claimants should be indemnified for their loss.[113] The sums involved have tended to be small. In the last year of the 1979 Act, 82 claims were settled at a total cost of £503,733,[114] although to this must be added a considerable amount of staff time as well as, in some cases, the payment of legal

---

104 Dunedin Report (n 18) 7–8 ('a well-known and necessary incident of registration of title'); Reid Report (n 28) para 114 ('It is an essential feature of any system of registration of title that the title should be guaranteed by the State'). In fact it is perfectly possible to have a fully-developed system of registration of title *without* indemnity, except in a case where the problem is caused by the fault of the registration department. The system in Germany is an example. So, unless the term is given a special meaning, indemnity is not a 'necessary' or 'essential' feature.
105 Land Registration etc (Scotland) Act 2012 part 7: see ch 13.
106 LR(S)A 1979 s 12(3).
107 For a review, and criticism, see SLC DP 128 paras 8.2–8.13.
108 LR(S)A 1979 s 12(3)(n). A proportionate reduction was made where the claimant's fraud or carelessness merely contributed to the loss: see s 13(4). Fraud or carelessness is not the same as bad faith: *Dougbar Properties Ltd v Keeper of the Registers of Scotland* 1999 SC 513 exposed a defect in the 1979 Act when it was held that indemnity was recoverable in respect of a pre-existing inaccuracy on the Register even although the claimant was aware of the inaccuracy at the time of acquisition. For discussion, see SLC DP 125 paras 7.3–7.6.
109 LR(S)A 1979 s 9(3)(a)(iii): see para 2.9 above.
110 LR(S)A 1979 s 12(2). An equivalent power exists in LR(S)A 2012 s 75. Unlike the 1979 Act, the 2012 Act makes provision as to the circumstances in which warranty (the equivalent of indemnity) can be limited or excluded.
111 LR(S)A 1979 s 10.
112 LR(S)A 1979 s 9(3)(a)(iv).
113 LR(S)A 1979 s 12(1).
114 Registers of Scotland, *Annual Report and Accounts, 2013–2014* (2014) 35. For earlier years, see Scottish Parliament, *Passage of the Land Registration etc (Scotland) Bill 2011* (2013, SPPB 174) (available at www.scottish.parliament.uk/parliamentarybusiness/Bills/44469.aspx) 155.

expenses.[115] Where indemnity was paid, the Keeper was subrogated to any rights of the claimant against others for recovery of the loss,[116] and in some cases recovery was indeed sought and made.

CRITICISM AND REFORM

2.11 The Scottish Law Commission project

Misgivings as to the 1979 legislation were quick to emerge. As early as the mid-1980s some harsh things were being said about the new system,[117] and many of these (and other) criticisms were borne out by subsequent experience as well as by a series of court decisions.[118] An initial approach to the Keeper by the Scottish Law Commission, in the late 1990s, was received without enthusiasm, but in due course it was agreed that the Law Commission should conduct a review of the law and practice of land registration. A member of the Keeper's staff[119] was seconded to the Law Commission and provided indispensable technical help, but the responsibility for the review lay with the Commission and not with Registers of Scotland.[120] The Law Commission started work in 2003, and issued three discussion papers for comment in 2004 and 2005.[121] The Commission's final report, containing recommendations for reform and a draft Bill, was published in 2010.[122] The present writers were the Law Commissioners successively in charge of the project, Professor Reid being responsible for the discussion papers and Professor Gretton for the report. The Law Commission's recommendations were largely implemented by the Land Registration etc (Scotland) Act 2012.

The Scottish Law Commission's work provides important background to the 2012 Act. The account which follows is necessarily selective. Among the most important themes were: (i) the protection of acquirers and the related issue of insecurity of title; (ii) the Keeper's 'Midas' touch and the difficulties to which it gave rise; (iii) the problem of completing the Land Register, ie of ensuring that all or substantially all properties in Scotland were transferred to the Land Register within a reasonable time; (iv) the problem that much of the way that land registration actually worked lacked a clear statutory basis, calling for what the Commission called 'pumping concrete into the foundations'; and (v) issues about competition of title, and the Commission's proposal to introduce 'advance notices'.

---

115 Due to what may have been a drafting accident, s 13(1) imposed primary liability for expenses on the Keeper, win or lose, provided that the claim had been *prima facie* well-founded. For background and analysis, see SLC DP 128 paras 9.43–9.50.
116 LR(S)A 1979 s 13(2). By s 13(3) the Keeper could require an assignation.
117 See in particular the series of articles by K G C Reid published in (1984) 29 JLSS 171, 212, and 260. See also K G C Reid, '*A non domino* conveyances and the Land Register' 1991 JR 79.
118 See eg A J M Steven, 'Problems in the Land Register: recent cases surveyed' 1999 SLT (News) 163.
119 Martin Corbett followed by John Glover.
120 The equivalent project in England and Wales was a joint project between the Law Commission and the Land Registry: see *Report No 271 on Land Registration for the Twenty-first Century: a Conveyancing Revolution* (2001).
121 Scottish Law Commission, *Discussion Paper No 125 on Land Registration: Void and Voidable Titles* (2004) ('SLC DP 125'); *Discussion Paper No 128 on Land Registration: Registration, Rectification and Indemnity* (2005) ('SLC DP 128'); *Discussion Paper No 130 on Land Registration: Miscellaneous Issues* (2005) ('SLC DP 130'). All Scottish Law Commission papers are available at www.scotlawcom.gov.uk.
122 Scottish Law Commission, *Report No 222 on Land Registration* (2010) ('SLC Report 222').

2.12 Protection of acquirers and insecurity of title

In adjudicating between 'true' owner and acquirer – between Colin and Eilidh (the innocent grantee of a forged disposition)[123] – the 1979 Act, as we have seen,[124] relied on the state of possession. If Eilidh possessed, she kept the property (the 'mud') and Colin had to make do with indemnity from the Keeper (the 'money'). If Eilidh was not in possession – which in practice usually meant that possession was with Colin – the result was the other way round, with Colin receiving the mud and Eilidh the money. There was a certain intuitive attractiveness to this approach, for not only did it avoid the unpleasantness of eviction but it gave the property to the person who, as possessor, might be assumed to have the greater stake in it. Experience, however, quickly brought out some of the difficulties.[125]

In assessing possession, the legislation took little account of history. What mattered was, not who had possessed the most, but who possessed *now*. The choice between money and mud thus turned on present and not on historic possession. There was, moreover, no requirement that the present possession be long-standing. Possession at the time when the dispute became live was sufficient; that that possession might be short-lived, or obtained by underhand means, appeared not to be a consideration. In one case involving forgery of a disposition, the dispute between the 'true' owner and the acquirer (both innocent of the fraud) was fought out by a scramble for possession. The acquirer, having lost possession when the 'true' owner, returning from abroad, broke into the property (a flat) and changed the locks, regained it by the same method in order to achieve the coveted status of 'proprietor in possession'.[126] In another case a dispute concerning a small area of river bed led to underwater marker posts being put into position by one of the parties and promptly removed by the other.[127] Some relief was provided in the later years of the 1979 Act when the courts began to disregard or at least play down the effect of 'wilful acts intended simply to assert possession in face of protest' and occurring when the parties were already locked in active dispute.[128] Nonetheless the difficulty of short-lived possession remained.

No less serious was the persistent advantage which the possessory rule gave to acquirers. For in practice acquirers usually took possession and did so at once (that being the reason for buying the property in the first place); and with that single act of possession, they destroyed any advantage which might have derived from the previous possession of the 'true' owner or, it may be, of past generations of his family. Far from being even-handed as between the parties, therefore, a rule which allocated the mud to the person in possession was a rule which usually favoured the acquirer.

But as well as being damaging to the position of Colin, the 'true' owner, such a rule was not wholly favourable to the position of Eilidh, the acquirer. Her security depended on continuing possession: lose that and she was vulnerable to

---

123 For the Colin/Eilidh example, see para 2.9 above.
124 Paragraph 2.9 above.
125 SLC DP 125 paras 4.22–4.28; SLC Report 222 paras 21.22–21.25.
126 *Kaur v Singh* 1999 SC 180.
127 *Safeway Stores plc v Tesco Stores Ltd* 2004 SC 29.
128 *Gray v Keeper of the Registers of Scotland* 2014 SLT (Lands Tr) 117, para 60. See also *Nicol v Keeper of the Registers of Scotland* 2013 SLT (Lands Tr) 56, para 26; *Burton v Keeper of the Registers of Scotland* 2014 SLT (Lands Tr) 69, para 61; *Van Eck v Keeper of the Registers of Scotland* 2014 SLT (Lands Tr) 117, para 27; *Mather v Keeper of the Registers of Scotland* 2015 GWD 3-68, para 40. Such acts were dismissed as part of a 'tennis-match' of claim and counterclaim.

rectification. Furthermore, what had happened to Colin could also, in the future, happen to Eilidh: 'To whatever extent ... [a person] can acquire an interest from a predecessor through error', Thomas W Mapp observed, 'he is vulnerable to losing that interest through the same error repeated after his registration.' 'Easy come' (the ready acquisition of the property by Eilidh) led inexorably to 'easy go' (the possibility of its subsequent loss to a future acquirer).[129] To make life easy for acquirers was also to make titles on the Land Register less secure. It was important, therefore, that life be made less easy.

In place of a crude possession requirement, the Scottish Law Commission proposed an approach which, as the first step, asked what type of error had occurred.[130] That acquirers should be able to rely on the Register was, of course, a key principle of registration of title, and the basis for the reduction in transaction costs to which it led. There should never (or almost never) be a need to look behind the Register at the underlying deeds,[131] and if the Register turned out to be wrong, acquirers must be fully protected. But 'transactional error' was not in the same position as 'Register error'. If the mistake lay not in what the Register said but in what the parties to the current transaction did, then there was no reason to favour the acquirer over the 'true' owner. On the contrary, it was the former, and not the latter, who was best placed to avoid or detect the mistake. So if Eilidh's disposition turned out to be forged, the property should stay with Colin (who had played no part in the transaction) and not pass to Eilidh (who had). On this scheme, money and mud would thus be allocated by type of error. If the error affected the transaction, the 'true' owner would take the property and the acquirer the money; if it affected the Register, the allocation would be reversed.

There remained the problem of knowledge.[132] The enhanced protection for the 'true' owner was of value only if he knew of the transaction which threatened his title. For a transactional error would, with the next transaction, become an error on the Register itself and so result in the loss of the property.[133] It was important that the 'true' owner had the opportunity to rectify the Register before this occurred. The Scottish Law Commission's solution was one of notification by possession. For an acquirer to take free from Register error – and defeat the 'true' owner's title – the person from whom he acquired must have been in possession for a year.[134] And for a 'true' owner to lose his property, therefore, he would first have to have

---

129 Mapp (n 90) paras 3.13 and 4.26. These remarks were made in the context of the Torrens system.
130 SLC DP 125 paras 3.15–3.41 and 4.44–4.46. Unknown to the Scottish Law Commission, a similar idea had been proposed 100 years earlier by the WS Society: see *Report of the Society of Writers to His Majesty's Signet with regard to Registration of Title* (1908) 6. As the *Report* explained: 'The whole virtue of Registered Title lies in the principle that, so far as onerous and *bona fide* third parties are concerned, the Register entries are conclusive, no matter what fraud or error or latent equity may lie behind them. The necessary consequence is that if a person not the rightful owner be allowed to appear on the Register as owner, the true owner may be dispossessed or deprived of his right. In a question with the first person wrongfully registered, the injured owner might get the Register rectified and his property restored to him.'
131 This is Ruoff's 'curtain principle': see Ruoff (n 12) 162.
132 SLC DP 125 paras 4.29–4.52; SLC Report 222 paras 21.30–21.34.
133 So for example from the point of view of a purchaser from Eilidh, what at the time of Eilidh's acquisition was a transactional error (ie a forged disposition) has become a Register error (ie the wrong person (Eilidh) named as owner): see para 12.4 below.
134 See now Land Registration etc (Scotland) Act 2012 s 86(3)(a). If the granter's possession was for less than a year, the balance could be provided by the acquirer's subsequent possession.

lost possession for this period. Owners who retained possession had nothing to fear for their title.

2.13 Title by registration and the Midas touch

The proposed withdrawal of the acquirer's protection from transactional error (other than by monetary compensation) facilitated[135] the abandonment of the principle of title by registration.[136] And, as the Scottish Law Commission pointed out, there were strong reasons for such abandonment.[137]

One was its indiscriminate nature. A rule so crude could not work well in every case. Unkindly if not unfairly, the Scottish Law Commission likened it to the 'touch' of King Midas: just as everything that the mythical King touched was changed into gold, even his food or his daughter, so everything that the Keeper registered was changed into 'valid', even where that result was undesirable, and indeed undesired by the Keeper.[138] So if a fraudster drew up a disposition and forged the owner's signature, registration would confer ownership on the fraudster, and hence take it away from the person whose signature had been forged. Or if a person, seeking to acquire ownership by prescription, registered an *a non domino* disposition, then he would become owner *at once*, even before he had embarked on the ten years of possession needed in order for prescription to run. Or again, if the Keeper allowed the same land to appear on two different title sheets, as sometimes (most unwisely) he did, its ownership would oscillate from one competitor to the other depending on which title sheet had changed proprietor most recently.[139] The Midas touch was inescapable: it operated even if, because of doubts about the title, the title sheet contained an exclusion of indemnity.

To ameliorate these difficulties the 1979 Act would sometimes allow the Register to be corrected ('rectified') on the basis of 'ordinary' property law.[140] In this way, having given too much too soon, the Act might seek to undo that which, unwisely, had previously been done. But this led to the complexity of bijuralism, as we have seen,[141] in cases where rectification was allowed, and to the unfairness of the 'wrong' result in cases where it was not.

Bijuralism in turn caused uncertainty as well as complexity, for it was never clear how far the idea should be taken. Take the identity theft case mentioned earlier.[142] The Register, no doubt, was 'inaccurate' in showing Eilidh (the grantee of the forged disposition) as owner rather than Colin (the 'true' owner). But what if Eilidh now disponed to Fergus? If 'ordinary' property law were to continue to be applied, the owner should still be Colin and hence the Register would still be inaccurate. But since the Midas touch had made Eilidh owner (albeit 'wrongly'),

---

135 It did not, however, make it inevitable, for it would have been possible to combine the Scottish Law Commission's proposals as to transactional error with a 'Midas' system of title registration: see SLC DP 125 para 5.7. Indeed those Torrens systems which operate a system of deferred indefeasibility do precisely that.
136 For title by registration, see para 2.7 above.
137 SLC DP 125 paras 5.14–5.39; SLC Report 222 paras 13.11–13.28.
138 SLC DP 125 para 5.34. The term has stuck.
139 Reid (n 72) para 685; K G C Reid and G L Gretton, *Conveyancing 2001* (2002) 108–15.
140 LR(S)A 1979 s 9.
141 Paragraphs 2.8 and 2.9 above.
142 Paragraph 2.9 above.

it was possible to argue that, even under 'ordinary' property law, Fergus must have become owner in turn. On that view the Register would then be perfectly accurate and rectification would be denied. Which answer was correct was never determined.[143]

The abandonment of Midas, the Scottish Law Commission pointed out, would allow the abandonment of bijuralism. And that in turn would allow acquirers to be protected from Register error by a simple *bona fide* acquisition rule of the type found in German law, and many other civilian systems, and indeed, in our own law, in s 25 of the Sale of Goods Act 1979.[144] The person shown on the Register as owner might not always, under this system, be owner; but a *bona fide* acquirer from such a person could proceed on the basis that what the Register said was true.

2.14 Completion of the Land Register

Viewed from the perspective of registration, Scotland is like an uncompleted jigsaw. At the most recent estimate, around 26% of the country is in the Land Register.[145] The figure calculated by individual title units is higher, at around 58%, because smaller properties tend to change hands more quickly than larger properties. Although the percentages have increased year by year, completing the jigsaw would, under the 1979 Act rules, have taken centuries. That is because properties moved to the Land Register only on sale,[146] and some properties could go unsold for generations, because they were owned by a juristic person (eg local authorities, companies and so on) on a long-term basis, or because, though owned by private persons, they were transferred inter-generationally by inheritance or donation, or held through trusts. Indeed, there are some properties that have yet to make their first appearance in the Register of Sasines, which was established in 1617, even though under the legislation applicable to that register all transactions, not just sale, require recording.

The position, as the Scottish Law Commission pointed out, was scarcely satisfactory.[147] The benefits of registration of title were too great to be withheld for so long from so many properties. Nor was it sensible to continue, apparently indefinitely, with two different systems of registration. Quite aside, moreover, from the interests of conveyancers and their clients, completion of the Register was also a matter of interest to the public at large. The Land Register, unlike the Register of Sasines, shows title boundaries, the names of owners, and a great deal else besides. Anyone, not just conveyancers, can use and understand it – and 'anyone' includes central government, local government, law enforcement agencies, or those just curious to know who owns what. The benefits of the Land

---

143 We would favour the first of the two views if only because under the second Colin would be denied not only the 'mud' but also (because the Register was not inaccurate) even the 'money', an unacceptable result.
144 The rule is found in s 86 of the LR(S)A 2012: see paras 12.8–12.17 below.
145 *Completion of the Land Register: Public Consultation* (n 53) paras 4, 16 and 17. These figures disguise substantial variation across Scotland caused by the length of time counties have been operational for registration of title, the liveliness of the conveyancing market, and the ratio of urban to rural properties. For the breakdown by county, see appendix 2 of the consultation document as well as the map on p 4.
146 Paragraph 2.5 above.
147 SLC Report 222 paras 33.17 and 33.18.

Register could be fully realised only if the pace of registration were to be greatly increased.[148]

To this end the Law Commission had three main proposals.[149] First, the triggers for first registration should be extended from dispositions on sale to all dispositions, and in due course to standard securities and other deeds as well. Secondly, voluntary registration should be encouraged, with the Keeper losing the discretion to turn applications down. And finally and more controversially, the Keeper should have the power to register unregistered properties on her own initiative and without need for the owner's consent; this is called Keeper-induced registration, or KIR.

All three proposals were enacted as part of the 2012 Act.[150] And shortly before the Act came into force the Scottish Government announced that it would seek to achieve completion of the Land Register by as early as 2024.[151] There seems no prospect of realising this ambitious target without a very great deal of Keeper-induced registration.

2.15 'Pumping concrete into the foundations'

So brief was the 1979 Act[152] that much was left uncertain and there were many points on which, in the absence of legislative guidance, Registers of Scotland had to develop policies of their own. An important aim of the Scottish Law Commission's project was to 'pump concrete into the foundations' of the system by providing the missing certainty and guidance.[153] Of the many examples in the Law Commission's draft Bill, and now in the 2012 Act, special mention may be made of the provisions on the component parts of the Register,[154] the criteria for accepting and rejecting applications for registration,[155] and the rules for *a non domino* dispositions.[156]

2.16 Competition of title and advance notices

Until the disposition or other deed can be registered, acquirers are vulnerable to a competing deed by the granter, and also to other dangers such as the granter's insolvency. And as there is an unavoidable time-period between even a last-minute search in the registers, on the strength of which the price is paid, and the moment of registration, acquirers must generally face a few days during which their position is at risk. In Scottish practice the risk had traditionally been covered by a letter of obligation by the granter's solicitors. In England and Wales, by contrast, there is a long-established system called 'search with priority' whereby an entry can be made at the Land Registry that will protect an acquirer provided that the deed

---

148 So it was that the *Policy Memorandum* which accompanied the introduction of the Land Registration etc (Scotland) Bill proclaimed (para 14) that 'Completion of the Land Register is considered to be the most important policy aim of the Bill'.
149 SLC Report 222 paras 33.24–33.67: see further ch 7.
150 LR(S)A 2012 ss 27–29 and 48.
151 See *Completion of the Land Register: Public Consultation* (n 53).
152 See para 2.1 above.
153 SLC Report 222 paras 3.5 and 3.6.
154 LR(S)A 2012 ss 2–15: see ch 4.
155 LR(S)A 2012 ss 21–26: see paras 8.6–8.9 below.
156 LR(S)A 2012 ss 43–45: see paras 17.12–17.20 below.

itself is registered within a certain defined period thereafter. The Reid Committee considered but rejected the introduction of such a system in Scotland on the basis that it would be a 'considerable innovation' whose absence had not hitherto 'led to difficulties'.[157] It was not, therefore, included in the 1979 Act.

Subsequent experience led the Scottish Law Commission to reconsider the matter.[158] Solicitors had become more risk-averse on behalf of their clients. There were two prominent cases, *Sharp v Thomson*[159] and *Burnett's Tr v Grainger*,[160] in which sellers actually did become insolvent before the buyer registered, although admittedly this would not have happened if the registration had not been delayed until many months after payment of the price. And, finally, the insurers behind the solicitors' master policy were showing increasing reluctance to cover letters of obligation. The Law Commission's solution was to recommend a system of 'advance notices'.[161] The future deed would be protected by the registration of a notice before settlement. This gave priority for 35 days. So long as the deed was registered within the priority period, the acquirer would be invulnerable to competing deeds or insolvency.[162] Advance notices are the most important single change in conveyancing practice introduced by the 2012 Act.

THE 2012 ACT

2.17 Parliamentary passage

The Scottish Law Commission's report was published in February 2010.[163] Thereafter the Scottish Government, in association with Registers of Scotland, moved quickly to implement its recommendations. Following a period of public consultation, a Bill was prepared and introduced to the Scottish Parliament on 1 December 2011.[164] This followed closely the recommendations of the Law Commission as to policy although, for reasons which were not always apparent, or perhaps wise,[165] there was quite extensive rewriting of the Commission's original draft Bill. A considerable amount of evidence, both written and oral, was presented to the Parliament's Economy, Energy and Tourism Committee, which was charged with the Bill's scrutiny at Stage 1, and there was vigorous discussion of matters such as *a non domino* conveyances, the future of ARTL, the completion of the Register, the proposed new offence for false or misleading acts or omissions in applying for registration, and common land.[166] For the most part, however, the Bill's parliamentary passage was untroubled. It was completed on 31 May 2012, and Royal Assent followed on 10 July 2012.

---

157 Reid Report (n 28) para 99.
158 SLC Report 222 paras 14.1–14.8.
159 1997 SC (HL) 66.
160 [2004] UKHL 8, 2004 SC (HL) 19. The overall result was a draw: in *Sharp* the buyer won the competition, in *Burnett's Tr* the seller's trustee in sequestration.
161 SLC Report 222 paras 14.9 ff.
162 This was implemented by LR(S)A 2012 pt 4 (ss 56–64): see ch 10.
163 Scottish Law Commission, *Report No 222 on Land Registration* (2010).
164 A full record of all the papers, evidence and debates is conveniently collected together in *Passage of the Land Registration etc (Scotland) Bill 2011* (n 114). Details of the pre-introduction public consultation can be found at pp 231–32.
165 See eg paras 12.22, 13.11 and 14.7 below. A number of other examples could be cited.
166 *Passage of the Land Registration etc (Scotland) Bill 2011* (n 114) 223–587.

2.18 Implementation and commencement

Much still needed to be done before the Act could be brought into force. New procedures were required at the Registers. Land Registration Rules had to be drafted and enacted.[167] Other delegated legislation was needed on a host of matters.[168] And Registers of Scotland, having produced a comprehensive and invaluable set of guidance materials,[169] took on the task of educating the legal profession by means of a nationwide series of seminars. After all this preparation the Act was brought fully into force on 8 December 2014.[170] Unsurprisingly, the first months were not easy, as both Registers of Scotland and the legal profession adjusted to the many changes in law and especially in practice which the new system involved.[171] Nonetheless, with the 2012 Act, imperfect as it will inevitably be discovered to be, Scotland finally has legislation which is equal to the ambition of its system of land registration.[172]

---

167 Land Register Rules etc (Scotland) Regulations 2014, SSI 2014/150.
168 Land Registration etc (Scotland) Act 2012 (Commencement No 1) Order 2012, SSI 2012/265; Fees in the Registers of Scotland (Consequential Provisions) Amendment Order 2013, SSI 2013/15; Land Registration etc (Scotland) Act 2012 (Commencement No 2 and Transitional Provisions) Order 2014, SSI 2014/41; Electronic Documents (Scotland) Regulations 2014, SSI 2014/83; Registers of Scotland (Fees) Order 2014, SSI 2014/188; Registers of Scotland (Information and Access) Order 2014, SSI 2014/189; Land Registration etc (Scotland) Act 2012 (Incidental, Consequential and Transitional) Order 2014, SSI 2014/190; Land Register of Scotland (Rate of Interest on Compensation) Regulations 2014, SSI 2014/194; Act of Sederunt (Rules of the Court of Session and Sheriff Court Rules Amendment No 2) (Miscellaneous) 2014, SSI 2014/291; Land Registration etc (Scotland) Act 2012 (Amendment and Transitional) Order 2014, SSI 2014/346; Land Register of Scotland (Automated Registration) etc Regulations 2014, SSI 2014/347; Lands Tribunal for Scotland Amendment (Fees) Rules 2015, SSI 2015/199; Registers of Scotland (Voluntary Registration, Amendment of Fees, etc) Order 2015, SSI 2015/265.
169 www.ros.gov.uk/about-us/2012-act/general-guidance.
170 Land Registration etc (Scotland) Act 2012 (Designated Day) Order 2014, SSI 2014/127.
171 K G C Reid and G L Gretton, *Conveyancing 2014* (2015) 153–60; J Edwards, 'Tools for today's titles' (2015) 60 JLSS April/12.
172 For an assessment of the position at the end of the first 18 months, see the articles collected in (2016) 142 Greens Property Law Bulletin.

Chapter 3

The Land Register and the Keeper

THE LAND REGISTER

3.1 From 1979 Act to 2012 Act

'There is to continue to be a public register of rights in land in Scotland (which is to continue to be known as the "Land Register of Scotland")', says s 1(1) of the Land Registration etc (Scotland) Act 2012, thus making clear that, however extensive the changes made by the Act, they are changes to an *existing* system. It is true that the 2012 Act repeals almost the whole of its predecessor legislation, the Land Registration (Scotland) Act 1979,[1] but that does not affect the fact of continuity. As an analogy, the successive Companies Acts have repealed earlier Companies Acts, but the Companies Register remains in continued existence and companies registered under, say, the Companies Act 1929 retain their registration even though that Act has long since been repealed. Likewise properties registered in the Land Register under the 1979 Act remain registered in the Land Register. The 1979 Act has gone, but the Land Register lives on. The 2012 Act was not a revolution; the revolution was the 1979 Act.[2]

3.2 A public Register

The passage quoted from the 2012 Act in the previous paragraph says that the Register is to be a *public* register of rights in land.[3] The word 'public' is significant. In Scotland registers relating to land have always been public,[4] but that is not the case everywhere. In some countries, such as Germany, the land register is non-public. The same was true in England until 1990. In such countries only persons who can demonstrate a legitimate interest can inspect the register, such as – to state the most obvious case – conveyancers.

Although the Register of Sasines has always been public, its use by non-lawyers has been limited, because obtaining useful information from it is slow and cumbersome, and indeed hardly possible for the non-expert. Obtaining information from the Land Register is much easier. A title sheet can be understood, at least in general terms, by any person of reasonable education and intelligence.[5] Conveyancers tend to think of the Land Register, like the Register of Sasines, as 'their' register, a register for the benefit of conveyancers and the work that they do for clients. Yet the range of people and organisations with an interest in

---

1 The unrepealed provisions are ss 15(4), 16 and 29, and sch 3.
2 See paras 1.13–1.17 above. For a comparison of the Register of Sasines and the Land Register, see eg G L Gretton and K G C Reid, *Conveyancing* (4th edn, 2011) para 8-07.
3 Land Registration etc (Scotland) Act 2012 s 1(1).
4 See para 1.3 above.
5 But non-experts – and indeed sometimes experts too – will often be baffled by the D (burdens) section.

the question 'who has what rights in which land?' is broad, including planning authorities, environmental authorities, tax authorities and numerous other public bodies as well as prospective lenders, unpaid creditors, local amenity associations, and pressure groups.[6]

3.3 Structure and contents

The Land Register comprises (a) the title sheet record; (b) the cadastral map; (c) the archive record; and (d) the application record.[7] The individual title sheets which make up the title sheet record are themselves divided – as they were under the 1979 Act – into four sections: property, proprietorship, securities, and burdens.[8] Full details as to the structure and contents of the Land Register can be found in chapter 4.

3.4 'Beneficial ownership' and 'controlling interest'?

The Land Register is a register of ownership (and certain other rights), and not of 'beneficial ownership' or 'controlling interest'. The idea that 'beneficial ownership' should be included in the Land Register was put forward when the Bill was going through Parliament, but did not meet with success.[9] Legislative provision, however, has since been made for the establishment of a separate public register of controlling interests in land, also under the charge of the Keeper of the Registers of Scotland.[10] This is intended to show, not who owns (or leases) land – which is the task of the Land Register – but rather who controls the person who owns (or leases) land. The main target is evidently trusts and juristic persons such as companies.[11] So far, only framework provisions have been enacted, and the details have been left to regulations which, at the time of writing, had yet to the published even in the draft form required for the purposes of the public consultation which the legislation requires.[12] 'Controlling interest' is an elusive concept and its definition is awaited with particular interest. It seems unlikely that the disclosure requirements will apply to all types of land or to all types of owner.

Whilst these new provisions are not contained in the 2012 Act itself, the 2012 Act is amended so as to allow the Keeper to seek additional information as to the categories of owners and lessees on the Land Register.[13] The 2012 Act provisions are discussed elsewhere.[14]

---

6 Scottish Law Commission, *Report No 222 on Land Registration* (2010) ('SLC Report 222') para 33.17.
7 LR(S)A 2012 s 2.
8 LR(S)A 2012 s 5.
9 For the Scottish Government's view, see Scottish Parliament, *Passage of the Land Registration etc (Scotland) Bill 2011* (2013, SPPB 174) (available at www.scottish.parliament.uk/parliamentarybusiness/Bills/44469.aspx) 580–81, 605 ff.
10 Land Reform (Scotland) Act 2016 ss 39–42. The new register does not, thus far, have a name.
11 With some exceptions, UK companies are already bound under the Companies Act 2006 pt 21A (ss 790A–790ZG), inserted by the Small Business, Enterprise and Employment Act 2015 sch 3 para 1, to maintain a public register of people with significant control over the company. The meaning of 'significant control' is elaborated on in sch 1A paras 1–6, and includes those who hold more than 25% of the company's shares or voting rights.
12 Land Reform (Scotland) Act 2016 s 41. A preliminary consultation was launched by the Scottish Government in September 2016: see *Improving Transparency in Landownership in Scotland*.
13 LR(S)A 2012 ss 48A and 48B, inserted by Land Reform (Scotland) Act 2016 s 43. The link between these new sections of the 2012 Act, on the one hand, and the new register provided for by the 2016 Act, on the other hand, is not expressly stated in the legislation, but may be inferred.
14 See para 8.20 below.

3.5 Private law and public law

Conveyancers naturally think of the Land Register (and the Register of Sasines) as a place where private-law deeds, such as dispositions and heritable securities, are registered. That indeed is its primary purpose. It was the reason that the Register of Sasines was established: the Registration Act 1617 mentions only private-law deeds.[15] But once the Register of Sasines had been established, it began, by force of various statutes over the centuries, to be used for some property-related rights of a public-law nature, and the same is equally true of the Land Register. Here is a random selection: tree preservation orders, suspension orders in relation to mineral workings, orders applying the code for the management of houses let as lodgings or occupied by members of more than one family and control orders (and notices of revocation of such control orders) in relation to such houses, and suspended forfeiture orders and forfeiture certificates in respect of the proceeds of crime.[16] The cynical bystander does not always find it easy to discern why some public-law matters are registrable and others are not. It seems inevitable that the list will continue to grow.

3.6 A land information system?

The Land Register provides much information about land, but much information must be found elsewhere. There are indeed what might be called parallel registers, such as the Register of Community Interests in Land,[17] the Register of Applications by Community Bodies to Buy Land,[18] and the Crofting Register,[19] all administered by the Keeper of the Registers of Scotland. A desire is often expressed that, following the digital revolution and the possibilities that it has created for linking data, there should be some sort of land information system, of which the Land Register might perhaps be the hub. At the time of writing, such ideas were under consideration by the Scottish Government.[20]

3.7 Paper or electronic?

'Subject to the provisions of this Act, the register is to be in such form (which may be, or be in part, an electronic form) as the Keeper considers appropriate'.[21] The provision just quoted is non-prescriptive: the Land Register can be on paper or electronic or a mixture, as the Keeper sees fit. Of course in fact it is kept in electronic form. There is an official seal,[22] and so where paper documents are issued, they can be sealed in the traditional manner.

---

15 For the Registration Act 1617, see paras 1.2–1.7 above.
16 For this list, and the statutory basis of the requirement of registration, see SLC Report 222 para 13.32.
17 Land Reform (Scotland) Act 2003 s 36.
18 Land Reform (Scotland) Act 2003 s 97F, inserted by the Community Empowerment (Scotland) Act 2015 s 74, amended by the Land Reform (Scotland) Act 2016 s 53; Land Reform (Scotland) Act 2016 s 52. At the time of writing, this register had yet to be set up.
19 Crofting Reform (Scotland) Act 2010 s 3.
20 S Brymer, 'Conveyancing: A Bright Digital Future?', in F McCarthy, J Chalmers and S Bogle (eds), *Essays in Conveyancing and Property Law in Honour of Professor Robert Rennie* (2015) 279. A task force set up by the Scottish Government recommended the creation of a system to be called ScotLIS (Scotland's Land Information System): see *A Digital Land and Property Information Service for Scotland: Report to the Deputy First Minister* (July 2015).
21 LR(S)A 2012 s 1(4).
22 LR(S)A 2012 s 1(3).

3.8 Cybercrime

The 2012 Act requires the Keeper to 'take such steps as appear reasonable to the Keeper to protect the Register from (a) interference, (b) unauthorised access, and (c) damage'.[23] No doubt this would be an implied duty in any case.[24] The reason for its introduction was that, since the Register is now electronic, there could be public concern about the risk of cybercrime. RoS are of course aware of that, so this provision can be read as a reassurance to the public that the risk of cybercrime is not being overlooked.

3.9 Registration areas

The Register of Sasines had 33 areas which, subject to one or two qualifications, were the traditional administrative counties.[25] Like the 1979 Act before it,[26] however, the 2012 Act does not mention these, so that their continuing role is a matter of administrative, rather than of legislative, decision. Their use is reflected in the title numbers – for instance Edinburgh Castle, the first property in Midlothian to have been registered, is MID1 – and there is an obvious convenience in a prefix which shows at a glance in which general part of Scotland the property is to be found. Nonetheless, the absence of a statutory basis means that the Keeper could decide tomorrow to divide Scotland into a hundred areas for the purpose of land registration, or indeed to have just a single area.

The following table shows the 33 registration counties,[27] with the three-letter codes, and with the dates when each became operational under the 1979 Act for the purposes of registration of title. The traditional number of 33 is in fact now 34, because the seabed round Scotland, within the 12 nautical mile limit, is, since 8 December 2014, a distinct registration 'county'.[28]

Table of registration counties

Renfrew	REN	6 April 1981	Kincardine	KNC	1 April 1996
Dunbarton	DMB	4 October 1982	Ayr	AYR	1 April 1997
Lanark	LAN	3 January 1984	Dumfries	DMF	1 April 1997
Glasgow	GLA	30 September 1985	Kirkcudbright	KRK	1 April 1997
Clackmannan	CLK	1 October 1992	Wigtown	WGN	1 April 1997
Stirling	STG	1 April 1993	Angus	ANG	1 April 1999
West Lothian	WLN	1 October 1993	Kinross	KNR	1 April 1999
Fife	FFE	1 April 1995	Perth	PTH	1 April 1999
Aberdeen	ABN	1 April 1996	Berwick	BER	1 October 1999

---

23 LR(S)A 2012 s 1(5).
24 There was no express provision in the LR(S)A 1979.
25 But not the modern local authority areas. For example, Edinburgh is in Midlothian, but the modern local authority area of that name excludes Edinburgh.
26 For the purposes of phasing in the introduction of registration of title, however, LR(S)A 1979 ss 11 and 30(2) used the idea of 'operational areas' which were in practice the same as the old Register of Sasines areas. See para 2.5 above.
27 The table follows the conveyancing convention of not using the -shire suffix.
28 See para 3.10 below.

East Lothian	ELN	1 October 1999	Nairn	NRN	1 April 2002
Peebles	PBL	1 October 1999	Banff	BNF	1 April 2003
Roxburgh	ROX	1 October 1999	Caithness	CTH	1 April 2003
Selkirk	SEL	1 October 1999	Moray	MOR	1 April 2003
Argyll	ARG	1 April 2000	Orkney & Shetland	OAZ	1 April 2003
Bute	BUT	1 April 2000	Ross & Cromarty	ROS	1 April 2003
Midlothian	MID	1 April 2001	Sutherland	STH	1 April 2003
Inverness	INV	1 April 2002	(Seabed)	SEA	8 December 2014

What proportion of properties remains outwith the Register depends, to state the obvious, mainly on how long the county in question has been operational, but even in the counties that have been operational for the longest period many properties remain outwith the Register.[29] The process whereby eventually all properties in Scotland will be registered in the Register is discussed in chapter 7.

3.10 Extent of the Register: the seabed

The territory of a coastal state extends to 12 nautical miles from the coast, measured by reference to 'baselines'.[30] The territorial seabed adjacent to Scotland is, speaking generally, subject to the same law of property as the dry land.[31] Almost all the territorial seabed is owned by the Crown, though the Crown can alienate it, and very occasionally has done so in respect of small areas. Moreover, the Crown, or other seabed owner, can grant non-ownership rights such as leases or maritime burdens.[32] It is therefore necessary that the Land Register should cover the seabed as well as dry land.[33] Accordingly, the 2012 Act provides that '"land" includes … (b) the seabed of the territorial sea of the United Kingdom adjacent to Scotland (including land within the ebb and flow of the tide at ordinary spring tides) …'[34] The territorial seabed is designated as a registration area in its own right (with the appropriate prefix of 'SEA') rather than being incorporated into the areas to which it happens to be adjacent.[35] It does, however, give rise to special mapping issues, which are considered later in this volume.[36]

29 For further details, see para 2.14 above.
30 This rule of modern international law is adopted into UK law by the Territorial Sea Act 1987 s 1(1). See also Scottish Adjacent Waters Boundaries Order 1999, SI 1999/1126. See further Scottish Law Commission, *Report No 190 on Law of the Foreshore and Sea Bed* (2003) para 2.3.
31 Cf *Shetland Salmon Farmers Association v Crown Estate Commissioners* 1991 SLT 166. For further details, see J Robbie, *Private Water Rights* (Studies in Scots Law vol 4, 2015) paras 3-08 – 3-13. Coastal states have an economic zone that goes beyond the 12 nautical mile limit, and this includes the North Sea oilfields. The land registration system does not extend to the oil fields, because the seabed beyond the 12-mile limit is not part of the *territory* of the United Kingdom.
32 Registration of Leases (Scotland) Act 1857 s 1(2) (inserted by LR(S)A 2012 s 52(3), sch 2 para 2(d)); Title Conditions (Scotland) Act 2003 s 44.
33 The point, nonetheless, had been left in a certain amount of doubt by the 1979 Act: see Scottish Law Commission, *Discussion Paper No 130 on Land Registration: Miscellaneous Issues* (2005) ('SLC DP 130') para 2.29.
34 LR(S)A 2012 s 113(1).
35 Registers of Scotland, *General Guidance: The Cadastral Map – the Land Register and land covered by water* (v.02, 2015) 1.
36 See para 5.17 below.

The Land Register 49

3.11 Access and searchability

Although the Register is public, the Act does little to define the ways in which it may be inspected or searched, or the types of data package that the Keeper can be asked to deliver.[37] Provision is, however, made for extracts, certified copies and plain copies (discussed below);[38] and requests for inspection of the Register, it is further provided, may be made '(a) in person at a Registers of Scotland Customer Service Centre; (b) in writing by (i) letter; or (ii) email; or (c) electronically by submitting the form on the Registers of Scotland website'.[39] This latter provision is somewhat skeletal. There seems to be no statutory obligation on RoS to offer, for instance, the possibility of searching by name of proprietor, or 'zoomability' for the cadastral map. As far as the law is concerned, such matters are at the Keeper's discretion. The Keeper provides legal reports[40] and plans reports[41] but these too appear to be offered on a discretionary basis.

3.12 Extracts, certified copies, plain copies[42]

Three different types of copy are available from RoS: extracts, certified copies, and plain copies. We begin with extracts. The Keeper must, on request and on payment of a fee (currently £30 plus VAT),[43] issue extracts of: (a) title sheets (either in whole or in part); (b) any part of the cadastral map; and (c) documents in the archive record (either in whole or in part).[44] There is a form on the RoS website but its use is not mandatory, and applications may also be made by letter, by email or in person.[45] In practice, those who want (a) will usually want (b) as well, but while a combined extract is available, it has to be specially requested.[46]

The first of the listed items, ie (a), corresponds to the land certificate or office copy of the previous law.[47] The wording of the second, ie (b), suggests that an extract can be obtained not only of a single cadastral unit but of a group of such units, such as the cadastral map for a whole street. That, however, is not the position: for technical reasons,[48] an application may only be made in respect of one cadastral unit number or title number.[49] The last, ie (c), represents a significant

---

37 For instance, to independent search firms.
38 Paragraph 3.12 below.
39 Registers of Scotland (Information and Access) Order 2014, SSI 2014/189, art 4(1). A footnote indicates that the only 'Registers of Scotland Customer Service Centres' are Meadowbank House, 153 London Road, Edinburgh EH8 7AU and Hanover House, 24 Douglas Street, Glasgow G2 7NQ.
40 See paras 10.31 and 10.32 below.
41 See para 5.23 below.
42 For background, see SLC Report 222 part 8.
43 Registers of Scotland (Fees) Order 2014, SSI 2014/188, sch 1 pt 7.
44 LR(S)A 2012 s 104(1), (3). Further provision about extracts and certified copies can be made by subordinate legislation (s 107), but at the time of writing this had not happened.
45 Registers of Scotland, *General Guidance: Extracts, Certified Copies and Plain Copies* (v.01, 2014) 2.
46 *General Guidance: Extracts, Certified Copies and Plain Copies* (n 45) 2.
47 For land certificates, see para 2.6 above. Office copies were available under LR(S)A 1979 s 6(5).
48 Registers of Scotland, *Consultation on Implementation of the Land Registration etc (Scotland) Act 2012: Post Consultation Report* (2014) para 11.5. The Keeper adds (para 11.6) that she will 'reconsider the position when the possibility of electronic extracts of the cadastral map becomes possible from her computer systems'.
49 Registers of Scotland (Information and Access) Order 2014, SSI 2014/189, art 3.

advance on the previous position. Under the 1979 Act, authenticated copies were restricted to documents referred to in a title sheet,[50] and while the Keeper would in practice issue a copy of any document,[51] such copies lacked evidential status. Now extracts can be obtained of any document in the archive record.

Extracts of a title sheet or from the cadastral map can be requested not only as at the present date but also as at some date in the past, although the Keeper need comply with the request only to the extent that it is reasonably practicable to do so.[52] The reason for the qualification is that in the earlier years of the land registration system superseded data were not always retained.[53] A difficulty for cadastral units (title plans in the older conception) is that the base map changes over time. The legislation allows the Keeper to issue an extract using the base map as at some earlier date.[54] In all cases the date of the base map must be stated.[55]

Extracts are only available for three of the component parts of the Land Register.[56] For the fourth – the application record – the Keeper will supply certified copies, which are functional equivalents.[57] Again the fee is £30 plus VAT.[58]

Both extracts and certified copies have privileged evidential status, and can be accepted for all purposes as sufficient evidence of the contents of the original.[59] In principle, they can be in paper or electronic form,[60] but at the time of writing electronic copies were not available. The reason is that the main use of extracts and certified copies is as productions in litigation, and at present the courts apparently have difficulty in handling electronic documents.[61]

Finally, a plain copy[62] is a simple copy that lacks the evidential status of an extract or certified copy. The availability of plain copies is co-extensive with the availability of extracts and certified copies, and subject to the same limitations.[63] There does not appear to be any definition of 'plain copy'.[64] A plain copy can be in either paper or electronic form. The fee is £16 plus VAT.[65]

In the unlikely event of a copy issued by RoS turning out not to be a true copy, the Keeper is liable for any loss suffered as a result.[66]

50 LR(S)A 1979 s 6(5).
51 This did not happen at first, but began to happen in the late 1990s.
52 LR(S)A 2012 s 104(4).
53 In this respect the wording in the LR(S)A 2012 perhaps imposes on the Keeper a less stringent requirement than the wording of the SLC draft Bill s 70, sch 6 para 20.
54 LR(S)A 2012 s 104(5)(a).
55 LR(S)A 2012 s 104(5)(b).
56 For the component parts of the Register, see para 3.3 above and para 4.1 below.
57 LR(S)A 2012 s 104(2), (3).
58 Registers of Scotland (Fees) Order 2014, SSI 2014/188, sch 1 pt 7.
59 LR(S)A 2012 s 105.
60 LR(S)A 2012 s 104(7).
61 *General Guidance: Extracts, Certified Copies and Plain Copies* (n 45) 4. In *Scottish Parliamentary Corporate Body v The Sovereign Indigenous Peoples of Scotland* [2016] CSOH 65, 2016 SLT 761, the court was content with a Registers Direct printout in order to vouch for the pursuer's title to the Scottish Parliament: see para 6.
62 A term that replaces the previous 'quick copy'.
63 The Registers of Scotland (Information and Access) Order 2014 arts 2, 3. Plain copies may also be requested from certain other registers, including copies of any deed recorded in the Register of Sasines.
64 The term is used in the Registers of Scotland (Fees) Order 2014 sch 1 pt 7, and in the Registers of Scotland (Information and Access) Order 2014 art 2.
65 Registers of Scotland (Fees) Order 2014 sch 1 pt 7.
66 LR(S)A 2012 s 106: for discussion, see para 14.8 below.

3.13 The PDF link

When the Keeper sends to the grantee of a deed, and also the granter, an email confirming that registration has been completed, the email contains a link to the 'landing page', which contains a PDF of the title sheet plus the relevant part of the cadastral map. The PDF itself is not an attachment to the email. The link is available for 50 days.[67] Applications for registration are the subject of a separate chapter.[68]

3.14 Access to past data

Information about land rights in the past can be of value. For example, a trustee in sequestration may wish to recover information about properties, which, though not owned by the insolvent person at the time of the opening of the sequestration, may have been owned in the recent past. This could be relevant, for example, in seeking to challenge gratuitous alienations made by the debtor. Investigative journalists, police detectives and so on may also have an interest in past data, as may genealogists and local historians (who have, indeed, long made use of the Register of Sasines). The legislation does not in express terms require the Keeper to retain past data, but does so indirectly by requiring the Keeper to issue, if so requested, extracts referring to dates in the past.[69]

THE KEEPER

3.15 The Keeper and RoS

The Keeper of the Registers of Scotland ('the Keeper') administers the Land Register.[70] Everything that happens, happens in her name.[71] Of course in reality the Keeper is a senior administrator: there exists a large department that carries out the work, known as Registers of Scotland (RoS).[72]

The Keeper and RoS are virtually synonyms. When speaking administratively 'RoS' is the natural term, while 'the Keeper' is the natural legal term, and that usage is reflected in the legislation, which almost invariably refers to 'the Keeper', though occasionally, when administrative matters are in question, to 'Registers of Scotland'.[73] But conveyancers often speak of 'the Keeper' in cases where others might speak of 'RoS'.

The Keeper administers a large stable of different registers,[74] and accordingly RoS are not solely concerned with the Register of Sasines and Land Register.

---

67 Registers of Scotland, *General Guidance: Notifications* (v.01, 2014) 2.
68 Chapter 8.
69 LR(S)A 2012 s 104(4): see para 3.12 above.
70 LR(S)A 2012 s 1(2).
71 At the time of writing the Keeper was Sheenagh Adams – hence the use of the feminine pronoun. All previous Keepers had been men.
72 www.ros.gov.uk. For the history of these administrative arrangements, see para 1.9 above.
73 For instance, the Registers of Scotland (Fees) Order 2014.
74 Currently 17. As well as the Land Register and the Register of Sasines, there are other land-related registers, notably the Register of Inhibitions, the Crofting Register and the Register of Community Interests in Land. But there are other registers in the Keeper's stable that have no, or no specific, connection with land, such as the Books of Council and Session. Some of the registers are little known, such as the Register of the Cachet Seal.

The position here is thus different from that which exists in many countries, where the department that manages the land registration system has no other responsibilities.[75] Moreover, in many countries land registration is done on a local or regional basis, whereas in Scotland there is today[76] a single department for the whole of the country.

3.16 Appointments and vacancies

Appointment to the office of Keeper is by the Scottish Ministers, but the decision is not theirs alone, for the Lord President's consent is required.[77] The Keeper is the holder of a non-ministerial office of the Scottish Government.[78]

Because everything is, in the eyes of the law, done by the Keeper, a problem would arise in the event of the Keeper's death or incapacity, for the appointment of a new Keeper could not happen instantly, with the result that doubts might arise as to the validity of registrations and other acts done by RoS in the interval. The issue is addressed by s 109 of the 2012 Act, which confers validity on acts done by RoS during a vacancy in office.

3.17 Keeper's *vires*

Before the 2012 Act, RoS sometimes carried on activities which lacked a clear legal basis in terms of the Keeper's legal *vires*, such as giving paid advice to foreign administrative bodies in relation to land registration. The position is clarified by the Act, which provides that the Keeper may provide 'commercial services' and may establish and invest in companies.[79]

3.18 Financial regime

The financial regime applicable to the Keeper is regulated by the Registers of Scotland Executive Agency Trading Fund Order 1996[80] and by the Public Finance and Accountability (Scotland) Act 2000.[81] RoS are self-funding, and hence not a burden on the taxpayer; most of the income comes from fees for registration.[82] Annual reports and accounts are published on the RoS website.

3.19 Keeper's role administrative, not judicial

In some countries the land registration office has a judicial as well as an administrative role. In Germany, for instance, the land registrar has the status of a

---

75 For instance in England and Wales, where Her Majesty's Land Registry (HMLR) deals only with land registration.
76 Relatively speaking, that is a recent development. Between 1617 and 1868 an applicant could register deeds either in a local ('particular') Register of Sasines or in the General Register of Sasines in Edinburgh. The particular registers were disbanded by s 8 of the Land Registers (Scotland) Act 1868. For details, see paras 1.7 and 1.8 above.
77 Public Registers and Records (Scotland) Act 1948 s 1(1).
78 Scotland Act 1998 s 126(8).
79 LR(S)A 2012 s 108.
80 SI 1996/1004.
81 Public Finance and Accountability (Scotland) Act 2000 s 9. See further para 14.14 below.
82 For details as to fees, see para 8.5 below.

judge. That is not the position in Scotland.[83] The Keeper does not hold a judicial office; indeed she does not even have to be legally qualified.[84]

In the course of the normal business of registering deeds, the Keeper must make decisions of fact and also, sometimes, of law. 'Where the issue is one of law, he can usually be expected to reach a decision; proceed on the basis of such decision; and leave it open to a dissatisfied party to seek to have the matter finally determined on appeal. Where the doubtful issue is one of fact, he may well be faced with a situation which he simply cannot resolve.'[85] The Keeper's decisions are made in an administrative, not a judicial, capacity. There exists no system at RoS for the judicial determination of parties' rights – no power to swear witnesses, to compel their attendance, and so on.[86] The Keeper does not hear and determine cases. To apply to the Keeper is not to litigate. Her decisions are not decrees, one of the consequences being that they cannot give rise to *res judicata*. Where parties are in irreconcilable disagreement about their rights, the matter can be resolved only by a court or the Lands Tribunal, or by arbitration.

3.20 Appeals

An appeal may be made to the Lands Tribunal, on fact or law, against any decision of the Keeper.[87] Although the legislation uses the term 'appeal', that does not mean that the Keeper's original decision is of a judicial nature. As already mentioned, the Keeper's office is administrative, not judicial. Thus if there is an appeal to the Tribunal, the Tribunal hearing is, as a *judicial* hearing, a first-instance hearing.

Under the 1979 Act, appeals, especially against the refusal of rectification, were often used to resolve what were in reality disputes between neighbours or other competing parties. Although notionally directed at the Keeper, therefore, such appeals raised issues which could only be determined by adjudicating between the warring parties.[88] Fortunately, the procedure was sufficiently flexible to accommodate this reality. The other party to the dispute entered the proceedings as an 'interested party' while the Keeper, at least in the later years of the Act, was not represented at the hearing at all (though might submit written answers).[89] No such subterfuge is needed under the 2012 Act. Where the real dispute is with a neighbour or other party, the appropriate course of action is likely

---

83 For background, see *Registration of Title to Land in Scotland: Report by a Committee appointed by the Secretary of State for Scotland* (Cmnd 2032, 1963) ('Reid Report') para 117.
84 Neither the current Keeper nor her immediate predecessor was legally qualified and both came from outside RoS. Before that the practice had been to appoint someone who had made a career working in the Registers. Reflecting that earlier practice, the Macmillan Committee thought that the person holding the office of Keeper needed 'an intimate knowledge of the technicalities of Scottish conveyancing': see Scottish Home Department, *First Report of the Committee on Land Registration in Scotland* (Cmd 7451, 1948) para 6. That that is no longer true reflects a change in the role of the Keeper who is in reality the chief executive of a large organisation.
85 *PMP Plus Ltd v Keeper of the Registers of Scotland* 2009 SLT (Lands Tr) 2, para 43.
86 See eg *Balfour v Keeper of the Registers of Scotland* 2015 SLT (Lands Tr) 185, para 10.
87 LR(S)A 2012 s 103(1). The position was the same under LR(S)A 1979 s 25(1).
88 For a general discussion, see SLC Report 222 part 31.
89 For one example of many, see *Burton v Keeper of the Registers of Scotland* 2014 SLT (Lands Tr) 69. As was observed in *PMP Plus Ltd* (n 85) para 49, 'the Keeper may have no real interest in the outcome'.

to be an application to the Lands Tribunal under its new jurisdiction to consider questions relating to the accuracy of the Register, or alternatively litigation before the ordinary courts.[90] And while the Keeper is entitled to appear and be heard in any civil proceedings concerning the accuracy of the Register, or what is needed to rectify such an inaccuracy,[91] she is likely to leave the parties to fight matters out for themselves. Under the 2012 Act, therefore, appeals against a decision of the Keeper will more often be used in cases where title matters have been resolved or are not at issue and where it the Keeper's decision alone that is under challenge.[92]

The Lands Tribunal is, under the Tribunals (Scotland) Act 2014,[93] prospectively merged into the new First-tier Tribunal. One of the chambers of the latter is expected to be, in substance, a continuation of the Lands Tribunal.[94] Appeal can, with leave, be made to the Upper Tribunal; thereafter there is, with leave, a further appeal to the Inner House of the Court of Session.[95]

In addition to a Lands Tribunal appeal, a decision of the Keeper, being administrative in nature, can be challenged by judicial review.[96]

3.21 The Keeper's discretion

The new legislation confers less discretion on the Keeper than did the previous legislation.[97] For instance, under the 1979 Act the decision whether to accept an application was essentially discretionary.[98] So was the decision whether to rectify an inaccuracy.[99] The general approach of the 2012 Act is against discretion. The Keeper has to make decisions, but the legislation generally states the rule that the Keeper is to apply. Of course, in specific cases the rule may be difficult to apply, but in theory at least a given set of facts should lead to only one possible decision. In the case of applications for registration, for example, if certain criteria are satisfied the Keeper *must* accept the application, and if they are not satisfied the Keeper *must* reject it.[100] Similarly, in the case of manifest inaccuracy the Keeper *must* rectify the Register.[101] Unavoidably, even the 2012 Act makes some use of discretion,[102] but as compared to the previous legislation its role is significantly curtailed.

---

90 See para 11.19 below. Before the ordinary courts the action will often be one of declarator or reduction, or both.
91 LR(S)A 2012 ss 82(2)(c) and 83.
92 An appeal, however, is not a judicial review, and it is entirely open to the Tribunal to consider matters of title. As the Tribunal observed in *Brookfield Developments Ltd v Keeper of the Registers of Scotland* 1989 SLT (Lands Tr) 105, 110J, 'the central issue before us is not … whether the Keeper has properly carried out his duties, but rather the simple question of whether there is an inaccuracy'. See also *PMP Plus Ltd* (n 85) paras 36, 39 and 42.
93 Tribunals (Scotland) Act 2014 ss 27–29.
94 T(S)A 2014 s 20.
95 T(S)A 2014 ss 46–50.
96 LR(S)A 2012 s 103(2). See eg *Short's Tr v Keeper of the Registers of Scotland* 1996 SC (HL) 14; *Foster v Keeper of the Registers of Scotland* 2006 SLT 513.
97 This indeed was one of the objects of the reform: see para 2.15 above.
98 LR(S)A 1979 s 4(1): see para 2.6 above.
99 LR(S)A 1979 s 9(1): see para 2.9 above.
100 LR(S)A 2012 s 21(2), (3).
101 LR(S)A 2012 s 80.
102 Some examples were mentioned in para 3.11 above. On discretion generally in this context, see *PMP Plus Ltd* (n 85) para 34.

Chapter 4

The Land Register: Structure and Contents

4.1 Introduction

The Land Register comprises four distinct parts: the title sheet record, the cadastral map, the archive record, and the application record. In substance that was already the position under the 1979 Act,[1] although it was not until the 2012 Act that a legislative basis was put in place.[2] This chapter is mainly about title sheets, although something will be said at the end about the other parts of the Register.[3] It is necessary to begin, however, with a concept introduced by the 2012 Act: the plot of land.

PLOTS OF LAND

4.2 Definition

A plot of land is 'an area or areas of land all of which are owned by one person, or one set of persons'.[4] The word 'area' is undefined. The primary meaning is a section of the earth's surface including the airspace above and the ground below; for, in principle, ownership of land extends *a coelo usque ad centrum*, forming a cone from the sky down to the centre of the earth. However, to this simple idea separate tenements form an exception. Under the Act a separate tenement is itself regarded as a 'plot' distinct from the plot in the normal sense:[5] this is a necessary consequence of the way that the common law conceptualises separate tenements.[6] Thus the cone just mentioned might have carve-outs for mineral rights, salmon-fishing rights, and so on. Each is a 'plot' for the purposes of the Act. So too is a tenement flat.[7]

The definition just quoted speaks of 'areas' in the plural. A plot could consist of two separate areas. An example would be a house with a garden on the other side of the street.[8] In such a case the Keeper could maintain two separate title sheets,

---

1 The Land Registration (Scotland) Act 1979 provided only for title sheets (in s 6): for discussion, see Scottish Law Commission, *Report No 222 on Land Registration* (2010) ('SLC Report 222') paras 4.2–4.4.
2 Land Registration etc (Scotland) Act 2012 s 2. Providing such a legislative basis was one example of the process of 'pumping concrete into the foundations', for which see para 2.15 above.
3 See paras 4.29–4.32 below.
4 LR(S)A 2012 s 3(4). The term 'plot' is a traditional one in Scottish conveyancing, and for that reason was the term adopted in the Act. In many English-speaking countries the term 'parcel' is used, and in Francophone countries *parcelle* is sometimes used in the same sense. The concept is similar to the German concept of *Grundstück* (a point of which the Scottish Law Commission was aware during its project): see C von Bar, 'Why do we need *Grundstücke* (land units) and what are they?' (2014) 22 Juridica International 3.
5 LR(S)A 2012 s 3(5).
6 As to which see K G C Reid, *The Law of Property in Scotland* (1996) paras 207–13.
7 More is said about tenements at para 4.25 below.
8 Quite a common example would be 'a farm bisected by a road: it is farmed as a single farm although the two parts are not contiguous': see Registers of Scotland, *General Guidance: The Cadastral Map* (v.01, 2014) 2, n 3.

but could alternatively treat the two areas, house and garden, as a single plot. For every plot there has to be unity of ownership, as the statutory definition makes clear. For instance if, in the example just given, Jack and Jill are co-owners, and Jack dispones his half share in the garden to Jill while remaining in co-ownership with her as to the house, the garden would then become a distinct plot.

4.3 Plots of land, title sheets, and cadastral units

Each registered plot of land has a title sheet of its own.[9] And, in the normal case, there is a one-to-one correlation between (i) plots of land, (ii) title sheets, and (iii) the individual units which make up the cadastral map ('cadastral units').[10] A single reference number is used for all three,[11] which in practice is a shortened version of the name of the registration country followed by a number (for example, 'MID77614').[12] Title sheets and cadastral units exist within the Register, whilst plots exist in the physical world.

To this one-to-one correlation there are two qualifications. One concerns leases: a long lease can (and in practice always does) have its own title sheet, but there is no cadastral unit for a lease.[13] The other qualification is that, although a tenement flat is a 'plot', nevertheless a tenement as a whole can constitute a single cadastral unit.[14]

4.4 A register of what?

Before the 2012 Act, it was common to say, for instance, that 'the disposition by Tom to Mary was registered in the Land Register on 2 February 2000', but the propriety of so speaking was questionable since under the 1979 Act registration was, strictly, of interests in land rather than of the deeds which vouched for their creation, transfer, variation or extinction.[15] Under the 2012 Act deeds are registered. But as well as being a register of title, and a register of deeds, the Register is, under the Act, also a register of plots of land, and it is correct to speak of land being registered.[16] Thus the Land Register is (i) a register of title, (ii) a register of deeds, and (iii) a register of plots of land.

TITLE SHEETS: IN GENERAL

4.5 Plot title sheets and lease title sheets

Every plot of land has its own title sheet, as already mentioned. But in addition to such 'plot title sheets' the Register also has title sheets for long leases ('lease title sheets').[17] The extent to which they are used is at the discretion of the Keeper:

---

9 LR(S)A 2012 s 3(1).
10 LR(S)A 2012 s 12(1): 'A cadastral unit is a unit which represents a single registered plot of land.' For cadastral units, see para 5.8 below.
11 LR(S)A 2012 ss 4(1)(a) and 12(5).
12 LR(S)A 2012 s 4(2) provides that title numbers must consist of numerals or of letters and numerals.
13 See para 4.5 below.
14 LR(S)A 2012 s 16(1). Tenemental buildings are discussed at para 4.25 below.
15 See para 2.2 above.
16 Eg LR(S)A 2012 s 27.
17 LR(S)A 2012 s 3(2). In effect, this follows the 1979 Act system under which there were title sheets for all primary interests in land, ie for ownership and long lease: see para 2.2 above.

either a lease title sheet can be created, or the details of the lease can be set out in the landlord's (plot) title sheet. The Keeper's policy, however, is that registered leases should have their own title sheets,[18] from which it follows that the total number of title sheets necessarily exceeds the total number of plots.[19]

A title sheet cannot be *both* a plot title sheet and a lease title sheet. If, therefore, a person holds one plot as owner and a neighbouring plot as tenant, it is necessary to have a plot title sheet in respect of the former and a lease title sheet in respect of the latter.[20]

Lease title sheets have their own number[21] but, since a lease is not a plot of land, this is not the number of any cadastral unit.[22] Although a lease does not have its own cadastral unit, a registered lease still has its extent[23] depicted on the cadastral map.[24] Its extent may be the same as that of a cadastral unit, as where the owner of a building grants a long lease of it; or it may be smaller, as where the owner of an industrial estate grants a long lease of one unit on the estate; or it may cover more than one cadastral unit, though this would be unusual.

A plot title sheet will refer to any registered lease in relation to that plot. But it will not refer to any short lease (ie lease for 20 years or under), for short leases cannot appear in the Land Register.[25] In this respect an acquirer runs a risk, although in practice the fact of the tenant's possession will usually be apparent.

The Keeper has the power to combine and divide cadastral units and consequently plot title sheets.[26]

4.6 Transitional: 1979 Act title sheets

Under the 1979 Act, title sheets were maintained for interests in land and not for (physical) plots of land.[27] But, whatever the theoretical differences that that might entail, the difference in practice was sufficiently small to allow the (roughly) one and a half million title sheets already created under the 1979 Act to be converted

---

18 Registers of Scotland, *General Guidance: Leases and Automatic Plot Registration* (v.02, 2015) 1–2. This is to avoid the 'practical problems' of deciphering a single title where, for example, both the plot and the lease are subject to a large number of encumbrances.
19 For further information as to lease title sheets, see Registers of Scotland, *Registration Manual* (https://rosdev.atlassian.net/wiki/display/2ARM/Home) Topics: Leases – lease title sheet. The only case where a lease will not, at first, have its own title sheet is where it is considered to be registered in the Land Register merely by virtue of being mentioned in the plot title sheet: see para 20.6 below.
20 *Registration Manual* (n 19) Topics: Leases – mixed ownership/leasehold titles.
21 LR(S)A 2012 s 4(1)(b).
22 LR(S)A 2012 s 12(1).
23 'Extent' is a term used in land registration practice to mean a defined area of land. The term (in that sense) is not used in the LR(S)A 2012, though it is used in the Land Register Rules etc (Scotland) Regulations 2014, SSI 2014/150 ('LRR 2014').
24 *General Guidance: Leases and Automatic Plot Registration* (n 18) 3.
25 Only leases that are long leases can be registered: see Registration of Leases (Scotland) Act 1857 (20 & 21 Vict c 26) s 1.
26 LR(S)A 2012 s 13(2)–(4). This follows the Land Registration (Scotland) Rules 2006, SSI 2006/485, r 8. The current rule is expressed in terms of cadastral units, whereas the rule under the previous legislation was expressed in terms of title sheets.
27 For the system under the 1979 Act, see para 2.2 above. An illustration of the difference, chosen more because it is striking than because the point has often cropped up, is that under the 1979 Act there could be, and occasionally was, registration of just one *pro indiviso* share of a property, the other share, or shares, remaining in the Register of Sasines, so that the property was, so to speak, partly registered and partly unregistered, like a half-transparent ghost. Under the 2012 Act, it is the plot of land that is registered.

automatically into 2012 Act title sheets. This happened on the designated day (8 December 2014), when title sheets in respect of the interest of ownership became plot title sheets, and title sheets in respect of the interest of tenancy became lease title sheets.[28] The Keeper is empowered (but not bound) to take such steps as may be necessary to bring converted title sheets into line with the requirements of the 2012 Act.[29] The changes that are needed include creating separate cadastral units and title sheets for common areas, removing conflicting overlaps, and adding in, for co-owners, the size of their respective *pro indiviso* shares.[30] Such changes may take many years to accomplish.

Where a development was, on the appointed day, partially sold off, the Keeper may register the remaining split-off deeds on the basis of the old law, and it is the practice to do so.[31] This does not, however, extend to permitting the registration of unmapped common areas.

4.7 Divisions of title sheets

Title sheets are divided into four sections: a property section, a proprietorship section, a securities section, and a burdens section.[32] These are often referred to by the letters A, B, C and D respectively. The A section identifies the property, the B section the proprietor (or, in the case of a lease title sheet, the tenant), the C section any securities over the property, and the D Section any other registered encumbrances, such as real burdens.

Individual sections can be divided at the Keeper's discretion.[33] For example, as the D (burdens) section encompasses a potentially very disparate set of encumbrances, the Keeper could have one subsection for servitudes, a second for real burdens, a third for public-law encumbrances,[34] and so on. Another possibility would be to make a division in the A (property) section, so that incorporeal pertinents had their own subsection. If appropriate, different title sheets can have different divisions. Such divisions are simply a matter of convenience, both for RoS and for those who read title sheets: they are shelves or drawers or pigeonholes where items can conveniently be grouped together.

4.8 Contents of title sheets

Detailed provision is made in the legislation as to (i) what *must* be included in a title sheet, (ii) what *may* be so included, and (iii) what *must not* be included. Any

---

28 LR(S)A 2012 sch 4 paras 1, 4, and 5. In respect of the first of these, the Keeper has to create a cadastral unit for each plot.
29 LR(S)A 2012 sch 4 paras 2, 3 and 7 ff.
30 See respectively: para 4.20 below; para 5.11 below; and LR(S)A 2012 s 7(1)(b).
31 LR(S)A 2012 sch 4 paras 9 and 10. RoS refer to this as the principle of 'the Keeper has started so she'll finish'. See generally Registers of Scotland, *General Guidance: The Cadastral Map – Mapping common areas* (v.02, 2015).
32 LR(S)A 2012 s 5(1). This is the same division as under the 1979 Act except that the securities section was called the charges section: see para 2.2 above. The Reid Report had recommended the use of the correct Scottish term, 'heritable securities': see *Registration of Title to Land in Scotland: Report by a Committee appointed by the Secretary of State for Scotland* (Cmnd 2032, 1963) para 94; but 'in the interest of brevity' the Henry Report recommended adoption of the English-law term, 'charge': see *Scheme for the Introduction and Operation of Registration of Title to Land in Scotland: Report by a Committee appointed by the Secretary of State for Scotland* (Cmnd 4137, 1969) Part I, para 4. The 2012 Act restores Scottish terminology without adding to the number of words.
33 LR(S)A 2012 s 5(2).
34 Such as tree preservation notices.

Title Sheets: in General 59

shortcoming in respect of (i) or (iii) (but not (ii)) has the effect of making the title sheet – and hence the Register – inaccurate and so in need of rectification.[35]

The first of these (mandatory content) is a large subject and is discussed separately in the next section.[36] Here we are concerned only with the other two.

4.9 Material that *may* be included

A title sheet 'must' include 'such other information (if any) as the Keeper considers appropriate'.[37] Although this is verbally a 'must' it is in substance a 'may'. The most obvious example of such supplementary data[38] is the postal address that is almost always set out in the property section. Other examples would be supplementary plans,[39] or the giving of variants as to an owner's name. Anything can be included, according to the Keeper's judgement,[40] with the exception of the material mentioned in the next paragraph.

4.10 Material that *must not* be included

No rights or obligations may be included in a title sheet except in so far as this is authorised by an enactment, whether the 2012 Act itself or (more usually) some other enactment.[41] At first glance this might seem to contradict the provision quoted above allowing 'such other information (if any) as the Keeper considers appropriate' to be entered. The explanation lies in the difference between 'information' on the one hand and 'rights or obligations' on the other. Inclusion of information is generally permissible, if relevant to the aims and objectives of land registration, but is not permissible if it is about rights or obligations, unless they are rights or obligations whose inclusion is authorised by an enactment.

For example, suppose that Tamsin sells part of her land to Stewart, and the disposition contains (a) servitudes and real burdens relating to the disponed area and the retained area, and (b) contractual terms. The servitudes and real burdens must be registered, but the purely contractual terms must not be registered. The function of the Register is to set out real rights, and rights similar to real rights, affecting immoveable property. Purely personal rights have no place there.[42] Although this was probably the law under the 1979 Act, the position was not wholly clear, and in practice purely personal rights were sometimes admitted to registration, either as pertinents in the A section or as encumbrances in the D section.

There are three reasons for this 'no admittance' rule. One is that the appearance of such rights and obligations in the Register could give the impression to non-expert users of the system that they affect third parties when in law they do not. A second reason is that the more the Register becomes clogged up with data that should not be there, the more the costs of conveyancing are increased, and

35 In respect of (i) this is inaccuracy by omission, in respect of (iii) inaccuracy by commission: see paras 11.2–11.4 below.
36 Paragraphs 4.13–4.19 below.
37 LR(S)A 2012 s 10(2)(e).
38 To use the term employed in LR(S)A 2012 s 11(1)(a), (8).
39 For which see para 5.18 below.
40 LR(S)A 2012 s 11(8).
41 LR(S)A 2012 s 10(4). For an account of registrable deeds, see ch 6.
42 They can indeed be registered but their registration home is the Books of Council and Session.

increased unnecessarily, for the simple reason that conveyancers have to spend time reading title sheets, and time is money – clients' money. The third reason concerns the 'offside goals' rule. In some circumstances, a right that is in itself simply a contractual right between the granter of a disposition or other deed and a third party can affect the grantee of the deed if the grantee has knowledge of it.[43] It would be undesirable if entries whose inclusion in a title sheet was unnecessary should be able to produce such an effect. Moreover, since the applicability of the offside goals rule to individual fact-situations is sometimes uncertain, the appearance of contractual rights in title sheets can push up conveyancing costs, with the law firm acting for the buyer having to take time to consider the offside goals issue, and sometimes having to obtain a professional opinion.

What if the Keeper does by mistake include a right or obligation whose inclusion is unauthorised? In the first place, such an inclusion constitutes an inaccuracy, and so the entry should be deleted.[44] In the second place, because of the worry about the inappropriate engagement of the offside goals rule, s 10(5) says: 'The entry or incorporation by reference in a title sheet of any right or obligation, in so far as not so authorised, (a) does not constitute notice of that right or obligation, and (b) is without any other effect.' That means that if there is a wrongful entry, it is treated as if it had not been made.[45]

4.11 Trusts

'Keeping trusts off the register', wrote the New Zealand Law Commission, has come to be regarded as 'one of the objects' of registration of title.[46] The idea is that if land is owned by Tom, Dick and Harry as trustees, only their names should appear in the register, not their status as trustees. Similar concerns can be found elsewhere in the common-law world, where beneficial rights tend to have the status of proprietary rights, and hence the potential to complicate conveyancing. The position in Scotland is different. In neither the Register of Sasines nor the Land Register is there any problem about revealing the fact of a trust, nor has this ever been a matter of controversy. The reason lies in the fact that the Scottish trust is conceptually rather different from the common-law trust.[47]

4.12 Mode of making entries

Not all entries in title sheets need to be in full.[48] It is permissible to incorporate by reference a document held in the archive record, or for that matter a deed in any other register that is under the management and control of the Keeper.[49]

---

43 The case law and literature are extensive. For an overview, see Reid (n 6) paras 695 ff.
44 Ie by rectification: see LR(S)A 2012 ss 65 and 80. This would be an inaccuracy by commission: see para 11.4 below.
45 Cf s 14(4) (discussed at para 4.31 below) which has a similar purpose.
46 New Zealand Law Commission, *Review of the Land Transfer Act 1952* (Issues Paper 10, 2008) para 8.1.
47 For further discussion see SLC Report 222 para 4.63.
48 On the other hand, there is no equivalent to s 6(2) of the LR(S)A 1979 which allowed the Keeper to enter a real right or real burden or condition 'by entering its terms or a summary of its terms'. Our impression is that the power to enter only a summary of terms was barely used.
49 LR(S)A 2012 s 10(3).

New entries must be accompanied by the date on which they are made.[50]

TITLE SHEETS: MANDATORY CONTENT

4.13 Introduction

The legislation makes detailed provision as to what a title sheet *must* contain and, in most cases, in which of the four parts of a title sheet it must appear.[51] In so far as anything which should be on the title sheet fails to appear there, the title sheet is inaccurate and hence in need of rectification.[52]

4.14 The A (property) section

The property section (A section) of a title sheet sets out the essential features of the plot of land in question. The plot itself must be described by reference to the cadastral map[53] and, while the legislation says nothing about further information, such as the property name or address or other descriptive words, such information can be added under the Keeper's general power to enter supplementary information.[54] In the case of seabed properties the OSGB36 coordinates are needed.[55] There must also be stated whether the title sheet is for the right of ownership or of lease;[56] the latter must give particulars of the lease.[57] If the plot is a separate tenement, the nature of the tenement (eg salmon fishing rights) is stated.[58] For properties entering the Register after the designated day, the area must be given if it is greater than half a hectare.[59] The date of the first registration of the plot must be stated, and also the date of the last entry in the title sheet.[60]

The property section must also set out the particulars of any incorporeal pertinents.[61] These are rights, typically in respect of some other property, which benefit the property in question. If known, details of the burdened property should also be given. Thus if the property is Blackmains, and the property enjoys the benefit of a servitude of way across the neighbouring property, Whitemains, that fact should be set forth in the property section of the Blackmains title sheet.

---

50 LR(S)A 2012 s 102.
51 In addition to the text that follows, more information can be found in the *Registration Manual* (n 19) Topics, where there are separate sections on each of the four parts of the title sheet.
52 This is inaccuracy by omission: see para 11.3 below.
53 LR(S)A 2012 s 6(1)(a)(i). See also para 5.9 below.
54 LR(S)A 2012 s 10(2)(e), discussed at para 4.9 above.
55 See para 5.16 below.
56 LR(S)A 2012 s 6(1)(a)(ii). Although this provision is awkwardly worded (especially the use of 'proprietor' which seems to indicate the right of ownership) and, viewed in isolation, hard to interpret, it seems to repeat the requirement of the Land Registration (Scotland) Rules 2006 r 4(1)(b) that the property section should show 'the nature of the interest in land'.
57 LR(S)A 2012 s 6(1)(e).
58 LR(S)A 2012 s 6(1)(a)(ii), (iii).
59 LRR 2014 r 12(1)(f). Under the previous legislation the rule was the same, but the figure was not half a hectare but two hectares: LR(S)A 1979 s 6(1)(a). For the change, see Registers of Scotland, *Consultation on Implementation of the Land Registration etc (Scotland) Act 2012: Post Consultation Report* (2014) paras 1.7 ff.
60 LRR 2014 r 12(1)(a)
61 LR(S)A 2012 s 6(1)(b). For pertinents, see para 4.24 below. For the practice in relation to KIR title sheets, see para 7.20 below.

(From the standpoint of Whitemains, the servitude is an encumbrance, and should appear in the D section of the Whitemains title sheet.[62]) The same is true of other pertinents, such as the benefit of a real burden.[63] In the case of prescriptive servitudes, it should be possible to show their extent on the cadastral map, as this information must be supplied by applicants for first registration.[64] Surprisingly, perhaps, there may be no corresponding duty on applicants in respect of servitudes constituted in writing, but in entering such a servitude the Keeper must give details of the deed.[65]

Where an area of land has more than one title sheet – as where the land is leased, or a part is broken off as a separate tenement – the property section of each is to mention the title number of the other.[66] The result is a cross-referencing system. A person who looks at, say, a salmon-fishing title sheet will see a reference to the main title sheet, and *vice versa*. In some cases the result will be a large number of references. For example, Jill might hold the mineral rights under land on which there are a thousand houses. Each house title sheet would have just one cross-reference, to the mineral rights title sheet, but the latter would have a thousand cross-references. Furthermore, a statement that minerals are reserved must be made in the title sheet of the surface plot (ie of the house title sheets in the example just given).[67]

The requirement to cross-refer does not apply in respect of flats, so that in a tenement the individual flat title sheets do not have to identify the others.[68] Whilst this exception makes sense within a tenement itself, its wording may mean that there do not have to be cross-references as between flats on the one hand and mineral rights title sheets on the other. That possible interpretation may not have been what was intended. Even if that interpretation is correct, the Keeper would be free to cross-refer by way of supplementary data.[69]

Finally, some specialities. Any caveat must be entered.[70] So must s 66 agreements made in respect of water boundaries.[71] And there are special requirements in respect of 'sharing' and 'shared' plot title sheets,[72] the latter representing a common area that is in multiple ownership.[73]

---

62 An incorporeal pertinent in favour of property X is an encumbrance over another property, Y (or in some cases, more than one other property). But the converse is not true. There are some encumbrances that are not the pertinents of another property. A standard security would be an example. A tree preservation notice would be another example, as would personal real burdens, for which see s 1(3) of the Title Conditions (Scotland) Act 2003.
63 Rather oddly, on first registration the applicant is required to say what servitudes benefit the property, but is not asked about other pertinents: see para 8.23 below.
64 LRR 2014 r 7, sch 1 pt 4. For prescriptive servitudes, see para 4.28 below.
65 LRR 2014 r 12(1)(c). We understand that it was intended that the Keeper should always be supplied with sufficient information to delineate the extent of the servitude on the cadastral map, but the application form in its current version makes no such requirement.
66 LR(S)A 2012 s 6(1)(f).
67 LRR 2014 r 12(1)(d). This is only of value where the minerals remain on a Sasine title and so there is no title sheet to refer to.
68 LR(S)A 2012 s 6(2).
69 For supplementary data, see para 4.9 above.
70 LRR 2014 r 12(1)(b).
71 LR(S)A 2012 s 6(1)(c). For s 66 agreements, see para 5.17 below.
72 LR(S)A 2012 ss 6(1)(d) and 18, sch 1 paras 6–10.
73 For shared and sharing plots, see paras 4.20–4.23 below.

4.15 The B (proprietorship) section

As might be expected, the proprietorship section (B section) contains the name and designation of the 'proprietor', or in other words of the owner or, in the case of a lease title sheet, the tenant of the property.[74] This is mandatory information except where, in Keeper-induced registration or automatic plot registration,[75] either or both of these cannot be determined with reasonable certainty.[76]

There are special rules for designation in the case of corporations and other juristic persons: this must include the legal system under which the juristic person is incorporated or otherwise established and either the person's registered number (if there is one) or some other identifier which is peculiar to the person.[77] In the case of UK companies, therefore, the company number is needed, which is a significant change in the law. At the time of the 1979 Act, usual conveyancing practice in respect of deeds was to give the company's name but not the number. This was hardly satisfactory since a company can change its name – can even swap its name with another company[78] – but its number cannot be changed.[79] Today of course the use, in conveyancing documents, of the company's number is almost universal.

No corresponding provision is made in the Act as to the designation of natural persons. The Scottish Law Commission had recommended that date of birth be required, as is now the international norm in conveyancing deeds, but this was not carried forward into the legislation.[80]

Where the proprietor holds in some special capacity, for instance as a trustee, this must be indicated,[81] although sometimes the Keeper will be unaware of the special capacity in question.[82] The deed or decree constituting the trust or other relationship should be mentioned.

In the case of property owned in common, other than tenement flats,[83] the B section must state the respective shares of the proprietors.[84] No such quantification statement is appropriate for property held by trustees because in joint property the owners do not have distinct shares.[85]

The B section must also include the consideration paid and the date of entry.[86] Both are in practice stated in dispositions presented for registration, though general law does not positively require this. It seems worth adding that whilst the date of entry may be useful information, it is not necessarily – indeed not usually – the date when ownership passes; ownership passes on the date of registration.[87]

---

74 LR(S)A 2012 s 7(1)(a). Where the title sheet is not a plot title sheet but a lease title sheet, the terminology is modified accordingly: LR(S)A 2012 s 113(3)(b). Thus what would be the 'proprietorship section' in an ordinary plot title sheet is the 'tenancy section' in a lease title sheet.
75 For which see respectively paras 7.9 and 7.20 below.
76 LR(S)A 2012 s 30(5).
77 LR(S)A 2012 s 113(1) (definition of 'designation').
78 For an example of a name swap, and the resulting confusion, see *F J Neale (Glasgow) Ltd v Vickery* 1973 SLT (Sh Ct) 88.
79 One might also note that natural persons can change their names, but not their dates of birth.
80 SLC Report 222 paras 4.20–4.24 and draft Bill s 92(1) (definition of 'designation'). It is to be hoped that Scottish Ministers will in due course add such a requirement in exercise of their power, in LR(S)A 2012 s 113(4), to amend the definition in the Act of 'designation'.
81 LR(S)A 2012 s 113(1) (definition of 'designation').
82 For trusts, see para 4.11 above.
83 LR(S)A 2012 ss 7(2) and 16(2)(b).
84 LR(S)A 2012 s 7(1)(b).
85 Reid (n 6) paras 20 and 35.
86 LRR 2014 r 12(2).
87 LR(S)A 2012 ss 36, 37(1) and 50(2).

Two types of entry which were found under the 1979 Act regime are now absent from the B section. One is proper liferents, which have relocated to the D section. The other is a statement about occupancy rights of spouses or civil partners, which no longer appears anywhere in the title sheet.[88]

Some special requirements, considered later,[89] affect 'sharing' and 'shared' plot title sheets,[90] the latter representing a common area that is in multiple ownership.

4.16 The C (securities) section

The Keeper must enter in the securities (formerly 'charges') section of the title sheet particulars of any heritable security burdening the plot (or lease) together with the name and designation of the creditor.[91] Floating charges, which were occasionally noted as overriding interests under the 1979 Act,[92] no longer appear on the Register. Designation was discussed above in connection with the proprietorship section,[93] and the rules are the same. The fact that the creditor in a standard security is a well-known bank does not alter the need for the company number. As for 'particulars', this could be a brief reference; the standard security itself will be in the archive record.[94]

Where there is a shared plot title sheet (eg in respect of an amenity area), standard securities over the sharing plots will automatically encumber the relevant shares of the shared plot, and the title sheet of the shared plot will not refer to such securities.[95]

4.17 The D (burdens) section

The burdens section is mainly for real burdens and servitudes or, in the case of a lease title sheet, leasehold conditions.[96] The legislation requires that the terms of such title conditions[97] are set out in full or by reference to a registered deed,[98] that a description is given of any benefited property (insofar as known to the Keeper), and that, in the case of personal real burdens such as conservation burdens, the

---

88 *Post Consultation Report* (n 59) para 1.27. Unlike their predecessors, the LRR 2014 make no provision for a statement on this topic.
89 For shared and sharing plots, see paras 4.20–4.23 below.
90 LR(S)A 2012 ss 7(2) and 18, sch 1 paras 6–10.
91 LR(S)A 2012 s 8(1). A lease title sheet thus no longer lists the securities burdening the plot: see *General Guidance: Leases and Automatic Plot Registration* (n 18) 2.
92 LR(S)A 1979 s 6(4); Land Registration Rules 2006 r 6(2).
93 Paragraph 4.15 above.
94 For the archive record, see para 4.31 below. In a few cases where property is registered in the Land Register subject to an undischarged standard security, the latter will still be in the Register of Sasines.
95 LR(S)A 2012 ss 8(2) and 18(3)(b), sch 1 para 8(b). See para 4.21 below.
96 Only encumbrances which affect 'the right in land to which the title sheet relates' are to be included: LR(S)A 2012 s 9(1)(a). Thus, the former practice of including in the lease title sheet real burdens and servitudes which affect the plot of land is discontinued, and such burdens and servitudes will be removed from existing title sheets in due course: see *General Guidance: Leases and Automatic Plot Registration* (n 18) 2. Nonetheless, the tenant will continue to be affected by the burdens and servitudes, and prospective acquirers should consult the plot title sheet.
97 The rule applies to all title conditions. LR(S)A 2012 s 113(1) adopts the definition of 'title condition' in s 122(1) of the Title Conditions (Scotland) Act 2003. Apart from the title conditions already mentioned, this includes conditions of agreements entered into under s 7 of the National Trust for Scotland Confirmation Act 1938 (rarely encountered in practice).
98 LR(S)A 2012 s 10(3). Compare LR(S)A 1979 s 6(2) which allowed the Keeper to make do with a summary of their terms.

name and designation of the holder is stated.⁹⁹ Except in KIR title sheets,¹⁰⁰ the practice is for the terms to be set out in full, but coupled with a reference to the deed by which the title conditions were constituted.

If the property is subject to a long lease – or, in the case of a lease title sheet, to a long sub-lease – this must be mentioned,¹⁰¹ and the A section will contain an appropriate cross-reference to the lease title sheet.¹⁰² Other encumbrances where an enactment¹⁰³ provides or allows for registration must also be included, together with the name and designation of the person who has title to enforce.¹⁰⁴ Typically, these derive from public law, such as tree preservation orders¹⁰⁵ or s 75 agreements,¹⁰⁶ but they also include such private-law encumbrances as proper liferents¹⁰⁷ or notices of potential liability for costs in tenements and other developments.¹⁰⁸ Many of these are rarely encountered in practice, and it would be hard to draw up a definitive list.¹⁰⁹

Finally, the burdens section must also contain certain encumbrances which were constituted off-register, namely prescriptive servitudes, public rights of way, and paths delineated by order under s 22 of the Land Reform (Scotland) Act 2003.¹¹⁰ This is an innovation¹¹¹ and also, for the Keeper, a considerable challenge, although in first registrations the applicant is asked to provide the necessary information.¹¹² It seems unavoidable that off-register rights will often be omitted, and for that reason they are excluded from the Keeper's warranty.¹¹³

In some cases an encumbrance may affect only part of the property: an example would be a servitude of way. If so, an applicant for first registration must provide the Keeper with sufficient information for it to be mapped.¹¹⁴

4.18 Cleansing the D section

In practice, D sections of title sheets often include encumbrances that were either invalid from the beginning¹¹⁵ or have become invalid with the passage of

---

99 LR(S)A 2012 s 9(1)(a). 'Designation' is defined in s 113(1): see para 4.15 above for discussion.
100 For which see para 7.20 below.
101 LR(S)A 2012 s 9(1)(b). There is no need to mention sub-leases, as these will appear in the title sheet of the lease.
102 See para 4.14 above.
103 This includes pre-1979 statutes, for such statutes, insofar as referring to registration in the Register of Sasines, are (with certain exceptions) deemed to refer equally to the Land Register: see LR(S)A 1979 s 29(2), (3), sch 3.
104 LR(S)A 2012 s 9(1)(f). 'Designation' is defined in s 113(1): see para 4.15 above for discussion.
105 Town and Country Planning (Scotland) Act 1997 s 161(2).
106 Town and Country Planning (Scotland) Act 1997 s 75. For further examples, see para 3.5 above.
107 LR(S)A 2012 s 51. Previously, proper liferents appeared in the proprietorship section of the title sheet.
108 Title Conditions (Scotland) Act 2003 ss 10 and 10A; Tenements (Scotland) Act 2004 ss 12 and 13.
109 But see para 6.3 below.
110 Respectively LR(S)A 2012 s 9(1)(a), (d), (e). For off-register rights, see paras 4.26–4.28 below.
111 Previously, 'overriding interests' only required to be 'noted' where they were disclosed in a document accompanying an application for registration: see LR(S)A 1979 s 6(4).
112 This is done by a question in the application form: see para 8.25 below.
113 LR(S)A 2012 s 73(2)(a)–(c): see para 13.4 below.
114 LR(S)A 2012 ss 23(1)(d), 25(1)(c) and 28(1)(b). See Registers of Scotland, *General Guidance: Encumbrances and Off-Register Rights* (v.02, 2015) 3 for RoS mapping requirements. To this rule pipe servitudes and servitudes by prescription are exceptions: see LR(S)A 2012 ss 23(4), 25(4) and 28(4).
115 Because of failure to comply with the rules about the form and content of real burdens contained, now, in ss 2–4 of the Title Conditions (Scotland) Act 2003.

time. In particular, a significant minority of real burdens have ceased to have a benefited property and hence to be enforceable, either because of the abolition of the feudal system on 28 November 2004, or because of the reformulation of implied enforcement rights which accompanied that abolition.[116] A similar issue arises with long leases which have been converted into ownership as a result of leasehold conversion.[117] This is a practical problem. Such encumbrances while they remain in the Register give the false impression of validity. They may increase the expense of conveyancing, because they have to be scrutinised. Sometimes a professorial opinion must be sought. The Keeper is under an obligation to delete such encumbrances on becoming aware that they are invalid, provided that the invalidity is clear to the 'manifest' standard,[118] but it is doubtful whether this will do much to solve the problem.[119] A provision in the Title Conditions (Scotland) Act 2003 which required the Keeper, 'where satisfied', to make a positive statement on the title sheet as to the applicability of the new rules of implied enforcement rights[120] was repealed by the 2012 Act,[121] primarily on the basis that RoS had found it to be unworkable.[122]

4.19 Further mandatory content

Four additional matters must be included in title sheets, but the choice of which section to use is left to the Keeper. These are: (i) statements that the Keeper's warranty is restricted or extended (both of which would be unusual);[123] (ii) particulars of any special destination;[124] (iii) a reference to any entry in the Register of Inhibitions that may affect the title;[125] and (iv) the terms of any caveat.[126] So for example if Hilary owns Blackacre, and Iona inhibits her, and later, the inhibition remaining in place, Hilary dispones to James, the title sheet, though it now shows James as owner, will also refer to the inhibition.[127]

---

116 Abolition of Feudal Tenure etc (Scotland) Act 2000 ss 17–19; Title Conditions (Scotland) Act 2003 ss 49–57. For details, see K G C Reid, *The Abolition of Feudal Tenure in Scotland* (2003) chs 2–7.
117 See para 20.8 below.
118 LR(S)A 2012 s 80(1), (2): see paras 11.13–11.19 below.
119 The Abolition of Feudal Tenure etc (Scotland) Act 2000 s 46 and the Title Conditions (Scotland) Act 2003 s 51 had provisions, now repealed (by LR(S)A 2012 sch 5 paras 39(4), 43(4)), about the cleansing of burdens rendered invalid by those statutes. In substance they said that there would be no cleansing for a period of ten years.
120 Title Conditions (Scotland) Act 2003 s 58.
121 LR(S)A 2012 sch 5 para 43(4).
122 See SLC Report 222 paras 10.19 ff.
123 LR(S)A 2012 ss 10(2)(a), 75(3), (4)(b) and 76(5)(a): see paras 13.11–13.14 below.
124 LR(S)A 2012 s 10(2)(b). If, as occasionally happens, the destination makes provision as to evacuation, this too should be included, as being part of the destination. For special destinations, see G L Gretton and K G C Reid, *Conveyancing* (4th edn, 2011) ch 26.
125 LR(S)A 2012 ss 10(2)(c) and 32(1), (2). This appears in the B (proprietorship) section.
126 LR(S)A 2012 s 10(2)(d). For caveats, see ch 18 below.
127 Inhibitions are considered further in para 9.19 below.

SHARED PLOTS

4.20 The basic idea[128]

It sometimes happens that an area of land is co-owned by neighbouring proprietors as pertinents of their properties. For instance a housing development may have areas, such as paths, car-parking, a play-park, planted areas and so on, which are held in co-ownership among the individual properties in the development. The 1979 Act made no provision for such cases, but it was the Keeper's practice to include the shared areas in each of the title sheets of the sharing properties.[129] Suppose, for example, that there were ten houses and that each had a tenth share of a common garden. The Keeper's practice was to create ten title sheets, not eleven, and each title sheet would be for both (i) the principal property and (ii) a one-tenth share of the common garden. A single area of land was thus included in ten separate title sheets. This worked well enough from an everyday conveyancing point of view, but it meant that when viewing the embryonic cadastral map there was a lack of clarity: if one zoomed in to the garden area its ownership status was less than clear.

The 2012 Act adopts a different approach. In general an area that is shared by other properties (a 'shared plot') will form a separate cadastral unit and have its own title sheet.[130] Thus in the example given, there will be eleven cadastral units and eleven title sheets. The Keeper then has a choice as to whether to treat this eleventh title sheet as an ordinary title sheet or as a 'shared plot title sheet'.[131] If it is an ordinary title sheet then the B section will list all ten owners,[132] and will need to be altered every time an individual property changes hands. Hence in practice the Keeper usually chooses the other type of title sheet, the shared plot title sheet.

4.21 Modifications to title sheets

The mandatory content of title sheets has already been described.[133] Inevitably, however, some modifications apply in the case of the title sheets both of a shared plot and also of the plots in association with which the shared plot is owned (the 'sharing plots').[134]

Only slight modifications are needed in the case of sharing plot title sheets. The A section of each will refer to the shared plot title sheet, so that it is obvious at a glance that the main property has a share in the common area.[135] Further, this must state the quantum of share, eg a one-tenth *pro indiviso* right.[136]

---

128 See also para 8.17 below.
129 This is still the position for other corporeal pertinents: see LR(S)A 2012 ss 3(7) and 12(3), discussed in para 4.24 below. It is thought that these provisions cannot apply to shared plots, otherwise they would undermine the rules just about to be discussed.
130 LR(S)A 2012 s 12(2). But s 12(3) permits a continuation of the practice under the 1979 Act.
131 LR(S)A 2012 s 17(2): 'the Keeper may, if the Keeper thinks it appropriate ...' The Keeper also has the power to change a shared plot title sheet into an ordinary title sheet: see s 19.
132 Or more, if some of the individual properties are themselves co-owned, for instance by a married couple.
133 Paragraphs 4.13–4.19 above.
134 The terminology is set out in LR(S)A 2012 s 17(3). For sample shared plot and sharing plot title sheets, see www.ros.gov.uk/services/registration/land-register/general-guidance/cadastral-map.
135 LR(S)A 2012 s 18(1)(a).
136 LR(S)A 2012 s 18(2)(a).

In the case of shared plot title sheets, the modifications are more extensive. Instead of listing the owners, the B section simply lists the sharing properties and the size of their share.[137] As a result, whenever one of the sharing properties changes hands, no alteration to the shared plot title sheet is needed. In the C section the Keeper inserts a statement to the effect that the shared plot may be subject to a heritable security registered against a sharing plot.[138] The security itself is not mentioned unless it is over the shared plot alone.[139] An equivalent rule applies in respect of the D section.[140] The result of these provisions is that a shared plot title sheet, once created, will remain unchanged indefinitely. It will only be in unusual cases that change is needed. One example would be where one of the sharing plots is divided into two plots, so that the total number of sharing plots increases from ten to eleven. In that case there would have to be a matching change in the B section of the shared plot title sheet.

4.22 Conveyancing shortcut

As in the case of ordinary pertinents,[141] if the principal property (ie a sharing plot) is mentioned in a document, this is taken to include the relevant share in the shared plot.[142] Thus suppose that ten houses share a central common garden. If a deed describes the property as 'All and Whole 7 Cameron Square, Balallan, Angus, title number ANG987654321' that will automatically carry with it the one-tenth share of the common garden, even though the garden has its own cadastral unit and plot number.

4.23 Shared and sharing: long leases

It can happen that properties held on long lease share an area also held on long lease, very much as in the ordinary case of shared areas, but with a lease title rather than an ownership title.[143] In such cases substantially the same rules apply.[144]

PERTINENTS AND TENEMENTS

4.24 Pertinents

Pertinents have already been mentioned, but a few more words may be appropriate.[145] There are two types of pertinent: corporeal and incorporeal. The latter consists mainly of the right to enforce servitudes and real burdens, and are included in the A section of a title sheet.[146] The former are physical areas that are deemed part of

---

137 LR(S)A 2012 s 18(1)(b), (2)(b), (3)(a).
138 LR(S)A 2012 s 18(2)(c).
139 LR(S)A 2012 s 18(3)(b).
140 LR(S)A 2012 s 18(2)(d), (4), (5).
141 For which see Reid (n 6) para 199.
142 LR(S)A 2012 s 17(4), enacting the rule at common law. See also s 17(5) which provides that 'Registration has the same effect in relation to a share in a shared plot which pertains to a sharing plot as it has in relation to the sharing plot'.
143 For recent litigation involving such a case (registered under the 1979 Act), see *Gyle Shopping Centre General Partners Ltd v Marks and Spencer plc* [2016] CSIH 19, 2016 GWD 10-205.
144 The provisions, however, are separate: see LR(S)A 2012 s 20, sch 1.
145 See generally Reid (n 6) paras 199–206.
146 See para 4.14 above.

the principal area. The main use of the concept of corporeal pertinent in modern law is in the context of tenemental properties.[147] Apart from that, the concept has little part to play in the land registration system, for if a physical area is part of a property, it should be mapped as such, and if it is not mapped, it will not normally be part of the property. So if Jack is the registered owner of a house and garden, and later claims that some adjacent or nearby ground is a pertinent of his property, his claim is not stateable in terms of land registration law (as it might have been in the Register of Sasines). At most he could argue that, at the time of first registration, it ought to have been included in his title sheet.

So far as mapping is concerned, the legislation gives the Keeper the choice between making up a separate cadastral unit (and hence title sheet) for a corporeal pertinent or including it within the cadastral unit (and title sheet) of the principal property.[148]

4.25 Tenements

Under the legislation the Keeper has a discretion, invariably exercised in practice, to represent the whole of a tenement (or a single-storey building with internal divisions)[149] as a single cadastral unit.[150] Each property within the tenement is nevertheless a distinct plot, so that the result is an exception to the 'one cadastral unit, one title sheet' principle:[151] in a tenement there is one cadastral unit but also separate title sheets for the individual flats. One implication is that, whereas in general the number of a title sheet is the same as the number of the cadastral unit, that is not so in tenements.[152] The verbal description in each title sheet is in the following form: 'Subjects, part of Cadastral Unit GLA12345 edged red on the Cadastral Map, being the westmost dwellinghouse on the first floor above the ground floor of the tenement 48 Craigpark, Glasgow G31 2LX'.[153]

The area of land on which a tenement building stands is known in RoS as the 'steading'. The steading includes both the ground immediately under the building itself, and the associated ground, most notably, in traditional tenements, the back green. It is the steading as a whole, not just the building, which is represented as a single cadastral unit.[154] But to this there is an exception for cases where the associated ground is unusually large: the special rules cannot apply to ground that is more than 25 metres from the building, measured to the nearest part.[155] If that is the position, the ground that is more than 25 metres away has to be constituted

---

147 Tenements (Scotland) Act 2004 s 3.
148 LR(S)A 2012 ss 3(7) and 12(3). SLC Report 222 para 5.28 (and draft Bill s 4(4)) would have restricted the second option to cases where the pertinent 'is so small that it cannot be readily delineated in the cadastral map'.
149 This is a 'subdivided building' which is treated by the legislation as being a type of 'flatted building': see LR(S)A 2012 s 16(4), (5).
150 LR(S)A 2012 s 16(1). Section 16 differs significantly from the equivalent provision (s 15) in the Scottish Law Commission's draft Bill. For further information on RoS practice, see *Registration Manual* (n 19) Further Guidance: Plans – mapping tenement properties.
151 As to which see para 4.3 above.
152 Except for the first flat registered after the designated day: see Registers of Scotland, *General Guidance: The Cadastral Map – Tenements and other flatted buildings* (v.04, 2015) 1.
153 *General Guidance: The Cadastral Map – Tenements and other flatted buildings* (n 152) 1.
154 This is because 'tenement' is defined to include land pertaining to the building: see Tenements (Scotland) Act 2004 s 26(1), imported by LR(S)A 2012 s 16(8).
155 LR(S)A 2012 s 16(3).

as a separate cadastral unit with its own title sheet (which would typically take the form of a shared plot title sheet). This exception operates prospectively only, ie to tenements which are constituted for the first time after 8 December 2014.[156]

Where an area within the steading belongs exclusively to one flat, the Keeper's policy is not to mark this on the cadastral map but to state it as supplementary data on the title sheet of the flat in question.[157] Supplementary data might also indicate the footprint of the individual flat, or common areas such as bin stores and garden areas.[158]

OFF-REGISTER RIGHTS

4.26 Overriding interests: farewell

'Overriding interests' was a term used in the 1979 Act, but it is not used in the Act of 2012. In a general sense the concept was straightforward: an overriding interest was an encumbrance that 'overrode' the terms of a title sheet, in that it was effective even though the title sheet did not mention it.[159] For example, Blackmains and Whitemains are neighbouring properties, and by reason of long usage a servitude of way came into prescriptive existence over the former in favour of the latter. From the point of view of Whitemains this was an off-register right, from the point of view of Blackmains an off-register encumbrance. Either way, it was fully valid and effective even though not mentioned in the Blackmains (or indeed the Whitemains) title sheet.

The same is true under the 2012 Act, and so in a very broad sense the concept of overriding interest could be said still to exist. But the term does not appear in the Act, for good reason. The 1979 Act attempted to enumerate all the types of overriding interest.[160] The list was long and had to grow longer over the years, as new types of right came into existence. Despite valiant attempts, the task was impossible, and there were all sorts of right which should have been overriding but which did not appear on the list.[161] A different overall approach to the legislation has allowed the 2012 Act to avoid the term and hence the task.[162]

4.27 Presence on the Register

Rights constituted off-register might nonetheless appear on the Register, not as a matter of validity and effect, but simply for information. Under the 1979 Act the rules were complex: sometimes the Keeper had to note overriding interests, sometimes there was a discretion whether or not to note them, and sometimes

---

156 LR(S)A 2012 sch 4 para 25. This will usually mean newbuilds, but sometimes an existing building will be converted into a tenement after 8 December 2014, and in that case the 25-metre rule will be applicable.
157 *General Guidance: The Cadastral Map – Tenements and other flatted buildings* (n 152) 1.
158 Registers of Scotland, *FAQs: Tenements* Qs 2 and 3.
159 See para 2.2 above.
160 The definition, in LR(S)A 1979 s 28(1), was frequently amended.
161 See further SLC Report 222 part 7.
162 In brief, the definition was needed under the 1979 Act because registration was declared to confer a real right subject only to encumbrances on the Register and overriding interests: see LR(S)A 1979 s 3(1)(a). By contrast, the 2012 Act does not attribute effects to registration but relies on the general law. See para 9.20 below, and also SLC Report 222 paras 7.13–7.15.

noting was forbidden.[163] The 2012 Act simplified the position. Apart from where legislation provides otherwise (typically in respect of public-law rights), the only rights constituted off-register that may, and indeed must, appear on the Register are prescriptive servitudes, public rights of way, and paths delineated by order under s 22 of the Land Reform (Scotland) Act 2003.[164] Where 1979 Act title sheets contain other off-register rights, the Keeper can delete them[165] and it is the intention that in due course they will be deleted.[166] Of course, even those rights which are supposed to appear on the Register will not do so if the Keeper does not know about them; and one prominent off-register right, the right of a tenant under a short lease, cannot so appear.

4.28 Prescriptive servitudes

Of those off-register rights which fall to be entered on the Register, the most important are servitudes constituted by prescription. Such a servitude is, of course, valid whether mentioned in the Register or not, but nowadays buyers of the benefited property will usually wish to see the servitude mentioned in the A section of the title sheet. Under the 1979 Act the Keeper's practice in this regard varied. At one time a prescriptive servitude would be entered if its existence was supported by affidavit evidence.[167] From 1997 the practice changed. The Keeper had experienced many cases in which the affidavit evidence had proved false. From 1997 servitudes would not be entered unless backed up by a court declarator or by the agreement of the owner of the burdened property.[168] This policy met with the approval of the Scottish Law Commission,[169] but when the 2012 Act came into force the Keeper changed approach. The current approach does not merely revert to the pre-1997 position: it is even more relaxed.[170] The Keeper does not wish to see any evidence of the existence of the servitude: the simple assertion of its existence is enough.[171] The applicant, however, must bear in mind the potentially serious consequences of asserting that a prescriptive servitude exists if this is not in fact the case.[172]

This laid-back approach applies to cases where there is a disposition to be registered, including first registrations. But if an owner wishes an alleged prescriptive servitude to be added as a pertinent at some other time, this can only be done by rectification, and its omission must be shown to be a manifest inaccuracy;[173] in practice a court declarator might be necessary.[174] It could be argued there is an

---

163 LR(S)A 1979 s 6(4).
164 LR(S)A 2012 s 9(1)(a), (d), (e): see para 4.17 above. For background, see SLC Report 222 paras 7.16–7.19.
165 LR(S)A 2012 sch 4 para 2.
166 *Post Consultation Report* (n 59) para 1.18.
167 But it appears that while it was then entered in the (allegedly) benefited property's title sheet, it was not always entered in the (allegedly) burdened property's title sheet.
168 I Davis and A Rennie (eds), *Registration of Title Practice Book* (2nd edn, 2000) para 6.55.
169 SLC Report 222 paras 10.7–10.18.
170 See para 8.23 below.
171 Registers of Scotland, *General Guidance: Rights and the Title Sheet* (v.01, 2014) 1–2. Application forms have provision for the assertion of prescriptive servitudes.
172 See in particular LR(S)A 2012 ss 111 and 112: see ch 15.
173 LR(S)A 2012 s 80(1), (2). For rectification, see paras 11.13–11.19 below.
174 *General Guidance: Rights and the Title Sheet* (n 171) 2.

inconsistency between these two approaches.[175] If the omission of a prescriptive servitude amounts to an inaccuracy, the 'manifest' evidentiary standard ought to be adopted in all cases, and it does not seem relevant whether the issue arises in connection with the registration of a disposition.

The Keeper, on entering a prescriptive servitude on the A section of a title sheet, must at the same time enter it on the D section of the corresponding burdened title sheet. This too looks like a rectification, regardless of whether there was a disposition of the first property. If it is a rectification of the burdened title sheet, that will, it seems, automatically engage the 'manifest' evidential standard for both title sheets.[176]

THE OTHER PARTS OF THE REGISTER

4.29 Introduction

Of the four parts which make up the Land Register,[177] we have so far concentrated on only one, the title sheet record. In this final section we consider the other three: the cadastral map, the archive record, and the application record.

4.30 The cadastral map

The cadastral map is a map of the whole of Scotland, showing title boundaries, or, as the Act puts it, 'the totality of registered geospatial data (other than supplementary data in individual title sheets)'.[178] The expression 'whole of Scotland' is true in the sense that a jigsaw puzzle whose picture is a map of Scotland is a map of the 'whole of Scotland' even if it is still on the kitchen table, unfinished. The assembled pieces are the registered properties; the gaps are properties that have yet to be registered. Conveyancers see title plans in isolation, as shown on land certificates, or extracts.[179] This is like having a map of Switzerland that shows the boundaries of Switzerland but no other national boundaries. The cadastral map is like a map of Europe that shows all national boundaries. More about the cadastral map and other mapping issues can be found in chapter 5.

---

175 The difference is justified in *General Guidance: Encumbrances and Off-Register Rights* (n 114) 6, in the following way: 'Where a prescriptive servitude is included in a title as a result of its disclosure in an application for registration the duty of care on parties and their solicitors is engaged and it is evidenced by certification of the application form. However, a rectification request is not subject to such certification and the Keeper will therefore require appropriate evidence of the existence of a servitude right in order to establish that a manifest inaccuracy exists in a title sheet.'
176 If what is happening is the first registration of the benefited property, it could not be said that the title sheet of that property is being rectified, since there is as yet no such title sheet. But even in this case the 'manifest' standard is arguably engaged assuming that the burdened property is on the Land Register.
177 LR(S)A 2012 s 2.
178 LR(S)A 2012 s 11(1)(a). The reason for the words in brackets is that title sheets may, and in practice always do, have supplementary data. Such data form part of the title sheet but not of the cadastral map. See para 5.18 below.
179 'Land certificate' is the terminology of the LR(S)A 1979, replaced by 'extract' in the LR(S)A 2012 (see s 104, and para 3.12 above).

4.31 The archive record

The archive record consists of copies of documents submitted to the Keeper and of such other documents as the Keeper considers appropriate.[180] As well as copies of deeds presented for registration, the archive record includes, for example, copies of application forms for registration and copies of advance notices. The provisions in the 2012 Act formalise an archive which had previously existed on a non-legislative basis.[181]

The archive record is open for public inspection,[182] and the Keeper issues extracts or plain copies of its contents on request and for a fee.[183] Online access, however, is not available, in the light of the personal information contained in some documents, and the potential risk that such information could be used for fraudulent and other criminal purposes;[184] the extent to which this will deter the committed must, however, be open to question. In practice, of course, most documents in the archive record will never be looked at again. They form the basis for what the title sheet record and the cadastral map say (or do not say)[185] about titles and their boundaries, and as such will not normally need to be consulted unless the accuracy of the Register is challenged. That happens only in a small minority of cases, but in that small minority of cases the existence of the archive record is of great importance. There may occasionally be other reasons too for consultation: for instance a trustee in sequestration might wish to examine a disposition for evidence as to whether it was a gratuitous alienation.

As the archive record is, relatively speaking, little consulted, its contents are declared not to be within the constructive knowledge of any person.[186] Suppose, for example, that the Keeper has misread a deed and that as a result the title sheet is inaccurate. The fact that a copy of the misread deed is in the archive record does not impose constructive knowledge on anyone that the title sheet is inaccurate. Or again, suppose that a deed contains contractual terms that are, quite properly, not reproduced in the title sheet, because they do not amount to servitudes or real burdens. Since there is no constructive knowledge, it would not be possible to argue that the presence of a copy of the deed in the archive record engages the 'offside goals rule' as against a purchaser.[187] There is, special cases apart, no

---

180 LR(S)A 2012 s 14(1). As well as this general provision, there are some specific provisions in ss 30(2)(c), 31(2)(d), 62(1)(b), 63(1)(a)(ii), and 80(4)(a). Section 14(3)(b) introduces an exception for documents comprised in any other register under the management and control of the Keeper or of the Keeper of the Records of Scotland, for example the Register of Sasines or Books of Council and Session. Some practical issues concerning the archive record are explored in *Registration Manual* (n 19) Further Guidance: Workflow – archive.
181 See SLC Report 222 paras 4.12–4.14. LR(S)A 2012 sch 4 para 12 says that the items that were in the *de facto* archive record on the eve of the designated day became part of the *de jure* archive record.
182 Registers of Scotland (Information and Access) Order 2014, SSI 2014/189, art 4.
183 LR(S)A 2012 s 104: see para 3.12 above. By s 14(2), the Keeper is directed to include in the archive record such information as is required for the purposes of s 104.
184 Registers of Scotland, *General Guidance: Archive Record* (v.01, 2014) 2.
185 For example, suppose that a property has a standard security over it, which is later discharged. The title sheet would as a result have a blank C section. The deed of discharge, now in the archive record, would be the deed that was the basis of that negative entry.
186 LR(S)A 2012 s 14(4). In this respect it is like the Books of Council and Session. Compare the title sheet record, the contents of which are (subject to s 10(5)) within constructive knowledge. See eg *Trade Development Bank v Warriner and Mason (Scotland) Ltd* 1980 SC 74. For discussion, see SLC Report 222 para 4.36.
187 For the offside goals rule, see para 4.10 above.

duty in a conveyancing transaction to look at anything in the archive record. This approach is, indeed, a necessary aspect of the 'curtain principle'.[188]

4.32 The application record

In an ideal world, all registration applications would be dealt with instantly on receipt. The Register would immediately be altered in accordance with the application, or, in the case of an invalid application, there would be an instant rejection. Items would no sooner arrive in the Keeper's in-tray than they would leave again. But the real world is not the ideal world. Applications may take some time to be processed, especially more complex applications such as first-registration cases and split-off cases. As a result, at any one time there are numerous pending applications. These pending applications make up the fourth part of the Land Register, the application record.[189] As with the archive record, the application record already existed but had no statutory basis; and as with the archive record, the 2012 Act placed it on a statutory basis for the first time.[190]

The particular importance of the application record lies in the fact that an application, if successful, takes effect from the date of the application, not from the date when the relevant title sheet is changed. Thus Eliza sells Bluemains to Fraser, and he applies for registration on 1 May, an entry in the application record being made on that day. On 5 May the application is accepted, Fraser's name being substituted for Eliza's on the B section of the title sheet. When does ownership pass from Eliza to Fraser? Ownership passes on registration, of course,[191] but when is registration? Under the Act, registration occurs on the date an entry in respect of a successful application is made in the application record (ie 1 May).[192] Although this is sound policy, it potentially creates a problem for those searching the Register. If a third party, Janet, examines the Bluemains title sheet on 3 May, she will see Eliza's name in the B section. That could mislead her. But if her search includes the application record, she will know of the pending application, though as of 3 May she cannot yet know whether or not it will be accepted.

In addition to placing the application record on a statutory basis, the 2012 Act made one substantial change to it. Advance notices, introduced for the first time by the Act, have to appear somewhere in the Register, and the Act allocates them to the application record.[193]

Entries in the application record are temporary. Once an application for registration has been dealt with – whether positively or negatively – it is removed from the application record.[194] The same is true of advance notices.[195] Copies of both are retained in the archive record.[196]

---

188 For which see para 2.12 n 131.
189 Together with advance notices, discussed below.
190 LR(S)A 2012 s 15.
191 LR(S)A 2012 s 50(2).
192 LR(S)A 2012 ss 36 and 37(1). By s 33(1), such an entry must be made 'as soon as reasonably practicable' after receipt of the application. See further paras 9.2 and 9.22 below.
193 LR(S)A 2012 s 15(b). For advance notices, see ch 10.
194 LR(S)A 2012 s 33(3).
195 LR(S)A 2012 ss 62(1) and 63(4).
196 See para 4.31 above.

Chapter 5

Plans and the Cadastral Map

5.1 Introduction

The cadastral map, as one of the four parts of the Land Register, has already been mentioned in the previous chapter.[1] This chapter looks at the cadastral map in more detail and also considers the identification of property in conveyancing practice.

THE BASE MAP

5.2 The Ordnance Map

The Ordnance Survey (OS) produces the 'Ordnance Map'.[2] It is a topographic map, and as such shows physical features.[3] It is a stylised representation of what someone would see when looking down from a balloon on that familiar Scottish phenomenon, a cloudless day. Its object is not to show legal boundaries. In fact it does include some boundaries of *public* law, such as constituency boundaries. But it never shows private-law boundaries – title boundaries. In practice, legal boundaries, whether of public or private law, commonly coincide with physical features such as walls, roads, rivers and so on. But physical features are often not legal boundaries, and legal boundaries may coincide with no physical features. By contrast, the purpose of the cadastral map is to show title boundaries – private-law boundaries.

5.3 The Ordnance Map as the base map

The 1979 Act adopted the Ordnance Map as the basis of the new land registration system.[4] The 2012 Act, however, is more circumspect, defining the 'base map' as '(a) the Ordnance Map, (b) another system of mapping, being a system which accords with such requirements as the Scottish Ministers may, by order, prescribe, or (c) a combination of the Ordnance Map and such other system'.[5] Thus unlike the previous law, the Ordnance Map does not now have a legally-enshrined monopoly

---

1 Paragraph 4.30 above. For the cadastral map in general, see Scottish Law Commission, *Report No 222 on Land Registration* (2010) ('SLC Report 222') part 5; Registers of Scotland, *General Guidance: The Cadastral Map* (v.01, 2014).
2 This term is used by the 2012 Act, as it was by the 1979 Act before it. It means 'a map made under powers conferred by the Ordnance Survey Act 1841': see Interpretation and Legislative Reform (Scotland) Act 2010 sch 1.
3 See R Hewitt, *Map of a Nation: A Biography of the Ordnance Survey* (2011). For technical information, see Registers of Scotland, *Registration Manual* (https://rosdev.atlassian.net/wiki/display/2ARM/Home) Further Guidance: Plans – basics of the Ordnance Survey Map.
4 LR(S)A 1979 s 6(1)(a): see para 2.3 above.
5 LR(S)A 2012 s 11(6).

as the base map. The Keeper could use another map as a base map. But at present no such change is in contemplation.[6]

The Ordnance Map is not the same as the cadastral map: the former underlies the latter. The cadastral map can be imagined as a transparent plastic sheet spread on top of the Ordnance Map. The cadastral map, unlike the base map, has title boundaries: that is its purpose. It is the cadastral map that is part of the Register. The base map is the Register's main source of topographic data, but it is itself not part of the Register.

5.4 The problem of scale

The Ordnance Map is not perfect.[7] One of its problems is that whilst some areas are surveyed at 1:1250, others are surveyed at 1:2500, and some remoter areas (usually described by the phrase 'mountain and moorland') only at 1:10,000. As the scale becomes less detailed, the suitability of the base map for land registration purposes declines. The third of these scales in particular is seriously inadequate. At such a scale, one centimetre on the map represents 100 metres on the ground. Whilst it is true that the number of land titles mapped at this worst scale is small,[8] it is not acceptable that even a single one should be mapped at this scale. Even the 1:2500 scale is unsatisfactory. It is possible to scale to 0.23 metres on a 1:1250 map, to 0.46 metres on a 1:2500 map, but only to 1.83 metres on a 1:10,000 map.[9] The limitations of scale are acknowledged in the statutory definition of 'inaccuracy': the cadastral map is not inaccurate 'in so far as it does not depict something correctly by reason only of an inexactness in the base map which is within the published accuracy tolerances relevant to the scale of map involved'.[10]

5.5 The base map in constant change

The Ordnance Survey constantly carries out new surveys, because topography is not static: there are new roads, new buildings, and so on, as well as new names or different or additional forms of names.[11] Moreover, features of the natural environment may change: ponds and lochs may be created, or existing ones expanded, or contracted, or wholly drained, rivers and burns may shift their course, coastal land may be eaten away by the sea, or land may be reclaimed from the sea whether by gradual natural process or by human activity.

---

6 Registers of Scotland, 'Mapping in the Land Register' (2011) 56 JLSS Aug/9: 'It is likely that the Ordnance Map will continue to provide the base map for the foreseeable future (except for the seabed, to which the Ordnance Map does not extend).'

7 It was subject to considerable criticism in the oral and written evidence given during stage 1 of the Land Registration Bill's progress through the Scottish Parliament. The evidence is conveniently summarised in paras 59–84 of the Economy, Energy and Tourism Committee's *Stage 1 Report* (2012), reproduced in Scottish Parliament, *Passage of the Land Registration etc (Scotland) Bill 2011* (2013, SPPB 174; available at www.scottish.parliament.uk/parliamentarybusiness/Bills/44469.aspx) 241–45.

8 About 1% of titles are mapped at 1:10000: see *Passage of the Land Registration etc (Scotland) Bill 2011* (n 7) 242 and 388.

9 I Davis and A Rennie (eds), *Registration of Title Practice Book* (2nd edn, 2000) para 4.26.

10 LR(S)A 2012 s 65(3): see para 11.4 below.

11 For the issue of Gaelic names, see www.ordnancesurvey.co.uk/about/governance/policies/gaelic-names.html.

RoS have a standing order for the new OS 'map tiles'[12] as and when they are available. Thus the cartographic layer beneath the 'transparent plastic sheet' that is the cadastral map is subject to gradual change which may or may not have significance for the cadastral map. The 2012 Act provides that 'on the base map being updated, the Keeper must make any changes to the Register which are necessary in consequence of the updating'.[13] An example would be where a physical feature which is also a title boundary comes to be more accurately represented on the base map.[14]

THE CADASTRAL CONCEPT

5.6 Cadastre

A cadastre or cadaster or cadastral map is, in its standard modern sense, a map showing title boundaries for a whole district or country.[15] Cadastral maps have sometimes been developed solely for fiscal purposes, for instance the Napoleonic cadastre, but generally they are used for conveyancing purposes too, and sometimes only for that purpose.[16]

A type of cadastral mapping existed in the Roman Empire, though information about it is sparse, and only a few fragments of such maps now survive, a notable instance being the fragments of the map for the Arausio district.[17] This is at a scale of 1:6000, better than what is available in some parts of Scotland in the twenty-first century.[18]

The term 'cadastral' has not been used in Scotland hitherto but, as a fairly standard international term,[19] its adoption makes Scottish land law more transparent from an international standpoint.

5.7 The cadastral map: a half-new idea

The 1979 Act did not have a conception of a cadastre. Its vision was that each title sheet should have its own title plan, and that when all properties were eventually in the Land Register there would then be (about) 2.5 million separate title plans. These might or might not dovetail. To keep track of things, there was to be an

---

12 A map tile is a set of digitised cartographic data representing a rectangle of ground.
13 LR(S)A 2012 s 11(7).
14 See Scottish Law Commission, *Report No 222 on Land Registration* (2010) ('SLC Report 222') vol 2, 425.
15 Some variant uses can be found in the past. For instance, single deed-plans have occasionally been called cadastral. Maps showing land use have sometimes been called cadastral. For a general account of cadastral maps, see R J P Kain and E Baigent, *The Cadastral Map in the Service of the State: A History of Property Mapping* (1992), a scholarly work, superbly illustrated, but whose approach is more cartographic than legal.
16 There was once, briefly, a fiscal cadastre for the UK, under the Finance (1909–1910) Act 1910. The legislation called for detailed land valuation (see s 26) without specifying that mapping should be used, but in fact the legislation was implemented by mapping. See generally B Short, *The Geography of England and Wales in 1910: An Evaluation of Lloyd George's 'Domesday' of Landownership* (1989). For some reflections on the Lloyd George cadastre from a Scottish standpoint, see A Wightman, *The Poor had no Lawyers* (2010) 96 ff.
17 Modern Orange, in southern France.
18 On this see http://orange.archeo-rome.com/orange01.html.
19 French *cadastre*, Dutch *kadaster*, German *Kataster*, Italian *catasto*, Polish *kataster*, Spanish *catastro*, and so on.

'index map',[20] but that was what its name indicated – just an index. The index map was secondary: the title plans were primary.

From an early stage RoS departed from that approach, creating a single electronic system, the Digital Mapping System ('DMS'), which was something like a single cadastral map of the whole country in so far as in the Land Register. There was thus a single map instead of 2.5 million individual ones. Title sheets, in their property section, contained an electronic link to the relevant dataset within the DMS. As from the opening of the Register in 1981, therefore, RoS have been gradually building a quasi-cadastral map of the whole country.

Nevertheless, the 2012 Act did more than just give a new and continental name to an existing reality. The idea of a cadastre is that of a single map that sets out every title unit, as a jigsaw. In particular, no piece of the jigsaw should overlap with any other, and no piece of the map should be blank. It should be possible to unroll the map of Scotland and see the complete jigsaw, with each cadastral unit linking to the matching title sheet.[21] Conversely each title sheet links to a single matching cadastral unit. More precisely, the Act defines the cadastral map as a map:[22]

(a) showing the totality of registered geospatial data (other than supplementary data in individual title sheets),
(b) showing for each cadastral unit –
    (i) the cadastral unit number,
    (ii) the boundaries of the unit, and
    (iii) the title number of any registered lease relating to the unit, and
(c) otherwise depicting registered rights in such manner as the Keeper considers appropriate.

5.8 Cadastral units

A cadastral unit is a unit that represents a single registered plot of land.[23] It is a single one of the (roughly) 2.5 million jigsaw pieces that make up (or will eventually make up) the cadastral map of Scotland. Each cadastral unit is numbered, the number being the same as the title number of the plot of land which the unit represents.[24] In general, there is a one-to-one correlation between cadastral units and title sheets, ie each cadastral unit has its own title sheet and, conversely, each title sheet has its own cadastral unit.[25] To this principle there are two qualifications. One is that a long lease can have its own title sheet but not its own cadastral unit.[26] The other is that a tenement can have a single cadastral unit, even though each flat within the tenement has a title sheet of its own.[27]

---

20 Land Registration (Scotland) Rules 2006, SI 2006/485, r 20, repeating a provision first found in the Land Registration (Scotland) Rules 1980, SI 1980/1412, r 23.
21 Of course the cadastral map is not physical. In its virtual form it can be inspected in RoS Customer Service Centres at Meadowbank House in Edinburgh or Hanover House in Glasgow. A representation of an extract from the map can be found in Registers of Scotland, *FAQs: Central mapping: overview*.
22 LR(S)A 2012 s 11(1).
23 LR(S)A 2012 s 12(1). For the meaning of 'plot' see LR(S)A 2012 s 3, discussed in para 4.2 above.
24 LR(S)A 2012 s 12(4), (5).
25 See para 4.3 above.
26 See para 4.5 above.
27 See para 4.25 above.

5.9 Title plans

The introduction of the cadastral map means that separate title plans no longer exist.[28] Instead of a plan, the A section of a title sheet has a reference to the relevant unit in the cadastral map.[29] But this is more a change in form than substance. Before the 2012 Act that was already the position in reality, albeit not in law. And today if a plain copy is obtained, or an extract, or a post-registration PDF,[30] what is issued includes a copy of the cadastral unit, so that the result is much the same as the old land certificate.

5.10 Nothing can be registered without being mapped

The 'no registration without mapping' principle might also be expressed as 'registration is only to the mapped extent'. The two formulations come to the same thing. In fact, the principle, or something like it, already existed in the 1979 Act,[31] although RoS did not apply it strictly until 2009. Until then, RoS would accept for registration deeds which described corporeal pertinents – most typically shares in common areas such as shared amenity areas – without a proper plan. As a result, the title sheet would identify the principal property by way of a plan but then copy out the 'together with…' clause of the deed for the pertinents, thus purportedly registering the applicant as owner of a share in unmapped property. As a result of the *PMP Plus* decision,[32] this practice ceased, and from 2009 the 'no registration without mapping' principle began to be applied with reasonable strictness. The 2012 Act makes it a mandatory rule,[33] in pursuit of the objective of a complete cadastral map; for otherwise there would always be blanks on the map – missing pieces of jigsaw – where there was a registered but unmapped title. Despite this, however, common areas may continue to be unmapped if the original descriptive deed was registered under the 1979 Act.[34]

5.11 But mapped once only: no overlaps

The 2012 Act forbids overlaps: 'the same area of land cannot be represented by more than one cadastral unit'.[35] There are two aspects to this rule: (i) shared-ownership overlaps, and (ii) conflicting overlaps.

A shared-ownership overlap is where, under the previous law, a shared area such as, say, an amenity area common to several properties, was included in the title sheets of each of the properties. Under the 2012 Act a separate cadastral unit (and title sheet) is created for the common area, and it will not appear in the title sheet

---

28 Under the previous law 'the Keeper shall include in the Property Section a plan of the land to which the interest relates': see Land Registration (Scotland) Rules 1980 r 4(2); Land Registration (Scotland) Rules 2006 r 4(2).
29 For the contents of the A section, see para 4.14 above.
30 After any registration the Keeper sends an email with a link to a PDF: see para 9.16 below.
31 LR(S)A 1979 ss 4(2)(a) and 6(1)(a).
32 *PMP Plus Ltd v Keeper of the Registers of Scotland* 2009 SLT (Lands Tr) 2. See also *Lundin Homes Ltd v Keeper of the Registers of Scotland* 2013 SLT (Sh Ct) 73. On these cases (which remain good law in respect of the 2012 Act), see K G C Reid and G L Gretton, *Conveyancing 2013* (2014) 105–16.
33 LR(S)A 2012 s 6(1)(a)(i).
34 See para 8.17 below.
35 LR(S)A 2012 s 12(2).

of the sharing properties.[36] For developments which were already completed and registered before the designated day (8 December 2014), the Keeper has the power but not the duty to detach the common area and allocate to it its own cadastral unit (and title sheet).[37] Where a development was partially completed as at the designated day, the Keeper can, and in practice does, complete the development on the basis of the old law.[38]

A conflicting overlap is where the same area of ground was, before the designated day, included in two distinct title sheets, not as common property, but as being *solely* part of each. It may seem strange that this was done, but done it sometimes was.[39] It cannot be done now.[40] An application for registration of a plot that would encroach on another registered plot is rejected. If an area included in a cadastral unit (and title sheet) ought not to be there, that is a problem to be resolved by rectification, not by registration. For instance, suppose that Blackmains is a registered property, and that there is a first-registration application for the neighbouring property, Redmains. If the latter application includes a strip of ground that is in the Blackmains cadastral unit the application will fail. The strip will remain in the Blackmains cadastral unit unless and until rectification takes place.[41]

What about 'legacy' cases, ie cases of conflicting overlaps that existed as at the appointed day? The 'no overlaps' rule, being prospective only, does not apply to them,[42] and there is no clear provision in the legislation for purging conflicting overlaps. We return to this difficult issue in a later chapter.[43]

5.12 Separate tenements

Separate tenements, such as mineral rights and salmon-fishing rights, are (following common law) considered as separate plots, and have their own cadastral units and title sheets. In that limited sense cadastral units can overlap: for instance a dozen farms, owned by a dozen different farmers, might have beneath them a single area of mineral rights owned by someone else entirely. But subject to that qualification, 'the same area of land cannot be represented by more than one cadastral unit'.[44]

---

36 For details, see paras 4.20–4.23 above.
37 LR(S)A 2012 sch 4 paras 7 ff.
38 LR(S)A 2012 sch 4 para 9.
39 The origins of the practice can be traced to a recommendation of the Reid Report: see *Registration of Title to Land in Scotland: Report by a Committee appointed by the Secretary of State for Scotland* (Cmnd 2032, 1963) para 104. See also *Scheme for the Introduction and Operation of Registration of Title to Land in Scotland: Report by a Committee appointed by the Secretary of State for Scotland* (Cmnd 4137, 1969) ('Henry Report') Part I, para 56(2).
40 Except by human error at RoS.
41 In practice, rectification may be difficult to achieve. For further discussion of cases such as this, see para 11.23 below.
42 LR(S)A 2012 sch 4 para 6.
43 See para 11.24 below.
44 LR(S)A 2012 s 12(2). Section 12 does not mention the qualification for separate tenements, which arises from the definitional structure of the legislation. It does however (at subsection (3)) mention the pertinents exception, which is of only limited practical significance: see para 4.24 above.

5.13 Alterations of cadastral units

The Keeper may (a) combine cadastral units, (b) remove a cadastral unit from the map, or (c) divide a cadastral unit.[45] An example of (a) would be site assembly by a developer: several adjacent plots are bought by the developer, thus creating a single larger unit. An example of (c) would be the converse: a developer acquires a substantial area, and sells it off bit by bit. Whether category (b) is necessary is perhaps arguable, since a cadastral unit represents a plot of land, and plots of land do not disappear, though they may be merged, which would be case (a). The word 'may' is used in the legislation. For example, where the owner of one property buys a neighbouring property, it is for the Keeper to decide whether to retain two cadastral units or whether to merge them. The component parts need not be contiguous: a farm bisected by a road might comprise a single cadastral unit.[46]

Alterations of cadastral units result in alterations of the corresponding title sheets. So if, for example, two units are merged, the title sheets are merged as well.

5.14 Real rights other than ownership

Cadastral units exist for plots of land, ie areas in separate ownership.[47] Subordinate real rights (ie rights other than ownership) do not result in separate cadastral units, nor (with the exception of long leases) in separate title sheets. But that does not mean that subordinate real rights can be found only in title sheets and not on the cadastral map.[48] If a subordinate real right affects only part of a property, then the extent of the subordinate real right will be shown on the cadastral unit in question.[49] For instance, Shania owns Redmains Farm. She grants a servitude of way to her neighbour, Theodore. The servitude will be registered, both in the A section of the title sheet of Theodore's property and in the D section of the Redmains title sheet, and the line will be depicted on the unit of the cadastral map that is for Redmains Farm. A year later Shania grants a long lease of half the farm to Ursula. The lease is registered. A new title sheet will be made up for the lease. No new cadastral unit will be created, but on the existing Redmains cadastral unit on the cadastral map the area covered by the lease will be marked (and the Redmains title sheet will be annotated accordingly).

5.15 Base-map boundaries versus cadastral-map boundaries

The cadastral map takes its title boundaries from the deeds which form their legal basis. Title boundaries, of course, do not always coincide with physical features shown on the OS map, such as walls, hedges, burns and so on. It is unfortunate that such physical features are often called 'occupational boundaries' when they may be no such thing. In some countries the law requires the land to be marked off on the ground before a new title unit can be registered; Scottish law does not have that requirement.

---

45 LR(S)A 2012 s 13(2). The previous law was the same: see Land Registration (Scotland) Rules 2006 r 8.
46 *General Guidance: The Cadastral Map* (n 1) 2.
47 LR(S)A 2012 s 3(4).
48 *General Guidance: The Cadastral Map* (n 1) 1.
49 *Registration Manual* (n 3) Further Guidance: Plans – plans references for specific rights, burdens and servitudes.

Sometimes in new developments the property as disponed to the purchaser does not match the property as built. This may be because the deed plans in the split-off dispositions are based on the original site-layout plan, whereas the development as subsequently built is not quite the same. For instance, all the physical boundaries might be built two metres north-east of where they are shown on the site-layout plan, or there may be overlaps. Further, the discrepancies may be undetectable (in a practical sense) by the purchaser or the purchaser's solicitors. At one time RoS tended to wait for the new OS map tile, typically a few months after the completion of the development, and then register the properties as they were built (or, to be precise, as the Ordnance Survey showed them to have been built) rather than as they were disponed, thus covering up for the failure of the developers to match up the properties as built with the terms of the split-off deeds. This practice, however, was dropped even before the introduction of the 2012 Act, in recognition of the fact that the Keeper's legal obligation is to register properties as they are disponed and that to do otherwise is to create inaccuracies in the Register.

THE CADASTRAL MAP: SOME SPECIAL ISSUES

5.16 Seabed

Under international law the territory of a coastal state extends to 12 nautical miles from the coast, measured by reference to 'baselines'.[50] Almost all the territorial seabed is owned by the Crown,[51] though the Crown can lease and even dispone it. Although the Land Register covers the territorial sea,[52] it faces the practical difficulty that the OS map does not extend significantly beyond the coastline. In depicting an area of seabed on the cadastral map, therefore, the Keeper is given discretion as to how to show the boundaries.[53] In practice, the same coordinate system ('OSBG36') is used as for OS maps;[54] and a deed relating to the seabed (such as a lease or a disposition of salmon-fishing rights) must describe the property by reference to the OSGB36 coordinates (preferably in the form of a table) and also by a verbal description and by a plan which shows the location of the plot in relation to the coastline.[55] OSGB36 coordinates need not

---

50 Territorial Sea Act 1987 s 1(1): see para 3.10 above.
51 At the time of writing administered on behalf of the Crown by the Crown Estate Commissioners but soon to be succeeded by the Scottish Ministers: see Scotland Act 1998 s 90B, inserted by Scotland Act 2016 s 36. This does not alter ownership, which remains in the Crown.
52 LR(S)A 2012 s 113(1) (definition of 'land'). The position under the 1979 Act had not been entirely clear: see Scottish Law Commission, *Discussion Paper No 130 on Land Registration: Miscellaneous Issues* (2005) ('SLC DP 130') para 2.29. For some of the resulting problems, see *Passage of the Land Registration etc (Scotland) Bill 2011* (n 7) 380.
53 LR(S)A 2012 s 13(1).
54 It is explained on the OS website (www.ordnancesurvey.co.uk/business-and-government/help-and-support/navigation-technology/os-net/surveying.html) that: 'OSBG36 National Grid (Ordnance Survey Great Britain 1936) is our national coordinate system for topographic mapping. It is used for Ordnance Survey mapping at all scales, and for many private topographic surveys. The OSBG36 part of the name refers to the geodetic datum (system of latitude and longitude) used, and the National Grid part refers to the map projection and grid referencing convention for eastings and northings.'
55 Land Register Rules etc (Scotland) Regulations 2014, SSI 2014/150, r 8; Registers of Scotland, *General Guidance – The Cadastral Map: The Land Register and land covered by water* (v.02, 2016) 1–3. See also Registers of Scotland, *FAQs: Seabed and natural water boundaries*; Registers of

be used, however, where the plot comprises a single area that straddles both land and sea.[56]

Rather than forming part of the 33 traditional registration areas,[57] the seabed has its own registration area (with the prefix 'SEA'), so that seabed off the coast of St Kilda is in the same registration area as the seabed off the coast of, say, Yell and Unst.[58] The SEA registration area has the low-water mark as its land-facing edge, the foreshore itself falling within the relevant county area.[59]

5.17 Water features as boundaries

Sometimes a boundary is a water feature such as a burn, river, pond, loch or the sea. The boundary line may be the near edge, or the middle, or some other line.[60] A difficulty is that the water feature may move over time. For example, in a burn or river there may be gradual erosion on one bank, whilst the opposite bank gradually extends through silting, consolidated by vegetation; or the line of the coast may change over time by erosion or the opposite. As a general rule, the legal boundary moves with the water boundary by virtue of the doctrine of alluvion, so that if two properties are bounded by the centre line of a river and the river changes course, the boundary becomes the centre line of the relocated river.[61] Indeed, this is presupposed by the 2012 Act, because it provides a mechanism, called a shifting boundary agreement, whereby the two proprietors[62] in question can, by a registered agreement, fix the title boundary permanently,[63] so that future movement of the water boundary will have no effect on the title boundary.[64] The existence of the agreement is noted both on the cadastral map and on the affected title sheets.[65] In the absence of such an agreement, the title boundary is taken to track the water boundary, thus making the cadastral plan and the title sheets inaccurate.[66] The Keeper's warranty does not extend to inaccuracies brought about by alluvion.[67]

Scotland, *General Guidance: Deed Plan Criteria* (v.05, 2016) 10. Where the seabed is bounded by foreshore or land, it is acceptable to describe that particular boundary by reference to the mean low water springs (which are themselves a defined feature on the OS map).

56 *General Guidance: The Cadastral Map – The Land Register and land covered by water* (n 55) 2. In such a case the result will normally be two separate cadastral units (and title sheets), with the seabed part being registered in the county of SEA and the land part in the appropriate land-based county.

57 For which see para 3.9 above.

58 *General Guidance: The Cadastral Map – The Land Register and land covered by water* (n 55) 1.

59 Tides vary: the foreshore is defined by 'ordinary spring tides', a definition that gives to the foreshore very nearly its maximum possible extent, for it is at spring tides that the high water is at its highest and low water at its lowest. See eg J Robbie, *Private Water Rights* (Studies in Scots Law vol 4, 2015) para 3-40.

60 All of this creates challenges for the cadastral map: see *Registration Manual* (n 3) Further Guidance: Plans – mapping natural water boundaries.

61 For alluvion, see Robbie (n 59) ch 4.

62 In the case of the coast, one of the two proprietors would normally be the Crown.

63 It appears that an agreement, once registered, cannot subsequently be revoked; certainly no provision for revocation is provided by the legislation.

64 LR(S)A 2012 s 66. Such an agreement must be registered against both properties: see *General Guidance: The Cadastral Map – The Land Register and land covered by water* (n 55) 4.

65 *General Guidance: The Cadastral Map – The Land Register and land covered by water* (n 52) 4.

66 This is the presupposition of s 66(3). For the thinking behind this provision, see SLC DP 130 paras 3.5–3.17 and SLC Report 222 paras 5.33–5.35.

67 LR(S)A 2012 s 73(2)(i): see para 13.3 below.

In her important study of *Private Water Rights*, Jill Robbie has challenged the assumptions underlying the provisions in the Act.[68] She argues that a title boundary tracks the movement of the water boundary if, but only if, the title states the water boundary to be the title boundary; if, by contrast, there is a precise plan of the property, or there are precise measurements of it, any change in the water boundary is irrelevant. In the Register of Sasines, both forms of description were commonly found: in other words, a title boundary could be defined as being the water boundary (in which case it would change with the water boundary itself) or it could be defined by precise plan or precise measurements (in which case, on Dr Robbie's view, the fact that it coincided, or initially coincided, with the water was essentially irrelevant). In the Land Register, however, property is necessarily defined by precise plan, from which Dr Robbie concludes that title boundaries can never move with the movement of water boundaries, and that accordingly the statutory provision about shifting boundary agreements is misconceived. On this view, shifting boundary agreements, though they do no harm, do no good either, because cadastral unit boundaries are fixed and unchangeable anyway.[69]

5.18 Supplementary plans and other data

Information as to boundaries that is too detailed to be conveniently represented on the cadastral map – for example, whether the title boundary is (or is not) the middle of a wall[70] – is entered in the A section of the title sheet.[71] This will be based on what appeared in the underlying deed or deeds, and in complex cases there is likely to be a reference back to the deed itself rather than an attempt at a summary.[72] Such information is one example of 'supplementary data' on the A section. A supplementary plan is another.[73] This is useful where a plan is available at a scale more detailed than that of the base map, or in order to show the vertical layout in a building.[74] Whether to include supplementary data is a matter for the Keeper's discretion,[75] and current practice is against the use of supplementary plans, at least in the normal case.[76] The fact that a deed contains a plan does not make that plan a supplementary plan. The deed, with its plan, enters the archive record; it becomes a supplementary plan only if it is incorporated into the A section, whether by being copied into it, or by reference.[77]

---

68 Robbie (n 59) paras 4-59–4-63.
69 Except of consent.
70 Compare shifting boundary agreements (for which see para 5.17 above) which *are* mentioned on the cadastral map.
71 LR(S)A 2012 s 11(1)(a) provides that the cadastral map is to show 'the totality of registered geospatial data (other than supplementary data in individual title sheets)'. For the A section, see para 4.14 above. Some of the practical issues are explored in *Registration Manual* (n 3) Topics: Boundaries.
72 Registers of Scotland, *FAQs: Cadastral Mapping: Deed Plan Requirements* Q 14. There is, however, no *obligation* to bring forward supplementary data from the deeds: see SLC Report 222 para 5.37.
73 For other examples, see paras 4.9 and 4.25 above.
74 Vertical data could, in principle, be part of the cadastral map itself but at present that does not happen, and accordingly a supplementary plan is the only possibility: see para 5.19 below.
75 LR(S)A 2012 s 10(2)(e).
76 This policy, and some exceptions to it, are set out in *Registration Manual* (n 3) Further Guidance: Plans – supplementary plans, SPLs and supplementary data to the title sheet.
77 For the latter, see LR(S)A 2012 s 10(3).

Data not included in the title sheet can still be consulted for various purposes.[78] The question has two aspects. One is where it is alleged that the Register is inaccurate and hence in need of rectification. The answer to that is that in principle the old deeds can, depending on the circumstances, be relevant to an assertion of inaccuracy.[79] The other aspect is whether the old deeds can be adduced to help resolve matters where the Land Register is simply not clear enough, ie not to contradict what the Register says but to supplement it, to explain it, and to give it better precision. We think that the position is the same as it (probably) was under the previous legislation: the old deeds are admissible for this purpose.[80]

Occasionally, supplementary data can lead to title disputes. For example, take two neighbouring properties. Their cadastral units dovetail neatly: as far as the cadastral map is concerned it is a happy and perfect union. But the title sheets contain supplementary data which conflict: for instance, they have conflicting textual statements as to whether the boundary is the middle of a field wall or one of its faces. Ideally, of course, the Keeper would always check such data to ensure that no conflict arises, but that does not appear to happen as standard practice. Conflicts, when they occur, may be hard to resolve, though sometimes they can be solved by realignment or by positive prescription, both of which allocate title according to the state of possession.[81]

There can also be internal conflict, ie conflict between different elements in the supplementary data within the same title sheet, or between the supplementary data in a title sheet and the cadastrally mapped extent for that title. As to the latter, what appears in the cadastral map has priority (though the fact of the conflict may itself be a symptom of an inaccuracy);[82] as to the former, there seems to be no general rule.[83]

5.19 Three dimensions?

Under the legislation, the cadastral map 'may (but need not) show the boundaries of cadastral units on the vertical plane'.[84] Up to now it does not do so. In a tenement building, for example, the cadastral map shows only the footprint of the building.[85] The flats in the tenement are verbally described, and may also be identified in the vertical dimension by the use of a supplementary plan, though the latter is unusual.

---

78 There is, however, no legislative provision on the subject.
79 For inaccuracies and their rectification, see ch 11.
80 *Stuart v Stuart*, 27 July 2009, Stonehaven Sheriff Court (unreported), discussed in K G C Reid and G L Gretton, *Conveyancing 2009* (2010) pp 176–77. In that case the sheriff (P P Davies) thought that: 'One can and should, where appropriate, examine prior titles to see how, if at all, they describe boundary lines. Such titles would be irrelevant to the issue of who currently owns any property, but relevant to the line of a disputed boundary.' For possible limitations, see *Willemse v French* [2011] CSOH 51, 2011 SC 576, paras 14–18 per Lord Tyre.
81 For realignment, see ch 12; for positive prescription, see ch 17.
82 This is not stated in the legislation, but seems implied by the conception of a cadastral map. Data in title sheets are merely 'supplementary'.
83 A series of rules was proposed in SLC DP 130 paras 2.11–2.13 but was not carried forward into the final Report or the legislation.
84 LR(S)A 2012 s 11(3).
85 It will also show the whole 'steading' of the tenement, ie the area of ground occupied by the building itself, plus associated ground, such as, in a traditional tenement, the back green, and so on. For details, see para 4.25 above.

But the cadastral map does not use the vertical dimension. That could, however, change in the future.[86]

Of course, in one sense the cadastral map is already three-dimensional, for it shows mineral rights. But it shows only that mineral rights exist (ie by separate title from ownership of the land in general) and does not attempt to show where, in terms of depth, any particular mineral deposits lie.

5.20 Mapping conventions

In the absence of legislative prescription, mapping conventions are a matter for the Keeper, and a useful guide to the Keeper's practice can be found on the RoS website.[87] For example, the cadastral map makes extensive use of colour tinting. Wherever possible, blue is used for the solum of buildings, pink for exclusive ground, yellow for paths or areas burdened by tree preservation orders, brown for drying greens or paths, and mauve for small areas such as bin stores. Coloured edging is also standard, with red generally denoting the extent of the property, and yellow for the landlord's interest where parts of the property have been leased. In relation to red edging, RoS warn that:[88]

> Occasionally, the edging will be applied 'externally' to the boundary defining the subjects: for instance, where a red edge covers another colour reference or important detail near to a boundary. For this reason, it should not be assumed that the registered extent includes up to the outer edge of the red, but rather see the registered boundary as being the line (firm or pecked) to which the red edge has been applied.

DEED PLANS AND PLANS REPORTS

5.21 Identifying the property

If a conveyancing transaction concerns the whole of a cadastral unit, no issues of identification arise apart from the need to specify the title number.[89] But issues of identification do arise on first registration or on a split-off. They also arise where a subordinate real right is to be registered over part only of a property, such as a servitude of way or a lease granted over a single field in a farm. In all these cases sufficient information must be given in the deed to allow the Keeper to 'delineate' the property (or the part of the property) on the cadastral map.[90] Failure to provide this information will result in the rejection of the application for registration.[91] RoS have issued detailed guidance on their website as to what is needed,[92] and, while the guidance is not mandatory,[93] it will usually be advisable to follow it.

---

86 See further J E Stoter and P van Oosterom, *3D Cadastre in an International Context: Legal, Organizational and Technological Aspects* (2006).
87 Registers of Scotland, *Agency Conventions Regulating Plans References*; *Registration Manual* (n 3) Further Guidance: Plans – mapping styles on the cadastral map. The information which follows in the text is drawn from these guides.
88 *Agency Conventions Regulating Plans References* (n 87) 2.
89 LR(S)A 2012 s 26(1)(c).
90 LR(S)A 2012 ss 23(1)(c), (d), 25(1)(b), (c), 26(1)(d), and 28(1).
91 LR(S)A 2012 s 21. The application will also be rejected if the property as described overlaps with another cadastral unit on the Register: see para 5.11 above.
92 *General Guidance: Deed Plan Criteria* (n 55). Examples of common errors are given in an appendix. See also *FAQs: Cadastral mapping: deed plan requirements* (n 72).
93 *General Guidance: Deed Plan Criteria* (n 55) 2.

For split-off deeds a new plan will usually be necessary.[94] In the case of first registrations, the existing description in the Sasine deeds will sometimes be sufficient: there may already be a plan of sufficient quality or a bounding description which is detailed enough for the Keeper to plot the boundaries on the cadastral map.[95] Any doubt as to sufficiency can be resolved by obtaining a level 2 or level 3 plans report, which will indicate whether the description is suitable for registration.[96]

Where a new plan is needed it must be used as the deed plan.[97] It is not acceptable for the plan to be stated as 'demonstrative', as opposed to 'taxative', and it seems best to avoid both terms.[98] Any new plan must correspond in scale to the OS map for the area being registered. If an actual OS map is to be used (such as the extract supplied with a plans report), the written permission of the Ordnance Survey is needed.[99] RoS offer their own plan drawing and plan assistance services, the former for straightforward cases, the latter for cases where it is unclear how a Sasine description or plan should be translated on to the OS map.

Deed plans must display a number of fairly obvious virtues.[100] They must show the scale of the map, preferably by a drawn or bar scale (which allows any distortion by copying to be identified), and also the compass orientation of north. They must contain sufficient surrounding detail (such as fences, neighbouring buildings, and road junctions) to enable the location and position of the plot to be fixed: a plan which shows a 'floating rectangle' will be rejected. The boundaries of the plot must be clearly marked, for example by coloured edging, tinting or hatching. Measurements are encouraged, and should be given in metric units to one decimal place. Boundaries which do not coincide with physical features must be accurately fixed to existing detail by measurements shown on the plan.[101] Additional digital data are competent but likely to be useful only in respect of large areas of ground or where the plotting is complex. The plan itself can be in digital form.[102]

The special rules for the seabed have already been discussed.[103] In the case of a tenement flat, the 'steading' (comprising the building and grounds) will need to be mapped if this has not been done already in respect of the registration of another

---

94 An exception is where a plan for the development has been approved in advance by RoS: see para 5.22 below.
95 *FAQs: Cadastral mapping: deed plan requirements* (n 72) Q 2.
96 For plans reports, see para 5.23 below.
97 This is because the application conditions for registration require that the plot be sufficiently described in the deed itself: see LR(S)A 2012 ss 23(1)(c), 25(1)(b) and 26(1)(d). Where there is no deed, as in the case of voluntary registration, the plan will be freestanding: see s 28(1).
98 *General Guidance: Deed Plan Criteria* (n 55) 8. For the difference between 'demonstrative' and 'taxative' plans, see G L Gretton and K G C Reid, *Conveyancing* (4th edn, 2011) para 12-18.
99 This, however, will be assumed by RoS to have been obtained: see Registers of Scotland, *FAQs: Reports Portal* Post-report Q 7.
100 *General Guidance: Deed Plan Criteria* (n 55) 2–8.
101 *General Guidance: Deed Plan Criteria* (n 55) 9.
102 In which case it must contain Geographical Information System ('GIS') or Computer-Aided Design ('CAD') data. For further guidance, see *General Guidance: Deed Plan Criteria* (n 55) 11.
103 See para 5.16 above.

flat in the same building; a plans report will disclose whether a cadastral unit for the steading already exists.[104]

As well as being used in respect of deeds, a plan may also be needed to support an application for an advance notice, where the property has not previously been mapped,[105] or indeed in an application for a plans report.[106] It may also be needed for the purposes of voluntary registration.[107]

5.22 Development plan approval

For new developments, whether residential or commercial, RoS provide a service known as development plan approval ('DPA').[108] Its primary purpose is to allow a proper check by RoS of the extent of the developer's title, thus reducing the risk that buildings will be erected beyond the boundary line.[109] But if DPA is sought after planning permission has been obtained, the plan submitted by the developer can include the internal layout of the development, thus allowing the Keeper to map the individual units, roads, common areas and so on.[110] No further plan is then needed for a subsequent deed of conditions, for an advance notice (whether over all or part of the development), or for the split-off dispositions of the units; it is sufficient to make reference to the development plan already held, in digital form, by RoS. In respect of the last of these, RoS have issued a style: 'All and Whole that plot of ground edged red and marked plot number 31 of the development plan approved by the Keeper for the development registered under ANG63461 on 1 December 2014'.[111] RoS will examine draft deed styles in advance of their submission for registration. As well as assisting developers, DPA is also of assistance to the purchasers of individual units, providing reassurance that the unit falls within the developer's title and removing the need for a plans report.[112]

DPA is limited to sites already on the Land Register or in respect of which an application for registration is pending. In addition, the site must be the subject of imminent development. Approval requires the submission of digital architectural drawings, geo-referenced to OS national grid co-ordinates.[113]

---

104 For the implications for applications for registration, see LR(S)A 2012 ss 23(2), 25(2), 26(3), and 28(2), discussed further in paras 8.8 and 8.9 below. For the implications for advance notices, see LR(S)A 2012 s 56(2). An account of the way in which tenements are represented on the Register is given at para 4.25 above.
105 See para 10.12 below.
106 For plans reports, see para 5.23 below.
107 See para 7.18 below.
108 See generally www.ros.gov.uk/services/dpa; *Registration Manual* (n 3) Further Guidance: Plans – development plan approval. See also Registers of Scotland, *FAQs: Development Plan Approval* which, in Q 1, contains the following definition: 'Development plan approval is where we take a developer's proposed layout in a digital format and compare it against a registered title or registered titles.'
109 As in the infamous case involving the 'Happy Valley' housing estate in Blackburn, West Lothian, as to which see *Consumer Protection in Conveyancing Cases: A Report to the Council of the Law Society of Scotland by Sheriff Principal Edward Bowen* (2015) paras 19–40. Sheriff Principal Bowen comments (para 37) that DPA 'raises awareness of the type of situation which arose at Happy Valley'.
110 Where plans change, a new layout can be substituted and approved: see *FAQs: Development Plan Approval* (n 108) Q 4.
111 (2015) 60 JLSS Feb/9.
112 Registers of Scotland, *FAQs: One Shot Rule* Q 10.
113 Ie OSGB1936 (for which see n 54 above). Digital data are acceptable in a number of formats, the most commonly used being AutoCAD .dwg files. For further details, see Registers of Scotland, *Development Plan Approval Guidance for Architects*.

Deed Plans and Plans Reports 89

5.23 Plans reports[114]

For first registrations it is always advisable to obtain a plans report, whether from RoS or from independent search firms.[115] Three levels of report are offered, escalating in £10 price bands from the simple level 1 report (£35) through level 2 reports (£45) to level 3 reports (£55). Plans reports serve three main purposes. One is to confirm that the property can be identified and to compare the legal boundaries, as disclosed by the Sasine description, with the physical boundaries on the OS map.[116] Another is to ensure that the description is sufficiently clear to allow the Keeper to plot the property on the cadastral map.[117] The third purpose is to check for overlaps with existing registered titles or, in other words, with existing cadastral units.[118] All levels of report disclose the last of these,[119] although only a level 3 report shows the extent of the overlap. The other matters are covered in level 2 and level 3 (but not level 1) reports. In addition, level 3 reports identify any servitudes, real burdens or other encumbrances which are plotted on the cadastral map. Typically, it is a level 3 report which is instructed, although if a new plan is being prepared anyway it is usually possible to make do with a level 1 report.[120] RoS restrict level 3 reports to plots which are to be transferred or leased.[121]

An important reason for obtaining a plans report is to receive advance warning of difficulties which could result in the application for first registration being rejected. Thus, boundary discrepancies might require corrective conveyancing[122] or an acceptance on the part of the applicant that less ground is being acquired than was previously thought.[123] The same is true of overlaps with an existing cadastral unit, although rectification to remove the overlap from the cadastral unit might be another way forward.[124] An unclear description will prompt the preparation of a new plan.

In principle, there is no need for a plans report where the property is already on the Land Register unless only a part of the property is to be affected by the

---

114 See generally: Registers of Scotland, *General Guidance: Reports* (v.03, 2015); *FAQs: Reports Portal* (n 99); F Rooney and J King, 'Plans reports: yes or no?' (2015) 60 JLSS July/10; J King and F Rooney, 'Plans reports: an evolving scene' (2016, available at bit.ly/25N1Wgh).
115 If the Sasine title is complex, involving many split-offs, it will usually be necessary to draw up a new plan before a plans report can be obtained: see Rooney and King (n 114) 11.
116 This is the same function provided under the 1979 Act regime by a P16 report.
117 See para 5.21 above.
118 For overlaps, see para 5.11 above. LR(S)A 2012 s 12(2) provides that 'the same area of land cannot be represented by more than one cadastral unit'.
119 As well, in many cases, as any competing application for registration: see King and Rooney (n 114).
120 In the year to the end of March 2016, RoS issued some 36,000 plans reports of which the vast majority were at level 3. See King and Rooney (n 114), who also express the view that too many level 3 reports are being ordered.
121 King and Rooney (n 114).
122 The little-used facility of a boundary agreement made under LR(S)A 1979 s 19 has been withdrawn, although existing agreements remain valid. For an explanation and an account of the difficulties with s 19, see SLC DP 130 paras 3.28–3.49 and SLC Report 222 paras 5.31 and 5.32. A replacement had been contemplated in DP 130 but was not proceeded with in Report 222.
123 For helpful guidance, see *FAQs: Reports Portal* (n 99) Post-report Qs 1–4. Q 6 deals with the case where, following the report, the applicant believes the OS map to be incorrect. Provided that the Keeper is persuaded on the point, and that the property can be plotted on the cadastral map, registration can proceed, and the Keeper will update the cadastral map as and when the OS map is updated.
124 See paras 11.23, 11.25 and 11.26 below.

transaction (as with a split-off disposition).¹²⁵ This is because a cadastral unit for the property already exists, and any overlaps should already be noted on the title sheet.¹²⁶ Anecdotal evidence, however, suggests that competing titles are *not* always apparent from the Register, and it may be that in high-value commercial transactions a plans report would be a sensible precaution.¹²⁷ As no overlap is possible under the 2012 Act, any overlaps which do exist must date from the days of the 1979 Act.

For deeds affecting part only of a registered property, a plans report provides assurance that there are no overlaps with another registered title. A level 1 report should normally be sufficient for this purpose, and even this can be dispensed with where the part is delineated on a development plan which has been approved by RoS.¹²⁸

Applications for a plans report from RoS must be made electronically, and any accompanying plan or deed must be uploaded as a PDF.¹²⁹ The application must be supported by a plan or by a full bounding description in words. Any bounding description relied on should by preference be reproduced in the 'additional information' field of the application form, although incorporation by reference to an (uploaded) deed is also competent. If a plan or verbal description relates to more than one area, it is necessary to make clear in respect of which area the report is being requested. Applications are normally processed within 24 hours, and a link sent to the (online) report which can be viewed for up to a year. It is possible and normal to combine a request for a plans report with one for a legal report.¹³⁰

---

125 Rooney and King (n 114); King and Rooney (n 114).
126 *FAQs: Reports Portal* (n 99) Pre-report Q 2.
127 See also A E A Stewart and E F F Sinclair, *Conveyancing Practice in Scotland* (7th edn, 2016) 302–03.
128 This is because RoS will already have checked for overlaps and other matters: see para 5.22 above.
129 But arrangements can be made to submit large or unusual plans by post in paper form: see *FAQs: Reports Portal* (n 99) Pre-report Q 8; *General Guidance: Reports* (n 114) 3.
130 *General Guidance: Reports* (n 114) 2–3. A combined level 1 plans report and legal report costs £55, a combined level 2 plans report and legal report costs £95, and a combined level 3 plans report and legal report costs £100. This represents a saving. For legal reports, see paras 10.31 and 10.32 below.

Chapter 6

Registrable Deeds

OVERVIEW

6.1 Introduction

The Land Register is at one and the same time a register of title, a register of deeds, and a register of plots of land.[1] This chapter deals with the second of these and asks: what types of deed can be registered in the Land Register? The focus is on deed types: other conditions about registrability, such as whether a document has been sufficiently executed, are considered elsewhere.[2]

The Land Registration etc (Scotland) Act 2012 has as one of its aims the final closure of the Register of Sasines to new transactions. Something that once would have been registrable in the Register of Sasines, but which cannot now be registered there, is in principle registrable in the Land Register.[3] The closure is progressive. Further detail is given in chapter 7.

6.2 Registrable only if an enactment so provides

The 2012 Act does not lay down what deeds can be registered.[4] Instead, the idea is that registrability should be addressed by sector-specific legislation;[5] it is not the role of a land registration statute to usurp policy-making in specific sectors.[6] Deeds are only registrable, therefore, where an enactment so provides.[7] No deeds are registrable at common law, for the Register of Sasines and the Land Register are statutory.[8]

---

1 See para 4.4 above.
2 See paras 8.6–8.9 below.
3 But there are exceptions: see para 6.4 below.
4 Compare here the approach of the 1979 Act, discussed in para 6.4 below. The word 'deed', used in LR(S)A 2012 s 49(1), is defined (by s 113(1)) to mean 'a document (and includes a decree which is registrable under an enactment)'. 'Document' is not defined in the Act, but it is a term that is often used in legislation, including the Requirements of Writing (Scotland) Act 1995 (where it is given a non-exhaustive definition in s 12(1)).
5 LR(S)A 2012 s 49(1). This 'look to other legislation for what is registrable' principle parallels the 'look to other legislation for the effect' principle set out in s 49(2) and discussed at para 9.7 below.
6 Scottish Law Commission, *Discussion Paper No 128 on Land Registration: Registration, Rectification and Indemnity* (2005) ('SLC DP 128') para 3.24. LR(S)A 2012 s 48(4) might be read as saying that any type of deed that was recordable in the Register of Sasines is registrable in the Land Register. That was not its intended meaning.
7 LR(S)A 2012 s 49(1) allows registration 'only if and so far as' registration is authorised by an enactment. The threefold list in subs (1) – ie (a) to (c) – is perhaps an over-elaboration, since all that needed to be said was 'an enactment' (as in s 17(1)(a) of the Scottish Law Commission's draft Bill). It is not clear why four statutes are singled out for mention in para (b) (and subs (3)).
8 Possibly there exist deed types which ought to be registrable but for whose registration no statutory provision exists. This is an issue that needs to be kept an eye on, and the Keeper proposes so to do. See Registers of Scotland, *Consultation on Implementation of the Land Registration etc (Scotland) Act 2012: Post Consultation Report* (2014) para 2.6.

The 2012 Act itself provides for the registration of certain types of deed, and these are considered later in the chapter.⁹ Many other enactments do likewise. For instance, the Conveyancing and Feudal Reform (Scotland) Act 1970 says that standard securities must be registered, and the Title Conditions (Scotland) Act 2003 says that real burdens must be registered. As well as public general statutes, provision for registration may also be made by private or local Acts, or by statutory instrument. In each case those framing the legislation made the decision to require registration. In other legislation the opposite decision was made, even though land is affected. For example, the planning legislation does not generally provide for the registration of planning conditions, with the exception of s 75 agreements.[10]

Many enactments, of course, were passed before the legislation setting up the Land Register in 1979. For such pre-1979 legislation,[11] provisions permitting or requiring recording in the Register of Sasines are, subject to some exceptions,[12] to be read as encompassing[13] registration in the Land Register.[14] In addition, two important statutes – the Registration of Leases (Scotland) Act 1857 and the Conveyancing and Feudal Reform (Scotland) Act 1970 – have been specifically amended to include references to the Land Register.[15]

6.3 A definitive list?

Conveyancers naturally think of the Land Register (and the Register of Sasines) as a place where private-law deeds, such as dispositions and heritable securities, are registered. That indeed is its primary purpose. But, as mentioned elsewhere,[16] some public-law documents affecting property are also registrable.

Given the mass of legislation, it would be a daunting task to draw up a definitive list of the deeds and other documents that are registrable in the Land Register. A provisional list published by RoS, and reproduced in an appendix to this chapter, names 93 documents.[17] Most deed types encountered in ordinary conveyancing

---

9 Paragraphs 6.6–6.16 below.
10 Town and Country Planning (Scotland) Act 1997 s 75.
11 'Pre-1979' is slightly inaccurate shorthand. As the wording makes clear, LR(S)A 1979 s 29(2) applies to some enactments of the year 1979 itself. An example is the Ancient Monuments and Archaeological Areas Act 1979, which received Royal Assent on the same day (4 April 1979) as the LR(S)A 1979. Section 1(10) of the former (which remains in force) provides that 'it shall be competent to record in the Register of Sasines' a notice saying that an ancient monument has been scheduled.
12 LR(S)A 1979 s 29(3), sch 3, as amended by LR(S)A 2012 sch 5 para 19(9).
13 That is the meaning and effect of the provision although the wording ('shall be construed as a reference to' the Land Register) would, on a literal reading, imply that registration can *only* be in the Land Register. In fact, for as long as the Register of Sasines remains open, some deeds will continue to be registrable there.
14 LR(S)A 1979 s 29(2). This is one of the few provisions of the 1979 Act to remain in force (the others being s 15(4) and s 16).
15 LR(S)A 2012 s 52, sch 2 (1857 Act), and sch 5 paras 17–25 (1970 Act). The former also includes amendments of a substantive nature: see ch 20.
16 Paragraph 3.5 above.
17 Registers of Scotland, *General Guidance: Registrable deeds under Section 49: List* (v.03, 2016). The list continues to grow: this is the third version, and further versions can be expected. See also Registers of Scotland, *Registration Manual* (https://rosdev.atlassian.net/wiki/display/2ARM/Home) Topics: Court orders that are registrable deeds. For a non-exhaustive list of documents that are *not* registrable, see *Registration Manual* Further Guidance: Examining deeds – what is a registrable deed? These include confirmation of executors, deeds of assumption and conveyance, and floating charges.

practice are included, as well as many that the typical law agent might not encounter in a lifetime. But there is no suggestion that the list is complete: it is prefaced by the cautious statement that 'the Keeper is satisfied that the following deeds are registrable in terms of s 49 of the Act'. Doubtless other deeds will come to be added to the list. Some will also drop off in the course of time.[18] Where an application is made to register a deed of a type not listed, the applicant is asked to specify the enactment that authorises registration.[19]

6.4 Differences from the 1979 Act

The approach just described differs from that of the 1979 Act, which had a general provision as to what was registrable.[20] This, however, created numerous difficulties and was not carried forward to the 2012 Act.[21] One result is that a small number of deeds and documents which were accepted by the Keeper under the 1979 Act are no longer registrable under the 2012 Act.[22] The documents affected are mainly midcouples (such as acts and warrant, certificates of confirmation, and docket transfers), or documents (such as death certificates) which speak to events such as the operation of a survivorship destination.[23] The change, however, is less significant than might appear. Although midcouples have ceased to be registrable, a notice of title will often be registered in their place.[24] And if the event vouched for by a document results in the title becoming inaccurate (as with the death of one of the owners holding on a survivorship destination), the document (in the example given, a death certificate and a statement of non-evacuation) will need to be produced to the Keeper in order to have the title rectified and a copy will then be preserved in the archive record.[25]

6.5 Language of the deed

The view of RoS is that only deeds in the English language[26] are registrable in the Land Register and, accordingly, that if deeds in any other language, such as Gaelic, are to be registered, that would require legislation.[27]

---

18 One already has. Notices under the Long Leases (Scotland) Act 2012, for example in order to convert leasehold conditions into real burdens, ceased to be registrable on 28 November 2015. For further details, see K G C Reid and G L Gretton, *Conveyancing 2013* (2014) 63–66 and 139–50.
19 Registers of Scotland, *General Guidance: Registrable deeds under Section 49: Questions* (v.01, 2014) 1. In the case of a private or local Act, it is also necessary to enclose a copy of the title page of the Act and of the relevant provision.
20 LR(S)A 1979 s 2.
21 See Scottish Law Commission, *Report No 222 on Land Registration* (2010) ('SLC Report 222') part 12 for discussion of the problems.
22 *General Guidance: Registrable Deeds under Section 49: Questions* (n 19) 2. Strictly, however, registration under the 1979 Act was of interests in land rather than deeds: see para 2.2 above.
23 Events were registrable under LR(S)A 1979 s 2(4)(c).
24 See para 6.9 below.
25 For rectification, see ch 11; for the archive record, see para 4.31 above. One of the aims of the 2012 Act was to provide a much clearer distinction between registration and rectification: see SLC DP 128 paras 3.20–3.23. If property is held by A and B and the survivor, the effect of A's death is for A's half share to pass to B (unless the destination has been evacuated). In continuing to show the owners as both A and B, the Register is inaccurate. Hence the appropriate method of altering the Register is rectification, not registration. A disadvantage from the Keeper's point of view is that there is no fee for rectification: see para 11.15 below.
26 Though a sprinkling of Latin is unobjectionable, at least on this ground.
27 See further SLC Report 222 para 34.36, n 35.

DEEDS REGISTRABLE UNDER THE 2012 ACT

6.6 Introduction

As already mentioned, a deed or document is registrable in the Land Register if and only if this is provided for by legislation.[28] The 2012 Act itself makes provision as to the registration of certain deeds, sometimes directly and sometimes by amending other legislation. These may now be considered in turn.

6.7 Dispositions: in general

Section 50 of the 2012 Act provides for the registrability of dispositions and spells out the substantive effects: 'Registration of a valid disposition transfers ownership. An unregistered disposition does not transfer ownership.'[29] The last of these is partly aimed at the decision of the House of Lords in *Sharp v Thomson*[30] which, on one reading at least, seemed to allow a form of ownership to pass when a disposition is delivered. As of the designated day (8 December 2014), dispositions can no longer be recorded in the Register of Sasines.[31] Section 50 applies to all land, including udal land.[32]

As s 50 reminds us,[33] there are a handful of other ways in which ownership of land can be acquired, including by notice of title,[34] by the registration of a decree of reduction of a voidable disposition,[35] by positive prescription,[36] by realignment,[37] by the first death when property is held on a survivorship clause, and by alluvion.

Normally, dispositions are granted by the heritable proprietor, but there can be cases where the granter, though not heritable proprietor, has a power to grant a valid and thus registrable disposition.[38] One example is a disposition by an unregistered holder (or, in feudal terminology, an uninfeft proprietor), ie by a

---

28 LR(S)A 2012 s 49(1), discussed in para 6.2 above.
29 Section 50 replaces s 4 of the Abolition of Feudal Tenure etc (Scotland) Act 2012, which was repealed by LR(S)A 2012 sch 5 para 39(2). For the (feudal) background to that provision, see Scottish Law Commission, *Report No 168 on Abolition of the Feudal System* (1999) paras 7.6–7.12. Dispositions were in any case registrable in the Land Register by virtue of LR(S)A 1979 s 2(1)(a), (4)(a).
30 1997 SC (HL) 66. Since *Burnett's Tr v Grainger* 2004 SC (HL) 19, the decision in *Sharp* is usually regarded as being confined to the interaction of dispositions with floating charges.
31 Prior to the designated day (8 December 2014) a disposition was registrable in the Register of Sasines (only) if no consideration was given and if the property in question was still in that Register. Today all dispositions fall to be registered in the Land Register: see LR(S)A 2012 s 48(1)(a), and see para 7.6 below.
32 LR(S)A 2012 s 50(5). For the background, see SLC Report 222 para 38.14.
33 LR(S)A 2012 s 50(4)(b), providing that subsections (1)–(3) are subject to 'any other enactment or rule of law by or under which ownership of land may pass'. This is taken from the Abolition of Feudal Tenure etc (Scotland) Act 2000 s 4(2), as to which see SLC Report 168 (n 29) para 7.11. Subsections (1)–(3) are also said (by s 50(4)(a)) to be subject to ss 43 and 86, which are both examples of where ownership passes under an *invalid* disposition. The provision as a whole is for information and has no substantive effect.
34 See para 6.9 below.
35 See para 6.12 below.
36 See ch 17.
37 See ch 12.
38 Invalid dispositions are not generally registrable: see para 8.7(4) below.

person who has a right to the property but whose title has not been completed by registration.[39] A clause of deduction of title is no longer needed.[40]

The legislation does not cover the effect of a clause of retention of title in a disposition. Such clauses seem to be unknown in practice. We incline to the view that such a clause would not be effective: either the clause would be disregarded or the whole deed would be invalid.[41] If parties wish for some reason to have a delayed-action arrangement, there are other means at their disposal.

6.8 Dispositions of souvenir plots

A 'souvenir plot' is a plot of 'inconsiderable size and of no practical utility' which does not already exist as a separate title unit.[42] The background here is that some companies (usually based outside Scotland and indeed outside the EU) offer for sale tiny areas of land, such as a square metre or even less. This practice has gone on for decades. The term 'souvenir' is a long-established one, though one might question how suitable it is, given that few buyers may have been to or even near the property that they are 'buying' or indeed have visited Scotland at all.[43] From a land registration point of view, souvenir plots are a nuisance, and their registration is forbidden.[44] This constitutes a restriction on the division of cadastral units. So if a company owns 10,000 square metres of moorland, and sells off plots of one square metre each, the cadastral unit for the 10,000 square metres cannot be divided. Furthermore, as ownership of land passes by registration, buyers of souvenir plot cannot become owners. The company that sells the plot thus receives payment but retains ownership. The only thing that the buyer obtains ownership of is a piece of paper. If the piece of paper states that the buyer is the owner of the plot, that is a false statement.

The term 'practical utility' has to be interpreted with common sense. Take this case: a public-spirited farmer has on his land a prehistoric standing stone. He donates this to the National Trust for Scotland, the disposition being of the small patch of ground where the stone stands. In our view this is not a souvenir plot and accordingly the disposition is registrable, provided of course that the other requirements of registrability are met.[45]

6.9 Unregistrable conveyances and notices of title

As well as dispositions, the law has long recognised the existence of certain other types of conveyance. Typically, these are court decrees such as confirmation of

---

39 Completion of title would normally require the registration of a notice of title: see para 6.9 below.
40 LR(S)A 2012 s 101. Previously, clauses of deduction of title were excused only in respect of land already on the Land Register and so continued to be required on first registration: see LR(S)A 1979 s 15(3).
41 Cf BGB (German Civil Code) § 925(2).
42 LR(S)A 2012 s 22(2). By 'separate title unit' is meant either a registered plot, or 'a plot the ownership of which has, at any time, separately been constituted or transferred by a document recorded in the Register of Sasines'. In practice tiny areas of land will be neither, not least because of LR(S)A 1979 s 4(2)(b).
43 On souvenir plots, see further: SLC Report 222 paras 12.82–12.85; Registers of Scotland, 'Caution the souvenir hunters' (2012) 57 JLSS Apr/10; J Robbie and M Combe, 'A square foot of old Scotland: ownership of souvenir plots' (2015) 19 EdinLR 393.
44 LR(S)A 2012 s 22(1)(b). The previous law was to the same effect: see LR(S)A 1979 s 4(2)(b).
45 For guidance as to how this topic is approached by RoS, see *Registration Manual* (n 17) Topics: Souvenir plots.

executors or the act and warrant in favour of a trustee in sequestration, although some ordinary deeds also fall into this category, an example being deeds of assumption and conveyance in respect of new trustees. Typically, too, they are 'general' conveyances (eg conveyances of all of the property of the bankrupt or of a trust) and do not enumerate or describe particular property.[46]

Under the 1979 Act conveyances of this kind were accepted by the Keeper for registration.[47] That is no longer the case. The 2012 Act, reverting to the system which always applied in respect of the Register of Sasines, requires the use of a notice of title.[48] The conveyance itself is simply an unregistered midcouple. Notices of title are also needed in respect of subordinate real rights such as standard leases and long leases.

A new form of notice of title is prescribed for the Land Register,[49] although not for the Register of Sasines where the existing, somewhat old-fashioned and cumbersome, forms continue in use.[50] But even in respect of Sasine land, it is possible to elect for the notice of title to be registered in the Land Register.[51] One difference from the old forms is that there is no clause of deduction of title, ie no specification of the last completed title or of the midcouples (ie links in title). The form is as follows:[52]

> Be it known that A.B. (*designation*) has right as proprietor to all and whole (*description*) conform to the last completed title and subsequent writ (*or* writs), which title and writ (*or* writs) have been examined by me, Y.Z. (*designation*), Notary Public (*or* Law Agent).
> [*Testing clause*.]

The form has attached to it four official notes. The first two say that the words 'as proprietor' will be changed in the case where title is being completed to a subordinate real right. Note 3 provides that 'If any writ by which A.B. acquired right contains a new title condition, whether burdening or benefiting the property, the condition is to be inserted in full after the description of the property'. Note 4 is about execution. Though the note does not make the point clear, the notice of title must be formally executed if it is to be accepted for registration.[53]

In applying for registration, the applicant certifies that 'appropriate links in title are in place'.[54] The deed (or deeds) on which the notice of title rests is neither examined by, nor even sent to, RoS.[55] It is only the notice of title that is registered. But the validity of the title depends on the midcouples. They must be

---

46 For full coverage of this topic, see G L Gretton and K G C Reid, *Conveyancing* (4th edn, 2011) ch 24.
47 LR(S)A 1979 s 3(6).
48 LR(S)A 2012 s 53, amending and inserting new provisions into the Conveyancing (Scotland) Act 1924. For the reasons for the reversion to notices of title, see SLC Report 222 paras 15.4–15.8.
49 Conveyancing (Scotland) Act 1924 s 4A, sch BA.
50 C(S)A 1924 s 4, sch B. There will come a time when a notice of title cannot be recorded in the Register of Sasines, even for property that is not yet in the Land Register: see LR(S)A 2012 s 48(3)–(5), and para 7.15 below.
51 C(S)A 1924 s 4A (which, unlike s 4, applies to all land whether held in the Register). See paras 7.7 and 7.14 below.
52 C(S)A 1924 sch BA.
53 Requirements of Writing (Scotland) Act 1995 ss 6 ar
54 Application form for registration, 5. The form is p (Scotland) Regulations 2014, SSI 2014/150, r 7, sch
55 See para 8.16 below. This is an application of the 'tel see para 8.11 below.

the right midcouples, in accordance with the traditional conveyancing law on the subject. They must remain available, in case the accuracy of the Register comes into question, so typically they should be registered in the Books of Council and Session.

6.10 Liferents

Section 51 of the 2012 Act makes provision for the registration of proper liferents.[56] A proper liferent can be created either by grant or by reservation: in other words, the owner of land can either grant a liferent to a second party, or dispone the land to a second party under reservation of a liferent. Either way the liferent is constituted at the moment of registration of the deed.[57] Normally registration must be in the Land Register, but the grant (though not the reservation)[58] of a liferent over land held on a Sasine title continues, for the time being, to be registrable only in the Register of Sasines.[59]

In a cautious spirit, s 51 is made 'subject to any other enactment or any rule of law by or under which a proper liferent over land may be created,'[60] but we know of no enactment or rule of law which allows liferents to be created without registration.[61]

6.11 Leases

Under the previous law, the registrability of long leases and deeds relating to long leases was governed in part by the Registration of Leases (Scotland) Act 1857 and in part by the Land Registration (Scotland) Act 1979. Following amendments made to the 1857 Act by the 2012 Act,[62] the position is now governed solely by the 1857 Act (as amended).[63] Details can be found in chapter 20.[64]

6.12 Decrees of reduction[65]

A decree of reduction might concern a deed that is void or one that is merely voidable. The effects are different. Reduction of a void deed does not alter the

---

56 This replaced s 65 of the Abolition of Feudal Tenure etc (Scotland) Act 2000, which was repealed by LR(S)A 2012 sch 5 para 39(6). The background is explained in SLC Report 168 (n 29) paras 7.38 7.40. A proper liferent (or usufruct) is a subordinate real right in the land. The classic study remains W J Dobie, *Liferent and Fee* (1941). In a trust (or improper) liferent, by contrast, ownership is vested in trustees, and the liferenter and fiar have merely beneficial interests under the trust. Section 51 does not apply to trust liferents.
57 LR(S)A 2012 s 51(2).
58 For dispositions can no longer be registered in the Register of Sasines: see LR(S)A 2012 s 48(1)(a).
59 As is expressly permitted by LR(S)A 2012 s 51(1)(b). This includes a grant completed by notice of title: see s 51(4). For further information as to registration and other matters in respect of liferents, see *Registration Manual* (n 17) Topics: Burdens section information – liferent, detail.
60 LR(S)A 2012 s 51(3).
61 Transmission, however, is possible without (further) registration, as in the case where a liferent is granted in favour of A and B and the survivor, and A then dies without having evacuated the destination.
62 See LR(S)A 2012 s 52 and also sch 2.
63 Thus, strictly, provision for registration of leases is not made by the 2012 Act: in other words, leases fall within LR(S)A 2012 s 49(1)(b) and not s 49(1)(a).
64 See paras 20.5 and 20.6 below.
65 For background, see SLC Report 222 part 28. The previous law as to how decrees of reduction should be dealt with on the Land Register was less than clear.

rights of the parties. For example, Serafina owns a house and lets it out to Frieda, a fraudster. Frieda impersonates the owner and sells the property to Bertie, who is in good faith. The disposition to Bertie (which bears to be signed by Serafina, the signature actually being forged by Frieda) is registered in the Land Register, the Keeper accepting it because to all appearances everything is in order. The disposition is a forgery and therefore void. Shortly after the sale, Serafina discovers what has happened and obtains a decree reducing the disposition. The decree does not alter the validity of the deed. It never was valid. The decree's role is evidential: it is in effect a declarator of nullity. The decree establishes that the title sheet, in showing Bertie as owner, was inaccurate from the beginning.[66] Since there is a decree to that effect, the inaccuracy is 'manifest', ie too clear for dispute. Accordingly, the Keeper must now rectify the title sheet by deleting Bertie's name and reinstating Serafina's.[67] This is not a case of registration but of rectification. Serafina never lost ownership:[68] the title sheet is changed not because the property rights of the parties concerned are changing (the normal reason why the Register is changed) but to reflect the fact that those rights have *not* changed.[69] Thus a decree of reduction of a void deed is not, as such, registrable.[70]

The position is different in respect of voidable deeds. A voidable deed is valid unless and until reduced. Reduction is merely an option for the prejudiced party, who in practice may decide never to exercise that option. Accordingly, a title sheet that reflects a voidable deed is accurate, not inaccurate. Suppose that Alice owns a house and Bella by fraud induces Alice to dispone it to her. Bella is now registered as owner. The Register is accurate, because a deed induced by fraud is not void, but voidable. A few months later, Alice, realising what has happened, raises an action and obtains decree of reduction. The decree, in and of itself, neither transfers ownership back to Alice nor makes the Register inaccurate.[71] It is only when Alice registers an extract of the decree that ownership is reacquired. Thus a decree of reduction of a voidable deed enters the Register by registration, not by rectification.[72]

A practical difficulty is that actions to declare void deeds to be void, and actions to set aside valid but voidable deeds, are both called actions of reduction, and occasionally it is less than clear, from the terms of the final decree, which type of reduction has taken place. This is not a new problem; the two types of reduction have always had different natures and different practical effects. There is now a special form of decree to be used for reduction of voidable deeds.[73]

66 LR(S)A 2012 s 65(1)(a).
67 LR(S)A 2012 s 80: see paras 11.13–11.17 below. Bertie will have the protection of the Keeper's warranty: see ch 13.
68 LR(S)A 2012 s 49(4): 'Registration of an invalid deed confers real effect only to the extent that an enactment so provides.' No enactment validates Bertie's title here.
69 For the registration/rectification distinction, see SLC Report 222 part 11.
70 But when the Register is rectified, the decree or a copy of the decree will be placed in the archive record.
71 LR(S)A 2012 s 65(4): see para 11.4 below.
72 Conveyancing (Scotland) Act 1924 s 46A, inserted by LR(S)A 2012 s 54. See also *Registration Manual* (n 17) Topics: Reduction of a deed, discussing among other things the treatment of reductions *ad hunc effectum* (notably at the instance of an inhibiting creditor).
73 Rules of the Court of Session r 105.5, form 105.5, inserted by Act of Sederunt (Rules of the Court of Session and Sheriff Court Rules Amendment No 2) (Miscellaneous) 2014, SSI 2014/291, para 3(3).

6.13 Judicial rectification of documents

Section 8 of the Law Reform (Miscellaneous Provisions) (Scotland) Act 1985 allows 'defectively expressed documents' to be 'rectified' by the court.[74] This sort of rectification, which is of documents, is not the same as rectification of the Land Register, though they are linked where the document being rectified is a deed which has been registered in the Land Register.

A court order for the rectification of a registered deed does not take real effect until it too has been registered.[75] Rectification orders thus enter the Land Register by registration, not by rectification. Further, while rectification of a document has retrospective effect,[76] where rectification is to be given effect to in the Land Register, the title change happens only as from the time of the new registration.[77]

In rectifying one document, the court is empowered to order the consequential rectification of other documents.[78] For example, Alice sells some fields to Billy. By mistake the disposition includes a field that was not part of the sale. Billy is registered as owner in the Land Register. A year later Billy sells what he owns to Carla, and Carla is registered as owner in turn. On discovering what has happened, Alice can seek judicial rectification of the disposition to Billy so as to have the additional field removed from the dispositive clause. But this is of little help to Alice unless she can also rectify the disposition by Billy to Carla.[79] In determining whether she should be allowed to do so, the legislation applies a test of good faith.[80] If Carla acquired in good faith, the disposition in her favour cannot be rectified without her consent; if, however, she knew about the mistake, rectification can go ahead and Alice will be restored (although not retrospectively) to her field. The rule is not limited to dispositions but applies to any registered deed. For instance, suppose that the deed in favour of Carla had been a standard security rather than a disposition. If Carla had acted in good faith, her security would remain effective over the extra field.[81]

---

74 For the form of decree, see Rules of the Court of Session r 105.6, form 105.6, inserted by Act of Sederunt (Rules of the Court of Session and Sheriff Court Rules Amendment No 2) (Miscellaneous) 2014, para 3(3). A full account of s 8 in the context of conveyancing deeds is given in Gretton and Reid (n 46) ch 20.
75 Law Reform (Miscellaneous Provisions) (Scotland) Act 1985 s 8A. This is one of a number of amendments made to the 1985 Act by LR(S)A 2012 s 55. For the background to the amendments, including an analysis of the unsatisfactory features of the previous law, see SLC Report 222 part 29.
76 LR(MP)(S)A 1985 s 8(4).
77 LR(MP)(S)A 1985 s 8A. The 2012 Act altered the 1985 Act provisions only in relation to land registration matters, but it may be that they ought to be reviewed more generally.
78 LR(MP)(S)A 1985 s 8(3).
79 As rectification of a registered deed is not retrospective, the rectification of the Alice/Billy disposition would, of itself, have no effect on the validity of the Billy/Carla disposition. At the time of the second disposition, Billy still had a good title to the additional field.
80 LR(MP)(S)A 1985 s 8(3A). The meaning of good faith in this context, however, is not entirely clear. In particular, it is unclear whether there is a role for constructive knowledge and, if so, to what extent. Under the previous law, it would have been necessary to show that Carla had relied on the disposition in its unrectified state. *Jones v Wood* 2005 SLT 655 shows the difficulties. The reliance test, which is set out in s 9, remains in place in respect of any document which has not been registered in the Land Register.
81 In such a case Alice could still register the order. The effect would be that she would recover ownership of the extra field, but subject to the security. By contrast, in the original example, where the Billy/Carla deed was a disposition, Carla's good faith would mean that the rectification of the Alice/Billy disposition could not be registered.

6.14 Ranking agreements

Free-standing ranking agreements for standard securities are registrable in the Land Register.[82] The legislation does not, however, state what the effects may be of registration or of an omission to register. If that question requires to be addressed at a legislative level, it would have to be in the context of a review of the law of heritable security.[83]

6.15 Caveats

Caveats, an innovation of the 2012 Act, can be put on the Land Register.[84] A caveat is a notice placed on a title sheet stating that there is currently a court action concerning that title sheet. Caveats are discussed further in chapter 18.

6.16 Advance notices

Advance notices may be mentioned here, though they are dealt with in detail in chapter 10. An advance notice is strictly speaking not 'registered' but it does enter the Register, in the application record, and later in the archive record.

APPENDIX: KEEPER'S LIST OF REGISTRABLE DEEDS

At the time of writing, the following was the list of deed types recognised by the Keeper as registrable.[85] It does not claim to be exhaustive.[86]

> agreement (nature conservancy)
> ancient monuments – schedule entry
> assignation and variation of lease
> assignation of lease
> assignation of standard security
> certificate granted by a private rented housing committee
> certificate of consignation
> certificate of exclusion of monuments
> charging order, Health and Social Services and Social Security Adjudications Act 1983
> charging order (repayment charge)
> compulsory purchase order
> contract of excambion
> countryside management agreement
> decree of adjudication in execution
> decree of adjudication in implement
> decree of reduction of voidable deed
> deed of conditions

---

82 Conveyancing and Feudal Reform (Scotland) Act 1970 s 13(4), inserted by LR(S)A 2012 sch 5 para 17(7). This removes a doubt which existed under the previous law: see SLC Report 222 paras 12.16 and 12.17.
83 Such a review will shortly be commenced by the Scottish Law Commission: see Scottish Law Commission, *Ninth Programme of Law Reform* (Scot Law Com No 242, 2015) paras 2.15–2.17.
84 LR(S)A 2012 s 67. The provision does not actually use the word 'register': rather, by subs (2), a person may apply to the court for warrant 'to place a caveat on the title sheet'.
85 *General Guidance: Registrable deeds under Section 49 (List)* (n 17). Notices of conversion under the Long Leases (Scotland) Act 2012 have been omitted because they ceased to be registrable on 28 November 2015.
86 See para 6.3 above.

Appendix: Keeper's List of Registrable Deeds

deed of variation of community burdens
deed of real burdens
deed of restriction
deed of servitude
determination discharging good neighbour agreement
determination modifying good neighbour agreement
determination discharging planning obligation
determination modifying planning obligation
Development Management Scheme (deed of application)
disapplication of Development Management Scheme
discharge of bond
discharge of burdens
discharge of charging order (repayment charge)
discharge of charging order, Health and Social Services and Social Security Adjudications Act 1983
discharge of community burdens
discharge of *ex facie* absolute conveyance
discharge of liferent
discharge of repayment order
discharge of servitude
discharge of standard security
disposition
disposition and discharge of servitude
disposition and grant of servitude
disposition reserving liferent interest
disposition incorporating deed of conditions
extract decree of foreclosure
extract decree of irritancy of lease
forestry dedication agreement
general vesting declaration
good neighbour agreement
guardianship order (incapacity)
intervention order under the Adults with Incapacity (Scotland) Act 2000
Lands Tribunal order in respect of variation etc of title conditions etc
Lands Tribunal order in respect of Development Management Scheme
lease
liferent (deed creating)
maintenance order
maintenance plan
management agreement
minute of extension of lease
nature conservation order
notice of cessor of improvement grant
notice of cessor of repairs grant
notice of conditions of grant under the Croft House Grant (Scotland) Regulations 2016
notice of decision to vary or revoke a repairing standard enforcement order
notice of discharge under the Title Conditions (Scotland) Act 2003
notice of discharge under the Tenements (Scotland) Act 2004
notice of liability for costs (Tenements (Scotland) Act 2004)
notice of liability for costs (Title Conditions (Scotland) Act 2003)
notice of payment of grant, s 84(1) Housing (Scotland) Act 2006
notice of payment of loan
notice of revocation of a maintenance plan

notice of termination
notice of title
order for rectification of defectively expressed document
partial assignation of lease
partial assignation of standard security
partial discharge
ranking agreement
receipt (under Industrial and Provident Societies Acts)
renunciation of lease
section 32 agreement, Enterprise and New Towns (Scotland) Act 1990
section 75 agreement, Town and Country Planning (Scotland) Act 1997
shifting boundary agreement
standard security
statutory conveyance
stopping-up order
sub-lease
tree preservation order
unilateral obligations (s 75(1)(b) of Town and Country Planning (Scotland) Act 1997 as amended)
variation of Development Management Scheme
variation of lease
variation of servitude
variation of standard security

Chapter 7

Completing the Land Register

THE COMPLETION OBJECTIVE

7.1 First registration

'First registration' happens when a plot of land enters the Land Register for the first time.[1]

This chapter deals with the objective of bringing all land into the new Register, with the set of measures that seeks to achieve that objective, and, correspondingly, with the phased closure of the Register of Sasines.

'First registration' is not a statutory term. It can mislead non-lawyers, because property that is the subject of first registration is almost always *already* in a register, namely the Register of Sasines. The term comes from England, where properties were almost wholly unregistered before the advent of the modern land registration legislation.[2]

Under the 1979 Act, the main trigger for first registration was the transfer of property on sale.[3] If some other type of transaction happened, there was no registration in the Land Register, the transaction being recorded instead in the Register of Sasines. Examples included non-onerous dispositions (donations, transfers to beneficiaries by trustees, transfers to legatees by executors, and so on) and standard securities. The grant of a long lease, and the assignation of an existing long lease, were trigger events for registration of the *lease*[4] but did not bring about the registration of the property itself.[5]

There was also the possibility of voluntary registration in which the owner of property applied to the Keeper for it to be registered in the Land Register,

---

1 This is the meaning under the LR(S)A 2012. Under the LR(S)A 1979 'first registration' was when one of the primary interests in land (ie ownership or long lease) entered the Land Register for the first time: see para 2.2 above. Registration of ownership resulted in what, in 2012 Act terms, is called a plot title sheet; registration of a long lease resulted in a lease title sheet: see para 4.6 above. Under the 2012 Act it is not possible to create a new lease title sheet unless a title sheet for the plot is also in existence, so that the creation of the former has the automatic consequence of bringing about the creation of the latter if no plot title sheet already exists: see para 7.10 below.
2 To be precise, a system comparable to the Register of Sasines was introduced for two counties, Middlesex and Yorkshire, in the eighteenth century. Although the first legislation on title registration was the Land Registry Act 1862, title registration did not begin in significant volume until the Land Transfer Act 1897: see para 1.14 above.
3 LR(S)A 1979 s 2(1)(a)(ii): see para 2.5 above. A 'transfer of the interest in consideration of marriage' was also a trigger: LR(S)A 1979 s 2(1)(a)(iii). A charitable – but alas improbable – explanation of this provision would be that it was a joke.
4 LR(S)A 1979 ss 2(1)(a)(v) and 3(3).
5 Of course, the property might already be on the Land Register. Under the 1979 Act the property could be unregistered and the lease registered, or the property registered and the lease unregistered, or both, or neither. Under the 2012 Act, if a lease is registered for the first time, the property too must be registered if this has not already been done; further, if the property is registered, the lease too is treated as being registered: see paras 7.10 and 7.11 below.

without any trigger event making that necessary.[6] The Keeper had what was, in substance, a discretion to accept or to decline such applications, but they were normally declined and it was not until the final years of the 1979 Act's life that the policy changed and applications were generally welcomed.[7]

First registration was and is a one-way process. Once a plot of land enters the Land Register, it stays there.[8] Thus the number of properties outwith the Land Register has been constantly shrinking since the Register opened for business on 6 April 1981.[9] But it remains significant, and the Register is to that extent incomplete.

7.2 An incomplete Register[10]

Property can remain in the hands of an organisation for decades or even centuries without being sold. Likewise, property may be held by a family, and be passed down the generations through donations, succession or trusts, without being sold. In fact, there are numerous properties round Scotland for which no sale has taken place since historical records began. As a result, completion of the Land Register – the inclusion in the Register of all land in Scotland[11] – had the potential, under the 1979 Act, to take hundreds of years. Indeed, although the Register of Sasines had more triggers than the Land Register under the 1979 Act (for instance any disposition, not just dispositions for value), even after nearly 400 years some properties had still not entered that register – for example, properties belonging to the Crown, to local authorities and to the old universities. On that basis, the completion of the Land Register could be expected to take much more than 400 years. It was true that the 1979 Act contained a provision allowing a compulsory registration scheme to be introduced,[12] but it was sketchily drafted and not a satisfactory basis for completing the Land Register. It was never used.

The state of affairs that existed under the 1979 Act, with many properties being in the Land Register and many properties not, and with the prospect of an indefinitely long period before the process was completed, was generally regarded as unsatisfactory. The Land Register makes conveyancing easier and cheaper. Moreover, its benefits go beyond conveyancing: it makes it possible for the ownership of land, and other major rights in land, to be readily discoverable by anyone with an interest, including central and local government and public agencies.[13] The land registration system is not only a tool for conveyancers.

Indeed, for politicians and land reform campaigners, the 'who owns Scotland?' question is a vitally important one, and they were aware that, without a completed

---

6   LR(S)A 1979 s 2(1)(b).
7   See F Ewing and S Adams, 'All Aboard the Land Register' (2011) 56 JLSS Oct/22. See further J King, 'Completion of the Land Register: the Scottish approach', in F McCarthy, J Chalmers and S Bogle (eds), *Essays in Conveyancing and Property Law in Honour of Professor Robert Rennie* (2015; available at www.openbookpublishers.com/reader/343#page/1/mode/2up) 317, 329–30.
8   LR(S)A 2012 s 48(1)(d).
9   The Land Register was introduced on a county-by-county basis, and it was not until 1 April 2003 that it extended to the whole country: see para 2.5 above.
10 See also para 2.14 above.
11 For the possible meanings of 'completion', see King (n 7) 321–3.
12 LR(S)A 1979 s 2(5).
13 For some discussion of the reasons for the drive to completing the Register, see King (n 7) 319–21.

Land Register, that question could never be fully and satisfactorily answered.[14] The aim of 100% coverage was the most important single reason why the Scottish Law Commission's recommendations for a new Act[15] were taken up by the Scottish Government. 'Completion of the Land Register is considered to be the most important policy aim of the Bill' said the Scottish Government on introducing to Parliament the Bill that became the 2012 Act.[16] And, through various mechanisms, the 2012 Act provides the possibility that such completion might be attained within a reasonable timescale.

7.3 Four mechanisms for completion

Under the 2012 Act, first registration happens either (a) where there is a registrable transaction (deed-triggered first registration), or (b) without any registrable transaction (no-deed first registration). In the first, what is being registered is both the plot and the deed. In the second, the plot is being registered but there is no accompanying deed. That does not mean, in the second case, that a cadastral unit is created, and nothing more; on the contrary, even when only a plot is registered, a title sheet is created in the usual way, with the appropriate entries in all four sections.

Each of these two types subdivides into two sub-types, producing four separate mechanisms for completion of the Register. In the table that follows they are listed as (1), (2), (3) and (4):

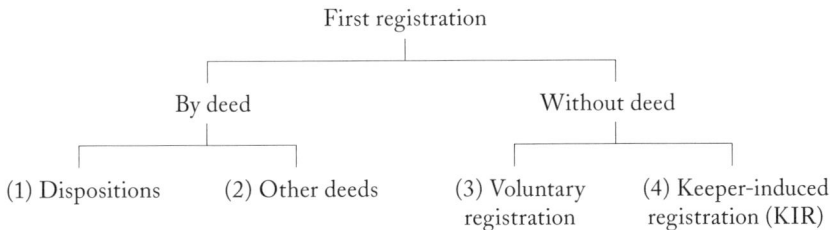

Of these four mechanisms, (1) and (3) already existed under the 1979 Act, although the scope of (1) was narrower, while (3) was little used in practice.[17] Neither (2) nor (4), however, had really existed before.[18] One thing to unite them is the non-participation of the person who owns the property. With (4), that is the very nature of the enterprise, registration being conducted by the Keeper without reference to the owner. With (2) the 'automatic plot registration' (APR), as it is called,[19] is the result of the registration of a deed other than a

---

14 Though valiant attempts had sometimes been made to provide at least a provisional answer to the question: see most recently A Wightman, *The Poor Had No Lawyers: Who Owns Scotland (And How They Got It)* (2010) ch 12.
15 Ie the recommendations set out in Scottish Law Commission, *Report No 222 on Land Registration* (2010) ('SLC Report 222').
16 *Policy Memorandum* para 14, reproduced in Scottish Parliament, *Passage of the Land Registration etc (Scotland) Bill 2011* (2013, SPPB 174; available at www.scottish.parliament.uk/parliamentarybusiness/Bills/44469.aspx) 180.
17 See para 2.5 above.
18 But see LR(S)A 1979 s 2(1)(a)(i), (v), (5). The first of these allowed, indeed required, the first registration of a long lease over unregistered land; but that is actually a somewhat different conception.
19 For APR, see para 7.9 below.

disposition. A detailed account of each of these mechanisms is given later in the chapter.[20]

7.4 Completion by 2024

Even with these new or enhanced mechanisms, completion of the Register would be, the Scottish Law Commission thought, a number of decades away.[21] It came as a considerable surprise, therefore, when in May 2014 the Scottish Government announced that it had 'asked Registers of Scotland to prepare to complete land registration within ten years'.[22] By 2014 the Land Register had been in existence for over 30 years[23] and in that time about 58% of all property titles and 26% of Scotland's land mass had been registered.[24] To attain completion in just ten years thus had the appearance of optimism. It should be stressed that the target is not imposed by legislation, and thus has no legal force.

For the target to be achievable, RoS estimate that it will be necessary to complete 113,000 first registrations per year for each of the ten years to 2024. This compares with an average of 45,000 registrations per year during the preceding ten years.[25] Much of the additional coverage will have to be attained through deed-triggered first registration and voluntary first registration, but significant use of Keeper-induced registration (KIR) will also be needed.

As an interim target, the Scottish Government asked that all public land – that is, land owned by the Crown and by public-sector bodies – be registered by 2019. This includes land held by the Scottish Government itself, by Forestry Commission Scotland,[26] by the Ministry of Defence, and by local authorities.[27] On one estimate, public land accounts for some 12% of rural Scotland,[28] as well as for a large number of urban properties. Relatively little of it is thought to be on the Land Register. The expectation is that public land will be brought on to the Register by voluntary registration, but voluntary registration is, to state the obvious, voluntary, and non-devolved bodies are beyond the reach of the persuasive powers of the Scottish Government.[29] Some public authorities, especially local authorities, are taking the view that they lack the resources to carry out voluntary registrations, and that accordingly the 2019 target, if it is to

---

20 Respectively at paras 7.5–7.7 (registration of dispositions), paras 7.8–7.15 (registration of other deeds), paras 7.16–7.18 (voluntary registration), and paras 7.19–7.24 (Keeper-induced registration).
21 SLC Report 222 paras 33.65–33.67.
22 See further Registers of Scotland, *Completion of the Land Register: Public Consultation* (2014).
23 Since April 1981.
24 *Completion of the Land Register: Public Consultation* (n 22) paras 4, 16 and 17. If compared to the position south of the border, this cannot be called slow. By 2015, ie after more than 150 years, land mass coverage for England and Wales had reached about 85%: see H M Land Registry, *Annual Report and Accounts 2014/15* (2015) 7.
25 *Completion of the Land Register: Public Consultation* (n 22) para 17.
26 This is really a subset of the previous category as all Forestry Commission land is vested in the Scottish Government: see Forestry Commission Scotland, *Annual Report and Accounts 2013–14* (2014) 64.
27 For the relative share of these and other public bodies, see Wightman (n 14) 108, table 4. By far the largest amount of public land is Forestry Commission land.
28 Wightman (n 14) 106, table 1c.
29 King (n 7) 342 points out that, at the time the 2019 target was set, the independence referendum had yet to be held, and that the enhanced control over public bodies that independence would have brought remained a live possibility.

be met at all, will have to be met primarily by KIR.[30] There are issues here whose solution is not yet easy to discern.[31]

The 2024 target is more challenging still. The contribution of deeds-based registration depends largely on the amount of activity in the property market. Voluntary registration will be attractive to some, in part because of a 25% fee discount,[32] and in part because a voluntary registration may have a better chance of producing a title sheet that is accurate (not least in respect of boundaries) than would KIR. Another motive for voluntary registration is where a proprietor of unregistered land intends to grant long leases. Such leases would trigger APR, and the proprietor is likely to prefer registration via voluntary registration than via APR.[33] KIR, largely untried so far, will also be crucial. Nonetheless, it seems improbable that the 2024 target can be met in full. As a senior RoS official has accepted, 'achieving absolute completion, in the sense that every area of land or separate tenement of land, be it large or small, is on the Land Register with an identified owner is unlikely'.[34] As the cadastral map moves towards completion, gaps will be identified which will be difficult to fill. Some will be in respect of property which has failed to reach even the Register of Sasines. Others, typically much smaller in area, will be land left behind on first registration where applicants settled for less generous boundaries than their Sasine deeds would have entitled them to.[35] Even if additional government funding is made available,[36] it may not be cost-effective, even where it is possible, to capture all such cases.

FIRST REGISTRATION BY DEED: DISPOSITIONS[37]

7.5 First registration by deed: in general

Any deed granted in respect of a plot of land or long lease already on the Land Register must itself be registered in that Register.[38] That has always been the position and does not, of course, increase the extent of Land Register coverage. More importantly for present purposes, certain deeds in respect of *Sasine* land or leases must likewise be registered in the Land Register. This is first registration by deed. The relatively short list of deeds which could have this effect in the 1979 Act was greatly expanded by 2012 Act.[39]

From a legislative point of view, two different kinds of provision are needed to achieve first registration by deed. First, and positively, the deed in question must

---

30 Registers of Scotland, *Completion of the Land Register: Report on the Public Consultation* (2015) paras 38 ff. Whilst we have no statistics for the proportion of land owned by public bodies that is in the Land Register, it is no doubt small. This makes the 2019 target particularly challenging.
31 But the view of one local authority, that voluntary registration would be *ultra vires*, because it would be a waste of money, is not one that would, we think, meet with general acceptance: see *Completion of the Land Register: Report on the Public Consultation* (n 30) para 48.
32 See para 7.17 below.
33 King (n 7) 342.
34 King (n 7) 341.
35 King (n 7) 322–3.
36 As some have suggested: see *Completion of the Land Register: Report on the Public Consultation* (n 30) para 51.
37 This is the first of the four mechanisms for completion of the Register set out in para 7.3 above.
38 LR(S)A 2012 s 48(1)(d). So a deed of servitude over registered land must be registered in the Land Register.
39 The 1979 Act list comprised: dispositions for valuable consideration, and leases and their assignation: see LR(S)A 1979 ss 2(1)(a) and 8(4).

be declared registrable in the Land Register.[40] Secondly, and negatively, the deed must be excluded from registration in the Register of Sasines, thus leaving the Land Register as the only available option. In the 2012 Act the second of these is achieved by s 48. This sets out a programme for the progressive closure of the Register of Sasines to a widening class of deeds, the final stage being the closure of the Register of Sasines to *every* type of deed.[41] At the time of writing, certain deeds had already been excluded: dispositions, standard securities, long leases and their assignations. All other deeds will follow at a date or dates yet to be determined. Thus the door of the Register of Sasines is gradually being pulled to, until finally it will be shut tight. And accompanying this phased closure will be a corresponding increase in the coverage of the Land Register.

In this and the next section the deeds which trigger first registration are considered in turn.

7.6 Dispositions

Already under the 1979 Act, dispositions of Sasine land fell to be registered in the Land Register if they were granted for consideration. The 2012 Act removed the requirement of consideration, so that today *any* disposition of as-yet unregistered land, including dispositions by way of donation, dispositions by executors to legatees, and dispositions by trustees to beneficiaries, results in first registration.[42] Enterprising conveyancers who seek to avoid this result by using the disposition as a midcouple for a notice of title will find that such a notice of title, too, can only be registered in the Land Register.[43] Nonetheless the effects on completing the Register are likely to be modest: the number of additional dispositions anticipated by RoS is between 8,000 and 10,000 per year.[44]

There is one qualification. Where a disposition creates real burdens and servitudes and so requires to be registered against both the property conveyed and also against some additional property (being the benefited or burdened property in the title condition),[45] the registration in respect of the additional property will be in the Register where title to that property is held.[46] Hence if the additional property is still held on a Sasine title, registration of the disposition will, to that extent, be in the Register of Sasines.

7.7 Notices of title: ownership

Intergenerational transfer of land need not involve a disposition. On the contrary, it is often carried out by docket transfer or, in a few cases, by a deed of assumption and conveyance in respect of trustees.[47] What is then registered is not the

---

40 As to which see paras 6.6 ff above.
41 For discussion, see SLC Report 222 paras 33.29 ff.
42 LR(S)A 2012 s 48(1)(a). This took effect from the designated day (8 December 2014): see s 123(2). It extends to the equivalent of dispositions in the case of acquisitions by compulsory purchase, ie to statutory conveyances and general vesting declarations: see s 46.
43 Conveyancing (Scotland) Act 1924 s 4B. This is an anti-avoidance provision.
44 *Completion of the Land Register: Public Consultation* (n 22) para 19.
45 Title Conditions (Scotland) Act 2003 ss 4(5) and 75(1).
46 LR(S)A 2012 s 48(6). For background, see SLC Report 222, vol 2, 470 (explanatory notes to s 64(9) of the SLC draft Bill).
47 See respectively Succession (Scotland) Act 1964 s 15(2); Trusts (Scotland) 1921 s 21.

conveyance itself but, subsequently, a notice of title in which the conveyance serves as a midcouple.[48] For the moment at least, such notices of title can continue to be registered in the Register of Sasines (if the land is Sasine land),[49] although there is also the option of registration in the Land Register.[50] The latter would induce first registration and so be functionally indistinguishable from registration of a disposition.[51]

FIRST REGISTRATION BY DEED: DEEDS OTHER THAN DISPOSITIONS[52]

7.8 Introduction

Under the 1979 Act, deeds relating to Sasine land (other than dispositions) had usually to be registered in the Sasine Register and not in the Land Register.[53] They did not, in other words, trigger first registration. One important reason was a practical one. Subordinate real rights, such as standard securities and servitudes, not having a title sheet of their own, require to be entered in the title sheet of the land to which they relate.[54] Thus it was, and is, not possible to register such rights until the relevant plot of land[55] has also been registered and a title sheet made up. If deeds other than dispositions are to be registered in the Land Register, therefore, it is necessary that the plot be registered too – if necessary, without the cooperation or consent of the plot's owner. This was a step which the 1979 Act was not willing to take.

The 2012 Act, in contrast, allows for 'automatic plot registration' ('APR'). Details are given below,[56] but the basic idea is that the registration of certain deeds has the 'automatic' consequence of registration of the plot of land as well. As with dispositions, therefore, there will be registration of both deed and plot. One reason for APR is to ensure the more rapid completion of the Register. But it also implements one of the foundational principles of the Act, namely the registration of plots of land. The idea of a registered right in an unregistered plot is contrary to that principle.[57]

APR is avoided if the registration of the deed is preceded or accompanied by registration of the plot by other means, whether by voluntary registration or by Keeper-induced registration ('KIR').[58] The former will sometimes be attractive to

---

48 See para 6.9 above.
49 Conveyancing (Scotland) Act 1924 s 4. In due course that will cease to be the case: see para 7.15 below.
50 Conveyancing (Scotland) Act 1924 s 4A. For background, see SLC Report 222 para 15.9. An alternative to registering a notice of title may be an application for voluntary registration: see para 7.16 below.
51 From another aspect it is a hybrid between a deed-triggered first registration and voluntary registration.
52 This is the second of the four mechanisms for completion of the Register set out in para 7.3 above.
53 LR(S)A 1979 s 2(3) allowed first registration of subordinate real rights only where the interest in land over which they were granted was itself already on the Land Register.
54 The special position of long leases is mentioned below.
55 Or 'interest in land' in the conceptualisation of the 1979 Act: see para 2.2 above.
56 Paragraph 7.9.
57 Although it is tolerated for a transitional period; assignations of registered leases do not lead to the registration of the plot of land: see para 7.11 below.
58 For voluntary registration, see paras 7.16–7.18 below; for KIR see paras 7.19–7.24 below.

owners who are unhappy at the loss of control which APR will necessarily involve; and there are indications that the latter may be used by RoS as 2024 approaches in order to facilitate the registration of the 'lesser' deeds for which, at the time of writing, the Register of Sasines continues to be available.[59]

Under the 1979 Act, long leases were in a special position. As, uniquely among the subordinate real rights, they had their own title sheet, it was possible to provide for mandatory first registration of the grant or assignation of a lease without at the same time requiring registration of the land to which they related.[60] The 2012 Act, by contrast, requires that the registration of a long lease be accompanied by the registration, through APR, of the plot of land itself.[61]

7.9 Automatic plot registration (APR)

Though not found in the legislation, 'automatic plot registration' (APR) has become an accepted term. It is used to describe what happens when the Keeper registers a plot of land as a response to an application to register certain deeds affecting an unregistered plot of land.[62] APR applies to most deeds, the main exceptions being dispositions (where registration of the plot happens anyway as a matter of course) and standard securities.[63] It involves the registration of the plot regardless of the owner's consent. Whilst APR is a deed-triggered first registration, the deed may not be the deed of the owner.

The mechanics of APR are as follows. In applying for registration of the deed, the applicant selects 'automatic plot registration' in response to the opening question on the application form (as to application type). The fee payable is that for the deed in question (only) and no additional fee is payable in respect of the APR.[64] As with any application for first registration, the applicant must provide the Keeper with the information – for example in relation to rights and burdens – which is needed in order to make up all four sections of the new title sheet;[65] and, on the principle of 'tell me don't show me', the Keeper will rely on the information so provided without making independent inquiry.[66] If the deed was one granted by the owner of the plot – as for example with a new long lease – then that owner can be expected to cooperate in providing information for the grantee (and applicant for registration). In other cases, however, the applicant may have to work without the owner's help or, it may be, knowledge. Indeed the first that some owners may

---

59 King (n 7) 336–7. For the (future) registration of such deeds in the Land Register, see para 7.15 below.
60 See para 7.1 above.
61 See para 7.10 below. Some assignations, however, are in a different position: see para 7.11 below.
62 APR requires that LR(S)A 2012 ss 21, 24, 25 and 30 (and 48) be read together. For an overview, see Registers of Scotland, *Registration Manual* (https://rosdev.atlassian.net/wiki/display/2ARM/Home) Topics: Leases – automatic plot registration.
63 APR does, however, apply to standard securities over unregistered subordinate real rights: see para 7.13 below.
64 Registers of Scotland: *FAQs: Leases and automatic plot registration* Q 24.
65 If, unusually, the owner cannot be traced, this should be indicated in the further information section of the application form. In making up the plot title sheet the Keeper will then use her power under LR(S)A 2012 s 30(5) to enter a statement that the name or designation to be entered in the B (proprietorship) section is unknown. Indemnity may be excluded from the plot (but not the lease) title sheet. See Registers of Scotland, *General Guidance: Leases and Automatic Plot Registration* (v.02, 2015) 13.
66 LR(S)A 2012 s 22(1)(a): see *General Guidance: Leases and Automatic Plot Registration* (n 65) 7–8. For 'tell me don't show me', see para 8.11 below.

find out about the registration of their plot is when the Keeper gives notification (as she must)[67] that the process is completed.

A title sheet created by APR contains a note that the Keeper's warranty is granted under s 74 of the 2012 Act (and not, as in standard cases, under s 73), and so can be readily identified.[68] The fact that warranty is granted at all can be presented as a windfall for the owner. For instance, suppose that a lease is assigned, the property itself having been until now unregistered. The resulting APR of the property will confer Keeper's warranty on its owner, even though the owner is uninvolved in the transaction and pays no fee.[69] The warranty, however, is likely to be qualified or excluded if the assignee was unable to obtain the titles or unrecorded links in relation to the landlord's plot.[70]

APR is limited to the property affected by the deed being registered.[71] For example, suppose that Blackmains extends to 50 hectares, and that a part of Blackmains, extending to 10 hectares, is subject to a 150-year lease created in 1969. Both the property and the lease are in the Register of Sasines. In 2015 the lease is assigned and, as the 2012 Act requires, the assignation is registered in the Land Register.[72] The result will be that both a plot title sheet and a lease title sheet are created, but the former as well as the latter will be limited to 10 hectares. Title to the balance of Blackmains (ie 40 hectares) will remain, for the time being, in the Register of Sasines. It is likely that the rights and burdens affecting Blackmains as a whole will also affect the 10-hectare plot, and, if so, they must be listed in the application form for registration, and so included in the resulting title sheet.[73]

7.10 Long leases

The grant of a long lease[74] must be registered in the Land Register even if it is in respect of land which is itself still held in the Register of Sasines.[75] So too must the grant of a long sub-lease,[76] or the variation of an existing lease which has the effect of increasing its extent.[77] Only 1000 or so leases are registered each year.[78] In the case of unregistered land, the registration of a lease is accompanied by the registration of the plot of land, by APR, the new title sheet showing the granter

---

67 LR(S)A 2012 s 41. This is done by email if the email address is known, otherwise by post. In the first case a PDF of the title sheet is included. See *General Guidance: Leases and Automatic Plot Registration* (n 65) 13–14.
68 *General Guidance: Leases and Automatic Plot Registration* (n 65) 12.
69 The same is true in respect of KIR: see para 7.24 below. The Keeper's warranty is the subject of ch 13.
70 See para 13.12 below.
71 LR(S)A 2012 s 25(5). Just occasionally, it may be more extensive. An example is given in *General Guidance: Leases and Automatic Plot Registration* (n 65) 6: 'where the tenant is granted a lease to a unit in a shopping centre, they may also be granted a *pro indiviso* share in a common area. Since this is part of the subjects of the lease, the APR plot will include this area.'
72 See para 7.11 below.
73 *General Guidance: Leases and Automatic Plot Registration* (n 65) 8.
74 A long lease is a lease of over 20 years: see Registration of Leases (Scotland) Act 1857 s 1. Short leases cannot be registered in the Land Register. Long leases are the subject of ch 20.
75 LR(S)A 2012 s 48(1)(b). This took effect from the designated day (8 December 2014): see s 123(2).
76 LR(S)A 2012 s 113(1) (definition of 'lease').
77 *General Guidance: Leases and Automatic Plot Registration* (n 65) 10.
78 King (n 7) 333.

as owner and the grantee as tenant.[79] In addition the Keeper may, and in practice will, create a lease title sheet to supplement the plot title sheet, but this is a point of practice rather than of substance.[80]

The position is the same in the less common case where the holder of a long lease grants a long sub-lease. The effect of the sub-lease is to trigger registration not only of the new sub-lease but of the plot itself, by APR.[81] Intermediate leases, however, are unaffected, so that, for example, a head lease which is recorded only in the Register of Sasines will remain for the moment in that Register.[82]

APR is limited to the extent of the lease or sub-lease.[83] So if a lease is granted over part of the landlord's property, only that part will be subject to APR and the rest will remain in the Register of Sasines. In the case of multi-level buildings such as (some) shopping centres, the lease of a unit on, say, the third floor will result in the registration of the *solum* immediately beneath that unit but not of any other part of the shopping centre.[84] The prospect of this patchwork arrangement may be sufficient to persuade the landlord to undertake a voluntary registration of the entire property.[85]

7.11 Assignation of long leases

All assignations of long leases fall to be registered in the Land Register.[86] Furthermore, if neither the lease nor the plot of land over which it is granted is on the Land Register, the registration of the lease results in the registration, by APR, of the plot of land.[87] A level 3 plans report will disclose to the assignee whether or not the plot is already registered.[88] On registration, title sheets will be made up for both the plot and for the lease. Equivalent rules apply to partial assignations.[89]

Conversely, and perhaps anomalously, if the lease was previously registered in the Land Register under the 1979 Act,[90] the registration of an assignation does not for the moment lead to APR so that the plot of land, if unregistered, will remain

---

79 LR(S)A 2012 ss 24(2) and 30(2)(a), (c). Compare the position under the 1979 Act where the lease was registered in the Land Register but the land itself remained, for the time being, in the Register of Sasines.
80 It is a matter for the Keeper's discretion whether just to include a long lease in the plot title sheet or whether, in addition, to create a lease title sheet: LR(S)A 2012 s 3(2). For lease title sheets, see para 4.5 above.
81 LR(S)A 2012 s 24(4).
82 *General Guidance: Leases and Automatic Plot Registration* (n 65) 10–11.
83 LR(S)A 2012 s 25(5)(a). See also para 7.9 above.
84 *General Guidance: Leases and Automatic Plot Registration* (n 65) 11–12. In applying for registration, the grantee of the lease would have to furnish the Keeper with details of any leases affecting any other unit which lies directly above the *solum* in question.
85 The Scottish Law Commission had recommended that the granting of a long lease should *always* be preceded or accompanied by voluntary registration, and that APR should not be available: see SLC Report 222 para 33.38. In the Act, this approach only survives in respect of standard securities: see para 7.12 below.
86 LR(S)A 2012 s 48(1)(c). This took effect from the designated day (8 December 2014): see s 123(2).
87 LR(S)A 2012 ss 24(3) and 30(a), (c). For APR, see para 7.9 above. Conversely, the registration of the plot of land leads to the lease being mentioned on the plot title sheet and hence being regarded as registered. This applies equally to leases in title sheets made up before the designated day. See *General Guidance: Leases and Automatic Plot Registration* (n 65) 3.
88 For plans reports, see para 5.23 above.
89 *General Guidance: Leases and Automatic Plot Registration* (n 65) 9.
90 If the lease was registered under the 2012 Act, the plot would have been registered too by APR: see para 7.10 above.

First Registration by Deed: Deeds other than Dispositions

on the Sasine Register.[91] This is a continuation of the previous practice under the 1979 Act.[92]

The table below summarises the position.

Registration of assignations of long leases

Lease registered in Land Register?	Plot of land registered in Land Register?	What the Keeper does in registering the assignation
No	No	Keeper registers both plot (APR) and lease.
Yes	No	Keeper registers assignation; plot remains unregistered.
Yes[93]	Yes	Keeper registers assignation.

With the conversion of ultra-long leases into ownership on 28 November 2015,[94] there has been some reduction in the number of long leases, and hence in the number of assignations.

7.12 Standard securities: in general

All new standard securities must now be registered in the Land Register. If the plot of land is held on a Sasine title, this will trigger first registration.[95] RoS expect around 50,000 such first registrations before the end of the completion period in 2024.[96] This will involve mainly voluntary registration,[97] because APR does not generally apply to standard securities.[98] An owner who wishes to grant a standard

---

91 No provision for APR is made by LR(S)A 2012 s 24.
92 According to *General Guidance: Leases and Automatic Plot Registration* (n 65) 8: 'Assignations of registered leases were intentionally excluded from the APR scheme in order to protect the efficiency of current processes, ensuring that such deeds continue to be registered as straightforward applications over the lease title sheet.' Registration of the assignation takes place under s 26 (deeds relating to registered plots) but with the adjustments made by sch 4 para 11B to take account of the fact that the plot is not, after all, registered. These adjustments will fall on the date when the Register of Sasines is finally closed by an Order made under s 48(3) (for which see para 7.15 below). If any unregistered plots still remain which are subject to registered long leases, it will presumably be necessary to make further legislative provision for the registration of assignations of such leases.
93 There is no fourth possibility, ie of an unregistered lease over a registered plot. This is because, as mentioned in n 87 above, in all cases where the plot is registered, the lease too is regarded as registered even although it may not yet have a title sheet of its own.
94 By the Long Leases (Scotland) Act 2012 s 4. The conversion was automatic. In order to qualify for conversion, a lease had to have been granted for more than 175 years and have an unexpired duration of more than 175 years or, in the case of a lease of a private dwelling house, more than 100 years. The Act was based on the Scottish Law Commission's *Report No 204 on Conversion of Long Leases* (2006). See para 20.8 below.
95 LR(S)A 2012 s 48(2); Registers of Scotland (Voluntary Registration, Amendment of Fees, etc) Order 2015, SSI 2015/265, art 3. This has been the law since 1 April 2016. Previously, a standard security granted over Sasine land was registered in the Register of Sasines.
96 *Completion of the Land Register: Public Consultation* (n 22) para 24.
97 As to which see paras 7.16–7.18 below.
98 Except standard securities over unregistered subordinate real rights, for which see para 7.13 below. The requirement for voluntary registration is not set out in the legislation; but if (i) standard securities can only be registered in the Land Register, (ii) registration cannot take place without registration of the plot of land, and (iii) APR is unavailable, then (iv) it must follow that voluntary registration of the plot is needed. The Scottish Law Commission thought that any inconvenience would be minimised by delaying the requirement to register standard securities in

security must therefore apply for voluntary registration either before or at the time the security is presented for registration.[99] The second will often be the more attractive option because no additional fee is charged for a voluntary registration which accompanies the registration of a standard security.[100]

The rule applies only to the registration of (new) standard securities. If there is an existing standard security over property in the Register of Sasines, and a further advance is made, the question of registration does not arise.

Occasionally a standard security is granted over only one part of a plot. In that case there could in theory be voluntary registration of that part only, but RoS policy is, understandably, to encourage registration of the whole property.[101]

7.13 Standard securities over leases or other subordinate real rights

A special rule applies to standard securities granted over a long lease (or other subordinate real right) where both lease and plot of land are still in the Register of Sasines. Voluntary registration of the plot is neither necessary nor, often, possible, for it is only the *owner* of land who can apply for its voluntary registration.[102] What happens in such a case, therefore, is that the grantee of the security applies for the security to be registered, and the Keeper will register the plot as well, under APR.[103] The lease will also be entered in the Register as part of that process.[104]

The rule is restricted to securities over Sasine leases. Where a lease is already registered in the Land Register, any security over the lease is likewise registered in that Register, but the registration status of the plot of land is left undisturbed.[105]

7.14 Notices of title: subordinate real rights

A notice of title that is prepared in respect of a subordinate real right registered in the Register of Sasines can be registered either in that Register or in the Land Register.[106] Where the Land Register is selected, registration of the notice of

---

the Land Register until only a small proportion of unregistered plots was left: see SLC Report 222 para 33.38. In fact, however, the requirement was introduced little more than a year after the designated day.
99 For details, see *Registration Manual* (n 62) Topics: Voluntary registration – voluntary registration as a result of the closure of the Sasine Register to standard securities. The Keeper's discretion to refuse applications for voluntary registration, contained in LR(S)A 2012 s 27(3)(b), was, as the Act required (s 48(7)), repealed with effect from the same date (1 April 2016) that mandatory registration of standard securities was introduced: see LR(S)A 2012 s 27(6)–(8); Registers of Scotland (Voluntary Registration, Amendment of Fees, etc) Order 2015, SSI 2015/265, art 2.
100 Registers of Scotland (Fees) Order 2014, SSI 2014/188, sch 1 para 1(11), inserted by the Registers of Scotland (Voluntary Registration, Amendment of Fees, etc) Order 2015 art 4(5). The standard security must relate to the whole extent of the plot of land.
101 *Completion of the Land Register: Report on the Public Consultation* (n 30) para 15.
102 LR(S)A 2012 s 27(2).
103 LR(S)A 2012 ss 24(7) and 30(2)(a), (c). For APR, see para 7.9 above.
104 As with the assignation of unregistered leases (for which see para 7.11), the underlying theory of the 2012 Act is that the registration of a subordinate real right must derive from the registration of the plot of land.
105 No provision for APR is made by LR(S)A 2012 s 24. Registration of the standard security takes place under s 26 (deeds relating to registered plots) but with the adjustments made by sch 4 para 11B to take account of the fact that the plot is not, after all, registered. These adjustments will fall on the date when the Register of Sasines is finally closed by an Order made under s 48(3) (for which see para 7.15 below). This is the same rule as applies to the assignation of registered leases: see para 7.11 above.
106 Conveyancing (Scotland) Act 1924 s 4A. This is the same rule as applies to notices of title in respect of ownership: see para 7.7 above.

First Registration by Deed: Deeds other than Dispositions 115

title is accompanied by registration, by APR, of the plot of land over which the subordinate real right subsists.[107] There is, however, no APR if the subordinate real right was already registered in the Land Register.

7.15 All remaining deeds

As completion of the Land Register advances, so the number of deeds which still fall to be registered in the Register of Sasines will diminish sharply. At some point the Register of Sasines will be closed to all remaining deeds: power to do so by statutory instrument is conferred by the legislation.[108] This could be done in phases, both as to type of deed and even as to registration county.[109] The expectation, however, is that the power of closure, assuming it is exercised at all,[110] will be exercised in respect of all deeds and all registration counties. The door of the Register of Sasines, open since 1617, will then finally be shut and locked.

Following closure of the Register of Sasines, deeds formerly registered there will become registrable in the Land Register.[111] But, as registration of a deed is generally possible only if the plot of land to which it relates is also registered, APR will operate, so that deed and plot are registered at one and the same time.[112] Suppose, for example, it is 2023 and Jemima is owner of property still held on a Sasine title. Her creditor, Lucretia, has obtained a decree of adjudication against her and wishes to make that decree effectual by registration. If the Register of Sasines has been closed, Lucretia must register the extract decree in the Land Register. It would be handy if Jemima were to smooth the way by applying for voluntary registration, but we can assume that such cooperation is unlikely to occur. It does not matter. When Lucretia lodges the extract decree with the Keeper for registration, APR operates and the Keeper also registers the land itself – regardless of whether Jemima consents or not. The newly-created title sheet will show Jemima as registered owner and Lucretia as registered adjudger.

When the Register of Sasines will finally be closed is not as yet clear. The Scottish Law Commission made the 'illustrative' suggestion of 2043, being forty years after the last counties became operational for the Land Register.[113] In an ideal world the time fixed would be many years after the commencement of the 2012 Act but also many years before the date when the Register is supposed to be completed. But since the latter date is planned to be as early as 2024, it is not easy to see the solution. The Keeper's current thinking on timing is influenced by a reluctance to use APR for the rather miscellaneous group of deeds that will be affected by final closure of the Register of Sasines, and by the idea that this could

---

107 LR(S)A 2012 s 24(6). For APR, see para 7.9 above. The reference in s 24(6)(b) to s 53(3) of the Conveyancing (Scotland) Act 1924 is a mistake; s 4A was inserted by s 53(3) of the LR(S)A 2012.
108 LR(S)A 2012 s 48(3).
109 LR(S)A 2012 s 48(9). As completion of the Register is much more advanced in some registration counties than in others, there might be some sense in closing the Register first in the more advanced counties.
110 For the suggestion that it might not be, see King (n 7) 337: 'if KIR is to be aggressively used it may be that this provision will never be used as it may have the effect of running counter to a planned programme of KIR'.
111 LR(S)A 2012 s 48(4).
112 LR(S)A 2012 ss 24(5) and 30(2)(a), (c). For APR, see para 7.9 above.
113 SLC Report 222 para 33.66. For the original programme of operational areas, see para 2.5 above.

be avoided by Keeper-induced registration ('KIR') of the remaining plots before any deed in relation to such plots needed to be registered.[114] If that is the approach which turns out to prevail, the moment of final closure is likely to be postponed until an intensive campaign of KIR can be put in place.

VOLUNTARY REGISTRATION[115]

7.16 Eligibility

Where land is still in the Register of Sasines,[116] the owner has the right to have it registered in the Land Register.[117] But only the owner – or, in the case of co-ownership, one of the owners – can apply for voluntary registration.[118] The application could not, therefore be made by the holder of some other right, such as a lease or a heritable security; nor is the consent of such parties needed if the owner decides to apply. It further follows that an application from someone with a bad title must be rejected.[119] An application is unlikely to be competent from a person who has right to the property as owner but has not completed title by registration;[120] instead, such a person should apply for registration of the conveyance under which the property is held or, where that conveyance is a general one, of a notice of title founded on the conveyance.

7.17 Applications for registration

The 'general application conditions' which apply to other registration applications apply equally to applications for voluntary registration.[121] In addition, s 28 of the 2012 Act imposes requirements as to the identification of the plot which are also found in respect of 'ordinary' applications for first registration.[122]

The application form must be accompanied by such deeds and evidence as will be needed by RoS in order to make up a title sheet for the property.[123] The main requirements are:[124] (i) the last recorded deed in favour of the

---

114 King (n 7) 336–7. For KIR, see paras 7.19–7.24 below.
115 This is the third of the four mechanisms for completion of the Register set out in para 7.3 above.
116 Or indeed, in the case of land in respect of which there has been no relevant transaction since 1617, not even in that register.
117 LR(S)A 2012 s 27. For details, see *Registration Manual* (n 62) Topics: Voluntary registration. An initial discretion conferred on the Keeper by s 27(3)(b) to refuse applications was repealed with effect from 1 April 2016 by the Registers of Scotland (Voluntary Registration, Amendment of Fees, etc) Order 2015, SSI 2015/265, art 2 (made under LR(S)A 2012 s 27(6)–(8)). In accordance with s 48(7), this took effect on the same day that the Register of Sasines was closed to standard securities (for which see para 7.12 above).
118 LR(S)A 2012 Act s 27(2).
119 However, the Keeper would be free to proceed with registration, but on the basis of KIR, not on the basis of voluntary registration.
120 LR(S)A 2012 s 27(2) provides that applications must be made by the 'owner'. It may or may not be significant that 'owner' is used here instead of the more usual 'proprietor'. 'Owner' is also used in s 74 in relation to the Keeper's warranty in respect of voluntary registration. 'Owner' is not defined in the Act. The definition of 'proprietor', in s 113(1), requires a completed title.
121 LR(S)A 2012 s 27(3)(a)(i). For the general application conditions, see s 22 of the Act, discussed in para 8.7 below.
122 Ie from LRS(A) 2012 s 23: see para 8.9 below.
123 LR(S)A 2012 s 22(1)(a), as applied by s 27(3)(a).
124 See www.ros.gov.uk/about-us/land-register-completion/voluntary-registration.

owner; (ii) a deed which identifies the extent of the plot, or alternatively a new plan;[125] (iii) any deed in which servitude rights in favour of the plot are constituted; (iv) a plan or full description of any servitude right created other than by deed (such as by prescription); (v) any deeds containing other incorporeal pertinents (such as the right to enforce a real burden) in favour of the property and, if there is a burdened property, the particulars of that property in so far as known; and (vi) a plan or full description of any lesser area within the plot in respect of which a registrable encumbrance is constituted (such as a servitude burdening the property, a real burden or a tree preservation order), as well as the deeds or documents setting out the terms of such encumbrances.[126]

To encourage voluntary registrations, a 25% discount on fees currently applies.[127]

7.18 New plans

Usually, the description in the titles will provide sufficient identification of the plot, and of the route of any servitude affecting the property,[128] to allow registration to proceed. Where it does not, it will be necessary to prepare a new plan. A plan may also be needed where the application includes a request for the inclusion of a servitude created by prescription.

RoS have issued guidance in relation to such plans.[129] Any plan must fulfil the Keeper's deed plan criteria (discussed elsewhere in this work).[130] The plan should be referred to in the application form (for example in the further information field), and it should be clear that the plan submitted is the plan referred to in the form. The purpose of the plan should also be clear. This is best done by a docket, which need not, however, be signed or certified.[131] RoS offer the following sample dockets:

> This is the plan of plot [*address or general description*] for which registration is sought, referred to in the application for voluntary registration by [*applicant's name*].

> This is the plan referred to in the application for voluntary registration by [*insert name of applicant or applicants*]. The boundaries of the plot [*describe nature of plot where separate tenement such as eg 'salmon fishing rights'*] for which registration is sought are [*edged red*].

> This is the plan of the route of the right of access for vehicular and pedestrian purposes created by prescription, referred to in the application for voluntary registration by [*applicant's name*] of [*description of plot transferred*].

---

125 LR(S)A 2012 s 28(1)(a). Special rules for tenement flats can be found in s 28(2), (3). For new plans, see para 7.18 below.
126 LR(S)A 2012 s 28(1)(b); for exceptions, see s 28(4).
127 Registers of Scotland (Fees) Order 2014, SSI 2014/188, sch 1 para 1(2)(b), (3)(b), amended by the Registers of Scotland (Voluntary Registration, Amendment of Fees, etc) Order 2015, SSI 2015/265, art 4(2), (7).
128 One of the conditions for voluntary registration in LR(S)A 2012 s 28 is that the Keeper must be furnished with a plan or description sufficient to identify any part of the plot which is affected by a registrable encumbrance (except for servitudes created other than by registration, or pipeline servitudes): see s 28(1)(b), (4).
129 www.ros.gov.uk/about-us/land-register-completion/voluntary-registration/voluntary-registration-and-certified-plans; *Registration Manual* (n 62) Further Guidance: Plans – certified plan procedure.
130 See para 5.21 above.
131 Nonetheless, the RoS guidance refers to the plan as a 'certified plan'.

KEEPER-INDUCED REGISTRATION ('KIR')[132]

7.19 Introduction

Keeper-induced registration ('KIR'), like APR,[133] has no parallel in the 1979 Act. It came into operation on 8 December 2014, but at the time of writing its use had been very limited.[134] The idea is straightforward: the Keeper identifies an unregistered property and proceeds to register it without the consent of the owner or of anyone else.[135] There is no application for registration, no deed requiring to be registered, and no fee payable by anyone. The cost of KIR is borne by RoS, although, since RoS is itself funded by registration dues, KIR will ultimately be funded by those who apply for registration in the years in which KIR is in operation.[136] The input of the owner is not sought,[137] nor is the owner contacted once registration is complete. Rather, the Keeper interprets her duty to notify[138] as meaning only that the fact of registration is available from a search of the Register.

Conceived originally as a device which was to be used only sparingly and perhaps not for some years,[139] KIR has now become central to achieving the 2024 target for completion of the Land Register. Initially it is to be used for the 58% of unregistered titles, some 700,000 titles in all, which lie within research areas. These areas comprise housing estates and other developments which are subject to uniform burdens.[140] In relation to such areas KIR is relatively straightforward because, in preparation for registration counties first becoming operational under the 1979 Act, RoS has already examined the titles and identified common burdens. The plan is to work through the research areas one by one, and to alert conveyancers and the general public to which areas are next by means of a timeline on the RoS website.[141] Registration in respect of the first three areas began in the autumn of 2016, with the intention of completing all research areas by the end of 2020.

---

132 This is the last of the four mechanisms for completion of the Register set out in para 7.3 above.
133 For APR, see para 7.9 above.
134 Among the early properties registered, with the co-operation of the National Trust for Scotland, was St Kilda: see Registers of Scotland, *Keeper-induced Registration Consultation Document* (2015) para 7. An analysis of the responses to the consultation was published by RoS in February 2016. See also, on KIR, F Rooney and S Duncan, 'The Keeper is coming' (2016, available at bit.ly/21z75nT).
135 LR(S)A 2012 s 29. For discussion, see SLC Report 222 paras 33.47–33.58.
136 That is why, in fixing the level of fees, the Scottish Ministers are directed by LR(S)A 2012 s 110(3)(b) to consult the Keeper as to the expenses being incurred in completing the Register. An early estimate was that each KIR registration would cost £395: see para 420 of the Financial Memorandum which accompanied the introduction to Parliament of the Land Registration Bill, reproduced in *Passage of the Land Registration etc (Scotland) Bill 2011* (n 16) 164.
137 In the interests, presumably, of speed and expense. The decision not to take account of the views or knowledge of owners was subject to criticism by those responding to the RoS consultation: see *Analysis of the responses* (n 134) esp Q11.
138 LR(S)A 2012 s 41.
139 SLC Report 222 para 33.49. During the Bill's stage 1 proceedings, the government gave a commitment that KIR would not be used for complex titles in the lifetime of the Parliament, ie before April 2016: see *Passage of the Land Registration etc (Scotland) Bill 2011* (n 16) 558.
140 *Keeper-induced Registration Consultation Document* (n 134) annex B; *Registration Manual* (n 62) Topics: Research Areas.
141 *Keeper-induced Registration Consultation Document* (n 134) paras 14, 15 and 51.

Whether, or to what extent, KIR will be used beyond the research areas remains unclear. Pilot studies conducted by RoS have been discouraging, even where the co-operation of the owner was sought.[142] Of course, in the coming years many properties will be registered through the other mechanisms described in this chapter so that by the time the Keeper has finished registering properties in research areas through KIR the number of remaining properties in other areas will have been much diminished. The further use of KIR might turn out to be problematic, primarily because many rural properties have titles where the boundaries are far from easy to determine.

7.20 Form of KIR title sheets

Title sheets issued as a result of KIR will differ in certain respects from standard title sheets, although at the time of writing the matter was still under discussion.[143] The differences will reflect both the absence of information on certain points, such as the off-Register creation or extinction of rights, and also the (necessary) limitations on the Keeper's own examination of title. In the A (property) section, for example, the Keeper is likely to take on trust, and so reproduce uncritically, the information in the Sasine deeds in respect of servitudes and other incorporeal pertinents, although it may not always be possible to depict the route of servitudes.[144] The D (burdens) section will list all possible burdens writs, with a hyperlink to the deed itself, but will not transcribe the burdens or attempt to be selective as to what is and is not included.[145] That practice in itself will indicate a KIR title sheet, although its status as such will also be noted in the property section of the title sheet.[146]

7.21 Identification of the owner

Sometimes the owner of property will prove difficult or impossible to identify, as for example where the last recorded title was 100 years ago or where the property has never entered the Sasine Register. In cases like this the legislation allows the Keeper to record, in the B (proprietorship) section, that the proprietor is not known, or not known with certainty.[147] This power is available even in respect of survivorship clauses: where the most recent disposition was granted in favour of Mr and Mrs Smith and survivor, the B section will give the names of both but add a note along the lines of: 'The current proprietor of the subjects in this title is not known with certainty as the Keeper has been unable to establish whether the survivorship destination has operated'.[148]

---

142 *Keeper-induced Registration Consultation Document* (n 134) paras 11–13.
143 For the contents of standard title sheets, see paras 4.13–4.19 above.
144 *Keeper-induced Registration Consultation Document* (n 134) paras 35–36. If no pertinents are disclosed in the titles, this will be noted.
145 *Keeper-induced Registration Consultation Document* (n 134) paras 43–46. The legislative basis is LR(S)A 2012 s 10(3). A significant minority of consultees had reservations about this way of going about things: see *Analysis of the responses* (n 134) Q9.
146 *Keeper-induced Registration Consultation Document* (n 134) para 22; *Analysis of the responses* (n 134) Q4. A mock-up of a KIR title sheet is given in annex C of the *Consultation Document*. The note is likely to be removed after the first transmission.
147 LR(S)A 2012 s 30(5).
148 *Keeper-induced Registration Consultation Document* (n 134) paras 38–40. The wording is taken from the mock-up of a title sheet in annex C.

It may turn out that many of the 'blank spaces', where ownership is difficult to ascertain, will in fact be Crown property, for one of two reasons. The first is that as a matter of property-law theory, albeit not as a matter of real history, all land is considered as having originally been owned by the Crown. Accordingly, if there is no evidence that a plot of land has ever been acquired by anyone else, continuing Crown ownership must be inferred. That is so even if there has been no possession by the Crown, for ownership of land cannot be lost by non-possession.[149] The second reason is that land that has at one time been owned by somebody other than the Crown can pass to the Crown under the doctrines of *bona vacantia* and *ultimus haeres*.[150]

7.22 Identification of boundaries

One reason for the decision to concentrate on property in research areas is that the boundaries in housing estates and the like are typically clear and undisputed. In cases where they are not, RoS promise a thorough investigation.[151]

One potential problem is title overlap, where the boundaries as set out in the target property's Sasine title overlap with a neighbouring property that is already in the Land Register. In such cases the Keeper's provisional intention is to take a practical approach which, depending on the state of possession, may involve rectification by removing some ground from the already-registered property.[152]

7.23 No alteration in substantive rights

KIR is (like voluntary registration) a migration of title data from the Register of Sasines to the Land Register. It does not alter the substantive rights of the owner, or of other parties having rights in the property in question. So suppose that Sophia owns Silvermains, her title being in the Register of Sasines. One day she is informed by the Keeper that her title is now in the Land Register. She was owner before, and she is owner now. No private-law right has changed.

What if the Keeper makes a mistake as to the boundaries of Silvermains, and as a result registers Sophia as owner of a smaller area than is correct? Even that has no effect in terms of private-law rights. The part of Silvermains that the Keeper wrongly excluded is still Sophia's, on the basis of her original Register of Sasines title.[153] What if the Keeper were to make the opposite mistake and register Sophia as owner of too large an area, including a strip of land that is actually part of the neighbouring property, Bluemains, whose owner is Balthasar?

---

149 Prescription and Limitation (Scotland) Act 1973 sch 3 para (a). Ownership of land can be acquired by someone else by possession, through the doctrine of positive prescription, but that requires a registered deed.
150 The Crown's entitlement in this respect was unaffected by the abolition of the feudal system: see Abolition of Feudal Tenure etc (Scotland) Act 2000 s 58.
151 *Keeper-induced Registration Consultation Document* (n 134) para 25. This is despite the fact that the Keeper's warranty does not extend to over-registration: see LR(S)A 2012 s 73(2)(ha), substituted by s 74(3)(a).
152 For details, see *Keeper-induced Registration Consultation Document* (n 134) annex D. For the treatment of overlaps more generally, see paras 11.20–11.26 below.
153 The omission is not an inaccuracy (a term defined in LR(S)A 2012 s 65). There is nothing that the Register says that is false. Hence, as and when the omitted area is brought into the Register, that will happen by one of the four mechanisms of first registration, and not by rectification, for it is only inaccuracies that can be rectified (ie under s 80).

What would the result be? Because under the 2012 Act the Keeper's Midas touch has disappeared,[154] the strip of ground would still belong to Balthasar, and the Register, being inaccurate as showing it as part of Silvermains, would be rectifiable. Meanwhile it would not be possible for Sophia to acquire ownership by positive prescription, because only a registered deed, and not an entry on a title sheet, can found prescription.[155]

What if the Keeper by mistake omits from the C section of the new title sheet a standard security over Silvermains? The standard security would not be extinguished by the omission, and so would still validly exist, and the Register would be rectifiable.

Costs reasonably incurred in securing rectification are met by the Keeper.[156] Mistakes can, however, be troublesome to correct, and may involve litigation unless the inaccuracy in the Register is 'manifest'.[157] Furthermore, in the absence of rectification, the effect of the first transfer of the property after KIR may be to 'realign' the legal position with the position as stated in the Register, and so result in a loss of rights.[158]

7.24 An overall benefit to owners?

From an owner's point of view, KIR provides a free upgrade from a Sasine to a Land Register title. Among other benefits this confers the benefit of the Keeper's warranty of title, although in some cases it will have to be limited or even excluded due to title concerns or, more typically, to absence of information.[159] In the end, of course, the value of KIR to an owner will depend on how well it is done. At the least, owners should check the new title sheet against the Sasine titles, and may incur legal fees in order to do so.[160] And some owners will conclude that the risk of mistakes in KIR is a risk not worth taking and that it is better to proceed by voluntary registration.

---

154 See paras 2.7 and 2.13 above.
155 Prescription and Limitation (Scotland) Act 1973 s 1(1)(b). That is a change in the law: see paras 17.3 and 17.4 below.
156 LR(S)A 2012 s 84: see para 14.7 below.
157 LR(S)A 2012 s 80(1), (2): see paras 11.13–11.26 below.
158 LR(S)A 2012 ss 86–92: see paras 12.8–12.20 below.
159 LR(S)A 2012 s 74. This applies equally to APR: see para 7.9 above. The Scottish Law Commission had recommended that there should be no warranty: see SLC Report 222 para 33.50. The Keeper expects the limitation or exclusion of warranty to be 'an unusual occurrence': see *Keeper-induced Registration Consultation Document* (n 134) para 18. That may be true of KIR in research areas; it may prove to be less true in other areas. The Keeper's warranty is the subject of ch 13.
160 This was a criticism which was frequently made when the Bill was in Parliament: see eg *Passage of the Land Registration etc (Scotland) Bill 2011* (n 16) 236 and 368.

Chapter 8

Applications for Registration

INTRODUCTION

8.1 Scope of the chapter

This chapter is about registration applications. The next chapter continues the story, dealing with the way in which the Keeper carries out registration, and what the effects of that are. Whilst all applications for registration are covered within the present chapter, the main treatment of first registration is in chapter 7. Rectifications, caveats, and advance notices are dealt with elsewhere in the book.[1]

8.2 Types of application

Applications for registration fall into two broad categories. On the one hand, there are applications in respect of deeds which relate to registered plots of land; on the other hand, there are applications which affect plots which are not yet on the Land Register – applications, in other words, for first registration. Although the two have much in common, each category of application raises special issues, and in this chapter is treated to some extent on its own.[2] It should be added that not all deeds in respect of unregistered plots trigger first registration: at the time of writing, a certain number of deed types affecting land still in the Register of Sasines continued to be registrable only in that register.[3]

Applications in respect of registered plots can themselves be divided into applications where the deed affects the whole of a registered plot and applications where part only of the plot is affected.

First registrations divide into three: (i) applications in respect of dispositions (or notices of title);[4] (ii) applications in respect of other deeds which bring about first registration, indirectly, by 'automatic plot registration' ('APR');[5] and applications for voluntary registration.[6] Only the last of these does not involve a transaction or, therefore, a deed.

---

1 In chs 11, 18 and 10 respectively.
2 See para 8.8 (applications in respect of a registered plot) and paras 8.9 and 8.22–8.25 (applications for first registration).
3 For details, see para 7.15 above.
4 Or indeed for the equivalent in the case of compulsory purchase, ie statutory conveyances or general vesting declarations: see LR(S)A 2012 s 46. For first registrations in respect of dispositions and equivalent, see paras 7.5–7.7 above.
5 See paras 7.8–7.15 above.
6 See paras 7.16–7.18 above. First registration can also be achieved by the Keeper acting on her own initiative – so-called 'Keeper-induced registration' ('KIR') – but in such cases there is, of course, no application for registration: see paras 7.19–7.24 above.

Introduction

The same form is used for all applications,[7] other than applications within the ARTL system,[8] but in response to the form's first question it is necessary to indicate which of the five categories[9] of application is involved. If more than one is engaged – as, for example, where a disposition conveys both registered and unregistered property[10] – this too must be indicated in the form.[11]

8.3 Who may apply?

Applications for first registration in respect of a disposition, notice of title, statutory conveyance, or general vesting declaration must be made by the person in whose favour the deed runs.[12] Applications for voluntary registration must be made by an owner of the plot of land in question.[13] Beyond this, the legislation gives no rule as to the identity of the applicant.[14] The silence is understandable. It would be difficult to find a form of words which covered the huge variety of deeds and documents that are potentially registrable,[15] and the matter seems best left to the sector-specific legislation which provides for the deed in the first place. Here, typically, the rule is given by implication rather than by express provision.[16] For instance, under the Conveyancing and Feudal Reform (Scotland) Act 1970 it is a matter of implication rather than express provision that registration is to be at the instance of the grantee of the standard security. In cases of registrable notices issued by a public authority it is an equally obvious implication that the application is to be by the public authority in question.

---

7 It is set out in the Land Register Rules etc (Scotland) Regulations 2014, SSI 2014/150 ('LRR 2014') r 7, sch 1 pt 4. Under the previous law, there were separate forms for first registrations (form 1), dealings (form 2), and transfers of part (form 3). In addition, all deeds being submitted or referred to were listed in a further form (form 4). See Land Registration Rules 2006, SSI 2006/485, r 9(1), (2); the forms themselves were set out in sch 1.
8 LRR 2014 r 7, as amended by the Land Register of Scotland (Automated Registration) etc Regulations 2014, SSI 2014/347, reg 8. For ARTL applications, see para 19.10 below.
9 Ie deed over an unregistered plot; automatic plot registration; deed over the whole of a registered plot; deed over part of a registered plot; and voluntary registration: see Registers of Scotland, *General Guidance: Application for Registration Form – Guidance Notes* (v.07, 2016) 3.
10 Such a disposition would be both a deed over an unregistered plot and a deed over the whole (or as the case may be, part) of a registered plot.
11 This can only be done using a paper application form; the drop-down menu in the electronic form insists on a single choice. In the highly unusual case of more than two categories applying, the additional categories can be added to the additional information sheet of the form. See generally, *General Guidance: Application for Registration Form* (n 9) 4.
12 Land Registration etc (Scotland) Act 2012 ss 23(1)(a) and 46.
13 LR(S)A 2012 s 27(1), (2).
14 Other than the uninformative statement in LR(S)A 2012 s 21(1) that applications may be brought by 'a person'. We are grateful to Dr Rebecca MacLeod for first drawing these matters to our attention.
15 For a list of registrable deeds, see the appendix to ch 6. The previous legislation provided that 'any application for registration shall be made by the person in whose favour a real right will be created or affected by registration' (see Land Registration Rules 2006, SSI 2006/485, r 9(1)), a provision which re-enacted, more or less, the rule in respect of warrants of registration for Sasine deeds, such warrants in turn having replaced instruments of sasine: see Titles to Land Consolidation (Scotland) Act 1868 (31 & 32 Vict c 101) s 15 (now repealed). Such a rule is, however, only of assistance for deeds which create, vary or discharge real rights.
16 But not always: an example of an express provision is s 69 of the Title Conditions (Scotland) Act 2003.

Where a deed requires dual registration because it creates real burdens or servitudes,[17] the application can normally be made by the owner of either the benefited or the burdened property,[18] or indeed by both acting together. But where the deed is a disposition which induces first registration, it appears that the disponee must be among the applicants in accordance with the rule mentioned earlier.[19] More is said about dual registration later in the chapter.[20]

In practice, applications are normally made by solicitors on behalf of their clients rather than by the parties themselves. In the unusual case of an application being made without a solicitor, an identity check is carried out on the applicant, which involves the applicant completing an additional form and producing two separate identifying documents, such as a passport, driving licence, or utility bill.[21]

8.4 Death or corporate dissolution[22]

The living can apply for registration; the dead cannot.[23] A parallel rule operates in respect of companies and other juristic persons, with dissolution being the equivalent of death. The dissolution of a juristic person happens when it ceases to exist; a company that is subject to an ongoing insolvency process, such as being wound up, still exists (for the time being) as a juristic person.

It is for the applicant's solicitors to be aware of the status of their client and, if death or dissolution strikes after the application has been despatched, to inform the Keeper. Deliberate or negligent failure to do so is a potential breach of the duty to the Keeper imposed by s 111 of the Act.[24] Nonetheless, applications are unaffected by death or dissolution occurring after the date of the application,[25] or in other words after the date on which the application is received by the Keeper and entered in the application record,[26] even if this means that the applicant was dead or dissolved by the time that the Keeper reaches a decision on the application. So if an application for registration of a disposition is received on 1 May, the disponee dies on 5 May, and the Keeper's decision on the application is made on 15 May, the Keeper must decide on the basis of the position as at 1 May[27] and hence, if the application is otherwise in order, must enter the (now deceased) disponee on the Register as proprietor.[28]

---

17 Title Conditions (Scotland) Act 2003 ss 4(5) and 75(1). In a case where dual registration is needed, it is not competent to register against only one of the properties: see TC(S)A 2003 s 120.
18 This was the previous law, without qualification: see Land Registration Rules 2006 r 9(3).
19 LR(S)A 2012 s 23(1)(a).
20 See para 8.19 below.
21 *General Guidance: Application for Registration Form* (n 9) 1. The form, known as the identification (ID) form, can be downloaded from www.ros.gov.uk.
22 For a discussion of some of the issues in this paragraph, see Scottish Law Commission, *Report No 222 on Land Registration* (2010) ('SLC Report 222') paras 12.78–12.81.
23 LR(S)A 2012 s 47(1).
24 For solicitors' post-application duty to the Keeper, see para 15.2 below.
25 LR(S)A 2012 s 47(1). A comparable rule applies for the Register of Sasines: see Titles to Land Consolidation (Scotland) Act 1868 s 142.
26 LR(S)A 2012 ss 36 and 37(1): see para 9.22 below.
27 LR(S)A 2012 s 21(2). This is what is sometimes known as 'the state of the legal universe principle': see para 9.8 below.
28 Registration itself is backdated to 1 May: see LR(S)A 2012 s 37(1), and also para 9.22 below.

Introduction 125

The position is more straightforward where it is the granter, rather than the grantee, of the deed who succumbs to death or dissolution. A deed, once delivered,[29] is unaffected by the granter's passing, though in theory there might then be a race to the register with whoever succeeds to the granter's right in the property.[30] At any rate, as the Act makes clear, the application for registration can go ahead.[31]

8.5 Fees

Most of RoS's income derives from the fees paid for registration.[32] The purpose of fees is not to make a profit for RoS, although substantial reserves are held against a rainy day,[33] but rather to ensure that the registration system pays for itself.[34] The statutory basis for fees, both for the Register of Sasines and for the Land Register, was formerly s 25 of the Land Registers (Scotland) Act 1868. This was repealed by the 2012 Act[35] and replaced with new provisions,[36] including a new Fees Order,[37] but the fees themselves remained largely unchanged.

The fee for the registration of a disposition or notice of title is a specified fraction of the purchase price or, if greater, of the value of the land.[38] The fee for voluntary registration is a fraction of the value of the land.[39] Leases and assignations of leases are charged on the basis of the consideration paid (if any) plus a figure representing ten times the largest amount of annual rent reserved by the lease, within the first ten years of its term, that is capable of being quantified or estimated.[40] In all cases the fee payable is calculated using the rates specified in the following table.[41] A discount on the normal rates is offered for use of the ARTL system and also for voluntary registration.

---

29 If the deed has been signed but not delivered, no right can be acquired by the grantee: see *Stamfield's Creditors v Scot* (1696) 4 Brown's Supp 344, where Sir James Stamfield signed a document and told the grantee that it was ready to be uplifted. Within a few hours his corpse was found floating in a river. It was held that the document was ineffective.
30 K G C Reid, *The Law of Property in Scotland* (1996) para 618.
31 LR(S)A 2012 s 47(2).
32 See para 14.14 below.
33 See para 14.14 below.
34 A principle which seems first to have been enunciated in the *Report of the Commissioners appointed to inquire as to the State of the Registers of Land Rights in the Counties and Burghs of Scotland* (1863) 44–45. The Commissioners had heard 'great complaints' as to the level of fees (13).
35 LR(S)A 2012 sch 5 para 5.
36 LR(S)A 2012 s 110. For some discussion of the replacement, see SLC Report 222 para 8.23.
37 Registers of Scotland (Fees) Order 2014, SSI 2014/188, as amended by the Registers of Scotland (Voluntary Registration, Amendment of Fees, etc) Order 2015, SSI 2015/265, art 4. See also Registers of Scotland, *General Guidance: Fees* (v.03, 2016).
38 SSI 2014/188 sch 1 para 1(1), (2).
39 SSI 2014/188 sch 1 para 1(1)(b), (2)(b).
40 SSI 2014/188 art 2(1) (definition of 'relevant rent'), sch 1 para 1(6), (7). *General Guidance: Fees* (n 37) 2 gives the following example: 'where the annual rent that would be payable in the first year of a lease would be £100 but the lease specifies that the rent that would be due on the 10th year of the lease would be £10,000 the fee would be based on 10 x £10,000'.
41 SSI 2014/188 sch 1 para 1(3).

Table of fees

Consideration paid or value	'Normal' fee	Fee for ARTL transactions	Fee for voluntary registration
£0–50,000	£60	£50	£45
£50,001–100,000	£120	£90	£90
£100,001–150,000	£240	£180	£180
£150,001–200,000	£360	£270	£270
£200,001–300,000	£480	£360	£360
£300,001–500,000	£600	£450	£450
£500,001–700,000	£720	£540	£540
£700,001–1,000,000	£840	£660	£630
£1,000,001–2,000,000	£1,000	£800	£750
£2,000,001–3,000,000	£3,000	£2,500	£2,250
£3,000,001–5,000,000	£5,000	£4,500	£3,750
£5,000,001 or more	£7,500	£7,000	£5,625

The higher fees for higher-value properties can be justified partly on the grounds of presumed complexity and partly because the Keeper's exposure under her warranty of title is correspondingly greater.[42] But we stress the word 'partly', because if that principle were to be carried out consistently, the fee would not be capped for transactions over £5 million. Fees for deeds inducing first registration are the same as those for deeds in respect of registered land (where much less work is involved), so that the latter cross-subsidise the former.[43]

In one case, the fee for dispositions is less than stated in the table of fees and in one case it is more. The fee is a mere £60 where the sole purpose of the disposition is to evacuate a survivorship destination, so that there is to be no change of proprietor.[44] A typical example would be a disposition by a couple who hold title on a survivorship destination in favour of themselves without the destination.[45] Conversely, the fee is increased if the disposition is to be registered against more than one title, as in the case of the dual registration needed for the creation of real burdens and servitudes.[46] The fee is augmented by £60 for each additional title sheet affected by the registration.[47]

Deeds other than dispositions, notices of title, leases, and assignations of leases attract a fixed fee of £60 (or £50 under the ARTL system), except for advance notices for which the fee is £10.[48] Thus the fee for standard securities or their discharge, for example, is £60 (or £50). Where a standard security is granted over Sasine land, no additional fee is charged for the voluntary registration of the plot which must accompany the registration of the security.[49]

42 For the Keeper's warranty, see ch 13 below.
43 Registers of Scotland, *Annual Report and Accounts 2014–2015* (2015) 56, 71, explaining that first registrations 'cost more to undertake than the fee charged', and that the loss on first registrations in the year in question was more than £2 million.
44 SSI 2014/188 sch 1 para 1(10).
45 G L Gretton and K G C Reid, *Conveyancing* (4th edn, 2011) para 26-20.
46 Title Conditions (Scotland) Act 2003 ss 4(5), 75(1) and 120.s
47 SSI 2014/188 sch 1 para 1(8) and 10.
48 SSI 2014/188 sch 1 paras 2, 3(2) and 9.
49 See para 7.12 above.

THE APPLICATION CONDITIONS

8.6 'General' conditions and 'particular' conditions

In order to be accepted for registration, an application must comply with certain 'application conditions'.[50] These come in two groups. First, there are the 'general' application conditions which, as the name suggests, apply to all applications for registration;[51] then there are what may be called the 'particular' application conditions (although the term is not used in the Act) which are slightly different as between first registrations and applications in respect of plots which are already on the Register.[52] These conditions are the sentries that command the entrance to the Register. To the extent that the applicant satisfies the Keeper that they are met, the Keeper is under a statutory duty to accept the application; to the extent that the applicant fails in this endeavour, the application must be rejected.[53] On the satisfaction of the conditions thus hangs the success or failure of the application.

In the paragraphs that follow, the application conditions are listed and explained. Yet that is far from being the whole story, for the whole practical business of applying for registration – the content of the application form, the manner in which it must be completed, and the very documents and information that must accompany its journey – is itself underpinned, indeed often determined, by the application conditions. That is the subject of much of the rest of the chapter.

8.7 General application conditions

Formally speaking, the legislation names only six general application conditions, but a further two conditions are also prerequisites for registration under the legislation and so can be added to the list. The eight conditions are:

(1) *The application is such that the Keeper is able to comply, in respect of it, with the Keeper's duties under part 1 of the 2012 Act.*[54] This refers mainly to the Keeper's duty, under ss 3–10 of the Act, to make up and maintain a title sheet for each registered plot of land. If a title sheet already exists, no further information is likely to be needed by the Keeper unless something has changed in the meantime (for example, the presence of a new inhibition),[55] or unless the entry which will result from the deed requires additional information (such as the number or place of incorporation of

---

50 LR(S)A 2012 s 21(2), (3). The former law was different. While LR(S)A 1979 s 4(2) set out a short list of circumstances under which an application must be rejected (absence of a proper description, no registration fee, and so on), there was no positive account of what was needed beyond the disconcertingly vague statement, in s 4(1), that 'an application for registration shall be accepted by the Keeper if it is accompanied by such documents and other evidence as he may require'.
51 The general application conditions are set out in LR(S)A 2012 s 22.
52 The particular application conditions are set out in LR(S)A 2012 ss 23, 25 and 28 respectively for the three types of application for first registration, and in s 26 for applications in respect of deeds relating to registered plots.
53 LR(S)A 2012 ss 21(2), (3) and 27(3), (4). For decision-making by the Keeper, see paras 9.7–9.11 below.
54 LR(S)A 2012 s 22(1)(a).
55 LR(S)A 2012 s 10(2)(c). See para 4.19 above and para 9.19 below.

a company).[56] This first condition, therefore, is mainly concerned with cases where a new title sheet is needed, ie with first registrations or – but to a far lesser degree – with split-off dispositions in respect of registered land. It is considered further in the context of first registrations.[57] In most cases, the relevant information will either be obvious from the deed being presented for registration, or will be prompted by particular questions in the application form.

(2) *The application does not relate to a souvenir plot.*[58] This condition bars very few applications or potential applications. It is considered further in chapter 6.[59]

(3) *The deed is registrable.*[60] This is the first of three conditions that concern the deed which is being presented for registration. None of these, of course, applies to voluntary registrations as such registrations do not involve a deed. In terms of this first condition, a deed cannot be registered unless it is 'registrable', and the Act further provides that a deed is only 'registrable' if its registration is authorised by legislation.[61] Registrability is the subject of chapter 6, and a list of registrable deeds is given at the end of that chapter. They range from dispositions and standard securities through advance notices and caveats to relative rarities such as good neighbour agreements, maintenance plans, and stopping-up orders. Except where ARTL is being used,[62] only 'traditional' (ie paper or equivalent) deeds can be registered, although legislative provisions are in place which will in due course allow the registration of electronic deeds and documents.[63]

(4) *The deed is valid.*[64] Only valid deeds can be registered.[65] In terms of the Act, a deed is valid 'if (a) by the registration applied for, a right would be acquired, varied or extinguished, or (b) the deed is certificatory of an acquisition, variation or extinction which has taken place'.[66] For practical purposes, a deed is likely to be valid if it is (i) granted by a person with title and capacity to grant; (ii) valid as to content; (iii) valid as to execution; and

---

56 LR(S)A 2012 ss 7(1)(a), 8(1), 9(1)(a)(iii), and 113(1) (definition of 'designation'): see para 8.13 below. The condition does not extend to information which the Keeper might need in order to bring a 1979 Act title sheet up to the standards of the 2012 Act, because this is something which the Keeper is empowered rather than bound to do, and in any event the relevant provisions are in sch 4 paras 2 and 3, and not in part 1 of the Act. See on this topic para 4.6 above.
57 See para 8.22 below.
58 LR(S)A 2012 s 22(1)(b).
59 See para 6.8 above.
60 LR(S)A 2012 s 21(1). The Act does not treat this as a registration condition as such.
61 LR(S)A 2012 s 49(1).
62 For ARTL, see paras 19.6 ff below.
63 Notably Requirements of Writing (Scotland) Act 1995 s 9G; LR(S)A 2012 s 100. For discussion, see para 19.5 below.
64 LR(S)A 2012 ss 23(1)(b), 25(1)(a) and 26(1)(a). Although this is a requirement for all applications for registration of deeds, just like the requirement of probativity, the Act, puzzlingly, treats it as a particular and not as a general application condition.
65 This was latterly the practice under the previous law, although its legislative basis was unclear. For this, and for the thinking behind the condition, see SLC Report 222 paras 12.42–12.51.
66 LR(S)A 2012 s 113(2). An example of the latter is a discharge of a fixed-sum standard security following repayment of the amount due.

(iv) in cases where delivery is necessary,[67] has been delivered by the granter to the grantee. A voidable deed is a valid deed until such time – which may never arrive – when it is reduced, and as such is eligible for registration.[68] The requirement of validity is waived, in certain circumstances, in the case of *a non domino* dispositions, or for deeds following on from such dispositions.[69]

(5) *The deed is probative.*[70] Not only must the deed be valid but it must also *appear* to be valid in respect of execution, or in other words it must be probative. Typically, this means that the granter's subscription must bear to have been authenticated by the signature of a witness,[71] although special rules apply where the granter is a company or other juristic person.[72] Electronic deeds are probative where the granter's electronic signature bears to have been certified by a qualified certificate;[73] such a certificate is embedded in the Law Society of Scotland's smartcard, meaning that deeds signed using the smartcard are probative as well as formally valid.[74] The requirement of probativity for registration is sometimes overridden by statute, as for example in the case of court decrees such as decrees of reduction.[75]

(6) *The prescribed application form is used.*[76] The use of this form is considered later in the chapter.[77] It is expected that this form will be replaced by a revised, non-statutory form.

(7) *Either the prescribed fee is paid or arrangements satisfactory to the Keeper are made for its payment.*[78] Legal firms have an arrangement to pay by direct debit; unrepresented applicants can pay by cash or cheque.[79] The amount of the fee must be correctly entered on the application form. More about fees is said elsewhere in the chapter.[80]

(8) *The deed or its registration is not prohibited by other legislation.*[81] It is uncommon, though not unknown, for the granting of a deed to be prohibited by legislation, as for example a disposition where the land is subject to a registered community interest.[82] Registration itself can also be prohibited by legislation, notably where the land and buildings transaction tax due on the transaction has not been paid.[83]

---

67 For delivery of deeds, see W W McBryde, *The Law of Contract in Scotland* (3rd edn, 2007) ch 4. This must now be read in the light of s 4 of the Legal Writings (Counterparts and Delivery) (Scotland) Act 2015, which provides for the electronic delivery of paper deeds.
68 For discussion in the context of the condition as to validity, see SLC Report 222 para 12.53.
69 LR(S)A 2012 s 43(1), (5): see paras 17.18 and 17.19 below.
70 LR(S)A 2012 s 22(1)(c), referring to ss 6 and 9G of the Requirements of Writing (Scotland) Act 1995. This reflects previous practice although not previous law.
71 RW(S)A 1995 s 3(1)(b).
72 RW(S)A 1995 sch 2.
73 RW(S)A 1995 s 9C.
74 For a discussion, see K G C Reid and G L Gretton, *Conveyancing 2014* (2015) 143–44.
75 RW(S)A 1995 ss 6(3)(a), (b) and 9G(6)(a), (b); Conveyancing (Scotland) Act 1924 ss 46(1) and 46A(1).
76 LR(S)A 2012 s 22(1)(d).
77 See paras 8.12–8.25 below.
78 LR(S)A 2012 s 22(1)(e).
79 *General Guidance: Application for Registration Form* (n 9) 3.
80 See para 8.5 above.
81 LR(S)A 2012 s 22(1)(c).
82 Land Reform (Scotland) Act 2003 s 40(1).
83 Land and Buildings Transaction Tax (Scotland) Act 2013 s 43(1); for LBTT see further para 8.18 below.

8.8 Particular conditions: deeds in respect of registered land

Two particular conditions apply to applications for the registration of deeds in respect of land which is already registered in the Land Register.[84] First, the deed must give the title number of each title sheet to which the application relates.[85] This has long been standard conveyancing practice. So if, for example, the deed is a disposition of subjects registered under title number REN123456, the subjects are described in the disposition by reference to the title number, as well as, in practice, by the postal address. The affected title number or numbers must also be listed in the application form. Secondly, in so far as the deed relates to part only of a registered plot (or the subjects of a registered lease) – for example, a split-off disposition or a deed of servitude – it must so describe the part as to enable it to be delineated on the cadastral map.[86] For this purpose a new plan will often be needed,[87] although it may be possible to make do with a (verbal) bounding description or to use existing colouring on the title plan.[88]

Each condition is subject to exceptions. Where a 'shared plot' title sheet has been created for an area of common property, typically in a housing estate or other development, there is no need to include its title number in a deed relating to one of the 'sharing plots', ie a plot to which a right of common property is attached.[89] This is because the A section of the sharing plot title sheet already includes a reference to the shared plot title sheet.[90]

To the statutory exception just mentioned there is added an extra-statutory exception for cases where no title number yet exists or the number is unknown. This particularly affects discharges of standard securities on the occasion of a first registration where, at the time the discharge is prepared, the title number of the affected plot is not available. The terms of the concession are that a deed will be accepted without a title number provided that it contains an otherwise sufficient description of the subjects (or, as the case may be, of the security being discharged), and it is executed before, or up to 28 days after, the title number is known.[91]

There are also exceptions to the second condition. For tenement flats, a description of location within the building (such as 'southmost flat on the first floor') is sufficient because the flat will not be individually delineated on the cadastral map;[92] only the boundaries of the building and attached land – of the 'steading' in RoS parlance – are shown on the map, where they form a single cadastral

---

84 LR(S)A 2012 s 26(1). This actually lists four conditions, but one (para (a)) is really a general condition and was listed as such in para 8.7 above (condition 4), while another (para (b)) simply states the ambit of the conditions.
85 LR(S)A 2012 s 26(1)(c).
86 LR(S)A 2012 s 26(1)(d). This condition is only included in the legislation for emphasis, for it is already implicit in the first of the general conditions (ie the condition, in s 22(1)(a), that the application is sufficient to enable the Keeper to comply with the Keeper's duties under part 1 of the Act): see para 8.7(1) above.
87 The requirements for such plans are considered in paras 5.21 and 5.22 above.
88 Eg 'the area tinted pink on the title plan for REN12345'.
89 LR(S)A 2012 s 26(2). For shared plots, see paras 4.20–4.23 above.
90 LR(S)A 2012 s 18(1)(a).
91 Registers of Scotland, *General Guidance: One-Shot Rule* (v.04, 2015) 3.
92 LR(S)A 2012 s 26(3). A minor drafting accident is that 'so depicted' is used instead of 'so represented': compare s 23(2)(b)(ii) where the correct word is used. The same exception applies to first registrations: see para 8.9 below.

unit.⁹³ It would still be necessary, however, to give the boundaries of any area of garden ground or other pertinent which attaches exclusively to the flat and is outwith the building.⁹⁴ So if a developer builds a block of flats, and the garden ground is to be owned in separate parts by the various flats, the split-off deeds will need to have a deed plan from which the individual parts of garden can be identified.

A second exception relates to deeds of servitude. Normally a plan is needed where the servient tenement is only part of a registered plot (such as an access right over a lane, the lane being part of a farm), but this requirement is waived, for practical reasons, in the case of pipeline servitudes.⁹⁵ The route of such servitudes will not, therefore, be mapped.

8.9 Particular conditions: first registrations

As well as the general application conditions, described above, a further three conditions apply to applications for first registration. All types of application are affected, except that the final condition does not apply to voluntary registration.⁹⁶

In the first place, the deed must so describe the property as to enable the Keeper to delineate its boundaries on the cadastral map.⁹⁷ This may or may not involve the preparation of a new plan: the Keeper's requirements as to descriptions are considered in chapter 5.⁹⁸ In the case of voluntary registrations, where no deed is involved, a plan or other description is to be submitted with the application.⁹⁹ Special rules apply to tenement flats. The Keeper's practice is to represent the whole tenement building and surrounding ground – the 'steading' – as a single cadastral unit.¹⁰⁰ Unless the current flat is the first to be registered, the cadastral unit will usually already exist,¹⁰¹ in which case the only information needed by the Keeper is a description in the deed of the flat's location within the building as well as a description, in words or by plan, of any garden ground or other area outwith the building which is exclusive to the flat.¹⁰² Where, however, the cadastral unit

---

93 See para 4.25 above.
94 LR(S)A 2012 s 26(4). The Keeper's policy, however, is not to mark such areas on the cadastral map but rather to give the information as supplementary data on the title sheet of the flat in question: see para 4.25 above.
95 LR(S)A 2012 s 26(5). Such servitudes are also exempt from the requirement of dual registration: see Title Conditions (Scotland) Act 2003 s 75(3)(b). See also para 4.17 above.
96 The conditions, however, are repeated in three separate provisions, corresponding to the three types of application: see ss 23 ('ordinary' first registrations), 25 (APR), and 28 (voluntary registrations).
97 LR(S)A 2012 ss 23(1)(c) and 25(1)(b). The rule is implicit in the first of the general conditions (ie s 22(1)(a)) and is included as a particular condition only for emphasis. In substance this is the same rule as formerly applied under LR(S)A 1979 s 4(1)(a). Where the application proceeds by APR, the applicant will have to produce a sufficient description of both the plot (under s 22(1)(a)) and, if different, of the land to which the deed relates (under s 25(1)(b), (5)).
98 See paras 5.21 and 5.22 above.
99 LR(S)A 2012 s 28(1)(a). Any plan should be mentioned in the application form and be appropriately docketed. For further details as to descriptions and plans in the context of voluntary registrations, see para 7.18 below.
100 See para 4.25 above.
101 That may not be the position where all previous registrations took place under the 1979 Act.
102 LR(S)A 2012 ss 23(2), (3), 25(2), (3), and 28(2), (3). In the case of voluntary registration, the plan or description will not, of course, appear in a deed; in other cases the use of the deed is mandatory.

does not yet exist, it falls to the applicant to provide sufficient information to allow the steading to be mapped. This can take the form either of a plan of the steading or of a bounding description.[103]

In the second place, where within the property there is a lesser area in respect of which a registrable encumbrance is constituted, there must be submitted with the application a plan or description sufficient to enable the Keeper to delineate the boundaries on the cadastral map.[104] A 'registrable encumbrance' is, presumably, an encumbrance which is capable of appearing on the Register,[105] and so includes standard securities, title conditions, long leases, proper liferents, and such public-law encumbrances as tree preservation orders and s 75 agreements.[106] The idea is that, in making up the title sheet, the Keeper should be able to give an accurate depiction of all encumbrances that appear on the Register. Many, of course, will encompass the whole property, in which case no action is required. That is likely to be true, for example, of almost all standard securities and of most long leases. The main target of the condition seems to be servitudes. Even so, the applicant is excused from having to identify the route of servitudes for pipelines, or of any servitude constituted other than by registration,[107] although the existence of such servitudes must be disclosed in the application form along with the other encumbrances.[108]

Finally, in all applications other than those for voluntary registration, there must be included a description of every public right of way (by whatever means) over or through the property in so far as known to the applicant.[109] The closing words take away much of the force of the rest: no duty is imposed to go hunting out public rights of way; rather the idea is just to gather as much information as possible for the Register. The words 'by whatever means' refer to the fact that a public right of way might be for pedestrian use only, or be a bridleway (pedestrians and riders), or be for all uses. In giving a 'description' of the public right of way, it is not clear whether the precise route is needed.[110]

---

103 This obligation arises out of the first of the general application conditions (ie s 22(1)(a)) and not out of the particular condition currently being discussed. For practical guidance, see Registers of Scotland, *General Guidance: The Cadastral Map – Tenements and other flatted buildings* (v.04, 2015) 2–3.
104 LR(S)A 2012 ss 23(1)(d), 25(1)(c), and 28(1)(b). The exception for tenement flats applies to this condition as it applies to the previous condition, although it is unlikely to be often invoked.
105 As opposed to the narrower category of encumbrances which have been the subject of a deed registered in the Land Register. Encumbrances may also have been created in other ways, most notably by the recording of a deed in the Register of Sasines or by positive prescription.
106 LR(S)A 2012 ss 8 and 9, and also paras 4.16 and 4.17 above. Not all encumbrances appear on the Register: see paras 4.26–4.28 above.
107 LR(S)A 2012 ss 23(4), 25(4), and 28(4).
108 See para 8.25 below.
109 LR(S)A 2012 ss 23(1)(e) and 25(1)(d). There is no equivalent requirement for applications in respect of registered land. Nor is such a requirement implicit in s 22(1)(a) because the Keeper's duty, under s 9(1)(d), is limited to including on the title sheet public rights of way 'in so far as known to the Keeper'.
110 No such stipulation is made in LR(S)A 2012 ss 23(1)(e) and 25(1)(d). On the other hand: (i) it appears that public rights of way qualify as 'encumbrances' under the Act (see s 9(1)(f) which talks of 'other encumbrances' after a list that includes public rights of way); (ii) encumbrances require to be plotted under the second of the particular conditions described above (ss 23(1)(d) and s 25(1)(c)); and (iii) unlike, say, prescriptive servitudes, public rights of way are not included among the exceptions to that requirement.

THE KEEPER'S DUTIES

8.10 The Keeper and the application conditions

To the extent that the Keeper is satisfied that the application conditions have been met, an application must be accepted; to the extent that the Keeper is not so satisfied, the application must be rejected.[111] The onus of satisfying the Keeper lies on the applicant, or in practice on the applicant's solicitor: it is for the applicant to give reason to the Keeper why the application should be accepted, not for the Keeper to give reason why it should not be accepted.[112] That is only to be expected. It is the applicant, or the applicant's solicitor acting on the applicant's behalf, who prepares the deed, answers the questions on the application form, and provides such further evidence and information as may be required. Nonetheless, unless the Keeper is to assume the infallibility, and honesty, of the applicant or the applicant's solicitor, the Keeper's role cannot be entirely passive. At the least, the staff at RoS must read the application form, and scrutinise the deed and supporting documentation. Need they do more? Should they look behind the paperwork and verify, so far as it is practicable to do so, that the application is in order, or should they, rather, take the applicant at his word and proceed to registration without further ado? In the Register of Sasines, being a mere register of deeds, the practice was largely to take the applicant at his word. In the Land Register, being a register of title, the practice under the 1979 Act was to treat the applicant with a degree of suspicion and hence, where possible, to double-check his work. 'As part of the process of registration', the *Registration of Title Practice Book* explained, 'the Keeper will re-examine all the title deeds and, therefore, the purchaser's solicitor's work will be subject to detailed scrutiny'.[113]

The general expectation was that this practice would continue under the 2012 Act. It came as a surprise, even as a shock, to discover that this was not to be the case. There had been no warning in the legislation itself:[114] in so far as the 2012 Act touches on the matter, it suggests even greater vigilance than before. On the one hand, the Keeper retains the duty, found in the 1979 Act,[115] to make up and maintain title sheets;[116] on the other hand, the 2012 Act is much more prescriptive than its predecessor as to the conditions which the applicant must meet, leaving the Keeper with much more as to which she must be satisfied before an application can be accepted.[117] The second of these would seem to imply an enhanced level of

---

111 LR(S)A 2012 ss 21(2), (3) and 27(3), (4).
112 This is made clear in the provisions just cited, which talk of 'the extent the applicant satisfies the Keeper'.
113 *Registration of Title Practice Book* (1st edn, 1981) para G.2.14. The Reid Report had, however, anticipated the principle of 'tell me don't show me' by suggesting that, where the value of a property was relatively low, the Keeper should have a discretion to follow the example of England and accept a certificate from the applicant's solicitor to the effect that the title was valid: see *Registration of Title to Land in Scotland: Report by a Committee appointed by the Secretary of State for Scotland* (Cmnd 2032, 1963) para 98(c). See also *Scheme for the Introduction and Operation of Registration of Title to Land in Scotland: Report by a Committee appointed by the Secretary of State for Scotland* (Cmnd 4137, 1969) ('Henry Report') 73–74. The suggestion was not adopted.
114 Although the (statutory) application form, issued in 2014, did provide for self-certification in respect of links in title: see para 8.16 below.
115 LR(S)A 1979 s 6.
116 LR(S)A 2012 ss 3(1), (2), 30 and 31.
117 Compare LR(S)A 2012 ss 21–23, 25, 26 and 28 (discussed at paras 8.7–8.9 above) with the extraordinarily brief requirements set out in LR(S)A 1979 s 4(1), (2).

scrutiny. As for the first, the Lands Tribunal said of the corresponding duty in the 1979 Act that:[118]

> We cannot see how the Keeper can discharge his duties under s 6(1) of the Act unless he investigates the progress of titles relevant to the application subjects to the extent necessary to reach a view on what entries should be made in the title sheet and what matters he might safely omit.

Under current practice, however, investigation of the progress of titles is exactly what the Keeper has ceased to do. In its place is a policy of 'tell me don't show me'.

8.11 'Tell me don't show me'

'Tell me don't show me' means relying on what the applicant says without asking for evidence or otherwise seeking to check its veracity.[119] Such reliance is, of course, far from universal. RoS look over the deed submitted for registration, as they have always done.[120] Equally, and crucially given the scope for error, plans and other descriptions are carefully scrutinised, on first registrations or split-offs, so as to allow the boundaries of the cadastral unit to be accurately plotted and to avoid overlaps with other units. In cases like these there is both 'show me' as well as 'tell me'. But what no longer occurs is an examination by RoS of an applicant's underlying title. That may not matter very much where the title is already on the Land Register and is easy to review as well as being, in all probability, irreproachable as to its validity. But it matters a great deal more in first registrations, where the title is a mere jumble of Sasine deeds. It is on the basis of these deeds that RoS must make up the new title sheet – the authoritative and warranted account of the state of the title, and the basis of all future transmissions. Yet the selection of deeds for this purpose, and the interrogation of their validity, is now a matter for the applicant and the applicant's solicitor alone.

In justification it might be said that examination of title is best left to the experts, ie to the solicitors engaged by applicants, and should not be usurped by the staff at RoS, few of whom are legally qualified. But that justification, such as it is, presupposes that every applicant has a solicitor,[121] and that every solicitor

---

118 *Brookfield Developments Ltd v Keeper of the Registers of Scotland* 1989 SLT (Lands Tr) 105, 109–10. See also *PMP Plus Ltd v Keeper of the Registers of Scotland* 2009 SLT (Lands Tr) 2, para 43: 'it was not disputed that, in exercise of his statutory duty, when presented with an application to register the Keeper is not merely acting administratively but has a duty to investigate the title. He must actively investigate the relevant circumstances to enable him to reach a sound decision'.
119 See generally K G C Reid, '"Tell Me Don't Show Me" and the Fall and Rise of the Conveyancer', in F McCarthy, J Chalmers and S Bogle (eds), *Essays in Conveyancing and Property Law in Honour of Professor Robert Rennie* (2015; available at www.openbookpublishers.com/reader/343#page/1/mode/2up) 15.
120 Registers of Scotland, *FAQs: One-shot rule* Q5: 'The Keeper will however continue to conduct basic checks for any errors on the face of the deed.' For details, see Registers of Scotland, *Registration Manual* (https://rosdev.atlassian.net/wiki/display/2ARM/Home) Further Guidance – Examining deeds.
121 See in this context the Opinion of the Professors of Conveyancing, published at 2005 JR 201, which took the view, in the context of the 1979 Act, that the acceptance without appropriate scrutiny of applications from those who are not professionally qualified (and thus probably not knowledgeable in the law of Scotland, not professionally regulated, and not professionally insured) would normally constitute an unlawful abdication by the Keeper of responsibility.

examines title. Neither, unfortunately, is always the case.[122] An incidental benefit of the new system has been to speed up the process of registration: now that the underlying title is no longer examined, it has been possible to halve the target times for completion of standard first registrations from 40 days to 20.[123]

The extent of the change should not be exaggerated. 'Tell me don't show me' was already in use under the 1979 Act although, except in ARTL transactions, only in relatively minor respects. More importantly, around half of the titles still unregistered are in 'research areas' – developments subject to uniform burdens in respect of which RoS have already done much of the applicant's work by examining the title and identifying the burdens.[124] In such cases, at least, there are plausible reasons why RoS should wish to be told, but not shown once again, that which they have already seen and checked. In respect of other unregistered titles, however, it is not possible to be so sanguine. It is not merely that, under the previous system, two sets of eyes were better than one, though undoubtedly they were. Nor is it that the Keeper's re-examination of title impelled conveyancers to be careful with their own examination, though undoubtedly it did. Rather the difficulty is that solicitors represent their clients and not the public interest, and will examine title, and complete the application form, accordingly. That private individuals and not public officials should have so large a say in determining the content of the Register is an unwelcome prospect. The likely result will be a higher incidence of error[125] and even of fraud.

THE APPLICATION FORM: ALL CASES

8.12 Introduction

An application form is prescribed by the Land Register Rules and must accompany every deed submitted for registration;[126] a non-statutory replacement form is under consideration. Where two or more deeds are presented at the same time, such as a disposition and a standard security, each requires its own form. An application form must also accompany an application for voluntary registration. In practice, the form is usually completed and signed by solicitors on behalf of their clients.[127]

The same form is used in respect of all types of application,[128] other than applications within the ARTL system.[129] It can be downloaded from the RoS

---

122 A solicitor may be instructed by a client *not* to examine title, eg in the case of donations or certain types of commercial transaction.
123 Registers of Scotland, *Corporate Plan 2016–2019* (2016) para 54.
124 For research areas, see para 7.20 above. The percentage is likely to diminish quite quickly, however, as these titles are at the forefront of KIR.
125 A result, it is to be feared, which may also be contributed to by Keeper-induced registration under s 29 of the 2012 Act, which likewise involves only a single examination of title (in this case, by the staff at RoS). Conceived by the Scottish Law Commission as a device of last resort (see SLC Report 222 paras 33.47–33.58), KIR will need to be used aggressively and, depending on resources, perhaps with insufficient scrutiny, if the ten-year target for completing the Land Register is to be met. See further paras 7.19–7.24.
126 Land Register Rules etc (Scotland) Regulations 2014, SSI 2014/150, ('LRR 2014') r 7, sch 1 pt 4.
127 Except, of course, where no solicitor has been engaged, in which case the applicant will be subject to identity checks: see para 8.3 above. For the meaning and effect of the certification which appears above the signature, see para 15.15 below.
128 For the different types of application, see para 8.2 above.
129 LRR 2014 r 7, as amended by the Land Register of Scotland (Automated Registration) etc Regulations 2014, SSI 2014/347, reg 8. For ARTL applications, see para 19.10 below.

website, printed, and then completed, or it can be completed online and then printed and signed. Either way it must be submitted on paper: for the present at least, only ARTL applications may be made electronically.[130] Because it is an omnibus form, not all questions apply to all types of application. In particular, a number of questions are restricted to first registrations. Furthermore, the questions are designed with the most common deeds in mind, especially dispositions, and may not be well suited to, for example, tree preservation orders or notices in respect of improvement grants.[131] When completed electronically, the form is 'dynamic' and passes over the questions which do not apply. For some of the questions there are drop-down menus, for ease of completion.

Although the form is based on the statutory application conditions, it does not seek to encapsulate them all. That means that, even after completing the form as conscientiously as possible, the applicant may still have to provide additional information to the Keeper, usually through the content of the deed or by way of a further document such as a plan.[132] In signing the application form, the applicant certifies that the application conditions have been complied with.[133]

In examining title and completing the application form, solicitors acting for applicants will be mindful of their duty, under s 111 of the 2012 Act, to take reasonable care to ensure that the Keeper does not inadvertently make the Register inaccurate as a result of the application. A prominent reminder, indeed, is displayed on the signature page of the form. The scope of the duty under s 111, and of the equivalent duty on applicants, is considered in chapter 15. It need only be said here that the duty may not be new, that, even if new, there was already indirect liability under the 1979 Act for 'careless' conveyancing,[134] and that solicitors have always owed a duty of care to their clients.[135] Under the 2012 Act, therefore, as before, it is the Keeper, not the applicant's solicitor, who underwrites the title,[136] and liability moves from the former to the latter only in the event that the solicitor has

---

130 At the time of writing a project was underway to allow digital dispositions and other deeds: see Registers of Scotland, *Digital Transformation: Next Steps* (Nov 2016).
131 For criticism of the form on this and other grounds in the early weeks of the new system, see Reid and Gretton (n 74) 157–58.
132 For a checklist of what is needed for registration, see para 8.27 below (applications in respect of registered plots) and para 8.28 below (first registrations).
133 This certification appears directly above the signature, and binds the applicant rather than the applicant's solicitor (though the latter may nevertheless be liable under LR(S)A 2012 s 111). For the meaning and scope of the certification, see para 15.15 below.
134 LR(S)A 1979 ss 9(3)(a)(iii) and 12(3)(n).
135 Take this example. Alan holds on a Sasine title. He grants a disposition to Beth, inducing a first registration. Beth's solicitor negligently fails to detect that Alan's title does not extend to a particular strip of ground. The Keeper registers Beth as owner of the whole subjects, including the strip of ground. The mistake is discovered, and the strip is removed from Beth's title. What then? Under the 2012 Act, (i) the Keeper warrants Beth's title; (ii) Beth's solicitor is in breach of his duty to the Keeper under s 111; (iii) that breach excuses the Keeper from paying compensation to Beth (s 78(c)(ii)); (iv) Beth recovers from her solicitor on grounds of professional negligence. Under the 1979 Act the result would have been the same. Thus: (i) the Keeper indemnifies Beth in respect of loss arising from rectification; (ii) Beth's solicitor was 'careless'; (iii) that carelessness excuses the Keeper from paying indemnity to Beth (s 12(3)(n)); (iv) Beth recovers from her solicitor on grounds of professional negligence. There will, however, be some cases where a solicitor's exposure is greater than under the previous law (assuming no common-law duty to the Keeper), but perhaps only where Beth sells on to Colin, Colin acquires a good title by realignment (under s 86), and the Keeper, having paid compensation to the former owner of the strip, looks to Beth's solicitor for compensation for breach of s 111.
136 LR(S)A 2012 s 73: see ch 13 below.

failed in his professional duty. From a solicitor's point of view, the more significant change may lie in registration practice rather than in the rules as to liability, for the Keeper's increased reliance on the applicant's solicitor through the 'tell me don't show me' principle is likely to increase the incidence of error or at least to reduce the opportunity for its early detection and correction.[137]

Detailed guidance has been issued by RoS as to the completion of the application form and is updated on a regular basis.[138] Here it will only be necessary to comment on matters of particular interest or difficulty. Consideration of those parts of the form that are applicable only to first registrations may be postponed until later in the chapter.[139]

8.13 Designation of parties

The application form is divided into two parts (A and B), the first of which is concerned with basic factual information (names and addresses of the parties, details of the property, and so on), and the second with matters of title. This is followed by an inventory of deeds and by an additional information sheet (itself split into: applicants, granters, property, title number, and other material).

The designation of parties is a matter for part A. The form provides separate sections for 'individuals' and for 'non-natural persons' such as companies, local authorities and other juristic persons. The choice between them is usually self-evident. Where, however, someone is acting in a fiduciary capacity – for example as an executor or guardian – it is the person who is being represented who is considered to be the 'true' party, and so determines which section of the form is used, even if that person is dead.[140] So if an application is made by Alan as executor of Beth, it is Beth's name and (former) address that are given in the section for the 'applicant details (individual)', and Alan's details are given only at the end of the form, in the relevant additional information sheet (with the words 'executor of Beth' included in the 'prefix' field).

So far as concerns juristic ('non-natural') persons, it may be necessary, and is usually advisable, to insert in the 'allocated number' field any number allocated to the person (such as a company number) together with the legal system under which the person is incorporated or established. For this the legal basis is rather intricate. Title sheets are required by the 2012 Act to include the 'designations' of all proprietors, heritable creditors, and holders of personal real burdens.[141] In the case of juristic persons, 'designation' is defined as including the legal system under which the person is incorporated or established, and any unique number or other identifier.[142] And as the Keeper needs this information for the purposes

---

137 See paras 8.10 and 8.11 above. So for example it is stated by RoS in their *FAQs: One-shot rule* (2014) Q15 that: 'The applicant's agent should satisfy themselves that the granter of the deed has legal title, and capacity to grant, in advance of submitting the application. The Keeper will rely on the agent's certification in this regard and it will no longer be necessary for the Keeper to conduct an extensive legal examination for applications made under the Act.'
138 At the time of writing, the guidance had reached version 7: see Registers of Scotland, *General Guidance: Application for Registration Form – Guidance Notes* (v.07, 2016). See also F Rooney, K Massie and C Kerr, 'Questions of form' (2015) 60 JLSS Sept/18; A E A Stewart and E F F Sinclair, *Conveyancing Practice in Scotland* (7th edn, 2016) 659–74.
139 See paras 8.22–8.25 below.
140 *General Guidance: Application for Registration Form* (n 138) 11.
141 LR(S)A 2012 ss 7(1)(a), 8(1), and 9(1)(a)(iii): see paras 4.15–4.17 above.
142 LR(S)A 2012 s 113(1).

of completing registration, it follows from the first of the general application conditions that the applicant must supply it.[143] Strictly, the information is only needed in respect of the applicant, as opposed to the party who is granting the deed, as only the applicant's name will be added to the title sheet as a result of the registration. Further, if the information is already given in the deed being presented for registration, as will often be the case, it is not necessary to repeat the information in the application form. Finally, RoS do not insist on a statement of the legal system of incorporation or establishment where this is obvious from other information which is supplied, such as the company number (eg a Scottish company number prefixed with 'SC') or from the address of the registered office.[144] Nonetheless, many applications were rejected in the first months of the new Act for failure to supply the necessary information.

8.14 Information relevant to fees

Some deeds, such as standard securities, attract a fixed registration fee of £60, but others attract a variable fee which, in the case of dispositions and notices of title, is based on the purchase price or, if greater, the value of the land, and in the case of leases and their assignation is based on the consideration paid plus a figure representing ten times the largest amount of annual rent during the first ten years of the term. Voluntary registrations also attract a variable fee tied to the value of the land.[145]

Where the fee is a variable one, it is necessary to provide sufficient information in the application form to allow it to be calculated.[146] For dispositions (or notices of title) it is normally sufficient to give the price or, if none was paid, the value of the property.[147] But where the price falls short of the full value, it is necessary to give the property's actual value, at least if the difference is significant and especially where this will move the fee into a higher fee band.[148] For leases and their assignation the information needed is the consideration and the relevant annual rent.

8.15 Title examination

The application form asks whether there has been any 'limitation or restriction on the examination of title'. This is a consequence of the 'tell me don't show me' principle.[149] Now that RoS have ceased to carry out their own examination of title, they are particularly anxious to ensure that an examination has been carried out by the applicant's solicitors. Assuming that it has, they will rely on it; if, unusually,

---

143 LR(S)A 2012 s 22(1)(a): see para 8.7(1) above.
144 *General Guidance: Application for Registration Form* (n 138) 8–10. This was a concession made after the initial weeks of the new Act. It seems worth adding that it can be dangerous to make hasty assumptions as to place of incorporation. For example, many companies in the Bank of Scotland group, which have 'Bank of Scotland' in their name, are incorporated in England and Wales, such as, to take a random example, Bank of Scotland Equipment Finance Ltd.
145 For all details, see para 8.5 above.
146 *General Guidance: Application for Registration Form* (n 138) 2–3. Rather oddly, the heading of the relevant field, which is in part A, is 'payment details'.
147 In the absence of a price it is also necessary to specify the non-monetary consideration, such as 'love, favour and affection' or 'in implement of will'. *General Guidance: Application for Registration Form* (n 138) 2–3 gives a list of non-monetary considerations recognised by the Keeper.
148 Rooney, Massie and Kerr (n 138) 21.
149 See para 8.11 above.

it has not, RoS may reject the application or at least limit or exclude the Keeper's warranty.[150] For if the granter's title is bad, the deed is bad too, and one of the application conditions is not complied with.[151] In relying on the examination of title by the applicant's solicitors, the Keeper is not to be taken to 'expect solicitors to underwrite or guarantee good title'.[152] The risk of the title being bad remains with the Keeper and is underwritten by the Keeper's warranty.[153] But it is the responsibility of solicitors to examine title to normal professional standards, and a failure to do so gives rise to potential liability to the Keeper under s 111 of the Act.[154]

Assuming that the 'usual' examination of title has taken place, the question as to limitation or restriction can be answered 'no'. There is no need to mention restrictions or limitations which are standard for the type of transaction involved or which could not affect the validity of the deed. Nor does it matter that the examination was carried out by another solicitor who then certified title to the applicant.[155] The existence of encumbrances, such as an undischarged standard security, is not relevant to the granter's title to grant and should not be mentioned.[156]

Sometimes a client's instructions may be for a limited examination of title only, as for example where in a portfolio of identical properties only a sample of the titles are to be examined. There may also be occasions on which there has been no examination of title at all, for example, with some gratuitous transactions such as donations and legacies. In such cases the answer to the form's question would be 'yes' and the circumstances would require to be explained. Obviously, a client will need to be warned of the risk of the application being rejected or the Keeper's warranty restricted. Where no examination of title has taken place, the probable outcome is rejection.

8.16 Links in title

'Is the granter of the deed the last recorded/registered proprietor?', asks the form.[157] In most cases the answer will be 'yes'.[158] RoS advise that an affirmative answer should be given if the granter is the survivor of two or more owners who held on a survivorship clause (assuming that the destination had not been evacuated).[159] It will equally be 'yes' if the granter is acting as the representative of the last person to be registered, as in the case, for example, of the liquidator or administrator of a company or a person acting under a power of attorney.

---

150 See *General Guidance: Application for Registration Form* (n 138) 14–15.
151 Ie the condition that the deed must be valid: see para 8.7(4) above.
152 F Rooney, K Massie and C Kerr, 'Examination question' (2015) 60 JLSS Aug/9.
153 See para 8.12 above.
154 For s 111, see paras 15.2 and 15.3 below.
155 Rooney, Massie and Kerr (n 152) 10.
156 Rooney, Massie and Kerr (n 152) 9–10.
157 See *Registration Manual* (n 120) Further Guidance: Legal – deeds not granted by recorded/registered proprietor. The question is not well-worded for the case where the granter is not proprietor but is the holder of a subordinate real right, eg long lease or standard security. Nor is the wording appropriate for cases where the deed is a public-law document, eg a charging order.
158 This is easy for RoS to check, and the practice is to check it: see *Registration Manual* (n 120) Topics: Who is Granting Deed?
159 *General Guidance: Application for Registration Form* (n 138) 15.

If the answer is 'no', this will be for one of two reasons. Either the granter has a right to the property but has not completed title, or the granter has no right to the property at all. The next question on the form is designed to determine which of the two applies.[160] Any further explanation deemed necessary can be included in the additional information sheet at the end of the form.

In the first case (incomplete title), it is for the applicant's solicitor to check the links in title (ie midcouples) and for the applicant to guarantee their validity under the pre-printed (and hence non-negotiable) warranty on the form: 'By signing this application form you [ie the applicant] are certifying to the Keeper that appropriate links in title are in place and that the granter has the legal right to grant the deed'.[161] No clause of deduction of title is needed in the deed.[162] The links should not be sent to RoS – 'tell me don't show me' applies[163] – and it is for the solicitor or the applicant to make appropriate arrangements for their preservation, for instance in the Books of Council and Session. It appears, however, that RoS will not reject the application merely because the links in title are sent, and they are then likely, and conveniently, to finish up in the archive record.[164] Where the granter is a statutory successor of the person or body with the last registered title, the links in title will be the relevant provisions in a statute or statutory instrument and they should be listed in the additional information sheet.[165]

In the second case (no title), the deed is *a non domino* and the application will be rejected[166] unless the onerous requirements for registration of *a non domino* dispositions can be satisfied. This subject is explored further in chapter 17.[167]

8.17 Common areas

In housing estates (and other developments), a split-off disposition will often convey a share in a common area as well as the house plot itself. If so, the 2012 Act requires the common area to be mapped by RoS in the same way as any other plot of land, and it will constitute a cadastral unit of its own. Unless the house being conveyed is among the first to be sold out of the development, the chances are that the cadastral unit (and title sheet) for the common area will already exist and can simply be referred to in the disposition. In terms of the 2012 Act the title sheet can either be an ordinary title sheet or a shared title sheet.[168] Where no cadastral unit exists, it is essential that the description in the deed is sufficiently clear to allow

---

160 The question is: 'If no, and the deed is a disposition, is the disposition to be treated as valid by virtue of section 43(1) (prescriptive claimants)?'
161 The warranty's wording is opaque: see para 13.10 below. Furthermore, despite its unqualified terms, it cannot be meant to apply to all or even to most cases. It cannot apply, for example, where, the question immediately following on the form having been answered 'yes', the application is avowedly one in respect of an *a non domino* disposition. Nor can it sensibly apply where there are no links in title in the first place.
162 LR(S)A 2012 s 101. For discussion, see SLC Report 222 paras 15.1–15.3 and 37.49. See also para 6.9 above.
163 See para 8.11 above.
164 Rooney, Massie and Kerr (n 138) 21.
165 Rooney, Massie and Kerr (n 138) 21, giving the example of the Scottish Ministers as statutory successors to the Secretary of State for Scotland.
166 Ie on the ground that the deed is invalid and hence the application conditions are not complied with: see para 8.7(4) above.
167 See paras 17.12 ff.
168 LR(S)A 2012 s 17(2): see paras 4.20–4.23 above.

one to be created; otherwise the application will be rejected.[169] A plan would be normal. In this respect there is no difference between a split-off disposition which induces first registration and a split-off disposition in respect of land which is already in the Land Register. Typically, the disposition will incorporate an earlier description from a deed of conditions.

As well as describing the common area, the disposition must indicate the size of *pro indiviso* share being conferred, as this is information that the Keeper is required to enter on the title sheet.[170] This is best done by giving a specific fraction or percentage, but it can also be achieved, indirectly, by stipulating the number of other co-owners.[171]

Less exacting standards were applied to descriptions of common areas under the previous law, although practice was tightened up after 3 August 2009,[172] following the decision in *PMP Plus Ltd v Keeper of the Registers of Scotland*.[173] Before that date, descriptions were sometimes accepted for registration which were too vague and uncertain to be capable of representation on the Ordnance Map or even, in some cases, of rational interpretation. Such descriptions continue to cause problems today when dispositions are presented for registration in reliance upon them. RoS's response is pragmatic, if not perhaps entirely within the letter of the legislation.[174] If the application is one which requires a new title sheet to be made up – if, in other words, it is a first registration or a transfer in part – the house plot will be entered on the title sheet in the normal way but the right to the common area will be omitted unless a fresh description (preferably a plan) is produced which allows the area to be shown on the cadastral map.[175] If, on the other hand, the deed that is being registered is a disposition of the whole of subjects in a title sheet which was made up under the 1979 Act, the Keeper will not remove a reference to a common area even if that area is unmapped.[176] The result, in either case, is subject to the possibility of future rectification – in the first case, to add a common right which, with appropriate evidence,[177] might turn out to be capable of being mapped (and hence is a valid and subsisting pertinent),

---

169 Registers of Scotland, *General Guidance: The Cadastral Map – Mapping common areas* (v.02, 2015) 1. This is required in order to comply with the application conditions, including the first of the general conditions (as to which see para 8.7(1) above).
170 LR(S)A 2012 s 7(1)(b). This information is required in order to comply with the first of the general application conditions (as to which see para 8.7(1) above).
171 This is because of the presumption of equality of size of share: see Reid (n 30) para 22. So if a common area is a pertinent of 140 houses, the presumption is that each house receives a 1/140 share.
172 Registers of Scotland, *Update 27: Creation, Identification, and Transfer of Rights in Common Area in Developments* (2009), as supplemented by *Update 27: Additional Information – Lundin Homes Ltd v Keeper* (2014).
173 2009 SLT (Lands Tr) 2. For an assessment, see K G C Reid and G L Gretton, *Conveyancing 2008* (2009) 133–49. Significant later cases are *Lundin Homes Ltd v Keeper of the Registers of Scotland* 2013 SLT (Lands Tr) 73, discussed in K G C Reid and G L Gretton, *Conveyancing 2013* (2014) 105–16, and *Miller Homes Ltd v Keeper of the Registers of Scotland* 2014 SLT (Lands Tr) 79, discussed in Reid and Gretton (n 74) 134–39.
174 The difficulty lies in the 'no registration without mapping' principle described in para 5.10 above. It is a requirement of LR(S)A 2012 s 6(1)(a)(i) that the A (property) section of the title sheet contains a description 'by reference to the cadastral map'.
175 *General Guidance: The Cadastral Map – Mapping common areas* (n 169); *Registration Manual* (n 120) Topics: Property section information – unmappable common areas.
176 We are grateful to Registers of Scotland for this information. See also (2016) 61 JLSS Sept/35. The *General Guidance* is not clear on this point, and seems to have misled Stewart and Sinclair (n 138) 420.
177 *General Guidance: The Cadastral Map – Mapping common areas* (n 169).

in the second case, to remove a common right which is incapable of being mapped (and hence is not a valid pertinent).[178]

From what has already been said, it is clear that applicants will sometimes need to provide particular information in respect of common areas. In addition, the application form has a general question asking whether the deed contains rights to a common area and, if so, whether that area has been included in any registered title, such as the title of another plot in the same development or, in cases where the common area forms a separate cadastral unit, in a registered title of its own. These questions apply only in respect of first registrations and transfers in part. Moreover, like one or two other questions in the form, they are characterised by RoS as 'not mandatory', although it will obviously be prudent to attempt to answer them.[179] If the answer given to the second question is that the common area has indeed been included in one or more registered titles, the form asks the applicant to list the title numbers. In the case of a large housing estate, that could require a significant amount of title investigation and expense. The current advice, however, is to go for the simple option of obtaining a plans report in respect of the common area and to rely on the title numbers which it lists.[180]

8.18 Land and buildings transaction tax

Land and buildings transaction tax replaced stamp duty land tax on 1 April 2015. LBTT is a tax on 'land transactions', that is to say, on 'the acquisition of a chargeable interest'.[181] The main example of a 'chargeable interest' is a real right in land.[182] As previously with SDLT (and before that with stamp duty), some real rights are exempt, notably 'security interests' such as standard securities,[183] while some transactions with (non-exempt) rights – in particular, lifetime gifts and other cases of acquisition without consideration[184] – are also exempt.

In principle, all land transactions must be notified to Revenue Scotland by means of an LBTT return, but again there are a number of exemptions, including for transactions without consideration or where the consideration is less than £40,000, and for leases granted for seven years or more where the consideration is less than £40,000 and the annual rent is under £1,000.[185] LBTT returns are usually made electronically, but can also be made in paper form. An arrangement is in place whereby RoS can receive paper returns on behalf of Revenue Scotland, allowing the LBTT return to accompany the application for registration.[186] The

---

178 It is not a valid pertinent because property which cannot be identified cannot be conveyed. In a case like this, the common area is likely to continue in the ownership of the original developer, even though the developer's intention was evidently that it should be conveyed to the owners of the houses. This is the result of cases such as *PMP Plus Ltd v Keeper of the Registers of Scotland* 2009 SLT (Lands Tr) 2.
179 *General Guidance: Application for Registration Form* (n 138) 13. Other questions said to be 'not mandatory' in the *General Guidance*, though not on the form itself, are those which relate to plans.
180 Rooney, Massie and Kerr (n 138) 18–19. For plans reports, see para 5.23 above.
181 Land and Buildings Transaction Tax (Scotland) Act 2013 ss 1(1) and 3.
182 LBTT(S)A 2013 s 4(2)(a).
183 LBTT(S)A 2013 s 5(1).
184 LBTT(S)A 2013 sch 1 para 1. This talks of 'no *chargeable* consideration' by which is meant, in the normal case, consideration in money or money's worth: see sch 2 para 1.
185 LBTT(S)A 2013 ss 29 and 30(1), (2)(a).
186 Registers of Scotland, *General Guidance: Land and Buildings Transaction Tax* (v.01, 2015).

tax due must normally be paid (or at least payment arranged) at the same time as the return is made;[187] in the case of paper applications this is by cheque, and a cheque can also be sent, to RoS but drawn in favour of Revenue Scotland, in the case of electronic returns.[188]

All of this must precede registration. Under the legislation the Keeper cannot accept an application for registration of a deed effecting or evidencing a notifiable transaction unless an LBTT return has been made and any tax due has been paid.[189] Appropriate questions on the application form are designed to find out whether this has been done.[190] Revenue Scotland provides the Keeper with details of all LBTT returns made online.

8.19 Dual registration

In the creation of real burdens and servitudes, the constitutive deed must be registered against both the burdened and the benefited properties: in other words, there must be 'dual' registration.[191] Take the case of a split-off disposition which imposes real burdens and servitudes on both the property being disponed and also on the property being retained. The disposition, of course, will fall to be registered in the Land Register, as is now the rule for all dispositions,[192] but if the retained property is still in the Sasine Register then registration in that register will be required as well.[193] Where both registers are involved, two application forms are needed, one for each register. But if both (or all)[194] properties are, or will as a result of the transaction be, in the Land Register, then only a single application form is used, which in practice will be prepared by the disponee's solicitors.[195] Consideration should be given to making both parties (ie both disponer and disponee) applicants, because only applicants receive the benefit of the Keeper's warranty.[196] If this course is followed, it may be convenient to give one of the solicitors authority to sign the form on behalf of both parties.[197]

The registration fee will be met by the firm of solicitors whose FAS number is given on the form, and it is for the parties to decide, for example by a provision in missives, whether the cost is to be shared. A fee of £60 is charged for each additional title sheet that is affected by the application,[198] and the title numbers in question must be listed on the form. This listing is used by the e-form to calculate

---

187 LBTT(S)A 2013 s 40(2), (4).
188 *General Guidance: Land and Buildings Transaction Tax* (n 186).The cheque must reach RoS by the third working day after submission of the online return. The unique ID generated by the online system should be written on the back of the cheque.
189 LBTT(S)A 2013 s 43(1).
190 They are: (1) 'Is the transaction to which this application relates a notifiable transaction in terms of section 30 of the Land and Buildings Transaction Tax (Scotland) Act 2013?' and (2) 'If yes, has a land transaction return been made, and have arrangements satisfactory to the tax authority been made for the payment of any tax in respect of the transaction?'
191 Title Conditions (Scotland) Act 2003 ss 4(5), 75(1) and 120.
192 LR(S)A 2012 s 48(1)(a). This will be a first registration if the disponed property is still in the Register of Sasines.
193 And permitted: see LR(S)A 2012 s 48(6), and para 7.6 above.
194 For there can be multiple benefited and burdened properties.
195 Rooney, Massie and Kerr (n 138) 18.
196 LR(S)A 2012 s 73(1): 'The Keeper, in accepting an application for registration, warrants to the applicant ...' The Keeper's warranty is the subject of ch 13.
197 F Rooney and K Massie, 'Application forms: should the seller adjust?' (2015) 60 JLSS May/10.
198 See para 8.5 above.

the fee; in the case of a split-off disposition, where no title number yet exists for the property being disponed, RoS ask that the parent title number be listed twice in order to ensure that the correct figure is calculated.[199]

8.20 Supplementary information

The applicant is asked to indicate which one of the following descriptions best indicates the primary use of the land: residential; agricultural; commercial; forestry; land only; other. If the choice may sometimes be hard to make, there is comfort in knowing that it has no bearing on the acceptability of the application. The field appears after the signature box on the form, and the information is collected only for statistical purposes for the benefit of RoS and the Scottish Government.[200]

In due course this information as to land use may come to be supplemented by information as to the category of person into which the owners and tenants of land fall. By provisions which were added to the 2012 Act by the Land Reform (Scotland) Act 2016, Scottish Ministers can make regulations providing for the obtaining of such information by the Keeper, and for its inclusion on the Register.[201] At the time of writing no regulations had been made. It is not clear whether all owners and tenants are likely to be included or only some.[202] Nor is it clear whether the information will be requested from existing owners and tenants, or simply collected at the time of registration of new owners and tenants by means of a question in the application form. Finally, it is uncertain what 'categories' of person will be identified.

8.21 Adjustments

Signed, usually, by a solicitor on behalf of the applicant, the application form is a matter for applicant and solicitor alone. No one else is entitled to see the form prior to submission, far less to adjust it, unless permission is given or the right to do so has been created in missives of sale or in some other contract. Practice, however, is less rigid than the law. The solicitors acting for the grantee/applicant may be keen to have the form adjusted by the solicitors for the granter in the hope of shifting some of the potential liability that can arise under s 111.[203] Or, with better reason, the solicitors for the granter might wish to see the form if the granter is to have a continuing connection with the property.

The view of the Law Society's Property Law Committee is against adjustment, at least in the normal case, but at the same time accommodating of exceptions.[204] Certainly adjustment seems unnecessary, or even unwise, where the transaction is a straightforward transfer. The position may be different, however, where the

---

199 *General Guidance: Application for Registration Form* (n 138) 4.
200 *General Guidance: Application for Registration Form* (n 138) 20.
201 LR(S)A 2012 ss 48A and 48B, inserted by the Land Reform (Scotland) Act 2016 s 43.
202 The wording is odd. Sections 48A(2) and 48B(2) provide that the regulations may apply to '(a) owners of plots of land, (b) proprietors of registered plots and registered leases, and (c) tenants of leases which are registered or registrable'. There are both 'owners' and 'proprietors'. Registered tenants seem to appear twice (though in one case they are called 'proprietors'). One possible interpretation is that (b) refers to those whose title is registered in the Land Register, while (a) and, on the whole, (c) do not.
203 The solicitors for both parties are subject to duties to the Keeper under LR(S)A 2012 s 111: see paras 15.2 and 15.3 below.
204 Rooney and Massie (n 197) 10.

granter, or a third party, is to retain a real right in the property. Thus adjustment is likely to be desirable in applications which lead to APR: indeed, the applicant's solicitors may be looking not just for adjustment from the solicitors acting for the owner of the property but also for positive help in the preparation of an application which will, after all, result in the first registration of the property.[205] In some cases involving the grant of subordinate real rights, too, the granter/owner may have an interest in seeing the account of the future real right which is being presented in the application form.

THE APPLICATION FORM: FIRST REGISTRATIONS

8.22 Introduction

As well as the questions considered in the previous section, the application form, in so far as it concerns first registrations, has three additional questions which are intended to assist the Keeper in making up a new title sheet. The questions concern servitudes, heritable securities, and burdens, and they refer respectively to the A (property), C (securities) and D (burdens) sections of the title sheet. Full answers and, where appropriate, supporting documentation are required. Anything less and there is a risk of non-compliance with the first of the general application conditions,[206] and hence of rejection of the application. Under the policy of 'tell me don't show me' the Keeper, by and large, relies on the applicant to provide the necessary information and to vouch for its accuracy.[207]

Strictly, the additional questions do not apply to voluntary registrations,[208] but as the Keeper's task is the same as in other cases of first registration there is much to be said for answering them. Even if the questions are not answered, the Keeper will still need to be furnished with the information to which they refer.[209]

8.23 Servitudes

The issue of servitudes occurs twice in the form and, potentially, in the future title sheet as well – once in respect of those servitudes which benefit the property and again in respect of servitudes which burden it.[210] The question which is headed 'Servitudes' is concerned only with the first of these; the second comes under the question headed 'Burdens', considered below.[211]

The servitudes question asks whether 'the plot of ground to which this application relates [is] the benefited subjects in relation to any servitude' and, if so, whether the servitude was created in a deed or by prescription. If the former, the deed must be specified and enclosed; if the latter, particulars must be given of

---

205 See para 7.9 above.
206 LR(S)A 2012 s 22(1)(a). This provides that the application must be such that the Keeper is able to comply with her duties under part 1 of the Act (which include the duty to make up and maintain title sheets). See para 8.7(a) above.
207 For 'tell me don't show me', see para 8.11 above.
208 This is because each is prefaced with the words: 'Only applicable where the deed being registered affects an unregistered plot'. In a voluntary registration there is no deed.
209 See para 7.17 above.
210 The former appear in the A (property) section of the title sheet and the latter in the D (burdens) section.
211 As to which see para 8.25 below.

the servitude together with a plan or description sufficient to enable the Keeper to delineate its extent on the cadastral map.[212] In not requesting a plan or description in the first case, the question appears to presuppose that deeds will always disclose the extent of a servitude to a standard sufficient for the Keeper; at any rate, there seems to be no duty on the applicant to supply additional information.[213]

Where, unusually, a servitude was created by implication, this is (presumably) classified as a servitude created by deed.[214] As well as naming the deed, the applicant should indicate the grounds for concluding that the servitude exists.

As mentioned elsewhere in the book, the Keeper's willingness to register prescriptive servitudes represents a major change from the practice latterly adopted under the 1979 Act.[215] Further, in accordance with the 'tell me don't show me' principle, the Keeper will take the applicant at his word and make no further inquiries.[216] Of course, as the guidance notes warn, applicants must 'satisfy themselves that the servitude has been created by prescription and the right is exempt from challenge',[217] an investigation which is likely to involve the seeking out of affidavits as to possession; and while there is no requirement to include such affidavits with the application, it may be worth doing so as they will then be preserved, albeit unread, in the archive register.[218]

Assuming the application is accepted, the Keeper will transcribe the servitudes listed in the form on to the A (property) section of the new title sheet. A matching entry, by way (presumably) of rectification, will be made on the title sheet of the burdened property, if the servitude does not appear there already.[219] The response of the burdened proprietor, when informed of the new servitude, as the Act requires him to be,[220] may be unenthusiastic or even hostile. This is a matter on which applicants and their solicitors will wish to reflect before laying claim to a prescriptive servitude. Of course, it is true that, where a prescriptive servitude exists, the application conditions require it to be included in the application.[221]

---

212 A servitude may affect all or only a part of the burdened property. It is open to question whether the Keeper would insist on mapping in the case of a pipeline servitude. In applications for registration of the burdened property, such servitudes do not require to be mapped: see para 8.9 above.
213 No application condition appears to be breached, including those most obviously relevant, ie LR(S)A 2012 ss 22(1)(a) and 23(1)(d) (which only apply to servitudes in respect of which the plot is the burdened property).
214 This is because the creation of the servitude is an implied term of the deed in question.
215 See para 4.28 above.
216 *Registration Manual* (n 120) Topics: Servitudes – prescriptive servitudes: 'There is no requirement for additional evidence, such as an affidavit or court decree to be exhibited with the application. The Keeper will accept the applicant certifying, by signing the application form, that a servitude has been properly constituted.'
217 *General Guidance: Application for Registration Form* (n 138) 17.
218 Rooney, Massie and Kerr (n 138) 20. Affidavits which accompany applications for registration must be made before a notary public: see LRR 2014 r 9.
219 See para 4.28 above. If the burdened property is not yet in the Land Register the issue does not arise.
220 LR(S)A 2012 s 80(4)(b). Even if the Keeper did not rectify the title sheet of the burdened property, it is arguable that she ought to notify its proprietor of the initial act of registration on the title sheet of the benefited property: see s 40(1)(d).
221 This follows from the first of general application conditions (para 8.7(1) above) because the Keeper is bound by LR(S)A 2012 s 6(1)(b) to include in the A section of the title sheet 'the particulars of any incorporeal pertinents'. In practice, the Keeper's attitude may be more relaxed than the legislation, strictly, requires: see Rooney, Massie and Kerr (n 138) 19 ('The ability to register unwritten servitudes is seen as permissive, so applicants do not necessarily have to tell RoS about them').

Furthermore, and as a practical matter, a servitude which is omitted on first registration can only be added later by rectification, where the threshold criteria are much higher.²²² But set against this is the risk of conflict with neighbours. In such a conflict, however, it is the applicant who is at an advantage for, once a servitude is on the Register, it can only be taken off again by rectification, and only then if its presence can be shown to be a manifest inaccuracy. Attempting so to show may be beyond the neighbour's strength or means.²²³

The right to a servitude is the most prominent of the incorporeal pertinents that the Keeper is required to include in the property section of title sheets, but it is not the only one.²²⁴ The application form, however, does not seek information as to others. The main omission is rights to enforce real burdens, although this may simply recognise the reality that applicants have often no ready means of discovering their existence.²²⁵ Nonetheless, strict compliance with the application conditions would require that such rights be tracked down and included as part of the application.²²⁶

8.24 Heritable securities

The application form asks for details of outstanding heritable securities. The information is readily available to applicants by means of a standard search of the Register of Sasines, and the form requests details of that search, including the date to which the search is certified. RoS will then monitor the gap period between the end of the search and the date on which the application is entered in the application record (which, if the application is accepted, will be the date of registration).²²⁷

Continuing heritable securities are mainly a feature of voluntary and Keeper-induced registration. Where first registration is prompted by a disposition, any existing security is likely to be discharged as part of the transaction.

8.25 Burdens

Finally, the application form asks for the information needed to populate the D (burdens) section of the title sheet: 'Is the plot of ground to which this application relates subject to any encumbrance within the meaning of section 9?' The mandatory content of the burdens section under s 9 was considered in chapter 4.²²⁸ By far the most important encumbrances that fall to be listed are servitudes and real burdens. The Keeper will rely on the answer given by the applicant and carry out only limited checks.²²⁹

---

222 For rectification, see ch 11.
223 Especially as litigation would be involved unless the inaccuracy is conceded by the applicant: see para 11.14 below. The inclusion of an alleged servitude in the Register does not establish its validity; if not valid, its inclusion does not make it so.
224 LR(S)A 2012 s 6(1)(b): see para 4.14 above.
225 This is because, prior to the introduction of dual registration in 2004, there was often no trace of the real burden in the title of the benefited (as opposed to the burdened) property.
226 See para 8.7(1) above.
227 *General Guidance: Application for Registration Form* (n 138) 17.
228 See para 4.17 above.
229 *Registration Manual* (n 120) Further Guidance: Legal – burdens section summary. If the property is in a research area where the Keeper has already identified the common burdens writs, these will be included in the title sheet even where they were omitted from the application: see *General Guidance: One-Shot Rule* (n 91) 2.

In first registrations, most encumbrances will have been created by recorded deed and so will be detectable from a Sasine search (not to say from the burdens deeds listed in the most recent disposition), but that is not true of prescriptive servitudes, public rights of way, and path orders, all of which are constituted off-register and yet all of which should, in theory at least, be included in the application form.[230] Some may escape the notice of even the most assiduous applicant.[231] Special issues arise in respect of encumbrances affecting former long leases which were converted to ownership by the Long Leases (Scotland) Act 2012.[232]

Only subsisting encumbrances should be included, but with real burdens,[233] at least, it may not be easy to know which burdens are still alive and which are not. As a starting point, it may be accepted that real burdens created on or after 28 November 2004, when the feudal system was abolished and the Title Conditions (Scotland) Act 2003 came into force, are presumptively valid and should normally be included in the application form. For real burdens created before that date, however, the position is complex and, sometimes, unclear. Many such burdens were extinguished by the abolition of the feudal system.[234] Many more were extinguished ten years later, on 20 November 2014, with the final abolition of the rule which had allowed land still owned by the disponer to serve, by implication, as the benefited property.[235] The difficulty lies in separating those burdens which are spent from those which are still in force. The details cannot be gone into here,[236] but in essence burdens created before 28 November 2004 are likely still to be alive only if: (i) they were imposed as part of a common scheme on a group of properties of which the current property is one;[237] (ii) they are concerned with the maintenance or management of common parts or some other 'facility';[238] (iii) they expressly nominate a benefited property; or (iv) they are the subject of a registered notice which preserves enforcement rights.[239] What this means in particular is that burdens in a stand-alone split-off writ, whether a disposition or feu disposition, are unlikely still to be enforceable.

All of this creates a practical problem for solicitors and their clients. If spent burdens are not excluded at the time of first registration, another opportunity is unlikely to arise.[240] Not to exclude, therefore, is to allow the title to be weighed down for the foreseeable future by ageing and unenforceable burdens – yet burdens which,

---

230 For off-register rights, see paras 4.26–4.28 above.
231 In the case of public rights of way, an applicant's duty is restricted to those rights of which the applicant knows: see para 8.9 above. Applicants for voluntary registration are not required to list public rights of way.
232 See para 20.8 below.
233 For suggestions as to how burdens that are to be omitted from the title sheet should be indicated on the form, see Stewart and Sinclair (n 138) 671.
234 Abolition of Feudal Tenure etc (Scotland) Act 2000 s 17.
235 Title Conditions (Scotland) Act 2003 s 49(2). For details, see K G C Reid and G L Gretton, *Conveyancing 2013* (2014) 131–39. The rule derived from the decision in *J A Mactaggart & Co v Harrower* (1906) 8 F 1101.
236 See further K G C Reid, *The Abolition of Feudal Tenure in Scotland* (2003); Gretton and Reid (n 45) paras 13-13–13-16; A Steven and S Wortley, 'Is that burden dead yet?' (2006) 51 JLSS June/46 and July/50.
237 This potentially engages one or both of Title Conditions (Scotland) Act 2003 ss 52 and 53.
238 TC(S)A 2003 ss 56, 122(1) (definition of 'facility burden') and 122(2), (3).
239 Such as, for example, a notice under s 18 of the Abolition of Feudal Tenure etc (Scotland) Act 2000 or s 50 of the Title Conditions (Scotland) Act 2003.
240 See para 4.18 above. In theory this could be done later on by rectification, but it would then be necessary to satisfy the 'manifest inaccuracy' test set out in LR(S)A 2012 s 80(1).

because of their very presence on the title sheet, will have to be read through and considered every time the property changes hands, and some of which may impede future plans for the property's use and development. Yet the act of exclusion is no easy task. It requires time and skill from the solicitor and, it may be, an additional fee from the client. And if a mistake is made – if a burden is dropped which should have been included – the burden is likely to be extinguished, by realignment, on the next occasion that the property changes hands,[241] leaving the burden-holder with a claim for compensation from the Keeper,[242] and the Keeper with a corresponding claim against the applicant's solicitor, under s 111, for negligent conveyancing.[243] Faced with these considerations, many solicitors and their clients may be inclined to take the 'safe' course[244] of listing all the burdens writs, indiscriminately, on the application form.[245] That would be understandable, but at the same time a lost opportunity to cleanse titles of the detritus of a bygone age.

Even without the applicant's intervention, RoS will omit any burdens which are obviously obsolete, such as feuduties (except to the extent that the figure is needed for the apportionment of common repairs), ground annuals, irritancy clauses, obligations to pay stipend or teind, and, in the case of titles created by leasehold conversion, obligations to pay rent.[246]

In listing encumbrances it is necessary to name the deeds in which they are contained, whether directly or by reference to the inventory of deeds found later on in the form. The fact that the same deeds may also be listed for burdens in the disposition which is being presented for registration does not remove the need to name them in the application form. The deeds themselves should normally accompany the application. But where the legal report discloses that the property lies in a 'research area' it may be assumed that RoS have already examined the common burdens writs up to the date when the research area was completed and will not need to see them again.[247]

Finally, where an encumbrance affects only part of the property, the application must include a plan or description sufficient to enable the Keeper to show the part on the cadastral map.[248]

GETTING IT RIGHT

8.26 Introduction

Applications with material errors are rejected by RoS without an opportunity for correction. This is the 'one-shot rule' discussed in the next chapter:[249] to the extent that the application conditions are not complied with, the 2012 Act requires that

---

241 LR(S)A 2012 s 91: see para 12.18 below.
242 LR(S)A 2012 s 94.
243 See paras 15.2 and 15.3 below.
244 'Safe' only in one sense: if burdens are included which are obviously spent, then the solicitor is in breach of the duty under LR(S)A 2012 s 111 to ensure that the Keeper does not inadvertently make the Register inaccurate. In practice, however, this breach seems unlikely to lead to financial liability on the part of the solicitor.
245 That, in substance, is the advice given in Rooney, Massie and Kerr (n 138) 20–21.
246 *Registration Manual* (n 120) Topics: Burdens section information – obsolete burdens.
247 *General Guidance: One-Shot Rule* (n 91) 2. For research areas, see para 7.20 above.
248 This is one of the application conditions: see para 8.9 above. There is an exception for pipeline servitudes.
249 See para 9.10 below.

the application be rejected.[250] So, having paid a rejection fee[251] and lost registration priority, the unsuccessful applicant must begin again by submitting a fresh application. In this final section of the chapter we reproduce some RoS guidance which is designed to help avoid that unhappy fate.

8.27 Applications in respect of registered land

The following are needed for applications in respect of land for which a title sheet already exists on the Land Register:[252]

- a completed application form;
- the deed to be registered;
- the appropriate fee or arrangements for payment;
- any other material information, eg where a registered proprietor has died and the survivorship destination has operated to give the survivor proprietor the legal right to grant the deed, or where new information has come to light, such as a house name.

8.28 Applications for first registration

The requirements for applications for voluntary registration are set out in chapter 7.[253] The following are needed for other applications for first registration:[254]

- a completed application form;
- the deed to be registered;
- the appropriate fee or arrangements for payment;
- a plan and/or deed containing full bounding description identifying the extent of the plot;
- deeds containing rights (such as servitudes) which benefit the plot (including, if there is a burdened property, the particulars of that property in so far as known);
- a plan or full description of the extent of any servitude right which benefits the plot and is constituted by prescription;
- any outstanding heritable securities;
- deeds containing burdens over the plot, including real burdens, servitudes, and long leases;
- the last recorded disposition or conveyance in favour of the owner of the plot (if current deed is not a disposition or notice of title);
- any other material information, eg where there has been a limitation or restriction on the examination of title, or where the applicant does not know with any certainty who the current landlord is in relation to an automatic plot registration.

---

250 LR(S)A 2012 ss 21(3) and 27(4).
251 Currently £30: see Registers of Scotland (Fees) Order 2014, SSI 2014/188, sch 1 para 3(1)(a).
252 This list is based on Registers of Scotland, *General Guidance: Application for Registration – Checklist* (v.01, 2014).
253 See para 7.7 above.
254 This list is based on *General Guidance: Application for Registration – Checklist* (n 252).

8.29 Some common errors

Experience shows that the following errors are common reasons for the rejection of applications:[255]

(1) *Application forms.* The application form is not signed; the correct application type is not selected; not all of the form has been completed; the information on the form fails to match the information in the deed in respect, for example, of names, subjects, title numbers, or deed type.

(2) *The deed being registered.* The deed is not valid, or it is not probative. In order for a deed to be valid, the granter must have title and capacity to grant; both granter and grantee must be named and designed; the deed must contain present-tense operative words (eg 'I hereby dispone'); the deed and any plan or schedule annexed must signed by the granter. In order for a deed to be probative, a witness must have signed and be named and designed and, for companies and other juristic persons, the deed must specify whether a signatory is a witness, director, secretary or authorised person.

(3) *Dual registration.* A deed creating new real burdens or servitudes is drawn up ineptly, or is not presented for registration against both the benefited and the burdened properties.

(4) *LBTT.* The requirements for notification and payment in relation to land and buildings transaction tax have not been met.

(5) *Registration fee.* The correct fee is not included (whether by direct debit or cheque).

(6) *New cadastral map entries.* In cases where a new entry in the cadastral map is needed (eg first registrations or split-offs) the information provided is insufficient. If a plan is used, it must provide sufficient surrounding detail (ie not be a floating shape), have clearly identifiable references (ie not monochrome), and be to an appropriate scale.

(7) *Tenements.* The tenement steading and common areas are not capable of being mapped. The application must contain sufficient information to identify the tenement steading extent unless RoS have already identified the steading.

(8) *First registrations: real burdens and servitudes.* There is a failure to submit all the deeds identified in the application form as creating servitudes and real burdens, or there is an inconsistency between the deeds and the answers on the form.

8.30 Application checking service

For standard first registrations[256] RoS offer a checking service prior to submission of the application.[257] This looks over the application, including the deed, much in

---

255 This list is, of course, non-exhaustive. It is based on Registers of Scotland, *General Guidance: One-shot Rule – Checklist* (v.02, 2015), and on a list of 'helpful tips' given at www.ros.gov.uk/right-first-time/helpful-tips. For some other errors, see K G C Reid and G L Gretton, *Conveyancing 2015* (2016) 93–94.
256 But not for voluntary registrations or APR.
257 www.ros.gov.uk/services/application-checking-service. See also F Rooney, 'Cutting the RoS bouncebacks' (2016, available at bit.ly/1JYbdFX).

the same way as will be done on submission. It checks that: the deed induces first registration; the deed is signed; the application form is signed; the information in the deed matches the information in the application form; the extent deed has been submitted; the deed for registration is *ex facie* valid and the execution is self-evidencing; the burdens and servitudes questions have been answered in line with the information contained in the deed; where the property falls within a research area, any burdens writs not on the Keeper's common deeds index have been submitted; the fee is correct. No investigation is made, however, beyond the documentation provided. Nor does the service check the plan or bounding description, or that LBTT has been paid. For that and other reasons, no guarantee is given that the application will ultimately be accepted, but the service will at least check for many of the mistakes which typically lead to rejection.

The service can be used whenever the necessary documentation has been assembled. That might only be after the transaction has settled and the disposition been delivered, but it might also be as early as before the conclusion of missives. The check takes around 24 hours, and at the time of writing cost £50 plus VAT.

Chapter 9

Acceptance, Rejection, Registration

9.1 Introduction

The previous chapter was concerned with how an application for registration is made. The present chapter takes the story up at the point when the application arrives at Registers of Scotland.

Unless it is obviously defective, the application is entered in the application record. Thereafter it is further considered on its merits. In a relatively small proportion of cases the application will be rejected. Usually, however, it will be accepted, and the Keeper will proceed to registration.

DEALING WITH APPLICATIONS

9.2 First steps

On receipt, an application is scrutinised for obvious errors.[1] If it passes this initial test, it is entered in the application record 'as soon as reasonably practicable'[2] – normally within a single working day[3] – and the applicant is informed by email.[4] The date of the entry in the application record is the 'date of the application'; assuming that the application is accepted, this will also be the date of registration.[5] A number is allocated to the application.[6]

---

1 Ie at the 'intake' stage: see Registers of Scotland, *FAQs: One-shot rule* Q 23. This should occur on the day on which the application is received. 'In practice, this is turning out to be a fairly rigorous check': A E A Stewart and E F F Sinclair, *Conveyancing Practice in Scotland* (7th edn, 2016) 653. A snapshot from one day in February 2015 showed that the main reasons for rejection at the intake stage were: (i) application form not signed or completed (31); (ii) error in deed or no deed provided (20); (iii) incorrect fee, where payment was by cheque (5); (iv) no SDLT certificate (4) (not required since 1 April 2015); (v) no or wrong plan (4). See K G C Reid and G L Gretton, *Conveyancing 2016* (2015) 95.
2 LR(S)A 2012 s 33(1). It is provided in s 33(2) that no entry need be made if it is immediately apparent to the Keeper that the application falls to be rejected. For the application record, see para 4.32 above.
3 Registers of Scotland, *Corporate Plan 2016–2019* (2016) para 54.
4 Land Register Rules etc (Scotland) Regulations 2014, SSI 2014/150 ('LRR 2004') r 11(1): see para 9.16 below. In terms of r 11(2) the acknowledgement must contain: (i) the type of deed; (ii) the names of the parties; (iii) the date of application; (iv) the application number; (v) the title number or provisional title number; and (vi) particulars of the plot of land (or subjects of lease). In the unusual event of no email address having been given in the application form, no acknowledgement is sent.
5 LR(S)A 2012 ss 36 and 37(1). For the date of registration, see para 9.22 below. If the application is not to be entered in the application record but is rather to be rejected, the date of the application – and hence the date as at which its validity is to be determined (see para 9.8 below) – is the date in which it would have been entered, but for the rejection.
6 LRR 2014 r 10(1), (2). The application number is 'a unique identifier consisting of numerals or of letters and numerals'.

The entry remains in the application record only for so long as the application is being considered, and serves as a warning to those consulting the Register that an application is pending. As soon as a final determination is made, the entry is removed from the application record. A copy of the application is retained in the archive record.[7]

Most applications do not lead to the creation of a new title sheet, but where they do, as with first registrations and split-off dispositions, the Keeper creates a provisional title number at the time of entry into the application record, and this will become the number of the title sheet if the application is accepted.[8]

9.3 Order of dealing: in general

The legislation says that 'the Keeper must deal with two or more applications for registration in relation to the same land in order of receipt'.[9] This common-sensical rule has always been the Keeper's practice.[10] The provision applies to applications received on different days, but it can also apply to applications received on the same day. If it is unclear which application was received first, the order of receipt is taken to be the order of the entries in the application record.[11]

The order in which the Keeper is to deal with applications is not quite the same concept as the order of registration because, although the date of registration is the date on which an entry is made in the application record,[12] all applications entered on the same day are equalised, with the *time* of registration being treated as the time of close of business on a given day.[13] Nevertheless, when two applications are received on the same day relating to the same property, the 'order of dealing with' rule can sometimes produce a priority effect.

Take two cases. In the first case, Susie grants two standard securities, to Larry and Laura, neither of whom knows about the other. Neither security is protected by an advance notice. Both are lodged for registration on the same day. Although the Keeper will deal with the one before the other, it does not in fact matter what the order is. Both standard securities are registered on the same day, and accordingly rank equally.

In the second case, Freddie sells his house to two different people, Brenda and Brian. Neither disposition is protected by an advance notice. Brenda and Brian apply for registration on the same day. Whichever application is dealt with

---

7 LR(S)A 2012 s 33(3). The entry is also removed if the application is withdrawn. For the archive record, see para 4.31 above.
8 LRR 2014 rr 10(3)–(5).
9 LR(S)A 2012 s 39(1). Here, as in a number of places, the Scottish Law Commission looked at German law. Section 39(1) tracks *Grundbuchordnung* § 17: 'Werden mehrere Eintragungen beantragt, durch die dasselbe Recht betroffen wird, so darf die später beantragte Eintragung nicht vor der Erledigung des früher gestellten Antrags erfolgen.' 'Deal with' is not defined but is interpreted by RoS as meaning 'examined and the conditions of registration and other rules of examination applied': see Registers of Scotland, *Registration Manual* (https://rosdev.atlassian.net/wiki/display/2ARM/Home) Topics: Date, Time and Order of Registration.
10 The 1979 Act, however, made no provision on the point.
11 LR(S)A 2012 s 39(2). In practice, this rule is less straightforward than it sounds. See *Registration Manual* (n 9) Topics: Date, Time and Order of Registration: 'the registration officer will require to assess which application was entered on the application record first using the available information from the LRS movement history of the applications (they should not rely on the title number as evidence of timing of entry on the application record)'.
12 LR(S)A 2012 ss 36 and 37(1): see para 9.2 above.
13 LR(S)A 2012 s 37(2): see para 9.22 below.

first will be accepted, and the second will be rejected. If it could be shown that Brenda's application arrived at 10.00 and Brian's at 14.00, Brenda's application would be dealt with first and Brian's will be rejected. Alternatively, priority will be determined by the order of entry in the application record.

It will be seen that in the first case the 'order of dealing' rule makes no difference to the two standard securities lodged for registration on the same day,[14] but in the second case, of the competing dispositions, it does make a difference. The reason for the distinction is that two standard securities can co-exist by means of the concept of equal ranking, but two conflicting dispositions cannot co-exist.[15] So once the first disposition is accepted, the second (assuming registration of the first) is or will be invalid[16] and falls to be rejected for failure to comply with the application conditions.[17] In this way the 'day unit' rule for registration[18] is made subject to a 'time-consecutive' rule in respect of dealing with the applications. Such an arrangement could hardly be avoided, for if both dispositions were to be accepted by the Keeper, the effect of the 'day unit' rule would be for them to be treated as having been registered simultaneously, with uncertain legal consequences.[19]

In practice, the order of priority is often determined by an advance notice rather than by the rules just described; for if one of the deeds is protected by an advance notice and the other is not,[20] it is the protected deed that prevails. In the case of the two dispositions, for example, if Brian's disposition arrives second but is protected by an advance notice, the Keeper must deal with Brian's application as if no application had been received from Brenda.[21]

9.4 Order of dealing: two exceptions

The rule that applications are to be dealt with in order of receipt is subject to two exceptions.

In the first place, if a deed to X and a deed by X are received on the same day, the Keeper must deal with the former before the latter.[22] Thus if Sally is selling to Boris, and Boris, to finance the purchase, is granting a security to a bank, normally the two deeds will be sent to the Keeper at the same time. But the exception just mentioned means that the Sally/Boris disposition is to be dealt with before the Boris/bank security. This is a sensible provision for a situation which often occurs. If the standard security were to be dealt with first, it would fall to be rejected as granted by a person (Boris) who was not (yet) the owner of the property.[23]

14 Had the two standard securities been lodged on consecutive days, then the first would have been dealt with first and the second dealt with second. Both securities would have been accepted for registration, but the first would have ranked ahead of the second.
15 A theoretically possible solution might be that Brenda and Brian end up as equal co-owners, but that is not the law.
16 Ie as granted by a person, Freddie, who is no longer the owner.
17 Notably, the condition that the deed must be valid: see para 8.7(4) above.
18 Ie the rule that equalises the time of registration by reference to the time, each day, that the application record closes for business.
19 See Scottish Law Commission, *Discussion Paper No 128 on Land Registration: Registration, Rectification and Indemnity* (2005) ('SLC DP 128') para 5.61.
20 Or is protected by a later advance notice.
21 LR(S)A 2012 s 59(2): see paras 10.21 ff below. Where both applications arrive on the same day, that means dealing with Brian's application first: see LR(S)A 2012 s 39(4), (5).
22 LR(S)A 2012 s 39(6), (8).
23 There would, in other words, be a failure to comply with the application condition which says that the deed must be valid: see para 8.7(4) above.

The other exception concerns first registrations. If there are received on the same day both (i) an application for voluntary registration and (ii) a deed relating to the property, then the Keeper is to deal with (i) before (ii).[24] In other words, the Keeper is first to make up a title sheet in respect of the application for voluntary registration before proceeding with the registration of the deed. This gives preference to voluntary registration over APR.[25] More significantly, it accommodates applications in respect of standard securities, which do not induce APR and which, for that reason, are often accompanied by an application for voluntary registration.[26]

9.5 Timescale

Delays in registration were a major issue in the past, though in the latter years of the 1979 Act the position improved considerably. Delay is problematic for the immediate parties involved. But it is also a problem for third parties, who, during the time that an application is pending, cannot know the outcome, and so cannot know (in the case of an application to register a disposition) who the owner is, because if an application is accepted, the registration is deemed to happen at the date of the application. Third parties might be, for example, creditors, or the tax authorities, or those involved in litigating a neighbour dispute. The shorter the 'application pending' period is, the less this is an issue, but if an application is pending for several years, as was once known to happen, there is a real problem.[27]

Echoing a provision which has long existed for the Register of Sasines,[28] the 2012 Act says that the Keeper must deal with an application 'without unreasonable delay'.[29] There is power to include precise timings in the Land Register Rules but, so far at least, this has not been done.[30] The latest corporate plan from RoS sets 20 working days as the target for registration in the case of most applications, including 'standard' first registrations,[31] but a much longer period is indicated for more complex first registrations (within six months) and for deeds affecting part of registered land (within nine months).[32]

9.6 Withdrawal

An applicant is free to withdraw a pending application at any time,[33] but withdrawal ceases to be possible once an application has been accepted or rejected. Withdrawal may be appropriate where the applicant realises that an item has been omitted or that there is an error in the application.[34] It does not require the Keeper's consent. A fee of £30 is charged.[35]

---

24 LR(S)A 2012 s 39(7), (8).
25 For voluntary registrations, see paras 7.16–7.18 above; for APR, see para 7.9 above.
26 See para 7.12 above.
27 For discussion of delay, especially the third-party aspects, see Scottish Law Commission, *Report No 222 on Land Registration* (2010) ('SLC Report 222') paras 12.86 ff.
28 Titles to Land Consolidation (Scotland) Act 1868 (31 & 32 Vict c 101) s 142.
29 LR(S)A 2012 s 35(3). There was no equivalent provision in the 1979 Act.
30 LR(S)A 2012 s 35(1), (2).
31 This much-shortened period for standard first registrations is attributable to the effects of 'tell me don't show me': see para 8.11 above.
32 *Corporate Plan 2016–2019* (n 3) para 54.
33 LR(S)A 2012 s 34(1)(a).
34 *FAQs: One-shot rule* (n 1) Q 16.
35 Registers of Scotland (Fees) Order 2014, SSI 2014/188, sch 1 para 3(1)(b).

# CONSIDERATION OF APPLICATIONS

9.7 Acceptance or rejection

Section 21 of the 2012 Act provides that the Keeper 'must' accept an application 'to the extent the applicant satisfies the Keeper' that the application conditions are met. Conversely, '[t]o the extent that the applicant does not so satisfy the Keeper, the Keeper must reject the application'.[36] As we will see shortly, the Keeper has a little more discretion than these rather stark rules suggest.[37] Nonetheless, the decision to accept or reject an application will often be a mechanical one based on a standardised examination of the application form and the accompanying deed.[38]

The words 'to the extent that' imply that deeds which are partially valid should be accepted in so far as they are legally effective. That was certainly the intention of the Scottish Law Commission.[39] But while RoS will sometimes accept partially valid deeds,[40] they will not do so where the invalidity is caused by absence of title. So if, for example, in an assignation of ten standard securities, the title number of one of the securities is given incorrectly, the assignation will be accepted and registered to the extent of the other nine securities.[41] But if a disposition purports to convey area A and area B, and the granter owns the former but not the latter, the disposition will be rejected.[42] The logic can be questioned.[43]

9.8 The 'state of the legal universe' principle

Applications stand or fall according to their validity as at the date of the application.[44] This is sometimes referred to as the 'state of the legal universe' principle because the Keeper, in making the accept/reject decision, must consider the state of the legal universe as at the date of the application and not as at the date of the decision.[45] If the principle seems a little artificial, it is a scarcely avoidable consequence of the backdating of registrations; for if registrations take effect on the date of the application, then the validity of the deed being registered must also be judged as of that date.[46]

The principle does not preclude the Keeper from taking account of new information coming to her attention between the date of the application and the

---

36 LR(S)A 2012 s 21(2), (3). For the application conditions, see paras 8.6–8.9 above.
37 This is because of the flexibility inherent in the word 'satisfy': see para 9.9 below.
38 See *Registration Manual* (n 9) Further Guidance: Intake and Application Forms; *Registration Manual* (n 9) Topics: Rejection policy and procedures.
39 SLC Report 222 para 12.54.
40 The validity of the deed is one of the application conditions: see para 8.7(4) above.
41 We are grateful to RoS for providing this example. For another example concerning common areas, see para 8.17 above.
42 See also para 11.23 below.
43 In correspondence with the authors, RoS have explained this position on the basis of LR(S)A 2012 s 43(1), (2) which, they say, requires the rejection of a disposition which is partially *a non domino* unless the requirements of s 43 (prescriptive claimants) are met (as to which see paras 17.12 ff below). We are unable to agree. Compliance with s 43 would allow the disposition to be treated as wholly valid (see s 43(1)). Non-compliance leaves it as partially valid and hence in the same position as the assignation of ten standard securities mentioned in the text.
44 Ie the date on which they are entered (or would have been entered) in the application record: see LR(S)A 2012 s 36.
45 LR(S)A 2012 s 21(2).
46 Nonetheless, the position under LR(S)A 1979 was unclear: see SLC Report 222 paras 12.67 and 12.68.

date of the decision, in so far as that information is about the state of the legal universe at the date of the application. Indeed the applicant and the applicant's solicitor have a positive duty to supply such information as may become available.[47] But what the Keeper must disregard, in making the accept/reject decision, is any new legal event[48] that has occurred since the application. A deed which was valid at the date of the application must be accepted for registration even if, by the time of the decision, it is no longer valid.[49]

Take the case of an action to reduce the deed which, to the Keeper's knowledge, is begun shortly after the application is submitted. If the ground of action is that the deed is voidable, the action is irrelevant so far as the Keeper's decision is concerned because such a deed was (at worst) voidable – and hence valid – at the date of the application. But if the ground of action is that the deed is void, the Keeper will need to consider as best she can whether the ground of action has been made out. Either way, the decision to accept or reject is made at once, without waiting for the outcome of the litigation.[50]

One consequence of the 'state of the legal universe' principle has been a change of practice in respect of standard securities granted by companies.[51] These require to be registered in the Charges Register at Companies House within 21 days of creation,[52] and the Keeper's previous practice was to postpone a decision as to registration in the Land Register until confirmation of registration in the Charges Register had been obtained. But since the latter can only occur after the date of the Land Register application,[53] such confirmation is now irrelevant and is no longer sought by the Keeper.

9.9 Degrees of 'satisfaction'

Section 21(3) of the 2012 Act says that 'to the extent the applicant does not … satisfy the Keeper, the Keeper must reject the application'. Section 75(1) says that 'the Keeper may … if not satisfied as to the validity of the [deed etc] … grant less extensive warranty than is so provided for, or exclude warranty'. There is considerable tension between these provisions.[54] If the Keeper is not satisfied, what should be done – reject, as s 21 indicates, or accept but with restriction or exclusion of warranty, as is indicated by s 75? What the provisions presuppose is that, in land registration practice as in life, there may be degrees of satisfaction. In most cases the Keeper will be fully satisfied as to compliance with the application conditions, the outcome being acceptance and full warranty. In a minority of cases the Keeper will be completely or predominantly unsatisfied, the outcome being rejection. But there may be intermediate cases, and in such cases the Keeper can accept the

---

47 LR(S)A 2012 s 111: see para 15.2 below.
48 Whether a juridical act or a juridical fact.
49 For some examples, see SLC Report paras 12.62–12.65. See also para 8.4 above for discussion of the case where the applicant dies (or is dissolved) after the date of registration but before the date on which the Keeper's decision is made.
50 Registers of Scotland, *Update 42: Keeper's policy on holding applications in abeyance* (2014).
51 *FAQs: One-shot rule* (n 1) Q 12.
52 Companies Act 2006 s 859A.
53 This is because the date on which the standard security is 'created' is the date of its registration, which in turn is the date of the application.
54 See para 13.11 below.

application but restrict or exclude warranty.[55] This is a matter on which there is RoS guidance.[56] The Keeper will accept the application but limit the warranty if, on a balance of probabilities, she considers the deed to be valid but 'significant doubt remains'. As to the meaning of 'significant doubt':

> There has to be more than simply a suspicion on the part of the Keeper. There requires to be some evidence to support a suspicion. An unsubstantiated telephone call from a member of the public alleging that a deed is void, for example, would not give rise to 'significant doubt'. But a letter from a person acting in an official capacity (a solicitor, the Law Society, the AiB, for example) setting out that there are reasons to believe that a deed presented for registration is flawed, would give rise to doubt significant enough to justify limiting warranty.

9.10 The one-shot rule

Inadequate applications cannot be improved by additional or corrected documentation. An application must comply with the application conditions at the time when it is made,[57] or face rejection under s 21. This is the 'one-shot rule'.[58] The system of Keeper's 'requisitions' is largely abandoned by the 2012 Act, as 'a waste of public resources'.[59] Instead, the principle is that 'applicants should get their applications right first time'.[60]

The name of the rule is perhaps imperfect, because applicants can have a second shot, or indeed as many shots as they wish. But repeat applications come at a price. There is in the first place a rejection fee of £30.[61] Then the applicant loses the registration priority which would have been created by acceptance of the original application. So if the first application was received and (where appropriate) entered in the application record on 1 May, and the second, corrected application was received and entered on 10 June, the date of registration is 10 June and not 1 May.[62] Finally, where the deed was protected by an advance notice, the applicant may struggle to register within the 35-day protected period.[63] In all of this, there is, and is intended to be, an incentive to reduce the error rate in applications. There are some signs that it is succeeding.[64] Already, after only three months of the new

---

55 SLC Report 222 para 12.66: 'In any case where the Keeper is satisfied on a standard of balance of probabilities, but nevertheless significant doubt remains, the solution is to accept but to exclude warranty.'
56 *Update 42* (n 50).
57 Or, more strictly, 'as at the date of application': see LR(S)A 2012 ss 21(2) and 36.
58 The expression does not appear in the 2012 Act, although it can be found in SLC Report 222 paras 12.71 ff.
59 SLC Report 222 para 12.73. The passage continues: 'It leads to delays in registration and it encumbers the application record – from which third parties may suffer because of the unnecessarily prolonged uncertainty as to title.'
60 Registers of Scotland, *General Guidance: One-Shot Rule* (v.04, 2015) 1.
61 Registers of Scotland (Fees) Order 2014 sch 1 para 3(1)(a).
62 LR(S)A 2012 s 37(1), and para 9.22 below.
63 For advance notices, see ch 10.
64 As well as causing resentment amongst solicitors, for which see eg the letter published at (2016) 61 JLSS Jan/6. One point that is made is that, whereas errors by solicitors are penalised, errors by RoS, eg in the course of carrying out registration, are not. Another is that the collection of fees for rejections is a 'money-making enterprise' on the part of RoS, though this appears not to be the case: see F Rooney, 'Cutting the RoS bouncebacks' (2016, available at bit.ly/1JYbdFX).

system, the rejection rate had dropped to 6%,[65] close to the rejection rate under the 1979 Act, and since then the downwards trend has continued. The main grounds for rejection are mentioned elsewhere in this book.[66] Most rejections are temporary rebuffs and the application will ultimately be accepted.

9.11 Amendment and requisitions

Notwithstanding the one-shot rule, s 34 of the 2012 Act allows the Keeper to consent to an amendment of an application. It further provides that the Land Register Rules may specify the circumstances in which such consent must be given, although in the event the Rules are silent on the point, and RoS's view is that such specification 'would not allow for any flexibility in practice'.[67]

The approach taken is that if an application as submitted falls to be rejected, the question of amendment cannot arise, but amendment is possible (if the Keeper consents) where the issue is not about the accept/reject decision but about the grant of Keeper's warranty or some other matter.[68] In practice, amendment often involves the 'requisition' by RoS of some additional or revised document from the applicant.[69] Thus requisitions, which were such a prominent feature of the 1979 Act arrangements,[70] survive under the 2012 Act, albeit in a much weakened form. RoS guidance gives the following examples of circumstances under which a requisition might be made:[71]

- to reinforce information provided in the application regarding the existence of a public right of way, a core path, or a servitude created by prescription;[72]
- where an extension of warranty is sought in terms of section 75(1)(a) the Keeper may require further evidence to that provided in the application, for example, to extend warranty to a right to mines and minerals;[73]
- further evidence may be required in relation to the requirements for evidence set out under section 43 for prescriptive claimants;[74]
- where the search in the Register of Inhibitions carried out by the Keeper discloses an entry, it may be necessary to request confirmation that the name match disclosed is not that of the party in the application;[75] and

---

65 Reid and Gretton (n 1) 94–95.
66 Paragraphs 8.29 and 9.1, n 1 above.
67 *FAQs: One-shot rule* (n 1) Q 20.
68 *FAQs: One-shot rule* (n 1) Qs 12–14; *Registration Manual* (n 9) Topics: Substitution or amendment – requisition policy and procedures. Quite properly, this approach is founded on LR(S)A 2012 s 21(3), which requires the rejection of an application where, at the date of the application, the application conditions are not satisfied.
69 This word itself, though standard, is not in fact used either in the current legislation or in the previous legislation.
70 See *FAQs: One-shot rule* (n 1) Q 14, which gives as examples of requisitions and amendments under the 1979 Act, 'where the deed has not been witnessed, where witnesses have not been designed, where the granter or grantee's names are misspelt, or where the deed plan does not conform to the Keeper's deed plan criteria'. All are breaches of the application conditions imposed by the 2012 Act and all would now lead to rejection of the application.
71 *FAQs: One-shot rule* (n 1) Q 12.
72 For these off-Register rights, see paras 4.26–4.28 above.
73 For extension of the Keeper's warranty, see para 13.13 below.
74 For prescriptive claimants, see paras 17.12 ff below.
75 For inhibitions, see para 9.19 below.

Consideration of Applications

- where a supporting deed has been submitted in error, it may be possible to substitute it for the correct one.

Of these, queries about inhibitions seem to be the most common.[76] Another use of requisitions is to make inquiries as to unexplained exceptions from warrandice in the deed being presented for registration.[77]

The period for responding to a requisition is 42 days.[78] As, however, requisitions are not concerned with the central question of acceptance or rejection, a late response to a RoS request, or even a failure to respond altogether, is unlikely to result in the application being rejected. At most, there will be a restriction or exclusion of the Keeper's warranty, or the omission of something from the title sheet.[79]

9.12 Wrongful rejection

As with any decision by the Keeper, a decision to reject an application can be the subject of an appeal to the Lands Tribunal.[80] But unless the rejection is on some fundamental point not susceptible to correction, the applicant is much more likely to submit a revised application than to go to the lengths of an appeal.

Rejections involve costs for applicants and may even result in a loss of priority to a rival deed. If the rejection was unjustified – if, on any reasonable view, the Keeper ought to have been satisfied as to compliance with the application conditions – then the applicant's loss may be recoverable from the Keeper on normal principles of delict.[81] Alternatively, the Keeper is sometimes willing to make *ex gratia* payments, for example in respect of the cost of additional legal work.[82]

9.13 Wrongful acceptance

From time to time an application might be accepted which, if the staff at RoS had been more alert, ought properly to have been rejected. Nonetheless, the legal effectiveness of the resulting registration would appear to be unimpaired. Arguably, the Keeper will have acted within her powers; indeed, having been 'satisfied', however carelessly, that the application principles were met, she had no choice but to accept the application.[83] But even if the Keeper's powers are deemed to have been exceeded, it would be hard to deny effect to a change to the Register made in the name of registration.

Where wrongful acceptance occurs, the initial consequences, at least, are likely to be slight. If the deed is valid, there can be no objection to its taking effect on registration. If it is invalid, no rights will be conferred or removed,[84] and the

---

76 Rooney (n 64).
77 Rooney (n 64). Although the application must have appeared sound in order to allow a requisition in the first place, a candid reply to the effect that warrandice is excluded due to the absence of title will lead to the application being rejected.
78 LRR 2014 r 13. The period under the previous legislation was 60 days.
79 *FAQs: One-shot rule* (n 1) Qs 18 and 19.
80 LR(S)A 2012 s 103: see para 3.20 above. Even if the appeal is successful, however, the original application is not revived and a new application will be needed: see s 103(3).
81 SLC Report 222 para 12.100; para 14.9 below.
82 See para 14.10 below.
83 LR(S)A 2012 s 21(2): see para 9.7 above.
84 As there is no Midas touch under the 2012 Act: see para 9.20 below.

resulting inaccuracy in the Register can be put right by rectification.[85] It is only if the property comes to be transferred that, depending on its nature, the inaccuracy might be cured by realignment.[86] Compensation would then be due by the Keeper to any person suffering loss as a result.[87]

NOTIFICATION

9.14 Acceptance of application

The legislation requires that applicants, and certain others, are kept informed of the application's progress. As soon as an application is received and entered in the application record, the applicant must be told by email, as already mentioned.[88] The Keeper must send further notification if and when the application is accepted and given effect to by an appropriate change in the Register.[89] If the application is in respect of a deed, as typically it is,[90] the deed's granter must be informed as well as the grantee/applicant.[91] This is a change in practice,[92] and a welcome one too because granters have an obvious interest in knowing that the deed has been registered. For instance, if Sally sells to Boris she will want to know that she has ceased to be owner, and when that has happened. The rule also has a minor anti-fraud role. For instance, Aeneas owns property, and a disposition or standard security or other deed is forged and registered. Notification to Aeneas may help bring the scam to light at an early stage. Of course, with some types of deed, such as charging orders and tree preservation notices, there is no granter and hence no duty to notify.

In addition to the applicant and the granter, acceptance of an application may also be notified to 'any other person the Keeper considers appropriate', although this would be unusual.[93]

Where registration results in APR,[94] and hence in the migration of a plot of land from the Sasine to the Land Register, notification must be made to the person who owns the plot.[95] Thus suppose that Duncan is Eilidh's tenant under a long lease and that all deeds have hitherto been recorded in the Register of Sasines. If Duncan assigns the lease to Findlay and Findlay applies for registration in the Land Register, there will be (first) registration both of Findlay's deed and of Eilidh's plot of land.[96] Duncan and Findlay must be notified as to the registration

---

85 LR(S)A 2012 s 80: see paras 11.13 ff below.
86 LR(S)A 2012 ss 86–93: see ch 12.
87 LR(S)A 2012 s 94: see paras 14.2 and 14.3 below.
88 See para 9.2 above.
89 LR(S)A 2012 s 40(1) talks only of 'an application being accepted', but acceptance in this context needs to be read as including making the necessary changes to the Register: see Registers of Scotland, *General Guidance: Notifications* (v.01, 2014) 1. For decisions as to whether an application should be accepted or rejected, see paras 9.7–9.10 above.
90 The exception is voluntary registration, for which see paras 7.16–7.18 above.
91 LR(S)A 2012 s 40(1)(a), (b).
92 Though not, possibly, in law: in terms of the Land Registration (Scotland) Rules 2006, SSI 2006/485, r 18(1), the Keeper had to notify 'any person whose interest appears from the register to be affected'; nonetheless, there was no notification to granters.
93 LR(S)A 2012 s 40(1)(d); Registers of Scotland, *FAQs: Notifications* Section B, Q 7.
94 Automatic plot registration: see para 7.9 above.
95 LR(S)A 2012 s 41(1), (2). These provisions also require notification to the owner in cases of KIR: see para 7.19 above.
96 For cases like this, see para 7.11 above.

of the assignation (and emailed a copy of the new lease title sheet), as granter and grantee/applicant respectively;[97] and separately, all three must be notified as to the registration of the plot of land (and emailed a copy of the new plot title sheet).[98]

Notification must happen for *each* application. Thus take the everyday case of a sale, where there is (i) a disposition by seller to buyer, (ii) a discharge by the seller's lender, and (iii) a standard security by the buyer to the buyer's lender. Each of these is a distinct transaction and each requires notification by the Keeper.

The legislation says that there 'must' be notification. Nonetheless, a failure to notify does not affect the competence or validity of the acceptance of the application or, in the case of APR, of the registration of the plot of land.[99]

9.15 Rejection or withdrawal of application

If an application for registration is rejected rather than accepted, the rejection too must be notified to the applicant and to the granter of the deed (if any), both of whom have an obvious interest in knowing of the rejection.[100] Applications can be rejected only if they fail to satisfy the application conditions,[101] and the rejection email will explain the nature of that failure.[102]

Applications can be withdrawn before the Keeper reaches a decision.[103] The application is then returned to the applicant, and an email sent to both applicant and granter confirming the withdrawal.[104]

9.16 Method of notification

The method of notification is at the Keeper's discretion,[105] and her practice is to notify by email, using the email addresses provided for that purpose in the application form.[106] These will usually be the addresses of the parties' solicitors rather than of the parties themselves. If email addresses are omitted from the form, no notification is sent to applicants or granters: the Keeper will not notify by post.[107]

Assuming that the application for registration was successful, the Keeper includes in the email a link to a PDF version of the updated title sheet together

---

97 This is just the rule, already described, that requires notification to both applicant and granter: see LR(S)A 2012 s 40(1).
98 The notification to Eilidh is under s 41(2)(a); the notification to Duncan and Findlay is under s 41(2)(b). See *General Guidance: Notifications* (n 89) 3.
99 LR(S)A 2012 ss 40(6) and 41(6).
100 LR(S)A 2012 s 41(1).
101 LR(S)A 2012 s 21(3): see paras 9.7–9.10 above and, for the application conditions, paras 8.6–8.9 above.
102 *General Guidance: Notifications* (n 89) 2. The email contains a link to a landing page where the PDF of the rejection letter is available.
103 LR(S)A 2012 s 34(1)(a): see para 9.6 above.
104 Although LR(S)A 2012 s 40(2)(a) only requires notification to the granter, it is the Keeper's practice to notify the grantee/applicant as well: see *General Guidance: Notifications* (n 89) 2.
105 LR(S)A 2012 s 40(4).
106 Part A of the application form includes a box ('Notification Details') which asks for the email addresses of the applicant and the granter.
107 *General Guidance: Notifications* (n 89) 2. The lawfulness of this approach may be open to question: while the 2012 Act certainly allows the Keeper to notify 'by such means as the Keeper considers appropriate' (s 40(4)), she is also under a duty to notify except where notification is not reasonably practicable (s 40(1), (3)). Notification by post seems eminently practicable.

with a copy of the unit on the cadastral map.[108] This is done in respect of all applications and not merely those involving dispositions. The link to the PDF works for 50 days after notification, and the PDF can and should be sent to the client. The former practice of issuing an authenticated land certificate (or, in the case of standard securities, a charge certificate) has been discontinued.[109] The applicant, or indeed anyone else, is free to request an official extract of the title sheet,[110] though this would involve additional expense. In the unlikely event of the PDF version, or the extract, not being a true copy, the Keeper is liable for any loss suffered as a result.[111]

An exception to the 'email only' policy is made in respect of notification to the owner of the plot where registration proceeds under APR. Unless the Keeper happens to know the owner's email address – and it will not appear on the application form – notification is sent by post to the last address disclosed in the deeds.[112]

9.17 Clyping

Where an application for registration of a disposition is rejected on the ground that the transfer is prohibited due to the existence of a registered community interest in land (or an application for the registration of such an interest),[113] the Keeper must inform the Scottish Ministers of the rejection and provide them with a copy of the application.[114]

The Keeper is also bound to notify certain persons when an application to register an *a non domino* disposition is received, and once again when a decision is made as to its disposal.[115] This topic is further discussed in chapter 17.

REGISTRATION

9.18 Altering the Register

What must be done to complete the registration process? For property already in the Land Register, the Keeper completes registration of a deed by making such change or changes to the title sheet as the deed may require.[116] If, for example, the deed is a disposition, the name of the new owner is entered in the B (property) section; if it is a standard security, the security is entered in the C (securities) section.

---

108 *General Guidance: Notifications* (n 89) 2. This is provided out of the goodness of the Keeper's heart: there is no legislative requirement.
109 The former practice is explained in para 2.6 above. The 2012 Act makes no provision for land and charge certificates.
110 LR(S)A 2012 s 104: see para 3.12 above.
111 LR(S)A 2012 s 106: see para 14.8 below.
112 *General Guidance: Notifications* (n 89) 3. Post is also used where the Keeper registers under KIR.
113 Land Reform (Scotland) Act 2003 ss 37(5)(e) and 40(1).
114 LR(S)A 2012 s 42. A minor exception is set out in s 42(2). No method of notification is prescribed. It may be that the notification requirement will come to be extended to the new community rights to buy created by part 3A of the Land Reform (Scotland) Act 2003, inserted by s 74 of the Community Empowerment (Scotland) Act 2015 (see especially s 97N), and by part 5 of the Land Reform (Scotland) Act 2016 (see especially s 61).
115 LR(S)A 2012 ss 40(1)(c) and 45(1)–(3).
116 LR(S)A 2012 s 31(1), (2)(a).

Registration 165

First registrations, however, require the creation of a new title sheet and a new cadastral unit.[117] In respect of the former, the Keeper tends to rely on the information provided in the application for registration,[118] supplemented, if the property is in a research area,[119] by information previously compiled for the area in question. But where first registration occurs without application (as in KIR),[120] or without the owner's involvement (as in some cases of APR),[121] the Keeper must manage as best she can. The legislation does not then insist on the owner (or other right-holder) being named and designed in the title sheet, but allows the Keeper, in appropriate cases, to enter a statement that the name or designation is not known, or not known with reasonable certainty.[122]

Registration may also require supplementary changes to be made to the title sheet record or cadastral map.[123] In addition, the Keeper must preserve in the archive record a copy of any deed being given effect to by registration as well as any other deed submitted to the Keeper which is relevant to the accuracy of the Register.[124] These documents need to be preserved because they are the basis for what the relevant title sheets say (as well as the cadastral map if that is changed), and accordingly may need to be looked at if the accuracy of the entries ever comes to be challenged.

9.19 Entering inhibitions

In registering a deed the Keeper must be alert to inhibitions and other entries in the Register of Inhibitions which might affect that deed.[125] To that end, the application form for registration asks whether the validity of the deed is capable of being affected by an entry in the Register of Inhibitions.

Suppose, for example, that Serafina owns Blackmains, and that Iona inhibits her. The inhibition enters the Register of Inhibitions, but it does not normally enter the Land Register. An inhibition is noted in the Land Register only in one situation, which is where (to keep to the example) Serafina, with the inhibition still in place, grants a deed (eg a disposition) to Dawn, which is registered in the Land Register. The inhibition does not prevent this from happening, but it makes the deed potentially voidable at Iona's instance.[126] When registering the Serafina/

---

117 LR(S)A 2012 s 30(1), (2)(a), (c). For the four types of case in which first registration might occur, see para 7.3 above. For the content of title sheets, see paras 4.13–4.19 above; for cadastral units, see para 5.8 above.
118 On the principle of 'tell me don't show me': see para 8.11 above.
119 As to which see para 7.19 above.
120 For KIR (Keeper-induced registration), see paras 7.17–7.24 above.
121 For APR (automatic plot registration), see para 7.9 above.
122 LR(S)A 2012 s 30(5).
123 LR(S)A 2012 ss 30(2)(b), (d) and 31(2)(b), (c). These may include cancelling a title sheet and cadastral unit or making up a new title sheet and creating a cadastral unit: see ss 30(4) and 31(4).
124 LR(S)A 2012 ss 30(2)(e) and 31(2)(d). In the case of first registrations proceeding by KIR or APR, this duty extends to any relevant document which is reasonably available to the Keeper. For the archive record, see para 4.31 above.
125 For RoS procedures, see *Registration Manual* (n 9) Topics: Register of Inhibitions and Adjudications.
126 The Keeper's duty to note under LR(S)A 2012 s 32(1)(b) applies where 'the validity of the deed to which the application relates might be affected by an entry in the Register of Inhibitions'. A deed that is voidable is not an invalid deed, either at general law or under LR(S)A 2012 s 113(2), so the provision must be taken to include a reference to future invalidity following upon reduction. The idea of future invalidity had been captured overtly by the equivalent provision

Dawn deed, the Keeper must note the fact of the Iona/Serafina inhibition in the Blackmains title sheet.[127] The same applies to any other entry in the Register of Inhibitions which might affect the validity of the deed.[128]

The inhibition remains in force even if overlooked by the Keeper, but it 'ceases to have effect (and is treated as never having had effect) in relation to property if a person acquires the property … in good faith and for adequate consideration'.[129] An erroneous silence in the title sheet may thus assist a plea based on this provision.

The legislation says nothing as to the removal of entries. Plainly, the Keeper should remove the entry from the title sheet as and when aware of the fact that the inhibition (or other process) ceases to have effect. But as she is unlikely to know of future discharge or recall, even though registered in the Register of Inhibitions,[130] spent inhibitions will often linger on in title sheets. As to negative prescription, although an inhibition itself prescribes after five years,[131] where a deed has been granted that is reducible on the ground of an inhibition, the right to reduce prescribes, not with the inhibition itself, but 20 years after the time of the deed in question.[132] So if the Iona/Serafina inhibition is in 2016, and the Serafina/Dawn deed is in 2018, it would seem that the entry (unless recalled or discharged) should remain in place until 2038.

EFFECT

9.20 Abolition of the Midas touch

Before considering what effect registration has it is well to consider what effect it does *not* have. The 1979 Act had a provision saying that registration was not only a necessary condition for obtaining a real right but also a sufficient condition.[133] In other words, the rule was not only 'if you don't register, you won't obtain a real right'[134] but also 'if you do register, you will obtain a real right'. This latter

---

(s 6(5)(c)) in the Scottish Law Commission's draft Bill ('… if it is an entry by virtue of which a change in the title sheet might come to be made'). It might be added that reduction of a deed on the grounds of an inhibition results only in partial invalidity: the reduction is *ad hunc effectum* only, ie the deed is fully valid except in respect of the reducer; but partial invalidity too must be taken to fall within s 32(1)(b).

127 LR(S)A 2012 s 32(2). The legislation does not say which section of the title sheet should be the home of this entry; in practice it appears in the B (proprietorship) section. For the background to this area of law, see SLC Report 222 paras 30.3 ff.

128 Eg sequestration, trust deeds for creditors, and company administration. For a list of possible entries as at 1996, see G L Gretton, *Law of Inhibition and Adjudication* (2nd edn, 1996) 20–21. LR(S)A 2012 s 32(3) excepts two types of entry in the Register of Inhibitions, namely a notice of land attachment and a notice of a signeted summons in an action of reduction of a deed granted in breach of inhibition. But these are not really exceptions, because other legislation separately provides for such notices to enter the Land Register: see, respectively, Bankruptcy and Diligence etc (Scotland) Act 2007 s 83(1); Titles to Land Consolidation (Scotland) Act 1868 s 159A. It might be added that the system of land attachment has yet to come into force, and accordingly the old system of adjudication remains in place.

129 Bankruptcy and Diligence etc (Scotland) Act 2007 s 159.

130 We are grateful to RoS for this information. This is due to the separate administrative arrangements for the two registers.

131 Conveyancing (Scotland) Act 1924 s 44.

132 Bankruptcy and Diligence etc (Scotland) Act 2007 s 161.

133 LR(S)A 1979 s 3(1)(a).

134 Which was the principle underpinning the Register of Sasines: see para 1.5 above.

rule, 'that everything that is registered turns into a real right', was dubbed by the Scottish Law Commission as 'the registration equivalent of a Midas touch';[135] and, as we saw in chapter 2, it created much difficulty and uncertainty.[136] The Midas touch is abandoned by the 2012 Act. The acquisition under the Act of a real right depends on the validity of the deed and not on the mere fact of registration. In other words, the ordinary rules of property law apply.[137] So in the case of dispositions, for example, it is the 'registration of a *valid* disposition' which, in terms of s 50(2) of the Act, 'transfers ownership'.[138]

Admittedly, there can be exceptions: s 49(4) explains that 'registration of an *invalid* deed confers real effect only to the extent that an enactment so provides'.[139] The most important enactment so providing is s 86 of the Act, which protects those acquiring on the faith of the Register. So if land belongs to Alan but the Register says, wrongly, that it belongs to Betty, a person taking a disposition from Betty will, if in good faith and provided certain other conditions are satisfied, receive a good title just as if Betty really had been the owner. This exception, which 'realigns' property law with the position as stated on the Register, is considered in detail in chapter 12.[140] But it remains an exception: the general rule is that deeds must be valid.[141]

9.21 Sector-specific rules

One consequence of this changed conceptual structure is that there is no general 'effect of registration' provision in the 2012 Act. For the most part, the Act leaves the question of effect to the sector-specific legislation that provides for the registration of the deed in the first place.[142] For example, the Title Conditions (Scotland) Act 2003 says that real burdens are created by registration of a constitutive deed.[143] The 2012 Act does not attempt to re-enact that, either in the same or, worse, in different terms.

There are in fact countless enactments (including local and personal legislation, and statutory instruments)[144] about registration of deeds in the Land

---

135 Scottish Law Commission, *Discussion Paper No 125 on Land Registration: Void and Voidable Titles* (2004) ('SLC DP 125') para 5.34.
136 See paras 2.7–2.9 and 2.13 above.
137 *Registration Manual* (n 9) Topics: Effect of registration.
138 LR(S)A 2012 s 49(4) further provides that 'Registration of an invalid deed confers real effect only to the extent that an enactment so provides' – which, usually, it does not.
139 In so far as the 2012 Act has an anti-Midas provision, this is it. Strictly, such a provision is unnecessary: the absence of a *pro*-Midas provision is sufficient by itself to allow the ordinary rules of property law to apply. But the new legislation has to be used not only by specialists in property law but also by non-specialists, and it was thought important to make sure that the new position was set out in clear and unmistakable terms.
140 See paras 12.8–12.17 below.
141 For a discussion of the position of dispositions which are void under s 19D(6) of the Crofters (Scotland) Act 1993 as transfers of part of an owner-occupied croft, see D Findlay, 'Perils of the owner-occupied croft' (2015) 60 JLSS June/34.
142 LR(S)A 2012 s 49(2). This 'look to other legislation for effect of registration' principle parallels the 'look to other legislation for what is registrable' principle, set out in s 49(1) and discussed at para 6.2 above.
143 Title Conditions (Scotland) Act 2003 s 4(1), (5).
144 It is not clear why four statutes are singled out in s 49(2)(b) (and subsection (3)), except perhaps to mark out that all were amended by the 2012 Act.

Register,[145] and the 2012 Act itself contains further provisions, notably in respect of dispositions and proper liferents.[146] Some lack an express statement as to the effect of registration, leaving that to be worked out by implication.[147] Enactments are in turn supplemented by the general corpus of property law (to a large extent of ultimately Roman origins) that does not have statutory form.[148] Being common law, it does not relate directly to registration, because the Land Register, like the Register of Sasines, is the creature of statute, but it often relates to registration indirectly, for instance because there are common-law rules about the interaction of real rights, and registration typically defines if and when a right is real.

Sometimes registration has no effect in respect of real rights. That is the case, generally speaking, where a deed is invalid, or where, by its nature, the deed is not concerned with real rights at all (for example, tree preservation orders or notices of potential liability for costs). But it is also the case in voluntary registration and in Keeper-induced registration, both of which involve merely a migration of title data into the Land Register.[149]

9.22 Date of registration

To the extent that registration has legal effects, these effects generally (though not invariably)[150] occur on the date of registration. In the case of registration of a plot by KIR or APR, that date is the date on which the new title sheet is made up. Where registration is in respect of a deed, registration is backdated to the date of the application,[151] by which is meant the date on which the application is entered on the application record.[152] The rule applies equally to transactions proceeding under ARTL.[153] Thus if an application is received by the Keeper on 15 March for registration of a disposition from Sally to Boris, but the application raises difficult issues, requiring time for consideration, and is not accepted until 15 June, the registration, though in fact it happens on 15 June, is deemed to have happened on 15 March.[154] There are good reasons for the rule, one being that an applicant should not suffer if there is delay at RoS. The rule makes the application record essential, for third parties searching the Land Register after 15 March but before 15 June will see a title sheet that shows Sally as owner, something that will later prove false. The application record enables third parties to see pending applications.[155]

---

145 Pre-1979 enactments refer (unless later amended) only to the Register of Sasines, but such enactments are (with certain qualifications) deemed also to refer to the Land Register by virtue of s 29 of the LR(S)A 1979, a section that is not repealed by the 2012 Act.
146 LR(S)A 2012 ss 50 and 51.
147 This is captured in the words 'whether expressly or not' near the start of LR(S)A 2012 s 49(2).
148 LR(S)A 2012 s 49(2)(d).
149 See, respectively, paras 7.16–7.18 above and paras 7.19–7.24 above.
150 There can be exceptions. For example, real burdens can take effect on a later date which is specified in the constitutive deed: see Title Conditions (Scotland) Act 2003 s 4(1); or where a title by realignment relies on a period of post-registration possession, ownership is not acquired until the period is completed: see LR(S)A 2012 s 86(4)(b). For a discussion of retention of title in dispositions, see para 6.7 above.
151 LR(S)A 2012 s 37(1).
152 LR(S)A 2012 s 36: see para 9.2 above.
153 As to which see ch 19.
154 The previous law was the same: see LR(S)A 1979 s 4(3). For discussion of why this rule was retained, see SLC DP 128 paras 4.1–4.3.
155 For the application record, see para 4.32 above.

The precise time of registration is deemed to be the moment at which the application record next closes.[156] What that means is that all applications received during the course of a day are deemed to be received at the close of business on that day. So an application received at 10.00, and another application received at 11.00, are deemed to have been received at the same time, namely at close of business that afternoon. An application received after close of business is considered as having been received at the close of business on the next business day.[157]

---

156 LR(S)A 2012 s 37(2). For the background, see SLC Report 222 paras 12.27 ff. The question of when the application record closes is at present a matter for the administrative decision of the Keeper. Rules on the subject can be set out by statutory instrument (LR(S)A 2012 s 115(1)(d)) but thus far that has not happened.

157 There is power in LR(S)A 2012 s 37(3), (4) to change the rule by statutory instrument. Thus it would be possible, for example, to replace the current 'day unit' system with an 'hour unit', or indeed a fully time-consecutive system. LR(S)A 2012 s 38 confers a similar power to change the position for the Register of Sasines, where the same 'day unit' system exists. Given that the Register of Sasines is being phased out, the provision's value may perhaps be questioned.

Chapter 10

Advance Notices

BACKGROUND

10.1 Gap risk

In typical conveyancing transactions there is nothing to fear from competing titles. But just occasionally there can be competition from a creditor of the granter, or from a third party receiving a rival deed such as a disposition or standard security. Against such risks a buyer (or other party) will wish to be secure.

Much depends on when the competing right comes into the picture. The following chart sets out the position (Boris being the buyer or other grantee, and Sally the seller or other granter):

PERIOD	EVENT
Period A (pre-legal report)	
	Legal report (ie search of Land Register and Register of Inhibitions)
Period B (from legal report to settlement)	
	Settlement of transaction
Period C (from settlement to Boris's application for registration)	
	Application for registration
Period D (after Boris's application for registration)	

Adverse deeds in period A will seldom be a significant risk to Boris because, although such a deed will (usually) trump Boris's, he has not yet paid, and so, on discovering the competing deed (which will happen when he searches), he can abort settlement and keep the money safe in his purse.[1] Equally, deeds in period D will seldom be a significant risk to Boris, because the date of his application is normally the priority point for the acquisition of his real right.[2] For example, if Sally has secretly granted a competing deed to Rita, and Rita applies for registration the day after Boris applies, *prior tempore potior jure est*, and thus Boris's deed trumps Rita's.[3] The main worry for Boris is about adverse deeds in periods B and C. For instance, suppose that the Sally/Rita deed is registered in one of these periods. If it is registered in period B, Boris still has the money in his purse, but unless he updates the legal report before settlement he will go ahead and step over the cliff by paying the price at settlement date. As for period C, even an updated search

---

1 He may still suffer some loss, but at least he has not paid over the price.
2 LR(S)A 2012 ss 36 and 37: see para 9.8 above.
3 This assumes that Boris's application is successful.

would not help, because Boris has already parted with his money; and Rita's deed, being registered first, normally has priority.[4]

Periods B and C represent 'gap risk', also called by other names such as 'competing-deed risk' or 'blind-period risk'. Because the gap normally lasts for just a few days, the risk is not great, but it is not wholly negligible. What sort of risk might there be? In broad terms, there are two kinds of risk. One is the risk that the seller might grant some inconsistent deed, such as a standard security, or even a disposition, to a third party. The other is the risk that some third party, such as a creditor, might on his own initiative register a deed against the seller.

Of course, Boris has personal rights against Sally, both under the missives and under the warrandice clause. But the concern is that Sally might not prove solvent. Indeed, third-party deeds commonly appear precisely because the seller is *vergens ad inopiam* (teetering on insolvency).

10.2 Letters of obligation[5]

To protect the buyer from gap risk it was long usual for the seller's law firm to grant a letter of obligation, guaranteeing the buyer against adverse deeds, provided that the buyer presented the disposition for registration within a stated period. In the years leading up to the 2012 Act, 14 days was standard. If there turned out to be a competing deed which was registered first, and if the seller did not promptly resolve the problem, the seller's law firm had to resolve it, either by 'buying out' the third party or by paying compensation to the purchaser. In theory the cost could be recovered from the seller, but if matters had reached this stage it was commonly because the seller was insolvent.

Law firms had insurance against potential liability under letters of obligation. Nevertheless they were unpopular.[6] Even though the insurers would ultimately pay, internal costs (staff time) were taken up in resolving the problem. Nor were letters of obligation popular from the standpoint of a buyer. A buyer wants a good title and wants it at once. A letter of obligation could not assure that. There was always delay, sometimes long delay, and the eventual solution might be compensation rather than good title. There were other problems, too. There could be issues about enforceability arising out of the wording of the letter of obligation. There were situations, such as sales on an owner's insolvency, where the selling law firm might decline to grant a letter of obligation. Finally, there was the concern that the insurers were unhappy about providing cover for letters of obligation and might withdraw it. The system of letters of obligation had for some years been approaching a state of crisis. It may be added that it appears that in no other country does such a system exist.[7] Advance notices, an innovation of

---

4 In the unlikely event that Rita was in bad faith, the possibility would arise of a challenge to her title under the offside goals rule: see para 10.30 below.
5 See G L Gretton and K G C Reid, *Conveyancing* (4th edn, 2011) paras 9-25–9-28.
6 A Stewart, 'A New Era in Conveyancing: Advance Notices and the Land Registration etc (Scotland) Act 2012', in F McCarthy, J Chalmers and S Bogle (eds), *Essays in Conveyancing and Property Law in Honour of Professor Robert Rennie* (2015; available at www.openbookpublishers.com/reader/343#page/1/mode/2up)141, 147.
7 Quite a common system internationally is the use of an independent party with whom the price is temporarily deposited, sometimes called the escrow system. In continental Europe notaries commonly perform this function.

the 2012 Act, were designed to make letters of obligation unnecessary, by making available a better system.

OVERVIEW

10.3 Advance notices in outline

In designing the system of advance notices, the Scottish Law Commission was influenced both by the English 'search with priority' and by the German *Vormerkung*.[8] Advance notices are dealt with in part 4 (ss 56 to 64) of the 2012 Act, and the Land Register Rules 2014 also have extensive provisions.

The details are discussed below, but the basic idea is that, before settlement, an advance notice is entered[9] in the Land Register (or, in some cases, the Register of Sasines), which creates in favour of the buyer a 'protected period' of 35 days. So long as the disposition (or other deed) is registered before the expiry of the protected period, the buyer has priority over competing deeds. Advance notices are designed to cover the risks that 'classic' letters of obligation previously covered and, as with letters of obligation, they turn out, in the great majority of transactions, to have been irrelevant because there is no adverse deed.

Advance notices are merely an option; the 2012 Act does not require their use. But since they became available, they have been adopted as a standard part of conveyancing practice, and the use of letters of obligation has largely (though not entirely)[10] been discontinued. Around 4,000 advance notices are registered every week.[11]

10.4 Terminology

It would be convenient to speak of Sally 'granting' an advance notice to Boris. But the legislation does not use that language. Instead, Sally 'applies' to the Keeper for a notice,[12] so that Sally is the 'applicant' rather than the 'granter'. Nevertheless, in what follows we shall sometimes say that she grants the notice to Boris. The legislation does not use any particular term to describe Boris: we shall refer to him as the 'beneficiary' of the advance notice.

An advance notice identifies a deed that is to be granted in the future: this is the 'intended deed' (from a future perspective) or the 'protected deed' (once the deed has in fact been granted).[13] The protection afforded by an advance

---

8 For the background, see Scottish Law Commission, *Report No 222 on Land Registration* (2010) ('SLC Report 222') part 14. The system adopted in the LR(S)A 2012 is the same, minor details apart, as the system recommended by the Scottish Law Commission.
9 The legislation speaks of an advance notice being 'entered' rather than 'registered': see eg LR(S)A 2012 s 57(4)(a)(i).
10 At the time of writing, letters of obligation continued to be used where timescales were too tight for an advance notice, or where an advance notice would not cover the point (as in an obligation to deliver the discharge of a standard security). 'Classic' letters of obligation were, for the moment, still covered by the master insurance policy. For details, see F Rooney and C Kerr, 'Advance Notices and Letters of Obligation' (2015) 60 JLSS Dec/34, 37. See also Law Society of Scotland, *Rules and Guidance* (www.lawscot.org.uk/rules-and-guidance/table-of-contents/) Section F, Division C: Letters of Obligation and Advance Notices, paras 1 and 2.
11 Private information from Registers of Scotland.
12 LR(S)A 2012 s 57(1).
13 These terms are not used in the LR(S)A 2012; the former term can be found in the Land Register Rules etc (Scotland) Regulations 2014, SSI 2014/150 ('LRR 2014').

notice lasts for a period of 35 days, known as the 'protected period'.[14] The term 'priority period' also has some currency, though it is not the term used in the legislation.

Finally, we use the term 'competing deed' or 'adverse deed' as shorthand for any deed that may be registered that is potentially prejudicial to the beneficiary of the advance notice. Such deeds may be voluntary (as where, during the gap period, Sally grants a standard security to a third party) or involuntary (as where a local authority registers a charging order). In this context, 'deed' has a broad meaning, and includes inhibitions against Sally, for advance notices also provide protection against adverse entries in the Register of Inhibitions.[15]

10.5 Location in the Register

Dying after 35 days, advance notices are too short-lived to merit inclusion in the title sheet. Accordingly they appear not there but in the application record.[16] The application record is part of the Land Register and so advance notices are public, and discoverable by anyone searching the Register. After its death the advance notice is interred in the archive record.[17] For as long as an advance notice is in the application record, a certified copy can be obtained; once it is in the archive record, it is possible to obtain an extract.[18] In practice, occasions when an extract or certified copy is needed will be uncommon.

In first-registration cases the advance notice appears in the Register of Sasines and not the Land Register,[19] and of course extracts from the Register of Sasines can be obtained if desired. As with other Sasine deeds, advance notices are not removed on their expiry.[20]

10.6 Advance notices and applications for advance notices

The legislation draws a clear distinction between (a) advance notices and (b) applications for advance notices.[21] An advance notice is what appears in the Register, and so is what a third party sees when searching the Register. It is not drafted by the applicant. The role of the applicant is to *apply* for an advance notice, by filling up, and submitting to the Keeper, the appropriate form on the basis of which the advance notice can then be made up. The reality, however, is rather different. For most purposes, the completed application form *is* the advance notice. It is the application form that is preserved in the Land Register's archive record, and it is the application form that, in the case of Sasine titles, is recorded in the Register of Sasines. It is only in the application record that the application form is not reproduced as such, but even here the entry is populated by extracting data from the form, and no new document is created.

In terms of the legislation, an advance notice must (i) state that a person intends to grant a deed to another person; (ii) describe the deed; (iii) give the name and

---

14 LR(S)A 2012 s 58(3).
15 LR(S)A 2012 s 61(1): see para 10.27 below.
16 LR(S)A 2012 s 57(4)(a)(i). For the application record, see para 4.32 above.
17 LR(S)A 2012 ss 62(1) and 63(4)(a).
18 LR(S)A 2012 s 104(1)(c), (2)(a). See para 3.12 above.
19 See para 10.17 below.
20 Registers of Scotland, *General Guidance: Advance Notice* (v.03, 2016) 2.
21 The former is the subject of s 56 of the LR(S)A 2012, the latter of s 57.

designation[22] of both persons; and (iv) identify the property.[23] And as notice and application form are barely distinguishable in practice, the requirements for the notice are also, in effect, the requirements for the form.[24]

USE

10.7 When competent?

An advance notice can be used to protect any type of registrable deed, provided that it has both a granter and a grantee.[25] Thus it could be granted to protect, for example, a disposition, or a long lease, or an assignation of a long lease, or a servitude, or a standard security, or an assignation of a standard security, and so on. But it is not available for deeds of conditions (which have no grantee) nor for short leases (which are not registrable). It is also unavailable for deeds which still fall to be registered in the Register of Sasines,[26] but it is available for deeds triggering first registration.

10.8 When appropriate?

It would be possible to have an advance notice for every deed in respect of which such a notice is competent. But this would involve bother and (modest) expense without, in some cases, any real gain. The question of when advance notices should, and should not, be used is a matter for the law agent's professional judgment, a position expressly confirmed, in relation to standard securities, by the CML *Lenders' Handbook*.[27]

As advance notices are intended to replace letters of obligation, a reasonable rule of thumb is to use them wherever, under former practice, a (classic) letter of obligation was used, but not otherwise. Indeed a statement to that effect has been made by the professors of conveyancing.[28] On that basis, advance notices should be used for dispositions on sale (and in practice missives of sale generally so provide).[29] But they would not be required, in a residential purchase, for the buyer's standard security if the same solicitor acts for both borrower and lender. Where, however, borrower and lender are separately represented, an advance notice would be needed

---

22 For the meaning of 'designation', see LR(S)A 2012 s 113(1), and also para 10.11 below.
23 LR(S)A 2012 s 56.
24 Though, on the whole, they are separately provided for: see paras 10.10–10.12 and 10.18 below.
25 LR(S)A 2012 ss 56(1)(a) and s 57(1). The meaning of 'registrable deed' is given in s 49.
26 This follows from the wording of LR(S)A 2012 s 57(1).
27 *CML Lenders' Handbook (Scotland)* para 14.1.2 (revision as of 8 June 2015).
28 The statement, which is by Professors Gretton, Paisley, Reid and Rennie, reads: 'There has been some uncertainty as to when it is and is not appropriate to use an advance notice. Whilst this must be a matter for professional judgement according to the circumstances of the individual case, we would suggest that, as a rule of thumb, an advance notice should be used where a classic letter of obligation would have been used, but that where a classic letter of obligation would not have been used one would not normally expect to see an advance notice. Accordingly, in the normal case we consider that there is no need to request an advance notice in a dual representation scenario when the solicitor is acting for both borrower and lender.' The statement was published at 2015 SLT (News) 8.
29 For the Property Standardisation Group style (www.psglegal.co.uk), see Offer to sell with vacant possession cl 7.6. For the Scottish Standard Clauses, 2nd edition (2016) (www.lawscot.org.uk/media/816883/Scottish-Standard-Clauses-Edition-2-.pdf), see cl 17. And see also Stewart (n 6) 155–57.

for the standard security if, under former practice, the borrower's solicitor would have granted a letter of obligation.

The purpose of the rule of thumb, just described, is to preserve essentially the same level of protection as was formerly provided by letters of obligation. Of course, it would be possible to seek enhanced protection by using an advance notice even where a letter of obligation would not have been used. On the other hand, the risks protected against by such a notice would often be remote and theoretical – which is why letters of obligation were not used in the first place. For example, it would be possible to use an advance notice for all 'purchase-money' standard securities in respect of residential property, and in theory that might give the lender additional protection against the borrower's insolvency or possible predilection (if he or she has one) for granting competing deeds such as other standard securities. But where there is already a clear personal search against the borrower, where the same solicitor acts for both borrower and lender, and where both disposition and standard security will in practice be registered of even date, it would require a fertile imagination to detect much in the way of danger for the lender.

There have been suggestions that, in the type of case just described, the lender might be at risk from an inhibition against the borrower.[30] But we do not find it easy to conceive of cases where there would be a real risk. An inhibition is ineffective against a deed that the inhibitee is, at the time of the inhibition, already bound to grant.[31] Moreover, an inhibition does not affect property that the inhibitee acquires after the date of the inhibition.[32] Hence, in the type of case just described, an inhibition against the borrower will be either too early or too late, or indeed both. Of course, in a sense the debate is of limited significance because, even if an advance notice confers no real benefit in this type of case, the cost is only a small registration fee plus a little paperwork. Some will consider this worth paying for peace of mind.[33]

Finally, at the risk of stating the obvious, it should be mentioned that the buyer's lender is already protected, through the advance notice by seller to buyer, in respect of (to use a traditional term) 'deeds and diligences' affecting the seller.

Example 1

There is an advance notice on 1 May, in respect of a W/X sale. The W/X disposition is registered on 15 May. Purchaser X is also granting a standard security to lender Z, which is also registered on 15 May. It turns out that a standard security by W to Y was registered on 13 May.

Analysis. The effect of the advance notice is that the Keeper will, on 15 May, simply delete the standard security granted in favour of Y. It will have existed for just two days. X obtains an unencumbered title. Since the W/Y standard security is now non-existent, the X/Z standard security is a fully effective first-ranking security. This is true not only if the X/Z standard security is registered of even date with the W/X

---

30 See eg letter by John Lunn in (2015) 60 JLSS Jan/6.
31 G L Gretton, *The Law of Inhibition and Adjudication* (2nd edn, 1996) 97. This doctrine was not altered by the Bankruptcy and Diligence etc (Scotland) Act 2007: see *Playfair Investments Ltd v McElvogue* [2012] CSOH 148, 2013 SLT 225.
32 Gretton (n 31) 75.
33 The 'overwhelming consensus', however, appears to be against the use of a second advance notice for standard securities of this type: see R Mackay, 'That's fine in theory, but...?' (2016) 142 *Greens Property Law Bulletin* 5, 6.

disposition, as would typically be the case, but even if the X/Z standard security were to be registered say two months later. All that is necessary, in the situation described, is that the W/X disposition be registered within the protected period.

10.9 Timing

An advance notice can be applied for, and can enter the Register, at any stage in a transaction prior to the registration of the protected deed. It is not necessary that missives have been concluded. The only general advice is that the advance notice should be timed so that the protected period begins before the final pre-settlement search and ends long enough after the expected date of settlement as to allow the grantee plenty of time to apply for registration. The Property Standardisation Group style offer says that the notice is to appear in the Register 'no earlier than 5 working days prior to the date of entry'.[34] The Scottish Standard Clauses say 'no earlier than 10 working days prior to the date of entry'.[35] In the interests of certainty it might be worth adding a finishing date to this starting date, such as 'and no later than 3 working days prior to the date of entry'.[36]

APPLICATIONS

10.9 To whom and by whom?

Applications for advance notices are made to the Keeper. Only the granter of the intended deed can apply.[37] The Act identifies two categories of eligible applicant: a person who is to grant a deed is eligible if '(a) the person may validly grant the intended deed, or (b) the person has the consent of such a person to apply'.[38] In the application form it is necessary to certify which category applies.

Category (a) is clear enough. For instance, X owns property and sells to Y. The disposition will thus be granted by X. So the person to apply for the advance notice is X. If the deed is to be granted by two (or more) persons, such as, for instance, by husband and wife, the application should be by both (or all), and the advance notice should run in the names of both (or all).

The meaning of category (b) is less easy to establish, partly because of the repeated use of the word 'person'.[39] The underlying intention was the following.[40] Sally is to dispone to Boris, and Boris intends, immediately on acquiring title, to grant a subordinate real right (eg a long lease) to Zoe. If there is to be a Boris/Zoe advance notice, there is a problem because, until Boris actually acquires title, he is not a category (a) person, ie a person who may *validly* grant the intended deed'. With the consent of Sally, however, he falls within category (b). Category (b) is therefore about a second transaction by the grantee of the first. It may be added that missives normally contain the seller's general consent to advance notices by the buyer in respect of any deed which the buyer wishes to grant.[41]

---

34 Property Standardisation Group, Offer to sell with vacant possession (n 29) cl 7.6.1.
35 Scottish Standard Clauses (n 29) cl 17.2.
36 See eg Rooney and Kerr (n 10) 35. Without a finishing date, there is a theoretical risk that the advance notice might be registered *after* settlement.
37 LR(S)A 2012 s 57(1).
38 LR(S)A 2012 s 57(2).
39 There is some useful discussion in Stewart (n 6) 153.
40 See SLC Report 222 para 14.22.
41 Scottish Standard Clauses (n 29) cl 17.3; Property Standardisation Group, Offer to sell with vacant possession (n 29) cl 7.7.2.

In practice, applications for advance notices are submitted by law firms on behalf of their (eligible) clients. This can be done in the normal course of a conveyancing transaction and without seeking specific authority.[42] As formerly with letters of obligation, the practice is for the application form to be prepared in draft by the granter's law firm and then revised by the grantee's law firm.

10.10 The application form

Three different application forms are prescribed, depending on whether the advance notice relates to (i) the whole of a registered plot, (ii) part only of a registered plot, or (iii) property which is still in the Register of Sasines.[43] The last of these is discussed later in the chapter;[44] the present concern is only with applications in respect of registered plots.

The forms prescribed for advance notices share features in common with the form prescribed for applications for registration of deeds, and the reader is referred to the discussion of that form in chapter 8. The absence of an accompanying deed, however, means that, in some respects, forms for advance notices need to provide fuller information. As with the advance notice itself, from which it is not truly distinct,[45] the application form for an advance notice must give details of the deed, the parties and the property. The deed will typically be a disposition, but may of course be some other deed such as a standard security or a long lease. More is said, below, as to the parties and the property.[46] If an error is made, it cannot be corrected once the form has been submitted; instead a new application will be needed.[47]

In general the application must be done using RoS's online submission system[48] and, assuming that the application record is open, will enter the record on the same day.[49] But where the advance notice relates to part only of a registered plot, the (electronic) application is printed and then submitted in paper form rather than electronically.[50] This is because it will in practice usually need to be accompanied by a plan.[51] The notice will not be entered in the application record until the paper application has been received, so, unless there is special delivery to RoS, this is slightly slower than an electronic submission. If the online system is down for more than 48 hours, applications (of any type) can be made wholly on paper.[52] Paper applications are also allowed for applicants who are not using a law

---

42 See Law Society of Scotland, *Rules and Guidance* (n 10) Section F, Division C: Letters of Obligation and Advance Notices, para 32.
43 LRR 2014 r 2(a), sch 1 pts 1 and 2 (registered plots); Register of Sasines (Application Procedure) Rules 2004, SSI 2004/318, r 2(b), sch pt 2, inserted by the Land Registration etc (Scotland) Act 2012 (Incidental, Consequential and Transitional) Order 2014, SSI 2014/190, art 7.
44 See para 10.18 below.
45 See para 10.6 above.
46 See, respectively, paras 10.11 and 10.12.
47 Registers of Scotland, *Registration Manual* (https://rosdev.atlassian.net/wiki/display/2ARM/Home) Further Guidance: Advance notices – acceptance/rejection. The guidance also contains a contents checklist for the different types of advance notice.
48 LRR 2014 r 3(1). For RoS procedures, see *Registration Manual* (n 47) User Guides: Other processes – advance notices.
49 *General Guidance: Advance Notice* (n 20) 6.
50 LRR 2014 r 3(3).
51 See para 10.12 below.
52 LRR 2014 r 3(1)(a), (3)(a).

firm;[53] indeed such applicants would not in any event have access to the online system.[54]

The prescribed forms call for signature, and where paper submission is used that is indeed what the Keeper requires. The application is signed, typically by the applicant's solicitor, and without a witness. In the case of online submission, the requirement for a signature is, however, excused.[55]

At the time of writing, the application fee was £10.[56] Payment is the responsibility of the applicant/granter. The responsibility as between granter and grantee – ie whether the granter can recover the cost from the grantee – is a matter for agreement. The normal practice is for the missives to provide that the seller must pay.[57]

10.11 Describing the parties

Both the granter and grantee of the prospective deed must be described in the application form. And as the advance notice must give the parties' designations,[58] and as 'designation' is defined in the Act as including special capacities (eg trustee) and, in the case of juristic persons such as companies, the company number and the legal system of incorporation,[59] this information too must be included in the application form if the advance notice is to be valid beyond doubt. The prompts on the form in this regard are not, however, as clear or as full as is desirable. Any special capacity should be included in the box for 'prefix', while the box for 'allocated number' should contain not only the company number but also the legal system of incorporation.[60]

Obviously, care must be taken in describing the parties because, depending on its nature, an error might invalidate the advance notice.

> *Example 2*
> Wilbur Bonaparte is selling a property that he holds through a company of which he is the sole shareholder and sole director. The advance notice is applied for by Wilbur Bonaparte Property (Airdrie) Ltd. Shortly thereafter it is noticed that a mistake has been made and that title to this property is held by another of his companies, Wilbur Bonaparte (Greengairs) Ltd, and accordingly the disposition is granted by that latter company.
>
> *Analysis.* The advance notice does not protect the disposition.

---

53 LRR 2014 r 3(1)(b), (3)(b). This is a gloss, for which see *General Guidance: Advance Notice* (n 20) 5. What the provisions actually say is that an applicant is excused electronic submission where the applicant '(i) has no computer facilities with access to the internet; or (ii) is the granter of the deed'. The wording is obscure, but capable of sensible interpretation. The latter – (ii) – must mean a granter who is applying personally, ie without a law firm; and as all law firms have internet access, (i) can, equally, only apply to applicants without law firms.
54 LRR 2014 r 3(2).
55 Strictly, this is contrary to what is stated in the prescribed form, notwithstanding RoS's airy explanation that electronic applications 'are deemed to be signed as they are received through a closed IT system dependent on the use of a FAS number with RoS': see Registers of Scotland, *FAQs: Advance Notice* System Processes, Q 2.
56 Registers of Scotland (Fees) Order 2014, SSI 2014/188, sch 1 para 3(2)(a). LR(S)A 2012 s 57(3) prevents the Keeper from accepting an application unless the fee has been paid or satisfactory arrangements have been made for payment.
57 See eg Property Standardisation Group, Offer to sell with vacant possession (n 29) cl 7.6.1.
58 LR(S)A 2012 s 56(1)(b): see para 10.8 above.
59 LR(S)A 2012 s 113(1).
60 This is by analogy with the rule for the application form for registration: see para 8.13 above.

Example 3
Missives are concluded for the purchase of property by Mr and Mrs Macdonald. The advance notice identifies the intended deed as a disposition to both Mr and Mrs Macdonald. The buyers then decide that title should be taken in the name of Mrs Macdonald, only.

Analysis. The disposition will not be protected, because of the discrepancy.[61] In such a case, if, when the change of parties is decided upon, the advance notice has already been put in place, the agents for the buyers should make sure to obtain a new advance notice, identifying the disponee as Mrs Macdonald, alone.

There will occasionally be room for debate as to whether a discrepancy is sufficient to invalidate the notice. For instance, suppose that the advance notice identifies the intended disponee as Alasdair James Christie but the disposition when granted identifies him as Alistair James Christie. Is that fatal? We offer no views here on what is potentially a large subject, but the practical importance of checking that the names and designations match up must be stressed.

10.12 Describing the property

The rules about describing the property in an application for an advance notice are much the same as the rules for describing the property in a registrable deed.[62]

Usually the identification of the property will be straightforward, because the property already exists as a registered unit. In that case the title number is given, together with the postal address (or failing such an address, a description of the property).[63]

Split-off cases are, necessarily, more complex.[64] Normally, an application for an advance notice in respect of part only of a registered plot must contain a plan, which in practice is a copy of the plan that will be used in the deed itself.[65] The consequence is that the deed plan must already be available at the time of the application for the advance notice. The plan should be signed and docquetted with reference to the advance notice.[66] In addition, the postal address must be given (or failing such an address, a description of the property) and also the title number of the plot from which the property is being split off.[67]

---

61 There might, however, be an argument that it is protected to the extent of a one half *pro indiviso* share on the basis that the deed described in the advance notice would have conveyed a half share to Mrs Macdonald.
62 Compare LR(S)A 2012 s 56(1)(d) with ss 23(1)(c) and s 26(1)(c).
63 LRR 2014 sch 1 pt 1. This corresponds to LR(S)A 2012 s 56(1)(d)(i) in respect of the advance notice itself. In the case of a registered lease which does not have a lease title sheet, s 56(1)(d)(ii) says that the advance notice must state the particulars of the lease, which means that this information would need to be included in the application form (although the form itself does not say so).
64 For first registration cases, see para 10.18 below.
65 LRR 2014 sch 1 pt 2 ('Submit a paper plan'). This corresponds to LR(S)A 2012 s 56(1)(d)(iii) in respect of the advance notice itself.
66 *General Guidance: Advance Notice* (n 20) 5.
67 LRR 2014 sch 1 pt 2. Usually there will be no need to give details of pertinents, although there might possibly be cases where this would be prudent: for discussion, see Rooney and Kerr (n 10) 36. See also n 69 below.

To this requirement of a plan for split-offs there are two exceptions, matching the exceptions for split-off dispositions themselves.[68] One is for tenement flats.[69] The other is where there has been development plan approval ('DPA'),[70] in which case all that is needed is a reference to the DPA. The style suggested by RoS is: 'All and Whole that plot of ground edged red and marked plot number 31 of the Development Plan approved by the Keeper for the development registered under ANG63461 on 1 December 2014.'[71]

In some cases a deed will affect two (or more) properties. That does not mean that there must be two (or more) applications. All it means is that both properties must be identified in the application for the advance notice. The only time that two applications are needed is where one of the properties is in the Land Register and the other in the Register of Sasines.[72]

10.13 Registration and notification

Following acceptance of an application, the Keeper must enter an advance notice on the application record 'as soon as reasonably practicable'.[73] All applications submitted electronically before 4 pm are entered on that day; later applications are entered the following day.[74]

In the case of a notice relating to a proposed split-off deed, the Keeper must also delineate the boundaries of the new property on the cadastral map,[75] except in the case where the property to be split off is a tenement flat. As a result, anyone searching the Register can see what property is potentially affected by the protected deed. For example, if a developer is building and selling houses, and several houses are being sold at about the same time, the advance notice for one sale shows to the buyer in another sale what property the first sale will affect.

Electronic applications are acknowledged by an immediate email.[76] A further email is sent in respect of all applications once they are entered in the application record. This gives details of the advance notice (parties, property, deed type) as well as the application and the advance notice numbers and the validation dates (ie the protected period) for the advance notice. Also included are PDFs of the application form and, in the case of split-off transactions, of the delineation of the advance notice on the cadastral map.[77]

---

68 For split-off dispositions, see para 5.21 above.
69 LR(S)A 2012 s 56(2), which is referred to in LRR 2014 sch 1 pt 1. For tenement flats, see para 4.25 above. Any exclusive pertinent outwith the flatted building (such as a car-parking space) must, however, be independently identified in an advance notice: see s 56(3). In practice a plan will be needed: see Registers of Scotland, *General Guidance: Guidance for plans and descriptions for advance notices for deeds affecting part of a registered plot* (v.01, 2014) 2.
70 See para 5.22 above.
71 *General Guidance: Guidance for plans and descriptions for advance notices for deeds affecting part of a registered plot* (n 69) 2.
72 *General Guidance: Advance Notice* (n 20) 4.
73 LR(S)A 2012 s 57(4)(a)(i). The entry consists of certain key data extracted from the application form: see para 10.6 above.
74 *FAQs: Advance Notice* (n 55) Key Information, Q 6.
75 LR(S)A 2012 s 57(4)(a)(ii).
76 *General Guidance: Advance Notice* (n 20) 6.
77 *General Guidance: Advance Notice* (n 20) 6–7. This goes beyond the requirements set out in LRR 2014 r 5.

DELETION AND RENEWAL

10.14 Deletion on expiry

After the 35-day period has passed, the Keeper deletes the notice from the application record.[78] This happens whether or not the intended deed has in fact been granted. Evidence that the notice existed survives, because it is retained in the archive record.[79]

For notices in respect of split-off deeds, a question also arises as to the delineation of the intended new area which was made on the cadastral map.[80] If the intended deed is in fact granted, that delineation becomes permanent, but if the intended deed is not granted (or at any rate, not granted within the protected period) the Keeper deletes the delineation.[81]

10.15 Deletion on applicant's request

Advance notices can be deleted prior to the expiry of the 35-day period by means of an application for discharge.[82] Usually, the application will, and often must,[83] be submitted electronically. The prescribed form requires information as to the advance-notice number, the parties, property, and deed type,[84] but, as soon as the number is typed in, the (electronic) form is automatically populated with the rest of the required information.[85] At the time of writing the fee for a discharge was £10.[86] Assuming that the application is accepted, the Keeper removes the advance notice from the application record and the notice is thereby extinguished.[87]

It might have been supposed that, since an advance notice is for the benefit of the grantee of the intended deed, the application for discharge would be by that person, not by the original applicant for the advance notice. That is not so: the application for discharge is made by the original applicant.[88] But the legislation requires that the beneficiary of the notice should consent to the discharge,[89] and the form contains the applicant's certification 'that the person to whom the intended deed would be granted consents to this application to discharge the advance notice'. The Keeper thus relies on the applicant's assurance that the beneficiary has consented. This gives rise to a risk, no doubt small, of a fraudulent discharge.[90] What the effect

---

78 LR(S)A 2012 s 62(1)(a).
79 LR(S)A 2012 s 62(1)(b). What is actually retained is a copy of the application form: see para 10.6 above.
80 As to which see para 10.13 above.
81 LR(S)A 2012 s 62(2) read with LRR 2014 r 6.
82 LR(S)A 2012 s 63.
83 Strictly, however, an electronic application is mandatory only for the discharge of advance notices which relate to the whole of a registered plot: see LRR 2014 r 3(1).
84 LRR 2014 r 2(b), sch 1 pt 3.
85 *General Guidance: Advance Notice* (n 20) 6.
86 Registers of Scotland (Fees) Order 2014, SSI 2014/188, sch 1 para 3(2)(b). LR(S)A 2012 s 63(3)(b) prevents the Keeper from accepting an application unless the fee has been paid or satisfactory arrangements have been made for payment.
87 LR(S)A 2012 s 63(4)(a), (5). The application form continues to be preserved in the archive record.
88 LR(S)A 2012 s 63(1).
89 LR(S)A 2012 s 63(3)(a).
90 The offence of making a 'materially false or misleading statement in relation to an application for registration' (LR(S)A 2012 s 112(1)(a)) does not apply here: see the definition of 'application for registration' in s 113(1) of the Act.

of an improperly discharged notice would be is a matter for speculation.[91] A third party relying on the absence of an advance notice would, we think, be protected. In practice, missives usually contain the buyer's advance consent to a discharge by the seller in the event that the seller rescinds the contract.[92]

It is assumed that discharges will be rare, for there will seldom be any reason for them. If the intention of granting the deed in question is abandoned, an advance notice has such a short lifespan (35 days) that in the normal case it can just be left to die naturally of old age.

10.16 Renewal?

In the ordinary case the period of 35 days is ample. But sometimes there can be a delay in settlement, and it may be that the rescheduled settlement date will be after the expiry of the protected period. Can an advance notice be renewed? The answer is both no and yes. An advance notice cannot be renewed as such. From a policy point of view it would be unacceptable if a notice could have its effect prolonged beyond 35 days and indeed potentially for ever.[93] But there is nothing to stop a fresh advance notice from being created, and that is what should happen in cases of delayed settlement.[94]

The difference between the renewal of a notice (which is not possible) and a new notice (which is) is brought out in the following example:[95]

> *Example 4*
>
> On 1 March an advance notice by X to Y is entered in the Register. Settlement was expected on 3 March but it does not take place. On 30 March a second notice is entered and settlement finally takes place on 5 April, with the deed by X to Y being lodged for registration on 10 April.
>
> *Analysis.* The deed is protected by the second notice, though not by the first (as it would have been if it had been possible to renew the notice). Thus, if a competing deed by X to Z had been registered on 4 March (ie within the protected period of the first notice, only), it would have had priority over the deed to Y. On the other hand, such a deed should have been detected by Y before settlement by means of an updated search.

PROPERTY STILL IN THE REGISTER OF SASINES

10.17 Deeds destined for the Land Register

The discussion so far has been on the basis that the property is in the Land Register. But advance notices are also available for property still in the Register of Sasines, provided that the deed to be granted is to be registered in the Land

---

91 LR(S)A 2012 s 63(5) provides, without qualification, that: 'On the advance notice being removed from the application record ... the advance notice ceases to have effect.'
92 See Scottish Standard Clauses (n 29) cl 17.4; Property Standardisation Group, Offer to sell with vacant possession (n 29) cl 7.7.3.
93 In particular, an advance notice has effect not only as against voluntary deeds *by* the owner, but also against third-party deeds *against* the owner: see para 10.23 below.
94 Missives usually have a provision requiring the seller to co-operate in a renewal if one is needed. See Scottish Standard Clauses (n 29) cl 17.5; Property Standardisation Group, Offer to sell with vacant possession (n 29) cl 7.7.4.
95 This is taken from SLC Report 222 para 14.35.

Register.⁹⁶ In most cases, the transaction in question will be a sale triggering a first registration in the Land Register. But since the property is still in the Register of Sasines at the time of the advance notice, and so no title sheet exists for it, the advance notice enters the Register of Sasines, not the Land Register.⁹⁷ If there were to be a competing deed, this could (depending on the type of deed) enter the Register of Sasines before the plot is registered in the Land Register.

> *Example 5*
> Benedict owns Blackmains, his title being in the Register of Sasines. On 1 June 2016, he concludes missives to sell to Constantia. On 15 June he applies for an advance notice in her favour, and this is recorded the same day in the Register of Sasines. On 20 June he delivers a deed of servitude to Hortensius, and this is recorded on 21 June. On 22 June Benedict delivers the disposition to Constantia and she presents it for registration on 23 June.
>
> *Analysis.* This will be a first registration, and the Keeper will accordingly create a title sheet for Blackmains. In the B section Constantia's name will be entered. Will the servitude appear in the D section? No. Even though the servitude existed as a real right on the eve of the registration of the plot, the effect of the registration of the disposition within the protected period is for the servitude to be extinguished.⁹⁸ The title sheet will therefore omit it.

10.18 Applications and discharges

In respect of the Register of Sasines, applications for an advance notice must be made in a prescribed form which is much the same as the form prescribed for advance notices for properties registered in the Land Register.⁹⁹ The only material difference lies in the method of describing the property. The overarching rule is the uncontroversial one that the description must be sufficient to enable the Keeper to identify the property.¹⁰⁰ In split-off transactions, a signed and docqueted plan is needed; otherwise it is sufficient to refer to a recorded deed in which the property is described and to give the postal address.¹⁰¹ If the search sheet number is known, this should be added in the appropriate box in the form.¹⁰² The form can be completed online¹⁰³ but must then be printed, signed and submitted

---

96 A deed granted over property in the Register of Sasines will normally trigger first registration, but, where it does not, an advance notice to protect the deed is not competent. This follows from the reference to 'registrable deed' in LR(S)A 2012 s 57(1) ('registrable' being defined in s 49(1)).
97 LR(S)A 2012 s 57(4)(b).
98 See paras 10.21 and 10.22 below for an explanation of why.
99 The form can be found in the Register of Sasines (Application Procedure) Rules 2004, SSI 2004/318, r 2(b), sch pt 2, as amended by the Land Registration etc (Scotland) Act 2012 (Incidental, Consequential and Transitional) Order 2014, SSI 2014/190, art 7, sch. Examples of completed applications can be found in *Registration Manual* (n 47) General Guidance: Advance notices – example advance notice for first registration. For application forms in respect of registered property, see paras 10.10–10.12 above.
100 LR(S)A 2012 s 56(1)(e), (4); LRR 2014 r 4(1). This is the rule laid down for the advance notice itself but, as might be expected, it is reflected in the requirements laid down in the prescribed application form.
101 Register of Sasines (Application Procedure) Rules 2004 sch pt 2, corresponding to the equivalent rules for the advance notice itself set out in LRR 2014 r 4(2), (3). The plan must satisfy the Keeper that the Keeper can delineate the boundaries on the cadastral map.
102 For search sheets, see para 1.8 above.
103 It is accessed by answering 'no' to the question, 'are the subjects registered in the Land Register?'.

on paper.[104] Manual amendments are not usually permitted, and if changes are needed a new form should be prepared.[105] Assuming that the application is accepted, it is recorded in the Register of Sasines on the day of receipt, and the applicant is informed of the recording date by letter.[106]

Once recorded, an advance notice cannot, of course, be removed from the Register of Sasines. But it ceases to have effect on the expiry of the 35-day protected period, and it is extinguished earlier than that if the original applicant (with the consent of the grantee of the intended deed) records a notice of discharge.[107]

EFFECT

10.19 The protected period

The protection conferred by an advance notice is limited to the 'protected period'.[108] The intended deed is therefore unprotected if it is registered after the end of that period. Unless interrupted by a discharge, the protected period lasts for 35 days.[109] That is comparable to the English rule of 30 'working days' but is more straightforward because it avoids potentially complex rules about how 'working days' are to be calculated.[110] The length of the period can be changed by statutory instrument, but there are no indications that this is likely to be done.[111]

The protected period begins on the day after the day when the notice enters the Register.[112] So if an advance notice in respect of an intended disposition by Sally to

---

104 *General Guidance: Advance Notice* (n 20) 5. The reason given in the *General Guidance* for the use of paper submission is the requirement, in s 14 of the Land Registers (Scotland) Act 1868 (31 & 32 Vict c 64), that every writ shall, in token of registration, 'be impressed with an office seal or stamp'.
105 See the policy statement by Registers of Scotland, reproduced in K G C Reid and G L Gretton, *Conveyancing 2015* (2016) 101–02.
106 *General Guidance: Advance Notice* (n 20) 6. What is recorded (and so will appear in the record volume) is the application form itself: see para 10.6 above. A typical entry in the minute book would be: 'ADVANCE NOTICE for Disposition by WILLIAM ADAM MACPHERSON, 24 Dunbar Street, Edinburgh to IRENE WILSON, 72 Gladstone Road, Edinburgh of 24 DUNBAR STREET, EDINBURGH, referred to in Disp by said William Adam Macpherson recorded 8 May 1999, with effect for 35 days from 9 Oct 2016. Dated 8 Oct 2016.'
107 LR(S)A 2012 s 63. The prescribed form can be found in the Register of Sasines (Application Procedure) Rules 2004, SSI 2004/318, r 2(c), sch pt 3, as amended by the Land Registration etc (Scotland) Act 2012 (Incidental, Consequential and Transitional) Order 2014, SSI 2014/190, art 7, sch. The form can be completed using the online system but must then be printed, signed and submitted by post: see *General Guidance: Advance Notice* (n 20) 6.
108 LR(S)A 2012 s 58(3).
109 LR(S)A 2012 s 58(1), (2). For discharges, see para 10.15 above.
110 See SLC Report 222 para 14.18. The Scottish Property Federation wanted the rule to be exactly the same as the English rule, 'as the majority of Scottish commercial property is owned and invested in by UK institutions' and this received some support in the Economy, Energy and Tourism Committee's *Stage 1 Report* paras 193 and 196, reproduced in Scottish Parliament, *Passage of the Land Registration etc (Scotland) Bill 2011* (2013, SPPB 174) (available at www.scottish.parliament.uk/parliamentarybusiness/Bills/44469.aspx) 38. The suggestion was, however, firmly rejected by the Scottish Government (*Passage of the Land Registration etc (Scotland) Bill 2011*, 577): 'Simplicity and certainty are key in the advance notice system and the 35-day period is simple and certain. The issue of determining what is or is not a business day would add unnecessary complexity to the system. Moreover, there are different public holidays in Scotland and England, which would make any attempt to align the systems around working days extremely complicated.'
111 LR(S)A 2012 s 58(6), (7).
112 LR(S)A 2012 s 58(1).

Boris enters the application record on 1 May, and a competing standard security by Sally to Rita enters the application record on the same day, Boris is not protected against it, even if it is later in the day; but if the standard security had entered the application record on 2 May he would have been protected against it. 2 May is thus the first day of the protected period. The last day of the protected period is 6 June. If Boris registers his disposition on that day he is safe, but if he applies for registration on 7 June he is outwith the protected period.

10.20 Some misconceptions: no freezing, no suspension, no backdating

It might be supposed that an advance notice works by 'freezing' the Register, ie by preventing any competing deed from being registered, for that property, during the protected period. That is not the case. Freezing the Register might be acceptable if only deeds by the owner were in question, but deeds by third parties would also be affected, such as charging orders. The Register remains open for registrations, just as if the advance notice did not exist. The effect of the advance notice makes itself felt not through freezing but through priority.

A second misconception is a variation on the first. It is that, whilst a competing deed can be accepted into the Register, its operation is suspended until whichever is the earlier of (i) the date when the protected deed has been registered, or (ii) the date when the protected period expires. For instance, suppose that the protected deed is a deed of servitude, for which an advance notice enters the Land Register on 3 June, and the competing deed is a disposition. The disposition is lodged for registration on 10 June and the servitude is lodged on 20 June. On the 'suspended effect' interpretation, the disposition lodged on 10 June would not take effect until 21 June. That is not so. The disposition (assuming it to be valid) passes ownership from the disponer to the disponee on 10 June. But from 20 June the property is subject to the servitude.

A third misconception might be that an advance notice achieves priority by a legal fiction, deeming the protected deed to have been registered as at the date of the advance notice. Such a disposition (or other deed) would thus be deemed to have been registered before it was delivered or even signed, and perhaps even before any contract existed. That would be a large-scale fiction, giving rise to a variety of problems. It is not the approach adopted in the legislation. An advance notice operates by way of priority, but without fictional backdating: the protected deed's date of registration is what it would have been even if there had never been an advance notice.

Creating a priority effect without either freezing the Register or fictional backdating was the main technical difficulty that the Scottish Law Commission had to solve when devising the advance notice system.

10.21 The main effect: competing deed non-opposable to protected deed

The solution of the Scottish Law Commission, and hence now of the legislation, lies in the principle of non-opposability: where a competing deed precedes[113] the protected deed on to the Register, but both are registered within the protected

---

113 If the protected deed is registered first, it has priority in accordance with normal principles, and without the aid of the advance notice.

period,[114] the former is 'non-opposable' to, or 'relatively invalid' as against, the latter. This principle can be reduced to two main rules. In the first place, the (later) protected deed has the same effect, on registration, as if the (earlier) competing deed had not been registered at all.[115] In the second place, the original effect of the competing deed is now adjusted to take account of the priority given to the protected deed, but in all other respects is unimpaired.[116] In this limited sense, therefore, the competing deed is now treated as if it had been registered after (and not before) the protected deed.[117] This altered legal effect, however, is not retrospective and so does not affect the rights of the parties prior to the registration of the protected deed. Nor does it change the date of registration for other purposes or affect the relationship of the competing deed with any other deed which is itself unprotected. So, for example, when s 859E(1) of the Companies Act 2006 provides that a standard security granted by a company must be registered in the Companies Register within 21 days of 'the date of its .. registration in the Land Register of Scotland', the 21-day period starts with the actual date on which the security was registered and not with the (later) date on which it was deemed to be registered in a competition with a deed protected by an advance notice.[118]

Either of these rules may result in an alteration in the Register, including, in some cases, the removal from the Register of the grantee of the competing deed. Such alteration is expressly authorised by the legislation.[119] And just as the Keeper must notify any person who is materially affected by rectification,[120] so the Keeper also notifies those who are affected by any alteration of the Register arising out of an advance notice.[121]

Necessarily, the rules just described are expressed at a high level of generality; the examples given below explain how they work in practice, both singly and in combination.

---

114 Sometimes the initial effect of the competing deed is to make the protected deed invalid. So if, for example, the competing deed is a disposition by A to B and the protected deed a disposition of the same property by A to C, registration of the competing deed would result in the invalidity of the protected deed because A no longer has title to grant. In principle, such invalidity would require the Keeper to reject the application for registration of the protected deed: see LR(S)A 2012 s 21(2), (3) read with ss 23(1)(b), 25(1)(a) and 26(1)(a). To avoid that result, ss 59(2) and 60(2) provide that, in deciding whether to register the protected deed, the decision is to be taken as if the competing deed had not been registered.
115 LR(S)A 2012 ss 59(3)(a) and 60(3)(a). Section 59 applies to advance notices in the Land Register and s 60 to advance notices in the Register of Sasines, but in substance they are the same.
116 See SLC draft Bill s 36(3)(b), which states this second rule succinctly. The equivalent provisions in LR(S)A 2012 (ss 59(3)(b) and 60(3)(b)) can be seen as explications of the SLC provision, which is not itself carried forward to the 2012 Act.
117 LR(S)A 2012 ss 59(3)(b) and 60(3)(b).
118 Or take this example. Land belongs to Alan and there is an advance notice, effective from 1 June, for a servitude that Alan is to grant. On 3 June a disposition by Alan to Billy is registered. On 7 June the deed of servitude itself is registered. Billy's ownership is subject to the servitude (being the protected deed). But suppose that there is also a 15-year lease granted by Alan to Carole on 5 June (Carole taking possession the same day). By 5 June the owner was Billy, not Alan, so the lease cannot confer on Carole a real right. The registration of the Alan/Billy disposition, on 3 June, is considered 'as if' it had been registered 'after' 7 June only as far as the servitude is concerned.
119 LR(S)A 2012 s 59(3)(b): 'the Keeper must amend the Register ... '. In practice, the alteration of the Register often arises as a matter of course as part of the registration of the protected deed (as to which see s 31(2)(a) and para 9.1 above).
120 LR(S)A 2012 s 80(4)(b); see para 11.15 below.
121 *General Guidance: Advance Notice* (n 20) 7. Unless alteration can be regarded as a type of rectification, such notification has no legislative basis.

10.22 Some examples[122]

In the examples that follow, two assumptions are made, for the sake of simplicity. One is that all grantees are in good faith.[123] The other is that there is only one advance notice. It is also possible for there to be two (or indeed more) advance notices in favour of different parties: that situation will be discussed later.[124]

Example 6: protected disposition trumps competing disposition

Sally owns Blackmains, which she is selling to Boris. She grants an advance notice to Boris, for the intended disposition. The notice is entered on the Register on 1 May. Fraudulently, and unknown to Boris, Sally grants a disposition to Rita and this disposition is registered on 15 May. The disposition that she grants to Boris is presented for registration on 25 May.

Analysis. In the absence of the advance notice, the Sally/Boris disposition would be rejected by the Keeper, because at the time of application the granter had no title. But because of the advance notice, and because the Sally/Boris deed was presented for registration within the protected period, the Keeper will accept it,[125] and will delete Rita's name from the proprietorship section of the title sheet. This change has no retroactive effect. Rita owns the property from 15 May to 25 May. Boris acquires ownership on 25 May.[126]

Example 7: the same as example 6, but with onward transaction by competing grantee

The case is the same as in example 6, but Rita grants a deed to another party, who applies for registration before Boris applies.

Analysis. This deed would be initially effective, but would become subject to Boris's deed. Thus if Rita grants a standard security to a bank, which is registered of even date with the Sally/Rita disposition, the bank's real right of security will, like Rita's real right of ownership, disappear on 25 May.

Example 8: the same as example 6, but with onward transaction by protected party

The case is the same as in example 6, but Boris grants a standard security to a bank.

Analysis. Just as an advance notice works *against* not only a first competing deed, but also against onward deeds (see previous example), so it also works *in favour of* not only the protected party's deed but also in favour of onward deeds. That means that the grantee of Boris's standard security automatically receives the protection that Boris receives. Thus if the standard security were presented for registration of even date with the presentation of the Sally/Boris disposition, it would trump Rita's deed, ie the bank would take a good and first-ranking security. The same would be true if the security granted by Boris were to be registered outwith the protected period, say on 25 June. For Boris obtains, on 25 May, a good title, and so can grant a good security.

---

122 Some of these are based on the examples in sch 3 to the SLC's draft Bill. It is perhaps to be regretted that the LR(S)A 2012 omitted these examples, because ss 59 and 60 of the LR(S)A 2012 are hard to understand purely in the abstract. Some other examples can be found at the end of *FAQs: Advance Notice* (n 55), and in *Registration Manual* (n 47) General Guidance: Advance notices – advance notice scenarios.
123 Though this assumption is not strictly necessary, for the issue of good faith and bad faith does not actually affect the workings of the advance notice system. For the relationship of advance notices to the offside goals rule, see para 10.30 below.
124 See para 10.26 below.
125 LR(S)A 2012 s 59(2).
126 Advance notices may thus be seen as producing a limited exception to the principle of *nemo plus juris ad alium transferre potest quam ipse haberet*.

Example 9: the same as example 6, but notice expired

The case is the same as example 6, with one difference: Boris applies for registration on 25 June.

Analysis. That is outwith the protected period. Accordingly, the advance notice does not help him. The position is therefore the same as it would have been had the advance notice never existed. Accordingly the Keeper will reject Boris's application, and Rita remains owner.

Example 10: protected disposition trumps competing standard security

Ophelia owns Whitemains, which she is selling to Prospero. She grants to him an advance notice and this is entered in the Register on 1 May. On 15 May the Ophelia/Prospero disposition is presented for registration. But it emerges that a standard security by Ophelia to Cordelia was registered on 13 May.

Analysis. Had the advance notice not existed, the Keeper would still have accepted the disposition and registered Prospero as owner, but his title would have been encumbered by the security. The effect of the advance notice is that the security, as a real right, ceases to exist on 15 May. The security existed as a real right for two days, from 13 May to 15 May. Prospero's title is unencumbered.

Example 11: protected servitude trumps competing disposition

Clement owns Greenmains, and grants an advance notice to his neighbour Keira in respect of a prospective servitude. This is entered into the Register on 1 May. The servitude is presented for registration on 15 May. But in turns out that on 8 May a disposition by Clement to Sophia was registered.

Analysis. In the absence of an advance notice, the position would be that the Keeper would decline to register the deed of servitude because, as at 15 May, the granter had no title. But the effect of the advance notice is that the servitude will be registered.[127] That does not alter the fact that Sophia is the owner, but it does mean that as from 15 May her title is encumbered by the servitude in favour of Keira.

Example 12: unregistrable right unaffected by advance notice

Caspar owns Bluemains, and grants an advance notice to Isadora in respect of a prospective disposition. This is entered in the Register on 1 May. On 15 May the Caspar/Isadora disposition is presented for registration. It turns out that on 8 May Caspar granted to Myfanwy a ten-year lease, and she entered into possession on the same day.

Analysis. The Keeper will register the disposition and Isadora becomes owner. The lease, being a short lease, does not enter the Register. But Isadora's title is encumbered by the lease. The lease will, at least in the typical case, be a real right by virtue of the Leases Act 1449. Being constituted prior to the registration of the Caspar/Isadora disposition, the latter is subject to it: *qui prior tempore est, potior jure est.* There is nothing in the advance notice provisions of the 2012 Act to protect Isadora.[128]

10.23 Voluntary and involuntary competing deeds

The examples above were examples where the owner voluntarily granted two inconsistent deeds. But the position is exactly the same in respect of involuntary competing deeds.[129]

---

127 LR(S)A 2012 s 59(2).
128 But equally a 'classic' letter of obligation would not have protected her either.
129 LR(S)A 2012 s 61(2).

Example 13: protected disposition trumps competing charging order

Ophelia owns Whitemains, which she is selling to Prospero. She grants to him an advance notice and this is entered in the Register on 1 May. On 15 May the Ophelia/Prospero disposition is presented for registration. But it emerges that a charging order was registered by the local authority on 13 May in respect of arrears of care expenses.[130]

Analysis. The analysis is the same as in example 10. Had the advance notice not existed, the Keeper would still have accepted the disposition and registered Prospero as owner, but his title would have been encumbered by the charging order. The effect of the advance notice is that the charging order, as a real right, ceases to exist on 15 May. The charging order existed as a real right for two days, from 13 May to 15 May. Prospero's title is unencumbered.

There could, however, be certain involuntary deeds against which an advance notice gives no protection, because their effect does not depend on who owns the property. In the example just given, the charging order can be placed on the property only so long as Ophelia is the owner. It can be compared to a standard security. But some registrable public-law notices are different: their effectiveness is not tied to any particular owner at the time of the notice. Suppose that a tree preservation notice is registered over the property that Boris is buying. The effectiveness of that notice is not time-sensitive: it would be effective if registered one month before Boris's title is registered, and also just as effective if registered one month after his title is registered. An advance notice works as if the registration dates of (i) the protected deed and (ii) the competing deed were rearranged so that the protected deed is treated as being registered first. Although that would apply to something like a tree preservation notice, the practical consequences of its so applying would seem to be nil.

Finally, two types of involuntary deed are expressly excluded from protection, and there is power, not so far exercised, to exclude others by delegated legislation.[131] The excluded deeds are notices of potential liability for costs under the Title Conditions (Scotland) Act 2003 and the equivalent notices under the Tenements (Scotland) Act 2004.[132] The reason for their exclusion is not known.[133]

10.24 Some practice issues

The above examples show the effect of an advance notice as against a competing deed. But of course the very presence of an advance notice will tend to ensure that there is no competing deed in the first place. An advance notice places in the public domain the fact that there is a pending transaction relating to a given property. Thus in example 6 if Rita sees from the Register that there is a Sally/Boris advance notice, it is likely that she will not enter into a transaction with Sally in the first place, or, if she has already begun, will not proceed further. Even if Rita has concluded missives, she would be entitled to refuse to settle, because the existence of the Sally/Boris advance notice would mean that Sally could not give to Rita a good and marketable title.

---

130 Health and Social Services and Social Security Adjudication Act 1983 s 23.
131 LR(S)A 2012 s 61(3), (4).
132 Title Conditions (Scotland) Act 2003 s 10(2A); Tenements (Scotland) Act 2004 s 12(3). For such notices, see Gretton and Reid (n 5) para 14-12.
133 They were not excluded in the draft Bill drawn up by the Scottish Law Commission.

Before the introduction of advance notices it was important to time the final search to be as near to the settlement date as possible. With an advance notice, some relaxation is possible. For example, suppose that on 8 May the Register is searched and shows nothing adverse. The transaction settles on 24 May. On 28 May Boris applies for the registration of the Sally/Boris disposition. Under previous practice the gap period (8 May to 28 May) would have been worryingly long. But suppose that on 1 May a Sally/Boris advance notice is entered in the Register. The effect is that Boris does not have to worry about any competing deed registered in the protected period (2 May + 34 subsequent days).

10.25 Does registration of the competing deed amount to an inaccuracy?

An advance notice does not bar the Register to new entries. On the contrary, if a third party seeks registration of a competing deed during the protected period the Keeper must make the registration decision without reference to the existence of the advance notice.[134] Take example 6. On 8 May the Keeper receives Rita's application and must accept it,[135] regardless of the Sally/Boris advance notice. At that stage it is not known whether there will ever actually be a Sally/Boris disposition, or, if there is, whether it will be lodged with the Keeper before the expiry of the protected period. Hence the registration in favour of Rita on 8 May is not an inaccuracy.

10.26 What if both deeds are notice-protected?

In the examples given above there was just one advance notice. The competing deed did not have its own notice. What if it had had? The answer is that the earlier advance notice will normally prevail, for the protective effect applies not only where the competing deed is unprotected, but also where the competing deed is protected by a *later* advance notice.[136]

> *Example 14*
>
> Sally owns Blackmains, which she is selling to Boris. She grants an advance notice to Boris, for the intended disposition. The notice is entered on the Register on 1 May. Fraudulently, and unknown to Boris, Sally grants a disposition to Rita and this disposition is registered on 15 May, an advance notice having previously been entered on 10 May. The disposition that she grants to Boris is presented for registration on 25 May.
>
> *Analysis.* This is like example 6. Rita becomes owner on 15 May, but the Keeper will accept the Sally/Boris disposition for registration on 25 May, whereupon Boris will become owner in place of Rita. That would not mean that the Sally/Rita advance notice is wholly without effect. It could happen that the Sally/Boris sale collapses and that Sally, who is a fraudster, grants a disposition to someone else, Cornelius. Cornelius lodges the Sally/Cornelius disposition for registration on 12 May and Rita lodges the Sally/Rita disposition for registration on 15 May. Rita prevails because both deeds were registered during her protected period.

---

134 LR(S)A 2012 ss 59(2) and 60(2).
135 Assuming that it is acceptable in other respects.
136 LR(S)A 2012 s 59(1)(b)(ii). Oddly, there is no equivalent provision in s 60 in relation to advance notices recorded in the Register of Sasines.

An earlier advance notice will not prevail over a later one, however, unless the (first) protected deed is registered within the (first) protected period.

Example 15

Cosmo grants an advance notice to Quentin on 1 August and another to Rowena on 4 August. Both are for intended dispositions. The Cosmo/Quentin disposition is presented for registration on 28 September, which is outwith the protected period.

Analysis. If the Cosmo/Rowena deed has been presented for registration at any time before 28 September, Rowena prevails, and Quentin's application will be rejected by the Keeper.

10.27 Protection against entries in the Register of Inhibitions

Like letters of obligation, advance notices offer protection against inhibitions and certain other adverse entries in the Register of Inhibitions, provided that the entry was made during the protected period.[137]

Of course, an inhibition against a granter may not be a problem for a grantee anyway, because an inhibition does not affect a disposition (or other deed) which the inhibitee is already (at the time of the inhibition) under an obligation to grant.[138] So for example if Vitruvius concludes missives to sell Yellowmains to Wendy on 1 March, and on 3 March he is inhibited by Ishbel, the inhibition cannot stop the transaction. But even in this case, the inhibition has the *appearance* of effectiveness against Vitruvius,[139] and he will be put to the trouble of persuading Wendy that it is not effective against him. Moreover, in some cases an inhibition against a granter may indeed affect a grantee, such as where missives are not concluded until the eve of settlement. For cases like this an advance notice gives valuable protection.

Example 16

Rufus owns Redmains, and is selling to Tara. An advance notice is entered on the Register on 1 May. The transaction settles on 5 May, and on 7 May Tara applies for registration of the Rufus/Tara disposition. Missives were concluded only on 4 May. On 3 May Rufus was inhibited by Iona.

Analysis. In the absence of an advance notice, the disposition would be reducible *ex capite inhibitionis* at Iona's instance. The advance notice, however, renders the inhibition ineffectual so far as the Rufus/Tara disposition is concerned.

There can also be entries in the Register of Inhibitions which, though not inhibitions, have inhibition-like effect, and these too are covered by an advance notice.[140] For instance the initial order or determination in a sequestration is registered in the Register of Inhibitions and, on being so registered, 'shall have the effect … of an inhibition'.[141] An advance notice protects against this. More is said about the relationship of an advance notice to insolvency in what follows.

---

137 LR(S)A 2012 s 61(1).
138 See Gretton and Reid (n 5) para 9-17.
139 Because the protection of the V/W disposition from the inhibition hangs on the effect of an unregistered private document, namely the V/W contract.
140 LR(S)A 2012 s 61(1)(b).
141 Bankruptcy (Scotland) Act 2016 s 26.

10.28 Sequestration, and trusts for behoof of creditors

As just mentioned, sequestration has an inhibition-like effect, against which an advance notice provides protection.

> *Example 17*
>
> A petition for the sequestration of Alan is made in the sheriff court on 4 June. A notice about that petition is registered in the Register of Inhibitions on 6 June.[142] At the time, Alan is selling to Barbara, and an advance notice, by him to her, is entered in the Land Register on 2 June. The Alan/Barbara missives are concluded on 7 June.
>
> *Analysis.* As missives are concluded after the deemed inhibition against Alan (which took effect on 6 June), any subsequent disposition granted by Alan to Barbara would normally be subject to the inhibition. However, the advance notice protects Barbara against the deemed inhibition provided that the disposition is registered within the protected period.

Also of concern to a buyer (or other grantee) is that the seller might be sequestrated about the time of the sale and the trustee in sequestration might take title away from the seller (either by transfer to another buyer, or by completing title in his own name) before the buyer can register. In fact the risk of this is slight, because a trustee in sequestration is subject to a 28-day handicap.[143] Nevertheless, in certain rare cases an advance notice could provide a buyer with protection that would not be provided by the 28-day handicap.

> *Example 18*
>
> Cosmo is selling to Dorabella, and grants to her an advance notice, which enters the Land Register on 3 March. On 5 March he delivers the disposition to her, and she presents it for registration on 6 April, ie just within the 35-day period. Cosmo is sequestrated with effect from 4 March, and his trustee in sequestration, Elfrieda, completes title, *qua* trustee, on 5 April, ie just outwith the 28-day handicap period.
>
> *Analysis.* The advance notice protects Dorabella. The Keeper, on receiving Dorabella's application, must accept it, and insert her name in the title sheet in place of Elfrieda's.

An advance notice can also protect against a trust deed for behoof of creditors. Trust deeds can give rise to a deemed inhibition,[144] and, depending on the timing, an advance notice may give protection against it. An advance notice may also protect against completion of title by the trustee, or a buyer from the trustee, as the following example illustrates.

> *Example 19*
>
> Janet is selling property to Keith and grants to him an advance notice which enters the Land Register on 1 May. On 4 May Janet grants to Theresa a trust deed, and Theresa completes title to the property by registration on 8 May. On 10 May the Janet/Keith disposition is lodged for registration.

---

142 B(S)A 2016 s 26.
143 B(S)A 2016 s 78.
144 B(S)A 2016 sch 4 para 3.

Analysis. Because of the advance notice, and because the Janet/Keith deed was presented for registration within the protected period, the Keeper will accept it,[145] and will delete Theresa's name from the proprietorship section of the title sheet.

10.29 Some things that an advance notice does not protect against

There are some things that an advance notice does not protect against.[146] It offers no protection against corporate insolvency affecting a seller (or other granter).[147] Nor does it protect against the risk that a floating charge might attach. It cannot help with the problem, wearisomely familiar to conveyancers, of the discharge of the standard security that is, for good reasons or bad (usually bad), unavailable at settlement. In such a case a solicitor's undertaking may be necessary. Finally, and at the risk of repetition, an advance notice can protect only against entries in the Land Register (or Register of Sasines) or the Register of Inhibitions; it offers no protection against anything else.

10.30 Advance notices and the offside goals rule

Under what is commonly called the 'offside goals rule',[148] if A grants a deed to B, contrary to an obligation that A owes to C, and B knew of that obligation, C can, in certain circumstances, reduce the A/B deed. The advance notice system is to a limited extent comparable with the offside goals rule.[149] In a sale by Sally to Boris, if Sally grants a competing deed to Freddie (who is in bad faith), which is registered before Boris applies for registration, then Boris, even without the benefit of an advance notice, may be able to reduce the Sally/Freddie deed. The system of advance notices means that in future the offside goals rule is less likely to be invoked.

There are, however, many differences, including the following. First, the protection afforded by an advance notice is limited to the protected period of 35 days; the offside goals rule is not limited in time. Secondly, the offside goals rule confers a right of court action; an advance notice operates immediately and automatically when Boris makes his application. Thirdly, the offside goals rule presupposes a personal right held by the protected person; an advance notice works whether or not Boris has yet acquired a personal right. Finally, the offside goals rule normally requires bad faith for it to be invoked; good or bad faith is not relevant to the workings of the advance notice system.

There could also be cases in which the two pull in opposite directions.

Example 20

On 1 June Sally contracts to sell to Boris. There is no advance notice. The disposition to Boris is delivered on 20 June and lodged with the Keeper on 22 June. On 2 June Sally

---

145 LR(S)A 2012 s 59(2).
146 Generally speaking, these would also not have been covered by a letter of obligation.
147 In contrast, an advance notice does provide some protection against the insolvency of sellers who are natural persons: see para 10.28 above.
148 The name derives from the comments of Lord Justice-Clerk Thomson in *Rodger (Builders) Ltd v Fawdry* 1950 SC 483. See eg K G C Reid, *The Law of Property in Scotland* (1996) paras 695 ff; J MacLeod, 'The Offside Goals Rule and Fraud on Creditors', in McCarthy, Chalmers and Bogle (n 6) 115.
149 Indeed the Scottish Law Commission considered, but rejected, the idea of abolishing the offside goals rule in relation to heritable property: see SLC Report 222 paras 14.61–14.65.

contracts to sell to Freddie. Freddie knows about Boris's contract. There is an advance notice in favour of Freddie, which enters the Register on 11 June. The disposition to Freddie is delivered on 21 June and lodged with the Keeper on 24 June.

Analysis. On 22 June Boris is registered as owner, but on 24 June Freddie is registered as owner, Boris's name being deleted. So the advance notice has enabled Freddie to prevail over Boris. But the offside goals rule will work the other way round. Boris has the right to reduce the Sally/Freddie disposition and so prevails in the end.

LEGAL REPORTS

10.31 Legal reports and advance notices

From a theoretical point of view, legal reports and advance notices are very different. They are also very different in their history, for whereas legal reports – more usually known as 'searches' – have always existed in one form or another, advance notices are a recent arrival, the creation of the 2012 Act. But from a practical point of view advance notices and legal reports are closely connected, both being pre-settlement steps aimed at protecting the grantee from title problems, and accordingly it is appropriate to cover legal reports in a chapter on advance notices.

10.32 Legal reports: some details

In respect of legal reports, little has changed, apart from nomenclature, from the system which was in operation before 8 December 2014. RoS offer legal reports of three types.[150] There is the legal report on unregistered property, as a preliminary to first registration.[151] This involves a search of the Register of Sasines and of the Register of Inhibitions, plus a search of the Land Register to confirm that the property is not already registered. The fee is currently £55. In practice this report will be combined with a plans report.[152] Then there is the legal report on registered property, which covers the Land Register and the Register of Inhibitions.[153] The fee is £50. Finally, there is the continuation report which updates either of the previous reports.[154] It can be obtained only within six months, after which period a new report would be needed. There is no fee, unless a repeat continuation report is sought, in which case the fee is £25.

As well as the deeds long familiar to conveyancers, legal reports now disclose advance notices and, in the relatively few cases in which they are used, caveats.[155]

Reports can be ordered through the RoS portal and are usually issued within 24 hours. Reports are certified to the end of the working day immediately before the day of despatch.[156]

---

150 See Registers of Scotland, *General Guidance: Reports* (v.03, 2015). Independent search firms offer similar reports.
151 This corresponds to the old form 10.
152 For plans reports, see para 5.23.
153 This corresponds to the old form 12.
154 This corresponds to the old forms 11 and 13.
155 For caveats, see ch 18.
156 Registers of Scotland, *FAQs: Reports* Pre-Report FAQs, Q 6.

Chapter 11

Inaccuracies and their Rectification

11.1 Inaccuracies and rectification

The Land Register seeks to show, for each plot of land, the boundaries of the plot, the name of the owner, the rights in security, real burdens and other encumbrances by which it is affected, and various other matters. Happily, the information provided is usually correct;[1] but even where it is not correct, acquirers in good faith can, by and large, rely on what the Register says (and does not say) and will be protected if it turns out to be wrong.[2] Where mistakes do occur, they are likely to come about in one of three ways. There can be an error in a deed presented for registration such as to make the deed invalid due, for example, to forgery or the absence of title in the granter.[3] Or there can be administrative error by the Keeper in giving effect to a deed, so that, for example, the wrong person is entered as owner in the title sheet, or a title boundary is shown incorrectly. Or, finally, an entry on the Register which is correct when first made can become incorrect due to a later event, such as the dissolution of a company named as owner, or the extinction of a right by negative prescription. Although statistics are not available, it appears that administrative errors are much more common than errors arising in any other way.[4] These occur particularly in first registrations, when unruly sets of Sasine deeds must be reduced to the bland certainties of a title sheet; as first registrations diminish and then disappear, so too will occurrences of this type of error.

Of course many errors, such as typing mistakes, are trivial and may seem hardly worth the trouble of correcting.[5] But some errors are serious and go to the very heart of the rights and obligations which affect a property. To the extent that the Register is 'inaccurate', it can – indeed under the 2012 Act it must – be 'rectified' by the Keeper;[6] for, whatever the position may have been under the previous law,[7] inaccuracies today are no longer perpetuated for the benefit of proprietors in possession. But the Keeper can only rectify an inaccuracy which is 'manifest'

---

1 Subject to a small number of off-Register rights such as short leases, as to which see paras 4.26–4.28 above.
2 Land Registration etc (Scotland) Act 2012 ss 86–93: see ch 12 below.
3 The Register is not inaccurate if the deed is merely voidable (as opposed to void): see para 11.4 below.
4 This has certainly been a matter of frequent complaint by solicitors: see eg the letters published at (2015) 60 JLSS Nov/6 and Dec/6. For possible *ex gratia* payments by RoS, see para 14.12 below. If this is correct, it is also not new. Lewis Ockrent, who was himself an employee of the Registers, observed that 'The history of litigation on registration goes to show that quite as much trouble had been caused to the lieges through carelessness on the part of those who were entrusted with the working of the registers as may be ascribed to defects in the primary Registration Act': see *Land Rights: An Enquiry into the History of Registration for Publication in Scotland* (1942) 84.
5 For a special mechanism for correcting such errors, see para 11.5 below.
6 LR(S)A 2012 s 80: see paras 11.13–11.19 below.
7 For which see para 2.9 above.

and beyond doubt,[8] a threshold requirement which, as we will see,[9] can be hard to meet. Where it is not met, the inaccuracy must perforce remain on the Register.

MEANING OF 'INACCURACY'

11.2 Introduction

Rectification is only possible in respect of 'inaccuracies' on the Register. The term, however, has a wide (statutory) meaning.[10] In essence, the Register is inaccurate when it 'misstates what the position is in law or in fact' – when, in other words, the Register says one thing and the true legal or factual position is something different.[11] So if the owner of Blackmains is Alan and the Register says that it is Barbara, the Register is inaccurate. It is no less inaccurate if Blackmains is subject to a standard security which the Register fails to disclose. As these examples show, the Register can be inaccurate either by commission or omission – by 'its wrongful utterances' or 'its wrongful silences'.[12] If the Register omits information which it is bound to include (such as the standard security), then it is inaccurate to that extent. But, equally, if it includes information which ought not to be included or which ought to be included but is not correctly stated, the Register is also inaccurate. Both senses of 'inaccuracy' are considered more fully below.

Only those parts of the Register concerned with the existence or non-existence of rights – only, in other words, the title sheet record and the cadastral map – can contain inaccuracies and so be subject to rectification.[13] The remaining parts of the Register, the archive record and the application record, do no more than store documents and cannot be inaccurate in this sense.

11.3 Inaccuracy by omission

The 2012 Act is prescriptive as to what must be included in title sheets and the cadastral map, and other legislation may add to these requirements. Where the Register omits that which is required to be included, whether as a right[14] or as an encumbrance,[15] the Register is inaccurate to that extent.[16] This is inaccuracy by omission.

The mandatory content of title sheets and the cadastral map was considered in chapter 4,[17] and is also set out fully and clearly in the legislation.[18] Here a

---

8 LR(S)A 2012 s 80(1).
9 Paragraph 11.14 below.
10 LR(S)A 2012 s 65: see Scottish Law Commission, *Report No 222 on Land Registration* (2010) ('SLC Report 222') paras 17.40–17.47.
11 LR(S)A 2012 s 61(1)(a). Whereas under the 1979 Act an accuracy could be either 'actual' or 'bijural' (see para 2.8 above), all inaccuracies under the 2012 Act are 'actual', ie the Register really is wrong.
12 SLC Report 222 para 17.41.
13 LR(S)A 2012 s 80(1). See also SLC Report 222 para 17.47. For the parts of the Register, see s 2, and ch 4 above.
14 In which case it has been omitted from the property section (A section) of the title sheet.
15 In which case it has been omitted from either the securities section (C section) or the burdens section (D section) of the title sheet.
16 LR(S)A 2012 s 65(1)(b), (2)(b).
17 See paras 4.13–4.19 and 4.30 above.
18 LR(S)A 2012 ss 3–13; Land Register Rules etc (Scotland) Regulations 2014, SSI 2014/150 ('LRR 2014') r 12.

summary must suffice. A title sheet must describe the plot of land, by reference to the cadastral map, and give the particulars of any servitudes and other incorporeal pertinents associated with it. It must also name and design the owner, and list all heritable securities, long leases, real burdens, servitudes, and public rights of way by which the plot is encumbered. The cadastral map in turn must show, for each cadastral unit, the cadastral unit number, the boundaries of the unit, and the title number of any registered lease relating to the unit.

Where inaccuracy by omission occurs, it is often because an encumbrance or a pertinent is overlooked at the time of first registration. But inaccuracy can also come about in other ways, such as from the registration of a forged discharge (leading to the deletion of a standard security or other encumbrance), or the off-register creation or extinction of rights of certain types.

Three types of off-register rights (viewed as encumbrances)[19] are required to be included in a title sheet (in the burdens section): servitudes created by prescription, public rights of way, and path orders made under s 22 of the Land Reform (Scotland) Act 2003.[20] The omission of any of these is an inaccuracy, and one which is likely to be more common than inaccuracies of any other kind. For if a servitude, for example, is created by prescription, there is no particular reason why the event should come to be recorded on the Register, and no dedicated mechanism by which this might be done. No doubt an applicant for registration might, in due course, draw attention to a prescriptive servitude, especially in cases of first registration and where the plot being registered is the benefited property.[21] But it is just as likely that the servitude, having been created off-register, will remain off-register for the foreseeable future. There is nothing surprising in this: the inclusion in the Register of rights which were created by means other than registration is an intractable problem for any system of land registration.[22] Whether included or not, the rights remain valid; but the Register is inaccurate.

Over time an inaccuracy by omission might cease to be an inaccuracy at all. That important topic is explored later in the chapter.[23]

11.4 Inaccuracy by commission

The Register can be inaccurate on account of what it says as much as on account of what it does not say. It is inaccurate if what it says is not true.[24] It is also inaccurate if what it says, while true, ought not to be on the Register at all.[25]

---

19 On off-register rights more generally, see paras 4.26–4.28 above.
20 LR(S)A 2012 s 9(1)(a), (d), (e): see para 4.17 above. Others, such as short leases, are not to be included. The qualification 'in so far as known to the Keeper' in respect of public rights of way is puzzling. No off-register right can be included if it is not known to the Keeper.
21 See paras 4.28 and 8.23 above. It would then enter the title sheet of the benefited property as part of the registration process (though not by actual registration of the right itself), and of the burdened property (if already on the Land Register) by rectification.
22 Under the 1979 Act a selection of such rights were 'noted' on the Register under s 6(4) but only where drawn to the Keeper's attention. The term 'noting' is not carried forward to the 2012 Act, but the entering on the Register of off-register rights is its exact functional equivalent.
23 Paragraphs 11.6–11.12 below.
24 LR(S)A 2012 s 65(1)(a).
25 LR(S)A 2012 s 65(1)(c): the Register is inaccurate if it 'includes anything the inclusion of which is not expressly or impliedly permitted by or under an enactment'. See also s 10(4): 'The Keeper must not enter or incorporate by reference in a title sheet any rights or obligations except in so far as their entry is authorised by an enactment.'

Only material whose registration is authorised by some enactment should be in the Register.[26]

Relatively speaking, the second of these is uncommon and causes little in the way of trouble. Certainly there is unlikely to be registration of a deed of a type that is not registrable, such as, say, a short lease,[27] although purported real burdens which, owing to some defect in creation,[28] are only contractual in effect do sometimes find their way into the D section of title sheets.

More important and troublesome is an entry which, while of a type eligible for inclusion, is simply wrong. If, for example, a deed is invalid, its registration can confer no rights;[29] hence to enter its grantee on the Register is to make the Register inaccurate. A deed can be invalid for many reasons, including forgery, lack of capacity, absence of title, errors in drafting, and defective execution. The result, however, is always the same: the deed is void and is not improved by registration. So if Alan owns land, and Betty, forging his signature on a disposition in her own favour, is registered as owner, the owner remains Alan and the Register is inaccurate in showing the owner as Betty.

But whereas a void deed results in inaccuracy, a deed that is merely voidable does not. For a voidable deed is valid until it is reduced and the extract decree of reduction registered;[30] before that moment arrives – and often it will never arrive – the deed is valid, and the Register is correct to show the grantee as holder of the right.[31]

Even a valid deed can lead to inaccuracy if the Keeper fails to give proper effect to its terms. In practice this is a significant cause of inaccuracies, especially in respect of the location of boundaries. So if a disposition conveys a one-hectare plot and the grantee is registered as owner of an additional 100 square metres, the Register is inaccurate to the extent of the additional area.[32] In one case, however, this is excused. In plotting boundaries the Keeper is subject to the limitations of the OS map on which the cadastral map is based. Accordingly, the legislation provides that there is no inaccuracy where an imprecision reflects the OS map itself, provided it is within the published accuracy tolerances relevant to the scale of the map involved.[33]

An entry can be accurate when made but become inaccurate due to a later event, such as the extinction, by negative prescription, of a registered servitude. But the opposite is much more common, that is to say, inaccurate entries that

26 For the reasons for this policy, see para 4.10 above.
27 Unlike eg prescriptive servitudes, a short lease (ie a lease of 20 years or less) is an example of an off-register right which is not to be included on the Register.
28 Typically, a failure to comply with the rules as to permissible content set out in the Title Conditions (Scotland) Act 2003 s 3.
29 The 2012 Act has no equivalent of the 1979 Act's Midas touch (for which see paras 2.17 and 2.13 above). See eg LR(S)A 2012 s 49(4) and s 50(2), and also para 9.20 above. Hence a transactional error of this kind is not cured by registration.
30 Conveyancing (Scotland) Act 1924 s 46A(1)(b).
31 LR(S)A 2012 s 65(4): see para 6.12 above. Equally, as s 65(4) makes clear, the Register is not inaccurate in giving effect to the original terms of a deed which has since been judicially rectified under s 8 of the Law Reform (Miscellaneous Provisions) (Scotland) Act 1985 until such time as the extract decree of rectification has been registered under s 8A of the 1985 Act. For the interaction of judicial rectification with land registration, see para 6.13 above.
32 See para 11.25 below.
33 LR(S)A 2012 s 65(3). For the tolerances in question, see para 5.4 above.

become, or at least form the basis of, accurate entries as a result of a future event. That topic is pursued in some detail below.[34]

11.5 Typographical errors

Typographical errors may be too trivial and obvious to reach the threshold for inaccuracy of misstating the position in law or in fact. Nonetheless they can still be corrected by the Keeper under a supplementary provision contained in the Land Registration Rules.[35] But while there is a power to correct errors of this sort, there is no duty to do so, ie no duty corresponding to the duty to rectify, and it is open to the Keeper to leave the error uncorrected. RoS guidance gives the misspelling of words such as 'disposition', 'right' or 'subjects' as examples of typographical errors, but considers that the misstatement of a person's name in the proprietorship or securities section would amount to an inaccuracy that must be amended by rectification.[36]

FROM INACCURACY TO ACCURACY

11.6 Introduction

Sometimes inaccuracies are resolved by means other than rectification. Three such routes can be identified. (i) First, by the operation of prescription, either positive or negative, an entry on the Register which was originally inaccurate can come to represent the true legal position and so be accurate. (ii) Secondly, certain inaccuracies can be cured by transfer of the property to an acquirer in good faith. (iii) Thirdly, many inaccuracies which existed under the 1979 Act were cured by force of law on 8 December 2014, the day on which the 2012 Act came into force. Each of these falls to be considered in turn.

11.7 Prescription

In some cases, inaccuracies by commission can be cured by positive prescription, and inaccuracies by omission by negative prescription.

A defective title can be cured by positive prescription provided that the requirements for that doctrine are met. These are considered more fully in chapter 17,[37] but in brief they are that the registered title-holder possesses for ten years on the basis of a registered deed which is sufficient in respect of its terms to constitute the real right in question.[38] So if, in 2016, Jean is registered as owner of John's land on the basis of an invalid disposition, no change in ownership occurs, and the Register is inaccurate in showing Jean as owner and not John. But if the disposition is sufficient in respect of its terms to found prescription,[39] and if Jean is in possession of the land, then in 2026 Jean will become owner (John at the same moment ceasing to be owner), and the Register will then be accurate.

---

34 Paragraphs 11.6–11.12 below.
35 LRR 2014 r 17. This power can only be used in respect of 'an error which is not an inaccuracy'.
36 Registers of Scotland, *General Guidance: Inaccuracy and Rectification* (v.02, 2015) 1.
37 Paragraphs 17.1–17.9 below.
38 Prescription and Limitation (Scotland) Act 1973 s 1.
39 A forged deed is not sufficient to found prescription if the registered proprietor (Jean) knew of the forgery at the time of registration: see PL(S)A 1973 s 1(2)(b).

An inaccuracy by omission is cured if the right omitted from the Register is extinguished by negative prescription due to its non-exercise. The usual period for negative prescription is twenty years,[40] but real burdens are extinguished after five[41] and can also be extinguished by acquiescence and by absence of interest to enforce.[42]

11.8 Transfer to a good-faith acquirer

Many inaccuracies by *omission* are cured on the first occasion, after the omission, that the property is transferred to a good-faith acquirer.[43] The scope of the rule varies depending on whether the title sheet relates to ownership (ie a plot of land) or long lease.[44] (i) A person acquiring ownership (ie a disponee) acting in good faith takes free of all omitted encumbrances other than leases and rights, such as prescriptive servitudes, which were constituted off-register.[45] (ii) A good-faith assignee of a long lease takes free of omitted heritable securities and leasehold conditions (other than an obligation to pay rent).[46] In both cases the effect of the transfer is for the omitted encumbrance to be extinguished.[47] Good faith is judged at the time of the acquisition, which normally means the time of registration.[48]

In the case of inaccuracies by *commission*, the position is more complex and less complete. There is no cure as such; but a person whose appearance on the Register as either owner or tenant under a long lease is an inaccuracy can (despite not being owner or, as the case may be, tenant) confer a valid title on a good-faith acquirer.[49] Certain other conditions must also be met, of which the most important is that the land was possessed for a year by the granter of the disposition or assignation, or by the granter and then by the grantee consecutively.[50] Take again the example of John and Jean.[51] Jean is registered as owner of John's land on the basis of an invalid disposition. John is the owner and the Register is thus inaccurate. But if Jean, having possessed for a year or more, dispones to Karen, who knows nothing about the infirmity of Jean's title, then Karen becomes owner on registration, John loses ownership,[52] and the Register is accurate in showing Karen as owner.

This 'realignment' rule is confined to ownership and long lease. If the wrong person is registered as holder of a standard security or proper liferent, the purported assignation of the right by such a person is ineffective, and the Register remains inaccurate as before.

---

40 PL(S)A 1973 s 8.
41 Title Conditions (Scotland) Act 2003 s 18.
42 TC(S)A 2003 ss 16 and 17.
43 For full details, see paras 12.18, 12.19 and 12.22 below.
44 All title sheets must relate to one or the other: see LR(S)A 2012 s 3(1), (2).
45 LR(S)A 2012 s 91.
46 LR(S)A 2012 s 92.
47 LR(S)A 2012 ss 91(1)(b) and 92(1)(b). Compensation is then paid by the Keeper to the (former) right-holder under s 94: see paras 14.2 and 14.3 below.
48 But could be later if the right were acquired by virtue of realignment (discussed below): see LR(S)A 2012 ss 86(4)(b) and 88(4)(b).
49 LR(S)A 2012 ss 86 and 88. The rule applies equally where the deed is granted on behalf of such a person, eg by the person's executor: see ss 87 and 89. For full details, see paras 12.8–12.17 and 12.21 below.
50 LR(S)A 2012 ss 86(3)(a) and 88(3)(a).
51 See para 11.7 above.
52 And is then entitled to compensation from the Keeper under s 94: see paras 14.2 and 14.3 below.

11.9 Transitional: the miracle of 8 December 2014

Transitional provisions applied in respect of inaccuracies that existed on the eve of the day when the 2012 Act came into force (8 December 2014). They were designed to bring an end to the complexities of bijuralism which resulted from the Keeper's Midas touch under the legislation of 1979.[53] In respect of any given inaccuracy, the starting point is this question: could the inaccuracy have been rectified immediately before 8 December 2014, ie under the law set out in the 1979 Act?

If the answer is that, due to the provisions of s 9 of the 1979 Act, the inaccuracy could *not* have been rectified, then it ceased to be an inaccuracy on 8 December 2014, the *de facto* position (no rectification, despite the inaccuracy) being thus elevated into the *de jure* position (no inaccuracy at all).[54]

If, conversely, the inaccuracy *could* have been rectified, then, on 8 December 2014, the real rights of the parties concerned became what they would have been had rectification in fact taken place.[55] Typically, this led to a reallocation of rights – for example, to a person not named on the Register becoming owner in place of someone else who was. Importantly, however, the Register was not *actually* rectified on 8 December.[56] Whatever else it can do, legislation cannot re-write Registers, and so the erroneous entry or omission remained in place as before. But, as the Register was now actually inaccurate,[57] the 2012 Act placed the Keeper under an obligation to rectify it.[58]

Following these events, indemnity became payable in the usual way (subject to the usual limitations) to those who had suffered loss, ie (i) to the person (formerly) entitled to seek rectification in the first case and (ii) to the person who had lost rights in the second.[59]

The miracle of 8 December 2014 operated more at the level of form than of substance. In cases where the inaccuracy was cured, the registered proprietor was unlikely to have been troubled by rectification anyway. But even in cases where the inaccuracy was not cured, the registered proprietor was hardly less secure than before. In theory, it is true, he had lost a right (in cases of inaccuracy by commission) or been made subject to a right (in cases of inaccuracy by omission). But the chances that the person entitled to do so would assert this against him were no higher than before.[60] Meanwhile the Register itself remained unaltered. No one was notified about the change. And as for the future (and depending on the type of inaccuracy), the prospect was now opened up, under the 2012 Act,

---

53 Scottish Law Commission, *Discussion Paper No 130 on Land Registration: Miscellaneous Issues* (2005) ('SLC DP 130') part 9; SLC Report 222 paras 36.9–36.15. For bijuralism and the Midas touch, see paras 2.8 and 2.13 above.
54 LR(S)A 2012 sch 4 para 22.
55 LR(S)A 2012 sch 4 para 17. This makes clear that the redistribution occurs only 'as from that day'. Rectification under the 1979 Act was not retrospective: see *Stevenson-Hamilton's Exrs v McStay* 1999 SLT 1175; *Keeper of the Registers of Scotland v MRS Hamilton Ltd* 2000 SC 271.
56 The expression 'deemed rectification' has occasionally been used.
57 As opposed to bijurally inaccurate (for which see para 2.8 above). In other words, the Register said one thing and the true legal or factual position was something different.
58 This is because, under LR(S)A 2012 s 80, the Keeper must rectify a manifest inaccuracy where what is needed to do so is manifest: see paras 11.13 and 11.14 below.
59 LR(S)A 2012 sch 4 paras 19–21 and 23–24: see paras 13.21–13.23 and 14.4 below.
60 Assertion would be by way of seeking rectification under LR(S)A 2012 s 80, ie by making the 'deemed rectification' an actual rectification. This is possible because the Register is inaccurate: see sch 4 para 17(b).

of being able to dispose of the property to a good-faith third acquirer free of the inaccuracy.[61]

11.10 Could the Keeper have rectified on 7 December 2014?

As the fate of an inaccuracy on 8 December 2014 depended on whether rectification could have taken place the day before, that inquiry must continue to be made today whenever a title contains an inaccuracy from that period.

Under the law in force immediately before 8 December 2014 the Keeper could rectify an inaccuracy unless – as was, however, typically the case – this was to the prejudice of a proprietor in possession.[62] By 'proprietor' was meant the person registered as such in the proprietorship section of the title sheet, or in other words the registered owner or (in the case of a leasehold title sheet) the registered tenant.[63] The holders of lesser rights were not 'proprietors' in this sense and so were not protected against rectification. The meaning of 'possession' was complicated and contested, and is discussed later in the chapter.[64]

Rectification was to the prejudice of a proprietor in possession where it was in respect of a 'bijural', but not an 'actual', inaccuracy.[65] An actual inaccuracy occurred where the Register was simply wrong about something (as for instance where it named as the holder of a right a company that had been dissolved), so that its correction did not change the legal or factual position. A bijural accuracy was where the Register was correct when judged by the law as laid down by the 1979 Act, and in particular by the Midas touch, but wrong where judged by the ordinary principles of property law.[66] So if the Register showed Jean as owner (Jean having registered an invalid disposition) and not John (who was the previous owner and should, under ordinary principles of property law, be owner still), the entry was a bijural (not an actual) inaccuracy. As only bijural inaccuracies involved the suppression of rights, it was only their rectification which could be to the prejudice of a proprietor in possession.[67]

Even where it was to the prejudice of a proprietor in possession, however, rectification could still go ahead if any one of five circumstances applied.[68] These were (i) where the purpose was to note or correct a right which was constituted off-register;[69] (ii) where all parties consented in writing;[70] (iii) where the inaccuracy was caused wholly or substantially by the fraud or carelessness of the proprietor in possession or a solicitor or other agent acting for that proprietor; (iv) where the

---

61 LR(S)A 2012 ss 86–92. See para 11.8 above and paras 12.8–12.18 below. Even where no disposal took place, the inaccuracy might be cured by positive prescription, although this would require the taking and keeping of possession for ten years.
62 LR(S)A 1979 s 9: see para 2.9 above.
63 *Kaur v Singh* 1999 SC 180; Scottish Law Commission, *Discussion Paper No 125 on Land Registration: Void and Voidable Titles* (2004) ('SLC DP 125') para 4.12.
64 Paragraph 11.12 below.
65 It is for that reason that paras 17–24 of LR(S)A 2012 sch 4 are headed 'bijural inaccuracies' (being the only occurrence of this expression in any legislation).
66 See para 2.8 above.
67 *Rivendale v Clark* [2015] CSIH 27, 2015 SC 558, paras 34 and 35 per Lord Drummond Young.
68 LR(S)A 1979 s 9(3): see G L Gretton and K G C Reid, *Conveyancing* (4th edn, 2011) para 8-16.
69 Or 'overriding interest' to use the terminology of the 1979 Act. For off-register rights, see paras 4.26–4.28 above.
70 In practice this would only have occurred on or before 7 December 2014 if an application for rectification was pending at that time. Consent given *after* that date does not count, as LR(S)A 2012 sch 4 paras 17 and 22 are concerned with whether there was power to rectify *on* that date.

rectification related to a matter in respect of which indemnity had been excluded;[71] and (v) where the rectification was consequential on the making of an order for judicial rectification of a deed under s 8 of the Law Reform (Miscellaneous Provisions) (Scotland) Act 1985.

11.11 Some examples

The rules described above are complex and the 1979 Act is increasingly forgotten and unfamiliar. It may therefore be helpful to give some examples of the operation of the transitional provisions.[72] All the events described should be read as having taken place prior to 8 December 2014.

Example 1
Anne owned land. She granted a disposition to Billy who was registered as owner. The disposition was void due to Anne's lack of legal capacity. Billy was in good faith.

Analysis. Billy became owner under the 1979 Act but, on the basis of ordinary property law, Anne should have been owner. Hence there was a bijural inaccuracy. If Billy was in possession, he would have been protected from rectification as a proprietor in possession. In that case his ownership ceased to be an inaccuracy on 8 December 2014, and no rectification can now take place. Conversely, if Billy was not in possession, ownership reverted to Anne on 8 December 2014. As a result, the bijural accuracy under the 1979 Act became an (actual) inaccuracy under the 2012 Act. Rectification can now take place to replace Billy's name with Anne's.

Example 2
Colin owned land. Stealing Colin's identity and forging his signature, his brother, David, granted a standard security over the land to the Edinburgh Bank and absconded with the money he had raised on the basis of the forged security. The security was registered.

Analysis. The Edinburgh Bank held a valid right in security under the 1979 Act but, due to the forgery, there was a bijural inaccuracy. As a heritable creditor could not be a proprietor in possession, the Bank had no protection against rectification. Hence the Bank lost the security on 8 December 2014, the bijural inaccuracy under the 1979 Act becoming an (actual) inaccuracy under the 2012 Act. Rectification can now take place to remove the security.

Example 3
Fergus, the owner of land, granted a standard security in favour of the Georgian Bank. The Bank registered the security. Later Fergus forged and registered a discharge, whereupon the security was removed from the title sheet.

Analysis. The security was extinguished under the system of the 1979 Act. But because the deed of discharge was a forgery, and so void, the omission of the security from the title sheet resulted in a bijural inaccuracy. Even if Fergus was in possession, the fact that his forgery caused the inaccuracy meant that he had no protection against rectification. Hence the security became valid again on 8 December 2014, the bijural inaccuracy under the 1979 Act becoming an (actual) inaccuracy under the 2012 Act.[73] Rectification to restore the security can now take place.

---

71 Ie under LR(S)A 1979 s 12(2).
72 For more examples, see SLC Report No 222 para 36.13.
73 This would not, however, be retrospective. If, therefore, another security had been granted before 8 December 2014, the restored security would be postponed to it: see *Santander UK plc v Keeper of the Registers of Scotland* [2013] CSOH 24, 2013 SLT 362 (where a security was restored by rectification under the 1979 Act).

11.12 The meaning of 'possession'

As already mentioned, the main barrier to the rectification of inaccuracies, before 8 December 2014, was where it would be to the prejudice of a proprietor in possession. The meaning of 'proprietor' has already been discussed.[74] In this section we consider the meaning of 'possession'.

In the absence of a definition in the 1979 Act, it took a long time to develop a clear idea of how a registered proprietor was to demonstrate the 'possession' needed to protect his title.[75] As case law began to accumulate, however, in the final years of the Act, it became possible to set out the rules with a reasonable degree of confidence. We list the eleven rules that appear to have emerged.

First, although the factual question to be determined, strictly, was whether the registered proprietor[76] was in possession, it was not usually possible to do this without considering the possessory status of the 'true' owner, ie of the person who would be owner if the inaccuracy on the Register were to be rectified.[77] So to ask whether the registered proprietor was in possession was often to ask which of the two parties – the registered proprietor or the 'true' owner – was in possession.[78]

Secondly, the relevant date for determining possession was 7 December 2014.[79] Nonetheless – and this is the third point – it was usually necessary to look at the state of possession *before* this time.[80] This was because, in order to *be* in possession, one first had to *acquire* possession, and the acquisitive act, or main acquisitive act, might have taken place some time before. In one case the Lands Tribunal was even prepared to consider the possession of the parties' predecessors.[81]

Fourthly, once possession had been acquired, a person was taken to remain in possession without further possessory acts.[82] So in one case, for example, the Lands Tribunal found that some earlier possessory acts, neither repeated nor challenged in the period that followed, were sufficient to constitute possession.[83]

Fifthly, it was sometimes difficult for the registered proprietor to demonstrate acquisition of possession. '[S]ome significant element of physical control' was required.[84] On the other hand – and this is the sixth point – possession was measured

---

74 Paragraph 11.10 above.
75 Though it should be noted that possession would not protect the title in every case: in particular, possession would provide no protection where there had been an exclusion of indemnity, or where the inaccuracy was the fault of the party in question: see para 11.10 above.
76 This is because 'proprietor' in this context meant, not the person who ought to be owner (the 'true' or 'should-be' owner) but rather the person who, because he was registered as owner, *was* the owner, because of the 1979 Act's gift to the Keeper of the Midas touch. See eg *Nicol v Keeper of the Registers of Scotland* 2013 SLT (Lands Tr) 56, para 25.
77 *Burr v Keeper of the Registers of Scotland*, 12 Nov 2010, Lands Tribunal, para 24; *Nicol* (n 76) para 28.
78 For a challenge to this approach, see *Gray v Keeper of the Registers of Scotland* 2014 SLT (Lands Tr) 117, discussed in K G C Reid and G L Gretton, *Conveyancing 2014* (2015) 168–69.
79 LR(S)A 2012 sch 4 paras 17 and 22.
80 *Safeway Stores plc v Tesco Stores Ltd* 2004 SC 29, para 80; *Rivendale v Keeper of the Registers of Scotland*, 30 Oct 2013, Lands Tr, para 60.
81 *Mathers v Keeper of the Registers of Scotland* 2015 GWD 3-68, para 40.
82 *Tesco Stores Ltd v Keeper of the Registers of Scotland* 2001 SLT (Lands Tr) 23, 36F.
83 *Rivendale* (n 80) para 60, affd [2015] CSIH 27, 2015 SC 558.
84 *Safeway Stores plc* (n 80) para 77. Lord Hamilton somewhat detracted from the effect of this statement by adding, later in the same sentence, that 'possession' suggests 'actual use or enjoyment, to a more than minimal extent'. In *Gray* (n 78) the Lands Tribunal (para 81) expressed 'some reservations about the reference to activities being "more than a minimal extent". That might be an appropriate requirement in some contexts but it may distract from the need for assessment to

by the nature of the property being possessed,⁸⁵ and in the case of uncultivated or open ground, the number of possessory acts needed might be rather small.⁸⁶

Seventhly, where, as often, it was only a part of the property in the title sheet which was in dispute, it was possible for possession of other parts of the same property to be regarded as possession of the disputed part – even if few or no acts had taken place on the disputed part itself. But for this rule to apply the disputed part must have been 'an integral element of the registered subjects viewed as a whole'⁸⁷ amounting to a single 'unit',⁸⁸ and whether that was so depended on the layout and use of the subjects.⁸⁹ In one case, for example, the area in dispute comprised two distinct elements – garden ground and a track – so that possession of one element could not be regarded as possession of the other.⁹⁰

Eighthly, civil possession – in other words indirect possession, through family members or tenants or the like – was the equal of ordinary (ie natural) possession.⁹¹

Ninthly, as well as the physical elements of possession, there had to be the necessary mental element. Possession, in Scots law as in Roman, requires *animus* as well as *corpus*.⁹² That mental element is possession as owner.⁹³ For that reason a person did not possess in the necessary sense if he was unaware that his registered title extended to the area in question.⁹⁴ But good faith was not needed: a proprietor was entitled to stand on his registered title even if he knew it to be incorrect.⁹⁵

Tenthly, each case turned on its own facts and circumstances. As the Lands Tribunal emphasised:⁹⁶

> There has in fact been some authoritative guidance from court cases, as well as one or two cases before this Tribunal, on what is meant by 'possession' in this context, although it is fair to say that the situations in which the issue has to be considered will be particular to every case.

Finally, there was a statutory presumption that the registered proprietor was indeed in possession on the relevant day, ie 7 December 2014.⁹⁷ In the absence of other

---

have regard to the extent of use appropriate to the nature of the subjects.' On the requirement for physical possession, see also *Campbell-Gray v Keeper of the Registers of Scotland* 2015 SLT (Lands Tr) 147, para 62.
85 *Gray* (n 78) para 81: 'The type of acting required to establish possession depends on the nature of the subjects.' See also para 83.
86 See *Gray* (n 78) but compare *Burton v Keeper of the Registers of Scotland* 2014 SLT (Lands Tr) 69 (which, however, seems to give too little weight to the possessory acts by the registered proprietor).
87 *Safeway Stores plc* (n 80) para 77.
88 *Gray* (n 78) para 80.
89 *Burr* (n 77) para 26.
90 *Rivendale* (n 80) paras 54 and 55. See also *Mathers* (n 81) paras 44 ff.
91 *Kaur v Singh* 1999 SC 180, 191G per Lord President Rodger; *Rivendale v Clark* [2015] CSIH 27, 2015 SC 558, para 32 per Lord Drummond Young.
92 See eg K G C Reid, *The Law of Property in Scotland* (1996) para 117.
93 *Gray* (n 78) para 82: 'if a person understands that the effect of the law is to make him owner of the land and he acts as if he was, we are entirely satisfied that is sufficient mental element to give his actings the character of possession'.
94 As for example during the period before he has received a copy of his title sheet on registration: see *Gray* (n 78) para 84.
95 *Gray* (n 78) paras 56–71; cf *McKenna v Keeper of the Registers of Scotland*, 21 Aug 2015, Lands Tr, para 25.
96 *Nicol* (n 76) para 26.
97 LR(S)A 2012 sch 4 para 18.

evidence, therefore, the proprietor would qualify for protection from rectification. As the years go by and 7 December 2014 becomes more distant (so that definite evidence about possession at that time may become increasingly hard to recover), this presumption will become of increasing importance.

RECTIFICATION

11.13 A duty to rectify

As a general rule, the Keeper must rectify any inaccuracy which comes to her attention. This, however, is subject to qualifications which, by contrast to the 1979 Act, are grounded only in practicalities.[98] The important requirement that the inaccuracy be 'manifest' is discussed in the next paragraph. A second, and minor, limitation connected with titles on which prescription is still running is discussed later, in the context of prescription.[99] A final restriction is where it is not clear – 'manifest' in the words of the Act – what must be done in order to carry out the rectification.[100] This has its origins in an apprehension by the Scottish Law Commission that 'occasionally it might not be clear what form the rectification should take'.[101] No example is suggested by the Law Commission, but RoS have managed to think of one. '[W]here the *pro indiviso* shares in a common area do not add up to one, it is obvious that an inaccuracy exists. However, since the Keeper will not necessarily know in which title or titles the problem stems from, it may not be obvious how to fix it.'[102] A more common example is where two title sheets overlap as to area, so that the fact of inaccuracy (competing titles to the same area) is manifest but not how it should be resolved.[103] In cases like this – and there will not be many – the Act directs the Keeper to enter a note identifying the inaccuracy in the title sheet or, as the case may be, the cadastral map.[104]

11.14 But only where the inaccuracy is 'manifest'

As the Keeper is not a member of the judiciary and does not conduct judicial proceedings, her ability to determine matters of fact is seriously limited.[105] Where the existence of an inaccuracy has neither been conceded by the parties involved, nor determined by a court, her position is evidently a difficult one, and even before the 2012 Act the practice had developed that, in the absence of such concession, or such judicial determination, she would not effect a rectification unless the evidence that the Register was inaccurate was incontestable.[106] The 2012 Act confirmed this long-standing practice by providing that an inaccuracy is to be rectified only

---

98 The main restriction under the 1979 Act was the desire to protect proprietors in possession against rectification: see para 2.9 above.
99 LR(S)A 2012 s 81: see para 17.6 below.
100 LR(S)A 2012 s 80(2).
101 SLC Report 222 para 18.12.
102 *General Guidance: Inaccuracy and Rectification* (n 36) 2.
103 Paragraph 11.24 below. Since the designated day it is no longer possible for the Keeper to create overlapping title sheets in this way: see LR(S)A 2012 s 12(2), and para 5.11 above.
104 LR(S)A 2012 s 80(4).
105 Paragraph 3.19 above.
106 See eg *Balfour v Keeper of the Registers of Scotland* 2015 SLT (Lands Tr) 185, para 10.

where it is 'manifest'. The Scottish Law Commission glossed the word 'manifest' as meaning where the inaccuracy is 'virtually certain' or 'perfectly clear' or 'not reasonably disputable'.[107] The issue is not about substance but about evidential standard.[108]

This means that where someone alleges that a title sheet is inaccurate, but this is not conceded by the other interested party (or parties), and the evidence available to the Keeper falls short of demonstrating to the Keeper, to the 'manifest' standard, that the allegation is correct, the next step for the person who desires rectification is to seek judicial determination of the issue. This can take place either in the ordinary courts or under the new jurisdiction conferred by the 2012 Act on the Lands Tribunal.[109] Once the matter has been judicially considered, then, if the decision is in favour of the person aggrieved, the fact of the inaccuracy thereby reaches the 'manifest' standard, and accordingly the Keeper will rectify. 'Any decree which clearly (whether expressly or not) said that the Register was inaccurate would normally amount to evidence at the "manifest" standard'.[110] The action would commonly be, or include, a declarator. In the 2012 Act system, unlike the 1979 Act system, conclusions directed against the Keeper to require rectification are not normally appropriate.[111]

What if the decree is in absence? The issue here is that a decree in absence is more susceptible than a decree *in foro* to a later challenge. Our view is that a decree in absence is, at least in the normal case, a sufficient basis for rectification of the Register.[112]

It might be thought that the 'manifest' standard adopted by the Act is too stringent. One argument is that to maintain a high threshold for rectification while having a lower one for registration[113] is to create a structural imbalance in the system. In other words, if it is easy for mistakes to enter the Register, it must not be too hard for them to be corrected.[114] This, however, is an area where views may differ and we do not pursue it further here.[115]

---

107 SLC Report 222 paras 7.21 and 18.17. In the equivalent provision in the SLC's draft Bill (s 54(1)), the Keeper is taken bound to rectify 'a manifest (and not merely a probable) inaccuracy'.
108 It may be that the RoS guidance does not properly make this distinction. For instance, it is said (*General Guidance: Inaccuracy and Rectification* (n 36) 2) that 'a manifest inaccuracy would exist where a void deed is given effect to'. But *any* inaccuracy is manifest if it is known to exist. The 'manifest' issue is about imperfect information available to RoS. It may be that Jack asserts that a disposition that bears to have been granted by him was forged, while Jill, the grantee, says that the deed is genuine. In such a case it is usually impossible for the Keeper to determine the matter. In the absence of concession by Jill, Jack will have to resort to litigation.
109 LR(S)A 2012 s 82, discussed at para 11.19 below.
110 SLC Report 222 para 18.18.
111 For more about litigation concerning the Land Register, see ch 18.
112 Cf SLC Report 222 paras 18.17 and 18.18.
113 Not least because of the reliance, in applications for registration, on the principle of 'tell me don't show me': see para 8.11 above.
114 See also para 11.25 below. In its Stage 1 Report, the Economy, Energy and Tourism Committee of the Scottish Parliament recorded the evidence it had heard 'that "manifest" sets the bar too high with the result that fewer disputes would be resolved by the Keeper and more people would have to undertake expensive and potentially prolonged litigation'. See Scottish Parliament, *Passage of the Land Registration etc (Scotland) Bill 2011* (2013, SPPB 174) (available at www.scottish.parliament.uk/parliamentarybusiness/Bills/44469.aspx) 262.
115 The authors themselves do not agree.

11.15 Requests for rectification

Only inaccuracies which come to the Keeper's attention can be rectified.[116] Many, unfortunately, will not. Chance discovery apart, the main way in which an inaccuracy will reach the Keeper's desk is when she is informed about it. Sometimes this will be almost as soon as the inaccuracy occurred. But as rectification declares existing rights rather than conferring new rights, no time limit applies and the Keeper's duty to rectify is exempt from negative prescription.[117] Delay, however, carries the risk that the inaccuracy will be cured by realignment of rights following disposal to a good-faith purchaser or by some other supervening event.[118]

Strictly, it is not possible to apply for rectification.[119] So strong is the Keeper's duty to rectify that a formal application process was thought to be out of place – it would be to ask a public official to do what that public official is already bound to do.[120] But RoS recognise the reality of the situation by providing a short form for the 'notification' of inaccuracies and by encouraging its use.[121] No fee is payable. The form requests information on matters such as whether the inaccuracy is manifest, whether it existed immediately before 8 December 2014, and whether it might have been cured by realignment. The Keeper's decision is made on the basis of the form. She will not call for further information from the person who submitted it, or enter into any sort of correspondence.[122] Nor will she seek comments from others who might be affected by the inaccuracy. Rather than choosing between competing submissions her task is simply to decide, on the basis of the information provided, whether the existence of a 'manifest' inaccuracy has been established. Where it has not, the person is informed accordingly, and has the option of making a second notification, supported this time by fuller information. If, conversely, the inaccuracy is found to exist, the Keeper makes the necessary correction to the Register, and retains in the archive record all supporting documentation.[123] It is only then that the Keeper gives notice, by email or more typically by letter, to any person who appears to be materially affected by the rectification.[124] In theory such a person might then

---

116 For RoS practice in this regard, see Registers of Scotland, *Registration Manual* (https://rosdev. atlassian.net/wiki/display/2ARM/Home) User Guides: Other processes – rectification of an inaccuracy in a title sheet.
117 Prescription and Limitation (Scotland) Act 1973 sch 3 para (i). Rectification under the 1979 Act had substantive effect and the right to rectify appears to have prescribed after 20 years: see SLC Report 222 para 35.11.
118 See paras 11.7 and 11.8 above.
119 As it was under the 1979 Act: see Land Registration (Scotland) Rules 2006, SSI 2006/485, r 17(1). It may be noted, however, that LR(S)A 2012 s 84(1)(a) comes close to the idea of application when it speaks of a person 'securing rectification'.
120 SLC Report 222 para 18.10.
121 *General Guidance: Inaccuracy and Rectification* (n 36) 2. The form (ILR) is available on the RoS website. The use of such a form had been anticipated in SLC Report 222 para 18.10.
122 This is comparable to the one-shot rule which applies to applications for registration (as to which see para 9.10 above). The justification given is the slightly odd one that it is no longer competent to disclose applications for rectification in the application record (which now has a statutory content prescribed by LR(S)A 2012 s 15): see *General Guidance: Inaccuracy and Rectification* (n 36) 3.
123 LR(S)A 2012 s 80(2), (4)(a).
124 LR(S)A 2012 s 80(4)(b). At the time of writing, the power in s 80(5) to make rules as to the persons to be notified and the method of notification had not been exercised. RoS's view is that the circumstances surrounding rectification vary too much to make a list worthwhile. See *General Guidance: Inaccuracy and Rectification* (n 36) 4, giving as examples

challenge the rectification as creating (rather than correcting) an inaccuracy; but if the Keeper has applied the 'manifest' test properly, such a challenge will rarely be upheld.[125]

Under the 1979 Act the Keeper received between 250 and 350 applications for rectification a year – as against more than 250,000 applications for registration.[126] If, owing to the 'tell me don't show me' principle, more mistakes are now made on first registration, requests for rectification may experience a corresponding rise.

11.16 Effect of rectification

Rectification, in and of itself, has no legal effect, in the sense that rights are neither conferred nor lost thereby.[127] Rather, rectification brings the Register into line with what was already the legal or factual position so that it is then, once more, a proper mirror of the title.

But if rectification does not *cause* legal effects, it can at any rate *prevent* them. An inaccuracy which is left unrectified may, over time, be cured by realignment or prescription.[128] If so, then instead of the Register coming to correspond with the legal or factual position, as with rectification, the legal or factual position comes to correspond with the Register.

11.17 Compensation from the Keeper

Naturally, no compensation is due in the event that rectification is refused.[129] And even if it is granted, the fact that rectification is, in and of itself, without legal effect might suggest that no compensation could be due then either. That, however, would be incorrect. Although a person whose position is worsened on the face of the Register has lost nothing by the rectification, the very fact that he had nothing to lose – the fact that, in other words, the Register was wrong all along – will often trigger a claim under the Keeper's warranty of title.[130] In addition, the person who secured the rectification is entitled to compensation for the cost of making the claim as well as for any loss which resulted from the inaccuracy.[131] Further details on compensation can be found in chapter 14.[132]

---

of those who might need to be notified 'the proprietor of the registered title in question, a heritable creditor, a neighbouring proprietor, the benefited proprietor in respect of a servitude, or a registered tenant'. By s 80(6) the validity of a rectification is unaffected by a failure to notify.
125 A challenge could be by way of appeal against the Keeper's decision under LR(S)A 2012 s 103. Or the challenger could complete form ILR, thus giving formal notice of the alleged inaccuracy. Assuming the Keeper refused to change her mind, the only avenue left would be an application to the court or Lands Tribunal.
126 *Passage of the Land Registration etc (Scotland) Bill 2011* (n 114) 393.
127 Compare here the 1979 Act where the rectification of a bijural inaccuracy resulted in the creation or extinction of rights.
128 See paras 11.7 and 11.8 above.
129 The position was different under the 1979 Act. As a refusal of rectification meant, in effect, that the right lost as a result of the inaccuracy could never be recovered, compensation was due for the loss: see s 12(1)(b), and para 2.10 above. Under the 2012 Act rights are lost, not by refusal of rectification, but by the realignment of rights under ss 86–92, and compensation under s 94 is due accordingly.
130 LR(S)A 2012 pt 7: see ch 13.
131 LR(S)A 2012 ss 84 and 85.
132 See para 14.7 below.

11.18 Applications or appeals pending on 8 December 2014

Any application for rectification under the 1979 Act which was pending on the day on which the 2012 Act came into operation (8 December 2014) fell on that day.[133] A fresh request for rectification then required to be made, with the provisions of the 2012 Act, described above, being applicable. It should, however, be borne in mind that if the inaccuracy was one which, under the 1979 Act, the Keeper was unable to rectify, the inaccuracy was cured on 8 December 2014 and there can be no question of future rectification.[134]

No corresponding provision is made for appeals, ie for the case where an appeal against the Keeper's decision as to rectification had been made before the designated day but the appeal was yet to be heard. The Lands Tribunal has decided, surely correctly, that such appeals do not fall but may continue to be heard.[135] In so far, however, as the Tribunal in such an appeal is determining what the rights of the parties are today, ie after the designated day, it will be necessary to apply the relevant provisions of the 2012 Act and in particular the transitional provisions in schedule 4.[136]

11.19 Referral to the Lands Tribunal

Under s 82 of the 2012 Act, the Lands Tribunal may determine any question relating to the accuracy of the Land Register or as to what is needed to rectify an inaccuracy. The idea is to provide an expert and relatively cheap forum for cases where an inaccuracy is alleged to exist but is not sufficiently 'manifest' to persuade the Keeper to rectify.[137] The jurisdiction is wide.[138] So long as the matter at issue is reflected in an entry on the Register, the Lands Tribunal can consider any dispute between neighbours or competing title-holders. The Keeper is entitled to appear and be heard but in most cases is unlikely to do so.[139] In addition, the Lands Tribunal has an appellate function in respect of any decision of the Keeper, including a decision to grant or refuse rectification.[140]

In either case, the initial application fee is £150 and a further £88 is due on the making of an order or determination. The daily rate for a Tribunal hearing is £155.[141] On making a determination the Tribunal must give notice to the applicant, to any other person appearing to have an interest, and to the Keeper.[142]

---

133 LR(S)A 2012 sch 4 para 14.
134 LR(S)A 2012 sch 4 para 22: see para 11.9 above.
135 *Wight v Keeper of the Registers of Scotland* 2015 SLT (Lands Tr) 195.
136 That was not, however, the view taken by the Tribunal in *Wight*; for criticism, see K G C Reid and G L Gretton, *Conveyancing 2015* (2016) 28–30.
137 This had been a matter of concern during Stage 1 of the Bill's parliamentary proceedings, and provision for the Lands Tribunal's (new) jurisdiction was added by backbench amendment (by Mike MacKenzie MSP) at Stage 2. See *Passage of the Land Registration etc (Scotland) Bill 2011* (n 114) 262–63, 307, and 615.
138 It does not, however, extend to reduction, and there may be cases where rectification cannot proceed without reduction.
139 LR(S)A 2012 s 83.
140 LR(S)A 2012 s 103(1): see para 3.20 above. An appeal may be made on both questions of fact and points of law. The position was broadly similar under LR(S)A 1979 s 25(1).
141 Lands Tribunal for Scotland Rules 1971, SI 1971/218, sch 2, as amended by the Lands Tribunal for Scotland Amendment (Fees) Rules 2014, SSI 2014/24.
142 LR(S)A 2012 s 82(2).

DISPUTED BOUNDARIES

11.20 Classification by cause

It may be helpful to examine in more detail one of the commonest examples of inaccuracy and rectification. This is where the owners of two adjacent properties (which we may call plot A and plot B) are in dispute as to the boundary line between them. Often latent for as long as the properties are still in the Register of Sasines, the issue is brought out, or in some cases caused, by the first registration of one or both of the plots. In practice, such disputes tend to come about in one of two ways. One is where the underlying Sasine titles are unclear, so that it is difficult to say with confidence where the boundary line truly lies. This is not uncommon, especially in rural areas, where titles may have no reliable plan or indeed no plan at all. But disputes as to boundaries can also arise where the Sasine titles are (tolerably) clear if, on first registration of one plot of land, the Keeper by mistake includes a strip of land which is actually part of another plot still on the Sasine Register. In principle these two cases are distinct, although it may sometimes be a matter of dispute which case applies. They are discussed separately below.

11.21 Uncertainty in Sasine titles

The topic is most easily approached by an example. Suppose that it is unclear from the Sasine titles whether a strip of land is part of plot A or plot B. And further suppose that plot B is being sold and that a disposition is being prepared for its transfer. The position of the purchaser of plot B will depend on whether either or both of the plots are on the Land Register. There are thus four possible cases: (i) the title to neither plot A nor plot B is on the Land Register; (ii) the title to plot A (only) is on the Land Register; (iii) the title to plot B (only) is on the Land Register; and (iv) the title to both plots is on the Land Register.

11.22 Case (i): neither plot on the Land Register

If both plots are still in the Register of Sasines, the position, for the moment at least, is relatively straightforward. As the strip is not yet part of any cadastral unit, the purchaser of plot B can lay claim to it in applying for first registration. This is done by including the strip in the deed plan, and by certifying the title as valid in the application form for registration. The strip will then be included within the (new) title sheet for plot B. If the Keeper has reservations as to the title, she might restrict her warranty in respect of the strip; what, apparently, she will not do is to reject the application, for that would be to take sides in a potential dispute between neighbours.[143] Of course, inclusion on the title sheet does not, of itself, make the strip part of plot B. Only a valid disposition can transfer ownership.[144] But it is, at any rate, a start.

Matters become more difficult when it is plot A's turn to be disponed and to enter the Land Register for the first time. But that is then case (ii)[145] and not case (i).

---

143 Registers of Scotland, *General Guidance: Competing Titles* (v.01, 2014) 2 ('Clearly it would be unacceptable for the Keeper to reject a first registration application based on the possibility of a competing title at a later date'). See also para 9.9 above.
144 LR(S)A 2012 s 50(2): see para 9.20 above. So ownership of the strip passes to the disponee only if it was previously owned by the disponer.
145 Although with different plot lettering. In case (ii) as described below, it is plot A which is already on the Register and plot B which is being acquired.

11.23 Cases (ii) and (iii): one plot on the Land Register

Assume now that plot A is on the Land Register and that plot B is not. A strip included within the title sheet for plot A cannot be acquired, in the course of ordinary conveyancing, by a purchaser of plot B. For under the 2012 Act the same area cannot appear in the title sheets of different plots of land;[146] and since it is already in the title sheet for plot A, the strip cannot now be added to the title sheet of plot B.[147] A plans report will alert the purchaser of plot B to the problem; and the purchaser must then either omit the strip from the disposition of plot B or, it seems, face rejection of the application in its entirety.[148]

For the purchaser of plot B the solution, if there is one, lies in rectification and not in registration. The strip, having once been allocated to plot A, cannot now be reallocated to plot B except by rectification. And rectification, in turn, presupposes that the Register is inaccurate. In other words, it must be shown that, despite appearing in the title sheet for plot A, the strip is actually owned by the proprietor of plot B.[149] Whether that is really so will depend on the state of possession. If or to the extent that the strip is possessed by the owner of plot B, its ownership is likely to have been acquired or secured by positive prescription.[150] But if or to the extent that the strip is possessed by the owner of plot A, it is likely to have become part of that plot either by positive prescription,[151] by the transitional provisions for titles held on the Register on 8 December 2014,[152] or by realignment.[153] Of course, unless the matter is conceded by the owner of plot A, the purchaser of plot B must either litigate or give up his claim. An alleged inaccuracy which depends on disputed possession can never be accepted by the Keeper as 'manifest'.[154]

The position is different, and much more favourable to a purchaser of plot B, if it is plot B and not plot A that is on the Land Register. Assuming the strip to be included within plot B's title sheet, the purchaser will be registered as owner of the strip as a matter of course; and assuming a year's possession on the part of the

---

146 LR(S)A 2012 s 12(2): see para 5.11 above. For the reasons behind this (new) policy, see SLC Report 222 paras 5.25–5.27.
147 As was the Keeper's practice under the 1979 Act: see para 11.24 below.
148 *General Guidance: Competing Titles* (n 143) 1. The legal basis of such rejection can be questioned. LR(S)A 2012 s 21(2) provides that the Keeper must accept an application *to the extent* that the applicant satisfies the Keeper that the application conditions are met. In the present case the conditions are met except in respect of the strip. That would argue for acceptance in respect of the rest of the plot. On this issue see para 9.7 above.
149 As the Keeper will not accept a disposition of plot B which includes the strip, this would actually be the *former* owner of that plot. One of the odd consequences of the Keeper's unwillingness to accept a disposition of plot B which includes the strip is that it is impossible for the former owner, assuming he owns the strip, to transfer it. In other words, it has become (for the time being) inalienable property.
150 Assuming a *habile* Sasine title followed by ten years' possession.
151 Assuming a *habile* Sasine or Land Register title followed by ten years' possession. For prescription, see paras 17.1 ff below.
152 Assuming that first registration of plot A had occurred before that date: see LR(S)A 2012 sch 4 para 22, and paras 11.9–11.12 above.
153 Assuming that the title to plot A was already on the Land Register at the time when the current owner acquired, and that the current owner was in good faith: see LR(S)A 2012 s 86, and paras 12.8–12.17 below.
154 As this example shows, the proprietor of a plot which is *second* to be registered in the Land Register is put in the difficult position of having to vindicate his (alleged) rights by litigation. This follows from what some would describe as the structural imbalance of a system where registration is easy and rectification difficult: see para 11.14 above.

seller, and good faith on the part of the purchaser, any underlying doubts as to title will be stilled by realignment.[155]

11.24 Case (iv): both plots on the Land Register

Where the second of the plots entered the Land Register on or after the designated day (8 December 2014), there is little or no difference between case (iv) and case (ii) (discussed above). For under the 2012 Act, the strip can be included in the title sheet of one of the properties but not of both;[156] and only rectification, typically following on from a judicial determination of inaccuracy, can change the Keeper's original allocation.

Where, however, both plots were registered before the designated day, the strip may turn out to appear in the title sheets of each.[157] In the case of the first plot to enter the Register (say, plot A), there will then be a note referring to the competition in title; in the case of the second (say, plot B), the note will be accompanied by an exclusion of indemnity.[158] Potential purchasers are alerted to the problem both by the legal report and by an inspection of the title sheet itself.[159] It will then be for the parties to decide whether to put up with the situation or to attempt to resolve it by agreement or litigation.

That an inaccuracy exists will, of course, be readily accepted by the Keeper, for the same strip of land cannot belong both to the proprietor of plot A and to the proprietor of plot B; but what the Keeper cannot know, until it is judicially established (or one party concedes), is *which* proprietor is the owner. In other words, this is one of those rare cases where the inaccuracy is manifest but it is not manifest what must be done for the inaccuracy to be rectified.[160] The Keeper will therefore enter a note of the inaccuracy on both title sheets,[161] and await further developments.[162] And in the meantime she will exclude her warranty in respect of the overlap for all future transactions concerning the plots, including that plot (plot A) in respect of which the 1979 Act indemnity was not previously excluded.[163]

---

155 LR(S)A 2012 s 86: see paras 12.8–12.17 below.
156 LR(S)A 2012 s 12(1).
157 As was envisaged by *Registration of Title to Land in Scotland: Report by a Committee appointed by the Secretary of State for Scotland* (Cmnd 2032, 1963) ('Reid Report') para 104, and *Scheme for the Introduction and Operation of Registration of Title to Land in Scotland: Report by a Committee appointed by the Secretary of State for Scotland* (Cmnd 4137, 1969) ('Henry Report') 53–54.
158 *General Guidance: Competing Titles* (n 143) 2. For an example, see *Safeway Stores plc v Tesco Stores Ltd* 2004 SC 29.
159 Registers of Scotland, *Essential Guide to the 2012 Act Changes* (2014) Reports Q2.
160 LR(S)A 2012 s 80(2), (3): see para 11.13 above.
161 The note is likely to be in the following terms: 'The Keeper considers that XXX represents a manifest inaccuracy in terms of section 80 of the Land Registration etc (Scotland) Act 2012 but what is needed to rectify the inaccuracy is not manifest.' See *General Guidance: Competing Titles* (n 143) 2.
162 What the Keeper will not do is to take steps to remove the overlap, notwithstanding the rule in LR(S)A 2012 s 12(2) that 'the same area of land cannot be represented by more than one cadastral unit'. Provisions in the draft Bill produced by the Scottish Law Commission had required the Keeper, within a period of ten years, to create a separate title sheet (a 'conflict title sheet') for the overlap area and to enter there the name of both competing proprietors, but these were not carried forward to the 2012 Act. See SLC draft Bill sch 6 paras 12–18, and also SLC Report 222 para 36.5.
163 *General Guidance: Competing Titles* (n 143) 2–3.

The substantive issue, as usual, is likely to be determined by the state of possession. If or to the extent that the strip is possessed by plot A's proprietor, then the strip is probably part of plot A. This is because, even if its inclusion in the title sheet was once an inaccuracy, the inaccuracy ceased on the designated day if, immediately before that day, the inaccuracy could not have been rectified by the Keeper;[164] and the Keeper could not generally rectify inaccuracies to the prejudice of a proprietor in possession.[165] This transitional rule could not operate for the benefit of plot B because the exclusion of indemnity would have allowed the Keeper to rectify even in the face of possession.[166] Nonetheless, if and to the extent that possession is with the proprietor of plot B, positive prescription can run, so that ownership is conferred or assured at the end of ten years.[167]

11.25 Error on first registration

The examples considered so far concern boundaries which were unclear from the Sasine titles. But boundary disputes can also arise where, despite the Sasine boundary being (tolerably) clear, that boundary is rendered incorrectly when the first of the plots comes to be admitted to the Land Register.[168] In such a case, first registration *causes* the boundary dispute rather than, as with the previous examples, simply bringing it to light.

The problem was anticipated more than a century ago. In its report published in 1910, the Royal Commission on Registration of Title in Scotland expressed concern about the likely difficulties of first registration.[169] On the one hand, observed Lord Dunedin, the Commission's chairman, neighbours would have to be notified about applications for first registration and given the opportunity to make representations, 'for if the register is to be conclusive of all questions of right, the establishment in it of the identity of any one property necessarily involves the fixing of conterminous boundaries of others'. Yet in the very act of notification lay the possibility, or even the likelihood, of challenge. 'Such calling of all parties into the field with the peremptory need at once to assert or for ever to forfeit all claims ... would undoubtedly promote strife, expense, and litigation, some part of which at any rate would never otherwise have arisen at all.'[170] Lord Dunedin's solution was to reject registration of title.[171] The solution of the Reid Committee,

---

164 LR(S)A 2012 sch 4 para 22 ('it ceases to be an inaccuracy'): see paras 11.9–11.12 above. The provision does not confer ownership as such, relying on the Midas touch to have done this already. With overlapping titles, however, a system of 'shuttlecock title' operated (see para 2.13 above), so that the proprietor of plot A would own the strip only if no transfer of plot B took place after his own acquisition. It seems, however, that para 22 must be read as conferring ownership in a case where this was needed.
165 LR(S)A 1979 s 9(3)(a): see paras 2.9 and 11.10 above. Four exceptions are listed in s 9(3)(a).
166 LR(S)A 1979 s 9(3)(a)(iv).
167 Prior to the designated day, prescription would have run by virtue of the exclusion of indemnity; after that day, it would have run because prescription now runs on all Land Register titles: see Prescription and Limitation (Scotland) Act 1973 s 1(1) in the versions which operated before and after the designated day respectively.
168 See para 11.20 above.
169 *Reports by the Royal Commission on Registration of Title in Scotland* (1910, Cd 5316).
170 *Reports by the Royal Commission* (n 169) 12.
171 See para 1.15 above. Unable to reach agreement, the Royal Commission produced four separate reports. That prepared by Lord Dunedin (with W J Dundas and John Prosser) was the only report to reject registration of title outright.

half a century later, was to reject the idea of notice.[172] Hence neither the 1979 Act nor, now, the Act of 2012 made provision for intimation to neighbours.[173] The decision is understandable. But it leaves owners vulnerable to title encroachment by those who precede them on to the Land Register. The result seems particularly troublesome where the encroachment is caused, not by underlying uncertainty as to boundaries – the subject of the previous discussion – but by simple error at Register House.

Errors in plotting boundaries are more common than, no doubt, they ought to be. Often the area in question is small or even trivial, but it can also be substantial, as in *Gray v Keeper of the Registers of Scotland* where the boundaries mapped on first registration included more than half an acre held by a neighbour on a Sasine title.[174] Whether small or substantial, however, such errors put the neighbour at a serious practical disadvantage.[175] For once a mistake enters the Register it can only be corrected if it can be shown to be an inaccuracy. If the mistake is obvious – if, in other words, the inaccuracy is 'manifest' – the Keeper must of course correct it by rectification.[176] But if its existence is contested, the issue can only be settled by the Lands Tribunal or the court.[177] The neighbour must then either accept the (generally uncompensated)[178] loss of the property or embark on an uncertain litigation that is likely to be costly to the loser.

11.26 And its rectification

The prospects for rectification, for those willing to pursue it, depend on whether the first registration of the encroaching plot took place before, or on or after, the designated day (8 December 2014).

For first registrations occurring before the designated day, the position is regulated by the transitional provisions contained in the 2012 Act.[179] Thus suppose

---

172 Reid Report (n 157) para 64(4): 'we would not favour any system which required intimation to neighbouring proprietors as a preliminary to such registration, because that would inevitably stir up disputes and involve expense in many cases in settling or litigating questions which are at present dormant'.
173 Applications are not notified as such. LR(S)A 2012 s 40 provides for the notification of the *acceptance* (or rejection) of an application to the applicant, the granter of the deed, and 'any other person the Keeper considers appropriate': see para 9.14 above. There is no requirement to notify acceptance to neighbours, and it is not the Keeper's practice to do so. For the law and practice before the 2012 Act, see SLC Report 222 paras 12.113 and 12.114.
174 *Gray v Keeper of Registers of Scotland* 2014 SLT (Lands Tr) 117. For other examples, see *Nicol v Keeper of the Registers of Scotland* 2013 SLT (Lands Tr) 56; *Burton v Keeper of the Registers of Scotland* 2014 SLT (Lands Tr) 69; *Van Eck v Keeper of the Registers of Scotland* 2014 SLT (Lands Tr) 117; *Mathers v Keeper of the Registers of Scotland* 2015 GWD 3-68.
175 The position under the 1979 Act was, however, considerably worse. Ownership was lost from the moment that the area of land was included in the neighbour's title sheet, and was irrecoverable if the neighbour was in possession: see LR(S)A 1979 ss 3(1)(a) and 9(3)(a). As the Lands Tribunal observed in *Gray* (n 174) para 4, 'some of the problems and apparent unfairness arising from the approach taken in the 1979 Act and illustrated by the present case have been addressed by the provisions of the Land Registration etc (Scotland) Act 2012'.
176 LR(S)A 2012 s 80(1), (2).
177 Paragraph 11.14 above. The approach taken by the Keeper is set out in *Registration Manual* (n 116) User Guides: Other processes – rectification of an inaccuracy in a title sheet: transitional rectifications, overlap.
178 Usually, compensation was and is due only if the fact of an inaccuracy is established (see LR(S)A 1979 s 12(1)(b); LR(S)A 2012 s 94); and for that to happen, the neighbour would have to embark on the very litigation which (in the context of rectification) he has decided to eschew.
179 For which see paras 11.9–11.12 above.

that Michael was registered as owner of a plot which included some land of Nicola's (a neighbour who held on a Sasine title). Registration would make Michael owner of Nicola's land, by virtue of the Keeper's Midas touch, but the Register would then be inaccurate.[180] What happens thereafter depends, under the transitional provisions, on whether the inaccuracy could have been rectified immediately before the designated day; and that in turn is likely to depend on whether Michael was a proprietor in possession in respect of the land.[181] If Michael was in possession, as is presumed,[182] ownership remains with Michael, the Register is deemed accurate on the designated day, and Nicola's claim is reduced to one for compensation from the Keeper.[183] If, however, Michael was not in possession, ownership reverts from Michael to Nicola on the designated day, the Register continues to be inaccurate, and Nicola's position is much the same as if the first registration had occurred after the designated day (for which see below).[184]

For first registrations occurring on or after the designated day, Michael's position is weaker and Nicola's correspondingly stronger. Nicola's ownership is unaffected by Michael's registration;[185] she is entitled to rectification if she can prove the inaccuracy, and the state of possession is, for the moment at least, irrelevant. Delay, however, can be perilous, for if Michael is in possession and Nicola does not rectify, Nicola is vulnerable to the loss of ownership, either by realignment (if Michael dispones to an acquirer in good faith) or by positive prescription (if Michael possesses for ten years).[186] Compensation is payable only in the event of the former.[187]

---

180 For an account of the operation of the 1979 Act in this respect, see paras 2.8 and 2.9 above.
181 For the meaning of 'possession' in this context, see para 11.12 above.
182 LR(S)A 2012 sch 4 para 18.
183 LR(S)A 2012 sch 4 paras 22–24.
184 LR(S)A 2012 sch 4 para 17. A third possibility is that Michael was once in possession but had lost possession by the time of the designated day. Nicola would become owner on the designated day – even if she had earlier been paid indemnity by the Keeper following the Keeper's refusal of a request for rectification on account of Michael's then possession. Whether she would be able to keep the 'money', having now received the 'mud', is another matter.
185 As there is no Midas touch under the 2012 Act.
186 See, respectively, paras 12.8–12.17 and 17.1 ff below.
187 LR(S)A 2012 s 94: see paras 14.2 and 14.3 below. No compensation is payable for losses arising as a result of positive prescription.

Chapter 12

The Guarantee of Title (1): Realignment of Rights

THE GUARANTEE OF TITLE

12.1 Content: positive and negative

On registration, the title of the acquirer is guaranteed. The guarantee has both a positive and a negative aspect, covering both what is on the Register and what is not. Positively, there is a warranty that the acquirer's title is good; negatively, there is a warranty that the title is free from encumbrances which have been omitted in error from the Register.[1] Put together, these warranties provide a high degree of protection. Title insurance offered by insurance companies, standard in some countries, is unnecessary in Scotland, apart from special cases.[2] The guarantee of title also reduces the importance of the granter's warrandice which, traditionally, has accompanied (and accompanies still) most conveyancing transactions.[3]

12.2 Form: 'money' and 'mud'

A guarantee of title can take one of two forms. Title defects can be compensated with money, or the defect can simply be overlooked or 'cured' so that the acquirer receives, after all, the property right which was originally sought. In other words, the guarantee of title can take the form of either 'money' or 'mud' (ie property).[4] Both types are found in the 2012 Act, as they were found before in the legislation of 1979. The distribution, however, is by no means the same. A guarantee by 'money' is used more often by the 2012 Act than it was by the Act of 1979. On the other hand, the 'mud', when it is awarded, is 'real mud', unlike under the 1979 Act where the title given to acquirers was not fully 'cured', and thus remained, at least in some situations, vulnerable to future rectification.[5] The present chapter is concerned with the guarantee by mud, the next with the guarantee by money.

---

1 In contrast, the Register of Sasines offers no more than a limited negative guarantee, namely that it contains all deeds creating real rights (but excluding those rights which can be created without registration).
2 On title insurance see eg Scottish Law Commission, *Report No 222 on Land Registration* (2010) ('SLC Report 222') part 26. The same was true even of conveyancing practice before the introduction of the Land Register. Low though the risk was in the old system, it is much lower now.
3 Warrandice remains of value for cases where, for one reason or another, the statutory (ie the Keeper's) warranty does not apply. Furthermore, on paying compensation the Keeper is subrogated to the acquirer's rights and so could pursue a claim in warrandice: see LR(S)A 2012 s 77(4), (5).
4 SLC Report 222 para 21.2: 'If a registered grantee keeps what the title sheet says, then that is title guarantee by way of "mud" and if the registered grantee does not keep it but is compensated instead, that is title guarantee by way of "money".'
5 SLC Report 222 para 21.36. As the Scottish Law Commission put it, the 1979 Act only conferred 'quasi-mud'.

Common to both is an adherence to the 'curtain' principle, ie to the principle that, in seeking to acquire property, there is no need to look behind the Register at the underlying deeds.[6] Acquirers can rely on what they see on the Register. In the unlikely event that the Register turns out to be wrong, there is usually protection from one or other of the guarantees.[7]

Whilst the title guarantee addresses a title problem by either 'mud' or 'money' but not both, the consequence will normally be that someone else will receive a matching and opposite protection.[8] For instance if Jack is registered as owner of Mary's property, and under the rules about to be discussed he takes the mud, Mary normally receives money as compensation,[9] and, conversely, if Jack does not obtain the mud, Mary keeps it, and Jack normally receives compensation.[10]

12.3 Determination of form

A guarantee by money is the default guarantee, applying except where it has become unnecessary due to the title being cured as a result of the guarantee by mud. In determining when the latter applies – and therefore the former does not – two main variables apply. One is the type of error. The other is the type of real right being sought.[11] The result, it should be stressed, is a series of determinate rules: unlike in some other countries, no discretion is given to the Keeper or to the courts as to which guarantee applies.[12]

12.4 Determination by type of error

Errors, for present purposes, can be divided into two types. There are errors which occur in the course of a transaction, and errors which pre-date the transaction and are, as a consequence, already present on the Register before the transaction begins. There are, in other words, both 'transactional' errors and 'Register' errors. If the acquirer's deed is forged, the error is 'transactional' in nature; if the person named on the Register as owner is not owner, the error is a 'Register' error.

Under the 2012 Act the form of guarantee is determined, in the first place, by the type of error. For transactional errors, the guarantee takes the form of compensation, using the mechanism of a warranty of title by the Keeper.[13] For Register errors, there can either be compensation ('money') or, in some cases, the overlooking of the error so that the acquirer receives a valid title ('mud'); as we will see shortly, the choice between them depends on the type of right which is being acquired.[14]

---

6 For the 'curtain' principle, see T Ruoff, 'An Englishman looks at the Torrens System' (1952) 26 ALJ 118.
7 The main exception is where an acquirer (or his solicitor) is at fault in his conduct of the transaction.
8 The position was the same under the 1979 Act: see para 2.9 above.
9 LR(S)A 2012 s 94: see paras 14.2 and 14.3 below.
10 Ie under the Keeper's warranty: see LR(S)A 2012 s 73. This is the guarantee by money discussed in ch 13.
11 For the policy reasons behind this method of determination, see para 2.12 above, and also K G C Reid, 'De-throning King Midas: The New Law of Land Registration in Scotland', University of Edinburgh Research Paper 2016/07 (http://papers.ssrn.com/sol3/papers.cfm?abstract_id=2746847).
12 On discretion, see para 3.21 above.
13 LR(S)A 2012 pt 7. This is the subject of ch 13.
14 See para 12.5 below.

It is worth observing that an error which begins life as 'transactional' will become a 'Register' error if the transaction is completed by the acquirer's registration as owner. The transformation will not benefit the acquirer, the legal position of whom is already determined, for better or for worse, by the act of registration, but it will benefit any person with whom the acquirer later transacts. So suppose that Rona grants Samira a disposition which is void (because, for example, of forgery or lack of capacity or title). From Samira's point of view, this is a transactional error; in the event that it comes to be discovered and founded upon, it will engage the guarantee by money. But suppose that the error is not discovered and founded upon and that Samira, now registered as owner on the basis of the void disposition, proceeds to dispone the property to Tom. The error is now in the Register, following the registration of Samira's disposition (ie the Register shows Samira and not Rona as owner); and what was a transactional error from the viewpoint of the first acquirer (Samira) has become a Register error from the viewpoint of the second (Tom). As a result, the guarantee by mud is potentially engaged in Tom's favour, and hence the error is potentially cured.[15] A further example is given later.[16] Systems of land registration which operate in this way – systems which forgive errors not at once but only on the second transaction – are often characterised in the international literature as involving 'deferred' (as opposed to 'immediate') indefeasibility of title.[17] A defect in the current transaction can be cured only in the course of the next. The cure, if it comes,[18] is thus 'deferred' rather than 'immediate'.

12.5 Determination by type of right

For Register errors, as just mentioned,[19] the guarantee is sometimes by way of money and sometimes by way of mud. Which guarantee applies depends on the type of right which is being acquired.[20] The 1979 Act restricted the guarantee by mud to the acquisition of ownership and long lease; a money guarantee applied to the acquisition of subordinate real rights such as standard securities and servitudes.[21] The approach of the 2012 Act is not quite the same.[22] The acquisition of ownership qualifies for the guarantee by mud, as it did before.[23] So too does the acquisition of a long lease by an assignee, although not by the original grantee.[24]

---

15 Whether it will be cured will depend on whether the conditions for LR(S)A 2012 s 86 are met: see paras 12.8 ff below.
16 See example 2 in para 12.7 below. See also para 2.12 above.
17 This terminology is particularly associated with the Torrens system: see eg P O'Connor, 'Registration of Invalid Dispositions: Who gets the Property?', in E Cooke (ed), *Modern Studies in Property Law* vol 3 (2005) 53–54. For a discussion, see SLC Report 222 paras 21.3–21.9.
18 Which it may not, for, before Samira has the chance to re-sell, Rona may become aware of the error and obtain the restoration of her title by rectification.
19 See para 12.4 above.
20 Although we speak of acquisition, discharges are also included.
21 In other words, only those acquiring ownership or a long lease were capable of being proprietors in possession and hence of being protected from rectification of the error by LR(S)A 1979 s 9(3)(a): see para 2.9 above.
22 For discussion, see SLC Report 222 paras 23.1–23.35.
23 LR(S)A 2012 ss 86, 87 and 91: see paras 12.8–12.20 below.
24 LR(S)A 2012 ss 88, 89 and 92: see paras 12.21–12.23 below. The reasons for excepting the grant (but not the assignation) of long leases are explained in SLC Report 222 para 23.29. For example, in the event that the legislation had made the lease valid, the Scottish Law Commission considered that there would be difficulty in determining whether the acquirer/tenant was in contractual relations with (i) the actual owner, (ii) the person appearing on the Register as owner, or (iii) both.

And so, finally, does the acquisition of a servitude.[25] Standard securities and other subordinate real rights are eligible for the guarantee by money.[26]

The rules just described are the outcome of difficult choices between the interests of acquirers and the interests of owners; for if the acquirer is to be awarded the right rather than the money, which is usually what he will want,[27] then the same right must be taken away from the owner. More precisely, if an acquirer (Alan) is awarded ownership on taking a disposition from the person wrongly entered on the Register as proprietor (Betty), then ownership is taken away from the true owner (Colin) even though Colin knows nothing about the transaction. Or if Alan, taking from Betty not a disposition but the grant of a subordinate real right such as a security or servitude, is awarded the security or servitude, then that security or servitude will be an unexpected and unwanted encumbrance on Colin's title.

Only in the case of securities does the choice between owner and acquirer seem self-evident, for, faced with an invalid deed, a bank will be satisfied by repayment of the loan, whether by the debtor or the Keeper, and has no need of a property right. A guarantee by money, in other words, is perfectly sufficient. In other cases, there is no incontestably 'right' approach and it would have been possible for the 2012 Act to draw the line between the types of guarantee in more than one place. As it is, the Act tends to favour acquirers over owners, a policy choice which acknowledges the importance of lowering transaction costs, facilitating acquisition, and removing the temptation to look behind the Register. It is also broadly consistent with legislation on registration of title in other countries. The implications for examination of title are explored in a later chapter.[28]

12.6 Rectification v realignment

A guarantee by 'money' acknowledges the inaccuracy on the Register and compensates the acquirer for its rectification. A guarantee by 'mud' cures the inaccuracy and compensates the (now former) right-holder for the loss of the chance to rectify.[29] The first involves rectification, the second what the Scottish Law Commission calls 'realignment'.[30] These work in opposite ways. Rectification brings the Register into line with the rights which affect the property; realignment brings the rights which affect the property into line with the Register.[31] The first

---

25 LR(S)A 2012 s 90: see paras 12.24–12.26 below.
26 This follows from the omission from the Act of any provision for realignment in such cases.
27 J Burns, 'Registration of Title to Land – Royal Commission's Reports' (1910–11) 22 JR 237, 239 ('money may be the universal solvent, but a man may not consider himself indemnified for the loss of a desired possession by a cheque, especially when the amount is fixed by a third party').
28 See ch 16.
29 'Money' is thus paid in both cases, but to a different party. Indeed the 'mud' is also allocated in both cases, also to a different party. So the first case allocates the 'money' to the acquirer and the 'mud' to the holder of the right in respect of which the inaccuracy exists (ie it allows the holder to keep the right); the second case allocates the 'money' to the right-holder (as compensation for loss of the right) and the 'mud' to the acquirer.
30 SLC Report 222 para 21.40. The word does not appear in the 2012 Act. Thus, while the heading to the relevant part (pt 6) of the SLC's draft Bill is 'Guaranteed title: realignment of rights', in the 2012 Act this becomes (pt 9) 'Rights of persons acquiring etc in good faith'. Nonetheless, the term 'realignment' is used by RoS, and in this book.
31 An 'overview' provision (s 44) in the Scottish Law Commission's draft Bill (not carried forward to the 2012 Act) stated that: 'Provision is made for rights relating to property to be realigned so that they conform with what is set out in the register'.

says that the Register is false and must be corrected, the second that it is (now) true and must be left as it is. The first applies the ordinary rules of property law, the second alters those rules in favour of an acquirer who satisfies certain conditions such as good faith.[32]

Realignment of rights is the subject of this chapter.[33] As previously mentioned, it can occur only where the transaction is the granting and registration of (i) a disposition, (ii) an assignation of a lease, or (iii) a deed of servitude. All three are considered in detail below.

12.7 Some examples

Finally, some examples may help to explain the rather complicated issues discussed above.

Example 1

Andrew owns land. Brian impersonates Andrew and dispones the land, in Andrew's name, to Carol, forging Andrew's signature on the disposition. Carol, who is in good faith, presents the disposition for registration and is registered as owner.

Analysis. This is a transactional error (ie an error in the transaction by which Carol acquired the property). The guarantee by money applies. Andrew remains owner and can seek rectification of the Register. Following rectification, Carol is entitled to indemnity under the Keeper's warranty.

Example 2

The facts of example 1 continue. Before Andrew can apply for rectification, Carol sells the land to David. David, who is in good faith, presents the disposition for registration and is registered as owner.

Analysis. At the time of David's transaction, the Register showed Carol as owner when the owner was actually Andrew. Although having its origins (in example 1) as a transactional error, this is now a Register error, and one to which the guarantee by mud applies.[34] David becomes owner on registration (provided certain conditions are met), due to realignment, and Andrew ceases to be owner. Andrew is entitled to compensation from the Keeper.

Example 3

Variation of example 2. Instead of disponing to David, Carol grants a standard security to the Edinburgh Bank. The Bank, which is in good faith, registers the security.

Analysis. At the time of the Bank's transaction, the Register showed Carol as owner when the owner was actually Andrew. This is a Register error, and one to which the guarantee by 'money' applies. The standard security is void and can be removed from the Register by rectification. Following rectification, the Bank is entitled to compensation under the Keeper's warranty for any loss it has suffered.

---

32 Registration of title must always alter property law rules to some extent, because an acquirer must be able to take title from the person named on the register as owner, regardless of the merits of the person's title. So, under the 1979 Act, registration cured any defect in the underlying title (subject to the possibility of future rectification). In a far less radical intervention, the 2012 Act merely provides protection for good-faith acquirers. See paras 2.7–2.9 and 2.12–2.13 above.
33 RoS have issued a certain amount of guidance on the topic: see Registers of Scotland, *General Guidance: Realignment of Rights* (v.02, 2014); Registers of Scotland, *Registration Manual* (https://rosdev.atlassian.net/wiki/display/2ARM/Home) Topics: Realignment of rights.
34 For this transformation of a transactional error into a Register error, see para 12.4 above.

Example 4

Fiona owns land which is burdened by a standard security in favour of the Glasgow Bank. Fiona forges and registers a discharge of the security, and then sells the land to Ian. Ian, who is in good faith, presents the disposition for registration and is registered as owner.

Analysis. At the time of Ian's transaction, the standard security continued to burden the land but, due to the forged discharge, was not shown on the Register. This is a Register error, and one to which the guarantee by 'mud' applies. On registration of Ian's disposition, the standard security is extinguished (provided certain conditions are met) as a result of realignment.

DISPOSITIONS

12.8 Reliance on the Register

Disponees can take the Register at its word, for, even if the Register was inaccurate, it ceases to be so at the moment of the disponee's registration. This the legislation achieves by 'realigning' the right in question so that it corresponds to what appears on the Register. Realignment operates whether the inaccuracy was caused by commission or omission.[35] Thus, positively, disponees can take to be the owner of the land the person named on the Register as owner (even if he is not).[36] Negatively, disponees can assume that all encumbrances which require registration for their constitution will appear on the Register and that no other such encumbrances affect the property.[37] Certain conditions, however, must first be met. Naturally, disponees must be in good faith, for a person cannot hold the Register to be correct while knowing all along that it is wrong. In addition, for the positive protection, there are a number of further conditions which must be satisfied.

12.9 Dispositions by the person named as proprietor

Provided certain conditions are met, a disposition by the person named on the title sheet as proprietor can take effect even though the granter's title was void. In other words, a disposition from that person will not fail for absence of title (although it may of course fail for other reasons).[38] So if John owns land but the title sheet shows the owner to be Jane, a disposition from Jane, if the conditions are met, would transfer ownership.[39] The rule is found in s 86 of the 2012 Act.[40] Such cases will,

---

35 For the distinction, see paras 11.2–11.4 above. The former concerns the A and B sections of the title sheet, the latter the C and D sections.
36 LR(S)A 2012 ss 86 and 87, discussed in paras 12.9–12.17 below.
37 LR(S)A 2012 ss 91 and 93, discussed in para 12.18 below.
38 LR(S)A 2012 s 86(2). Section 86(3)(d) indeed expressly provides that the disposition must have been otherwise valid. Possible other causes of invalidity are manifold but include forgery, lack of capacity, and errors of execution. Such 'transactional' errors are covered by the Keeper's warranty but are not cured by registration of the deed: see para 12.4 above.
39 In principle, a disposition by John would also transfer ownership, because John is the owner. But as Jane is the registered proprietor, any person taking a disposition from John would need to satisfy the Keeper that John really was the owner (and hence that the Register was inaccurate) before the disposition would be accepted for registration. This is because the Keeper is empowered to register only if she is satisfied that the deed is valid: see para 8.7(4) above.
40 For discussion of this provision, see D L Carey Miller, '*Bona Fide* Acquisition: New in Scottish Land Law?', in F McCarthy, J Chalmers and S Bogle (eds), *Essays in Conveyancing and Property Law in Honour of Professor Robert Rennie* (2015; available at www.openbookpublishers.com/reader/343#page/1/mode/2up) 165.

of course, be rare, for if Jane is named on the Register as proprietor then, almost certainly, she is the proprietor, and the disponee has no need of protection. But just occasionally the Register will be wrong. This can arise in respect of 2012 Act titles, where there was no Midas touch to confer ownership on Jane, but it can also apply under the transitional provisions which apply in respect of 1979 Act titles.[41]

That a disposition from Jane is valid is, of course, an exception to the rule that only owners can transfer land.[42] It can be seen as the equivalent for heritable property of s 25 of the Sale of Goods Act 1979 for moveable property.[43] Of course, there is no transfer by Jane as such, for Jane has nothing to transfer. Rather s 86 of the 2012 Act provides that the disponee becomes owner notwithstanding that the disponer was not the owner, and hence that the disponee's right is realigned with what is stated on the Register. This might be classified as a case of original acquisition, ie where the law extinguishes John's title and confers a new title on the disponee, albeit a title subject to the same encumbrances as before;[44] or it might be seen as a case where, through Jane's actions, John's title is transferred to the disponee. Either way the result is the same: the disponee becomes owner, and John ceases to be owner.

Section 86 is concerned with *void* titles, ie with the case where Jane has no title at all, and not with *voidable* titles, ie with the case where Jane is owner but there are grounds for setting her title aside. Where Jane's title is voidable rather than void, the position continues to be governed by the general law, a subject to which we will return later.[45]

12.10 Dispositions by representatives of the person named as proprietor

The disposition need not be by the registered proprietor (Jane). It could also be granted by any person 'who would have had power to dispone the land were A [ie Jane] the proprietor, or (where A has died) had A been the proprietor'.[46] So for the purposes of realignment the granter can be an agent acting for Jane under a power of attorney, or Jane's executor or trustee in sequestration, or a heritable creditor exercising a power of sale in respect of a standard security granted by Jane.[47]

12.11 Transfers other than by disposition

Section 86 is restricted to dispositions, and does not apply where a person completes title on the basis of some other deed. For instance, if Scott (whose registered title

---

41 More precisely, it arises where, on the designated day, ownership is taken from the person registered as proprietor because (i) the entry was inaccurate and (ii) immediately before that day, the Keeper could have rectified the inaccuracy: see LR(S)A 2012 sch 4 para 17, discussed in para 11.9 above.
42 *Nemo plus juris ad alienum transferre potest quam ipse haberet.*
43 Section 25 confers (subject to exceptions) a good title on someone who buys in good faith from a seller in possession even if the seller is not yet the owner. But as the seller must have been in the process of becoming owner by buying from the person who was the owner, s 25 is much narrower in scope than s 86 of the 2012 Act.
44 On one view, a properly original title could not be subject to the previous encumbrances, but that is not the case here.
45 See para 12.17 below.
46 LR(S)A 2012 s 87(1).
47 Of course it is possible in such cases that the representative has already completed title in his own name. In that case, a disposition by the representative is a disposition by the registered proprietor, and so s 87 is not relevant.

is latently void) dies, and his executrix, Tara, confirms and completes title in her own name as executrix by registration of a notice of title, s 86 is not engaged and Tara's title will be void. But if Tara thereafter dispones, s 86 will apply in favour of the disponee, provided that the various conditions are met.

If, following Scott's death, the property is to be transferred to a third-party beneficiary, the beneficiary might prefer to receive a disposition from Tara, thus engaging s 86, as opposed to receiving a docket transfer under s 15 of the Succession (Scotland) Act 1964.

12.12 The conditions that must be met for s 86 to apply

A number of conditions must be met in order for s 86 to apply. These may be grouped into major conditions, of which there are two (good faith and possession), and some minor conditions. The implications of these conditions for examination of title are explored in a later chapter.[48]

One condition that does not apply is that the disposition be for value. Thus, for instance, a disposition by way of donation by a parent to a child, or a disposition by an executor to a beneficiary, could potentially engage the realignment provisions. Similarly, the Keeper's warranty applies regardless of whether the deed being registered is onerous or gratuitous.[49]

12.13 The first major condition: possession

In order to alert the true owner to the threat to his title,[50] s 86 imposes two distinct possessory requirements for realignment. In the first place, the disponer must be in possession when he 'purports to dispone the land'.[51] No further guidance is given as to timing, but as dispositions are not effective until they are delivered, it is thought that the relevant date is the date of delivery rather than the, possibly much earlier, date of execution.[52]

In the second place, the disponer must also have been in continuous possession for a period of a year.[53] Such a period cannot begin before the disponer was himself registered as proprietor, so that earlier periods of possession on a different basis, such as as a tenant, must be discounted.[54] As to when the period ends, it is not entirely clear whether *any* period of a year will do or whether the year must immediately precede the date of the disponee's registration. The purpose of the requirement, which is to alert the owner (John) to the rival claim (by Jane), would be served by either interpretation.[55] The Scottish Law Commission's policy, however, was that the possession should come immediately before registration[56]

---

48 Chapter 16.
49 See para 13.1 below. For discussion of this issue, see Scottish Law Commission, *Discussion Paper No 125 on Land Registration: Void and Voidable Titles* (2004) ('SLC DP 125') paras 7.21–7.35; SLC Report 222 para 19.29.
50 See para 2.12 above.
51 LR(S)A 2012 s 86(1).
52 The date on which the disposition is registered is excluded by LR(S)A 2012 s 86(5)(b), which allows for possession by the disponee on that date.
53 LR(S)A 2012 s 86(3)(a).
54 This is because s 86(3)(a)(i) requires the possession to be 'of A', and 'A' is defined in s 86(1)(a) as a person who 'is entered in the proprietorship section of the title sheet as proprietor'.
55 SLC DP 125 paras 4.46–4.52; SLC Report 222 paras 21.30–21.34.
56 SLC DP 125 para 4.49.

and, on the whole, the wording of s 86 supports that position.[57] This is especially apparent from two of the minor conditions in s 86, which impose requirements (in relation to caveats and to the state of the Keeper's knowledge) in respect of the one-year period, and which would hardly be workable if they did not refer to a *fixed* period of one year (as opposed to *any* period nominated by the disponee), nor indeed unless that period ended on the date of registration.[58] Of course, the issue will rarely be a live one because the disponer's possession will usually have been continuous and uninterrupted from the moment that his title was first registered.

Possession includes civil (indirect) possession, for example through a tenant,[59] and it is further provided that possession by a representative (such as an executor) is to be treated as possession by the registered proprietor.[60] Any shortfall in the disponer's year of possession can be made up for by possession by the disponee, provided that this follows, rather than precedes, the disponer's possession.[61] So if the disponer has been registered as proprietor, and in possession, for only nine months, the missing three months can be provided by the disponee. To the extent that those missing months occur after registration of the disponee's disposition, the acquisition of ownership is postponed until the months have been completed.[62] This, of course, assumes that the disponer was not owner and hence that s 86 was needed; if the disponer owned, as almost always, the disponee becomes owner immediately on registration. An example illustrates. Suppose that Jane is (mistakenly) registered as proprietor on 1 January and takes possession at that time. A few months later she dispones to Patrick, who registers his disposition on 16 July and takes possession. Under s 86 Patrick becomes owner, not on 16 July when he registers the disposition, but on 1 January of the following year when the year of possession has been completed. Deeds granted by Patrick between those two dates, such as, say, standard securities, will, in the normal case at least, be validated, as from 1 January, by the doctrine of accretion.[63]

As with positive prescription,[64] the land must be possessed openly, peaceably, and without judicial interruption.[65] Although s 86 does not say so, it may be assumed that 'judicial interruption' carries the same meaning as in the Prescription Act, namely the making by a person with an interest to do so of a claim in court or arbitration proceedings which challenges the possession in question.[66] Where the absence of title affects only a part of the subjects disponed, it may sometimes be difficult to show possessory acts in relation to that precise part; but if the part

---

57 Apart from what is said in the text, attention may also be drawn to the link between s 86(2) (with its reference to 'acquires ownership of land') and s 86(3)(a) ('the land has been in the possession'), and especially to s 86(5) ('where, as at the date of registration, the land has been in the possession').
58 LR(S)A 2012 s 86(3)(b), (e): see para 12.16 below.
59 LR(S)A 2012 s 113(1).
60 LR(S)A 2012 s 87(2).
61 LR(S)A 2012 s 86(3)(a)(ii).
62 LR(S)A 2012 s 86(3), (4)(b), (6). This date, however, will not be apparent from the title sheet.
63 For accretion, see K G C Reid, *The Law of Property in Scotland* (1996) para 677.
64 But s 86 is not a form of positive prescription, not least because the possession is not, or at least not primarily, by the acquirer. See also Carey Miller (n 40) 173–77.
65 LR(S)A 2012 s 86(3)(a). Assistance in the interpretation of these terms may be obtained from the case law and literature on positive prescription. For the second, see in particular D Johnston, *Prescription and Limitation* (2nd edn, 2012).
66 Prescription and Limitation (Scotland) Act 1973 s 4.

forms an integral element of the whole subjects, possession of other parts of the subjects may be treated as possession of the part in question.[67]

12.14 Possession: four cases

It may be helpful to say more about four cases involving possession which may appear to present difficulties.

Case 1

For several years Jane has been the registered owner[68] and possessor of a house. She now sells to Patrick. On 1 July (being the date of entry) the disposition is delivered and the price paid, and Patrick takes possession. On 14 July the disposition is registered.

Analysis. Both possessory requirements of s 86 are satisfied. (i) Jane possessed when, on 1 July, she purported to dispone. (ii) Jane followed by Patrick possessed for the year immediately prior to registration.[69]

Case 2

For several years Jane has been the registered owner and possessor of a house. She now sells to Patrick. On 1 June she relinquishes possession to Patrick. On 1 July the disposition is delivered and the price paid. On 14 July the disposition is registered.

Analysis. Both possessory requirements of s 86 are satisfied. (i) Jane was in civil possession, through Patrick, when she purported to dispone on 1 July. This is because, until delivery of the disposition, Patrick's entitlement to possess derived from Jane's entitlement.[70] (ii) As in case 1, Jane followed by Patrick possessed for the year immediately prior to registration.

Case 3

For several years Jane has been the registered owner and possessor of a house. Due to deteriorating health, she leaves the house on 1 February and moves into a care home. The house is marketed and sold to Patrick. It remains unoccupied until, on 1 July (being the date of entry), the disposition is delivered and the price paid, and Patrick takes possession. On 14 July the disposition is registered.

Analysis. Both possessory requirements of s 86 are satisfied. (i) Although the house was by then unoccupied, Jane possessed when she purported to dispone. This is because, having initially taken possession, Jane remained in possession (although the house was unoccupied) unless she was dispossessed by someone else (which did not occur).[71] (ii) As in case 1, Jane followed by Patrick possessed for the year immediately prior to registration

Case 4

For several years Jane was the registered owner and possessor of a house. Following her death, on 1 February, the house is marketed and sold to Patrick by her executor, James (who is confirmed as executor on 1 May). It remains unoccupied until, on 1 July (being the date of entry), the disposition is delivered and the price paid, and Patrick takes possession. On 14 July the disposition is registered.

---

67 Reid (n 63) para 119; and see also para 11.12 above.
68 By 'registered owner', here and below, we mean the person whose name appears as proprietor in the B section of the title sheet. Although registered, such a person might not actually be owner; it is for such occasional cases that s 86 is needed.
69 As permitted by LR(S)A 2012 ss 86(3)(a)(ii) and 86(5)(b).
70 Reid (n 63) para 121.
71 This is possession *animo solo*: see Reid (n 63) para 122; C Anderson, *Possession of Corporeal Moveables* (Studies in Scots Law vol 3, 2015) paras 4-06–4-14.

Analysis. (i) The first possessory requirement of s 86 is satisfied. Although the house by then was unoccupied, James possessed when he purported to dispone. This is because, having initially taken such possession as was necessary to sell the house, James remained in possession (although the house was unoccupied) unless he was dispossessed by someone else (which did not occur). (ii) The second possessory requirement is more troublesome. Jane's possession ended with her death on 1 February. James – whose possession is treated under the Act as equivalent to Jane's[72] – may not have taken up possession at once and, on one view, could not have done so for the purposes of s 86 until he was confirmed as executor on 1 May.[73] If that is correct, the period of continuous possession did not begin until 1 May, leaving a shortfall of more than nine months when the disposition was registered on 1 July.[74] That shortfall could be made up by Patrick's subsequent possession, but the one-year period would not then expire until 1 May of the following year.

Admittedly this case may also be capable of a different analysis. Odd though it may sound, it is not impossible that legal possession does not automatically terminate at death, and moreover there exists some authority that an executor is for certain purposes (which might include the present circumstances) the 'same person' as the deceased.[75] Thus it is possible that there was no discontinuity of possession.

12.15 The second major condition: good faith

The disponee must be in good faith.[76] The term is not defined by the Act but probably refers to subjective rather than objective good faith, so that disponees remain in good faith except where they know, as a positive fact, that the Register is wrong.[77] Thus a disponee who merely suspects that all is not well does not, it seems, have any duty to make further inquiries and is not deemed to have done so. Nor is the disponee deemed to know the contents of the archive record, which contains the deeds on which the entries in the Register are based.[78] Indeed to impose a duty of inquiry would be to infringe the 'curtain' principle of registration of title, ie the principle that the Register is the sole source of information about the title. All the same, there is no requirement that the disponee actually relied

---

72 LR(S)A 2012 s 87(2).
73 This is because 'A' for the purposes of s 87 is a person with the power to dispone the land, and James may not have acquired such power until he was confirmed as executor. If, however, there was a will in which James was appointed executor, and if it is accepted that executors can deduce title through wills (as to which see G L Gretton and K G C Reid, *Conveyancing* (4th edn, 2011) para 25-04), then James would have acquired the power to dispone the land at the moment of Jane's death.
74 The problem would disappear, of course, if s 86 can be read as not requiring that the one-year period immediately precede the date of registration; for, before her death, Jane was in possession for a continuous period of more than a year.
75 *Eadem persona cum defuncto.*
76 LR(S)A 2012 s 86(3)(c). This replaces the requirement of absence of fraud or carelessness which applied for the protection of purchasers (and others) under LR(S)A 1979 s 9(3)(a)(iii). A difficulty with that requirement was that it could sometimes be satisfied even where the purchaser was in bad faith: see *Dougbar Properties Ltd v Keeper of the Registers of Scotland* 1999 SC 513. See further SLC Report 222 paras 23.8–23.14.
77 SLC DP 125 paras 7.8–7.11. Compare, however, SLC Report 222 paras 23.16 and 23.17 which suppose otherwise. One might argue that the very existence of the provisions about caveats and restriction of the Keeper's warranty, referred to in these paragraphs, presupposes that objective good faith was *not* intended. Note that the equivalent provision in respect of the Keeper's warranty (s 78(b)) is worded quite differently and extends to objective knowledge, but that (presumably) is because the warranty covers transactional error and not just Register error: see para 13.17 below.
78 LR(S)A 2012 s 14(4).

on the Register. A disponee who ignores the Register and is ignorant as to what it contains is as much protected by s 86 as one who has pored anxiously over its contents.[79]

For the purposes of assessing good faith, the knowledge of an agent such as the solicitor acting in the purchase is, presumably, to be attributed to the principal.[80] So if a solicitor knows the title to be bad but cannot bring himself to tell his client, the client is denied the protection of s 86 (and indeed of the Keeper's warranty) and must seek his remedy against the solicitor.

Although the drafting is not as clear as one would wish,[81] it seems that the relevant date for good faith is the date on which ownership is acquired.[82] In the normal case that would be the date of registration, which is also the date on which the application is entered in the application record.[83] Where, however, the disponee's possession is needed to supplement possession by the disponer in order to achieve the required one-year period, ownership is not acquired until the end of that period.[84] Thus, and especially in the second case, disponees are at risk of unwelcome bad news even after the transaction has been settled and the price paid.[85]

12.16 The minor conditions

As well as the two major conditions (possession and good faith) there are four further conditions in s 86.[86] All are relatively minor and all concern indications, generally from the face of the Register, that the disponer's title may be open to question.

In the first place, the Keeper must have warranted, or be taken to have warranted, the disponer's title.[87] The Keeper does not warrant the title to minerals,[88] or

---

79 See SLC Report 222 para 19.27: 'Making an exception for those who do not actually rely on the Register would have little effect since almost everyone does in fact rely. Moreover, it would drag the system into messy and expensive disputes as to whether there had been actual reliance in any given case.' Reliance was not required under the 1979 Act.
80 As was the case for the equivalent (fraud and carelessness) requirement under the 1979 Act: see SLC DP 125 para 7.9.
81 In setting out the conditions that have to be satisfied, subs (3) of s 86 gives no indication as to timing. However, subs (2) ('The disponee acquires ownership of the land provided that the conditions in subsection (3) are met') can be taken to imply that the relevant time is the date on which ownership is acquired. That was certainly the Scottish Law Commission's policy: see SLC Report 222 para 23.5, and also s 45(3)(a) of the SLC draft Bill. LR(S)A 2012 s 91(2) makes the position clear in respect of the good-faith requirement in that provision. One might add that it is hard to think of a plausible alternative to the date of registration other than, perhaps, the date of delivery of the disposition: see SLC DP 125 paras 7.17–7.19.
82 SLC DP 125 para 7.19: 'if an acquirer is to be protected by the Register, then he ought to register with clean hands'.
83 LR(S)A 2012 ss 36 and 37(1): see para 9.22 above.
84 LR(S)A 2012 s 86(4)(b), (6), discussed at para 12.13 above.
85 In the second case but not the first, a claim would still lie under the Keeper's warranty: see LR(S)A 2012 s 78(b).
86 Strictly, there is a fifth, namely that the disposition is otherwise valid (s 86(3)(d)), but this is implicit in the idea that s 86 cures only absence of title.
87 LR(S)A 2012 s 86(3)(f). This is the successor of the rule in LR(S)A 1979 s 9(3)(a)(iv) which left even a proprietor in possession unprotected against rectification in the event that the Keeper had excluded indemnity.
88 LR(S)A 2012 s 73(2)(f); but there is power to grant such a warranty, in which case it will be mentioned on the title sheet: see para 13.13 below.

titles in which the entry as proprietor is marked as 'provisional',[89] or titles to the extent that they include land which the registered deed did not bear to include.[90] Otherwise,[91] the Keeper automatically warrants all titles registered under the 2012 Act unless, at the time of the registration,[92] the Keeper took steps to qualify or exclude the warranty and made an entry to that effect on the title sheet.[93] A qualification or exclusion is based on misgivings as to the title's validity;[94] unless obviously irrelevant, either will prevent the operation of s 86.[95] Though the drafting might have been clearer, the reference in the provision to 'be taken to' have granted warranty covers titles registered under the 1979 Act where the equivalent to the Keeper's warranty was registration with an indemnified title.[96]

In the second place, the Keeper must not since have 'become aware', during the one-year period of possession, that the disponer was not the owner.[97] It is hard to see why this condition was thought necessary, or indeed why it is tied to the one-year period.[98] If the Keeper knows that the disponer is not the owner, she must reject the application for registration on the ground of the disposition's invalidity, and no question of realignment can arise.[99] She will also be taking steps to have the entry on the title sheet rectified.[100] Of course, there is an element of risk here for acquirers, who might pay the price at settlement only to find that the application is rejected. The risk, however, seems a small one. If the Keeper has not uncovered the inaccuracy before (and rectified), it is unlikely that she will do so at the precise moment that the transaction is taking place. Furthermore, as RoS guidance makes plain, 'the Keeper cannot be considered to be aware of an inaccuracy until such time as she has fully satisfied herself as to its existence, ie that an inaccuracy is manifest in terms of s 80(1). Accordingly, an unsubstantiated claim of inaccuracy intimated to the Keeper would be insufficient in itself to prevent realignment.'[101] If the disponer's absence of title is a matter of doubt rather than certainty, the Keeper will accept the application for registration and,

---

89 LR(S)A 2012 s 73(2), (5). These are the result of the registration of *a non domino* dispositions: see para 17.18 below.
90 LR(S)A 2012 s 73(2)(h); of the three qualifications mentioned, this is the only one which will not be visible from an inspection of the title sheet. So if A dispones 5 acres to B, and B is by mistake registered as proprietor of 6 acres, when B comes to dispone the 6 acres to C, s 86 will not operate in respect of the sixth acre. In practice, of course, it is unlikely that B would be in possession of the sixth acre, a fact that ought to be apparent to C.
91 Section 78 lists a number of further cases where the Keeper's liability is excluded, but these are cases where 'the Keeper has no liability to pay compensation' rather than, as in s 73(2) and (5), cases where 'the Keeper does not warrant'.
92 That is, the registration in favour of the registered proprietor.
93 LR(S)A 2012 s 75(1), (3): see paras 13.12 below.
94 Qualification or exclusion is permitted only where the Keeper is 'not satisfied as to the validity of the acquisition': see LR(S)A 2012 s 75(1)(b).
95 SLC DP 125 para 7.12; SLC Report 222 para 23.17.
96 LR(S)A 1979 s 12. Indemnity could be excluded in whole or in part under s 12(2).
97 LR(S)A 2012 s 86(3)(b).
98 The condition did not appear in the equivalent provision (s 45) of the Scottish Law Commission's draft Bill.
99 See para 8.7(4) above. Alternatively, if the inaccuracy was discovered by the Keeper only after registration of the disposition, but realignment had yet to operate because some months of possession by the disponee were still needed, under s 86(3)(a)(ii), to complete the one-year period, the Keeper could rectify the Register before the one-year period expired.
100 LR(S)A 2012 s 80.
101 *General Guidance: Realignment of Rights* (n 33) 2.

at worst, restrict or exclude her warranty.[102] Such exclusion or restriction would not prevent realignment from taking place.[103]

The third condition is that there should be no caveat on the title sheet relevant to the acquisition.[104] That would not include a caveat which has expired but has yet to be removed from the Register.[105] A caveat indicates ongoing litigation in relation to the title.[106] Logically, the condition should concern only caveats on the title sheet at the time of acquisition of ownership, as indeed the Scottish Law Commission's draft Bill provided.[107] It is puzzling,[108] therefore, that s 86 extends the period to a full year prior to acquisition.[109] For on the one hand, a caveat which was on the title sheet at the start of the year but has since lapsed[110] or been recalled or discharged[111] is unlikely to refer to current litigation; and on the other hand, it is not obvious how information as to the previous state of the title sheet is to be discovered.[112] There is also another sense in which the condition is over-inclusive. It applies to any caveat 'relevant to the acquisition', a form of words which, since it is also used in s 91 in respect of the extinction of encumbrances,[113] must presumably be read quite broadly. If that is correct, it means that realignment could be prevented by a caveat in respect of litigation which has nothing to do with the validity of the disponer's title – for example, an action of reduction of a standard security.

The final condition concerns the (rare) case where the title sheet states that a particular name or designation is not known or is not known with reasonable certainty.[114] This can arise only from first registrations other than by application, that is to say, for Keeper-induced registration or automatic plot registration.[115] This condition too is over-inclusive. The condition is not met if the statement is found on the title sheet at any point during the year before the disponee's potential acquisition.[116] Nor is it met even if (as would admittedly be most unusual) the statement concerned, not the name or designation of the owner but the name or designation of someone with a lesser right such as a heritable security.

---

102 See para 9.9 above.
103 As explained above, LR(S)A 2012 s 86(3)(f) only requires the Keeper to have warranted the title of the *disponer*.
104 LR(S)A 2012 s 86(3)(e)(i).
105 Such caveats are often slow to be removed: see para 18.5 below.
106 LR(S)A 2012 s 67. For caveats, see ch 18 below.
107 SLC draft Bill s 45(3)(c)(i).
108 Indeed it may simply be a mistake. The equivalent provision in s 91(2)(b) refers only to caveats 'as at the date on which ownership is acquired'.
109 This is done by reference to the one-year period of possession which in turn (see para 12.13 above) seems to refer to the year immediately before the acquisition of ownership (ie, normally the year immediately before registration).
110 Unless renewed, a caveat expires after 12 months: LR(S)A 2012 ss 68 and 69.
111 LR(S)A 2012 ss 71 and 72.
112 It is true that LR(S)A 2012 s 104(1), (4) envisages that an extract of the title sheet can be obtained, subject to practicalities, 'as at a particular date', but an acquirer can hardly ask for title sheets for each of 365 days: see para 3.12 above.
113 For s 91, see para 12.18 below. Compare s 90 where, in the context of the grant of servitude, the wording is properly narrow ('a caveat relevant to the creation of the servitude').
114 LR(S)A 2012 s 30(5).
115 As to which see paras 7.9 and 7.19–7.24 respectively.
116 Again, the SLC draft Bill s 45(3)(c)(ii) refers only to the date of acquisition.

12.17 Voidable titles

Section 86 protects acquirers against titles that are void, not against those that are voidable. This is because protection against voidable titles is already provided for under the general law.[117]

As voidable titles are good unless and until set aside by reduction, a disponer, being the owner, can confer ownership on the disponee. A purchaser in good faith takes free of the voidability, while even a purchaser in bad faith or a donee becomes owner, albeit on a title which is voidable as before. With voidable titles as with void, therefore, a purchaser can rely on the Register. So long as the disponer is shown as owner, there need be no anxiety as to the title which is to be conferred.

The position is different if the voidable deed has already been reduced. But as a decree of reduction does not obtain real effect without registration,[118] and as registration will lead to a change of registered proprietor, there is no danger of an acquirer being misled.

Finally, something should be said about compensation, or its absence. A person who loses ownership to a *bona fide* acquirer under s 86 is compensated by the Keeper for his loss.[119] But a person who loses the right to reduce a voidable title under the general law has no claim for compensation but must pursue whatever remedy he may have against the person whose wrongdoing led to the initial transfer. Here the common law is less generous than the 2012 Act. Yet although the result is thus different, the fact-situations are sometimes quite close. So if the disponer became registered as owner by forgery, the victim of the forgery will be compensated by the Keeper for the loss of the property to the disponee. But if the disponer became registered as owner by fraud, resulting in a title which was voidable rather than void, no compensation will be due.[120]

12.18 Omitted encumbrances extinguished

Section 86 (discussed above) concerns errors by commission. Its companion provision, for errors by omission, is s 91. The linkage is conceptual rather than factual, for an acquirer in need of s 91 will rarely also be in need of s 86, or vice versa.

By s 91 an acquirer takes free of encumbrances which ought to appear on the Register but do not. Again, the idea is that the Register can be taken at face value. Under s 91 any omitted encumbrance is extinguished,[121] leaving its (former) holder with a claim for compensation from the Keeper.[122] Whether there was an omission on the title sheet is judged as at the date on which ownership is acquired

---

117 Reid (n 63) para 692. Equally, voidability is not protected under the Keeper's warranty: see para 13.6 below.
118 Conveyancing (Scotland) Act 1924 s 46A. An unregistered decree of reduction does not (as under the 1979 Act) make the Register inaccurate: see LR(S)A 2012 s 65(4)(a) and, for a discussion of the policy, SLC Report 222 part 28. See also para 6.12 above.
119 LR(S)A 2012 s 94; for details, see paras 14.2 and 14.3 below.
120 At first sight this difference between void and voidable titles may seem odd. For discussion, see para 13.6 below.
121 LR(S)A 2012 s 91(1)(b). The position under the 1979 Act, by contrast, was that an omitted encumbrance was suppressed for as long as there was a proprietor in possession, but remained capable of re-entering the Register by rectification.
122 LR(S)A 2012 s 94.

– which, almost always, will be the date of the acquirer's registration.[123] But if an encumbrance was absent then, it is likely to have been absent earlier as well, at the time when the acquirer was examining title.

Unlike s 86, s 91 is not confined to acquisition by disposition but applies to all acquisitions which involve registration, including acquisitions by notice of title.[124] Furthermore, as there is no requirement that a title sheet exist *before* the date of registration, s 86 applies to first registrations as well as to dealings with (already) registered land.

There are two conditions for the operation of s 91, both already familiar from s 86. First, acquirers must be in good faith,[125] by which seems to be meant subjective good faith or in other words an absence of actual knowledge of the encumbrance in question.[126] And secondly, the title sheet must not be subject to a caveat relevant to the acquisition; caveats are an indication of ongoing litigation.[127] The possessory requirements of s 86 are absent from s 91 for, as there is no quarrel with the disponer's title to possess, the fact of his possession would contribute nothing to alerting the holder of an encumbrance to its omission from the Register.[128]

Section 91 applies to any encumbrance which was constituted by registration, such as standard securities and real burdens.[129] It does not, therefore, apply to off-register rights such as public rights of way or prescriptive servitudes, or indeed to any servitude which was not constituted by dual registration.[130] Equally, it does not apply to leases, regardless of their duration. The exclusion of long leases[131] may seem surprising for, unlike short leases, they can only be constituted, as real rights, by registration;[132] but if a lease had indeed been registered and had a title sheet of its own, it was presumably thought unacceptable for it to be extinguished merely because of a missing cross-reference in the title sheet of the plot of land.[133] In the, no doubt tiny, number of cases where this occurs, an acquirer will have to be alerted to the lease by the tenant's possession, as in the case of a short lease.[134]

---

123 Except where the acquisition is by virtue of s 86 and the disponee needs extra time to complete the possession of the disponer: see ss 86(4)(b) and 91(1).
124 Of course, acquisition of land is almost invariably by registration. An exception is where ownership is acquired by operation of a survivorship clause.
125 LR(S)A 2012 s 91(2)(a).
126 See para 12.15 above.
127 LR(S)A 2012 s 91(2)(b). For caveats, see ch 18. By contrast to s 86, for a caveat to be relevant it must appear on the title sheet on the date on which ownership is acquired. Nonetheless the provision is still over-inclusive in respect that the caveat might relate to litigation which has nothing to do with the encumbrance in question: see para 12.16 above.
128 The giving of notice is the purpose of the possessory requirement in s 86: see para 2.12 above.
129 In fact the definition in LR(S)A 2012 s 91(4) is one by exclusion, and para (e) excludes 'an encumbrance the creation of which does not require registration of the constitutive deed'. 'Encumbrance' is not further defined but includes, though is wider than, subordinate real rights. For the encumbrances that must appear in the D (burdens) section of title sheets, see para 4.17 above.
130 These are two of the three examples listed in s 91(4)(a)–(c) (the other example being a path delineated by order under s 22 of the Land Reform (Scotland) Act 2003); this is the same as the list in s 73(2)(a)–(c), giving exclusions from the Keeper's warranty: see para 13.4 below. For off-register rights, see paras 4.26–4.28 above.
131 Ie leases for more than 20 years.
132 See para 20.4 below.
133 It should appear in the burdens section: see LR(S)A 2012 s 9(1)(b). The omission of long leases is, however, covered by the Keeper's warranty: see ss 73(1)(b) and 74(1)(b).
134 A standard security which appears in the securities section of a sharing title sheet but not of the shared title sheet is equally, and understandably, exempt from the extinctive effect of s 91: see LR(S)A 2012 s 91(3). For shared and sharing title sheets, see paras 4.20 and 4.21 above.

The most likely time for the omission of encumbrances is when a new title sheet is being made up on first registration, particularly as heavy reliance is now placed on what appears (or does not appear) in the application form for registration.[135] If omissions occur thereafter this will usually be due to a void discharge, resulting in the erroneous deletion of an encumbrance.[136] Such a deletion, it should be emphasised, does not of itself extinguish the encumbrance; but if the land is transferred before the error is noticed and the title sheet rectified, the encumbrance is extinguished when the transferee becomes the owner.[137]

12.19 Certain floating charges extinguished

Section 91 is concerned with encumbrances that ought to be on the Register but are not. It offers no protection against off-register encumbrances such as short leases and prescriptive servitudes.[138] Such encumbrances are simply outwith the land registration system.

But there is an exception for certain categories of floating charge. A floating charge can affect an acquirer only where it has crystallised (attached) before the acquirer takers delivery of the disposition.[139] Those acquiring from a company, therefore, must search the companies register for floating charges and, where one is found, obtain a certificate of non-crystallisation from the chargeholder.[140] In practice an acquirer can only search against the person currently registered as proprietor, for the Register gives no information as to previous owners. Yet if a previous owner had granted a floating charge, and that charge had crystallised before the owner parted with the property, the crystallised charge will continue to burden the property. For this practical difficulty the 2012 Act provides a simple solution.[141] By s 93 an acquirer in good faith is unaffected by a floating charge granted by a predecessor in title of the current disponer.[142] The floating charge is thus restricted so that it no longer burdens the property.

12.20 Compensation

Inevitably, the gain to acquirers by realignment is accompanied by a corresponding loss to those whose rights have now been extinguished. For that loss, compensation is due from the Keeper.[143] If the 'mud' is no longer to be available, there is at

---

135 Due to the 'tell me don't show me' rule: see paras 8.11 and 8.25 above.
136 As in *Santander UK plc v Keeper of the Registers of Scotland* [2013] CSOH 24, 2013 SLT 362 (decided under the 1979 Act).
137 LR(S)A 2012 s 91(1).
138 See para 12.18 above.
139 Registration is not needed: see the controversial decision in *Sharp v Thomson* 1997 SC (HL) 66. The Scottish Law Commission has recommended that the attachment of a floating charge should involve registration: Scottish Law Commission, *Report No 208 on Sharp v Thomson* (2007) part 5. It is to be regretted that nothing has been done to give this effect.
140 See eg Gretton and Reid (n 73) para 28-09.
141 There was none under the 1979 Act. For background, see Scottish Law Commission, *Discussion Paper No 130 on Land Registration: Miscellaneous Issues* (2005) ('SLC DP 130') paras 8.29 and 8.30; SLC Report 222 para 30.12.
142 Section 93 applies to any case where a person in good faith 'acquires ownership of land' regardless of the method of acquisition used. There is no corresponding provision for the acquirers of a registered lease.
143 LR(S)A 2012 s 94.

least the consolation of the 'money'. The compensation arrangements are explored further in the chapter 14.[144]

ASSIGNATIONS OF REGISTERED LEASES

12.21 Assignations by the person named as tenant

The rules just discussed for dispositions apply, with appropriate modifications, to assignations of registered leases.[145] Like a disponee, therefore, a good-faith assignee is protected against latent errors on the Register.

Section 88[146] is the equivalent for assignations to s 86 for dispositions. On registration, the acquirer becomes tenant under the lease.[147] The conditions which must be met for acquisitions under s 86 apply equally to those under s 88,[148] and the reader is referred to the account given earlier.[149] One additional condition applies: the acquirer becomes tenant only if the lease is extant.[150] This is unsurprising.[151] If the lease was invalid from the beginning, or was valid but has since been terminated, it would be strange indeed if it could be brought into existence without the consent of the putative landlord.[152]

12.22 Omitted encumbrances extinguished

Section 92 is the parallel provision for assignations to s 91 for dispositions, and we will not repeat here what we have already said in relation to s 91.[153] The broad principle is that assignees in good faith take free of encumbrances which ought to appear on the Register but do not.[154] On the assignee's acquisition of the lease, any omitted encumbrances are extinguished. The encumbrances in question are listed in s 92(4): heritable securities over the lease;[155] such terms of the lease as concern the property, and so are binding on future tenants, other than the obligation to pay rent or an obligation of relief in relation to such payment; and real conditions created in an assignation or deed of conditions. In line with s 91, subleases are excluded, whether they are of short duration (and so not registrable) or for more than 20 years (in which case registration is required for their constitution).

In function and scope, s 92 is broadly equivalent to the extinctive words which occurred at the end of s 3(1)(a) of the 1979 Act, providing that, on receiving a

---

144 See paras 14.2 and 14.3 below.
145 Except that there is no equivalent for registered leases of s 93 (floating charges).
146 As supplemented by s 89 in respect of assignations made by a representative of the person named as tenant.
147 LR(S)A 2012 s 88(1), (2).
148 LR(S)A 2012 s 88(3). There is, however, no equivalent to s 86(3)(e)(ii) because registration of a lease interest can only occur by application.
149 See paras 12.12–12.16 above.
150 LR(S)A 2012 s 88(3)(d).
151 Indeed it is arguable that the result would be the same even without a formal condition, for s 88 would simply make the assignee the acquirer of something which does not exist.
152 The Scottish Law Commission emphasised that off-register changes in rights are risks that an acquirer must simply take and are not the proper subject of protection by a system of land registration: see SLC Report 222 para 23.28.
153 See para 12.18 above.
154 LR(S)A 2012 s 92(1), (2).
155 But not over the land itself: such securities appear only in the title sheet for the plot of land: see para 4.16 above.

real right on registration, a person took subject only to those encumbrances which were listed on the Register and to overriding interests (ie off-register rights);[156] encumbrances which should have appeared on the Register but did not were not capable, under s 3(1)(a), of affecting acquirers.[157] For reasons explained in chapter 20, the 2012 Act amended the Registration of Leases (Scotland) Act 1857 by inserting a provision – s 20B(1)(a) – which was modelled closely on s 3(1)(a) of the 1979 Act.[158] In what was evidently an oversight, however, s 20B(1)(a) includes the extinctive words from s 3(1)(a), notwithstanding that extinction of omitted encumbrances is now separately provided for by s 92 of the 2012 Act. Thus the effect of registering a deed in respect of a long lease, s 20B(1)(a) provides, is for the acquirer to take the right 'subject only to the effect of any matter entered in that register so far as adverse to the entitlement'.

None of this would matter very much if the extinctive words in s 20B(1)(a) covered the same ground as s 92. Unfortunately, however, shorn of the context of the 1979 Act (which, in other provisions, added a requirement of good faith and allowed for the payment of compensation),[159] and adjusted so as to exclude any reference to overriding interests,[160] s 20B(1)(a) goes considerably further than s 92, at least if read at face value. It appears to allow for the extinction of omitted encumbrances even where the assignee was in bad faith and knew of the omission. More importantly, it seems to provide for the extinction, without compensation,[161] of all off-register rights[162] (such as subleases of 20 years or less) on every occasion on which the lease is assigned or some other deed in respect of it is registered.

It is plain that s 20B(1)(a) needs to be amended so as to remove the extinctive words. Until such time as this is done, however, it will be necessary to read the provision so as to comply as far as possible with the policy set out in s 92 of the 2012 Act. In fact it should not be too difficult to imply into s 20B(1) a duty of good faith on the part of acquirers; nor, in construing the words 'subject only to the effect of any matter entered in that register' should it be beyond normal interpretative principles to confine them to matters which are able to appear on the Register in the first place and hence as excluding encumbrances (such as short leases) which are constituted off-register.

12.23 Compensation

As with other cases of realignment, a person who suffers loss is entitled to compensation from the Keeper.[163] The details are considered in chapter 14.[164]

---

156 For off-register rights, see paras 4.26–4.28 above.
157 Scottish Law Commission, *Discussion Paper No 128 on Land Registration: Registration, Rectification and Indemnity* (2005) ('SLC DP 128') part 5 and especially paras 5.33–5.44. See also para 2.7 above.
158 LR(S)A 2012 s 52(2): see para 20.7 below.
159 LR(S)A 1979 ss 9(3)(a)(iii) and 12(1).
160 This adjustment, which is the source of most of the difficulty, was not present in the SLC draft Bill which, in sch 4 para 18, had been careful to exclude overriding interests.
161 This is because the compensation provisions of the 1979 Act have been repealed, while those in the 2012 Act (ie s 94) only apply, in this context, to encumbrances extinguished by s 92.
162 Ie overriding interests.
163 LR(S)A 2012 s 94.
164 See paras 14.2 and 14.3 below.

GRANTS OF SERVITUDE

12.24 Realignment and subordinate real rights

Realignment does not usually apply to subordinate real rights.[165] If the granter of, say, a standard security or lease is not the owner of the land (despite being registered as such), the grant is ineffective and the land remains unburdened. The grantee receives, at most, the 'money' and not the 'mud': there will be a claim under the Keeper's warranty, as well as under the warrandice clause in the deed; but the grant itself will not be good, even if the grantee was in good faith. To this rule the grant of servitudes forms a lone exception. In view of the potential value of servitudes to those seeking to acquire them, it was felt preferable to validate the servitude and compensate the owner of the (now) servient tenement rather than the other way around.[166] Section 90 (discussed below) so provides. With servitudes, therefore, it is the grantee who receives the 'mud' and the servient proprietor the 'money' in the form of compensation from the Keeper.[167]

12.25 Grants of servitude by the person named as proprietor

Section 90 validates grants of servitude from a person who, though not the owner of the property to be burdened, is named on the Register as its owner. The grantee can thus rely on what the Register says and need do nothing to verify its accuracy. As with s 86, however (which makes equivalent provision for dispositions), certain conditions must first be met.

The two central conditions concern the granter's possession and the grantee's good faith.[168] The grantee must be in good faith, in the sense of not knowing the Register to be wrong.[169] And the granter must be in possession at the time of the grant, and for the year prior to the grant's registration.[170] Any shortfall in the possession before registration can be made up by the granter's possession after registration, but the servitude is then not acquired until the one-year period of possession is completed.[171] Possession may be either natural or civil.[172]

---

165 See para 12.5 above.
166 SLC DP 130 para 4.18. Whether the same logic should have been applied to the grant of long leases will not be discussed here.
167 Where s 90 operates to create a servitude, the owner of the (now-servient) property is entitled to compensation from the Keeper under s 94: see paras 14.2 and 14.3 below.
168 A fuller discussion of both conditions can be found at paras 12.13–12.15 above in the context of s 86.
169 LR(S)A 2012 s 90(3)(c). The relevant time for good faith is probably the date of registration or, if post-registration possession is needed to complete the one-year period, at the end of the year of possession.
170 LR(S)A 2012 s 90(1), (3)(a). A grant of servitude normally requires to be registered against both the dominant and the servient tenements: see Title Conditions (Scotland) Act 2003 s 75.
171 LR(S)A 2012 s 90(4)(b), (6). Unlike with s 86, the post-registration possession must also be by the granter, reflecting the facts (i) that the granter remains as owner, and (ii) that the grantee of a servitude has only intermittent possession of the land.
172 LR(S)A 2012 s 113(1).

Certain additional conditions apply, and follow closely the equivalent conditions in s 86.[173] As they are discussed fully in that context,[174] the treatment here can be brief. In the first place, the Keeper must have warranted, or be taken to have warranted, the granter's title.[175] Secondly, during the one-year period of possession there must have been no caveat on the Register which was relevant to the creation of the servitude.[176] Finally, during the same period the Keeper must not have become aware that the Register was inaccurate.[177]

Section 90 makes no stipulation as to type of deed so that the provision applies, for example, to a grant by freestanding deed of servitude or as part of a split-off disposition. In the case of a disposition, s 90 will work hand-in-hand with s 86 (to validate the actual transfer). Servitudes in a split-off disposition can be created either by grant (so that the part granted is the benefited property) or by reservation (so that the part retained is the benefited property). The former is plainly covered by s 90; the position of the latter is less certain and is considered separately below.

For the purposes of s 90 the grant must be by the registered owner; by contrast with s 86, there is no provision for grants by representative such as agents or executors.[178] Further, the grant of servitude must presumably be express; implied servitudes can thus only be granted by the person who really is the owner.

12.26 Servitudes by reservation

Does s 90 apply to servitudes by reservation? Take the following example. Jane is registered as proprietor of land that belongs to John. She grants a disposition of part of the land to Patrick, reserving a servitude right of way. Patrick, if the conditions for s 86 are met, will become owner on registration. But what of the servitude? As Patrick bought subject to the servitude, it seems only just that the servitude should be good. And the establishment of a servitude is, for John, some small consolation for the loss of his land. Yet if the result which is desired seems clear, it is less clear that it can be achieved by s 90.

Among the conditions set by s 90 is the condition that 'the proprietor of what is to be the benefited property is in good faith'.[179] Good faith is thus required, not of Jane (who granted the disposition), nor of Patrick (who received the grant), but of John (who in all probability knew nothing about the transaction).[180] So if John knew that the Register was wrong in showing Jane as owner, the servitude will fail; and if he did not know what the Register said, or knew what it said but not that it was wrong, the servitude succeeds. Which of those is the case will be a

---

173 There is, however, no equivalent of s 86(3)(d) ('the disposition would have conferred ownership on B had A been proprietor when the land was disponed'). Nonetheless it is thought that the grant of servitude (like a disposition) must be valid in all respects other than the absence of title in the granter, for absence of title is the only mischief that s 90 is seeking to cure. In this connection it should be noted that s 90(1) only applies where the registered proprietor 'purports to create a servitude', wording which may seem to presuppose an otherwise valid grant.
174 See para 12.16 above.
175 LR(S)A 2012 s 90(3)(e).
176 LR(S)A 2012 s 90(3)(d).
177 LR(S)A 2012 s 90(3)(b). This condition is not found in s 50 of the SLC draft Bill.
178 See para 12.10 above.
179 LR(S)A 2012 s 90(3)(c).
180 As s 90(1) makes clear that Jane is '*not* the proprietor', 'proprietor' in s 90(3)(c) must be given its natural meaning as the person who really does own the benefited property.

matter of chance. That it should determine the existence of the servitude is hardly satisfactory.

Another analysis is possible if contestable. A servitude by reservation, it might be argued, is created by the grantee of a disposition (Patrick) and not by the granter (Jane), because the property to be burdened is the grantee's and not the granter's; and since registration of the disposition makes Patrick owner of that property, then so too, on this view, does it bring the servitude over that property into life. The 'right' result is then achieved, and without recourse to s 90.

Chapter 13

The Guarantee of Title (2): The Keeper's Warranty

SCOPE

13.1 Introduction

In registering a title, the Keeper warrants its validity as at the date of registration.[1] This is the guarantee by 'money', as opposed to the (more limited) guarantee by 'mud' considered in the previous chapter.[2] The warranty is given to the applicant[3] or, if a plot was registered without application as a result of Keeper-induced or automatic plot registration,[4] it is given to the person who is being registered as owner.[5] It applies to registrations in respect of real rights occurring on or after 8 December 2014; registrations prior to that date are covered by the indemnity system contained in the 1979 Act or by a modified version of the 2012 Act system (for which see below).[6] No distinction is drawn between onerous and gratuitous transactions, so that, for example, a title based on a disposition by way of gift is warranted in the same way as one based on a disposition by way of sale. But an entry on the Register resulting from an *a non domino* disposition and marked as 'provisional' is not warranted.[7]

The Keeper's warranty applies automatically, by force of statute, unless excluded or restricted by an express statement on the title sheet, or by the legislation itself. Where the warranty is breached, the Keeper must compensate the person registered as owner or, as the case may be, as holder of a subordinate real right, in respect of any losses which result.[8] In effect the warranty is a form of title insurance, comparable to private insurance, paid for by a notional levy exacted as part of the registration dues.[9] It also resembles the obligation of warrandice found in most conveyancing deeds;[10] but whereas warrandice guarantees the title only at the start

---

1 LR(S)A 2012 ss 73 and 74: see para 13.5 below. For the meaning of date of registration, see para 9.22 above.
2 For the distinction, see paras 12.1–12.7 above.
3 LR(S)A 2012 s 73(1). Successors also potentially take the benefit of the warranty: see para 13.8 below.
4 As to which see, respectively, paras 7.19–7.24 and 7.9 above.
5 LR(S)A 2012 s 74(1): see para 13.8 below.
6 See paras 13.21–13.23 below.
7 LR(S)A 2012 s 73(5): see para 13.12 below.
8 See paras 13.15 ff below.
9 In 2010/11, the amount paid out in indemnity (a mere £272,513) corresponded to 0.8% of the registration fees: see Financial Memorandum accompanying the Land Registration (Scotland) Bill, para 385, reproduced in Scottish Parliament, *Passage of the Land Registration etc (Scotland) Bill 2011* (2013, SPPB 174) (available at www.scottish.parliament.uk/parliamentarybusiness/Bills/44469.aspx) 156. In the most recent year for which figures are available, 2014/15, a total of £344,000 was paid out as indemnity under the 1979 Act or compensation under the 2012 Act: see Registers of Scotland, *Annual Report and Accounts 2014–2015* (2015) 25.
10 For warrandice, see K G C Reid, *The Law of Property in Scotland* (1996) paras 702–714; G L Gretton and K G C Reid, *Conveyancing* (4th edn, 2011) paras 19-04–19-14.

of a transaction (ie the title of the granter), the Keeper's warranty guarantees the title at its conclusion (ie the title acquired by the grantee). In other words, it covers 'transactional' error as well as 'Register' error.[11]

Not everything on the Register is covered by the warranty.[12] But the Keeper guarantees those things that are likely to be important to acquirers of real rights. Thus, positively, there is a warranty that the acquirer's title is good, and, negatively, there is a warranty that the title is free from encumbrances other than those which appear on the Register. In other words, there is both a warranty as to title and a warranty as to encumbrances;[13] the former concerns the A and B sections of the title sheet, the latter the C and D sections.[14] This duality is another respect in which the Keeper's warranty resembles ordinary grants of warrandice.

13.2 The first warranty: validity of title

So far as title is concerned, the Keeper warrants the accuracy of the title sheet 'in so far as it shows an acquisition, variation or discharge[15] in favour of the applicant'.[16] In respect of the first of these, acquisition, this amounts to a guarantee (i) that the right exists; (ii) that it is held by the acquirer (now shown on the title sheet as the holder of the right); and (iii) that it is a right over the land described in the A (property) section of the title sheet, including the pertinents of that land.[17] In respect of variations and discharges, it guarantees their legal effectiveness. So if a disposition is registered in the Land Register, the Keeper warrants that the disponee is owner; if it is a standard security that is registered, the guarantee is that the security exists and is held by the creditor in question;[18] and if a discharge of the security is registered, the guarantee is that the security is extinguished.

In the creation of real burdens and servitudes, registration requires the making of an entry in two separate title sheets, ie the title sheets of both the benefited and the burdened properties (in the A[19] and D sections respectively).[20] Such dual registration does not affect the working of the warranty. Thus the title condition is warranted to exist and to be held by the person named as proprietor of the benefited property.[21]

---

11 Ie errors which occur in the course of a transaction as well as errors which pre-date the transaction and are already present on the Register: see para 12.4 above.
12 Compare here the apparently universal approach taken by the 1979 Act, which partly explains the large number of exceptions contained in s 12(3): see Scottish Law Commission, *Discussion Paper No 128 on Land Registration: Registration, Rectification and Indemnity* (2005) ('SLC DP 128') para 7.9.
13 Or, to put it another way, a warranty in respect both of the Keeper's commissions and omissions.
14 For the different sections of a title sheet, see paras 4.7 and 4.14–4.17 above.
15 A discharge is not 'shown' in the sense of being listed on the title sheet. Rather, when a standard security or other encumbrance is discharged, it is simply removed from the title sheet.
16 LR(S)A 2012 s 73(1)(a). Where registration occurs without application, the equivalent warranty, in s 74(1)(a), is that the Register is accurate 'in so far as it shows the owner to be the proprietor or proprietor in common'.
17 For this gloss, see proposal 25(2) in SLC DP 128 para 7.29.
18 But there is no warranty as to the amount owed.
19 This is likely to be only a glancing reference in the case of real burdens, with the details of the burdens being set out in the D section.
20 For dual registration, see para 8.19 above.
21 As LR(S)A 2012 s 73(4) acknowledges, that is not necessarily the applicant for registration but might be someone else. For example, when a real burden or servitude is created by reservation in a disposition, it is the disponer, not the disponee, who is the holder of the right.

13.3 Some matters not covered

Some qualifications to the title warranty should be mentioned. In the creation of servitudes and real burdens, the guarantee that the right exists does not cover the possibility that the right might not be recognised as a servitude or real burden in the first place;[22] in the assignation of long leases, the possibility of off-register variations or extinction is not covered.[23] The former is left to the professional judgment of the applicant's lawyers, the latter to due diligence.

There are also qualifications in respect of the land over which the right is being acquired. In principle, this is guaranteed to be such land, and associated pertinents, as are described in the A (property) section of the title sheet. But there is no guarantee that mines and minerals are included (even if expressly mentioned),[24] that a boundary has not been altered by alluvion,[25] or even, where the base map[26] was inaccurate, that the boundaries of the plot as shown on the cadastral map are correct.[27]

Nor is there a guarantee that (incorporeal) pertinents in the A section, such as servitudes, are of a kind recognised in law or that their content or existence is unaffected by off-register events (such as negative prescription).[28] So an incoming owner cannot place complete reliance on the fact that a servitude is mentioned in the A section of the title sheet; depending on its importance, he may feel the need to make inquiries. Even where the Keeper's warranty does apply, this is not the same thing as receiving the servitude itself, and the (slight) risk that it may not exist may be a further reason for making inquiries.[29]

Occasionally, a person is registered with more extensive rights than is justified by the deed or, where the registration proceeds without application, by the underlying title.[30] If so, the excess is not warranted; nor, assuming the registration

---

22 LR(S)A 2012 s 73(2)(d), discussed in Scottish Law Commission, *Report No 222 on Land Registration* (2010) ('SLC Report 222') para 22.27. Both servitudes and real burdens are subject to rules as to content: see Title Conditions (Scotland) Act 2003 ss 2, 3 and 76, and also Gretton and Reid (n 10) para 13-07.
23 LR(S)A 2012 s 73(2)(g): see SLC Report 222 para 9.31.
24 LR(S)A 2012 s 73(2)(f). This, and the equivalent provision in the SLC draft Bill (s 39(1)(b)(vi)), do not correspond to the recommendation in SLC Report 222 para 22.31, which excluded the warranty only where the title did not expressly mention mineral rights. That had been the position under the LR(S)A 1979 s 12(3)(f). It is, however, open to an applicant to request that the warranty be extended to minerals: see s 75(1)(a) and para 13.13 below.
25 LR(S)A 2012 s 73(2)(i). For alluvion, see para 5.17 above.
26 The base map is, and is likely to remain, the OS map: see LR(S)A 2012 s 11(6), and para 5.3 above.
27 LR(S)A 2012 s 78(a), which is based on LR(S)A 1979 s 12(3)(d). One might have expected this provision to appear, with the other qualifications, in s 73, and not in s 78 which is otherwise concerned with defences particular to a claim. For the qualification to apply, the Keeper's reliance on the OS map must have been reasonable, as would normally be the case. The cadastral map is not considered to be inaccurate if the error in the OS map is within the published tolerances relevant to the scale of map involved: see s 65(3) and para 11.4 above.
28 LR(S)A 2012 s 73(2)(d), (e): see SLC Report paras 22.27 and 22.28.
29 While the initial constitution of an express servitude benefits from realignment in the event that the granter turns out not to be owner (see LR(S)A 2012 s 90, discussed at paras 12.24–12.26 above), there is no equivalent protection in respect of later transmission. For the implications for examination of title, see para 16.9 below.
30 LR(S)A 2012 ss 73(2)(h) and 74(2), (3): see Scottish Law Commission, *Discussion Paper on Land Registration: Void and Voidable Titles* (2004) ('SLC DP 125') paras 3.35–3.41; SLC Report 222 para 22.24. Under the 1979 Act the disponee was likely to receive a windfall benefit, in the form either of the 'mud' (if he was in possession) or the 'money' (if the Register came later to be rectified).

is on or after 8 December 2014, are any rights conferred.[31] Such 'over-registration', where it occurs, arises typically on the making up of a new title sheet. For example, if a disposition inducing first registration conveys four hectares and the new title sheet shows the disponee as owner of five, title to the additional hectare is not warranted (nor does the disponee become its owner).

Finally, it should be mentioned that not all deeds presented for registration are concerned with real rights. The compendious list of registrable deeds includes quite a number whose function is entirely different.[32] For documents like these – many not often encountered – the warranty as to title is of no application.

13.4 The second warranty: freedom from undisclosed encumbrances

The warranty as to title is supplemented by a warranty in respect of encumbrances.[33] This concerns the C (securities) and D (burdens) sections of the title sheet. The Keeper warrants the accuracy of the title sheet 'in so far as there is [not] omitted from it any encumbrance the inclusion of which is permitted or required by or under an enactment'.[34] In other words, all encumbrances affecting the land which ought to be on the title sheet are guaranteed to be present; other encumbrances fall outside the warranty. The distinction is, roughly, between those encumbrances which are constituted by registration and those, such as short leases and floating charges, which are not. The former are (or should be) on the title sheet (where they will appear in the C or D sections); the latter, with some exceptions, are not. And the warranty, in effect, is that the property is subject only to (i) those encumbrances which are listed on the title sheet, and (ii) such further encumbrances, if any, as may have been constituted off-register.[35] In keeping with this division, the small class of encumbrances which, though constituted off-register, are meant nonetheless to be referred to in the D section of the relevant title sheet – public rights of way, prescriptive servitudes, and paths delineated by order under s 22 of the Land Reform (Scotland) Act 2003[36] – are excluded from the warranty.

Servitudes are in a special position. Prescriptive servitudes lie outside the Keeper's warranty, as just mentioned. But so too do registered servitudes except those constituted by dual registration.[37] This is because such servitudes might be registered against the benefited property only and hence would not appear on the title sheet of the burdened property.[38] Dual registration only became mandatory on

---

31 Under the 2012 Act there is, of course, no Midas touch: see para 9.20 above.
32 The list is reproduced as an appendix to ch 6.
33 'Encumbrance' is not defined, but includes, though is wider than, subordinate real rights.
34 LR(S)A 2012 ss 73(1)(b) and 74(1)(b). The 'which is permitted or required' formula derives from s 9(1)(f), listing the encumbrances to be included in the D section of title sheets. Encumbrances are 'required' to be included where either registration is needed for their constitution or, despite being constituted off-register, they fall within one of the other heads in s 9(1): see para 4.17 above. There does not seem to be any example of an encumbrance which is 'permitted' to be included in the title sheet but not 'required'.
35 Compare s 91(4)(e) (on realignment in respect of omitted encumbrances), where the exclusion of off-register encumbrances is made explicit. The ambit of ss 73(1)(b) and 91 appears to be the same, but, for reasons which are unclear, they are drafted in different ways.
36 LR(S)A 2012 s 73(2)(a)–(c). The same list appears in s 91(4)(a)–(c). See, for these encumbrances, para 4.17 above.
37 LR(S)A 2012 s 73(2)(c), excluding from the warranty all servitudes other than those registered under s 75(1) of the Title Conditions (Scotland) Act 2003 (which provides for dual registration).
38 See *Balfour v Kinsey* 1987 SLT 144.

28 November 2004.[39] The possible existence of servitudes created before that date is thus excluded from the Keeper's warranty.

Although the warranty extends to all transactions, it will be useful mainly for registrations in respect of acquisitions, whether of ownership or of subordinate real rights.

The warranty as to encumbrances is purely negative in character. While all relevant encumbrances are guaranteed to be listed on the title sheet, there is no accompanying guarantee that the encumbrances are themselves valid and enforceable. No doubt, indeed, a person acquiring the encumbered property would much prefer that they were not. However, the same encumbrances, or more precisely the matching right to enforce them, will often have been covered by a (positive) warranty as to title at the time of their initial registration or subsequent transmission.[40] Take the case of a servitude. If Anna, the owner of Whitemains, grants a servitude of way to Boris, the owner of Blackmains, the servitude will be registered in the A section of the title sheet for Blackmains and in the D section of the title sheet for Whitemains.[41] On registration, the Keeper warrants the validity of the servitude to Boris, the owner of the benefited property, but not to Anna, the owner of the burdened property. And if Boris then dispones Blackmains to Ciaran, the Keeper equally warrants the servitude's validity to Ciaran. Finally, if Anna dispones Whitemains to Dora, the Keeper, in addition to warranting the title to Whitemains, also warrants that there are no undisclosed encumbrances. So far as the servitude is concerned, however, the latter warranty is not needed because the servitude is already disclosed on the D section of the title sheet.

13.5 Subsequent events

Although not made explicit in the legislative text, the manner in which the provisions are framed causes some further matters to fall outside the Keeper's warranty. One is inaccuracy attributable to later events, ie events later than the grant of warranty. As with the warrandice clause in conveyancing deeds, the Keeper's warranty is a guarantee as at a particular date, namely the date of registration, and it does not cover infirmities of title subsequently arising.[42] So if a right, good at the time of registration, comes to be lost by prescription,[43] or by creditors' diligence, or by sequestration, there could be no claim under the warranty. 'Events which are the responsibility of the acquirer should not, in general, be paid for by the Keeper'.[44]

13.6 Voidability

Another matter not covered by the warranty is voidability of the acquirer's title. A registered title may be voidable for one of two reasons. (i) The granter's title

---

39 Title Conditions (Scotland) Act 2003 s 75(1). Even then, there is an exception for pipeline servitudes: see s 75(3)(b).
40 That will not generally be true of encumbrances entered into the title sheet under s 30(2) at the time of first registration: see para 13.7 below.
41 By no means all encumbrances involve two properties. Those without a benefited property – for example, standard securities, personal real burdens, and registrable public-law encumbrances – are registered (only) in the title sheet of the burdened property.
42 SLC Report 222 paras 22.17–22.21.
43 Either by negative prescription or by positive (ie, where someone else establishes a prescriptive title to the property).
44 SLC DP 128 para 7.38.

was voidable, and that voidability transmits also to the grantee's title.[45] (ii) The granter's title was perfectly good, but some problem associated with the transaction means that the grantee's title is voidable. The Keeper's warranty covers neither possibility.[46]

It might at first sight seem surprising that the warranty covers the more serious danger to the grantee (voidness) but not the less (voidability). In fact, it is not so surprising. Voidability at the time of registration does not breach the Keeper's warranty because a voidable title is good unless or until reduced; and if the title later is reduced this, equally, is not a breach because reduction is a subsequent event.[47] Suppose, for example, that there is a gratuitous disposition by Darius, who is absolutely insolvent at the time, to Elfrieda. Under insolvency law that disposition is voidable: persons who are absolutely insolvent should be conserving their assets and not giving them away, generosity being the privilege of the solvent.[48] But the title sheet, in showing Elfrieda as owner, is wholly accurate. She is the owner. Therefore there is no breach of warranty. It may be added that voidability is merely an option (for instance to Darius's subsequent trustee in sequestration) to recover property, an option that may never be exercised.[49] Whilst the juridical nature of voidability is problematic, it is nearer to belonging to the law of personal rights (with which the land registration system is generally not concerned) than the law of real rights.

Although the warranty does not apply, acquirers may often be protected in other ways. The general law protects grantees who act in good faith and for value against the voidability of the granter's title; the grantee's title is then absolutely good.[50] That remark refers to case (i) above. In case (ii), where the granter's title is perfectly good but some problem exists concerning the transfer to the grantee, it is not usually possible for this situation to arise without the grantee being at fault or at least knowing how matters stand.[51]

13.7 Entries made other than by registration

The warranty is confined to registrations. An entry consequent on rectification is not covered by the Keeper's warranty. Nor are entries which are incidental to applications for registration and do not arise directly from the applicant's deed. The main example of the latter is information taken from Sasine titles in order to populate a title sheet on first registration.[52] On the other hand, an entry which is not warranted by the Keeper when first made may come to be warranted on a future transmission of the right in question. These points are best explained by some examples.[53]

---

45 It would transmit if the grantee was either in bad faith or gave no consideration: see below.
46 For background, see SLC Report 222 paras 20.8–20.12.
47 See para 13.5 above.
48 Bankruptcy (Scotland) Act 2016 s 98.
49 Indeed Darius's trustee in sequestration could seek payment from Elfrieda, rather than reduction, and it would be strange if that were to end up as being underwritten by the Keeper.
50 Reid (n 10) para 692. See also para 12.17 above. The person whose right of reduction is lost cannot claim compensation from the Keeper because the loss is not attributable to realignment or any other rule of land registration; rather the loss occurs as a matter of general law.
51 Fraud on the part of the grantee is the typical case.
52 The same would be true, on a split-off of a registered title, of information that migrates to the new title sheet from the old.
53 See also SLC Report 222 paras 22.9–22.14.

Example 1

Anne owns land. Stealing Anne's identity and forging her signature, Anne's sister, Beth, grants a disposition to Colin. Colin is registered as owner. Later, the fraud is uncovered and the Register is rectified to show Anne as owner in place of Colin.

Analysis. As Colin entered the Register by registration, his title attracted the Keeper's warranty, and he is likely to be entitled to compensation when he is displaced by Anne. No warranty is granted in respect of Anne's title because she entered the Register by rectification. However (i) Anne's original registration will have been warranted (or indemnified under the 1979 Act), unless her title was still held in the Register of Sasines; (ii) as and when Anne eventually comes to dispone the property, the Keeper will warrant the disponee's title on registration.

Example 2

David dispones land to Eilidh. This is a first registration. In making up the new title sheet, the Keeper (i) enters Eilidh's name in the B section as owner; (ii) enters an undischarged standard security (in favour of Falkirk Bank) in the C section; and (iv) enters a number of real burdens in the D section.

Analysis. Of the three separate entries made by the Keeper, only the first (of Eilidh's name) is made as a result of registration, and it alone has the benefit of the Keeper's warranty (ie to Eilidh). The deeds creating the standard security and real burdens had previously been registered in the Register of Sasines (creating the rights in question), and are not registered afresh merely because their contents are now added to the title sheet in the Land Register.[54] However, if Falkirk Bank later assigns the standard security, the Keeper will (in the normal case at least) warrant the assignee's title on registration.

Example 3

Grant dispones land to Heather. This is a first registration. In making up the new title sheet, the Keeper (i) enters Heather's name in the B section as owner; (ii) enters in the A section (ie as a pertinent) a servitude right of way over neighbouring land which, in the application form, Heather said had been constituted by positive prescription; and (iii) enters a number of real burdens in the D section.

Analysis. As in the previous example, the first entry is covered by the Keeper's warranty (to Heather) and the last is not. Although the subject of the second entry, the servitude, was not registered as such, it is a pertinent of the property which Heather is acquiring; hence it is included in Heather's warranty.[55]

13.8 Warranty to whom?

The Keeper's warranty is given to a particular person or persons, not to the public at large. In the normal case the beneficiary of the warranty is the applicant or applicants for registration, but where registration occurs without application (ie by

---

54 But while the holder of the encumbrances receives no warranty, their listing in the C and D sections forms part of the warranty as to encumbrances given to Eilidh on registration.
55 The result would be the same if, rather than having been constituted by prescription, the servitude had been constituted by express grant recorded in the Register of Sasines. It is the servitude's inclusion in the A section, as a pertinent, which allows it to be covered by the warranty given, on registration, to the new owner (Heather).

automatic plot or Keeper-induced registration) the warranty is given to the person who is registered as owner.[56]

Section 73(3) extends the warranty 'to persons to whom the benefit of warrandice by the granter of a deed would extend', or in other words to singular successors.[57] In the case of warrandice in deeds, successors benefit because the right is assigned by virtue of the (implied) clause of assignation of writs found in dispositions and standard securities.[58] Whether s 73(3) similarly envisages an assignation is unclear; if it does, then the original right-holder would be divested by the disposition or other transmission and could not make a claim against the Keeper without the right being retrocessed.[59]

Potentially, s 73(3) gives rise to a choice of claims. So if Alan's title is inaccurate but warranted by the Keeper, and if the Keeper (not knowing of the inaccuracy) warrants the title for a second time on the right being transferred by Alan to Beth, the transferee (Beth), in the event that the inaccuracy is rectified, can claim under her own warranty or, it may be, under the warranty previously given to the transferor (Alan). In practice, however, it is hard to see why Beth would not just use her own warranty, unless that warranty was restricted in some way, for example by Beth's own prior knowledge of the inaccuracy.[60] Furthermore, the very act of transfer may have cured the original inaccuracy, by realignment, so that no question of a claim can arise.[61]

Normally, it is only Beth who will have suffered loss; but if Alan has also suffered loss – for example, because the Keeper takes over and enforces Beth's warrandice claim against him[62] – Alan could claim from the Keeper in turn although, if the warranty is regarded as having been assigned to Beth, it would need to be reassigned by Beth to Alan.[63]

The Keeper's warranty would also extend, for example, to the executor of a deceased owner who held on a warranted title, or to the trustee in sequestration of a bankrupt owner, but that would be true on general principles and without the aid of s 73(3).[64]

13.9 Interaction with realignment

To the extent that realignment applies, the Keeper's warranty is not relevant. Take the case of dispositions. Realignment protects *bona fide* disponees against the possibility that the disponer, though registered as owner, was not owner.[65]

---

56 LR(S)A 2012 s 74(1). The provision actually says the warranty is to 'the owner' but, for the warranty as to title to have any value, this must mean the person registered as owner (thus covering the possibility that the person might not be owner).
57 For this aspect of warrandice in deeds, see Reid (n 10) para 712; Gretton and Reid (n 10) para 19-14.
58 Conveyancing and Feudal Reform (Scotland) Act 1970 s 10(4); LR(S)A 1979 s 16(1). Other deeds might, of course, have an express clause of assignation of writs, in which case the result would be the same.
59 *Cobham v Minter* 1986 SLT 336.
60 For warrandice in dispositions, the insolvency of the disponer would make it attractive to enforce the warrandice granted by the disponer's author. But in the case of the Keeper's warranty, the debtor is always the same.
61 LR(S)A 2012 ss 86–93: see para 13.9 below.
62 As the Keeper is entitled to do under LR(S)A 2012 s 77(4), (5).
63 SLC Report 222 paras 24.12–24.15.
64 SLC Report 222 para 22.15.
65 LR(S)A 2012 s 86, discussed in paras 12.8–12.17 above.

Equally, it protects against the possible incompleteness of the Register in its listing of encumbrances.[66] In the first case, it enables a disposition by a non-owning disponer to confer a good title; in the second, it extinguishes any encumbrances which ought to have been listed but were not. As a result, neither the warranty as to title (for the first case) nor the warranty as to encumbrances (for the second) will be needed; the original defects are cured by realignment, and so there is no loss that requires to be compensated.

But that will not always be the case, even for dispositions. Realignment offers no protection against transactional error,[67] while protection against Register error depends on the fulfilment of certain conditions, one or more of which (typically the disponer's possession for a year) may not be met.[68] Furthermore, as realignment is restricted to dispositions, assignations of registered leases, and the grant of servitudes,[69] there are many transactions to which it does not apply, including the grant of leases, the grant or assignation of standard securities, and all deeds of variation or discharge. In such cases it is the Keeper's warranty and not realignment which protects the grantee.

13.10 Interaction with the applicant's counter-warranty to the Keeper

To the Keeper's (statutory) warranty there is opposed a counter-warranty by the applicant contained in the application form for registration.[70] For in signing the form or (as almost always in practice) in authorising it to be signed on the applicant's behalf by a solicitor, the applicant is taken to certify to the Keeper 'that appropriate links in title are in place and that the granter has the legal right to grant the title'.[71] This counter-warranty is both important and, unfortunately, obscure. It is important because any warranty given by the applicant diminishes, to that extent, the over-arching warranty given by the Keeper. It is obscure because, while it can be read as giving a blanket guarantee as to the granter's title, a much more plausible reading, based both on the first half of the warranty and on the heading under which the warranty is found ('Certification in relation to links in title'), is as a guarantee restricted to the validity of the links in title (which are not now produced to the Keeper). On that reading, it would have no application in the large majority of cases where no links in title are involved. Other factors support this view of things. It would be surprising if much of the Keeper's warranty as to title were to be taken away by the applicant's counter-warranty, leaving only a warranty in respect of transactional error. It would be even more surprising if a statutory warranty could thus be undone by a few words on the application form, and without any notice being given in the statutory provision itself. To undermine the statutory warranty in this way would be to depart both from the policy as to indemnity in the 1979 Act and from the replacement warranty which was envisaged by the Scottish Law Commission and on which the 2012 Act provisions

---

66 LR(S)A 2012 s 91, discussed in para 12.18 above.
67 Ie error in the disposition itself. For the distinction between transactional error and Register error, see para 12.4 above.
68 See paras 12.12–12.16 above.
69 LR(S)A 2012 ss 86–93.
70 Somewhat similar issues arise with the warranty in the signature box to the effect that the application conditions have been complied with: see para 15.5 below.
71 See para 8.16 above.

were based.⁷² And, most seriously of all, it would destroy one of the fundamental principles of registration of title, the curtain principle, by forcing acquirers in transactions not protected by realignment to embark on a full examination of the deeds lying behind the entry of the granter's name on the Register. We understand that the Keeper's interpretation is the same as our own. It is to be hoped that, in due course, the wording of the counter-warranty will be changed and clarified.⁷³

EXCLUSIONS AND UPGRADES

13.11 Exclusion or limitation of warranty: the statutory provisions

Under the 1979 Act, the Keeper could restrict or exclude indemnity at the time of registration,⁷⁴ and the evident intention is that the Keeper should be able to do the same, under the 2012 Act, in respect of the Keeper's warranty. The actual provisions, however, are unsatisfactory in their drafting, and it is to be hoped that as and when they come before the courts, a sensible and workable interpretation will prevail.

That general continuity with the 1979 Act rules was being sought is clearly explained by the Scottish Law Commission:⁷⁵

> The practice of the Keeper [under the 1979 Act] is in broad terms that indemnity is excluded only if there is material doubt about some aspect of the title. The draft Bill has an express provision to that effect. If the title is not merely subject to doubt but is actually bad (on balance of probabilities), the application for registration should not be accepted in the first place.

This distinction between titles that are thought to be bad and titles where there is merely a degree of doubt was reflected in the Scottish Law Commission's draft Bill. On the one hand, in what has come to be known as the 'one-shot rule', the Keeper was bound to reject an application if the applicant failed to 'satisfy the Keeper' that certain conditions were met, including the condition that 'the deed sought to be registered ... is valid'.⁷⁶ On the other hand, the Keeper could restrict or exclude her warranty (but accept the application) 'if in doubt as to the validity of the acquisition, variation or discharge in question'.⁷⁷ Thus, under these draft provisions the power to restrict the warranty arose where the Keeper, while satisfied on a balance of probabilities that the title was good, continued to harbour some doubts on the point.

The 2012 Act, however, departs from the Scottish Law Commission draft, and in doing so appears to have eliminated the space between 'not satisfied'

---

72 No suggestion can be found in SLC Report 222 part 22 (or indeed anywhere else in the Report) of any such restriction in the Keeper's warranty. On the contrary, the SLC's position (para 22.8) was that 'The Keeper's warranty remains, as it is under current law [ie the 1979 Act], an extensive one'.
73 That would require fresh subordinate legislation as the application form, including the counter-warranty, is provided for by the Land Register Rules etc (Scotland) Regulations 2014, SSI 2014/150, ('LRR 2014') r 7, sch 1 pt 4.
74 LR(S)A 1979 s 12(2).
75 SLC Report 222 para 22.39. In accordance with one of the policies behind the reform, however, the criteria for the exercise of the Keeper's decisions as to warranty were now to be set out in the legislation.
76 SLC draft Bill s 20(2), (3)(a)(i).
77 SLC draft Bill s 39(2)(b)(ii).

(leading to rejection) and 'satisfied but in doubt' (leading to acceptance subject to a restriction of warranty). The change occurs in the provision on restriction of warranty, s 75(1)(b), where the 'in doubt' test is abandoned in favour of a 'not satisfied' test: warranty may be restricted if the Keeper is 'not satisfied as to the validity of the acquisition, variation or discharge'. At first sight, this might seem to be a change with little or no substantive difference. But there is a difficulty. The 'not satisfied' test is also used, as it was in the Scottish Law Commission's draft, in the provision on acceptance or rejection of applications for registration. Under the Act the Keeper must reject an application if the applicant 'does not … satisfy the Keeper' that the application conditions are met,[78] including the condition that 'the deed is valid';[79] and a deed is valid only if, 'by the registration applied for, a right would be acquired, varied or extinguished'.[80] Thus the Keeper can only exclude or restrict warranty in the very circumstances – not being satisfied as to the validity of the acquisition, variation or discharge – where the application must be rejected in the first place. And if, conversely, the Keeper accepts the application, this is permissible only where she is satisfied as to the validity of the acquisition, variation and discharge, with the result that she is not able to restrict her warranty. Of course, the Keeper is still able to restrict the warranty in cases where the registration occurs without application (ie by automatic plot registration or Keeper-induced registration),[81] but this affects only a minority of cases.

13.12 Exclusion or limitation of warranty: the Keeper's practice

Notwithstanding the precarious legislative basis,[82] the Keeper's practice is to exclude or restrict warranty where it seems appropriate to do so. A possible justification lies in the idea that there may be degrees of 'satisfaction', so that warranty can be limited or excluded where the Keeper is sufficiently satisfied as to validity as to accept the application but not so completely satisfied as to have overcome all doubts on the matter.[83] Preliminary guidance from RoS provides a (non-exhaustive) indication of when this might occur:[84]

- Where the applicant has failed to comply with a requisition under s 34(1)(b).[85]
- Where there is an existing caveat on the title sheet.[86]

---

78 LR(S)A 2012 s 21(3): see paras 9.7–9.11 above.
79 LR(S)A 2012 ss 23(1)(b), 25(1)(a), and 26(1)(a): see para 8.7(4) above.
80 LR(S)A 2012 s 113(2).
81 Situations expressly contemplated at the end of s 75(1)(b).
82 It seems that the Keeper's understanding of the law follows the SLC Bill rather than the 2012 Act. See Registers of Scotland, *General Guidance: Warranty* (v.01, 2014) 3 ('… the Keeper can only consider limiting or excluding warranty where the application is acceptable for registration purpose but where some element of doubt exists').
83 See para 9.9 above.
84 *General Guidance: Warranty* (n 82) 3, supplemented by Registers of Scotland, *Registration Manual* (https://rosdev.atlassian.net/wiki/display/2ARM/Home) Topics: Warranty – limitation or exclusion of warranty.
85 The one-shot rule means that requisitions are rarely made, but they are competent under s 34(1)(b), and must then be met within 42 days (LRR 2014 r 13). For the use of requisitions, see para 9.11 above.
86 The Keeper is expressly directed by s 75(2) to have regard to relevant caveats on the title sheet: see para 18.4 below.

- Where the application form indicates that the parties are not content to certify that the registrable deed is valid, including where they think the land affected might be common good land.[87]
- Where a statement under s 30(5) is added to any name or designation entered in the plot title sheet following an automatic plot registration or a Keeper-induced registration. This section can be used where, for instance, the name of the proprietor cannot be determined with any certainty.[88]
- Where the Keeper becomes aware of a competing title in the Register of Sasines whilst completing registration of an unregistered plot.
- Where the applicant has indicated on the application form that examination of title has been limited or restricted in some way.[89] For instance, where automatic plot registration has taken place but the applicant has been unable to obtain the titles or unrecorded links in relation to the landlord's plot.[90] In such cases warranty may be granted on the lease title sheet but excluded on the plot title sheet.
- Where there is an existing exclusion of indemnity on the title sheet of continuing relevance (for example, an exclusion of indemnity concerned with the validity of the proprietor's title but where positive prescription cannot yet have remedied the issue may need to be converted into an exclusion or limitation of warranty).
- Where there is an existing exclusion or limitation of indemnity on the title sheet and a new deed is being registered, eg a standard security.
- Where on the basis of additional information provided on the application form it is appropriate to do so (for example, an applicant indicates uncertainty as to the validity of a midcouple or the actual authority of an attorney who has executed the registrable deed under the power of attorney).

Where warranty has been restricted or excluded, the Keeper informs the applicant on returning the documentation submitted with the application.[91]

A restriction or exclusion of warranty must be noted on the title sheet by statements such as 'Warranty is excluded [or limited] in terms of section 75(1)(b) of the Land Registration etc (Scotland) Act 2012 in relation to XXX [or in terms that XXX]' or 'As regards XXX on the cadastral map, warranty is excluded in terms of section 75(1)(b) of the Land Registration etc (Scotland) Act 2012 in relation to XXX'.[92] Silence, with one exception, means that the title is fully warranted.[93] The exception is for titles founded on *a non domino* dispositions and marked as 'provisional'.[94] Such titles are not warranted, even without a statement to that effect, but if the Keeper comes to be satisfied that the ten years of possession needed for positive prescription have been completed, she will remove the provisional marking and, by express statement, grant warranty.[95]

---

87 For certification, see para 15.5 below.
88 See para 4.15 above.
89 See para 8.15 above.
90 See para 7.9 above.
91 *General Guidance: Warranty* (n 82) 2. There is, however, no statutory obligation to do so.
92 LR(S)A 2012 s 75(3). The suggested wording comes from *General Guidance: Warranty* (n 82) 3.
93 SLC Report 222 para 22.36: 'the Keeper warrants, but warrants silently'.
94 LR(S)A 2012 s 44(1): see para 17.18 below.
95 LR(S)A 2012 ss 44(2) and 75(4).

13.13 Upgrades

It is sometimes possible to have the warranty upgraded, either at the time of registration or later.[96] An application is needed, and the Keeper will have to be furnished with appropriate evidence. For requests at the time of registration, the answer 'yes' should be given to the relevant question in the application form ('Are you applying for an extension of warranty under section 75(1)?'); for subsequent requests a separate form is prescribed,[97] and there is a fee of £60.[98] The type of evidence needed will depend on the nature of the upgrade; further guidance has been promised by RoS[99] but, at the time of writing, had not yet appeared. Where the upgrade request is part of an application for registration, this is one of the few occasions on which the Keeper's power to requisition documents may sometimes be used;[100] as the nature of the evidence can be complex, RoS have indicated that a strict application of the one-shot rule is inappropriate.[101]

Upgrades sought at the time of registration[102] are likely to be directed at the removal of one of the exceptions given in s 73(2) to the ordinary or default warranty set out in s 73(1); indeed RoS guidance says that they are confined to such a case and cannot lead to a warranty more extensive than the default warranty,[103] although this view is not supported by the legislation.[104] A standard example of an upgrade at the time of registration would concern minerals. Among the matters excepted from the default warranty is any guarantee that 'the applicant has by registration acquired a right to mines or minerals'.[105] This applies both to pure mineral titles (ie where minerals are held as a separate tenement, without ownership of the surface) and also to cases where the plot is thought to include the minerals beneath the surface. The supporting evidence would probably have to include evidence of possession, ie some degree of working of the minerals.[106]

Subsequent requests for upgrades are likely to be directed at the removal of a restriction on the default warranty which was imposed at the time of registration. So for example if the Keeper, on the basis of the titles and other evidence submitted in the application for registration, restricts her warranty in some respect, then it is open to the applicant to seek to have the restriction removed by the provision of further evidence. If that evidence in turn proves insufficient, the request will be rejected, but this would not prevent another application being made on the basis of fresh evidence.[107]

Unless the effect of the upgrade is simply to restore the default warranty, the Keeper must include a statement of its scope on the title sheet.[108]

---

96 LR(S)A 2012 ss 75(1)(a) and 76.
97 LRR 2014 r 6, sch 1 pt 6. This asks in what respect a variation of warranty is sought, as well as for an explanation of 'why it is appropriate for the Keeper to vary the warranty currently provided for'.
98 Registers of Scotland (Fees) Order 2014, SSI 2014/188, sch 1 para 3(4).
99 *General Guidance: Warranty* (n 82) 2.
100 LR(S)A 2012 s 34(1): see para 9.11 above.
101 *General Guidance: Warranty* (n 82) 2.
102 Ie by virtue of LR(S)A 2012 s 75(1)(a).
103 *General Guidance: Warranty* (n 82) 2.
104 Which empowers the Keeper, without qualification, to 'grant more extensive warranty than is provided for in section 73 or 74': see LR(S)A 2012 s 75(1)(a).
105 LR(S)A 2012 s 73(2)(f): see para 13.3 above.
106 *General Guidance: Warranty* (n 82) 2.
107 *General Guidance: Warranty* (n 82) 5.
108 LR(S)A 2012 ss 75(3) and 76(5).

13.14 Downgrades

Once granted, warranty cannot be revoked or restricted by the Keeper.[109] As the Scottish Law Commission explains, 'the Keeper gives warranty of title to a particular person at a particular time, and so the question of downgrade cannot arise. The Keeper cannot walk away from the guarantee, once it has been given, any more than any other guarantor can.'[110] Of course, the Keeper could restrict the warranty when the property is next transferred, and a fresh application for registration is made. That would be an appropriate response if a supervening defect had emerged. But for defects already present when the original, unqualified warranty was given and only now come to light, this would be of little help to the Keeper because successors have the benefit of the original warranty and can rely on it for the purposes of recovering compensation.[111]

While warranty cannot be downgraded, if the applicant obtained the warranty unfairly, that unfairness can be used by the Keeper as a defence to a subsequent claim based on the warranty. This issue is discussed below.[112]

CLAIMS

13.15 The need for rectification

Although what the Keeper warrants is the accuracy (in certain respects) of the Register,[113] inaccuracy does not by itself give rise to a claim for compensation. The trigger event for a claim is rectification of the Register, and inaccuracies which are left unrectified are also left uncompensated.[114] There is a close analogy here with the warrandice of title in deeds, where eviction is needed before a claim can be made.[115]

If an inaccuracy is unrectified this is usually because it is latent and undetected. But even where an owner has come to know of an inaccuracy, he is unlikely to suffer loss unless or until there is rectification. For, unless an inaccuracy is insisted on, the owner can use the property unhindered and even sell it; and if he does sell, the acquirer (if in good faith) will often take the property free of the inaccuracy due to realignment.[116]

One situation, however, which may cause difficulty is where the person whose right is denied by the inaccuracy takes steps to assert it but without going to the trouble and expense of rectification – which, as the Keeper requires to be satisfied

---

109 LR(S)A 2012 s 76(3).
110 SLC Report 222 para 22.43.
111 LR(S)A 2012 s 73(3): see para 13.8 above.
112 See paras 13.17 and 13.18 below.
113 LR(S)A 2012 ss 73(1) and 74(1).
114 LR(S)A 2012 s 77(2): see SLC Report 222 para 22.45. Earlier, in SLC DP 128 paras 7.49–7.51, the Scottish Law Commission had suggested that, as in warrandice, the trigger should be eviction, which includes but is wider than rectification. So for example there would be eviction if the person whose right was denied by the inaccuracy sought to assert that right either judicially or in circumstances where no reasonable defence could be advanced. The eventual rule, that claims require rectification, is based on the view that an alleged title defect which does not sufficiently satisfy the Keeper as to lead to rectification would be an unsatisfactory basis on which to award compensation. The rule also has the merit of simplicity.
115 Reid (n 10) para 707. But eviction is not required for warrandice claims in respect of encumbrances.
116 LR(S)A 2012 ss 86–93: see ch 12 above.

that the inaccuracy is 'manifest', would often involve litigation.[117] Where, for example, part of a garden owned by Olive is included by mistake in the title of a neighbour, Peter, Olive might prefer simply to occupy (or continue to occupy) the part in question rather than go to the trouble of seeking to have the Register rectified. In that situation the neighbour, Peter, could not repel the occupation by litigation (for, despite what the Register says, he is not the owner), nor could he claim compensation from the Keeper (for there has been no rectification), nor could he sell in a manner that would confer a good title on the purchaser (because there has not been the possession needed for realignment). Peter might be well advised to bring the inaccuracy to the Keeper's attention, yield to rectification, and then claim compensation under the warranty.[118]

On rectification occurring, the person rectified against has an immediate claim against the Keeper, without having to seek recovery first from elsewhere.[119] And in most cases a claim against the Keeper will be more attractive than pursuing the person from whom the property was originally acquired, under warrandice, especially if a number of years have since elapsed. It is, however, open to the Keeper, having paid the claimant, to enforce any of the claimant's rights against third parties, and the Keeper can require an assignation of such rights.[120] In addition, the Keeper might have a direct claim against a third party by virtue of the duty of care created by s 111.[121]

13.16 Defences

To claims for compensation the Keeper has a number of possible defences. Obviously, no compensation is due where the subject-matter of the claim lies outside the scope of the Keeper's warranty.[122] Claims, originally good, are extinguished if they are not made within twenty years of rectification, something that one imagines would very seldom happen.[123] The principal defence, however, turns on the absence of good faith. A claimant who, at the time of applying for registration, knew or ought to have known of the inaccuracy is denied compensation by the Keeper.[124] In this

---

117 LR(S)A 2012 s 80(1), (2): see para 11.14 above.
118 This assumes that the Keeper will regard the inaccuracy as 'manifest' if it is conceded by the person whom it affects. Whilst we think that that is correct, at the time of writing the Keeper's approach to the 'manifest' requirement was not yet fully apparent
119 LR(S)A 2012 s 77(3). The reasons for this policy include: (i) consumer expectations; (ii) continuity with the existing law; (iii) the fact that the Keeper's guarantee is not free but is paid for by a (hidden) premium in the registration fee; and (iv) the practical and psychological cost of having to claim from or litigate against third parties. See SLC DP 128 para 8.24.
120 LR(S)A 2012 s 77(4), (5). This more or less reproduces the position under LR(S)A 1979 s 13(2), (3) except that (for reasons given in SLC Report 222 para 24.16) the mechanism of subrogation has been dropped (a change of technique rather than substance.) The third party, if a former owner, might have a counterclaim against the Keeper on the ground that the inaccuracy (if present at the time) breached his own warranty from the Keeper.
121 See generally SLC Report 222 paras 24.4–24.11. For s 111, see paras 15.2–15.4 below.
122 As to which see paras 13.3–13.7 above.
123 Prescription and Limitation (Scotland) Act 1973 s 7, sch 1 para 2(e), as amended by LR(S)A 2012 sch 5 para 18(7)(b). The 20-year period begins when the obligation becomes enforceable (s 7(1)). Admittedly, s 11(1), (4) further provides that obligations to pay reparation become enforceable when the loss occurred, which, on one view, might be before rectification; but it is thought that prescription cannot begin to run until the day on which recovery from the Keeper first became possible (ie the date of rectification), for otherwise the right could be extinguished before recovery was possible.
124 LR(S)A 2012 s 78(b).

important respect the guarantee by 'money' mirrors, without being precisely the same as, the guarantee by 'mud'.[125] More is said about the need for good faith in the next paragraph.

13.17 The need for good faith

As just mentioned, a claimant must have been in good faith in respect of the inaccuracy. The relevant point in time, in this respect, is not when the transaction settles, by delivery of the deed, but later, at the date of registration,[126] or in other words at the date on which the application for registration is received by the Keeper and entered in the application record.[127] The policy is that 'if an acquirer is to be protected by the Register, then he ought to register with clean hands'.[128] Of course, since examination of title will have been completed before settlement, there is a risk that, having handed over the money in the belief that the title was good, an acquirer might then be alerted to a defect in the brief week or so before the disposition is registered. The risk, however, seems slight. An advance notice will protect against supervening events, ie against insolvency, diligence or competing deeds;[129] and if a defect was already present, undetected, at settlement, it is most unlikely to surface in the period before registration. If it did the acquirer would have a remedy against the granter in warrandice.

Both subjective and objective good faith are needed. In other words, the claimant must not have known of the inaccuracy, nor must it be an inaccuracy of which he ought to have had knowledge: there must be neither actual knowledge nor constructive knowledge.[130] The first is a simple factual test: what did the claimant know? The second turns on fault on the part of the claimant (or in practice the claimant's legal adviser), thus continuing the policy of the 1979 Act, which barred a claim for indemnity in respect of loss caused by the claimant's 'carelessness'.[131]

The meaning of 'carelessness' under the 1979 Act was considered by the Inner House in *Wilson v Keeper of the Registers of Scotland*.[132] In concluding that the test was essentially one of professional negligence, the court said this:[133]

> In a matter of the present kind, where any carelessness would apparently have to be on the part of the solicitors rather than the actual proprietor in possession, there would evidently have to be material indicating that the solicitors departed from a usual and normal professional practice or that the alleged failure to discover alleged flaws in the title … was a failure which no professional conveyancer of ordinary skill would have committed if acting with ordinary care.

125 For the requirement of good faith in the guarantee by 'mud' (ie realignment), see LR(S)A 2012 ss 86(3)(c), 88(3)(c) and 90(3)(c). Unlike in the guarantee by 'money', however, it is thought that good faith is restricted to subjective good faith: see para 12.15 above.
126 LR(S)A 2012 s 78(b). A slight awkwardness in this formulation is that, on the (actual) day of registration, the changes to the title sheet have yet to be made so that the applicant cannot know, without the aid of clairvoyance, what they may turn out to be. The intention behind the provision is, however, clear enough: any knowledge of a title defect which the applicant has, or ought to have, by the date of registration will prevent a claim in respect of that defect.
127 LR(S)A 2012 ss 36 and 37(1): see para 9.22 above.
128 SLC DP 125 para 7.19, a passage which contains further justifications.
129 For advance notices, see ch 10.
130 LR(S)A 2012 s 78(b).
131 For which see LR(S)A 1979 ss 12(3)(n) and 13(4).
132 2000 SLT 267, 276 F–G per Lord McCluskey. See also *Dougbar Properties Ltd v Keeper of the Registers of Scotland* 1999 SC 513, 532–33 per Lord Macfadyen.
133 At 276 F–G per Lord McCluskey.

Much the same seems likely to be true for the purposes of constructive knowledge under the 2012 Act. Under the relevant provision, claimants are visited with the constructive knowledge of their solicitor or other legal adviser;[134] and the solicitor or adviser may be taken to know that which could have been discovered by due diligence, or in other words by a normal examination of title conducted without negligence, and by the preparation of the new deed with normal professional care.[135] In the case of first registration, this would imply a full examination of the Sasine title. But where the title is already on the Land Register, its accuracy can be taken on trust, and there is no need to consult the deeds on which the entries are based.[136] This follows from the 'curtain principle' on which much of the value of registration of title depends.[137] As with the guarantee by 'mud', therefore, so with the guarantee by 'money', the acquirer's investigations can be confined to transactional error; the Register itself can be taken to be accurate, unless it is known as a positive fact that it is not.[138]

If, however, constructive knowledge imposes much the same duties on solicitors as the 'carelessness' provisions of the 1979 Act did formerly, the Keeper's extension of the 'tell me don't show me' principle removes the comfort of the second examination of title which RoS used to provide.[139] The client, however, remains protected as before. If the solicitor has been properly vigilant, there will be a claim against the Keeper; if not, there will usually be a claim against the solicitor for professional negligence.[140] This is because it seems that a solicitor can only be fixed with constructive knowledge (thus denying his client a claim under the Keeper's warranty) if he has lapsed into professional negligence.[141]

Finally, it should be observed that, while bad faith subverts the claimant's own entitlement to warranty,[142] it has no effect on the warranty granted to a predecessor in title that has now come into the claimant's hands on principles already considered.[143] For instance Cosmo is registered as owner on the basis of a disposition ostensibly from Barnaby. Unknown to Cosmo, the deed is a forgery. Shortly thereafter Cosmo dispones to Dorabella, and the disposition is registered with no restriction of warranty. The Keeper is unaware of the fact that the deed

---

134 LR(S)A 2012 s 78(b)(ii).
135 SLC DP 125 paras 7.14 and 7.15.
136 These deeds are contained in the archive record, and it is expressly provided, by s 14(4), that there is no constructive knowledge of its contents: see para 4.31 above.
137 SLC DP 125 para 7.11; SLC DP 128 para 7.42: 'An applicant should be able to rely on the Register without further inquiry. If it discloses that Mr and Mrs Smith became owners on 12 February 2005, that information may be accepted as correct unless known to be wrong ... Another way of expressing the point is to say that constructive knowledge is relevant for transactional error but not for Register error.'
138 SLC Report 222 para 21.38: 'No model is tenable ... that necessitates going behind the Register and inspecting prior conveyances. The new scheme preserves the curtain principle. Title is guaranteed, and whilst the guarantee will sometimes take the form of money rather than mud, that is already true of the current law.'
139 See para 8.11 above.
140 SLC DP 128 paras 8.26–8.28.
141 This is on the assumption that the passage quoted above from *Wilson v Keeper of the Registers of Scotland* represents the current law.
142 LR(S)A 2012 s 78(c)(i) refers to bad faith on the part of the 'applicant' for registration at the time the warranty was granted. The switching between 'applicant' and 'claimant' in the different parts of s 78 must be assumed to have been deliberate. In the case now being considered there is bad faith on the part of the 'claimant' but not of the (original) 'applicant' for registration at the time when the warranty in question was granted.
143 See para 13.8 above.

in favour of Cosmo was forged. But Dorabella did know. The Register is rectified, ie Dorabella's name is erased from the B section of the title sheet and Barnaby's is reinstated. Does Dorabella have a claim against the Keeper? She has no claim based on the Keeper/Dorabella warranty. But it would appear that she does have a claim against the Keeper under the Keeper/Cosmo warranty. That may seem odd, but the opposite outcome would also be odd. For otherwise the Keeper would have a windfall gain by the chance circumstance that Cosmo (against whom there would have been no defence) had disponed to Dorabella.

13.18 Non-compliance with s 111

There is also a second conduct-based defence. No liability to pay compensation arises 'in so far as the inaccuracy is attributable to a failure of the applicant, or any person acting as solicitor or other legal adviser to the applicant, to comply with the duty owed to the Keeper under section 111'. Section 111, which is discussed more fully in another chapter,[144] imposes a duty of reasonable care 'to ensure that the Keeper does not inadvertently make the register inaccurate' as a result of a change made in consequence of the deed presented for registration. That no compensation should be due in respect of inaccuracies caused by the claimant's lack of care is a principle too obvious to require defending. Yet it is hard to see what the actual provision adds to the requirement of good faith discussed in the previous paragraph.[145] A solicitor who causes an inaccuracy by negligently presenting an invalid deed, or an application form containing mistakes, would almost certainly be regarded as having constructive knowledge of the deficiencies in question and hence of the resulting inaccuracy on the Register. Indeed it is the requirement of good faith that is the wider of the two defences, turning as it does on knowledge and not on causation. It applies to any inaccuracy of which the claimant has (or ought to have) knowledge, even if the inaccuracy is caused by a predecessor in title of the claimant or by the Keeper herself.

The conduct-based defences concern the behaviour of applicants for registration, and their legal advisers. Neither defence, therefore, applies to claims under warranties granted in respect of registrations which occurred without application (ie to Keeper-induced or automatic plot registration).

13.19 Quantum

The basis of compensation is the 'loss incurred as a result of a breach of the Keeper's warranty';[146] and the Keeper, it will be recalled, warrants the accuracy of the Register in so far as it shows (i) the acquisition of a right; (ii) its variation or discharge; and (iii) the absence of encumbrances (with some exceptions) other than those which are listed in the title sheet.[147] In respect of (i) the loss is the failure to acquire the right which the Register states to exist;[148] in respect of (ii) and especially (iii), it is the fact that a right is burdened by an unexpected

---

144 See paras 15.2–15.4 below.
145 SLC Report 222 para 22.64.
146 LR(S)A 2012 s 77(1).
147 LR(S)A 2012 s 73(1): see paras 13.2 and 13.4 above.
148 It is not the loss of the right itself because, notwithstanding its appearance on the Register, the right was not acquired (there being no Midas touch under the 2012 Act).

encumbrance. The measure of loss in the first case is the value of the right which was not, after all, acquired;[149] the measure in the second is likely to be the diminution in the right's value due to the encumbrance, although it may be possible to make a case for the cost of cure, ie the cost of obtaining a discharge of the encumbrance.[150] Although the warranty is granted, and also breached, at the time of registration,[151] the loss is quantified at the time of rectification which, in some cases, might be a number of years later.[152] This is partly because rectification is the trigger for the claim, and partly because, in practical terms, the loss may only be felt if and when rectification occurs.[153]

Consequential loss may also be claimed.[154] So, for example, the claimant is likely to be able to recover for the cost of preparing the claim against the Keeper (including the taking of professional advice),[155] for the loss of a sale or purchase of property consequential on the emergence of the defect, and – if the claimant has had to move out of the property – for relocation costs including legal and other fees for the purchase of a replacement property.[156] Where the inaccuracy leads to litigation, whether against the Keeper (for compensation) or against someone else (in order to determine the state of the title), reasonable pre-litigation expenses are recoverable from the Keeper;[157] judicial expenses, however, are a matter for the court in the usual way.[158] To count as 'consequential', expenditure must of course follow, not precede, the occurrence of the principal loss, or in other words the date of registration.[159]

Consequential loss cannot be recovered where it is too remote,[160] remoteness being judged, it seems, by reference to the test of reasonable foreseeability used in the law of delict.[161] There will be marginal cases. For example, if the right 'lost' by

---

149 Registers of Scotland, *General Guidance: Compensation* (v.02, 2014) 2: 'Where compensation is payable, the loss to be compensated will be the value, at the date of rectification, of the right lost'. For the special position of standard securities, see para 13.20 below.
150 SLC DP No 128 para 9.3. Depending on the circumstances, however, the cost of cure might be a ransom figure.
151 As the Keeper warrants the position as at the time of registration, the warranty cannot be breached by later events. To put it another way, the Keeper breaches the warranty at the same moment as she grants it.
152 LR(S)A 2012 s 79(1)(a).
153 See para 13.15 above. No reasons for the choice, however, are given in SLC Report 222 para 22.55
154 LR(S)A 2012 s 79(1)(b)(ii). The position was the same under the 1979 Act: see SLC DP 128 para 9.22. Identical rules on this and other aspects of compensation can be found in ss 94(6) and 95, which provide for compensation for loss due to realignment: see paras 14.2 and 14.3 below.
155 In so far as these are legal expenses, they may be covered by s 79(1)(b)(i) ('extra-judicial legal expenses').
156 SLC DP 128 paras 9.25–9.29.
157 LR(S)A 2012 s 79(1)(b)(i) allows the recovery of 'extra-judicial legal expenses', an expression which includes, but may be wider than, pre-litigation expenses. The general law would exclude pre-litigation expenses: see *Shanks v Gray* 1977 SLT (Notes) 26. For present purposes, they seem best categorised as the expenses of preparing a claim; and, thus viewed, it would seem wrong to allow such expenses generally, as consequential losses, but to exclude them where the claim happened to lead to litigation. See SLC DP 128 para 9.54; SLC Report 222 para 27.11.
158 This departs from LR(S)A 1979 s 13(1) which, apparently due to legislative accident, allowed recovery of the cost of litigation against the Keeper in respect of indemnity, regardless of success. See SLC DP 128 paras 9.43–9.56; SLC Report 222 paras 27.7–27.10.
159 SLC DP 128 para 9.32.
160 LR(S)A 2012 s 78(e). Although there was no express provision in the 1979 Act, the previous law is thought to have been the same.
161 SLC Report 222 paras 22.61 and 22.62.

rectification is the sole means of access to another property owned by the claimant, it is unclear whether compensation is confined to the value of the access strip or includes the diminution in value of the other property due to the loss of the means of access. The latter is certainly consequential on the former, but it might, or might not, be too remote.

Compensation does not extend to non-patrimonial loss, notably solatium in respect of disturbance and distress.[162] This follows the position in the law of warrandice.[163] The restriction was deemed reasonable by the Scottish Law Commission in view of the fact that the Keeper's warranty (like warrandice) is not based on fault.[164]

Claimants, as might be expected, are required to minimise their loss by taking whatever measures might reasonably be adopted for that purpose.[165] This is more likely to affect consequential rather than the principal loss, which will usually be a fixed sum. So for example a person who is evicted from the home which, until rectification, he was registered as owning, and who as a result must find temporary accommodation, should do so at an appropriate cost and standard, and for an appropriate period, and not spend a year living a life of luxury in the most expensive hotel in town.

Interest is payable on the total amount due at the rate of 1% above the Bank of England base rate.[166] Interest runs from the date of rectification or, in the case of consequential loss, from the date on which the loss was sustained.[167]

13.20 Claims by heritable creditors

In contrast to other real rights, a standard security has no value for its own sake but only as a means of recovery of a sum due under a (separate) contract of loan. In most cases, that sum will be paid in accordance with the contract, and the standard security will prove to have been unnecessary. It is only if the debtor defaults on the loan that the creditor can enforce the standard security, usually by selling the property and recovering the sum due from the proceeds of sale.

These unique qualities affect claims under the Keeper's warranty. Suppose, for example, that a standard security which was registered and warranted by the Keeper is found to be void for reasons which are not the fault of the heritable creditor. Can the creditor claim under the warranty? In the first place, no claim arises until rectification,[168] and in practice rectification may not occur, if only because no one is willing to take on the burden of persuading the Keeper of the

---

162 LR(S)A 2012 s 78(f).
163 *Palmer v Beck* 1993 SLT 485.
164 SLC Report 222 para 22.59.
165 LR(S)A 2012 s 78(d): see SLC DP 128 para 9.33; SLC Report 222 para 22.60. Again, the position under the 1979 Act seems to have been the same, although an express provision was lacking. The new provision is wide enough to cover steps which might have been taken to avoid the inaccuracy itself, such as registering with greater expedition, but matters such as these would normally be caught by the good-faith defence in s 78(b).
166 LR(S)A 2012 s 79(2); Land Register of Scotland (Rate of Interest on Compensation) Regulations 2014, SSI 2014/194.
167 LR(S)A 2012 s 79(1),(3). In the case of reimbursement of extra-judicial legal expenses, interest runs from the date on which the claimant paid the sum in question.
168 LR(S)A 2012 s 77(2).

error.[169] But even if rectification does occur, it does not follow that compensation will be due. Compensation is due only in respect of loss,[170] and there is no loss for as long as the debtor continues to pay the loan instalments in accordance with the contract.

Even where loss does occur, the date on which it is to be quantified is problematic. The legislation provides for quantification as at the time of rectification.[171] But in the case of a standard security there is no loss until the debtor defaults, as already mentioned, and the date of default (if any) is likely to be after, or even long after, the date of rectification. The legislation here seems not capable of being applied literally, and a constructive approach seems unavoidable. We suggest that the Keeper's liability is to be quantified only after debtor default has happened. The amount would be the difference between (i) the amount that the heritable creditor would have recovered had the security been valid and (ii) the amount actually recovered by the heritable creditor. In other words, the amount payable by the Keeper would be the loss to the creditor caused by the non-existence of the security. A different approach would be to say that the Keeper is liable to the heritable creditor immediately on rectification, the amount due being the value of the loan, or the amount of the secured debt, whichever is the less.[172] In return, the lender would assign the debt to the Keeper. This second approach seems less appropriate than the first. It has many practical drawbacks, one of which would be that the assignation would disrupt the commercial relationship between the lender and its customer, a relationship that may be a long-standing and mutually satisfactory one.

Taking the first approach to be correct, there is further difficulty as to whether the creditor can claim from the Keeper immediately on the debtor's default, or whether the creditor must first seek to recover the money by enforcing the loan agreement. As a general rule the legislation does not require alternative remedies to be pursued prior to making a claim under the Keeper's warranty.[173] Nonetheless, in this particular case there are two reasons for concluding that the loan agreement must be tried first. One is the need for claimants to minimise their loss.[174] The other is the need to establish the loss in the first place. It is not until the creditor has tried, and in whole or part failed, to recover the sums due from the debtor that the amount of the loss can be known. It is only at this point that a claim under the warranty becomes possible, and only at this point that alternative remedies for recovering that (now ascertained) loss, such as the warrandice granted under the standard security, can be ignored.[175]

---

169 Rectification requires the Keeper to be satisfied that the supposed inaccuracy is 'manifest': see LR(S)A 2012 s 80(1), and also para 11.14 above.
170 LR(S)A 2012 s 77(1).
171 LR(S)A 2012 s 79(1)(a). A similar issue arises in respect of claims for compensation for loss of a standard security by realignment where, again, the date set for quantification (the date of realignment: see LR(S)A 2012 s 95(1)(a)) is likely to precede the date of the loss itself: see para 14.3 below.
172 For instance, if the lender is owed £1,000,000 and was granted security over property worth £600,000, it is clear that the latter figure is the maximum possible amount for which the Keeper could be liable.
173 LR(S)A 2012 s 77(3).
174 LR(S)A 2012 s 78(d). This is different from seeking to recover that loss from some third party, which is what s 77(3) excuses.
175 Ie by virtue of LR(S)A 2012 s 77(3).

TRANSITIONAL: 1979 ACT TITLES

13.21 Two types of indemnity

The designated day (8 December 2014) marked the shift from the 1979 Act to the 2012 Act. Titles registered before that day were registered under the 1979 Act; titles registered on or after the designated day were registered under the 2012 Act. Thus far in this chapter the concern has been with 2012 Act titles, but this final section considers titles registered under the 1979 Act. The subject is important, because properties which have not changed hands since the designated day – and there will be many – continue to be founded on the 1979 Act.

In terms of the 1979 Act, the Keeper was liable to pay indemnity, following an inaccuracy on the Register, both (i) where there was rectification, and also (ii) where there was no rectification (for under the 1979 Act the fact of an inaccuracy did not necessarily lead to the rectification of the inaccuracy).[176] In the first case, payment was due to the person against whom rectification proceeded; in the second, payment was due to the person in whose favour rectification would have been made, had it been made.[177] The changed model of land registration introduced by the 2012 Act separates these two types of claim. The first is the equivalent of the Keeper's warranty, which, equally, awards compensation on rectification;[178] the second is the equivalent of compensation for loss of property by realignment, and can be left over until the discussion of that topic in the next chapter.[179]

13.22 Compensation for rectification

Where the Register was rectified before the designated day, any person suffering loss as a result had a claim against the Keeper for indemnity.[180] Such claims are unaffected by the 2012 Act; subject to negative prescription,[181] a person with a claim before the designated day can enforce the claim after that day. It makes no difference for this purpose whether the claim had been intimated to the Keeper but not disposed of or whether it had not yet been started.[182] The claim will be governed by the 1979 Act, and nothing more need be said about it here.

The position is different for rectifications on or after the designated day. Under the transitional provisions in the 2012 Act, where, immediately before the designated day, the Keeper had power to rectify an inaccuracy, then, on that day, the property rights of the parties concerned automatically became what they would have been had a rectification actually taken place.[183] As, however, nothing has changed on the Register, the title sheet remains inaccurate unless or until an actual

---

176 Typically because rectification would prejudice a proprietor in possession: see LR(S)A 1979 s 9(3)(a). This was one of the many criticisms of the 1979 legislation: the Register was, in some types of case, required to remain inaccurate.
177 LR(S)A 1979 s 12(1)(a), (b): see para 2.10 above.
178 LR(S)A 2012 ss 73–79, discussed earlier in the chapter.
179 LR(S)A 2012 ss 94 and 95, discussed at paras 14.2 and 14.3 below.
180 LR(S)A 1979 s 12(1)(a).
181 The 20-year prescription applies assuming (which is not certain) that the Keeper's obligation is an 'obligation relating to land': see Prescription and Limitation (Scotland) Act 1973 s 7, sch 1 paras 1(d) and 2(e); SLC Report 222 para 35.12.
182 LR(S)A 2012 sch 4 para 15.
183 LR(S)A 2012 sch 4 para 17. If, conversely, the Keeper had no power to rectify, the entry in question ceased to be an inaccuracy, and so future rectification is prevented: para 22. See further paras 11.9–11.12 above.

rectification occurs. It is only actual rectification which gives rise to an entitlement to compensation. Subject to some qualifications mentioned below, compensation is paid on the same basis as if, at the time of the claimant's original registration, the Keeper had granted warranty.[184] In other words, although the title was registered under the 1979 Act, compensation is regulated by the 2012 Act.

An example makes the position clearer.[185] On a first registration, in 2013, Anton is registered as owner of a house and garden which, in error, includes a strip of garden belonging to a next-door neighbour, Barbara. Due to the Midas touch, Anton becomes owner of the whole subjects on registration, including the strip taken from Barbara's garden.[186] Barbara is accordingly divested. But if Barbara continues to possess, as is not unlikely in a case like this, then, on the designated day, ownership reverts to Barbara.[187] This is because, as Anton is not a proprietor in possession in respect of the strip of garden, the Keeper could have rectified the inaccuracy immediately before the designated day.[188] The Register, however, will continue to show Anton as owner of the strip unless or until Barbara seeks rectification or the inaccuracy is otherwise drawn to the Keeper's attention.[189] If and when rectification occurs, Anton can claim compensation for his loss under the (deemed) Keeper's warranty.[190]

13.23 Quantum and defences

In most respects, the rules as to compensation under the deemed Keeper's warranty[191] are the same as those already described in respect of the actual Keeper's warranty.[192] The idea is that rectifications occurring after the designated day should be treated alike, regardless of whether the title in question was acquired under the 1979 Act or the 2012 Act.[193] But no compensation is recoverable under the deemed warranty where it would not also have been recoverable under the indemnity provisions of the 1979 Act.[194] In other words, as well as being subject to the defences listed in the 2012 Act (with one exception mentioned below), the claim for compensation is also subject to the defences in the 1979 Act.[195] For the most part they are similar or the same[196] but, to the extent that they are not, the claimant may be in a worse position in respect of rectifications after the designated day than he would have been if the rectification had occurred before that day.

A defence found only in the 2012 Act excludes any claim in respect of a rectification which corrects over-registration, that is to say, the situation where

---

184 LR(S)A 2012 sch 4 para 19. See also Scottish Law Commission, *Discussion Paper No 130 on Land Registration: Miscellaneous Issues* (2005) ('SLC DP 130') para 9.10.
185 For other examples, see SLC Report 222 para 26.13, examples (2), (3) and (5).
186 LR(S)A 1979 s 3(1)(a): see para 2.7 above.
187 LR(S)A 2012 sch 4 para 17. Note, however, that possession is presumed unless the contrary is shown: para 18.
188 LR(S)A 1979 s 9(1).
189 In general, the Keeper must rectify an inaccuracy that is manifest: see LR(S)A 2012 s 80(1), (2), and paras 11.13 ff above.
190 LR(S)A 2012 sch 4 para 19.
191 Ie for post-designated day rectifications of 1979 Act titles.
192 Ie for post-designated day rectifications of 2012 Act titles. See paras 13.16–13.20 above.
193 LR(S)A 2012 sch 4 para 19.
194 LR(S)A 2012 sch 4 para 20(a), (b).
195 As to which see LR(S)A 1979 ss 12(2), (3) and 13(4).
196 For a detailed review of the 1979 Act defences, see SLC DP 128 paras 8.2–8.21.

the Register 'shows an acquisition, variation or discharge more extensive than the deed registered bore to effect'.[197] The transaction involving Anton and Barbara, mentioned above, may be an example, although that would depend on whether the inclusion of part of Barbara's garden in Anton's title was an innovation of the Keeper or whether it was already present in the disposition in favour of Anton.[198]

The only 2012 Act defences which do *not* apply are those based on the conduct of the claimant, ie the defences based on knowledge and on breach of s 111.[199] The thinking, presumably, was that a claimant should not be subject to a statutory duty, under s 111, which did not exist at the time of his application for registration;[200] nor should he be penalised for knowledge which would not have prevented a claim under the 1979 Act. The claimant's conduct will, however, still be relevant because, under the 1979 Act, loss was irrecoverable to the extent that it was caused by the fraudulent or careless act or omission of the claimant.[201]

---

197 LR(S)A 2012 s 73(2)(h)(i): see para 13.3 above.
198 Either way, there would probably not be compensation, in the first case because of LR(S)A 2012 s 73(2)(h)(i), in the second because of LR(S)A 1979 s 12(3)(n) (fraud and carelessness). See also SLC Report 222 para 26.13, example (2), but note that the analysis appears to be wrong in stating that compensation is payable.
199 LR(S)A 2012 sch 4 para 20(c) excludes s 78(b), (c). For those conduct-based defences, see paras 13.17 and 13.18 above.
200 Although there may possibly have been a common-law equivalent: see para 15.2 below.
201 LR(S)A 1979 ss 12(3)(n) and 13(4); LR(S)A 2012 sch 4 para 20(a), (b).

Chapter 14

Liabilities of the Keeper

14.1 Introduction

The 2012 Act imposes certain liabilities on the Keeper as well as on those who make use of the land registration system such as applicants for registration and their legal advisers. Liability may also arise under the general law. This chapter considers the liabilities of the Keeper, and the next chapter the liabilities of users of the Register.

LIABILITIES FOR THE LOSS OF RIGHTS

14.2 Liability in respect of realignment: in principle

To confer rights on good-faith acquirers by realignment is also, necessarily, to remove rights from other – generally, equally blameless – persons. Such persons are entitled to compensation from the Keeper in respect of their loss.[1] So, for example, if Alex, registered (wrongly) as owner of Betty's property, purports to dispone the property to Colin, Colin becomes owner (provided the conditions for the relevant realignment provision[2] are satisfied) and Betty ceases to be owner. Betty is then entitled to compensation from the Keeper. In other words, while the acquirer receives the 'mud', the other party is entitled to receive the 'money'.

Compensation is payable under this head wherever rights are lost due to realignment, or in other words wherever, as a result of rights being conferred on someone else, and without having taken part in any transaction, (i) a person ceases to be owner of land; (ii) a person ceases to hold the tenant's interest in a registered lease; (iii) a person loses a subordinate real right, or the benefit of some other encumbrance, which had been omitted from the Register in error; or (iv) a person loses the benefit of a floating charge.[3] It is also payable where, due to s 90 of the 2012 Act, an owner finds that his land is subject to a servitude which he did not grant.[4]

There will often be an interval of time – sometimes a substantial one – between the occurrence of the loss and its discovery by the person who suffered that loss.[5] After all, a person who fails to notice the loss of possession for a year (a prerequisite for realignment under ss 86 and 88) is unlikely to be immediately alive to the loss of title which then follows. No doubt partly for this reason, a claim for compensation is subject to the long (and not the short) negative prescription, and

---

1 LR(S)A 2012 s 94. This is the equivalent of LR(S)A 1979 s 12(1)(b).
2 LR(S)A 2012 s 86.
3 LR(S)A 2012 ss 86–93 and 94(2)(a). For realignment, see ch 12 above.
4 LR(S)A 2012 s 94(2)(b).
5 This did not arise under the equivalent provision in the 1979 Act (s 12(1)(b)) because there it was the refusal of an application for rectification which gave rise to the claim.

so will survive for 20 years.[6] It is no bar to a claim that the claimant could also have pursued a remedy against other parties, such as the person who was responsible for the inaccuracy on the Register;[7] but the Keeper, having paid the claimant, can take over these remedies,[8] and may also have a direct claim by virtue of the duty of care created by s 111.[9]

14.3 Liability in respect of realignment: quantum and defences

The amount payable by the Keeper is the value of the right lost or, as the case may be, the diminution in value of the claimant's land due to the existence of the servitude.[10] This is quantified as at the date of the loss (ie on the date of realignment), but interest runs thereafter at the rate of 1% above the Bank of England base rate.[11] Of course, by the date of realignment the value might have changed since the property was last under the claimant's control. Be that as it may, it is the value at the date of realignment that counts. So if, for example, a new building has been erected or the property has been otherwise improved[12] then the claimant will receive from the Keeper what amounts to a windfall benefit. The valuation of standard securities raises some difficult issues which were considered in a previous chapter.[13]

Consequential loss is also recoverable, for example the cost of preparing the claim against the Keeper, including the taking of professional advice.[14] Where realignment leads to litigation, whether against the Keeper (for compensation) or against someone else (in order to determine the state of the title), reasonable pre-litigation expenses are recoverable from the Keeper;[15] judicial expenses, however, are a matter for the court in the usual way.[16] To count as 'consequential', expenditure must of course follow, not precede, the occurrence of the principal loss, or in other words the date of realignment.[17] Consequential loss cannot be recovered where it is

6 Prescription and Limitation (Scotland) Act 1973 s 7. The five-year prescription is excluded by sch 1 para 2(e), as amended by LR(S)A 2012 sch 5 para 18(7). By s 11(1), (4), prescription begins to run on the date when the loss occurred.
7 LR(S)A 2012 s 94(3).
8 LR(S)A 2012 s 94(4), (5). The Keeper is entitled to an assignation from the claimant of any rights of recovery against third parties.
9 See generally Scottish Law Commission, *Report No 222 on Land Registration* (2010) ('SLC Report 222') paras 24.4–24.11. For s 111, see paras 15.2–15.4 below.
10 LR(S)A 2012 s 94(1), (2). See also Scottish Law Commission, *Discussion Paper No 128 on Land Registration: Registration, Rectification and Indemnity* (2005) ('SLC DP 128') paras 9.2 and 9.3.
11 LR(S)A 2012 s 95(2), (3)(a), (4); Land Register of Scotland (Rate of Interest on Compensation) Regulations 2014, SSI 2014/194.
12 At any rate there is nothing in the legislation to prevent a claim for improvements. A provision to that effect had been suggested in SLC DP 128 para 9.12, but the idea was not followed up in SLC Report 222.
13 See para 13.20 above.
14 LR(S)A 2012 s 95(1)(b) (which specifically mentions 'reimbursement of reasonable extra-judicial legal expenses'). Identical rules on this and other aspects of compensation can be found in ss 78(d)–(f) and 79, which provide for compensation for breach of the Keeper's warranty: see para 13.19 above.
15 LR(S)A 2012 s 95(1)(b)(i).
16 This departs from LR(S)A 1979 s 13(1) which, apparently due to legislative accident, allowed recovery of the cost of litigation against the Keeper in respect of indemnity, regardless of success. See SLC DP 128 paras 9.43–9.56; SLC Report 222 paras 27.7–27.10.
17 SLC DP 128 para 9.32. So, for example, the claimant could not recover from the Keeper in respect of any period of lost possession prior to the date of realignment; but a claim, in unjustified enrichment, might be available against the person who was in possession. This is perfectly logical: the loss of possession was a cause of realignment, not a consequence.

too remote,[18] remoteness being judged, it seems, by reference to the test of reasonable foreseeability used in the law of delict.[19] Nor can a claim be made in respect of non-patrimonial loss, notably solatium in respect of disturbance and distress.[20]

Finally, recovery is barred 'in so far as the claimant's loss could have been avoided by the claimant taking certain measures which it would have been reasonable for the claimant to take'.[21] This means that the claimant must minimise his loss, in the usual way.[22] More than that, it means that the claimant must have sought to avoid the loss in the first place, or in other words sought to prevent realignment, if the circumstances were such that it was reasonable to expect him to have done so.[23] What these circumstances might be is less clear. However, it should be borne in mind that realignment, though it happens at a precise moment, needs some time for its conditions to emerge. It requires an initial inaccuracy on the Register which is followed, sometimes years later, by the transfer of the property to a *bona fide* acquirer.[24] A claimant who discovered the inaccuracy in time is probably expected to have alerted the Keeper before any transfer – and hence realignment – could take place. Actual knowledge of the inaccuracy is probably required for this purpose, or at any rate a suspicion so strong that further investigation would be the only reasonable and prudent response. Loss of possession, by itself, cannot be sufficient; otherwise it would exclude compensation in the most common case of realignment.[25]

14.4 Liability for loss of the chance to rectify: 1979 Act titles

There was no realignment to cure inaccuracies under the 1979 Act. Instead, the entry or omission on the Register remained inaccurate and, hence, vulnerable to rectification, despite one or more transmissions of the land.[26] This unsatisfactory state of affairs as to inaccuracies built up under the 1979 Act was altered by transitional provisions in the 2012 Act, which provided for a one-off redistribution of rights on the designated day (8 December 2014). Where, immediately before that day, the inaccuracy was one which the Keeper had power to rectify, the parties acquired (or lost) the rights which a rectification would have given them (or deprived them of).[27] Where, conversely, there was no power to rectify the inaccuracy – typically because to do so would have been to the prejudice of a proprietor in possession[28] – the inaccuracy was cured and the right to rectify was lost for ever.[29] Compensation in the first case (for loss of property rights) is covered by the Keeper's indemnity and was discussed in the previous chapter,[30]

---

18 LR(S)A 2012 s 94(6)(b). Although there was no express provision in the 1979 Act, the previous law is thought to have been the same.
19 SLC Report 222 paras 22.61 and 22.62.
20 LRS)A 2012 s 94(6)(c).
21 LR(S)A 2012 s 94(6)(a).
22 SLC DP 128 para 9.33; SLC Report 222 para 22.60.
23 SLC DP 128 paras 7.56–7.58; SLC Report 222 para 23.40. The 1979 Act achieved much the same effect by reference to fault: indemnity could not be recovered in respect of a refusal to rectify where the loss was caused by the claimant's fraud or carelessness (ss 12(3)(n) and 13(4)).
24 Or, in the case of s 90, the granting of a servitude.
25 Ie the case where the transferor, though registered as proprietor, is not the proprietor but has possessed for a year: see LR(S)A 2012 ss 86 and 88.
26 See paras 2.9 and 2.13 above.
27 LR(S)A 2012 sch 4 para 17.
28 LR(S)A 1979 s 9(3)(a).
29 LR(S)A 2012 sch 4 para 22: see paras 11.9–11.12 above.
30 LR(S)A 2012 sch 4 paras 19–21: see paras 13.21–13.23 above.

compensation in the second case (for loss of the chance to rectify) is the subject of the present discussion.

Any person whom rectification would have benefited but whose prospects of rectification were extinguished on the designated day is entitled to claim compensation from the Keeper.[31] The rules are best approached through an example. Alan owned land. In 2013 Betty registered a disposition that purported to be from Alan but on which Alan's signature was (unknown to Betty) forged. Betty took possession.[32] Despite the fact of forgery, Betty became owner on registration, due to the Keeper's Midas touch,[33] and Alan ceased to be owner. But although the Register was inaccurate (ie in showing Betty as owner),[34] it could not be rectified for as long as Betty was in possession. On the designated day, therefore, the Register ceased to be inaccurate. Alan became entitled to compensation from the Keeper. From a functional point of view, Alan's loss and Betty's gain resemble realignment. But whereas realignment takes ownership from Alan and gives it to Betty, the provision being discussed left Betty with the ownership she already had and removed from Alan any prospect of getting it back.

As the loss incurred, in both cases, is the value of the property, broadly the same rules apply in assessing compensation, including rules as to consequential loss and defences.[35] These rules have already been explained.[36] Two differences, however, should be noted. First, although the loss was incurred on the designated day, compensation is quantified as at the date – often much earlier – on which the Register first became inaccurate.[37] In most cases this is unlikely to be to the advantage of the claimant,[38] even taking account of the running of interest, at the rate of 1% above the Bank of England base rate.[39] Secondly, no compensation is recoverable which would not have been recoverable under the equivalent provisions in the 1979 Act.[40] In other words, as well as being subject to the defences in the 2012 Act, the claim is also subject to the defences in the 1979 Act[41] – a less

---

31 LR(S)A 2012 sch 4 para 23.
32 The typical way that this fraud is carried out is that the fraudster first takes a tenancy of the target property, using, of course, a fake identity. This enables him to show the property to viewers, give possession at settlement, and so on. See K G C Reid and G L Gretton, *Conveyancing 2015* (2016) 174–76.
33 LR(S)A 1979 s 3(1)(a): see para 2.7 above.
34 Although, as a result of the Midas touch, Betty was indeed owner, she ought not to have been owner, and that was one of the two forms of inaccuracy under the 1979 Act, ie bijural inaccuracy: see para 2.8 above.
35 LR(S)A 2012 sch 4 para 24.
36 The rules are set out in LR(S)A 2012 ss 94(3)–(6) and 95, and summarised in para 14.3 above.
37 LR(S)A 2012 s 95(1)(a), inserted by sch 4 para 24. In the example, this would be the date on which Betty's disposition was registered and Betty entered on the Register as owner.
38 The thinking may have been that, from the moment that the inaccuracy was in place, the claimant had not only lost the right but also, in practice, any real prospect of its return. Even so, this is a different and generally less favourable rule than operated under the 1979 Act, where quantification was as at the date of refusal of rectification: see *M R S Hamilton Ltd v Keeper of the Registers of Scotland* 2000 SC 271. In some circumstances, however, the earlier date will be more favourable, notably where the loss is in respect of (past) income rather than capital: see SLC DP 128 paras 7.14–7.16.
39 LR(S)A 2012 s 95(2)–(4), applied by sch 4 para 24; Land Register of Scotland (Rate of Interest on Compensation) Regulations 2014, SSI 2014/194.
40 Ie LR(S)A 1979 s 12(1)(b): see LR(S)A 2012 sch 4 para 23.
41 As to which see LR(S)A 1979 ss 12(2), (3) and 13(4). For a detailed review of the 1979 Act defences, see SLC DP 128 paras 8.2–8.21. The most important was where the loss was caused or contributed to by the claimant's fraud or carelessness.

favourable position than if the claim had been made, before the designated day, under the 1979 Act.

Any claims that were already outstanding under the 1979 Act on the designated day continue to be processed in the normal way.[42] So if, in the example given above, Alan had sought and been refused rectification in November 2014, he would be entitled to indemnity under the 1979 Act rules, and not under the transitional provisions in the 2012 Act, even though, as at the appointed day, nothing had yet been paid to him by the Keeper.[43]

14.5 No liability for rights lost for other reasons

Naturally, the compensation scheme for loss of rights is confined to rights lost as a result of the legislation on land registration, and has no application to rights lost in some other way. So if Betty acquires Alan's land by positive prescription, Alan has no recourse against the Keeper or, probably, against anyone else, for the loss of ownership. The same is true where the right to reduce a voidable title is lost on the title-holder conveying the property to a *bona fide* acquirer for value. In the first case, the loss is by virtue of legislation,[44] in the second by virtue of the common law;[45] in neither case is there provision for compensation.

OTHER LIABILITIES

14.6 Liability for failure to acquire rights: the Keeper's warranty

As well as compensating those who lose rights, the Keeper sometimes compensates those who fail to acquire rights in the first place. For in registering a title, the Keeper will usually warrant its validity, and so pay compensation in the event that the title is successfully challenged by means of rectification.[46] This is compensation due to inaccuracy and not, as with realignment, compensation due to the Register being accurate. In the first case the Register inaccurately records an acquisition, variation or discharge; in the second it accurately records an acquisition which has as its corollary the loss of a right in the claimant. A full account of the Keeper's warranty was given in the previous chapter.

14.7 Liability to those securing rectification of the Register

The Keeper's warranty compensates the losing party in a battle over rectification. But the winning party, too, is likely to be out of pocket, for to secure rectification will usually involve costs.[47] Except in the simplest of cases, there will be representations to the Keeper, the assembling and scrutiny of evidence, and, where the Keeper is still not satisfied that an inaccuracy is 'manifest', the cost of the litigation needed to have the inaccuracy established.[48] Much or all of this may require the services

---

42 LR(S)A 2012 sch 4 para 15. It makes no difference whether a claim for compensation had actually been made; the test is merely whether the entitlement to indemnity was already present.
43 LR(S)A 1979 s 12(1)(b).
44 Prescription and Limitation (Scotland) Act 1973 ss 1 and 5(1A).
45 K G C Reid, *The Law of Property in Scotland* (1996) para 692.
46 LR(S)A 2012 ss 73 and 74. This is the equivalent of LR(S)A 1979 s 12(1)(a).
47 For rectification generally, see paras 11.13 ff above.
48 The Lands Tribunal has now jurisdiction to deal with such questions: see LR(S)A 2012 s 82.

of a lawyer. In principle, such expenses are recoverable from the Keeper: having compensated the vanquished, the Keeper must also compensate the victor. Provided that the efforts expended result in rectification, the Keeper must reimburse all 'reasonable extra-judicial legal expenses' which have been incurred;[49] and so long as rectification itself took place on or after the designated day,[50] it does not seem to matter that some or all of the expenses were incurred before that day. Expenses of any actual litigation will be dealt with by the Tribunal or court in the usual way.

That is not all. The Keeper must also pay compensation for any loss caused by the (now-rectified) inaccuracy, if patrimonial in character and not too remote.[51] As usual, there is a duty to minimise the loss.[52] It is easy to see how such loss might occur.[53] Suppose that, on first registration, Alice is registered (inaccurately) as owner of a piece of ground which actually belongs to a neighbour, Bert. If Alice asserts her (apparent) title and occupies the ground, Bert will lose the benefit of possession. If Alice does not occupy the ground, Bert may be entirely unaware of the problem, perhaps discovering it only when he comes to sell his property, at which point the projected sale might fall through.

The actual provision (s 84(1)), however, is in danger of being more restrictive than was presumably intended. The Scottish Law Commission's proposal was that compensation should be available to 'the person in whose favour the rectification is made',[54] and the Commission's draft Bill so provided.[55] Section 84(1), however, rearranges the Commission's draft and in doing so restricts compensation to 'a person *securing* rectification'.[56] It is suggested that 'securing' must here be interpreted as including 'benefiting from'; otherwise, where rectification was carried out by the Keeper on her own initiative and without the participation of the person who stood to benefit, no compensation would be due to that person.

Inaccuracies are seldom the fault of their victims. But where that is not so – where or to the extent that the inaccuracy was caused by the person now claiming compensation under either of the heads identified above – the entitlement to compensation is reduced or even excluded altogether.[57] It seems doubtful whether a mere failure to take possession or otherwise exercise a right is sufficient to trigger this defence, for in general the law does not require owners to exercise their rights.[58] But if, for example, a person facilitates the inaccuracy by wrongly

---

49 LR(S)A 2012 s 84(1)(a). This repairs an omission in the 1979 Act: see SLC Report 222 paras 27.13–27.15. In oral evidence to the Economy, Energy and Tourism Committee of the Scottish Parliament during the passage of the Bill, some solicitors complained about having to carry out additional work on account of mistakes by RoS without any prospect of remuneration: see *Official Report* cols 777–78 (11 January 2012), reproduced in Scottish Parliament, *Passage of the Land Registration etc (Scotland) Bill 2011* (2013, SPPB 174) (available at www.scottish.parliament.uk/parliamentarybusiness/Bills/44469.aspx) 318.
50 For s 84 is not retrospective in effect.
51 LR(S)A 2012 ss 84(1)(b) and 85(f), (g). It seems that remoteness is judged by reference to the test of reasonable foreseeability used in the law of delict: see SLC Report 222 paras 22.61 and 22.62.
52 LR(S)A 2012 s 85(e).
53 SLC Report 222 para 27.16.
54 SLC Report 222 para 27.15.
55 SLC draft Bill s 55(1).
56 This is because, unlike with the Scottish Law Commission's provision, para (b) of s 84(1) (which provides for compensation) is tied in with para (a) (which provides for reimbursement of the costs of securing rectification).
57 LR(S)A 2012 s 85(d).
58 It is for this reason that the ownership of land cannot be lost by negative prescription: see Prescription and Limitation (Scotland) Act 1973 sch 3 para (a).

asserting the correctness of a certain state of facts (such as that he does not own a particular area of ground), then the defence would come into play.

Not all inaccuracies qualify for compensation. The inaccuracy must affect a title sheet or the cadastral map and not some other part of the Register.[59] Inaccuracies in the cadastral map are excluded if they were caused by an error in the OS Map.[60] Excluded also is the (patent) inaccuracy of a prescriptive title,[61] such title being marked on the Register as 'provisional'.[62] Finally, the inaccuracy must have come about by act of the Keeper rather than by an off-Register event such as prescription.[63]

An immediate claim lies against the Keeper; after paying, the Keeper is at liberty to seek recovery from such other parties as the claimant might have pursued.[64] The Keeper may also have a direct claim under s 111.[65] Interest runs on the sum due from the date on which the expenses to be reimbursed were paid by the claimant or, as the case may be, from the date on which any loss from the inaccuracy was sustained.[66] The rate of interest is 1% above the base rate of the Bank of England.[67] The right to claim compensation is subject to the five-year negative prescription.[68]

14.8 Liability in respect of information provided or documents lost

In various ways, the Keeper provides information as to the state of the Register. If that information contains an error, the Keeper must compensate anyone who suffers loss as a result.[69] More precisely, the Keeper must compensate in respect of a mistake in (i) an extract of (or of any part of) a title sheet, the cadastral map, or a document in the archive record;[70] (ii) a certified copy of an application for

---

59 Ie the archive record and the application record: see LR(S)A 2012 s 85(a). For the different parts of the Register, see para 4.1 above.
60 Except where it was unreasonable to rely on the OS map: see LR(S)A 2012 s 85(b). An equivalent exclusion is found in respect of the Keeper's warranty: see s 78(a).
61 LR(S)A 2012 s 85(c).
62 LR(S)A 2012 s 44(1). For prescriptive titles generally, see paras 17.1 ff below.
63 LR(S)A 2012 s 85(a). The scope of this provision is not entirely clear. The following may be an example. Arthur is registered as owner of Whitemains. A year or two later, following usage for 20 years, a servitude over Whitemains is constituted in favour of Blackmains. The title sheets of both properties are inaccurate in failing to disclose the servitude: see LR(S)A 2012 ss 6(1)(b) and 9(1)(a). The provision removes the possibility of a claim under s 84(1)(b) by Arthur (assuming, which is far from clear, that Arthur was a person otherwise entitled to make such a claim). Note that the claim would not have been for the existence of the servitude but for its failure to appear on Arthur's title sheet – which might, for example, have led him to do certain things (such as erecting a building over the route of the servitude) which he would not have done had he been aware of the servitude's existence. In principle, a claim in respect of the existence of the servitude might have been made under the Keeper's warranty, but this is excluded by s 73(2)(c).
64 LR(S)A 2012 s 84(2)–(4). For this purpose the claimant is bound to assign to the Keeper any rights against third parties in respect of the loss compensated.
65 See paras 15.2–15.4 below.
66 LR(S)A 2012 s 84(5), (6).
67 LR(S)A 2012 s 84(7); Land Register of Scotland (Rate of Interest on Compensation) Regulations 2014, SSI 2014/194.
68 Prescription and Limitation (Scotland) Act 1973 s 6, sch 1 para 1(ad), inserted by LR(S)A 2012 sch 5 para 18(6).
69 LR(S)A 2012 s 106. For background, see SLC DP 128 para 7.62; SLC Report 222 paras 27.4–27.6. This follows the spirit, if not the letter, of LR(S)A 1979 s 12(1)(c), (d), and also of ss 72 and 73 of the SLC draft Bill (though s 72 took the form of a warranty by the Keeper).
70 Provided under LR(S)A 2012 s 104(1): see para 3.12 above.

registration, an advance notice, or any other document in the application record;[71] and (iii) any other information as to the contents of the Register which is provided in writing (such as a legal report or plans report).[72] In so far as mistakes occur, they are likely to be found only in the last of these. It should be noted that liability concerns misinformation as to what the Land Register actually says; so long as the Keeper gives correct information there is no liability, under these provisions, if what the Register says is wrong.[73]

Compensation is also due in the event of a document being lost, damaged, or destroyed while lodged with the Keeper.[74]

Liability to compensate is excluded in so far as the claimant's loss is too remote, is non-patrimonial in nature, or could have been reduced or avoided by the claimant taking certain measures which it would have been reasonable to take.[75] Although liability extends to anyone who suffers loss and not just to the person to whom the information was provided or, as the case may be, from whom the lost document was received,[76] some claims will fail as being too remote. The right to claim compensation is subject to the five-year negative prescription.[77]

LIABILITY AT COMMON LAW

14.9 Introduction

The statutory compensation scheme, just described, is unlikely to be the only basis on which the Keeper might incur liability. In its *Report on Land Registration* the Scottish Law Commission said that:[78]

> The listing of specific grounds of liability[79] is not intended to exclude other possible grounds of liability. For example, if the Keeper wrongfully rejects an application, or carries out an under-registration, and loss results, then *prima facie* the Keeper is liable. We see this as a matter of general law. The 1979 Act adopted the same approach. There is no point in re-inventing the wheel by attempting to set out the general law, and indeed any such attempt as well as being useless would be likely to become out of date.

---

71 Provided under LR(S)A 2012 s 104(2): see para 3.12 above.
72 For reports provided by the Keeper, see paras 5.23, 10.31 and 10.32 above. There is no (statutory) liability for information given otherwise than in writing (eg over the telephone), although s 106(1)(b) does include information given 'in such other manner as provision is made for in an order under section 107(1)(a)'; no order has so far been made.
73 The wording of s 106 makes clear, as LR(S)A 1979 s 12(1)(d) did not, that the error for which liability arises is an error in the transmission of information and not an error in the source itself (ie in the Register). In the event, s 12(1)(d) came, surely correctly, to be interpreted in that way: see *M R S Hamilton Ltd v Keeper of the Registers of Scotland* 2000 SC 271.
74 LR(S)A 2012 s 106(1)(c).
75 LR(S)A 2012 s 106(2). It seems that remoteness is judged by reference to the test of reasonable foreseeability used in the law of delict: see SLC Report 222 paras 22.61 and 22.62.
76 This is consistent with LR(S)A 1979 s 12(1)(c), (d), but is contrary to the normal tendency of liability under the 2012 Act to be restricted to a particular person or group of persons.
77 Or at least so it seems. Unlike other cases of compensation by the Keeper (for which see LR(S)A 2012 sch 5 para 18(6), (7)), this is not the subject of express provision. Nonetheless, as liability in cases to which s 106 applies must usually involve fault on the part of the Keeper, it is thought that it is subject to the five-year prescription as a liability to make reparation: see Prescription and Limitation (Scotland) Act 1973 s 6, sch 1 para 1(d); D Johnston, *Prescription and Limitation* (2nd edn, 2012) para 6.25.
78 SLC Report 222 para 27.17.
79 That is to say, in the draft Bill attached to the SLC Report.

Liability at Common Law

In some cases, additional liability might be a matter of the law of contract. But the main source of liability is likely to be the law of delict.

14.10 Liability for inaccuracies

Consider the question of mistakes, or in other words inaccuracies,[80] on the Register. The Land Register is under the management and control of the Keeper,[81] a public official who holds a non-ministerial office of the (devolved) Scottish Government.[82] Among the Keeper's many obligations under the 2012 Act are duties to take such steps as appear reasonable to protect the Register from interference, unauthorised access, and damage, as well as to register deeds, if they are valid, and to rectify inaccuracies, if the inaccuracy is manifest.[83] In registering a deed, the Keeper must evaluate and interpret it, or in other words make representations as to its meaning and legal effect; and the Register, taken as a whole, can be seen as a series of representations by the Keeper as to who owns what property, and subject to which encumbrances. Finally, the Register is open to the public, without limit, and can be accessed in person or electronically through Registers Direct (or its intended replacement, ScotLIS) or through a professional searcher.

Suppose, now, that the Register contains a mistake, and that the mistaken entry (or omission) is relied on by a person to that person's financial detriment. Is the Keeper liable for the resulting loss? The Act, of course, contains a scheme of compensation in respect of inaccuracies for those whose interactions with the Register result in changes to its content – in other words, for applicants for registration, and for those who procure (or at least benefit from) rectification.[84] That scheme, though comprehensive in nature, contains certain exclusions designed to protect the Keeper (for example in respect of minerals, or off-register events),[85] and it seems unlikely that exclusions which were mandated by Parliament can be circumvented by recourse to the law of delict.[86] But what of those who are not covered by the scheme at all? Might they have a claim, not under the Act, but under the general law of delict? Overwhelmingly, these will be people consulting the Register for information; and, depending on the reasons for the inquiry, a mistake in the information provided may result in financial loss. That might be true, for example, of a creditor who decides to lend on an unsecured basis on the footing of what the Register discloses as to the assets and liabilities of the potential debtor.[87]

Generalisation on this topic is difficult because so much depends on the facts and circumstances of particular cases. But it is plausible to argue that there might sometimes be liability. The *Caparo* test, for example, posits three indicators for

---

80 Defined in LR(S)A 2012 s 65.
81 LR(S)A 2012 s 1(2).
82 Scotland Act 1998 s 126(8): see paras 1.9 and 3.15–3.19 above.
83 LR(S)A 2012 ss 1(5), 21–28, and 80(1), (2).
84 LR(S)A 2012 ss 73–79, 84, and 85: see ch 13 and para 14.7 above. There is also liability for loss of rights due to realignment: see ss 94 and 95, discussed at paras 14.2 and 14.3 above.
85 LR(S)A 2012 s 73(2)(a)–(c), (e)–(g).
86 This is likely to fail the 'fair, just and reasonable' leg of the *Caparo* test: see *Braes v Keeper of the Registers of Scotland* [2009] CSOH 176, 2010 SLT 689, para 88 per Temporary Judge M G Thomson QC; D Brodie, 'Searching for *Gorringe*' (2013) 111 Greens Reparation Bulletin 5.
87 A creditor who takes a heritable security will be protected by the Keeper's warranty.

the existence of a duty of care: foreseeability of damage, proximity between the parties, and whether it is fair, just and reasonable to impose a duty upon the one party for the benefit of the other.[88] Foreseeability would often be present, at least if the mistake on the Register concerned the existence and scope of real rights, as opposed to some relatively trivial matter such as the middle name or occupation of the person registered as owner. Proximity is more problematic, although in at least one case (concerning representations by a regulator on its website), a court in England has decided that representation occurs when the material is consulted, not when the statement is first published, thus giving rise to sufficient proximity.[89] The law, however, continues to develop, and it is unclear whether this view of things will become established.[90] The final criterion, that the imposition of a duty would be fair, just and reasonable, might include a consideration of matters such as the role and status of the Register, the importance of its accuracy, the incidence of error, the cost to the Keeper (and hence ultimately to the users) of introducing additional checks, and so on.[91] Also relevant would be the exclusion of third-party liability from the statutory compensation scheme; but while this might suggest an intention to withhold any form of compensation,[92] it might also be explained by the difference between the strict liability of the statutory scheme (which, being generous, needs also to be restricted) and the fault-based liability of the common law (which, being narrower in scope, can safely be left to look after itself). The Scottish Law Commission appears to have adopted the second of these views.[93]

Even if a duty of care can be established, it would still be necessary to show that the duty had been breached, and that the breach caused the loss. There are errors on the Register that cannot be regarded as being due to the Keeper's fault – errors that could not have been detected by any system of scrutiny of applications which

---

88 *Caparo Industries plc v Dickman* [1990] 2 AC 605, 617H–618B per Lord Bridge of Harwich.
89 Accordingly, it did not matter that 'carelessness occurred at a time when the person to whom the representation was made was not personally in contemplation of the defendant and its employees': see *Schubert Murphy v The Law Society* [2014] EWHC 4561 (QB), [2015] PNLR 15, para 21 per Mitting J. In this case, a law firm listed on the Law Society's website turned out not to exist, causing loss to the claimant, itself a law firm, which had completed a conveyancing transaction with the non-firm in reliance on the website. The court refused an application to strike out the claim. See Reid and Gretton (n 32) 172–73.
90 Thus in *Sebry v Companies House* [2015] EWHC 115 (QB), [2015] 4 All ER 681, decided shortly after *Schubert Murphy*, while the court accepted that Companies House had a duty of care to an individual company which had been wrongly shown on the Companies Register as being in liquidation, it was careful not to extend the duty to outside third parties. In the words of Edis J, at para 111: 'It appears to me that where the Registrar undertakes to alter the status of a company on the Register which it is his duty to keep, in particular by recording a winding up order against it, he does assume a responsibility to that company (but not to anyone else) to take reasonable care to ensure that the winding up order is not registered against the wrong company ... This special relationship between the Registrar and the company arises because it is foreseeable that if a company is wrongly said on the Register to be in liquidation it will suffer serious harm.' See also para 106.
91 In *Santander UK plc v Keeper of the Registers of Scotland* [2013] CSOH 24, 2013 SLT 362 the pursuer's standard security was deleted from the Register, following the registration of a discharge forged by the debtor, and then reinstated by rectification too late to rank before a new standard security in favour of another creditor. As the statutory compensation scheme under the 1979 Act did not cover the situation, a claim in delict was made against the Keeper. This was rejected as being not fair, just and reasonable, mainly because the loss was caused by the criminal act of the pursuer's customer. For discussion, see K G C Reid and G L Gretton, *Conveyancing 2013* (2014) 178–82.
92 A view which is supported by SLC DP 128 paras 7.60 and 7.61.
93 SLC Report 222 para 27.17.

the Keeper could reasonably be expected to adopt. On the other hand, whether the required standard of care is met by the principle of 'tell me don't show me', with its uncritical reliance on the representations of interested parties, may be a different matter.[94]

14.11 Liability for wrongful decisions and other matters

So far the discussion has focused on mistakes on the Register. The example singled out by the Scottish Law Commission, however, was the wrongful rejection of an application.[95] A duty of care will be easier to establish in cases such as this because, applying the *Caparo* test, there is evidently foreseeability of loss and also proximity between applicant and Keeper, while it may well be fair, just and reasonable to impose a duty of care on the Keeper.[96] The same would be true of some other direct interactions between Keeper and customer, such as a wrongful refusal of rectification or a failure to process an application for registration with the reasonable despatch required by the legislation.[97]

14.12 *Ex gratia* payments

Ex gratia payments are sometimes made in respect of losses attributable to the Keeper's acts or omissions. Full details can be found on the RoS website.[98] Eligible losses can include the cost of additional work by solicitors due to mistakes on the title sheet, wrongful rejections of applications for registration, or other errors by RoS staff. The Keeper's policy, however, is to make payment only in 'exceptional circumstances', and in determining whether such circumstances exist, the Keeper has regard in particular to the following factors:

(a) whether an act or omission complained of was in accordance with the Keeper's policy at the relevant time;
(b) the availability of any other legal or administrative remedy;
(c) whether any other available remedy has been exhausted;
(d) whether the applicant has taken all reasonable steps to minimise their loss;
(e) the extent to which the applicant or any relevant third party has shown good faith.

---

94 For 'tell me don't show me', see para 8.11 above.
95 As to which see para 9.12 above.
96 The Scottish Law Commission had no doubt on the matter (SLC Report 222 para 12.100): 'If one [ie wrongful rejection] does happen, and if loss results, then in our view the general law imposes on the Keeper an obligation to make good that loss. The draft Bill has no specific provision on this, because we do not think it appropriate for this statute to attempt to codify, just for the Land Register, a more general principle of public law.' The only example of which we are aware is *Davidson v Mackenzie* (1856) 19 D 226, in which the Keeper was held liable to an inhibiting creditor for failure to register an inhibition properly (the sum due being mis-transcribed). The basis of the action was, not the common law of negligence, but the Act of 1693 (APS ix 271 c 23, RPS 1693/4/64), which provided for the keeping of minute books, for registration in the order specified in those books, and made 'the saids keepers not observing the premisses lyable to the damage of the parties prejudged by the not due observing of this present act'. The relevance of this Act to the Keeper's blunder is not, however, obvious. See also R Campbell, *The Law of Negligence* (2nd edn, 1879) 45.
97 LR(S)A 2012 s 35(3) provides that 'The Keeper must deal with an application without unreasonable delay'.
98 www.ros.gov.uk. See also a letter published at (2016) 61 JLSS Jan/6. For entitlement to legal expenses in connection with successful applications for rectification, see LR(S)A 2012 s 84(1)(a), discussed at para 14.7 above.

There is no prescribed form, but claims should give detailed information as to the nature and circumstances of the loss as well as addressing the issue of why, exceptionally, it is appropriate for a payment to be made. The Keeper will not consider a claim in respect of losses of less than £500, and will not necessarily cover the whole amount of a loss even where that amount is fully vouched for. Normally, claims will be processed within six weeks. No correspondence will be entered into about the merits of the decision..

FINDING THE MONEY

14.13 Liability without limit

The Scottish Law Commission considered, but in the end rejected, a cap on the amount which could be claimed from the Keeper under the 2012 Act provisions.[99] As it is, while the risk of a multi-million pound claim cannot entirely be discounted, the experience under the 1979 Act suggests that the Keeper's exposure is likely to be manageable. Indeed the sums paid out over the years have been surprisingly small. In the decade ending on 31 March 2011, the total amount paid by the Keeper was £3.5 million, an average of £350,000 a year.[100] Since then the annual amounts paid have been £161,934 (2011/12),[101] £400,000 (2012/13),[102] £503,733 (2013/14),[103] and £344,000 (2014/15).[104] The largest single amount paid out under the equivalent legislation in England and Wales was £8 million.[105] Only a very small percentage of registrations result in claims. In 2010/11, for example, the claims comprised 0.03% of the total of Land Register cases.[106]

These figures, of course, refer mainly to indemnity payments made under the 1979 Act, and it may be some years before the pattern produced by the 2012 Act becomes clear. The working hypothesis of the economic impact assessment prepared for the Scottish Law Commission was that the new legislation would actually reduce pay-outs, by 10%.[107]

14.14 Balancing the books

Registers of Scotland is required to balance the books. A non-ministerial department of the Scottish Administration, it operates as a trading fund under the

---

99   SLC DP 128 paras 9.39–9.42; SLC Report 222 paras 22.49–22.54. This was in the context of the Keeper's warranty.
100 *Financial Memorandum* accompanying the Land Registration etc (Scotland) Bill, para 381, reproduced in *Passage of the Land Registration etc (Scotland) Bill 2011* (n 49) 155. For slightly older figures, see SLC Report 222 para 27.20.
101 Registers of Scotland, *Annual Report and Accounts 2011–2012* (2012) 21.
102 Registers of Scotland, *Annual Report and Accounts 2012–2013* (2013) 26.
103 Registers of Scotland, *Annual Report and Accounts 2013–2014* (2014) 34.
104 Registers of Scotland, *Annual Report and Accounts 2014–2015* (2015) 25.
105 This figure was disclosed in oral evidence given by the Keeper to the Economy, Energy and Tourism Committee of the Scottish Parliament: see Scottish Parliament, *Official Report* col 866 (25 January 2012), reproduced in *Passage of the Land Registration etc (Scotland) Bill 2011* (n 49) 390.
106 Financial Memorandum (n 100) para 385. The percentage for 2008/09 was the same: see SLC Report 222 para 27.19.
107 SLC Report 222 vol 2, 583. This was said to be due to the simplification of the compensation system and the enhanced clarity of the rules.

Public Finance and Accountability (Scotland) Act 2000,[108] and its funds derive from the fees charged for registration and for information services.[109] Over the years it has accumulated substantial reserves – just under £83 million according to the most recent annual accounts[110] – which are intended to cover shortfalls in income resulting from a possible downturn in business as well as unexpectedly large claims for compensation.[111] There is no right of recourse to the Scottish Consolidated Fund.[112] A 'potentially significant proportion' of the reserves is likely to be used to pay for the costs of completion of the Land Register, scheduled to be accomplished by 2024.[113]

---

108 See in particular s 9 of that Act.
109 *Financial Memorandum* (n 100) para 363. See also para 3.18 above. There is also the possibility of income for services provided under LR(S)A 2012 s 108.
110 *Annual Report and Accounts 2014–2015* (n 104) 55.
111 *Annual Report and Accounts 2013–2014* (n 103) 20.
112 'Why are reserves necessary? First, because the Keeper cannot have access to consolidated funds; she must balance her budget. She does not have recourse to knock on Mr Swinney's door and ask for a top-up because things are not going well': Scottish Parliament, *Official Report* col 7201 (14 March 2012; Fergus Ewing MSP, Minister for Energy, Enterprise and Tourism), reproduced in *Passage of the Land Registration etc (Scotland) Bill 2011* (n 49) 552.
113 *Annual Report and Accounts 2013–2014* (n 103) 13. For completion of the Register, see ch 7.

Chapter 15

Liabilities of those using the Land Registration System

15.1 Introduction

The previous chapter considered the liabilities of the Keeper. The present chapter considers the liabilities of others involved in the registration process. The main category of such persons is applicants for registration and their legal advisers, but liability can also fall on the granters of deeds intended for registration. This chapter is chiefly about civil liability to the Keeper, but the legislation includes a provision for criminal liability which will also be discussed.

CIVIL LIABILITY

15.2 Solicitors: liability under s 111 – duty of care

As well as owing a professional duty to their clients, solicitors have a duty of care to the Keeper. This may already have been the rule at common law, although the position was unclear.[1] At any rate, the duty is now a matter of express provision in s 111 of the 2012 Act,[2] so that, if not new, it is a great deal more prominent than before and hence more likely to be enforced. A new statutory duty was regarded as acceptable by professional bodies representing solicitors,[3] although the Law Society thought that it should be matched by a reciprocal duty on the part of the Keeper[4] – something which, in the event, is largely achieved by the provisions already described in the previous chapter.

In terms of s 111, solicitors (and other legal advisers) who act for the granter or grantee of a deed presented for registration must 'take reasonable care to ensure that the Keeper does not inadvertently make the [land] register inaccurate as a result of

---

1 Scottish Law Commission, *Report No 222 on Land Registration* (2010) ('SLC Report 222') paras 12.101 and 12.102. See also *McCoach v Keeper of the Registers of Scotland*, 19 December 2008, Lands Tribunal ('… the client, acting through the solicitor, is under a duty of care in relation to the application for registration of the title. That duty specifically relates to the accuracy of the register entry.') An equivalent duty has gained tentative recognition in England and Wales: see *Chief Land Registrar v Caffrey & Co* [2016] EWHC (Ch) 161, [2016] PNLR 23.
2 Section 111 applies to the parties as well as to their solicitors, but we consider the latter first.
3 The Law Society of Scotland and the Scottish Law Agents Society, in oral evidence given to the Economy, Energy and Tourism Committee of the Scottish Parliament: see *Official Report* cols 776–77 (11 January 2012), reproduced in Scottish Parliament, *Passage of the Land Registration etc (Scotland) Bill 2011* (2013, SPPB 174) (available at www.scottish.parliament.uk/parliamentarybusiness/Bills/44469.aspx) 317–18. For the Law Society, Ross MacKay thought that s 111 'reflects what we understand to be the law anyway. We have always assumed that, if we make an honest mistake as part of the process, the Keeper may revert to us to seek compensation. As a matter of principle, we could not object to that'.
4 *Passage of the Land Registration etc (Scotland) Bill 2011* (n 3) 480. The Law Society thought that the duty should cover matters such as errors in P16 reports (ie plans reports) and delays in entering applications into the application record.

a change made in consequence of' the deed or the application for registration. To the extent that the Keeper relies on solicitors during the registration process, those solicitors must conduct their business with reasonable care. The standard of care is not further specified, but is presumably the same as that already owed to clients.[5] The guidance issued by RoS strikes a reassuring note:[6]

> The duty of care is not intended to impose on solicitors a higher standard of competence than the existing professional requirement but rather is to enforce a degree of responsibility and accountability. It is ROS' view that section 111 does not place a more onerous duty on conveyancers. A law firm could only be held accountable for an inaccuracy in the Land Register if it had fallen below the acceptable standard of reasonable care. What is deemed as reasonable will depend on the circumstances, and what is regarded as meeting that standard could change over time. The duty of care does not make law firms involved in conveyancing transactions in any sense absolute guarantors for their clients or their clients' titles.

In practice, the Keeper relies on solicitors in two respects: the preparation and execution of the deed being presented for registration, and the completion of the application form.[7] The first is the responsibility, in different ways, of both sets of solicitors, the second only of the solicitors who act for the grantee (and applicant for registration).[8] So far as the deed is concerned, the duty to the Keeper matches the long-established duty to the client to prepare a deed which is valid as to form and content, and executed by a person with title and capacity to grant. The novelty of s 111, if there is one, concerns completion of the application form. Here the applicant's solicitor must negotiate a series of questions and must do so with the appropriate degree of care.[9] In the case of applications for first registration, this involves making a professional judgment on matters such as which real burdens continue to affect the property, and whether evidence as to possession is sufficient to claim a prescriptive servitude.[10] In addition, if the solicitor has doubts as to any aspect of the title, these doubts should be shared with the Keeper in the 'further information' or 'additional information' parts of the form; indeed the first of these expressly asks for details of 'any other information material to this application that has not already been disclosed in this application or its accompanying documents'.

At what point in time does the duty of care end? On the making of the application, or perhaps later, at the time when the application is accepted? In practice the difference will seldom matter. But the issue was a matter of controversy during the passing of the legislation.[11] A provision in the Scottish Law Commission's draft Bill,[12] which brought the duty to an end on submission of the application form,[13] was removed from the Bill prior to its introduction to Parliament and, despite a request to reconsider the position made in the Parliament's Stage 1 Report, was

---

5 SLC Report 222 para 12.103. This is essentially the standard laid down in *Hunter v Hanley* 1955 SC 200. See R Rennie, *Solicitors' Negligence* (1997), and R Rennie, *Opinions on Professional Negligence in Conveyancing* (2004).
6 Registers of Scotland, *General Guidance: Section 111 – Duty of Care* (v.01, 2014) 1.
7 *General Guidance: Section 111 – Duty of Care* (n 6) 1.
8 For application forms are not usually revised by the granter's solicitors: see para 8.21 above.
9 See paras 8.12 ff above.
10 See paras 8.23 and 8.25 above.
11 It had also been a matter on which the Scottish Law Commissioners were not unanimous: see SLC Report 222 para 12.104, n 119.
12 SLC draft Bill s 27(2). For discussion, see SLC Report 222 paras 12.105 and 12.106.
13 Or, in the case of the duty on the granter or the granter's solicitor, on delivery of the deed.

not reinstated.[14] An amendment to restore the provision at stage 2 was no more successful, attracting only the vote of the MSP putting it forward,[15] and s 111 was passed without it. In its absence, it seems that the duty of care continues up to the point when it ceases to matter, that is to say, when the Keeper makes her final decision as to the application for registration.[16] For as long as this post-application period lasts, the parties' solicitors must inform the Keeper of new information which might have a bearing on the title.[17] In practice, there will usually be nothing to tell, and only a short period in which (not) to tell it.[18]

15.3 Solicitors: liability under s 111 – causation and loss

Breach of the duty of care imposed by s 111 does not, by itself, give rise to liability to the Keeper. For that to happen, two further requirements must be met.

One concerns causation. It must be shown that the breach caused the Keeper 'inadvertently' to make the Register inaccurate.[19] No liability arises, therefore, in respect of a deed or form, however negligently prepared, which does not result in an inaccuracy on the Register. Nor is there liability for mistakes made by the Keeper in the full knowledge of the facts, or at any rate for a reason that cannot be attributed to something done or not done by solicitors. However, the heightened use of 'tell me don't show me' means that the Keeper relies much more on the word of solicitors than was previously the case, increasing the likelihood that the causation requirement can be satisfied.[20]

The other requirement is that the Keeper should have suffered loss. Often there will be none. Even serious defects of title tend to lie undiscovered once they have found their way into the persuasive environs of the Land Register. Usually, what is on the Register is accepted at face value and without further inquiry. But even where a defect comes to light and – what is less common still – is pursued to the point of successful rectification, it may not be the Keeper who suffers loss.

Consider the following example. Andrew, whose title is still on the Register of Sasines, dispones land to Beth. Due to negligence on the part of Beth's solicitors, the disposition includes a strip of land which is actually the property of Calum,

---

14 Economy, Energy and Tourism Committee of the Scottish Parliament, *Stage 1 Report* paras 157–59, reproduced in *Passage of the Land Registration etc (Scotland) Bill 2011* (n 3) 259–60; and see p 572 for the Government's response.
15 Murdo Fraser MSP, who is a solicitor: see *Passage of the Land Registration etc (Scotland) Bill 2011* (n 3) 596 (amendment 2), 618–19.
16 *Land Registration etc (Scotland) Act 2012: Explanatory Notes* para 247; *General Guidance: Section 111 – Duty of Care* (n 6) 1. Compare here the requirement of good faith under LR(S)A 2012 s 86 which appears to last until the date of registration: see para 12.15 above. As this is backdated to the date on which the application appears in the application record (ss 36 and 37(1)), it is earlier than the date on which the Keeper makes her decision.
17 New information but not new events: the effect of the 'state of the legal universe' principle is that, in making a decision as to registration, the Keeper must disregard events occurring after the date of the application: see para 9.8 above.
18 In proposing the reinstatement of the SLC's provision, Murdo Fraser MSP warned that, due to possible delays in registration, a solicitor's duty of care might follow him long into his retirement: see Scottish Parliament, *Official Report* col 1404 (2 May 2012), reproduced in *Passage of the Land Registration etc (Scotland) Bill 2011* (n 3) 618. LR(S)A 2012 s 35(2), however, places the Keeper under a duty to deal with applications 'without unreasonable delay', and it is assumed that significant delays will be correspondingly rare.
19 LR(S)A 2012 s 111(1), (3).
20 For 'tell me don't show me', see para 8.11 above.

a neighbour, who also holds on a Sasine title.[21] Beth is registered as owner of the whole property included in the disposition and enters into possession. If Calum reclaims the strip and the Register is rectified by its removal from Beth's title, it is Beth who suffers loss and not the Keeper; for no compensation is payable, to Beth, under the Keeper's warranty for an inaccuracy caused by a breach of s 111.[22] It is only if (Calum having been inactive) Beth dispones to Donald, a *bona fide* acquirer, that the Keeper would have to pay compensation – not to Donald, who would normally acquire a good title by realignment,[23] but to Calum, who has now lost ownership of the strip.[24] Either way, it is the negligent solicitors who will finish up paying the bill. In the first case they are liable to Beth for professional negligence,[25] in the second to the Keeper for breach of s 111.[26]

In principle, all loss directly arising from a breach of s 111 is recoverable by the Keeper provided it is not too remote.[27] The Keeper is required to minimise her loss.[28] RoS guidance suggests the following, non-exhaustive, heads of loss: compensation payments made;[29] legal expenses for claiming compensation; interest paid on compensation and legal expenses; District Valuer's fees; legal opinions; and litigation costs.[30] Following the loss, the Keeper has five years to make a claim before it is extinguished by negative prescription.[31]

15.4 Parties to the deed: liability under s 111

Liability under s 111 is not confined to solicitors. The parties to a deed, too, must take reasonable care to prevent the Keeper from making inaccurate entries on the Register.[32] Breaches, however, are likely to be rare.[33] From time to time, no doubt, a careless answer to a solicitor's inquiry will result in false statements being

---

21 This was the issue which arose in *McCoach v Keeper of the Registers of Scotland*, 19 December 2008, Lands Tribunal.
22 LR(S)A 2012 s 78(c).
23 LR(S)A 2012 s 86: see paras 12.8 ff above.
24 LR(S)A 2012 s 94. For compensation under this provision, see paras 14.2 and 14.3 above.
25 As this example shows, if conduct by solicitors amounts to a breach of s 111, it will usually also amount to negligence in relation to the professional duty owed to the client. That would not, however, be true if the solicitors' actions in breach of s 111 (notably in preparing the application form) were specifically and knowingly authorised or instructed by the client: in that case the solicitors would be in breach of their duty to the Keeper but not in breach of their duty to their client.
26 If the facts had occurred before the designated day, the result would have been the same in the first case, because the Keeper's obligation to pay indemnity would have fallen away if Beth's loss was caused by her, or her solicitors', fraud or carelessness: LR(S)A 1979 s 12(3)(n). Whether it would have been the same in the second case would depend on whether Beth's solicitors were under a common-law duty of care to the Keeper (or, alternatively, to Calum, giving rise to a claim which the Keeper could enforce due to subrogation).
27 LR(S)A 2012 s 111(5), (6). By contrast to other compensation provisions in the Act, nothing is said as to recovery of consequential loss, perhaps because loss of that kind is unlikely to arise in this context.
28 LR(S)A 2012 s 111(6)(a).
29 In practice, this is likely to be either compensation under the Keeper's warranty (see ch 13) or compensation for loss following realignment (see paras 14.2 and 14.3 above).
30 *General Guidance: Section 111 – Duty of Care* (n 6) 2.
31 Prescription and Limitation (Scotland) Act 1973 ss 6 and 11(1), sch 1 para 1(ae), inserted by LR(S)A 2012 sch 5 para 18(6).
32 LR(S)A 2012 s 111(2)(a), (4)(a). Under the heading of 'Warnings', the application form for registration draws express attention, in the signature box, to s 111.
33 Full details of the operation of s 111 can be found in paras 15.2 and 15.3 above.

unwittingly made by the solicitor in the application form for registration, and thereafter to an inaccuracy on the Register. Otherwise, short of actual fraud, it is hard to envisage circumstances under which a client could influence the content of the Register. And if fraud does occur, the Keeper would often have a remedy against the fraudster at common law, whether directly,[34] or as assignee of a person to whom compensation has been paid under the statutory scheme.[35]

It is uncertain whether or in what circumstances a party might be liable under s 111, not for his own misdemeanours, but for those of his law agent.[36] The answer has little practical significance because the Keeper is likely to pursue the solicitor, who is insured, in preference to the solicitor's client, who is not.

15.5 Applicants for registration: liability under the application form

In practice, application forms for registration are signed, not by the applicant in person, but by a solicitor on the applicant's behalf. The effect, however, is to bind the applicant and not the solicitor.[37] Two certifications appear in the signature box, immediately before the signature. These are:

> I/we apply for registration of the deed identified in Part A of this form and certify that this application complies with the general application conditions in section 22, and the particular application conditions in section 21(2).[38]

> I/we certify that the information given in this form and the answers to the above questions are complete and correct to the best of my/our knowledge and belief.

It is thought that the second certification must be read as qualifying the first, for if that were not the case, the applicant would be giving a warranty to the Keeper so extensive in character as largely to negate the Keeper's statutory warranty of title to the applicant.[39] In particular, the applicant would be giving an absolute guarantee as to the validity of the deed,[40] or in other words a guarantee that 'by the registration applied for, a right would be acquired, varied or extinguished'.[41] As qualified by the second certification, however, the guarantee becomes one merely to the best of the applicant's knowledge and belief. And when the certifications

---

34 SLC Report 222 para 12.102 gives the example of a person who steals the identity of an owner and proceeds to grant a standard security to a bank.
35 Continuing the example in the previous footnote, the Keeper, after paying compensation to the bank under the Keeper's warranty, could take an assignation of the bank's delictual claim against the fraudster.
36 For a full discussion, see L Macgregor, *The Law of Agency in Scotland* (2013) paras 13-10 ff. To the extent that principals are liable for the delicts of their agent, Professor Macgregor categorises this as a matter of direct liability (the agent having acted within the authority, actual or apparent, of the principal) and not of vicarious liability.
37 Assuming, of course, that the solicitor is acting within his authority as agent.
38 This is the certification in respect of ordinary applications. For voluntary registrations (where there is no deed) it reads: 'I/we hereby apply for the registration of an unregistered plot of land. I/we certify that this application complies with the requirements of sections 27 and 28.' For the application conditions, see paras 8.6–8.9 above.
39 For a similar argument in respect of a warranty, earlier in the form, on links in title, see para 13.10 above.
40 LR(S)A 2012 ss 23(1)(b), 25(1)(a), and 26(1)(a).
41 LR(S)A 2012 s 113(2)(a). This almost exactly matches the Keeper's warranty as to title under s 73(1)(a), which is that, at the time of registration, 'the title sheet to which the application relates is accurate in so far as it shows an acquisition, variation or discharge in favour of the applicant'.

are taken together, they are (broadly) consistent with the obligation under s 111 in respect of standard of care, although wider in respect that they are not limited to matters which result in an inaccuracy on the Register.

A further certification, in respect of links in title, appears earlier in the form, and was discussed in a previous chapter.[42]

CRIMINAL LIABILITY

15.6 Background

Section 111 of the 2012 Act, providing for civil liability,[43] is accompanied by s 112 which, in certain limited circumstances, provides for criminal liability.[44] The details can be found in the next paragraph, but in essence it is an offence to make false or misleading statements in relation to an application for registration, or to fail to disclose material information.[45] The offence can be committed either by the applicant for registration or by the applicant's legal adviser. The provision's aim, according to the Government Minister in charge of the legislation,[46] was 'to disrupt serious organised crime and to criminalise individuals who knowingly use the Land Register to facilitate criminal behaviour'. The offence was not intended, the Minister added, 'to criminalise honest solicitors who make genuine errors in applications for registration'.[47] The Law Society, however, was far from reassured by statements such as these and conducted a vigorous campaign of opposition.[48] In the event, no provision in the Land Registration Bill was more controversial, or took up more time during its Parliamentary passage.[49]

The objections raised by the Law Society, and others, were threefold.[50] First, the provision was too wide in scope, penalising recklessness as well as intentional wrongdoing. Secondly, the defence of due diligence was too vaguely drawn for solicitors to know what they must do to be sure of avoiding liability. If, for example, 'we ask a client whether a third party uses their property, do we then have to go

---

42 See para 13.10 above.
43 For which see paras 15.2–15.4 above.
44 The draft Bill attached to the SLC Report did not contain such a provision.
45 For the policy background, see paras 76–80 of the *Policy Memorandum* which accompanied the introduction of the Bill to Parliament, reproduced in *Passage of the Land Registration etc (Scotland) Bill 2011* (n 3) 193.
46 Fergus Ewing MSP, the Minister for Energy, Enterprise and Tourism.
47 Scottish Parliament, *Official Report* cols 7174–75 (14 March 2012), reproduced in *Passage of the Land Registration etc (Scotland) Bill 2011* (n 3) 538–39. These remarks were made during the stage 1 debate. For further official pronouncements intended to reassure solicitors, see *Passage of the Land Registration etc (Scotland) Bill 2011* (n 3) 424 ('honest solicitors, who are the overwhelming majority, have absolutely nothing to fear'), 434 ('No solicitor who acts in good faith will be accused of acting recklessly').
48 For its written evidence, see *Passage of the Land Registration etc (Scotland) Bill 2011* (n 3) 325–28.
49 Scottish Parliament, *Official Report* col 1405 (2 May 2012; Murdo Fraser MSP), reproduced in *Passage of the Land Registration etc (Scotland) Bill 2011* (n 3) 619. The provision featured in most of the stage 1 hearings of the Economy, Energy and Tourism Committee and, in view of the controversy it aroused, the final session, on 22 February 2012, was devoted solely to questioning the Solicitor General for Scotland and officials from the Crown Office. See *Official Report* cols 1003–18, reproduced in *Passage of the Land Registration etc (Scotland) Bill 2011* (n 3) 433–40.
50 A convenient summary of the views expressed can be found in paras 138–56 of the *Stage 1 Report* by the Economy, Energy and Tourism Committee of the Scottish Parliament (reproduced in *Passage of the Land Registration etc (Scotland) Bill 2011* (n 3) 256–59.

on a site visit to look for evidence of third-party occupation?'[51] And finally the whole thing was unnecessary anyway, given existing statutory penalties in respect of money-laundering[52] and the common-law offence of fraud.

The Scottish Government was unmoved by the first and last of these points. Indeed, the inclusion of recklessness was 'exactly what makes this offence go further than the other statutory and common-law offences';[53] without it, it would, argued the Scottish Government, be considerably harder to obtain convictions for mortgage fraud and organised crime involving the Land Register.[54] On the defence of due diligence, however, the Scottish Government eventually agreed to drop a requirement on the part of the accused to show that 'all such steps as could reasonably be taken to ensure that no offence would be committed' had been taken.[55] Shorn of this requirement, the defence is undemanding, and should be easily met by a solicitor acting with ordinary professional care. But in any case prosecutions under s 112, at least of solicitors, are likely to be exceedingly rare.

15.7 The offence

Section 112 applies to applicants for registration of a deed and to their solicitors or other legal advisers.[56] It is an offence to make a false or misleading statement in relation to an application for registration.[57] It is equally an offence to fail to disclose material information.[58] The act or omission can concern the application form itself[59] or some related document or communication.[60] To qualify as an offence, there must be deliberate falsehood or at least recklessness as to the truth.[61]

---

51 Scottish Parliament, *Official Report* col 775 (11 January 2012; Fiona Letham), reproduced in *Passage of the Land Registration etc (Scotland) Bill 2011* (n 3) 317.
52 See Proceeds of Crime Act 2002 pt 7.
53 Scottish Parliament, *Official Report* col 1409 (2 May 2012; Fergus Ewing MSP, Minister for Energy, Enterprise and Tourism), reproduced in *Passage of the Land Registration etc (Scotland) Bill 2011* (n 3) 621.
54 Scottish Parliament, *Official Report* col 1004 (22 February 2012; Lesley Thomson QC, the Solicitor General for Scotland), reproduced in *Passage of the Land Registration etc (Scotland) Bill 2011* (n 3) 433. The requirement of common-law fraud that knowledge of the fraud must be proved was said to be particularly troublesome.
55 This was para (c) of what is now LR(S)A 2012 s 112(4). It had been strongly criticised by the Law Society: see *Passage of the Land Registration etc (Scotland) Bill 2011* (n 3) 328. The paragraph was removed by Government amendment at stage 2. For this and other amendments concerning s 112 (then numbered as s 108), see *Official Report* cols 1405–15 (2 May 2012), reproduced in *Passage of the Land Registration etc (Scotland) Bill 2011* (n 3) 619–24.
56 LR(S)A 2012 s 112(2). Crown employees are included but not the Crown itself, although the Court of Session has power, on the Keeper's application, to declare unlawful any act or omission of the Crown which would contravene s 112: see s 121.
57 LR(S)A 2012 s 112(1)(a).
58 LR(S)A 2012 s 112(1)(b).
59 The signature box in the application form contains a reminder of potential criminal liability ('It is an offence to knowingly or recklessly make a materially false or misleading statement, or to intentionally or recklessly fail to disclose material information, in relation to this application (see section 112)').
60 All that is required of the act or omission by s 112(1) is that it is made 'in relation to an application for registration'. See also Registers of Scotland, *General Guidance: Section 112 – Offence relating to applications for registration* (v.01, 2014) 2: 'The term "in relation to an application" ensures that statements made in both the initial application for registration and in associated deeds and documents are covered by the offence provision. Section 112, therefore, captures any document supplementary to the application itself, such as, any evidence submitted to the Keeper in response to a requisition.'
61 LR(S)A 2012 s 112(1). The inclusion of recklessness was controversial: see para 15.6 above.

The provision is silent as to the recipient of the communication, but it is assumed that it must be the Keeper or one of the Keeper's officials or, in the case of a communication by the applicant, the applicant's legal adviser. Loose talk in the pub does not engage s 112.

A single defence is provided. Acts or omissions are excused if the person in question took all reasonable precautions and exercised all due diligence to avoid the offence.[62] Fortunately, the (non-exhaustive)[63] example which the provision goes on to give is more indulgent than this demanding formulation might suggest. This declares the defence to be established if the person acted in reliance on information supplied by another person, and did not know, and had no reason to suppose, that the information was false, misleading, or incomplete.[64] Solicitors, therefore, can rely on what their clients tell them unless there are plausible grounds for suspicion.[65] None of this suggests a heightened duty of inquiry; solicitors were already alert as to the possible criminality of their clients.[66] When the relevant Minister[67] was pressed in Parliament as to 'what practical steps does an honest solicitor require to take, over and above what they are required to do under the money laundering regulations, to ensure they do not face criminal prosecution if acting in good faith?', the terse answer given was 'None'.[68]

A person who is prosecuted under s 112 must give notice if he intends to employ the defence of reliance on information provided by someone else, or alternatively must obtain leave from the court.[69] The purpose of the notice is to provide the prosecutor with information as to the identity of the person whose information was relied on.

The maximum penalty under s 112 is imprisonment for up to two years,[70] or a fine not exceeding the statutory maximum, or both.[71]

---

62 LR(S)A 2012 s 112(3).
63 LR(S)A 2012 s 112 (5).
64 LR(S)A 2012 s 112(4).
65 *General Guidance: Section 112 – Offence relating to applications for registration* (n 60) 2: 'the offence aims to deter solicitors from "turning a blind eye" to questionable actions by their clients'.
66 G L Gretton and K G C Reid, *Conveyancing* (4th edn, 2011) paras 1-08 and 1-09.
67 Fergus Ewing MSP, the Minister for Energy, Enterprise and Tourism.
68 Scottish Parliament, *Official Report* col 980 (8 February 2012), reproduced in *Passage of the Land Registration etc (Scotland) Bill 2011* (n 3) 426. It is noteworthy that this reply was given *before* para (c) of s 112(4) was dropped (as to which see para 15.6 above) and the defence made considerably less demanding.
69 LR(S)A 2012 s 112(6)–(8). Subsection (7) sets out the timetable for notice, and subs (8) excuses separate notice in cases where a defence statement has been lodged.
70 Or up to one year in the case of summary convictions.
71 LR(S)A 2012 s 112(9).

Chapter 16

Examination of Title

16.1 Introduction

This chapter is concerned with titles that are already on the Land Register, not with those that are still held in the Register of Sasines.[1] Even so, it does not seek to provide a comprehensive account of examination of such titles. That must be left to textbooks on conveyancing. Instead the chapter concentrates on those aspects of title examination that depend on the Land Register legislation.

Since the designated day (8 December 2014), registration has been governed by the Land Registration etc (Scotland) Act 2012. But the title of the person who, in the current transaction, is to grant the deed may pre-date that day and hence have been registered under the different regime of the Land Registration (Scotland) Act 1979. The first question to consider in examination of title is thus: under which Act was the granter's title registered. Does the granter have a 1979 Act title or a 2012 Act title?[2] The nature and scope of the title examination will depend on the answer.

If things go wrong, grantees will usually have a claim under the Keeper's warranty,[3] or the warrandice clause in the deed,[4] or both. One purpose of examination of title, however, is to avoid things going wrong and hence the need for such claims: the idea is to procure for the acquirer the 'mud' and not the 'money'.[5] Furthermore, if things do go wrong, a failure to examine title properly may lead to a claim under the Keeper's warranty being denied.[6] Hence, examination of title is necessary for both types of title guarantee (ie both 'mud' and 'money').

In this chapter examination of title is discussed in the context of the following transaction types: (i) the transfer of ownership;[7] (ii) the creation of a long lease;[8] (iii) the assignation or sublet of a long lease;[9] (iv) the creation of a servitude;[10] and (v) the creation of a standard security.[11]

1 For the examination of titles still held on the Register of Sasines, see G L Gretton and K G C Reid, *Conveyancing* (4th edn, 2011) paras 7-13 ff; A E A Stewart and E F F Sinclair, *Conveyancing Practice in Scotland* (7th edn, 2016) pp 317 ff.
2 As time goes on the number of the former will decline, and of the latter will grow, in part because of first registrations taking place after 8 December 2014 and in part through the transfer, after that date, of properties registered under the 1979 Act.
3 See ch 13.
4 For warrandice, see Gretton and Reid (n 1) ch 19.
5 See para 12.2 above.
6 LR(S)A 2012 s 78(b), (c): see paras 13.17 and 13.18 above. If the Keeper was aware, at the time of the original application, that title had not been examined, then warranty would be likely to have been excluded from the outset (if, indeed, the application was not simply rejected): see para 8.15 above.
7 Paragraphs 16.2–16.13.
8 Paragraphs 16.14 and 16.15.
9 Paragraphs 16.16–16.22.
10 Paragraphs 16.23–16.25.
11 Paragraphs 16.26 and 16.27.

TRANSFER OF OWNERSHIP

16.2 Seller as owner: 2012 Act titles

We begin with acquisition of ownership by transfer, which in the great majority of cases means acquisition by sale.[12] The first duty of examination of title is to check that the seller owns the property being sold or has power to grant on some other basis.[13] Otherwise ownership cannot be transferred to the buyer.[14] Where the seller was registered as owner on or after 8 December 2014, the title is governed wholly by the 2012 Act. Subject to what is said below, the person named on the title sheet as proprietor can be taken to be the owner without further inquiry. A legal report will be needed to update the title sheet; provided it shows the advance notice for the current transaction, and nothing untoward or unexpected, the buyer can proceed to settlement on the agreed date of entry.[15]

Section 86 of the 2012 Act (on realignment) gives full title protection to the buyer in the unlikely event that the person registered as proprietor was not, after all, the owner.[16] To qualify for the protection, however, a number of conditions must be complied with; and, while the likelihood of s 86 being needed is slim, the buyer's solicitors should nonetheless seek to verify the conditions so far as they are able to do so.[17] The conditions themselves were considered in detail in an earlier chapter,[18] and only a summary is needed here. The conditions are that:[19]

(i) the buyer is in good faith at the time of registration of the disposition;
(ii) the land is possessed by the seller at the time of delivery of the disposition;
(iii) the seller, or the seller followed by the buyer, is in possession of the land openly, peaceably, and without judicial interruption for the year immediately before the disposition is registered;
(iv) at no time during this one-year period (a) did the Keeper become aware that the seller was not the owner, (b) was the title sheet subject to a caveat, or (c) did the title sheet state that a particular name or designation is not known or known with reasonable certainty; and
(v) the Keeper has not restricted her warranty of title.

The good faith of one's client can usually be taken for granted (condition (i)). In this connection it should be borne in mind that the solicitor's knowledge of a title defect will be attributed to the client. A number of the other conditions can be checked from the title sheet (conditions (iv)(b) and (c) and (v)). A restriction in warranty

---

12 Other possibilities are donation, and transfer by an executor to a legatee.
13 As to the latter, see LR(S)A 2012 s 87, which extends the protection of s 86 to dispositions granted by the proprietor's representatives. The wording would include, for instance, a heritable creditor exercising power of sale.
14 LR(S)A 2012 ss 49(4) and 50(2). Unlike the position under the 1979 Act, there is no Midas touch to validate void dispositions: see para 9.20 above.
15 For legal reports, see paras 10.31 and 10.32 above; for advance notices, see ch 10.
16 Even if s 86 is not engaged, a buyer has the protection of the Keeper's warranty.
17 The advice given in Stewart and Sinclair (n 1) 51 is: 'Since it will never be apparent from the title sheet whether or not Dermot's [ie the seller's] title is "bad", in practice one should always check, as a matter of course, that a seller with a 2012 Act title has possessed for at least one year.' It is not suggested by the authors that the other conditions should be checked. This is one of a number of areas in which practice will no doubt evolve.
18 See paras 12.8–12.17 above.
19 LR(S)A 2012 s 86(1)(b), (3).

would of course stop the transaction in its tracks for reasons which have nothing to do with s 86.[20] The issue of possession is discussed separately below (conditions (ii) and (iii)).[21] Finally, if the Keeper is aware that the seller is not the owner, she is likely to have made the necessary change to the Register already (condition (iv)(a)).

The position adopted by RoS is that realignment will normally be assumed to have occurred, following registration of the buyer's disposition, unless a judicial determination to the contrary is obtained by a competing party.[22]

16.3 The possessory requirements

In relation to possession, s 86 imposes two separate requirements. First, the seller must be in possession at the time of delivery of the disposition.[23] Secondly, the seller (or the seller followed by the buyer) must have been in possession for the year prior to the disposition's registration.[24] Unless registration is long delayed, the second requirement will encompass the first. Possession includes civil possession so that if, for example, the property is leased, the seller will be considered to possess through the tenant.[25]

To verify that the seller is in current possession is in most cases not difficult. But to verify possession for the previous year is harder, and from the point of view of everyday conveyancing practice probably out of the question.[26] The issue is familiar from Sasine conveyancing where the validity of the title rests on the seller, and predecessors, having possessed, not for one year but for ten.[27] Yet in practice no one worries about this: if the seller possesses now, his previous possession is taken for granted.[28] The same is true in respect of s 86. Only three checks seem to be required, namely (i) that the seller possesses now; (ii) that by the date of registration the seller will have owned the property for at least a year, and so has presumptively possessed for the necessary one-year period;[29] and (iii) that no information has been disclosed which might suggest that the seller has not been in possession. From (i) and (ii) it can reasonably be inferred that the seller will have possessed for the necessary year; and unless there is positive evidence to the contrary, this is as far as the buyer's solicitor needs to inquire.

It is common for sellers to be asked to warrant their possession in the missives. For example, clause 28 of the Scottish Standard Clauses provides that:[30]

---

20 For the Keeper's warranty, see ch 13.
21 See paras 16.3 and 16.4 below.
22 Registers of Scotland, *Registration Manual* (https://rosdev.atlassian.net/wiki/display/2ARM/Home) Topics: Realignment of rights.
23 LR(S)A 2012 s 86(1)(b).
24 LR(S)A 2012 s 86(3)(a). As buyers normally take entry before registration, the year will include a few days' possession on the part of the buyer.
25 LR(S)A 2012 s 113(1).
26 Scottish Law Commission, *Report No 222 on Land Registration* (2010) ('SLC Report 222') para 37.54. The Scottish Law Commission saw 'no reason why examination of title, or any other aspect of conveyancing practice, should change'.
27 For it is only ten years' possession which allows positive prescription to run.
28 Gretton and Reid (n 1) para 7-22.
29 For where the seller has not owned for a year, see para 16.4 below.
30 Scottish Standard Clauses, 2nd edition (2016) (www.lawscot.org.uk/media/816883/Scottish-Standard-Clauses-Edition-2-.pdf) cl 28. See also cl 7.4 of the Property Standardisation Group's Offer to Sell – Vacant Possession (www.psglegal.co.uk): 'The Seller confirms that it is currently in possession of the Property and has been in possession of the Property openly, peaceably and without judicial interruption for a continuous period of at least one year.'

28.1 The Seller warrants that he has owned the Property for at least 6 months[31] prior to the date of the Offer or other document incorporating reference to these Clauses. This provision shall not apply where the Seller is a personal representative or executor of the proprietor; or is an institutional heritable creditor exercising its power of sale; or is a receiver, trustee in sequestration, administrator or liquidator.

28.2 The Seller warrants that the Property has been possessed openly, peaceably and without judicial interruption by the Seller since the Seller's acquisition of same.

There is no harm in this, of course. But it is doubtful whether there is much benefit. The seller is already bound to give a good and marketable title, and the clause adds nothing substantive to that obligation. The most that can be said is that the clause might smoke out cases where there has been insufficient possession; a seller whose possession falls short will, if he is honest, seek to qualify the warranty.

Where the sale is not by the owner but by someone whose title derives from the owner, such as a heritable creditor or a trustee in sequestration, possession by the heritable creditor or trustee is treated as possession by the owner, although of course the owner may simply have retained possession all along.[32] The position is trickier in sales by executors.[33] As the deceased's possession probably[34] ends with death, and the executor's probably cannot be regarded as having begun until confirmation (at least), there will have been an interruption in possession with the result that the one-year period is unlikely to have been completed by the time the disposition is registered. This is just one example of a more general problem, to which we now turn.

16.4 Possession for less than a year

If the seller has possessed for less than a year, it is usually because he has owned for less than a year. What then? The shortfall in the seller's possession can be made up by possession on the part of the buyer, even if that possession occurs *after* the disposition is registered.[35] So suppose that, by the time of registration, the seller has owned (and therefore presumptively possessed) for only nine months.[36] To make up the full year, the buyer must continue that possession for a further three months. That means that, at the time of settlement, it cannot be said for sure that s 86 will apply. For that a further three months' possession, this time on the part of the buyer, will be needed. Meanwhile there is a theoretical risk that, during this three-month period, evidence of a title defect will emerge, and s 86 will be halted in its tracks. Often, there is little or nothing that the buyer's solicitor can sensibly

---

31 A year might make more sense than six months. The latter period presumably derives from para 5.1.1 of the CML *Lenders Handbook for Scotland* which requires 'that the seller has been the owner of the property for at least six months'. See also n 36 below.
32 LR(S)A 2012 s 87(2).
33 For this and some other examples, see para 12.14 above.
34 It is, however, possible to argue that a deceased person retains a measure of passive legal personality and so can be treated as having remained in possession.
35 LR(S)A 2012 s 86(3)(a)(ii): see para 12.13 above. If the assistance of s 86 turns out to be needed, the buyer does not become owner until the period of missing possession has been completed: see s 86(4)(b), (6).
36 If the period is shorter than six months (taking the period to begin with the seller's date of entry), CML rules require that the buyer's lender must be informed, subject to certain exceptions (such as sales by executors, heritable creditors, or trustees in sequestration): see CML *Lenders Handbook for Scotland* cl 5.1.1. This requirement has nothing to do with s 86 but rather is intended to discourage certain types of mortgage fraud: see K G C Reid and G L Gretton, *Conveyancing 2012* (2013) 88–90.

do here to make matters better:[37] the risk must simply be borne. Fortunately, it is a very slight risk, for the following reasons. First, titles are rarely defective. If the seller was named on the Register as owner, then, almost certainly, he was indeed the owner. Secondly, if the seller only acquired a few months ago, then the chances are that the transaction by which he so acquired was itself one which had the benefit of s 86, thus eliminating any title defects other than defects arising out of the actual deed by which he acquired.[38] That deed could be examined,[39] in a spirit of caution, although it should be borne in mind that it will already have been examined by RoS at the time of registration.[40] Admittedly, s 86 would not apply if the previous transaction was a first registration, but as the years go by first registrations are becoming less common. Finally, even if the worst fears are realised and a title defect does emerge during the few months in which the buyer is making up the year of possession, then the buyer will normally be entitled to payment from the Keeper under the Keeper's warranty.[41] In other words, having been deprived of the 'mud', he will at least have the consolation of the 'money'.

16.5 Titles not covered by s 86

Occasionally it will be apparent that s 86 cannot apply to a transaction – for example, because the title sheet contains a relevant caveat, or a limitation or exclusion of the Keeper's warranty. Either might well be enough to stop the transaction in its tracks, for reasons unconnected with s 86. It should certainly lead to anxious inquiry on the part of the buyer. If, however, the transaction is to carry on, the question arises as to how title should be examined.

It would, of course, be possible just to take the seller's title at face value,[42] although the presence of a caveat or limitation of warranty might argue otherwise. Assuming, however, that the buyer chooses to venture behind the title sheet, the obvious way of proceeding is to examine sufficient of the prior dispositions as to satisfy the requirements of positive prescription which, largely unavailable for 1979 Act titles,[43] was reintroduced by the 2012 Act.[44] In order for a deed to found prescription it must either have been recorded in the Register of Sasines or registered in the Land Register whether under the 1979 or the 2012 Acts.[45] Once

---

37 To go behind the Register and examine the seller's underlying title would, in most cases, be an extravagant and unjustified reaction.
38 In other words, s 86 would have protected the seller against Register error (ie the risk that the disponer was not the owner despite being registered as such) but not against transactional error (ie a defect in the disposition itself). For this terminology, see para 12.4 above.
39 A copy is held in the archive record, and an extract could if necessary be obtained: see LR(S)A 2012 ss 14(1)(a) and 104(1)(c).
40 In this respect, at least, RoS do not rely on 'tell me don't show me' (as to which see para 8.11 above).
41 LR(S)A 2012 s 73: see ch 13.
42 As would often be appropriate in the different circumstances of the creation of a long lease: see para 16.15 below.
43 Positive prescription only applied where indemnity had been excluded. The justification was that such exclusion made the registered title vulnerable to rectification even against a proprietor in possession (LR(S)A 1979 s 9(3)(a)(iv)). In examining title, therefore, an acquirer had to go behind the title sheet and rely on prescriptive possession based on prior writs, in much the way we suggest in this paragraph for cases of exclusion of warranty and other instances where s 86 does not apply. In this sense, therefore, there is continuity with the previous law.
44 LR(S)A 2012 s 119, sch 5 para 18. On prescription, see generally paras 17.1 ff below.
45 Prescription and Limitation (Scotland) Act 1973 s 1(1). 1979 Act registrations are included because of the transitional arrangements set out in LR(S)A 2012 s 120(1): see para 17.11 below.

the foundation writ is identified, examination of title proceeds much as under the Sasine system.[46] Only *ex facie* validity[47] is required of the foundation writ (though it must not be forged),[48] but the subsequent deeds linking the foundation writ to the current seller must be absolutely valid. There must also be ten years of continuous possession, following the foundation writ,[49] although in practice this is taken for granted. Assuming that prescription operates, the effect is for the foundation writ to be conclusively validated, so that the seller's title is assured provided that any intermediate deeds are valid.[50]

If a disposition within the prescriptive period was registered in the Land Register under the 1979 Act, the examination of title can probably stop there and prior deeds be ignored. This is because the title obtained on registration of such a disposition can usually[51] be taken to be good, due to the Midas touch,[52] meaning that the seller's title will also be good provided that any intermediate disposition or dispositions are valid. The examination of title is thus limited to checking the disposition or dispositions that link the last holder of a 1979 Act title to the current seller.

16.6 KIR titles

While considerably easier to deal with than a Sasine title, a title which entered the Land Register by Keeper-induced registration ('KIR') may be less satisfactory than one registered as a result of a conventional application. We say 'may' because at the time of writing KIR had scarcely begun and the extent of the difficulties likely to be encountered by RoS in achieving first registration without the owner's input was unclear.[53] But it is possible that KIR title sheets will omit certain things which ought ideally to be included while including certain other things which would be better omitted.[54] Into the first category may come prescriptive servitudes, the delineation of the route of other servitudes,[55] and even, in some cases, the name of the owner;[56] into the second may come spent real burdens, for staff at RoS are unlikely to carry out the filleting exercise which might be expected of an applicant

---

46 For which see Gretton and Reid (n 1) paras 7-13 ff.
47 This, however, is not expressly required where the writ is registered in the Land Register: for a discussion, see para 17.7 below.
48 PL(S)A 1973 s 1(2), which, however, allows prescription on a forged deed registered in the Land Register provided the forgery was unknown to the prescriber at the time of registration of the deed in his favour.
49 PL(S)A 1973 s 1(1).
50 PL(S)A 1973 ss 1(1) and 5(1A).
51 This assumes that the transitional provisions did not invalidate the title on the designated day, as to which see para 16.7 below.
52 LR(S)A 1979 s 3(1)(a): see para 2.7 above.
53 See, however, Registers of Scotland, *Keeper-induced Registration Consultation Document* (2015).
54 See para 7.20 above. A mock-up of a KIR title sheet is given in annex C of the *Consultation Document*.
55 For the inclusion of servitudes in the A (property) section of a 'normal' title sheet, see para 4.14 above.
56 So if, for example, the most recent disposition was in favour of Mr and Mrs Smith and the survivor, it will not be possible for RoS to know whether one, or both, of them have died, thus potentially triggering the survivorship destination. If the mock-up KIR title sheet is any guide, the B (proprietorship) section will name both Mr and Mrs Smith as proprietors but add a note along the following lines: 'The current proprietor of the subjects in this title is not known with certainty as the Keeper has been unable to establish whether the survivorship destination has operated.'

for first registration.⁵⁷ What this means is that the first transaction after KIR may have to be characterised as lying somewhere between a first registration and a dealing with registered land. Depending on the state of the title sheet, the buyer might wish to look at prior Sasine deeds and, in appropriate cases, ask the Keeper to make adjustments.⁵⁸ A possible difficulty is that any changes to the title sheet would be classified as rectification rather than as registration, and so would have to satisfy the 'manifest inaccuracy' standard required by the former.⁵⁹

Like any other registered title, a KIR title will normally be fully warranted by the Keeper. Furthermore, the buyer will be protected by s 86 of the 2012 Act in the usual way.⁶⁰

16.7 Seller as owner: 1979 Act titles

As with 2012 Act titles, just discussed, the first duty in examining a 1979 Act title⁶¹ is to check that the seller owns the property being sold or is acting on behalf of the person who does. Otherwise ownership cannot be transferred to the buyer.⁶² Where the seller's title was registered before 8 December 2014, his acquisition of ownership would have been governed by the 1979 Act, although the 2012 Act will apply in respect of the current transaction. Subject to what is said below, the person named on the title sheet as proprietor can be taken to be the owner. A legal report will be needed to update the title sheet; provided it shows the advance notice for the current transaction, and nothing untoward or unexpected, the buyer can proceed to settlement on the agreed date of entry.⁶³

For 1979 Act titles too, s 86 protects the buyer in the event that the person registered as proprietor was not, after all, the owner.⁶⁴ But that eventuality will usually be too remote for it to be necessary to consider s 86 further. This is because the seller will have become owner on registration, due to the 'Midas touch' which operated under the 1979 Act,⁶⁵ and having thus become owner, the seller will remain owner today unless the transitional provisions in the 2012 Act had the

---

57 For that filleting exercise, see para 8.25 above. Rather than the burdens being transcribed, as in standard title sheets, it is possible that there will just be a hyperlink to the relevant deeds.
58 F Rooney and S Duncan, 'The Keeper is coming' (2016, available at bit.ly/21z75nT): 'for a KIR title, it may be safest … to examine the sasine title too'. In response to the RoS consultation on KIR, 'there was almost unanimous support for the proposition that the Keeper should provide guidance on post KIR activity, highlighting areas in which parties to the first transaction after KIR may wish to provide additional or more up-to-date information': see Registers of Scotland, *Keeper-Induced Registration: Analysis of the responses to the Public Consultation* (2016) Q12. At the time of writing it was unclear whether RoS would adopt such a course.
59 LR(S)A 2012 s 80(1): see para 11.14 above.
60 As to which see paras 16.2–16.4 above. We do not agree with the suggestion in Rooney and Duncan (n 58) that a buyer who relies without further inquiry on a KIR title sheet might not be regarded as being in good faith for the purposes of s 86. Apart from anything else, Registers of Scotland are on record as having said that 'we do not consider there is any greater risk of the register being inaccurate following a KIR than as a result of any other registration': see *Keeper-Induced Registration Consultation Document* (2015) para 57.
61 By '1979 Act titles' we mean cases where the current owner is registered under that Act, and by '2012 Act titles' we mean cases where the current owner is registered under the latter Act, even though first registration may have taken place under the 1979 Act.
62 LR(S)A 2012 ss 49(4) and 50(2). Unlike the position under the 1979 Act, there is no Midas touch to validate void dispositions: see para 9.20 above.
63 For legal reports, see paras 10.31 and 10.32 above; for advance notices, see ch 10.
64 See paras 16.2–16.4 above.
65 LR(S)A 1979 s 3(1)(a): see para 2.7 above.

effect of taking that ownership away on 8 December 2014.[66] That is unlikely. It will only have occurred if (i) the seller should not have become owner in the first place (ie because the disposition in his favour was invalid), with the result that the Register was inaccurate, *and* (ii) either (a) he was not in possession immediately before 8 December 2014, and so not protected against rectification as a proprietor in possession[67] or (b) despite being in possession, the Register could have been rectified against him either because indemnity was excluded or because he had caused the inaccuracy through his fraud or carelessness.[68] The chances of both (i) and (ii) applying are slight, and the odds are improved further by a statutory presumption that the registered proprietor was in possession immediately before 8 December 2014.[69] As a practical matter, if the seller is in possession now, he can probably be taken to have been in possession immediately before 8 December 2014; and that being the case, and in the absence of contrary evidence, his title can reasonably be accepted as good without further inquiry.

16.8 Corporeal pertinents: rights of common property

As well as describing the land in question, the A (property) section of the title sheet may list certain pertinents.[70] There is no difference here between 1979 Act and 2012 Act titles, and the account that follows applies to both.

Pertinents can be either corporeal (typically, a *pro indiviso* right to a common area in a tenement or housing estate) or incorporeal (typically, a right to servitudes and real burdens).[71] As well as those pertinents listed in the A section, the plot of land may carry the benefit of unlisted pertinents such as servitudes constituted by prescription or, in the case of a tenement flat, rights of common property in the common passage and stair and other parts of the tenement which are made pertinents by statute.[72]

More is said about incorporeal pertinents in the next paragraph. As for corporeal pertinents, the seller's title to an area owned in common is governed by the same principles as his title to the plot itself.[73] But if the common area is unmapped and insufficiently described, no rights in respect of it can be carried by the title.[74] This is a particular problem for housing estates developed before 2009[75] where the common areas were sometimes described too vaguely (eg

---

66 LR(S)A 2012 sch 4 para 17: see paras 11.9–11.12 above.
67 Ie under LR(S)A 1979 s 9(3)(a).
68 LR(S)A 1979 s 9(3)(a)(iii), (iv). If (i) is satisfied but not (ii) (ie the Register is inaccurate in showing the seller as owner but it could not be rectified), the inaccuracy was cured on 8 December 2014 and the seller now has an unchallengeable title: see LR(S)A 2012 sch 4 para 22.
69 LR(S)A 2012 sch 4 para 18.
70 LR(S)A 2012 s 6(1)(b), (f): see para 4.14 above.
71 On pertinents, see generally K G C Reid, *The Law of Property in Scotland* (1996) paras 199–206.
72 Tenements (Scotland) Act 2004 s 3.
73 As to which see paras 16.2 and 16.7 above. That means, eg, that LR(S)A 2012 s 86 applies, for a corporeal pertinent comprises a 'plot of land' within s 3(4), (5).
74 The buyer may have statutory access rights to the common area under s 1 of the Land Reform (Scotland) Act 2003, but these would be no greater than those held by any member of the public.
75 After 2009 descriptions of common areas were made subject to the more exacting standards set out in Registers of Scotland, *Update 27: Creation, Identification and Transfer of Rights in Common Areas in Developments*, as amended by *Update 27: Additional Information: Lundin Homes Ltd v Keeper*.

by reference to a future uncertain event) for a delineation of boundaries to be possible.[76]

Since the 2012 Act came into force, newly-constituted common areas[77] have usually been given a title sheet of their own – a 'shared plot' title sheet – which is then incorporated by reference into the A (property) section of those plots of which the common area is a pertinent.[78]

What has been said requires some qualification in respect of tenemental properties. Here a verbal description of common parts (eg the stair, the roof and the back green) will generally suffice, and for such common parts a shared plot title sheet is not used.

16.9 Incorporeal pertinents: rights to real burdens and servitudes

Real burdens and servitudes appear either in the A (property) section or the D (burdens) section of a title sheet depending on whether the plot is benefited by the title condition or is burdened by it. Before 2004 servitudes were only an intermittent presence in the A section, and real burdens did not appear there at all. Since 2004 it has been mandatory for all real burdens and servitudes, newly and expressly created by deed, to be registered against both the benefited and the burdened properties and hence, in relation to the former, to appear in the A section of the title sheet.[79]

The status of entries in the A section depends on when they were first made. Title conditions might reach the A section by ordinary registration, by being transcribed from a Sasine title on first registration, or, in the case of prescriptive servitudes, by being added to the Register on the Keeper being satisfied as to their validity.[80] However it came about, however, a servitude or real burden which was added to the A section of a title sheet before 8 December 2014 can usually be taken to be valid without inquiry, whereas one added on or after that date, while also usually valid, will only definitively be so if the rules of constitution were fully complied with at the time of creation. The reason for the difference is that in the first case, but not the second,[81] the title condition was provisionally made

---

76 *PMP Plus Ltd v Keeper of the Registers of Scotland* 2009 SLT (Lands Tr) 2; *Lundin Homes Ltd v Keeper of the Registers of Scotland* 2013 SLT (Lands Tr) 73; *Miller Homes Ltd v Keeper of the Registers of Scotland* 2014 SLT (Lands Tr) 79. For commentary, and a discussion as to whether the problem can be solved by positive prescription, see K G C Reid and G L Gretton, *Conveyancing 2008* (2009) 133–49, *Conveyancing 2013* (2014) 105–16, and *Conveyancing 2014* (2015) 134–39. Further discussion can be found in paras 5.10 and 8.17 above.
77 In other words, where there is a new development that has been sold off by the developer after the designated day.
78 LR(S)A 2012 ss 17–19: see paras 4.20–4.22 above.
79 Title Conditions (Scotland) Act 2003 ss 4(1), (5) and 75(1). There is an exception for pipeline servitudes: see s 75(3)(b).
80 For many years prior to the 2012 Act coming into force, the Keeper would only be satisfied as to the validity of servitudes if they were supported by a court declarator. Current practice, however, is to include such servitudes provided an applicant for registration is prepared to vouch for them: see paras 4.28 and 8.23 above.
81 Scottish Law Commission, *Discussion Paper No 130 on Land Registration: Miscellaneous Issues* (2005) ('SLC DP 130') paras 4.18–4.26 was in favour of having an equivalent rule under the 2012 Act but the idea was rejected by SLC Report 222 para 23.33. LR(S)A 2012 s 86 is confined to plots of land and so does not extend to a right to a real burden or servitude.

good by the Midas touch on registration,[82] and would usually have been made unchallengeable, on 8 December 2014, by the transitional provisions in the 2012 Act.[83] From the point of view of examination of title, however, the difference is likely to be of only theoretical interest. Unless the servitude or real burden is of vital importance to the buyer, the buyer's solicitor seems justified in taking the title sheet at face value and inquiring no further. After all, if the title sheet turned out to be wrong, there will usually be a claim for compensation under the Keeper's warranty.[84]

Occasionally a servitude or real burden shown in the A section will have been extinguished by some off-register event such as negative prescription or acquiescence;[85] or a right which is described as a servitude or real burden might, by its nature, not be capable of being so constituted.[86] In neither case is there is a claim under the Keeper's warranty.[87]

16.10 Real burdens, standard securities, and other encumbrances

The previous paragraph discussed real burdens and servitudes from the viewpoint of the benefited property, ie as pertinents in the A (property) section of the title sheet. The present paragraph discusses them from the viewpoint of the burdened property, ie as encumbrances in the D (burdens) section of the title sheet. Also discussed are other encumbrances such as heritable securities, which appear in the C (securities) section of the title sheet.

Few properties are free from encumbrances. But buyers will be anxious that the property is at any rate free from *unknown* encumbrances. In that respect, the Land Register serves acquirers reasonably well. Subject to the exceptions mentioned below, all encumbrances must be set out in the securities or burdens section of the title sheet.[88] An encumbrance which has been omitted or deleted in error will be

---

82 LR(S)A 1979 s 3(1)(a): see SLC DP 130 paras 4.7–4.12 and 4.38. Entering a title condition on first registration, or on coming to the Keeper's attention, was not registration; but there would have been registration, and hence the operation of the Midas touch, on the next occasion that the plot was transferred.
83 LR(S)A 2012 sch 4 paras 17, 18 and 22: see paras 11.9–11.12 above. The vast majority of title conditions would, of course, have been perfectly valid. But where they were not, so that the Register was inaccurate in showing them, the inaccuracy was cured if, immediately before 8 December 2014, the Keeper could not have rectified the inaccuracy. Although the case law was divided, the dominant view was that a servitude-holder was eligible as such to be a 'proprietor in possession': see *Yaxley v Glen* [2007] CSOH 90, 2007 SLT 756 and *Orkney Housing Association Ltd v Atkinson* 2011 GWD 30-652, but compare *Griffiths v Keeper of the Registers of Scotland*, 20 December 2002, Lands Tribunal (unreported, discussed K G C Reid and G L Gretton, *Conveyancing 2003* (2004) 88 ff). The same reasoning would apply to real burdens. Assuming this view to be correct, rectification could not have taken place if, as would be normal, the proprietor of the benefited property was in possession of *that property* (NB not of the servitude or real burden), unless indemnity was excluded or the inaccuracy was caused by the proprietor's fraud or carelessness: see LR(S)A 1979 s 9(1), (3)(a).
84 LR(S)A 2012 s 73(1). For the Keeper's warranty, see ch 13.
85 Prescription and Limitation (Scotland) Act 1973 s 8; Title Conditions (Scotland) Act 2003 ss 16–18.
86 Registration cannot improve its validity. This was true even under the 1979 Act; s 3(1)(a) of the Act was qualified by the words 'insofar as the right or obligation is capable, under any enactment or rule of law, of being vested as a real right, of being made real or, as the case may be, of being affected as a real right'.
87 LR(S)A 2012 s 73(2)(d), (e).
88 LR(S)A 2012 ss 8 and 9: see paras 4.16 and 4.17 above. For the impossibility of showing everything on the Register, see SLC DP 130 paras 5.6 and 5.7.

extinguished on registration of the buyer's disposition provided that the buyer was in good faith.[89]

The exceptions are encumbrances which can be constituted off-register – what were known under the 1979 Act as 'overriding interests'.[90] Three such encumbrances – off-register servitudes (typically constituted by prescription),[91] public rights of way, and path orders made under s 22 of the Land Reform (Scotland) Act 2003 – must be included on the Register if drawn to the Keeper's attention but are valid whether included or not.[92] The others cannot appear on the Register.[93] Whether registrable or not, however, all continue to burden the land and will affect even buyers in good faith. Apart from those already mentioned, the most important off-register rights are short leases (ie leases for 20 years or less) and public access rights of various kinds including access rights under s 1 of the Land Reform (Scotland) Act 2003. No claim lies under the Keeper's warranty in respect of off-register rights.[94]

Three encumbrances merit special mention. First, long leases (ie leases for more than 20 years). Until the 1979 Act came into force, a long lease could be created, as a real right, either with or without registration, and a few such leases have still not been registered. Nonetheless they continue to burden the property.[95] Where registered, a lease usually has a title sheet of its own[96] but is also mentioned in the burdens section of the landlord's title sheet so as to alert potential acquirers.[97] But even if, in error, it fails to appear in the burdens section, the lease will still affect the property.[98] Most ultra-long leases (ie leases for more than 175 years and with an unexpired duration of more than 100 years in the case of dwellinghouses and 175 years in other cases) were converted into ownership on 28 November 2015, and the landlord's interest was extinguished.[99]

Second, floating charges. A floating charge will not appear in the title sheet, even where it has attached to the property by crystallisation,[100] though a charge granted by the seller (if a company, LLP etc) can be discovered from the Companies Register. On registration of the buyer's disposition, however, any floating charge granted by a *predecessor* of the seller – and for that reason difficult to discover – ceases to affect the property provided that the buyer was in good faith.[101] That rule, in combination with a company search against the seller and, where necessary, a certificate of non-crystallisation or of discharge, removes any risk for a buyer.[102]

---

89 LR(S)A 2012 s 91: see para 12.18 above. Indeed, if the property has been transferred since the omission took place, the encumbrance will already have been extinguished by s 91, or by its 1979 Act equivalent, s 3(1)(a).
90 See paras 4.26–4.28 above.
91 Other possibilities, at least in theory, are implied servitudes and servitudes constituted by unregistered deed (which was permissible up until 2004).
92 LR(S)A 2012 s 9(1)(a), (d), (e).
93 SLC Report 222 paras 7.16–7.19.
94 LR(S)A 2012 s 73(1)(b), (2)(a)–(c).
95 See paras 20.3 and 20.4 below.
96 See para 4.5 above. A lease which is only 'deemed' to be registered because the plot of land to which it relates is registered will not have its own title sheet: see para 20.6 below.
97 LR(S)A 2012 ss 3(2) and 9(1)(b).
98 LR(S)A 2012 s 91(4)(d). This is an exception to the principle that, on registration, an acquirer takes free of omitted encumbrances.
99 Long Leases (Scotland) Act 2012 ss 1–7: see para 20.8 below.
100 The 2012 Act changed the law. Floating charges could be noted under LR(S)A 1979 s 6(4).
101 LR(S)A 2012 s 93: see para 12.19 above.
102 Gretton and Reid (n 1) paras 28-06 ff.

Finally, occupancy rights of non-entitled spouses or civil partners.[103] Their presence is not disclosed on the Land Register; nor is their absence now mentioned there, the Keeper having abandoned her previous practice of stating that there are no subsisting occupancy rights.[104] In cases where the seller is both a natural person and also sole owner, a buyer must, as usual, obtain a declaration, renunciation, or consent. On the other hand, a buyer in good faith is not affected by occupancy rights arising in respect of a predecessor of the seller.[105]

16.11 Inhibitions and caveats

If the disposition by which the seller became owner was potentially affected by an inhibition or other entry in the Register of Inhibitions, this should be indicated on the title sheet,[106] and may also be accompanied by a qualification of the Keeper's warranty. The issue will then require investigation. Buyers are protected from inhibitions if, acting reasonably and in good faith, they are unaware of them.[107] A personal search will of course be needed for the current transaction in the usual way.[108]

A caveat on the title sheet warns of current litigation in relation to the title.[109] This too requires investigation. The presence of a caveat prevents the operation of realignment under ss 86 and 91.[110] It is also likely to result in a qualification of the Keeper's warranty to the buyer.[111]

An outstanding inhibition will in the usual case mean that the title is not a good and marketable one, in the sense of a title that the buyer is bound to accept, and the same is true where there is an outstanding caveat.[112]

16.12 Minerals

Minerals are often held separately from the ownership of the surface, in which case they have a title sheet of their own. In the purchase of land it would be rash to assume that the minerals are included.[113] Sometimes the position will be made

---

103 See generally Gretton and Reid (n 1) ch 10.
104 There is no equivalent in the Land Register Rules etc (Scotland) Regulations 2014, SSI 2014/150, ('LRR 2014') of r 5(j) of the Land Registration (Scotland) Rules 2006, SSI 2006/485. Even before this change in practice the Keeper had ceased to check the relevant documentation, relying instead on a 'tell me don't show me' question in the application form for registration of the disposition.
105 Matrimonial Homes (Family Protection) (Scotland) Act 1981 s 6(1A); Civil Partnership Act 2004 s 106(1A).
106 LR(S)A 2012 ss 10(2)(c) and 32: see para 9.19 above. The equivalent provision in LR(S)A 1979 (s 6(1)(c)) was of broadly similar effect although its scope was not entirely clear: see SLC DP 130 paras 8.1–8.10; SLC Report 222 paras 30.3–30.5.
107 Bankruptcy and Diligence etc (Scotland) Act 2007 s 159. While all reasonable steps must be taken to discover the existence of the inhibition (s 159(4)(b)), a buyer would not be expected to obtain a personal search against a predecessor of the seller (the identity of whom is in any case likely to be unknown).
108 As to which see Gretton and Reid (n 1) paras 9-15 ff.
109 LR(S)A 2012 s 67. Caveats appear in the property section of the title sheet: see LRR 2014 r 12(1)(b). For caveats, see ch 18.
110 LR(S)A 2012 ss 86(3)(e)(i) and 91(2)(b). The implications for examination of title are considered at para 18.5 above.
111 LR(S)A 2012 ss 75(2) and 76(4): see para 18.4 below.
112 For good and marketable title, see Gretton and Reid (n 1) ch 6.
113 On minerals generally, see R Rennie, *Minerals and the Law of Scotland* (2001).

clear, positively or negatively, in the property section of the title sheet;[114] just as often it will be unclear. The Keeper's standard-level warranty does not cover mineral rights,[115] although a procedure exists to request that it be extended to minerals on production of appropriate evidence as to title.[116]

16.13 Validity of the disposition

Finally, the buyer's solicitors must, so far as reasonably possible, ensure that the disposition granted to their client is valid in all respects. There is no Midas touch under the 2012 Act, and so only a valid disposition can transfer ownership.[117] If, later, it turns out that the disposition was invalid, a claim lies under the Keeper's warranty, but no compensation will be due if the invalidity ought to have been known to the buyer or the buyer's law agent, or if either fell short in the duty of reasonable care to the Keeper.[118]

LONG LEASES: CREATION

16.14 In general

All grants of long lease[119] fall to be registered in the Land Register, and a real right cannot be obtained in any other way.[120] A new title sheet will be created for the lease.[121] Where the lessor's title is still in the Register of Sasines, registration of the lease will be accompanied by (first) registration of the lessor's plot of land by virtue of automatic plot registration.[122]

As registration does not validate a lease which is otherwise invalid,[123] it is for the lessee or the lessee's legal advisers to take such steps and make such inquiries as seem reasonable to ensure that a valid lease is obtained. In the next paragraph we say something of the lessor's title to grant and how it might best be examined.

In common with other real rights, the title to leases registered in the Land Register is warranted by the Keeper except where, at the time of registration, the warranty is excluded or qualified.[124] Furthermore, while no compensation will be due in respect of defects which ought to have been known to the lessee or the lessee's law agent, or where either fell short in the duty of reasonable care

---

114 LRR 2014 r 12(1)(d): see para 4.14 above.
115 LR(S)A 2012 s 73(2)(f). This goes further than the Scottish Law Commission's recommendation (SLC Report 222 para 22.31) or indeed LR(S)A 1979 s 12(3)(f), which covered by indemnity a statement on the title sheet that minerals were included. See further para 13.3 above.
116 LR(S)A 2012 ss 75(1)(a) and 76: see para 13.13 above.
117 LR(S)A 2012 ss 49(4) and 50(2): see para 9.20 above. Invalidity in the disposition is a 'transactional' (as opposed to a 'Register') error, and so qualifies for a guarantee by 'money' rather than a guarantee by 'mud': see para 12.4 above.
118 LR(S)A 2012 s 78(b),(c): see ch 13 and especially paras 13.6–13.8.
119 Ie, a lease for more than 20 years: see Registration of Leases (Scotland) Act 1857 s 1.
120 LR(S)A 2012 s 48(1)(b): see paras 20.4 and 20.5 below. The rule applies equally to subleases.
121 See para 4.5 above.
122 LR(S)A 2012 ss 24(2): see para 7.10 above.
123 Registration of Leases (Scotland) Act 1857 s 20B(3): see para 20.7 below. The Midas touch does not apply under the 2012 Act: see para 9.20 above.
124 LR(S)A 2012 s 73: for details, see ch 13. Thus, the grant of a lease is guaranteed as to 'money' if not as to 'mud': see para 12.2 above.

owed to the Keeper,[125] lessees who, acting reasonably and in good faith, take a lease from the person named on the Register as proprietor have done enough to benefit from the Keeper's warranty. So far as concerns the warranty, at least, there is no need to look behind the Register.[126]

16.15 Examining the lessor's title

Nothing will be said here about examination of title where the lessor still holds on the basis of deeds recorded in the Register of Sasines.[127] Where the lessor is registered as proprietor in the Land Register, there is a high degree of probability that the Register is accurate, that the lessor really is the proprietor,[128] and hence that the lessor has title to grant the lease.[129] If the lessor's title was registered under the 2012 Act this is due above all to s 86 of that Act (realignment protecting good-faith acquisition);[130] if the title was registered under the 1979 Act it is because of the Midas touch.[131]

Of course, even titles registered in the Land Register may occasionally turn out to be bad. If so, any lease then granted would be bad also, because grantees of long leases are not among those who are protected by realignment.[132] The lessee would, however, have a claim under the Keeper's warranty. Why might the lessor's title be bad? In the case of 2012 Act titles, this could be due to a historical title defect coupled with a failure, at the time of the lessor's acquisition, to comply with the requirements for realignment in s 86; in the case of 1979 Act titles it would be because, under the transitional arrangements which operated on the designated day (8 December 2014), the lessor's right of ownership was extinguished on the ground that, immediately before that day, it was a right which the Keeper would have been empowered to remove by rectification.[133] Neither is likely. Nonetheless, it would be open to the lessee's solicitor to go behind the Register and conduct an examination of the prior dispositions for the period of positive prescription, much as in the examination of a Sasine title.[134] Whether this will actually be done is likely to depend on matters such as the duration and value of the lease and the wishes of the client.

---

125 LR(S)A 2012 s 78(b),(c): see paras 13.16–13.18 above.
126 This is because it is a key policy assumption of the 2012 Act that the curtain principle should be preserved, and that it should not normally be necessary to go behind the Register to examine the underlying deeds.
127 For such examination, see standard works on conveyancing such as Gretton and Reid (n 1) paras 7-13 ff, and Stewart and Sinclair (n 1) pp 317 ff.
128 The same comment applies, *mutatis mutandis*, to cases where a long lease is granted, not by the proprietor, but by the holder of a registered lease, ie where the new lease is a sublease. See para 16.18 below.
129 There is, however, no formal presumption as such. A presumption was recommended by SLC DP 128 para 5.32 but this was not carried forward to SLC Report 222.
130 See paras 12.8–12.17 above. Section 86 does not, however, apply to first registrations.
131 LR(S)A 1979 s 3(1)(a): see para 2.7 above.
132 Unlike assignees of long leases: see LR(S)A 2012 s 88, discussed at para 16.19 below. The Scottish Law Commission considered, but rejected, extending protection to the grantees of long leases; the reasoning is explained in SLC Report 222 para 23.29.
133 See para 16.7 above.
134 For more details, see para 16.5 above. Alternatively, steps could be taken to investigate the operation of s 86 or, as the case may be, the Midas touch at the time when the lessor's title was registered.

In respect of other aspects of examination of the lessor's title, such as pertinents and encumbrances, reference is made to what was said earlier in the chapter.[135] In addition to encumbrances on or forming part of the lease itself, the lessee is also subject to any negative real burdens and servitudes that affect the plot, although these will only appear on the plot title sheet.[136]

LONG LEASES: ASSIGNATION AND SUBLETTING

16.16 Introduction

This section is concerned with the assignation and subletting of long leases which are registered in the Land Register. It is not concerned with long leases which are still in the Register of Sasines.

Examination of title on the part of the potential assignee or subtenant is likely to involve a consideration of (at least) the following matters: (i) the validity of the lease; (ii) the validity of the granter's title as tenant; and (iii) whether the terms of the lease are satisfactory. The last of these is not a matter for land registration and will not be discussed further here. In considering the other two, it is necessary to distinguish between leases registered under the 2012 Act and those registered under the 1979 Act.

16.17 2012 Act leases: validity of the lease

A lease is registered under the 2012 Act if it was registered on or after 8 December 2014.

As registration would not of itself have made the lease valid,[137] it should be checked for content and for execution.[138] It may also be prudent to inquire as to the title of the landlord to make the initial grant. That is straightforward enough if the lease has been registered for more than ten years, for in that case its validity will be vouched for by positive prescription provided that the tenant has been in possession.[139] If, however, the lease has been registered for less than ten years – as will always be the case in the early years of the 2012 Act – a separate check would be needed of the landlord's title, much in the same way as the tenant will have done at the time when the lease was being granted.[140]

16.18 2012 Act leases: validity of the granter's title as tenant

In addition to the validity of the lease, it is also necessary to verify that the person who is to grant the assignation or sublease has good title as tenant. In practice,

---

135 See paras 16.8–16.12 above.
136 This follows from their status as real rights, but it is also the subject of express provision in the case of negative burdens: see Title Conditions (Scotland) Act 2003 s 9(2)(a).
137 Registration of Leases (Scotland) Act 1857 s 20B(3): see para 20.7 below. Note that LR(S)A 2012 s 88 (discussed below), which confers certain protections on assignees, does not protect against the possibility that the lease is invalid: see s 88(3)(d).
138 Inquiry may also have to be made of the landlord to ensure that the lease has not been terminated eg by irritancy. The law is unclear as to whether off-register variation and extinction is effective: see SLC Report 222 paras 9.24–9.30. In accordance with the SLC's recommendations, the new s 20B(2) inserted by LR(S)A 2012 s 52 into the Registration of Leases (Scotland) Act 1857 retains the ambiguity of the previous provision.
139 Prescription and Limitation (Scotland) Act 1973 s 1.
140 As to which see para 16.15 above.

that means that either he is the person named as such in the B (tenancy) section of the lease title sheet or that he otherwise has power to grant, for example as a heritable creditor or liquidator. Section 88 (discussed below) gives protection to assignees just in case the Register is wrong and the person so named is not in fact the tenant. However, s 88 is not needed if the granter is the original tenant,[141] and it is not available for grants of sublease (as opposed to assignations). If further investigation is thought necessary in the case of a sublease, this would involve an examination of the assignation or assignations that link the current granter to the original tenant.[142]

16.19 Section 88

Section 88 of the 2012 Act (on realignment) protects assignees in the event that the title sheet is mistaken in showing the assigner as the tenant under the lease. To qualify for the protection, a number of conditions must be complied with; and, while the likelihood of s 88 being needed is slim, the assignee's solicitors may wish to verify the conditions so far as they are able to do so. The conditions themselves were considered in detail in an earlier chapter,[143] and only a summary is needed here. The conditions are that – [144]

(i) the assignee is in good faith at the time of registration of the assignation;
(ii) the land is possessed by the assigner at the time of delivery of the assignation;
(iii) the assigner, or the assigner followed by the assignee, is in possession of the land openly, peaceably, and without judicial interruption for the year immediately before the assignation is registered;[145]
(iv) at no time during this one-year period (a) did the Keeper become aware that the assigner was not the tenant, or (b) was the title sheet subject to a caveat; and
(v) the Keeper has not restricted her warranty of title.

The good faith of one's client can usually be taken for granted, though it should be borne in mind that the solicitor's knowledge of a title defect will be attributed to the client (condition (i)). A number of the other conditions can be checked from the title sheet (conditions (iv)(b) and (v)). A restriction in warranty would often stop the transaction for reasons which have nothing to do with s 88.[146] If the Keeper is aware that the assigner is not the tenant, she is likely to have made the necessary change to the Register already (condition (iv)(a)). The nature of the possession needed (conditions (ii) and (iii)), and the extent to which it requires investigation, were considered earlier in the chapter.[147] Where the assignation is not by the tenant but by someone whose title derives from the tenant, such as a heritable creditor or trustee in sequestration, possession by the heritable creditor

---

141 If the lease is valid, so must be the right of the original tenant.
142 If these stretch back for more than ten years, positive prescription will remove the need to examine assignations prior to the first assignation outside the ten-year period.
143 See para 12.21 above.
144 LR(S)A 2012 s 88(1)(b), (3).
145 If the one-year period is not completed by the time of registration, it can be completed after registration, but in that event the protection conferred by s 88 does not operate until the full one year has run: see s 83(1)(a), (4)(b).
146 For the Keeper's warranty, see ch 13.
147 This was in the context of s 86: see paras 16.3 and 16.4 above.

or trustee is treated as possession by the tenant, although of course the tenant may simply have retained possession all along.[148]

The position adopted by RoS is that realignment will normally be assumed to have occurred on registration of the assignation unless a judicial determination to the contrary is obtained by a competing party.[149]

16.20 1979 Act leases: validity of the lease

The focus now shifts from 2012 Act leases to 1979 Act leases. A lease was registered under the 1979 Act if it was registered before 8 December 2014. It is no less a 1979 Act lease if the title of the current tenant was registered under the 2012 Act.

A 1979 Act lease can normally be accepted as valid without further inquiry. This is because the lease would have been validly created on registration due to the Midas touch which operated under the 1979 Act;[150] and the lease will remain valid today unless the transitional provisions in the 2012 Act had the effect of making it invalid on the designated day (8 December 2014).[151] That is unlikely. It will only have occurred if (i) the lease should not have been created in the first place (ie because the deed constituting the lease was invalid), with the result that the Register was inaccurate, *and* (ii) either (a) the tenant was not in possession immediately before 8 December 2014, and so not protected against rectification as a proprietor in possession[152] or (b) despite being in possession, the Register could have been rectified against him either because indemnity was excluded or because he had caused the inaccuracy through his fraud or carelessness.[153] The chances of both (i) and (ii) applying are slight, and the odds are further improved by a statutory presumption (which can however be rebutted) that the registered tenant was in possession immediately before 8 December 2014.[154]

16.21 1979 Act leases: validity of the granter's title as tenant

In addition to the validity of the lease, it is also necessary to verify that the person who is to grant the assignation or sublease has good title as tenant. In practice, that means that either he is the person named as such in the B (tenancy) section of the lease title sheet or that he is acting on behalf of the person who is. As the Register is unlikely to be wrong, no further inquiry is needed if either the granter was the original tenant,[155] or if the granter, though a successor, acquired under the 1979 Act.[156] In the case of the granter having acquired under the 2012 Act, the position is as described in a previous paragraph.[157]

---

148 LR(S)A 2012 s 89(2).
149 *Registration Manual* (n 22) Topics: Realignment of rights.
150 LR(S)A 1979 s 3(1)(a): see para 2.7 above.
151 LR(S)A 2012 sch 4 para 17: see paras 11.9–11.12 above.
152 Ie under LR(S)A 1979 s 9(3)(a).
153 LR(S)A 1979 s 9(3)(a)(iii), (iv). If (i) is satisfied but not (ii), the inaccuracy was cured on 8 December 2014 and the validity of the lease is unchallengeable: see LR(S)A 2012 sch 4 para 22.
154 LR(S)A 2012 sch 4 para 18.
155 If the lease is valid, so must be the right of the original tenant.
156 Acquisitions under the 1979 Act have the protection of the Midas touch: see para 16.20 above. In theory, LR(S)A 2012 s 88 (discussed at para 16.19 above) could also be prayed in aid, in respect of assignations, but in practice it will rarely be needed.
157 See paras 16.18 and 16.19 above.

16.22 Assignees and encumbrances

Heritable securities over the lease[158] will be disclosed in the securities section of the lease title sheet, and leasehold conditions in the burdens section. As well as the terms of the lease itself, the latter may include conditions added when the lease was assigned.[159] Subleases for 20 years or less, however, are not registrable and so will not appear in the title sheet; long subleases should appear (although they normally have a title sheet of their own)[160] but are not extinguished if, by accident, they are omitted.[161] Assignees are also subject to any negative real burdens and servitudes affecting the plot, although these will only appear on the plot title sheet.[162]

In the unlikely event of a heritable security or leasehold condition having been omitted from the title sheet, it is extinguished on registration of the assignation provided the assignee was in good faith.[163]

CREATION OF SERVITUDES

16.23 Introduction

This section is concerned with the creation of servitudes where the title to the servient tenement is held on the Land Register. It is thus not concerned with Sasine titles. Nor is it concerned with the transmission of servitudes which already bear to exist; that subject was covered earlier in the chapter.[164]

Servitudes may be created either in a split-off disposition or in a freestanding deed. The validity of the first of these is hardly separable from the validity of the disposition itself, a topic which was considered earlier.[165] This present section, therefore, is confined to freestanding deeds of servitude.

The main concern of examination of title will be to ensure that the granter owns the property over which the servitude is to be granted; and the method to be employed will depend upon whether the property is held on a 2012 Act or a 1979 Act title.

16.24 2012 Act titles

Where the title of the granter of the servitude was registered on or after 8 December 2014, the acquisition of that title will have been governed by the 2012 Act. The very fact of the granter being registered as proprietor is a strong, if not absolutely conclusive, indication that he owns the property. Section 90 of the 2012 Act (on realignment) protects the grantee against the eventuality that the Register in this

---

158 As opposed to over the plot of land. Securities over the plot are no longer listed in lease title sheets: see Registers of Scotland, *General Guidance: Leases and Automatic Plot Registration* (v.02, 2015) 2.
159 Registration of Leases (Scotland) Act 1857 s 3.
160 LR(S)A 2012 ss 3(2) and 9(1)(c).
161 This is because LR(S)A 2012 s 92 does not extend to subleases.
162 This follows from their status as real rights, but it is also the subject of express provision in the case of negative burdens: see Title Conditions (Scotland) Act 2003 s 9(2)(a).
163 LR(S)A 2012 s 92: see para 12.22 above (which also considers the scope in this connection of s 22B(1)(a) of the Registration of Leases (Scotland) Act 1857). Indeed, if the lease has been assigned since the omission took place, the encumbrance will already have been extinguished by s 92, or by its LR(S)A 1979 Act equivalent, s 3(1)(a).
164 See para 16.9 above.
165 See paras 16.2 ff above.

respect is wrong. To qualify for the protection, a number of conditions must be met; and, while the likelihood of s 90 being needed is slim, the grantee's solicitors may – depending on the importance and value of the servitude – wish to verify, so far as possible, that the conditions are complied with.

The conditions themselves were considered in detail in an earlier chapter,[166] and only a summary is needed here. The conditions are that:[167]

(i) the grantee is in good faith at the time of registration of the deed of servitude;
(ii) the land is possessed by the granter at the time of delivery of the deed;
(iii) the granter is in possession of the land openly, peaceably, and without judicial interruption for the year immediately before the deed is registered;[168]
(iv) at no time during this one-year period (a) did the Keeper become aware that the granter was not the owner, or (b) was the title sheet subject to a caveat; and
(v) the Keeper has not restricted her warranty of title.

The good faith of one's client can usually be taken for granted, though it should be borne in mind that the solicitor's knowledge of a title defect will be attributed to the client (condition (i)). A number of the other conditions can be checked from the title sheet (conditions (iv)(b) and (v)). A restriction in warranty would of course stop the transaction for reasons which have nothing to do with s 90.[169] If the Keeper is aware that the granter is not the owner, she is likely to have made the necessary change to the Register already (condition (iv)(a)). The nature of the possession needed (conditions (ii) and (iii)), and the extent to which it requires investigation, were considered earlier in the chapter.[170]

16.25 1979 Act titles

Where the title of the granter of the servitude was registered before 8 December 2014, his acquisition of ownership would have been governed by the 1979 Act, although the 2012 Act will apply in respect of the current transaction. The granter can normally be taken to be owner if he is named on the title sheet as such. This is because the granter will have become owner on registration, due to the 'Midas touch' which operated under the 1979 Act;[171] and having thus become owner, the granter will remain owner today unless the transitional provisions in the 2012 Act had the effect of taking that ownership away on the designated day (8 December 2014).[172] That is unlikely. It will only have occurred if (i) the granter should not have become owner in the first place (ie because the disposition in his favour was invalid), with the result that the Register was inaccurate, *and* (ii) either (a) he was not in possession immediately before 8 December 2014, and so not

---

166 See paras 12.25 and 12.26 above.
167 LR(S)A 2012 s 90(1)(b), (3).
168 In the event that the one-year period is not completed by the time of registration, it can be completed after registration, but the protection conferred by s 90 does not then operate until the full one year has run: see s 90(4)(b), (6).
169 For the Keeper's warranty, see ch 13.
170 This was in the context of s 86: see paras 16.3 and 16.4 above.
171 LR(S)A 1979 s 3(1)(a): see para 2.7 above.
172 LR(S)A 2012 sch 4 para 17: see paras 11.9–11.12 above.

protected against rectification as a proprietor in possession[173] or (b) despite being in possession, the Register could have been rectified against him either because indemnity was excluded or because he had caused the inaccuracy through his fraud or carelessness.[174] The chances of both (i) and (ii) applying are slight, and the odds are further improved by a statutory presumption (which can however be rebutted) that the registered proprietor was in possession immediately before 8 December 2014.[175] As a practical matter, if the granter is in possession now, he can probably be taken to have been in possession immediately before 8 December 2014; and that being the case, and in the absence of contrary evidence, his title can normally be accepted as good without further inquiry.

CREATION OF STANDARD SECURITIES

16.26 Introduction

An initial distinction falls to be made between (i) purchase-money securities, and (ii) standalone securities granted in respect of property that the borrower already owns. In a standalone security, the lender's concern will be with the title of the borrower; in a purchase-money security, the concern will be with the title of the person from whom the borrower is buying and with the validity of the borrower's acquisition. Indeed in residential conveyancing the same solicitor will typically act for both borrower (in his purchase) and lender (in its standard security); but whether the lender is separately represented or not, the task of the lender's solicitor in examining title is hardly different from the task of the solicitor for the borrower/purchaser. Examination of title in the context of purchase was discussed earlier in the chapter and nothing further need be said here.[176] The current section, therefore, considers only standalone securities.

16.27 Examining the borrower's title

The main concern of examination of title is to ensure that the borrower owns the property over which the standard security is to be granted.[177] If that property is still held on a Sasine title, there must first be voluntary first registration before the security can be granted. This is because standard securities can no longer be registered in the Register of Sasines, and hence no longer granted in respect of Sasine property.[178]

The starting-point for examination of title, therefore, is to ensure that the borrower is named as proprietor in the title sheet of the intended security subjects. Assuming that to be so, there is a high degree of probability that the Register is accurate, that the borrower really is the proprietor, and hence that the borrower

---

173 Ie under LR(S)A 1979 s 9(3)(a).
174 LR(S)A 1979 s 9(3)(a)(iii), (iv). If (i) is satisfied but not (ii) (ie the Register is inaccurate in showing the granter as owner but it could not be rectified), the inaccuracy was cured on 8 December 2014 and the granter now has an unchallengeable title: see LR(S)A 2012 sch 4 para 22.
175 LR(S)A 2012 sch 4 para 18.
176 See paras 16.2 ff above.
177 Here, for convenience of terminology, we assume that the standard security is being granted over the borrower's property and not over the property of a third party.
178 LR(S)A 2012 s 48(2): see para 7.12 above.

has title to grant the security.[179] If the borrower's title was registered under the 2012 Act this is due above all to s 86 of that Act (realignment protecting good-faith acquisition);[180] if the title was registered under the 1979 Act it is due to the Midas touch.[181]

Of course, even titles registered in the Land Register may occasionally turn out to be bad. If so, any security then granted would be bad also, because grantees of standard securities are not among those who are protected by realignment. Why might the borrower's title be bad? In the case of 2012 Act titles, this could be due to a failure, at the time of the borrower's acquisition, to comply with the requirements of s 86; in the case of 1979 Act titles it would be because, under the transitional arrangements which operated on the designated day (8 December 2014), the borrower's right of ownership was extinguished on the ground that, immediately before that day, it was a right which the Keeper would have been empowered to remove by rectification.[182] Neither possibility is likely to worry a lender, for lenders who, acting reasonably and in good faith, take a security from the person named on the Register as proprietor have done enough to benefit from the Keeper's warranty.[183] The loan will therefore be repaid even if, due to the failure of the security, it has to be repaid by the Keeper.[184]

For other aspects of examination of the borrower's title, such as pertinents and encumbrances, the reader is referred to what was said earlier in the chapter.[185]

---

179 There is, however, no formal presumption as such. A presumption was recommended by SLC DP 128 para 5.32 but this was not carried forward to SLC Report 222.
180 See paras 12.8–12.17 above. Section 86 does not, however, apply to first registrations.
181 LR(S)A 1979 s 3(1)(a): see para 2.7 above.
182 See para 16.7 above.
183 Ie in the event of the granter not being owner, this would not be a case where the absence of ownership ought to have been known by the grantee: see LR(S)A 2012 s 78(b), and paras 13.17 and 13.18 above. This is because it is a key policy assumption of the 2012 Act that the curtain principle should be preserved, and that it should not normally be necessary to go behind the Register to examine the underlying deeds.
184 See further para 13.20 above.
185 See paras 16.8–16.12 above.

Chapter 17

Positive Prescription and *a non domino* Dispositions

POSITIVE PRESCRIPTION

17.1 Introduction

Positive prescription was largely excluded by the 1979 Act,[1] on a mistaken view as to the infallibility of the Land Register.[2] Quite properly, it was reintroduced by the 2012 Act.[3] But it will not often be needed; for, whereas prescription remains central to the examination of titles still held on the Register of Sasines,[4] a person seeking to acquire Land Register property is usually protected by the doctrine of realignment and can take the Register at its face value.[5] Nonetheless, prescription has a role to play in a number of cases, including (i) where the conditions for realignment are not met (for example, because of exclusion of the Keeper's warranty);[6] (ii) where realignment is not available (for example, in the granting of a lease);[7] (iii) in respect of transactional error (that is to say, a defect in the deed used in the current transaction);[8] (iv) in respect of *a non domino* dispositions;[9] and (v) in respect of voidable (as opposed to void) titles.[10]

17.2 Requirements

As amended by the 2012 Act,[11] s 1(1) of the Prescription and Limitation (Scotland) Act 1973 provides, in relation to Land Register titles, that:

1 It could apply only where the Keeper had excluded indemnity: see LR(S)A 1979 s 10, amending Prescription and Limitation (Scotland) Act 1973 s 1.
2 In fact the Midas touch did not result in infallibility because an entry in the Register which was inaccurate was vulnerable to the possibility of rectification: see paras 2.8 and 2.9 above.
3 Scottish Law Commission, *Discussion Paper No 125 on Land Registration: Void and Voidable Titles* (2004) ('SLC DP 125') paras 3.4–3.8; Scottish Law Commission, *Report No 222 on Land Registration* (2010) ('SLC Report 222') para 35.3. For a contrary view, based on opposition to the very idea of prescription, see A Wightman, *The Poor Had No Lawyers: Who Owns Scotland (And How They Got It)* (2010) 299–300.
4 See eg G L Gretton and K G C Reid, *Conveyancing* (4th edn, 2011) paras 7-17 ff.
5 LR(S)A 2012 ss 86–90: see ch 12.
6 LR(S)A 2012 ss 86(3)(f), 88(3)(g), and 90(3)(e).
7 See paras 16.14 and 16.15 above.
8 For this terminology, see para 12.4 above. The protection given by realignment is limited to Register error, or more precisely to the possibility that the person named on the Register as owner might not be owner.
9 For which see paras 17.12 ff below.
10 Realignment, when it applies, secures a grantee against the possibility that the granter's title is void. It offers no protection against the possibility that the title is voidable: see para 12.17 above. Much the same was true of the Midas touch under the 1979 Act, at least in cases where the transmission of the voidability to the grantee was due to the grantee's bad faith (as opposed to absence of consideration). This is because many cases of bad faith (probably) fell within the fraud and carelessness exception (LR(S)A 1979 s 9(3)(a)(iii)), allowing rectification even against a proprietor in possession.
11 LR(S)A 2012 sch 5 para 18(2).

If land has been possessed by any person, or by any person and his successors, for a continuous period of ten years openly, peaceably and without any judicial interruption and the possession was founded on, and followed ... the registration of a deed which is sufficient in respect of its terms to constitute in favour of that a person a real right in –

   (i) that land; or
   (ii) land of a description habile to include that land,

then, as from the expiry of that period, the real right so far as relating to that land shall be exempt from challenge.

The requirements set by this provision are the familiar ones of possession for ten years on the basis of a sufficient title. But whereas the former requirement (possession) is unchanged by the 2012 Act, the latter requirement (title) has been substantially and unexpectedly re-cast. Nothing further will be said here about possession – the matter is fully covered in standard works on prescription[12] – but the new requirement as to title will need to be considered in some detail.

17.3 The requirement as to title

As the Sasine Register is a repository of deeds and the Land Register, primarily, a repository of titles,[13] so the requirement as to title for the purposes of prescription involves deeds in the case of the Sasine Register and – until the changes made by the 2012 Act – involved registered title in the case of the Land Register. More precisely, while for Sasine titles there must be a recorded deed sufficient in respect of its terms to constitute the right in question,[14] for Land Register properties the requirement under the 1979 Act was of the 'registration of a real right ... in the Land Register of Scotland'.[15] The 1979 Act approach was followed in the Scottish Law Commission's draft Bill,[16] but was abandoned in the 2012 Act itself, which instead applies to Land Register titles much the same rule as already applies to Sasine titles. The focus is thus on deeds and not on registered titles: what the legislation requires is 'the registration of a deed which is sufficient in respect of its terms to constitute in favour of that person a real right in (i) that land; or (ii) land of a description habile to include that land'.[17]

A number of implications flow from this shift from title sheet to underlying deed. First, the curtain principle is disregarded. A person seeking to rely on prescription must now look behind the title sheet to the underlying deeds. Secondly, if there is a discrepancy between the deed and the title sheet, it appears that it is the deed which is to prevail.[18] One possible consequence – and this is the third point – is that there may no longer be notice from the title sheet itself that a person has a title on which prescription might run. In some

---

12 See in particular D Johnston, *Prescription and Limitation* (2nd edn, 2012) ch 18.
13 Under the 2012 Act, however, the Land Register is also a repository of deeds, because the archive record is one of the constituent parts of the Register: see LR(S)A 2012 ss 2(c) and 14, and also para 4.31 above.
14 Prescription and Limitation (Scotland) Act 1973 s 1(1)(a).
15 PL(S)A 1973 s 1(1)(b), inserted by LR(S)A 1979 s 10.
16 Draft Bill s 86(1), inserting s 1A(1)(b) into the PL(S)A 1973 ('the possession is founded on, and follows, registration of the person in the Land Register of Scotland as being the person holding a real right in that land').
17 PL(S)A 1973 s 1(1)(b), inserted by LR(S)A 2012 sch 5 para 18(2). No public justification appears to have been given for the change, and the reasons for it are unclear.
18 See para 17.4 below.

circumstances the prescriber's title will be invisible. In so far as the purpose of the requirement of title is to alert third parties to prescriptive claims, therefore, this purpose is to some extent defeated.[19] Finally, the accommodating rules as to deeds which are merely *capable* of including the land in question – *habile* titles, in other words[20] – now apply to Land Register titles as well as to Sasine titles. The point, however, is largely theoretical, for (with some exceptions)[21] no deed will be – indeed *can* be – accepted for registration unless the boundaries are, or (in the case of first registrations) are capable of being, delineated on the cadastral map.[22] By contrast with Sasine deeds, therefore, there must generally be a fixed boundary beyond which prescription cannot operate. More is said about some of these points below.

17.4 Discrepancy between deed and title sheet

There is a discrepancy between deed and title sheet where the latter fails to give full effect to the former. So far as dispositions are concerned, such a discrepancy will either give the grantee too much land or too little.

Where too much land is included in the title sheet, ie more land than the deed purported to convey, prescription cannot run on the additional area because the basis of prescription is the deed, not the entry on the Register, and the deed does not encompass the area in question. This exposes a degree of tension between prescription on the one hand and realignment on the other. If the grantee possesses for a year and then dispones to a *bona fide* acquirer, the acquirer will become owner by virtue of realignment (which operates on the basis of what the title sheet says);[23] but if the grantee does not dispone, title to the area will be unchanged, even after ten years, because prescription (which operates on the basis of the deed) cannot run.

Where too little land is included in the title sheet, it might be supposed that prescription would run on the disposition to the effect of giving the grantee title to the shortfall. So if a disposition purports to convey area A and area B, and the grantee is registered as owner of area A alone, the grantee may be able to prescribe to area B on the basis that area B, though not on the title sheet, nonetheless falls within the registered deed. This conclusion, however, appears to be unsound for, while the disposition is registered in respect of area A, it seems that it remains unregistered in respect of area B; and an unregistered deed cannot found prescription.

Strong support for this position can be found in the 2012 Act itself.[24] Under the general heading of 'completion of registration', ss 30 and 31 enjoin the Keeper to 'make such changes to the title sheet ... to which the application relates as are necessary to give effect to the deed' or, where no title sheet yet exists (as in first

---

19 See para 17.5 below.
20 As for which see Johnston (n 12) paras 17.40 ff; Colin M Campbell, *Positive Prescription of Landownership in Scots Law: The Requirement for a written deed, with particular reference to the concepts of* ex facie *validity and hability* (PhD thesis, University of Edinburgh, 2015).
21 Notably tenement flats.
22 LR(S)A 2012 ss 23(1)(c), 25(1)(b), and 26(1)(c): see paras 8.8 and 8.9 above.
23 LR(S)A 2012 s 86: see paras 12.8–12.16 above.
24 Apart from the provisions mentioned in the text, attention might also be drawn to s 50(2) ('Registration of a valid disposition transfers ownership'). It is hard to accept that the transfer of area B might occur without the grantee being entered in the Register as the proprietor.

registrations or dealings in part), to 'make up a title sheet for the plot'.[25] If area B is omitted from the title sheet, then registration is presumably not 'completed' in respect of that area. The point is reinforced by s 114(2) which provides that, unless the context otherwise requires, 'any reference, however expressed, in any enactment to "registering" a document in the register, is to be construed as including a reference to giving effect to that document in accordance with either section 30 or section 31'. In so far, therefore, as land conveyed by a disposition is not included in the title sheet, the disposition is not, to that extent, registered.

17.5 Invisible titles

The shift from what the title sheet says to what the underlying deed says creates the risk that the prescriber's title may be invisible to third parties. For while the disposition on which prescription is founded must be registered in the Land Register, there is no requirement in the legislation that the grantee must remain on the Register as owner in order for prescription to carry on running. Thus a person (X) might cease to be shown as owner either due (i) to the granting and registration of a disposition in favour of Y or (ii) due to rectification; yet in either case it would seem that the original disposition in X's favour would continue to provide X with a good title for prescription, provided, of course, that the necessary possession existed.

Case (i) is well established in the context of Sasine titles.[26] Now that the statutory wording is the same, presumably the same will in future be true of Land Register titles as well. So suppose that Billy owns the farm of Blackmains, following a disposition to him from Alice, and is entered on the Land Register as such. He sells one hectare of his land to Carole. By mistake the disposition's plan includes, in the area being conveyed, a strip measuring two metres by 20 metres that the parties did not intend to convey and which Billy, unsurprisingly, continues to possess. On the registration of the disposition, Carole becomes owner of the whole area in the plan, including the strip. Thus she owns the strip but does not possess it, while Billy possesses it and thinks he owns it but does not own it. If this state of affairs continues for ten years, Billy will reacquire ownership of the strip. This is because the original disposition from Alice to Billy provides a basis for prescription in Billy's favour.

What is true of voluntary conveyance (case (i) above) is presumably likewise true of rectification (case (ii) above). Suppose that David registers a disposition in the Land Register and enters into possession, and that, six years later, it turns out that the disposition was void and the owner of the land is Eilidh and not David. At the time of this discovery, David has already possessed for six years on the basis of his disposition. Even if the Register is now rectified to show Eilidh (and not David) as proprietor, David, to the extent that he is able to possess, would be able to complete the four years still needed for prescription, again on the basis of the disposition, and so acquire ownership of the property. Of course, such a case would be rare in practice, for even if Eilidh did not possess for the first six years, it is likely that she would do so thereafter, given the rectification in her favour.

---

25 LR(S)A 2012 ss 30(2)(a) and 31(2)(a): see para 9.18 above.
26 Hume, *Lectures* vol IV, 549–50; *Wallace v University of St Andrews* (1904) 6 F 1093; *Love-Lee v Cameron of Lochiel* 1991 SCLR 61. See also Gretton and Reid (n 4) para 7-24.

The consequences of the above would seem to be unfortunate. In the Register of Sasines, there is no title sheet, but rather a collection of deeds, and accordingly a third party searching will see all the relevant deeds. But in the Land Register, what is searched is the title sheet, and the title sheet does not show the deeds.[27] The result is that prescription may be running in a way that is invisible to third parties, and in favour of a person whose name does not appear on the Register.[28]

17.6 Section 81

The result just described is, however, contrary to what may be the presupposition behind s 81 of the Act. As set out in subsection (1), s 81

> applies where it appears to the Keeper that rectification of an inaccuracy would interrupt a period of possession –
> (a) which is current, and
> (b) which, if uninterrupted, would, under section 1(2) or 2(1) of the Prescription and Limitation (Scotland) Act 1973 (c 52) (sections which provide for positive prescription), affect a real right.

Where s 81 applies, the Keeper is not allowed to rectify unless the existence of the inaccuracy has been judicially determined (or the parties consent).[29] The idea, presumably, is to prevent prescription being interrupted by rectification except where the Keeper is sure of her ground.[30] Instead of rectifying, the Keeper must mark the relevant entry in the title sheet as 'provisional' and add the name and designation of the true holder of the right in question.[31]

Section 80's statement that 'rectification of an inaccuracy' could 'interrupt a period of *possession*'[32] is a drafting slip, for possession is unaffected by the state of the Register.[33] The intended meaning is that rectification interrupts the running of *prescription*. The difficulty, however, is that rectification appears to have no such effect.[34] Admittedly, in the Bill as drafted by the Scottish Law Commission interruption would indeed have occurred, for prescription under that Bill, being founded on a registered right, required the continuing presence of the prescriber on the Register. Indeed the explanation for s 81 may simply be that it was imported

---

27 Of course, a copy of the deeds, including the prescriptive disposition, will be retained in the archive record (which is part of the Register: see LR(S)A 2012 s 2(c)), but there will be nothing in the title sheet to direct third parties to it.
28 In the case of (potential) rectification, LR(S)A 2012 s 81 (discussed at para 17.6 below) may prevent the person from disappearing from the Register.
29 LR(S)A 2012 s 81(2), (3). As to who must consent, 'the Keeper will only require consent from persons who can demonstrate that they would have title and interest to be heard in court on the issue. Persons whose consent may be required will depend on the circumstances of each individual case but may include heritable creditors, benefited proprietors in respect of a servitude, neighbouring proprietors or registered tenants.' See Registers of Scotland, *General Guidance: Inaccuracy and Rectification* (v.02, 2015) 4.
30 The explanatory note to s 54(5) of the Scottish Law Commission's draft Bill states simply: 'Subsection (5) is a limited qualification to the Keeper's duty to rectify. Where rectification would prevent the running of positive prescription, the Keeper should not rectify unless and until the fact of the inaccuracy has been determined by decree.'
31 LR(S)A 2012 s 81(3). This will already have been done in the case of a disposition which was identified as *a non domino*: see s 44, discussed in para 17.18 below.
32 LR(S)A 2012 s 81(1). This is copied from s 54(5) of the Scottish Law Commission's draft Bill.
33 There would, of course, be judicial interruption of possession in the sense of Prescription and Limitation (Scotland) Act 1973 s 4 in the event that an inaccuracy was judicially declared. But that is the very situation in which the restraint on rectification imposed by s 81 does not apply.
34 See para 17.5 above.

from the Scottish Law Commission's Bill without realising that, with the move from registered right to registered deed, its basis had disappeared.[35] As it is, s 81 will at least ensure, in cases where it applies, that the prescriber's title is manifest from the Register. But at a substantive level the provision does not seem to achieve anything useful.

17.7 *Ex facie* validity?

In one respect the provisions on prescription for Land Register titles depart from those for Sasine titles. Subsection (2) of s 1 of the Prescription and Limitation (Scotland) Act 1973 provides, in relation to Sasine titles, that prescription is not to run where the deed founded on is invalid *ex facie*. No equivalent provision is made for Land Register titles.[36] In many cases, the omission will make no difference. To qualify for prescription a deed must already be 'sufficient in respect of its terms' to constitute the real right in question.[37] An additional requirement of *ex facie* validity would not add much to this, although the relationship between the two requirements has been little explored.[38] In particular, a deed which states, plump and plain, that it is granted by a person who has no power to do so is likely to be insufficient in respect of its terms as well as *ex facie* invalid. Some aspects of *ex facie* invalidity, however, may not be tied to the 'terms' of a deed. That is likely to be true in respect of mode of execution, so that a deed which, for example, was granted by A but signed by B (being a person with no connection with A) would seem to qualify for the purposes of prescription on the Land Register (because it is sufficient in respect of its terms) but not for the purposes of prescription on the Register of Sasines (because it is invalid *ex facie*).[39]

17.8 Good faith?

By contrast with realignment,[40] there is no requirement that a person seeking to acquire by prescription must do so in good faith.[41] This, however, is subject to s 1(2)(b) of the Prescription Act which excludes prescription where 'possession was

---

35 Section 81 is taken from s 54(5) of the SLC draft Bill.
36 Johnston (n 12) para 17.19 takes the omission to be deliberate, on the generous (but we think improbable) basis that 'if there is *ex facie* invalidity, this should presumably be noticed by the Keeper and lead to the rejection of the deed' – a point which might equally well be made in respect of deeds presented to the Register of Sasines. In fact, oversight seems a more probable explanation. For as long as the title for prescription in the Land Register was determined by registered right rather than registered deed, the requirement of *ex facie* validity had no place. It was absent from the Scottish Law Commission's draft Bill just as it had been absent previously from the 1979 Act. It is tempting to suppose that the framers of the 2012 Act, having made the switch from registered right to registered deed, but otherwise relying on the SLC draft, failed to pick up the point.
37 PL(S)A 1973 s 1(1)(b).
38 But see W M Gordon and S Wortley, *Scottish Land Law* vol I (3rd edn, 2009) paras 12-29–12-39; Johnston (n 12) paras 17.31 and 17.40–17.54; Campbell (n 20) 109 ff. The absence of attention is no doubt because, with both included in PL(S)A 1973 s 1 so far as it applies to Sasine titles, there has hitherto been no real need to distinguish between them. At any rate, they plainly overlap, and it is possible to see the requirement of *ex facie* validity as qualifying the more general requirement of sufficiency in respect of terms: see K G C Reid and G L Gretton, *Conveyancing 2014* (2015) 138–39.
39 Of course, deeds which are *ex facie* invalid will not usually survive the scrutiny of RoS and so will not make it on to the Register at all. In principle, only valid deeds can be registered in the Land Register: see para 8.7(4) above.
40 LR(S)A 2012 ss 86(3)(c), 88(3)(c), and 90(3)(c).
41 Johnston (n 12) para 18.04.

founded on registration in the Land Register of Scotland proceeding on a forged deed and the person appearing from the Register to have the real right in question was aware of the forgery at the time of registration in his favour'. This provision might usefully have been updated to refer to possession being founded on a deed, as the legislation otherwise requires,[42] rather than 'on registration'.[43] More significantly, it departs from the equivalent provision for Sasine titles, which disallows prescription on forged deeds regardless of the parties' state of knowledge.[44]

It may be taken that the deed referred to in s 1(2)(b) is the deed on which possession is founded, although, if the person currently registered as proprietor is a successor of the grantee of that deed, it may also include the deed by which the successor acquired. If that reading is correct, it means, in a straightforward case at least, that prescriptive acquisition is excluded where (i) the deed on which possession is founded is forged, and (ii) the person seeking to acquire[45] was aware of the forgery at the time when that person was registered as proprietor.[46]

17.9 Changing registers

If prescription begins to run on a disposition registered in the Register of Sasines, it seems that it will continue to run in the event that the title migrates to the Land Register before the ten-year period of possession is completed.[47] The Scottish Law Commission had recommended that the matter be put beyond doubt by express provision,[48] of which it provided a draft,[49] but the provision was not included in the 2012 Act. Nonetheless, it seems improbable that prescription is interrupted by a change of registers.

Certainly there seems to be no difficulty where, due to voluntary or Keeper-induced registration, it is the original grantee who comes to be registered as proprietor in the Land Register. Where, however, the migration was caused by a fresh disposition, triggering first registration, the issue becomes whether the disponee can be treated as a 'successor' of the grantee and hence, under s 1(1) of the Prescription Act, eligible to continue the grantee's possession in order to complete the necessary ten years. The answer appears to be 'yes'.[50]

A practical difficulty is that, before applying for registration of a disposition which is obviously *a non domino*, the disponee will have to notify the person who owns the land (or, if none can be identified, the Crown).[51]

---

42 PL(S)A 1973 s 1(1)(b): see para 17.3 above.
43 That this was not done may be because it was not reworded in the SLC's draft Bill (for the good reason that prescription under that Bill continued to be on the basis of a registered right).
44 PL(S)A 1973 s 1(2)(a).
45 The expression in s 1(2)(b) is 'the person appearing from the Register to have the real right in question'. Almost always, this will be the person seeking to acquire by prescription, although that would not be so where the prescriber had lost registered title to someone else whether by registration or rectification (see para 17.5 above). In the case of an *a non domino* disposition, the person seeking to acquire may not be the only person who is named as proprietor (see para 17.18 below); yet it would seem strange if bad faith on the part of the other person could block prescription.
46 If the person seeking to acquire is a successor, this refers to awareness of the forgery of the foundation writ and, possibly, of the disposition in favour of the successor.
47 That is the Keeper's view: see Registers of Scotland, General Guidance: *Prescriptive Claimants* (v.05, 2016) 8.
48 SLC DP 125 paras 3.10 and 3.11; SLC Report 222 para 35.4.
49 SLC draft Bill s 86(1), inserting s 1B(4) into the PL(S)A 1973.
50 For a discussion of the meaning and scope of 'successor', see Johnston (n 12) paras 18.05–18.07.
51 LR(S)A 2012 s 43(1)–(4): see para 17.15 below.

On the migration of a title to the Land Register, therefore, the prescriptive clock will not return to zero. The basis of prescription remains the original Sasine deed.[52]

17.10 Effect of prescription

Positive prescription has the effect of making 'exempt from challenge' the prescriber's title as it was at the *start* of the ten-year period of possession.[53] Title defects older than ten years can be thus disregarded;[54] and with each successive day, the ten-year period continues to advance (assuming continuing possession), thus beginning to eliminate any later defects. Under s 1 of the Prescription Act as first enacted, doubts were expressed as to whether a title being 'exempt from challenge' was the same as an actual acquisition of title; the thought was that, if the foundation writ was void, the prescriber might receive a title which could not be challenged but which nevertheless failed to confer ownership (or other real right).[55] These doubts are stilled by an amendment made by the 2012 Act.[56] Section 5(1A) of the Prescription Act now provides that any reference to a real right's being exempt from challenge is to be construed 'as including reference to the acquisition of the real right by the possessor'.[57]

The reason that the provision just quoted uses the word 'includes' is that positive prescription cures not only void titles but also voidable ones. Take two cases. (i) A void disposition by P to Q is registered. Being void, it does not confer ownership on Q. But if positive prescription runs, then after ten years Q acquires ownership, and P loses it. (ii) A voidable disposition by R to S is registered. Being voidable rather than void, the result is that S becomes owner on the day of registration. If positive prescription runs, then after ten years R's right of challenge is extinguished.[58] But that extinction does not alter the state of ownership, for S was already owner. In cases of this sort, positive prescription is in fact operating as a form of negative prescription, by extinguishing a right rather than by conferring a right, but that is an oddity of the law that cannot be discussed here.

---

52 And therefore the relevant provision is PL(S)A 1973 s 1(1)(a).
53 PL(S)A 1973 s 1(1) renders exempt from challenge 'the real right', which refers back to the 'deed which is sufficient in respect of its terms to constitute in favour of that person a real right'.
54 Of course, in order for prescription to run in the first place, the deed on which the possession is founded, though older than ten years, must satisfy certain requirements: see para 17.7 above.
55 See in particular D Johnston, *Prescription and Limitation* (1st edn, 1999) paras 14.13 and 14.14.
56 LR(S)A 2012 sch 5 para 18(5). For background, see SLC Report 222 paras 35.5–35.9; Johnston (n 12) paras 16.06–16.08.
57 The wording of s 5(1A), however, is not ideal. The references to 'immediately before that expiration' and to the 'acquisition of the real right by *the possessor*' suggest an acquisition which overcomes the infirmities of the past ten years rather than one which has to live with such infirmities. Read literally, it would mean that if Angus possesses on the basis of a void disposition and then, after six years, dispones to Betty by a disposition which is independently void (ie not just on account of Angus's absence of title), then after a further four years of possession, Betty will become owner. That would be contrary to the normal understanding of the operation of positive prescription.
58 The example assumes that after ten years S is still owner. If S had, within the ten-year period, disponed to a good faith disponee, the latter would, on general principles of property law, have acquired a title unchallengeable by R: see K G C Reid, *The Law of Property in Scotland* (1996) para 692. Thus the loss of a right to challenge a title on the basis of voidability may disappear faster than positive prescription can operate.

If Q becomes owner by prescription, then, necessarily, P must cease to be owner of the property.[59] Unlike with realignment, however, no compensation is paid for the loss of ownership.[60] Nonetheless, it seems that positive prescription is compliant with the European Convention on Human Rights.[61]

17.11 Transitional arrangements for Land Register titles

The amended version of s 1 of the Prescription Act, with its new rules for Land Register titles,[62] came into force on the designated day (8 December 2014). But title and possession which preceded that day qualify for the purposes of the amended provision provided that some part of the possession, however small, occurred on or after the designated day.[63] So if possession is lost before the designated day, the operation of prescription is governed solely by the previous version of s 1; but if possession runs forward to the designated day, the new version of s 1 applies.

Take the following case.[64] Sarah was registered as proprietor in the Land Register on 30 June 2004 on the basis of a voidable disposition. Indemnity was not excluded. Sarah took and maintained possession. Prescription could not run because, under the version of s 1 then in force, only titles in which indemnity was excluded could found prescription.[65] At the end of ten years (ie on 30 June 2014), therefore, Sarah's position was exactly as it had been at the outset. But on 8 December 2014 (assuming continuing possession), Sarah's title was fortified by prescription under the new version of s 1 and ceased to be voidable.[66] This is because (i) she had possessed for ten years; (ii) that possession continued beyond the start of the designated day; and (iii) the possession was founded on a registered, if voidable, disposition which, under the new (but not the old) version of s 1, is a sufficient title for prescription.[67] It will be observed from this example that possession which, at the time it occurred, did not qualify for prescription[68] is found, after the designated day, to have qualified after all.

In the example, Sarah's disposition was voidable. Titles that are based on deeds which are void are subject to further transitional provisions in the Act which may

---

59 This is because the law of property in Scotland is unititular, meaning that in respect of any one thing at any one time, only one title of ownership is capable of recognition: Reid (n 58) para 603.
60 For compensation in respect of realignment, see LR(S)A 2012 s 94, discussed at paras 14.2 and 14.3 above.
61 And in particular Art 1 of the First Protocol: see *J A Pye (Oxford) Ltd v United Kingdom* (2006) 43 EHRR 3 and (2008) 46 EHRR 45. For discussion, see further G L Gretton, 'Private law and human rights' (2008) 12 EdinLR 109; SLC Report 222 paras 35.32–35.41; Johnston (n 12) paras 16.17–16.19.
62 As to which see para 17.3 above.
63 LR(S)A 2012 s 120(1).
64 See also SLC Report 222 paras 35.28 and 35.29.
65 PL(S)A 1973 s 1(1)(b), inserted by LR(S)A 1979 s 10.
66 PL(S)A 1973 s 1(1), inserted by LR(S)A 2012 sch 5 para 18(2).
67 On a strict view the 2004 disposition was not 'registered' because, under the 1979 Act, registration was of interests in land rather than of deeds themselves. That in turn would prevent it from qualifying as a title under the new version of s 1(1) of the 1973 Act. But this view is incompatible with LR(S)A 2012 s 120(1) which, by implication, applies the new version of s 1(1) to periods of possession which began before the designated day, and hence also – since possession must *follow* the registration of a deed – to deeds 'registered' in the Land Register before that day. To maintain this view, therefore, would be render s 120(1) meaningless. (It could not be rescued by applying it to deeds registered before the designated day in the Register of Sasines because such deeds are governed by para (a) of s 1(1), which was not amended by the 2012 Act and which is not therefore covered by s 120(1).)
68 Due to the absence of a suitable title (ie an entry on the Register subject to exclusion of indemnity).

cure the title on the designated day, thus rendering prescription unnecessary.[69] So suppose that the disposition registered on 30 June 2004 in Sarah's favour was void and not voidable. On registration Sarah would still have become owner, due to the 1979 Act's Midas touch, but the Register would have been (bijurally) inaccurate, leaving Sarah vulnerable to future rectification.[70] Assume that no rectification occurred. Under the transitional provisions, Sarah's status on the designated day would depend on whether, immediately before that day, the Keeper *could* have rectified the inaccuracy. If no rectification would have been possible, Sarah's title was cured on the designated day and the Register ceased to be inaccurate. If, conversely, rectification could have occurred (for example, because indemnity was excluded or the inaccuracy was caused by Sarah's fraud or carelessness),[71] Sarah was stripped of ownership at the start of the designated day but, it appears,[72] would have immediately reacquired it by positive prescription as a result of some part of her possession occurring on or after the designated day.[73] In a case like this there is thus no difference between a disposition which was void and one which was voidable.

A NON DOMINO DISPOSITIONS

17.12 For and against

It is not necessary to view prescription as a form of theft – as some do[74] – to accept that restrictions are needed in respect of the use of *a non domino* dispositions;[75]

---

69 LR(S)A 2012 sch 4 paras 17 and 22: see paras 11.9–11.12 above.
70 See paras 2.7–2.9 above.
71 LR(S)A 1979 s 9(3)(a)(iii).
72 A possible counter-argument would be the following. (i) If, just before the designated day, Sarah had disponed the property to a third party but retained possession, the prescriptive clock would have needed to begin again: see eg *Love-Lee v Cameron of Lochiel* 1991 SCLR 61. (ii) This is because ten years of further possession is needed to cure a new title defect (ie the new disposition): see para 17.10 above. (iii) The statutory stripping away of Sarah's title on the designated day is a new title defect, akin to a voluntary disposition to a third party. (iv) Hence the prescriptive clock restarts, and Sarah needs a further ten years of possession if she is to reacquire ownership. This argument is certainly stateable, but we doubt whether it is correct. In reality there is no new title defect but merely a title defect which existed all along, namely the voidness of the disposition in Sarah's favour. All that happened on the designated day was a re-characterisation of the legal effect of the title defect (ie from being one which made Sarah's ownership challengeable by rectification to one which denied Sarah ownership at all). If the argument were correct, it would mean that a person with a title on which prescription was running before the designated day (ie a title from which indemnity was excluded) would lose the benefit of all possession which occurred before the designated day. That result is contrary to the policy behind LR(S)A 2012 s 120(1), and should not be accepted unless required by an express provision.
73 See SLC Report 222 para 35.27.
74 See eg Wightman (n 3) 251–52.
75 '*A non domino*' means 'by a non-owner', and an *a non domino* disposition is one which is granted by someone who does not own the property in question and does not act with the authority of the person who does. As such, the disposition cannot confer ownership on registration and will confer ownership later only if it is fortified by positive prescription. The term is well established but strictly speaking less than perfect. (i) In some types of case a non-owner can indeed give a good title, an example being a disposition by a standard security holder who has obtained a warrant for sale under s 24 of the Conveyancing and Feudal Reform (Scotland) Act 1970. No one would in practice describe such a deed as *a non domino*. (ii) More importantly in the present context, this chapter and the statutory provisions that it considers deal with the case of dispositions which both the applicant and the Keeper know to be granted by someone without power to grant it. There can be cases where the fact that a disposition is *a non domino* is simply not realised by those involved, because the problem is latent. Such cases are not in practice usually called *a non domino* cases and are not considered in this chapter.

for otherwise a device which is useful for adjusting boundaries, replacing missing deeds, and for getting unclaimed land into circulation can be used, unscrupulously, as a means of wresting property from unwary or inattentive owners. It was just such unscrupulous conduct which led the Keeper, in the mid-1990s, to introduce a policy of rejecting 'speculative' dispositions, or in other words 'deeds for which no obvious reasons exist and which conflict with existing title'.[76]

This policy is continued, and considerably extended, by the 2012 Act. As first drafted by the Scottish Law Commission, the relevant provisions largely sought to follow the criteria already operated by the Keeper (albeit without any solid statutory basis).[77] Before the Bill's introduction to Parliament, the Government added a requirement of notice to the owner (or the Crown), amounting to a substantial toughening of the criteria. Even this, however, was not enough for the Economy, Energy and Tourism Committee which, in its Stage 1 Report on the Bill, criticised the way in which *a non domino* dispositions encouraged a first-come first-served approach and suggested that applications in respect of such dispositions should trigger a process of advertising in order to attract rival claims, which could then be adjudicated on the basis of which of the proposed uses would confer the greatest benefit on the community.[78] This suggestion was rejected by the Government as being unsuitable for cases where the disposition was intended to replace missing deeds, and more generally as being unworkable in practice.[79] It did not find its way into the Bill as enacted.

17.13 Two requirements

In their final form, the provisions impose two[80] requirements for the registration of *a non domino* dispositions.[81] First, the land must have been possessed openly,

---

76 A M Falconer and R Rennie, 'The Sasine Register and dispositions *a non domino*' (1997) 42 JLSS 72. See also I Davis and A Rennie (eds), *Registration of Title Practice Book* (2nd edn, 2000) para 6.4. Rejection was based, rather precariously, on LR(S)A 1979 s 4(2)(c), which required an application to be rejected where it was frivolous or vexatious. For discussion, see Scottish Law Commission, *Discussion Paper No 128 on Land Registration: Registration, Rectification and Indemnity* (2005) ('SLC DP 128') para 4.56.
77 While generally supportive of the Keeper's approach, the Scottish Law Commission thought that the criteria served to 'narrow the class of "legitimate" cases too much: the door is almost shut': see SLC Report 222 para 16.9. One purpose of the SLC's provisions, in s 21 of its draft Bill, was to prise the door a little further open.
78 Stage 1 Report paras 112–132, reproduced in Scottish Parliament, *Passage of the Land Registration etc (Scotland) Bill 2011* (2013, SPPB 174) (available at www.scottish.parliament. uk/parliamentarybusiness/Bills/44469.aspx) 252–54. The idea originated with land reformers such as Andy Wightman: see Wightman's written evidence to Parliament (*Passage of the Land Registration etc (Scotland) Bill 2011*, 373–74). The only lawyer on the Committee, Murdo Fraser, was one of two dissenters.
79 *Passage of the Land Registration etc (Scotland) Bill 2011* (n 78) 567–68.
80 The Scottish Law Commission recommended that there should also be another requirement, namely that for a continuous period of seven years immediately preceding the application the land was not possessed by the proprietor. In effect, the land had to have been abandoned by its owner. See SLC Report 222 para 16.21, and s 21(1)(b)(i) of the SLC's draft Bill. Although included in the Bill at introduction to Parliament, this requirement was later dropped after evidence as to the difficulty, particularly for those new to the property, of proving a negative over so long a period. See Stage 1 Report paras 114–118, reproduced in *Passage of the Land Registration etc (Scotland) Bill 2011* (n 78) 251–52.
81 *A non domino* deeds other than dispositions can no longer be registered. They were never common. Only dispositions are eligible for the special procedure in s 43 which gives an exemption, through s 43(1), from the standard requirement that a deed presented for registration must be valid (as to which see para 8.7(4) above).

peaceably and without judicial interruption, for the year immediately preceding the date of application, by the disponer or the applicant for registration (or by the disponer followed by the applicant); and secondly, the prospective application must have been notified to the person who is proprietor of the land (or if there is no proprietor, to the Crown).[82] These requirements are taken seriously by the Keeper: while the statutory language is exactly the same as in respect of ordinary applications for registration – so that the applicant must 'satisfy' the Keeper that the requirements have been met – the Keeper, discarding the 'tell me, don't show me' approach,[83] polices the requirements with unyielding vigilance.[84] The details are given below. The reasons why can only be a matter of speculation but must probably include a desire to discourage the registration of *a non domino* dispositions by ranging a series of obstacles in their way. Full compliance with the requirements is needed even where the person entitled to the property has disclaimed any interest in it, and evidence to this effect can be produced.[85]

17.14 The first requirement: possession for the preceding year

The first requirement is intended to discourage speculative applications from those with no prior connection with the property.[86] The evidential standard set by RoS is high.[87] Affidavit evidence as to possession, sworn before a notary public,[88] is needed from the applicant or the disponer and, 'in many cases', from neighbouring proprietors as well. In 'certain cases' this will include *all* bounding neighbours. The wording of affidavits must be clear as to the nature and extent of possession, as well as to the area possessed. A plan should usually be attached, and should comply with the RoS deed plan criteria.[89] According to RoS, the key information that an affidavit should contain is as follows:[90]

- a sworn statement by the relevant party that the land has been possessed openly, peaceably and without judicial interruption;
- the duration of the applicant's and/or disponer's possession. Where possession extends back further than the required one-year period, and an accurate duration cannot be given, an approximate start date may be acceptable provided the required one-year period is covered;
- details of the type of land it is, eg garden ground, parking place, grazing land, overgrown space, etc;
- a detailed statement as to the specific nature of the possession, ie not a bald statement. For instance, that the land has been used as garden ground for a house, and that a shed has been constructed on it;

---

82 LR(S)A 2012 s 43(1), (3), (4).
83 For which see para 8.11 above.
84 See *General Guidance: Prescriptive Claimants* (n 47); Registers of Scotland, *Registration Manual* (https://rosdev.atlassian.net/wiki/display/2ARM/Home) Topics: Prescriptive claimants.
85 For example, a notice of disclaimer issued by the Queen's and Lord Treasurer's Remembrancer: see *Registration Manual* (n 84) Topics: Prescriptive claimants – evidential requirements, prescriptive claimants.
86 SLC Report 222 para 16.17.
87 *General Guidance: Prescriptive Claimants* (n 47), where full details can be found.
88 Land Registration Rules etc (Scotland) Regulations 2014, SSI 2014/150, ('LRR 2014') r 9.
89 As to which see para 5.21 above. The reason given for the requirement is that 'the plan may be used for other documentation also, for example, annexed to the disposition *a non domino*': see *General Guidance: Prescriptive Claimants* (n 47) 2.
90 *General Guidance: Prescriptive Claimants* (n 47) 2.

- a plan that clearly identifies the extent of the land possessed, unless relating to the whole of a registered title;
- confirmation of who has access to the land, who uses the land, and who maintains the land;
- confirmation of the apparent age and nature of the boundary features surrounding the ground, eg stone walls, wire fencing etc, and details of any maintenance provisions in place for these boundaries.

But even this may not be enough. The RoS guidance states that additional evidence may be required 'depending on the circumstances of the case. For instance, in order to better demonstrate the nature and extent of possession the Keeper may require photographic evidence showing the age and nature of boundaries or the use of the land in question. Evidence from local authority records or utility providers may also be useful in certain circumstances.'[91]

17.15 The second requirement: notification to the proprietor

Traditionally, the fact of ten years' adverse possession was thought to be sufficient notice to whoever owned the land. Under the 1979 Act, the Keeper was actually forbidden from telling the owner about *a non domino* applications.[92] The Scottish Law Commission, too, was against notification although it did not go so far as to forbid it.[93] The 2012 Act, however, takes a radically different approach.[94] The owner ('proprietor') is to be notified by the applicant and then notified again by the Keeper. If there is no owner, or none that can be identified, the notification must be sent to 'any person who appears to be able to take steps to complete title as proprietor'. Finally, failing both of the first two classes, there must be notification to the Crown, by which is meant the Queen's and Lord Treasurer's Remembrancer ('QLTR') or, in the case of the foreshore, seabed and other *regalia minora*, the Crown Estate Commissioners.[95] In such cases the property is assumed either to be *bona vacantia* (ie to have been formerly owned but now without a traceable owner)[96] or – as especially with the *regalia minora* – not to have left Crown ownership in the first place. In relation to the former, the QLTR asks that the notification be accompanied, or preferably preceded, by provision of the relevant titles, searches, and an explanation of why it is considered that the property may be *bona vacantia*.[97]

The first of the notifications, by the applicant, must be made in the prescribed form[98] and sent by recorded delivery[99] not later than 60 days before submitting

---

91 *General Guidance: Prescriptive Claimants* (n 47) 2.
92 Land Registration (Scotland) Rules 2006, SSI 2006/485, r 18(2). There was an exception for the foreshore, where notice had to be given to the Crown Estate Commissioners: see LR(S)A 1979 s 14.
93 SLC Report 222 paras 16.22–16.25. Section 21(8)–(12) of the SLC's draft Bill required the Keeper to notify the owner (whether or not the Crown) of any application made in respect of the foreshore or seabed.
94 LR(S)A 2012 ss 43(4) and 45.
95 LR(S)A 2012 s 43(4). The gloss as to the meaning of the 'Crown' comes from *General Guidance: Prescriptive Claimants* (n 47) 3.
96 Such property falls to the Crown on the principle *quod nullius est fit domini regis*. See eg Bankton I.8.9 and II.1.8; Erskine II.1.11. In cases where a person dies without heirs or disposing of property by will, the Crown is considered to succeed as last heir (*ultimus haeres*).
97 QLTR, *Policies* (www.qltr.gov.uk) 7.
98 LRR 2014 r 18(2), sch 2.
99 '… by a postal service which provides for the delivery of the notification to be recorded …'.

the application for registration.[100] The explanatory note which must accompany notification warns that the applicant 'is seeking to register a disposition in their favour in the Land Register of Scotland which, on certain criteria relating to possession being met, will result in them becoming the owner of the land in question', and advises that 'if you consider that you do own or are capable of becoming owner of the land in question and you wish to challenge the prescriptive claim or to negotiate a sale you are advised to contact your solicitor or other adviser'.

As with the one year's possession, the Keeper is vigilant in monitoring whether the notification requirement has been properly met. Evidence that notification has taken place is straightforward enough in itself, but the Keeper also requires to be satisfied that notification was sent to the right person, and that the person is still alive or, in the case of a company or other juristic person, has not been dissolved.[101] So if the applicant has notified the person whom he believes to be owner, it will be necessary to demonstrate that person's ownership to the Keeper. In the case of a Sasine title, 'such evidence may include copies of the relevant search sheets and perhaps copy deeds. Where the applicant has instructed searches from a private searching company then details of those instructions, and records of the results, should be submitted to the Keeper'.[102] Proof that the person is still alive might involve 'the result of searches of the electoral roll or searches of other local authority registers, evidence of contact with local solicitors (eg the last solicitor to act), and even local newspaper advertisements'.[103]

If, rather than notify the owner, the applicant has notified either of the two postponed classes of person (a person able to complete title or the Crown), the applicant must be able to justify why and how he failed to find persons in the earlier class or classes. So if for example the applicant has notified the Crown, the evidence required in respect of the two earlier classes will 'include details of failed searches, evidence showing that a proprietor was traced but they have died, and evidence of attempts to trace individuals able to complete title, such as letters to last known addresses, contact with local solicitors or advertisements in local newspapers'.[104] Faced with these kinds of demands, few applicants may be willing to stay the course. And, as we will see in the next paragraph, there is usually little incentive to do so.

17.16 Submitting the application

Following notification, a period of 60 days must elapse before the application can be submitted. In principle, the application proceeds in the normal way.[105] But the applicant must indicate on the application form the *a non domino* status of the disposition,[106] and must include with the application, and list on the

---

100 LRR 2014 r 18(1).
101 *General Guidance: Prescriptive Claimants* (n 47) 3–4.
102 *General Guidance: Prescriptive Claimants* (n 47) 4.
103 *General Guidance: Prescriptive Claimants* (n 47) 4.
104 *General Guidance: Prescriptive Claimants* (n 47) 4.
105 For applications for registration, see ch 8.
106 There are two relevant questions under the heading 'Certification in relation to links in title': see para 8.16 above. The applicant must answer 'no' to the first ('Is the granter of the deed the last recorded/registered proprietor?') and 'yes' to the second ('If no, and the deed is a disposition, is the disposition to be treated as valid by virtue of section 43(1) (prescriptive claimants)?').

inventory page, the evidence as to possession and notification already described. RoS ask that the additional information page of the form should include: (i) information as to who has been notified; (ii) a statement that copies of all correspondence generated by the notification are enclosed; and (iii) a statement as to which items in the inventory concern notification and which the one-year period of possession.[107] Due to the potential complexity of applications, the one-shot rule is not strictly applied and the Keeper may request further information by way of requisition,[108] although this is likely to be limited to a single requisition and will only be allowed where the application substantially complies with the evidential requirements.[109]

If the disponer's title is partly good as well as partly bad, it is necessary to use two separate dispositions and to make two separate applications. Any attempt to combine the good with the bad will result in the rejection of the application on the ground of the disposition's (partial) invalidity.[110]

17.17 Re-notification by the Keeper

On receipt of the application, the Keeper must notify again the person previously notified by the applicant.[111] There is no prescribed form,[112] and the Keeper can employ whatever means of communication she considers appropriate.[113] In practice notification is done by letter except for notifications to the QLTR where email is used.[114] As the letter (or email) explains, the person notified has 60 days to object, in writing, to the application.[115] No grounds need be stated: the right to object is absolute. If an objection is received, the Keeper must reject the application.[116]

It would be surprising if owners did not object, if only to provide leverage for striking a bargain with the applicant. Indeed an indication of a likely future objection may often be enough to cause the application to be abandoned. In the absence of any other owner, the decision to object will rest with the QLTR or, as the case may be, the Crown Estate Commissioners. The QLTR's policy is to object to applications except where persuaded that the disposition cures some previous

---

107 *General Guidance: Prescriptive Claimants* (n 47) 9.
108 LR(S)A 2012 s 34: see paras 9.10 and 9.11 above.
109 *Registration Manual* (n 84) Topics: Prescriptive claimants – one shot rule and supplementary evidence, prescriptive claimants.
110 C Kerr and J King, 'Lessons learned and new initiatives' (2016) 142 Greens Property Law Bulletin 4. The approach adopted here by RoS can be questioned: see para 9.7 above.
111 LR(S)A 2012 s 45(1) (which is modelled on s 21(8)–(12) of the Scottish Law Commission's draft Bill, provisions which, however, only applied to the foreshore and seabed and were not preceded by the applicant's own notification). This has been said to be 'essentially an anti-fraud measure': see *General Guidance: Prescriptive Claimants* (n 47) 5. Although s 45(1) repeats the same three-part list found in s 43(4), the Keeper will in practice notify the same person as the applicant, since after all 'the application can only proceed where the Keeper is satisfied that appropriate notification by the applicant has been made': see Registers of Scotland, *General Guidance: Notification* (v.01, 2014) 4.
112 LR(S)A 2012 s 45(6) states that land register rules may make further provision about the Keeper's notification, but the subject is not touched on in the current Rules of 2014.
113 *General Guidance: Notification* (n 111) 4.
114 For this and other aspects of notification by the Keeper, see *Registration Manual* (n 84) Topics: Prescriptive claimants – notification by the Keeper, prescriptive claimants.
115 Although no form is provided for re-notification by the Keeper, the explanatory note which must accompany the original notification promises that 'The Keeper's notification will contain guidance on how to respond'.
116 LR(S)A 2012 s 45(1)–(5).

conveyancing error affecting the parties.[117] And having thus objected to an application in respect of property of which, in all likelihood, there was no previous knowledge, the QLTR will then sell it, whether to the applicant[118] or, if there is competition, on the open market.[119] Few applications, therefore, will survive the notification procedures imposed by the Act, and successful registrations in respect of *a non domino* dispositions are likely to be correspondingly rare.[120]

17.18 Acceptance and entry on the Register

If no objection is made, and things are otherwise in order, the application will be accepted by the Keeper. It is true that the disposition, being granted *a non domino*, is invalid, but in the case of 'prescriptive claimants' (as a person registered under these provisions is called)[121] the usual requirement of validity is waived.[122] Of course, entry of the claimant's name on the Register as owner does not confer ownership: now that the Midas touch has gone, an invalid disposition cannot confer ownership.[123] The Keeper will therefore mark the entry as 'provisional',[124] and also include the name of the actual owner, if known.[125] Nor can a subsequent disponee acquire ownership under s 86 (realignment) for, standing the marking as 'provisional', such a disponee could not be in good faith.[126] Finally, and as one would expect, the Keeper's warranty is automatically disapplied.[127]

All that registration really achieves, therefore, is the necessary title in order to acquire the property by positive prescription. For that to occur, possession for the usual ten years is needed.[128] As possession must *follow* registration, the mandatory one year of possession prior to making the application does not count for this purpose. Assuming that the ten years of possession are completed, and that the Keeper is satisfied that this is so (for which she will require the same kind of evidence as for the previous one-year period of possession),[129] the provisional marking will be removed from the Register and the normal warranty restored.[130]

---

117 QLTR, *Policies* (n 97) 8. If the QLTR decides not to insist on its rights, an administration fee is payable.
118 At a price fixed by the District Valuer.
119 QLTR, *Policies* (n 97) 4–5. It is made clear that 'The QLTR does not undertake to deal with a property in any particular way, and does not undertake to dispose of a property to any particular person at any particular time or for any particular price, or at all' (4).
120 Of course, dispositions will continue to be registered which are latently *a non domino*, ie where, unknown to the Keeper (and possibly to the applicant), the disponer's title to all or part of the property is bad. Indeed, the incidence of such deeds is likely to increase due to the extension of 'tell me don't show me' to questions of title (as to which see para 8.11 above).
121 LR(S)A 2012 Act s 43(6)(a). By para (b) of s 43(6), the term also includes a person who did not go through the special procedure for *a non domino* dispositions but, on being later discovered by the Keeper to have no title, – and rectification being stayed so as not to interrupt the running of prescription – has his title marked as provisional under s 81(3)(a)(i). For s 81, see para 17.6 above.
122 LR(S)A 2012 s 43(1).
123 LR(S)A 2012 ss 44(3) and 49(4). It follows that the Register is inaccurate, but s 81 prevents the Keeper from rectifying in this situation except where the existence of the inaccuracy has been judicially determined: see para 17.6 above.
124 LR(S)A 2012 s 44(1).
125 *General Guidance: Prescriptive Claimants* (n 47) 7.
126 See para 12.15 above.
127 LR(S)A 2012 s 73(5).
128 Prescription and Limitation (Scotland) Act 1973 s 1: see para 17.2 above.
129 *General Guidance on Prescriptive Claimants* (n 47) 7.
130 LR(S)A 2012 ss 44(2) and 75(4).

The name of the (now former) owner will be removed by rectification. Even before the Register changes, however, the claimant will have become owner due to the operation of positive prescription.[131]

17.19 Completion of possession by a successor

The rules of prescription allow successors to complete a period of possession left unfinished by the grantee of the deed on which possession is founded.[132] So if the grantee (Anna) possesses for six years on the basis of an *a non domino* disposition, a person to whom Anna now dispones (Bill) can become owner by possessing for a further four. An important practical question is whether Bill, in applying for registration of the disposition granted by Anna, must give notice to the owner of the property (or the Crown) under the provisions described above;[133] for the giving of notice might trigger an immediate and hostile response which would prevent the completion of the prescriptive period.[134]

No notice is needed if notice was given at the time of the original application for registration by Anna; on that the legislation is clear. To notify the owner for a second time would be a pointless formality. Accordingly, a disposition – or other deed such as a standard security – by a prescriptive claimant, though invalid for lack of title, will be accepted for registration without further inquiry or procedure.[135] As before, the title of the grantee (Bill) is marked as 'provisional'.[136] As we will see, this special dispensation for prescriptive claimants is also capable of wider use.

The position is different where no previous notice was given, that is to say, where Anna's disposition was registered before the designated day (8 December 2014), whether in the Land Register or the Register of Sasines. In principle, notification will be required under the 2012 Act because (i) Anna's disposition to Bill is granted by a non-owner, and (ii) *a non domino* dispositions are subject to the procedure already described.[137] Nonetheless, the policy operated by RoS is directed at avoiding notification in cases such as this. Among other reasons this is intended to recognise the fact that any title insurance policy in operation is likely to include a condition prohibiting notification.[138]

Avoidance is easily achieved where the title is already on the Land Register (ie where Anna's disposition was registered, before the designated day, in the Land Register). Section 81 requires the Keeper to mark the title as 'provisional' in cases where prescription is continuing to run;[139] and this having been done, Anna

---

131 The effect of positive prescription is to make the possessor's title 'exempt from challenge' which is defined (by s 5(1A), which was added by LR(S)A 2012 sch 5 para 18(4)) as 'including reference to the acquisition of the real right': see para 17.10 above.
132 See paras 17.9 and 17.11 above.
133 Ie LR(S)A 2012 s 43(4).
134 No notice, of course, would have to be given if Anna chose to sit out the ten years of possession herself.
135 LR(S)A 2012 s 43(5). Unlike s 43(1), this exception to the need for a valid deed is unconditional.
136 LR(S)A 2012 s 44(1).
137 LR(S)A 2012 s 43(1)–(4).
138 Registers of Scotland, *FAQs: Prescriptive Claimants* (2014) Q 16: 'The Keeper is mindful, in particular, of the implications of the notification requirements at section 43(4) on obligations contained in existing title insurance provisions'. See also A E A Stewart and E F F Sinclair, *Conveyancing Practice in Scotland* (7th edn, 2016) 327.
139 LR(S)A 2012 s 81(3)(a)(i). What the Keeper cannot do, under s 81, is rectify the Register, unless the inaccuracy is judicially determined (or all those affected consent).

becomes a 'prescriptive claimant'[140] and so able to grant Bill a disposition which can be registered without notification, as explained above.

Avoidance, however, seems hardly possible where the title remains on the Register of Sasines (ie where Anna's disposition was recorded there before the designated day). RoS suggest (i) that Anna should move the title to the Land Register by means of a voluntary registration, whereupon (ii) Anna will be a 'prescriptive claimant' (the Keeper having marked her ownership as 'provisional') and so able to grant Bill a disposition which can be registered without notification, as already described.[141] There is no difficulty with (ii).[142] But the Act restricts applications for voluntary registration to those who are owners, and Anna, *ex hypothesi*, does not own the land.[143] It appears, therefore, that the stratagem devised by RoS cannot be made to work. We are unable to think of any other.

17.20 Competing applications

Nothing in the legislation prevents the Keeper from accepting competing applications in respect of *a non domino* dispositions. On the contrary, if the requirements of a year's possession and notice to the owner have been met, and the applications are otherwise in order, the Keeper is bound to accept them both.[144] Which of the claimants eventually becomes owner will then depend on which (if any) manages to achieve ten years of continuous and exclusive possession.

---

140 LR(S)A 2012 s 43(6)(b).
141 *General Guidance: Prescriptive Claimants* (n 47) 8.
142 LR(S)A 2012 s 43(5), (6)(b).
143 LR(S)A 2012 s 27(1), (2). The RoS *General Guidance* refers to Anna as 'the current a non domino owner' (8), which is self-contradictory. For voluntary registration, see paras 7.16–7.18 above.
144 LR(S)A 2012 s 21(2) read with s 43(1).

Chapter 18

Caveats

18.1 Scope

A caveat is an entry on a title sheet warning of an action in court that might affect the title to the property. Caveats were introduced by the 2012 Act.[1] They are not available in respect of property still held in the Register of Sasines, where matters continue to be regulated by notices of litigiosity.[2]

Caveats may be used for one or other of three kinds of civil proceedings, namely: (i) proceedings for the reduction of a registered deed on the ground that it is voidable; (ii) proceedings that could result in a judicial determination that a title sheet is inaccurate;[3] and (iii) proceedings under the Law Reform (Miscellaneous Provisions) (Scotland) Act 1985 which could result in an order for rectification of the Register.[4]

A few words may be helpful on the distinction between cases (i) and (ii). Suppose that there is a registered disposition that is alleged to be voidable, and an action of reduction is raised. That falls under case (i). A voidable deed is valid unless and until reduced, which may never happen. For instance, there is a voidable disposition by Clement to Isolde, and it is registered. The title sheet, in showing Isolde as owner, is accurate, and remains accurate unless a decree of reduction is obtained and registered in the Land Register.[5] But if the disposition had been void, the title sheet would have been inaccurate from the beginning: an action to reduce a void deed thus falls within case (ii).

In practice caveats will normally be sought by pursuers, but there is no reason why they should not be sought by another party, provided that there are appropriate pleadings in the cause. For instance, a defender might seek a caveat to support a counterclaim concerning title to the pursuer's property that is declaratory or reductive or both. It is competent (but unusual) for separate parties, whether in the same or different actions, to seek to place a caveat on the same title sheet.

Caveats are available for proceedings before any 'court', a word which, in context, can be taken to include the Lands Tribunal.[6] That is just as well because,

1 LR(S)A 2012 pt 6 (ss 67–72). For background, see Scottish Law Commission, *Report No 222 on Land Registration* (2010) ('SLC Report 222') part 32. The development of the idea of the caveat was influenced by the German *Widerspruch*.
2 Titles to Land Consolidation (Scotland) Act 1868 (31 & 32 Vict c 101) s 159(1) (with registered land now being excluded by s 159(2)); Law Reform (Miscellaneous Provisions) (Scotland) Act 1985 s 8(7) (with registered land now being excluded by s 8(8A)).
3 This replaces the previous rule by which the Keeper noted on the title sheet the existence of proceedings which might result in an order for rectification: see Land Registration (Scotland) Rules 2006, SSI 2006/475, r 17(2).
4 LR(S)A 2012 s 67(1). It may be observed that, quite properly, none of these is defined as an action directed against the Keeper.
5 Conveyancing (Scotland) Act 1924 s 46A: see para 6.12 above.
6 Registers of Scotland, *General Guidance: Caveats* (v.01, 2014) 1. Compare LR(S)A 2012 s 83 which, in a different context, refers to 'any civil proceedings, whether before a court or tribunal'. Express provision has been made for fees in respect of Tribunal applications regarding caveats: see

323

in addition to its normal appellate function in respect of decisions by the Keeper, the Tribunal has specific jurisdiction to determine questions as to the accuracy of the Register.[7] There is an argument that arbitrations are also included, on the basis that arbitrators comprise a 'tribunal' and, furthermore, that they are empowered in certain circumstances to order the rectification or reduction of deeds.[8]

18.2 Obtaining a warrant

The procedure is initiated by an application for a warrant for a caveat, made to the court that is hearing the case. If granted, the warrant is lodged by the applicant with the Keeper, who then enters the caveat into the title sheet in question.

In the sheriff court and Court of Session the application is by way of motion. It must contain a description of the registered plot of land, the title number, and the name and address of the proprietor. Where the caveat is to apply to part only of a plot of land, the motion is to be accompanied by a plan indicating the part so affected.[9]

The grounds for granting a warrant can be compared, in broad terms, with the grounds for an interim interdict or the grounds for diligence on the dependence. Indeed, the wording of the provisions is based to a substantial extent on the wording of the legislation concerning diligence on the dependence.[10] The applicant must satisfy the court that:[11]

(a) the applicant has a prima facie case on the merits of the proceedings,
(b) were warrant for placing the caveat not granted, there is a real and substantial risk that enforcement of any decree or order in the proceedings granted in favour of the applicant would be defeated or prejudiced by reason of the other party being likely to deal with the plot of land, and
(c) in all the circumstances, including the effect which granting the warrant may have on any person having an interest, it is reasonable to make the order granting it.

The form of warrant is set out in the relevant rules of court.[12] It is addressed to the Keeper, and grants warrant to place a caveat on the title sheet of a specified plot of land, which is identified by description, by title number, and by the name and address of its proprietor.

18.3 From warrant to caveat

What the court grants is a warrant for a caveat. The caveat itself does not come into existence until the appropriate entry is made on the title sheet, the reason

---

Lands Tribunal for Scotland Amendment (Fees) Rules 2015, SSI 2015/199. The Lands Tribunal was mentioned by name in a comparable rule under previous legislation: see Land Registration (Scotland) Rules 2006 r 17(2). The SLC draft Bill s 78(1) also expressly mentioned the Lands Tribunal.

7 LR(S)A 2012 ss 82 and 103.
8 Arbitration (Scotland) Act 2010 s 2(1), (3), sch 1 r 49(c).
9 Ordinary Cause Rules 1993 r 51.2; Rules of the Court of Session 1994 r 105.2. The former are set out in the Sheriff Courts (Scotland) Act 1907 sch 1, the latter in the Act of Sederunt (Rules of the Court of Session 1994) 1994, SI 1994/1443. The rules in respect of caveats were added by the Act of Sederunt (Rules of the Court of Session and Sheriff Court Rules Amendment No 2) (Miscellaneous) 2014, SSI 2014/291.
10 Bankruptcy and Diligence etc (Scotland) Act 2007 s 169.
11 LR(S)A 2012 s 67(3), (4). As s 67(5) makes clear, the onus is on the applicant to satisfy the court.
12 Ordinary Cause Rules 1993 r 51.3, form 51.3-A; Rules of the Court of Session r 105.3, form 105.3-A.

being that public notice is central to the nature of a caveat. Having obtained a warrant, the applicant must thus apply to the Keeper on the prescribed form to place the caveat on the title sheet.[13] The fee is £60.[14] There is no time limit within which an application must be made, but it is in the interests of the applicant to act as quickly as possible.

The legislation does not say in which part of the title sheet a caveat should appear;[15] the practice is to use the A (property) section.[16] The entry is in the following terms:[17]

> The plot of land/subjects of the lease in this title is affected by a caveat in terms of section 67(2) of the Land Registration etc (Scotland) Act 2012 granted by [*name of court*] in relation to [action raised under s 67(1)] in favour of [*name and designation of person in whose favour order granted*] for a period of 12 months from [].

Applications can be rejected although this would be unusual. RoS guidance gives the 'only' grounds of rejection as the following:[18]

(i) if the description of the property is at variance with the title number(s) quoted;
(ii) all of the title numbers affected are not included;
(iii) there is no completed title sheet available ie a caveat can only be placed against a registered title and is not appropriate for subjects in the Register of Sasines or still in the Land Register application record pending registration;
(iv) the original caveat has expired and an order for renewal, recall or restriction is submitted after the reference to the caveat has been removed from the title sheet;
(v) details of the warrant as prescribed in the Act of Sederunt are omitted from the court order.

18.4 Effect

A caveat gives notice of the proceedings to those who may, or ought to, consult the Register. One result may be to visit them with knowledge of the underlying cause of action. So for example if Alan's title sheet discloses that the disposition in his favour is subject to an action of reduction on the ground of voidability, a person (Barbara) seeking to buy from Alan would need to make inquiries and form her own view as to the action's merits. If she decides to proceed with the purchase nonetheless, but the action is later successful, she will be treated as being in bad faith in the sense of having known that Alan's disposition was (or might be) voidable, with the result that her own disposition will be voidable in turn.[19]

Two specific effects are provided for in the legislation. In the first place, the existence of a caveat must be taken into account by the Keeper in deciding on warranty.[20] Thus, while a caveat has no effect on warranty already granted by the Keeper, it is likely to affect warranty in a subsequent registration made at

---

13 Land Register Rules etc (Scotland) Regulations 2014, SSI 2014/150, ('LRR 2014') r 15(a), sch 1 pt 5.
14 Registers of Scotland (Fees) Order 2014, SSI 2014/188, sch 1 para 3(3)(a)(i).
15 LR(S)A 2012 s 10(2)(d).
16 *General Guidance: Caveats* (n 6) 2.
17 *General Guidance: Caveats* (n 6) 3. There is a second, modified, form for use in the case where the caveat applies only to part of the property.
18 *General Guidance: Caveats* (n 6) 4.
19 K G C Reid, *The Law of Property in Scotland* (1996) para 692.
20 LR(S)A 2012 ss 75(2) and s 76(4): see para 13.12 above.

a time when the caveat is still in place. Suppose Sally is the registered owner of Blackmains, with full warranty. Tina raises an action against her, and the Blackmains title sheet is caveated.[21] Three months later Sally grants a standard security to Ulysses. The caveat has no effect on the Keeper/Sally warranty, but it will have an effect on the Keeper/Ulysses warranty. Any restriction on warranty which is tied to a caveat will lapse when the caveat itself lapses or is discharged.

The second effect is that a caveat will normally remove the protection otherwise given to acquirers by the principle of realignment.[22] The question of whether this goes further than is necessary is discussed elsewhere.[23]

Finally, it should be stressed that a caveat does not freeze the title sheet. It does not forbid the Keeper to accept applications for registration.[24] Nor does it work as an interdict against the other party in the action, forbidding that party to enter into transactions. What a caveat does is to add a 'subject to ... ' proviso to any such transactions. In practice third parties will thus think twice before dealing with a caveated title sheet.

18.5 Restriction and extinction

A caveat lapses after 12 months, the time running from the date of entry into the Register.[25] This happens automatically, even where the caveat remains on the title sheet. Suppose that Jemima raises an action against Keith, the registered proprietor of Bluemains. She obtains warrant from the court and a caveat is entered into the Register on 29 November 2016. Although caveats can be renewed, as we will see,[26] this is not done. On 3 December 2017, while the Jemima/Keith litigation is still ongoing, Keith grants a standard security over Bluemains to Lucia. As the caveat has lapsed, Lucia's security has the same effect as if there had never been a caveat in the first place.

It is desirable that lapsed caveats should be removed from the title sheet immediately on the expiry of the 12-month period.[27] But, unfortunately, no mechanism for doing so is currently in place, and lapsed caveats are likely to linger on in title sheets, with the unintended consequence of alerting third parties to litigation which may still be ongoing, and potentially putting them in bad faith in respect of the matters being litigated. If the litigation is still ongoing at the end of the 12 months, it is likely that the holder of the caveat will wish the caveat to continue. But in that case the policy of the legislation is clear: there should be an application to renew the caveat.[28]

There are other ways in which a caveat might come to an end. The person who obtained the caveat can discharge it in whole or (probably) in part.[29] Alternatively,

---

21 A word more convenient than elegant.
22 LR(S)A 2012 ss 86(3)(e)(i), 88(3)(f), 90(3)(d), 91(2)(b), and 92(2)(b).
23 See para 12.16 above.
24 There is a comparison here with advance notices, which also do not freeze a title sheet: see para 10.20 above.
25 LR(S)A 2012 s 68(1). Section 68(3) enables the Scottish Ministers to substitute a different period.
26 See para 18.6 below.
27 SLC Report 222 para 32.20: 'A caveat would have a blighting effect on a title and so it is important that caveats do not persist after they have become inappropriate ... Accordingly we take the view that caveats should self-destruct after a fixed period, such as one year'.
28 For renewal, see para 18.6 below.
29 LR(S)A 2012 s 72. Partial discharge is not expressly mentioned in the provision.

those at whom a caveat is directed can seek its recall, on application to the court, on the basis that the grounds for it do not exist, or exist no longer.[30] Both must be followed up with an application to the Keeper, and payment of a fee of £60, if the caveat is to be removed from the Register.[31] Finally, a caveat falls if the action fails, just as diligence on the dependence or interim interdict falls if the action fails. In such a case the Keeper would be bound to delete the caveat, on seeing decree in favour of the defender.[32]

On application by a person with an interest, the court can also 'restrict' a caveat, by which is meant the lifting of the caveat in respect of part of the caveated title.[33] The court order forms the basis of an application to the Keeper to give effect to the restriction on the Register.[34]

18.6 Renewal

Caveats may be renewed,[35] and this may be done more than once,[36] which is important given how protracted litigation often is. The criteria for a warrant for renewal are the same as those for the original grant,[37] and the warrant, once granted by the court, forms the basis of an application to the Keeper to have the renewal placed on the Register.[38] A renewal does not extend the original caveat: rather, it is really a separate and independent caveat, which will itself expire at the end of 12 months.[39] There are, therefore, no rules as to when a renewal can or cannot be sought. There might thus be a gap in time between the original caveat and the renewal; or if, as is obviously desirable, an uncaveated period is to be avoided, the renewal might overlap by a few days or weeks with the original caveat.

18.7 Giving effect to the final decree

It may be that the action to which the caveat relates is unsuccessful. In that case the story ends, and the Keeper should simply delete the caveat.[40] If, however, the

---

30 LR(S)A 2012 s 71. This is done by motion: see Ordinary Cause Rules 1993 rr 51.2(3)(c) and 51.3(3), and form 51.3-C; Rules of the Court of Session rr 105.2(3)(c) and 105.3(3), and form 105.3-C.
31 LRR 2014 r 15(b), (e), sch 1 pt 5; Registers of Scotland (Fees) Order 2014 sch 1 para 3(3)(a)(iv), (b).
32 What is said here seems not to have a specific basis in either the primary or secondary legislation.
33 LR(S)A 2012 s 70. Something seems to have gone wrong with the wording of this provision, as the court is directed to restrict the caveat only where it is 'satisfied' as to the merits of the original grounds for the caveat; compare s 71(2) (recall), where the court is to be 'no longer satisfied'. The provision will not be much used, and where it is used the court will no doubt be able to make it work. Application to the court is by motion: see Ordinary Cause Rules 1993 rr 51.2(3)(b) and 51.3(2), and form 51.3-B; Rules of the Court of Session rr 105.2(3)(b) and 105.3(2), and form 105.3-B.
34 LRR 2014 r 15(c), sch 1 pt 5. The fee is £60: see Registers of Scotland (Fees) Order 2014 sch 1 para 3(3)(a)(iii).
35 LR(S)A 2012 s 69.
36 LR(S)A 2012 s 69(5).
37 LR(S)A 2012 s 69(2), (3). Application is by motion: see Ordinary Cause Rules 1993 rr 51.2(3)(a) and 51.3(1), and form 51.3-A; Rules of the Court of Session rr 105.2(3)(a) and 105.3(1), and form 105.3-A.
38 LRR 2014 r 15(b), sch 1 pt 5. The fee is £60: see Registers of Scotland (Fees) Order 2014 sch 1 para 3(3)(a)(ii).
39 LR(S)A 2012 s 68(2).
40 See para 18.5 above.

action succeeds, the successful party will need to take the appropriate steps to give effect to the decree in the Land Register. As previously mentioned, caveats are available in respect of three different kinds of civil proceedings.[41] In respect of the first (actions for the reduction of a registered deed on the ground that it is voidable) and the third (actions under the Law Reform (Miscellaneous Provisions) (Scotland) Act 1985), the decree is given effect to by registration.[42] As for the second (actions which could result in a judicial determination that a title sheet is inaccurate), the procedure to give effect to the decree is rectification rather than registration.[43]

---

41 See para 18.1 above.
42 See paras 6.12 and 6.13 above.
43 See paras 11.13 ff above.

Chapter 19

Electronic Conveyancing

PRELIMINARY MATTERS

19.1 Two elements

In automated registration of title to land – 'ARTL', in the acronym universally used – Scotland has an electronic system with the potential to transform the manner in which conveyancing and registration are conducted. Thus far, however, the potential is yet to be properly realised.

ARTL may be said to comprise two distinct elements. One is the use of deeds in electronic form, authenticated by electronic signature, in place of the paper or 'traditional' deeds[1] which have been a feature of the Scottish system of land registration since its inception in the early sixteenth century. The other is the provision of a closed electronic system – the 'ARTL system' – within which the relevant deed is prepared and authenticated, an application form for registration is completed, and registration is effected.[2] Both elements are considered below. But first it is necessary to mention some preliminary matters.

19.2 Origins and development

ARTL was first introduced, for standard securities and their discharge, in August 2007, and extended to dispositions and certain other deeds in February 2008. This marked the culmination of almost a decade of research, consultation, and preparation.[3] The long lead-in time, necessary as it was, may be partly responsible for technology which many have dismissed as old and slow.[4] In oral evidence to the Scottish Parliament in 2012, the Keeper was candid in her assessment:[5]

---

1 This term comes from s 1A of the Requirements of Writing (Scotland) Act 1995.
2 The creation of electronic documents, the electronic generation and communication of applications for registration in the register, and automated registration are the three functions identified in LR(S)A 2012 s 99(1).
3 The history is summarised in R Rennie and S Brymer, *Conveyancing in the Electronic Age* (2008) ch 5. An important initial step was the research project undertaken by Ian Burdon and published as *Automated Registration of Title to Land: A Report for the Government Study Fellowship* (1998, available at www.ros.gov.uk/__data/assets/pdf_file/0019/3790/ianburdon_artl.pdf). See also S Brymer, G Gretton, R Paisley and R Rennie, 'Automated Registration of Title' 2005 JR 201.
4 See for example the oral and written evidence given to the Economy, Energy and Tourism Committee of the Scottish Parliament in 2012 as part of the Stage 1 consideration of the Land Registration Bill, and summarised in paras 85–104 of the Committee's *Stage 1 Report* (conveniently reproduced in Scottish Parliament, *Passage of the Land Registration etc (Scotland) Bill 2011* (2013, SPPB 174, available at www.scottish.parliament.uk/parliamentarybusiness/Bills/44469.aspx) 245–50). Even the Council of Mortgage Lenders, which was involved in the development of ARTL and whose members are its main users, has lost heart, commenting that 'the ARTL system has had limited use and questions are regularly raised of whether it is fit for purpose': see *Passage of the Land Registration etc (Scotland) Bill 2011*, 455.
5 Scottish Parliament, *Official Report*, 25 Jan 2012, cols 879–80, reproduced in *Passage of the Land Registration etc (Scotland) Bill 2011* (n 4) 397.

The problem with ARTL is that it is not Amazon – its operation is extremely clunky. The system was developed in close partnership between Registers of Scotland and the Law Society. In many ways the problem with ARTL is that it reflects what lawyers wanted at that time. The legal business and IT have moved on considerably since then and ARTL is now behind the times in how it operates and what it offers.

Whether for this or for other reasons, such as the conservatism of the legal profession or its reluctance to take on tasks which it may feel properly belong to RoS, the take-up of ARTL has been disappointing. The latest figures indicate that ARTL is used in well under 10% of eligible cases.[6] Remortgages have dominated, and there has been little use of ARTL for transfers of ownership. Of the 15,860 ARTL applications made in 2011, 53% were in respect of standard securities, 25% in respect of discharges of securities, and a further 16% were for notices of payment of improvement or repairs grants. Applications in respect of dispositions contributed only 5% of the total. This weak performance has not been for want of trying on the part of RoS, who have been zealous in promoting the system and encouraging its use. Nor is it due to the intrinsic undesirability of automated registration itself. On the contrary, it is plain that a system like ARTL, provided that it is, and is seen to be, secure, offers significant benefits in terms of speed, cost, customer-control, and overall efficiency. For as long as the current technology is in place, however, it seems unlikely that take-up rates will improve. Meanwhile the considerable sums expended in creating and developing the system – some £6.6 million to the end of 2011[7] – do not yet seem like value for money.

The 2012 Act is laconic on the subject of ARTL. Section 99, the single provision on the topic, empowers the Keeper to enable the generation of electronic documents and applications for the purposes of automated registration 'by means of a computer system under the Keeper's management and control'. ARTL is not named as such,[8] and it would be open to the Keeper to abandon the current system in favour of something else. Plans are currently in place for the digital registration of dispositions, standard securities and discharges.[9]

19.3 Legislative basis

ARTL was originally introduced by delegated legislation made under s 8 of the Electronic Communications Act 2000.[10] This amended the Requirements of Writing (Scotland) Act 1995 (to allow electronic deeds) and the Land Registration (Scotland) Act 1979 (to allow electronic registration). In addition, the Keeper

---

6 Registers of Scotland, *Annual Report and Accounts 2014–2015* (2015) 9, recording 10,380 ARTL registrations as compared with 203,174 registered dealings with whole. This represents a falling back from the 15% of eligible transactions recorded in *Passage of the Land Registration etc (Scotland) Bill 2011* (n 4) 508–09.
7 *Passage of the Land Registration etc (Scotland) Bill 2011* (n 4) 405, which gives a break-down of the expenditure.
8 Unlike in the equivalent provision (s 77) of the Scottish Law Commission's draft Bill.
9 C Kerr and J King, 'Lessons learned and new initiatives' (2016) 142 *Property Law Bulletin* 4–5; Registers of Scotland, *Digital Transformation: Next Steps* (Nov 2016).
10 This was the Automated Registration of Title to Land (Electronic Communications) (Scotland) Order 2006, SSI 2006/491.

was empowered to make binding 'directions' in respect of certain matters,[11] and did so on two occasions.[12] This rather slender legislative base was overhauled and replaced in the course of 2014. Today there is a whole new part of the 1995 Act (part 3), added by the Land Registration etc (Scotland) Act 2012, which is devoted to electronic documents, including but not restricted to documents within the ARTL system;[13] and this is supplemented by delegated legislation, most notably by the Land Register of Scotland (Automated Registration) etc Regulations 2014.[14] While the opportunity was taken to make some changes, the new provisions largely reproduce the substance of the old, and the mechanics of making an ARTL application, in particular, were little altered. A small number of further changes were consequent on the coming into force of the 2012 Act.[15]

19.4 Qualifying deeds

ARTL is only suitable for transactions which are straightforward and routine. It cannot therefore be used for first registrations, for split-off dispositions, or for any other deed the registration of which requires a new title sheet to be created. Subject to those limitations, ARTL can be used for dispositions, standard securities and their assignation or discharge, and for assignations of long leases,[16] although even here there will be cases where complexities in the deed (eg the need for links in title or a reference to *pro indiviso* shares) will disqualify it from ARTL.[17] Furthermore, ARTL can only accommodate changes to the B (proprietorship) and C (securities) sections of the title sheet, so that, for example, a disposition which creates real burdens or servitudes cannot be registered under ARTL.

As well as these standard deeds, ARTL can also be used for notices and other documents in respect of improvement and repair grants.[18]

Regardless of the deed used, a small number of registered titles are themselves unsuitable for ARTL, for example because they contain an exclusion of the Keeper's warranty or a reference to an entry in the Register of Inhibitions. Users are immediately alerted to such titles by an on-screen message to the effect that the title is not suitable for ARTL processing.[19]

---

11 Requirements of Writing (Scotland) Act 1995 s 2B and LR(S)A 1979 s 5(2C), in each case as amended by SSI 2006/491.
12 Both in March 2007. They are reproduced in Rennie and Brymer (n 3) 169–71.
13 This largely came into force on 11 May 2014.
14 SSI 2014/347. This came into force on 8 December 2014 (ie on the designated day for the LR(S)A 2012). Certain transitional provisions contained in the Land Registration etc (Scotland) Act 2012 (Commencement No 2 and Transitional Provisions) Order 2014, SSI 2014/41, art 3 applied during the period between 11 May and 8 December 2014.
15 Full details are given in Registers of Scotland, *General Guidance: Changes to ARTL screens from December 8th 2014* (v.01, 2014). The most important are (i) a revised application form (see para 19.10 below); (ii) a requirement to provide the company number and jurisdiction of incorporation where the buyer or lender is a company or other juristic person: see LR(S)A 2012 ss 7(1)(a), 8(1), 9(1)(a)(iii), 22(1)(a), and 113(1) (definition of 'designation') (see paras 4.15–4.17 and 8.13 above); and (iii) the provision of email addresses so as to allow the Keeper to notify applicants and granters when a deed has been registered (see paras 9.14–9.16 above).
16 A complete list is set out in the Land Register of Scotland (Automated Registration) etc Regulations 2014, SSI 2014/347, reg 2.
17 For a (long) list of such cases, see Registers of Scotland, *ARTL Compatibility Guidelines*.
18 As to which, see Housing (Scotland) Act 2006 pt 2.
19 *ARTL Compatibility Guidelines* (n 17) 1–2.

ELECTRONIC DEEDS

19.5 Electronic deeds in general

While electronic deeds have been allowed within the confines of the ARTL system since 2007, it was not until 2014 that they became available more generally as alternatives to paper or 'traditional' deeds.[20] For the moment, however, electronic documents created outside ARTL are not eligible for registration in the Land Register or Register of Sasines,[21] and until such time as that changes,[22] they will only be used for rights not registrable in the Land Register, such as missives of sale and short leases. It is intended that the registration of electronic discharges of standard securities should become possible by the end of 2016, and that electronic standard securities and dispositions will follow in due course.[23]

The 2014 provisions, which are contained in a new part 3 inserted into the Requirements of Writing (Scotland) Act 1995, apply to ARTL and non-ARTL electronic deeds alike.[24] As with traditional deeds, a distinction is made between what is needed for formal validity and what is needed for self-proving status (probativity). An electronic document is formally valid if it is 'authenticated' by the granter and probative if it bears to be so authenticated and also to be 'certified' by a 'qualified certificate'.[25] Authentication is thus the equivalent of subscription in traditional documents, and certification is the equivalent of witnessing. An additional requirement for probativity, in both traditional and electronic deeds, is that nothing on the face of the deed should indicate that it was *not* subscribed or, as the case may be, authenticated.[26] This is because probativity is about appearance: a deed is probative if it *bears* to be subscribed and witnessed or, as the case may be, authenticated and certified – even if it has not been.

Something more should be said about authentication and certification. An electronic document is authenticated by being signed by means of an 'advanced electronic signature',[27] which must be 'incorporated into, or logically associated

---

20 Requirements of Writing (Scotland) Act 1995 pt 3. See further K G C Reid, *Requirements of Writing (Scotland) Act 1995* (2nd edn, 2015) 31–40; K G C Reid and G L Gretton, *Conveyancing 2014* (2015) 140–46.
21 This is because, by RW(S)A 1995 s 9G(3), registration is possible only where Scottish Ministers prescribe the form and type of document, electronic signature, and certification. At the time of writing this had only been done in respect of ARTL deeds: see Electronic Documents (Scotland) Regulations 2014, SSI 2014/83, reg 6, inserted by the Land Register of Scotland (Automated Registration) etc Regulations 2014, SSI 2014/347, reg 9(3).
22 LR(S)A 2012 s 100 empowers the Scottish Ministers to make provision by regulations for the recording or registration of electronic documents in any register under the management and control of the Keeper.
23 Registers of Scotland, *Digital Transformation: Next Steps* (Nov 2016).
24 The provisions in the Requirements of Writing (Scotland) Act 1995, which previously applied to ARTL deeds, have been repealed: see LR(S)A 2012 sch 3 paras 5, 7 and 13.
25 RW(S)A 1995 ss 9B and 9C.
26 RW(S)A 1995 ss 3(1)(c) and 9C(1)(b).
27 RW(S)A 1995 s 9B(1), (2); Electronic Documents (Scotland) Regulations 2014 regs 1 and 2. Self-evidently, as s 9B(2)(b) says, the electronic signature must be 'created by the person by whom it purports to have been created' and so not be a signature which is stolen or used without authority.

with' the document.[28] An 'advanced electronic signature' is one:[29]

(a) which is uniquely related to the signatory,
(b) which is capable of identifying the signatory,
(c) which is created using means that the signatory can maintain under his sole control, and
(d) which is linked to the data to which it relates in such a manner that any subsequent change of data is detectable.

The final criteria brings out a key advantage of electronic over handwritten signatures: an advanced electronic signature evidences not merely the assent of the granter at the time of signing ('authenticity', in the terminology used for electronic signatures) but also that the document has not been altered after execution ('integrity'). The signature is applied by the granter of the deed or by a person acting for the granter;[30] as with traditional deeds there are special rules for who is to sign in cases where the granter is a company or other juristic person.[31]

An electronic signature is 'certified' by means of a statement, incorporated into or logically associated with the document, that the signature is a valid means of establishing the document's authenticity or integrity.[32] For the purposes of the 1995 Act, the certification must be by a 'qualified certificate' provided by a certification-service-provider.[33] At the time of writing, the only certification-service-providers active in the Scottish legal market were the Keeper of the Registers of Scotland (in respect of ARTL deeds) and the Law Society of Scotland (in respect of non-ARTL deeds), and only the latter's certificate satisfied the requirements needed to count as 'qualified'. In practice, both electronic signature and certificate are held on a single chip embedded within a PIN-protected smartcard which, in the case of the smartcard issued by the Law Society, also embodies the practising certificate and a number of other functions.[34] A deed authenticated with a smartcard is thus both formally valid and also, in the case of the Law Society smartcard, probative.

19.6 Electronic deeds under the ARTL system

In addition to complying with the rules just described as to authentication,[35] an electronic deed made under the ARTL system is subject to three additional

---

28 RW(S)A 1995 s 9B(2)(a). This uses what has become standard terminology for the connection between electronic signature and electronic document: see Directive 1999/93/EC of the European Parliament and of the Council on a Community framework for electronic signatures (the E-Signatures Directive) art 2 (definition of 'electronic signature'); Electronic Communications Act 2000 s 7(2)(a). 'Incorporated' speaks for itself. A signature is 'logically associated' with an electronic document if there is a link or connection between the data which comprise the document and the data which comprise the signature (in the same way as, to take a familiar example, between an email and one of its attachments).
29 The definition comes from reg 2 of the Electronic Signatures Regulations 2002, SI 2002/318, and is in turn taken from the E-Signatures Directive (Directive 1999/93/EC).
30 RW(S)A 1995 s 12(3).
31 Electronic Documents (Scotland) Regulations 2014 reg 5, inserted by the Land Register of Scotland (Automated Registration) etc Regulations 2014 reg 9(3).
32 RW(S)A 1995 s 12(1) (definition of 'certification'). For the meaning of 'authenticity' and 'integrity', see s 12(4).
33 Electronic Documents (Scotland) Regulations 2014 reg 3(b). This is defined by reg 2 of the Electronic Signatures Regulations 2002 as 'a certificate which meets the requirements in schedule 1 and is provided by a certification-service-provider who fulfils the requirements in schedule 2'.
34 See www.lawscot.org.uk/smartcard.
35 If it did not so comply, the deed would fail to satisfy RW(S)A 1995 s 1(2) and so could not be used for standard conveyancing deeds.

requirements.[36] In the first place, it must be in the form of a PDF created within the ARTL system.[37] Secondly, the electronic signature must be created by unique data, such as codes or private cryptographic keys,[38] associated with a digital certificate supplied by the Keeper and certifying the signature. Thirdly, the digital certificate, while not a 'qualified certificate', must conform to exacting technological standards, employing advanced encryption techniques.[39] Both signature and certificate are based on what is known as an asymmetric key-pair public-key infrastructure ('PKI').[40] As certification-service-provider, the Keeper enables a 'key pair' (two extremely large numbers), one 'public' and the other 'private'.[41] The (unique) private key is used by the signatory to create electronic signatures and is unknown to recipients of the executed deed, or to anyone else;[42] the public key is publicly available in the form of the certificate, which confirms that signatures created by the private key were created by the identified individual. The identity of that individual is vouched for by the Keeper through personal interview by her staff or other checks, supplemented by independent evidence of identity.[43] To ensure that the private key is known only to its authorised user, the key pair is not 'grown' on the smartcard until after the user has taken possession of it and changed the PIN.[44]

If the technical details are complex, the practicalities are reassuringly straightforward. Approved signatories are issued by the Keeper with a PIN-protected smartcard, and can sign and certify deeds within the ARTL system

---

36 Electronic Documents (Scotland) Regulations 2014, SSI 2014/83, reg 6, inserted by the Land Register of Scotland (Automated Registration) etc Regulations 2014, SSI 2014/347, reg 9(3). Although the opening words of reg 6 are not as clear as one would wish, it appears (not least from the explanatory note at the end of SSI 2014/347) that reg 6 is intended to be an enactment within s 9G(6)(a) of the Requirements of Writing (Scotland) Act 1995, thus overriding the rule in s 9G(1), (2) by which a deed cannot be registered unless it is probative. ARTL deeds are not probative because the certificate by which they are certified is not a 'qualified certificate'.
37 A footnote to this provision in SSI 2014/347 reads: 'Portable document format – ISO 32000-1: 2008'.
38 Regulation 6(b) talks of 'signature-creation data', defined in reg 1(2) as having the meaning given in Art 2(4) of Directive 1999/93/EC of the European Parliament and of the Council of 13 December 1999 on a Community framework for electronic signatures, ie, 'unique data, such as codes or private cryptographic keys, which are used by the signatory to create an electronic signature'.
39 Electronic Documents (Scotland) Regulations 2014 reg 6(c). This long list of technical requirements is an updated version of the list that appeared in the Keeper's Direction No 1 of 2007.
40 Rennie and Brymer (n 3) para 8-03; SLC Report 222 paras 34.65–34.70.
41 As the definitions of 'public key' and 'private key' in reg 1(2) of the Electronic Documents (Scotland) Regulations 2014 make clear, the keys are intrinsically linked, 'although it is computationally infeasible to determine one key from knowledge of the other key'.
42 A private key 'is kept private to be used, in combination with data from an electronic document, to create a digital signature which is uniquely linked to both the signer of the document and the document itself': see the definition of 'private key' (n 41).
43 Rennie and Brymer (n 3) para 8-02. For the role of the local registration authority in this regard, see para 19.8 below.
44 The details are as follows. During the session with the Keeper's staff where a user registers for his or her digital certificate, a request is sent to the smartcard to generate a key pair. The private key is stored in a secure area in the smartcard chip, and the public key is transmitted up to the certification authority where it becomes an integral part of the digital certificate. The certificate itself is sent back to the smartcard once it has been signed by the private key of the certification authority. We are grateful to Kevin Ramsay of Registers of Scotland for information on this and other matters concerning digital signatures.

by using the smartcard in association with a smartcard reader, which provides the interface from smartcard to computer via a USB cable. The signature then works like a seal or watermark over the whole electronic document.[45] Obviously, it is essential to the security of the system that only the person issued with the smartcard should use it; to allow an assistant or a secretary to use it instead is to license forgery.[46]

19.7 Mandate to sign

As granters are unlikely to have electronic signatures of their own, or at least signatures of the kind that can be used within the ARTL system, electronic deeds must be executed on their behalf by those, generally solicitors,[47] who do have such signatures.[48] A solicitor will need clear and unequivocal authority to sign. Originally, this matter was regulated by Law Society rules,[49] which required a signed mandate from the granter which was then scanned and sent to RoS for retention in the archive record.[50] The relevant rule was repealed with effect from 1 September 2016, on the basis that it 'conveys no benefit to clients and may increase costs; is no longer effectively enforced; is unnecessary given the increased awareness of the ARTL system; and its maintenance is inconsistent with progress by the Registers towards e-enablement.'[51]

This change is perhaps more limited in scope than may appear. The validity of a deed, and hence the validity of the resulting title, will of necessity depend on the validity of the authorisation from the client. This is true regardless of whether the deed in question is one used in the ARTL system or not. The law firm acting for the granter will wish to have and retain clear authorisation, if only for its own protection. As for the grantee, the usual practice, where a deed is signed by an agent, is to ask to see the authorisation (eg power of attorney) linking the granter with the signatory: to the extent that that practice is either good or in fact superfluous, it is presumably equally good practice, or equally superfluous, for electronic deeds.

---

45 SLC Report 222 para 34.70.
46 For solicitors it may also give rise to conduct as well as service complaint issues: see Law Society of Scotland, *Rules and Guidance* Section F Division C: Registration of Deeds – ARTL.
47 A law firm could also sign. The legal argument used to resist this conclusion in Rennie and Brymer (n 3) paras 8-11–8-16, which was itself based on a supplementary Opinion by Professor Rennie for the Law Society, has fallen away in view of reg 5 of the Electronic Documents (Scotland) Regulations 2014, inserted by the Land Register of Scotland (Automated Registration) etc Regulations 2014 reg 9(3) (which makes provision for electronic signature by partnerships, LLPs, and other juristic persons). However, as Rennie and Brymer point out, there may be policy reasons for preferring individual solicitors to law firms.
48 Requirements of Writing (Scotland) Act 1995 s 12(3) contemplates authentication on behalf of the granter.
49 Law Society of Scotland, *Rules and Guidance* r B8.2.
50 This practice did not emerge without prolonged negotiation. For the background, see Rennie and Brymer (n 3) paras 8-05 and 8-06.
51 This was the justification for the repeal given by the Law Society of Scotland in its consultation exercise on 23 February 2016.

THE ARTL SYSTEM[52]

19.8 Authorisation

A person with access to the ARTL system can draw up deeds, sign them digitally, and procure their registration by means not requiring further human intervention. With so much power at stake, control over access is a key issue.[53] Access is regulated partly by an authorisation arrangement involving the Keeper and partly by internal organisational rules for those entities which have been authorised.

No entity can use the ARTL system without being authorised by the Keeper to do so.[54] Authorisation is obtained by written application and, with the active encouragement of RoS, the majority of law firms involved in conveyancing have signed up, as well as many lenders and local authorities.[55] The Keeper has power to suspend or revoke an authorisation on certain grounds, such as the provision of false information. There is a right of appeal to Scottish Ministers against suspension and revocation as well as against an initial refusal of authorisation.[56]

Within each law firm or other authorised entity, at least one 'local registration authority' ('LRA') – a person rather than the body suggested by the name – must be appointed to have oversight of the issue and withdrawal of smartcards.[57] An initial 'identity verification meeting' takes place with a member of the Keeper's staff at which the LRA is issued with the LRA smartcard, complete with digital certificate, which is needed to authenticate requests for digital certificates on behalf of staff within the firm. Thereafter the LRA can authorise members of staff to be users of the system, issue smartcards to them, and set up digital certificates. The day-to-day management of the system is in the hands of a practice administrator, who will decide matters such as the level of permissions to

---

52 'ARTL system' is defined in reg 1(2) of the Land Register of Scotland (Automated Registration) etc Regulations 2014, SSI 2014/347, as 'the computer system managed and controlled by the Keeper to facilitate the creation of electronic documents and the electronic generation and communication of an application of a deed relating to a registered plot in the Land Register of Scotland and automated registration of that deed in accordance with section 99(1) of the Land Registration etc (Scotland) Act 2012'.
53 As SLC Report 222 put it (para 34.58): 'the ARTL system must have entry control. It is an online dance-floor that needs bouncers.'
54 Land Register of Scotland (Automated Registration) etc Regulations 2014 reg 3. Regulations 3–6 go some way (no more) towards meeting the Scottish Law Commission's criticism of the previous absence of legislative provisions as to the method of authorisation, the criteria to be applied, the manner in which the system is to be used, and the revocation of authorisation: see SLC Report 222 para 34.60.
55 The figures as at 2012 were 686 law firms (out of 896 known to practise conveyancing), 29 lenders, and 13 local authorities: see *Passage of the Land Registration etc (Scotland) Bill 2011* (n 4) 509. Although reg 3(1) lists as prospective authorised persons 'any firm of solicitors (including a sole practitioner or partnership), firm of licensed conveyancers, commercial lender (within the meaning of section 75(5) of the Housing (Scotland) Act 2006), local authority', it is also made clear that any 'other person' may also apply for authorisation.
56 Land Register of Scotland (Automated Registration) etc Regulations 2014 regs 5 and 6. The procedure for appeals is set out in sch 1.
57 Land Register of Scotland (Automated Registration) etc Regulations 2014 reg 4(1)–(3). See also Rennie and Brymer (n 3) paras 9-21–9-25. A person cannot be appointed who has been convicted for fraud or suspended or disqualified as a solicitor (reg 4(5), (6)).

be allocated to individual users.[58] Only the LRA need be a solicitor.[59] Particularly in a small law firm, the practice manager may be the same person as the LRA.

Before the ARTL system can be entered for the first time, a user must accept the Keeper's terms and conditions by ticking the appropriate online box. These are designed 'to protect the security, integrity or stability' of the system, and may be altered unilaterally by the Keeper, acting reasonably, from time to time.[60]

19.9 Scope

The ARTL system allows for (i) the drafting, execution and delivery of the deeds such as dispositions and standard securities; (ii) the completion of the application for registration; and (iii) the registration of the deed.[61] Different people in a law firm may have permissions to deal with different tasks within the system.[62]

Earlier stages of the conveyancing transaction, such as negotiating and concluding the contract, examining title, instructing an advance notice, and obtaining a legal report, are conducted outside the ARTL system. The contract, however, can be concluded electronically, although it must then be signed with the Law Society's smartcard and not with the smartcard provided for ARTL. Applications for advance notices are usually made online.[63]

19.10 Deeds and their registration

Once certain key data as to property, parties, consideration, type of deed, type of warrandice, and so on have been entered into the system by the grantee's law firm,[64] an electronic deed is generated which bears a reassuringly close resemblance to a paper deed.[65] This can be printed, if desired, and sent to the client. Where the parties are separately represented, the deed can pass from the control of one law firm to the other, as in paper transactions, by clicking on a 'pass control' button. Once the digital signature has been added, the deed remains in the domain of the granter's agent until the money is paid (or, as the case may be, advanced), whereupon the deed is delivered by being passed back into the domain of the grantee's agent.[66] It can then be registered.

---

58 Rennie and Brymer (n 3) paras 9-26–9-35; Law Society of Scotland, *Rules and Guidance* Section F Division C: Registration of Deeds – ARTL. There is no mention of a practice manager in the 2014 Regulations.
59 This is a requirement, not of the 2014 Regulations, but of the Law Society's *Rules and Guidance* Section F Division C: Registration of Deeds – ARTL.
60 Land Register of Scotland (Automated Registration) etc Regulations 2014 reg 4(3), (4).
61 There is much useful material on the RoS website (www.ros.gov.uk) about the use of the ARTL system, including step-by-step guides to different types of transaction.
62 Rennie and Brymer (n 3) paras 9-31–9-33.
63 LRR 2014 r 3(1): see para 10.10 above.
64 This involves completing (i) the draft application and (ii) the transaction information. Different employees within a firm may complete the two stages. The core information to be provided is set out in part A of the ARTL application form: see Land Register of Scotland (Automated Registration) etc Regulations 2014 sch 2.
65 In the case of standard securities, the styles of all of the main lenders are held within the ARTL system, so that a style of security will be produced which is appropriate to the lender in question. The CML *Lenders' Handbook (Scotland)* pt 1 para 18.2.1 states that: 'Where we have more than one style of standard security held on ARTL you should check your instructions to see which style you should use.'
66 Ie, delivery is by electronic means: see Requirements of Writing (Scotland) Act 1995 s 9F. The common law was probably the same (see Rennie and Brymer (n 3) para 6-09), but s 9F has removed any lingering doubts.

ARTL applications are subject to the same rules as any other application, and so must satisfy both the general application conditions (in s 22 of the 2012 Act) and the special conditions (in s 26).[67] In addition, the grantee's agent must complete an application form, within the ARTL system, for each deed. This is based on the form for paper applications,[68] but with an additional question as to whether the granter has given authority for the deed to be authenticated on his behalf.[69] Where the parties are separately represented, the answers can be revised by the granter's agent, if desired;[70] indeed it is only the granter's agent who can answer the question about authority to authenticate.[71] As with the paper equivalent, the form concludes with a certification that the information given is correct 'to the best of my knowledge and belief' and that the application complies with the application conditions.[72] After signing the form (digitally), the grantee's agent applies for registration by clicking on the 'proceed' button. A message within ARTL will confirm the application number, and, following certain checks (notably in the Register of Inhibitions), registration will generally occur within 24 hours.[73] A confirming email is sent by RoS to the agents for the granter and grantee.

19.11 LBTT and registration fees

Deeds which effect transactions which are notifiable for the purposes of land and buildings transaction tax cannot be registered until a land transaction return has been made and any tax due paid.[74] Both matters are the subject of questions in the application form. In the case of ARTL transactions, a link is provided to Revenue Scotland's online system.[75]

The fee for registration is collected by direct debit. Fees for ARTL applications are lower than for paper applications, partly to encourage the use of ARTL and partly in recognition of the substantial reduction in staff time which ARTL involves.[76]

---

67 See paras 8.7 and 8.8 above.
68 Stripped of the questions which are relevant only to first registrations (which are not possible under ARTL).
69 The form is prescribed in sch 2 of the Land Register of Scotland (Automated Registration) etc Regulations 2014. Part A asks for the basic information which is used to create the deed (see above); part B comprises a series of questions. See paras 8.12–8.20 above for the paper equivalent.
70 See on this topic para 8.21 above.
71 For this reason the screen displays the following notice at the end of the questions: 'You may wish to leave the question regarding the mandate to sign the disposition blank. The selling agent will be responsible for signing the disposition and he/she will confirm they have a mandate when they revise the application questions.'
72 For liability under these certifications, see para 15.5 above.
73 See Registers of Scotland, *Annual Report and Accounts, 2014–2015* (2015) 9, reporting that in the year in question all ARTL applications were processed within 24 hours.
74 Land and Buildings Transaction Tax (Scotland) Act 2013 s 43(1). Section 30 determines whether a transaction is notifiable. For further details, see para 8.18 above.
75 It is no longer the case, as it was with stamp duty land tax, that the land transaction return is completed as part of the ARTL transaction; nor does RoS now collect the tax on behalf of the Revenue.
76 Registers of Scotland (Fees) Order 2014, SSI 2014/188, sch 1 pts 1 and 3. For example, the ARTL fee for registering a disposition with a consideration of £400,000 is £450 (as compared with £600 for a paper application). The ARTL fee for a standard security or its discharge is £50 (as compared with £60). For full details, see para 8.5 above.

Chapter 20

Leases

20.1 Introduction

Much of what is said in this book applies to long leases[1] as it applies to other real rights in land which are registrable in the Land Register. Furthermore, to the extent that leases raise special considerations, these have usually been discussed in the appropriate chapter. That is the position, for example, in respect of lease title sheets,[2] title sheets for shared and sharing leases,[3] first registrations and automatic plot registration,[4] standard securities over leases,[5] realignment,[6] and examination of title.[7] In this brief final chapter we consider the few topics concerning leases that have not already been covered in earlier chapters. The focus, it need hardly be added, is on the *registration* of leases, and relatively little will be said about the law of leases more generally.[8]

20.2 Maximum duration

The maximum duration of a lease executed on or after 9 June 2000 is 175 years.[9] Before that date there was no limit on duration; but existing leases for more than 175 years were automatically converted into ownership on 28 November 2015 provided that they were registered, that the annual rent was £100 or less, and that they had an unexpired duration of more than 175 years (100 years in the case of leases of private dwellinghouses).[10] The result is that hardly any leases today have an unexpired duration exceeding 175 years; in most cases the duration is much shorter.

20.3 Registration of Leases (Scotland) Act 1857[11]

The legislation which established the Register of Sasines in 1617 made no provision for the registration of leases, and leases remained unregistrable until

---

1 That is to say, leases for more than 20 years. Only long leases are registrable: see para 20.3 below.
2 See paras 4.5 and 4.14–4.17 above.
3 See para 4.23 above.
4 See paras 7.10 and 7.11 above.
5 See para 7.13 above.
6 See paras 12.21–12.23 above.
7 See paras 16.14–16.22 above.
8 For the law of leases, see A McAllister, *Scottish Law of Leases* (4th edn, 2013); R Rennie et al, *Leases* (2015).
9 Abolition of Feudal Tenure etc (Scotland) Act 2000 s 67. This was one of the package of measures which accompanied the abolition of the feudal system; its evident intention was to prevent the creation of a new feudal system through the use of leasehold tenure: see Scottish Law Commission, *Report No 168 on Abolition of the Feudal System* (1999) paras 9.40–9.42.
10 Long Leases (Scotland) Act 2012. The criteria for conversion are set out in s 1(3), (4). There were exceptions for leases of harbours and leases granted for the sole purpose of allowing the tenant to install and maintain pipes or cables. It was also possible to opt out of conversion (ss 63 and 64) but only five lessees chose to do so. See further para 20.8 below.
11 Registration of Leases (Scotland) Act 1857 (20 & 21 Vict c 26).

the Registration of Leases (Scotland) Act 1857.[12] That Act provided for the registration of 'long' leases, that is to say, leases for a term exceeding 31 years, a period later reduced to 20 years.[13] The main purpose was to allow leases to be used as collateral for secured finance, something that had previously been effectively impossible. The Act enabled a tenant to grant a security over the lease by recording the lease in the Register of Sasines, and then granting a security that would itself be recorded in that register. This limited purpose probably explains the sloppy drafting of the Act: the drafter was concerned with only one objective.

When the Land Register came to be introduced, county by county, in the last two decades of the twentieth century,[14] registration there replaced recording in the Register of Sasines. The legislative basis, however, was scarcely satisfactory. Instead of amending the 1857 Act, the Land Registration (Scotland) Act 1979 provided that references in the 1857 Act (and other Acts) to recording in the Register of Sasines should be read as including a reference to registration in the Land Register.[15] If the result was not readily intelligible, the defect was, fortunately, made good by the Land Registration etc (Scotland) Act 2012. Following amendments made by that Act to the 1857 Act,[16] provisions of the 1857 Act that apply to the Land Register (such as s 3) say so expressly. Conversely, provisions (such as s 12) that refer only to the Register of Sasines are not applicable to the Land Register.[17] The 1857 Act is itself in need of a thorough review, but that is a matter which goes far beyond issues of land registration.[18]

20.4 Real rights and registration

Leases are contracts, but contracts in which the right of the tenant is capable of being made real.[19] A long lease (ie a lease of more than 20 years) must be

---

12 A minor exception was the provision made in the Act of 1617 (APS iv 531 c 4, RPS 1617/5/18) for registration with the Clerk Register of certain classes of lease granted by prelates ('prelatis'). For the background to the 1857 Act, see W Guy, 'Registration of Leases' (1908–09) 20 JR 234, 234–37.
13 Registration of Leases (Scotland) Act 1857 s 1, as amended (in respect of the length of lease) by the Land Tenure Reform (Scotland) Act 1974 s 18, sch 6 para 1.
14 See para 2.5 above.
15 LR(S)A 1979 s 29(2), (3), sch 3.
16 LR(S)A 2012 s 52(3), sch 2. This includes providing styles for assignations and renunciations which are suitable for registered leases: see sch 2 paras 17 and 22 (inserting, respectively, schs ZA and ZG into the 1857 Act). At the same time, what is left of the LR(S)A 1979 is amended by adding the 1857 Act to the list of enactments in sch 3 to which the 'conversion' provision in s 29 is not to apply: see LR(S)A 2012 sch 5 para 19(9)(b), which replaces the particular provisions of the 1857 Act listed in LR(S)A 1979 sch 3 para 5(a)–(c) with the words 'The Whole Act' (ie the whole of the 1857 Act). In what is evidently a slip, albeit a harmless one, the amendment leaves in place the original para 5(d), so that sch 3 para 5 now excludes from s 29 both the whole of the 1857 Act and also the particular provision of that Act (s 16) which is mentioned in para (d).
17 Here, the distinction between 'recording' and 'registering' is crucial. Where the RL(S)A 1857 (as amended) refers only to 'recording', that means that the provision applies only to the Register of Sasines.
18 A review of aspects of the 1857 Act is included in the Scottish Law Commission's current programme of law reform: see *Ninth Programme of Law Reform* (Scot Law Com No 242, 2015) paras 2.21–2.25.
19 If the lease is not registered, it is still valid as a contract binding the parties and is thus, as between them, of the same effect as a registered lease, but it will not bind the landlord's singular successors.

registered in the Land Register if it is to be a real right and bind successors of the landlord.[20] By contrast, short leases (ie leases for 20 years or less) cannot be registered or even mentioned in the Register,[21] and so are among the off-register rights of which acquirers of land must be wary.[22] They are made real by the tenant taking possession, in accordance with the Leases Act 1449 (as interpreted).[23]

The 20-year threshold for registration refers to the contracted term (including renewals)[24] rather than to the term which happens to remain unexpired at the time when registration is sought.[25] There are sound reasons for requiring a reasonable duration of leases before they become registrable. The trouble and expense of registration would be disproportionate in the case of very short leases. In any case, tenants would often fail to register and so, if the protection of the 1449 Act were to be withdrawn, would not obtain a real right.[26] There is also an argument that ephemeral rights should not clutter up the Register (although some already do).[27] Whether 20 years is the correct threshold is, however, another matter. It excludes all but a small number of leases granted, so that only 1000 leases or so are registered each year.[28] In England and Wales, leases are registrable if the unexpired duration exceeds seven years.[29] In many Torrens systems the threshold is lower still.[30] It may be that the position in Scotland ought to be reconsidered.[31]

---

20 Registration of Leases (Scotland) Act 1857 ss 1 and 20C (the former enabling registration in the Land Register, the latter removing the alternative of becoming real under the Leases Act 1449); LR(S)A 2012 s 48(1)(b) (closing the Register of Sasines to leases). The previous law was the same: see LR(S)A 1979 ss 2(1)(a) and 3(3). Prior to the 1979 Act, possession under the Leases Act 1449 was available for long leases as an alternative to registration (ie in the Register of Sasines).
21 This emerges not by positive legislative statement but negatively: registrability in the Land Register requires a statutory basis, and there is none. The Scottish Law Commission considered but rejected the idea that short leases might be noted on the Register in the same way as, for example, prescriptive servitudes: see Scottish Law Commission, *Report No 222 on Land Registration* (2010) ('SLC Report 222') para 7.19, departing from Scottish Law Commission, *Discussion Paper No 130 on Land Registration: Miscellaneous Issues* (2005) ('SLC DP 130') para 5.57.
22 For off-register rights, see paras 4.26–4.28 above.
23 Leases Act 1449 (APS ii 36 c 6, RPS 1450/1/16–17).
24 Registration of Leases (Scotland) Act 1857 s 17.
25 RoS policy on the calculation of the length of leases for the purposes of registration is set out in Registers of Scotland, *Registration Manual* (https://rosdev.atlassian.net/wiki/display/2ARM/Home) Topics: Leases – examination of applications relating to a lease. For example, in RoS's view while a period expressed by reference to calendar dates (eg 15 May 2016 to 15 May 2036) exceeds 20 years with the result that the lease is registrable, the same is not true where the period is expressed by reference to term days (eg Whitsunday 2016 to Whitsunday 2036). No reason for the different treatment is given.
26 Of course, the shorter the lease, the less likely it is to matter whether there is real effect.
27 See the list of registrable deeds given in the appendix to ch 6.
28 J King, 'Completion of the Land Register: the Scottish approach', in F McCarthy, J Chalmers and S Bogle (eds), *Essays in Conveyancing and Property Law in Honour of Professor Robert Rennie* (2015; available at www.openbookpublishers.com/reader/343#page/1/mode/2up) 317, 333.
29 Land Registration Act 2002 s 3(3). To this figure would fall to be added long leases that the lessee does not register, but it is thought that the number of these is small.
30 See the statutory provisions cited in SLC DP 130 para 5.25, n 50.
31 The Scottish Law Commission considered that this was a matter for the law of leases and not the law of land registration. It may be that the Commission will consider this issue as part of the review of the law of leases mentioned at n 18 above.

20.5 Registrable leases

In principle, any lease or sublease for more than 20 years is registrable in the Land Register.[32] It cannot, now, be registered in the Register of Sasines.[33] In addition to leases of 'normal' land, registrable leases include leases of the seabed,[34] of separate tenements[35] such as salmon fishings and minerals,[36] and of those sporting rights (only 65 in number) which were preserved by registered notice at the time of the abolition of the feudal system.[37] If something is neither land nor a separate tenement, it cannot normally be leased, but statute has made an exception for freshwater fishings,[38] and there is Outer House authority in support of shooting leases although the matter cannot perhaps be regarded as settled.[39] Be that as it may, RoS practice is to accept both shooting leases and also, more controversially, 'leases' of the roofs of buildings in connection with solar panels for generating electricity.[40]

20.6 Other registrable deeds

Assignations of long leases are registrable in the Land Register, and cannot now be registered in the Register of Sasines.[41] The same is true of standard securities over long leases.[42] If both lease and plot are held on Sasine titles, registration of an assignation or a standard security will also result in the registration of the plot of land by APR.[43]

The registrability of other deeds depends on the registration status of the lease which is to be affected. If the lease is registered in the Land Register, then the deed must likewise be registered in the Land Register,[44] and may not have real effect unless it is.[45] But if the lease is not so registered, the deed falls to be registered in the Register of Sasines. A lease is regarded as registered if it was constituted by registration in the Land Register or if it has since migrated there as a result of having been assigned. But a lease is also treated as being registered if the plot of land to which it relates has been registered, even if the lease itself is not (yet) the

---

32 RL(S)A 1857 s 1(1). Although subleases are not expressly mentioned in the Act, it has always been the Keeper's practice to accept subleases for registration.
33 LR(S)A 2012 s 48(1)(b).
34 Now the subject of express provision: see RL(S)A 1857 s 1(2), inserted by LR(S)A 2012 s 52(3), sch 2 para 2.
35 For separate tenements, see K G C Reid, *The Law of Property in Scotland* (1996) paras 207–212.
36 For mineral leases, see Rennie et al (n 8) paras 9-20 ff.
37 Abolition of Feudal Tenure etc (Scotland) Act 2000 s 65A: see K G C Reid, *The Abolition of Feudal Tenure in Scotland* (2003) paras 8.6–8.10.
38 Salmon and Freshwater Fisheries (Consolidation) (Scotland) Act 2003 s 66; RL(S)A 1857 s 20D, inserted by LR(S)A 2012 s 52(3), sch 2 para 16.
39 *Palmer's Trs v Brown* 1989 SLT 128.
40 *Registration Manual* (n 25) Topics: Sporting rights – fishing and rights to take game; Topics: Leases – examination of applications relating to a lease. For discussion of leases of roofs, see K Swinton, 'Perils of solar panels' (2013) 81 SLG 4; K G C Reid and G L Gretton, *Conveyancing 2013* (2014) 155–56. In our view, rent-a-roof solar contracts cannot competently be registered.
41 RL(S)A 1857 s 3; LR(S)A 2012 s 48(1)(c).
42 Conveyancing and Feudal Reform (Scotland) Act 1970 s 9(2); LR(S)A 2012 s 48(2).
43 LR(S)A 2012 s 24(3), (7): see paras 7.11 and 7.13 above.
44 LR(S)A 2012 s 48(1)(d).
45 RL(S)A 1857 s 20B(2), inserted by LR(S)A 2012 s 52(2). This obscure provision is a deliberate copy-out of part of LR(S)A 1979 s 3(3). For discussion of its possible meaning, see SLC Report 222 paras 9.24–9.28.

subject of a title sheet of its own.[46] This is because, under the 2012 Act, the status of subordinate real rights is determined by the status of the plot of land over which they are granted.[47]

As amended by the 2012 Act,[48] the 1857 Act makes express provision for the registration in the Land Register of assignations of lease,[49] variations,[50] reductions,[51] and renunciations.[52] Nothing is said about decrees of irritancy, but RoS regard them as registrable,[53] as certainly they ought to be, and it seems likely that they fall within the provision of the 1857 Act which allows registration of any 'deed ... terminating the lease'.[54]

Something more may be said about renunciations.[55] Where a lease title sheet exists, a deed of renunciation should narrate this number (only), and will be registered against the lease title sheet, resulting in its closure.[56] Where, however, no lease title sheet exists – where, in other words, the lease is classified as registered only because the plot of land is registered – the deed should narrate the number of the plot title sheet, and the deed will be registered there.

20.7 Effect of registration

The 1857 Act has always made provision as to the effect of the registration of leases ('shall ... be effectual against any singular successors in the lands and heritages thereby let') and as to the effect of assignations ('shall fully and effectually vest the assignee with the right of the granter thereof').[57] No corresponding provision, however, was made in respect of ancillary deeds such as renunciations. For as long as the 1979 Act was in force, the lacuna was filled by the general provision as to the effect of registration found in s 3(1) of that Act, although its meaning and

---

46 This is sometimes referred to as 'deemed registration'.
47 Registers of Scotland, *General Guidance: Leases and Automatic Plot Registration* (v.02, 2015) 3, 4, 11. The precise legislative basis of this position is, however, unclear.
48 As well as the addition of references to the Land Register, mentioned in para 20.3 above, LR(S)A 2012 s 52(2) also added a new s 20A, which provides for registration of variations and deeds of termination. One reason for the addition was the repeal without replacement of LR(S)A 1979 s 2(4)(c) which, expressed in very general terms, had allowed for the registration of 'any other transaction or event which (whether by itself or in conjunction with registration) is capable under any enactment or rule of law of affecting the title to a registered interest in land but which is not a transaction or event creating or affecting an overriding interest'. Indeed the version of s 20A proposed in the SLC draft Bill sch 4 para 16 had largely reproduced this provision. For background, see SLC Report 222 paras 9.15–9.30.
49 RL(S)A 1857 s 3. There are mandatory forms of assignation in schs ZA and A, but there is some flexibility as to compliance: see *Rodger v Crawford* (1867) 6 M 24; *Crawford v Campbell* 1937 SC 596.
50 RL(S)A 1857 s 20A. The provision applies to deeds 'extending the duration of the lease' and 'otherwise altering the terms of the lease'.
51 RL(S)A 1857 s 14.
52 RL(S)A 1857 ss 13 and 20A(2)(a). Non-mandatory styles can be found in schs ZG and G.
53 *Registration Manual* (n 25) Topics: Court orders that are registrable deeds. Extract decrees of irritancy are included in the Keeper's list of registrable deeds which is reproduced at the end of ch 6.
54 RL(S)A 1857 s 20A(2)(a). This involves taking a broad meaning of the word 'deed'. The difficulty was avoided by the much more general wording employed by the version of s 20A which was proposed by the SLC draft Bill sch 4 para 16.
55 See *Registration Manual* (n 25) Topics: Leases – termination of lease.
56 The deed is registered only in the Land Register, even if the title to the plot of land is still held in the Register of Sasines: see LR(S)A 2012 s 48(1)(d).
57 RL(S)A 1857 ss 2 and 3.

scope were far from clear.[58] And while there is no equivalent general provision in the 2012 Act,[59] the s 3(1) approach is retained for leases and for deeds accessory to leases.[60] The 2012 Act does this by inserting a provision – s 20B – into the 1857 Act which uses substantially the same wording as s 3(1), troublesome as that wording was found to be.[61] At first sight this approach seems surprising. The reason for it is that it was considered unclear precisely what the effect of registration of ancillary deeds ought to be, and that in the context of reforming the law of land registration that issue could not be addressed.[62] As a result it was thought sensible to leave the law essentially as it was under the 1979 Act. That will presumably remain the position until such time as the 1857 Act is reviewed and reformed. There was, however, one important change. Section 3(1) of the 1979 Act brought with it the Keeper's Midas touch, so that, for instance, if a forged assignation of a lease were to be registered, the lease would be fully vested in the assignee, notwithstanding the deed's nullity.[63] The Midas touch was abandoned by the 2012 Act,[64] and, as s 20B(3) makes clear, that abandonment applies equally to deeds in respect of registered leases.[65]

20.8 Leasehold conversion

As previously mentioned,[66] all leases for more than 175 years were automatically converted into ownership on 28 November 2015 provided that they were registered, that the annual rent was £100 or less, and that they had an unexpired duration of more than 175 years (100 years in the case of leases of private dwellinghouses).[67] And because tenants thus became owners, landlords lost their ownership rights but could claim compensation in respect of loss of rent and certain other matters.[68]

The legislation – the Long Leases (Scotland) Act 2012 – made detailed provision as to the future of encumbrances which had previously burdened either the lease or the plot of land, now owned by the former tenant, over which the lease had been granted.[69] Encumbrances over the land continued to burden the land, other than

---

58 For discussion and criticism, see Scottish Law Commission, *Discussion Paper No 128 on Land Registration: Registration, Rectification and Indemnity* (2005) ('SLC DP 128') paras 5.1–5.7.
59 The policy of the 2012 Act is to leave the effect of registration to be determined by sector-specific legislation (see para 9.21 above), as indeed is now done, for leases, by the new s 20B of the RL(S)A 1857, discussed below.
60 In the case of leases and assignations of leases, this is unnecessary because, as already mentioned, express and targeted provision as to the effect of registration was made in the 1857 Act as enacted. But LR(S)A 1979 s 3(1) applied equally to leases and assignations.
61 RL(S)A 1857 s 20B, inserted by LR(S)A 2012 s 52(2). For an apparent oversight in this connection, see para 12.22 above.
62 See SLC Report 222 paras 9.21–9.30.
63 See paras 2.7 and 2.13 above.
64 See para 9.20 above.
65 RL(S)A 1857 s 20B(3) provides that, subject to the provisions in part 9 of the 2012 Act about realignment, 'registration of an invalid deed confers no real effect'.
66 See para 20.2 above.
67 Long Leases (Scotland) Act 2012 ss 1–4. Some minor exceptions are mentioned at n 10 above.
68 LL(S)A 2012 s 4(1)(b), pt 4 (ss 45–61).
69 For a more detailed account than the one that follows, see K G C Reid and G L Gretton, *Conveyancing 2013* (2014) 139–50; Rennie et al (n 8) paras 13-10 ff. Helpful background to this and other aspects of leasehold conversion can be found in the report by the Scottish Law Commission which led to the legislation: *Report No 204 on Conversion of Long Leases* (2006).

standard securities and proper liferents, both of which were extinguished.[70] The fate of encumbrances over the lease was more complex. Standard securities over the lease became standard securities over the land.[71] Conditions of the lease were generally extinguished with the lease itself,[72] unless they regulated the maintenance and management of common facilities, related to the provision of services to other property, or were imposed on a group of related properties under a common scheme, in which case they became real burdens over the land.[73] In theory, it was open to landlords to preserve certain other classes of leasehold condition by service and registration of a notice, but only five such notices were ever registered.[74] Finally, provision was made for the automatic creation of such servitudes as would have existed, by positive prescription or implication, if all leases and partial assignations had instead been conveyances.[75] The idea was to create now the servitudes that would have been created if neighbouring properties had been in separate ownership all along rather than in the same ownership but subject to one or more long leases.

Following leasehold conversion, it may be no simple matter to work out which encumbrances apply to a plot of land and which do not. The task is similar to the one required in respect of real burdens following the abolition of the feudal system,[76] and indeed the provisions of the Long Leases Act are modelled on those of the Abolition of Feudal Tenure etc (Scotland) Act 2000. As might be expected, RoS rely here on a policy of 'tell me don't show me'.[77] It is for the applicant for registration to determine which encumbrances have fallen and which have survived, and in the absence of a clear steer, RoS will simply include all the former leasehold conditions, other than the obligation to pay rent, in the D (burdens) section of the title sheet.[78] The issue arises, of course, on first registration, but for registered leases it arises equally on the first occasion on which the former lease, now ownership, is transferred on or after 28 November 2015.

Where a lease title sheet already existed for the converted lease, it becomes a plot title sheet and the previous plot title sheet (if there was one) will be closed. Where the lease was deemed to be registered in the Land Register only because the plot of land was registered, and there was no lease title sheet,[79] it is the plot title sheet which will be used for the former lease. The necessary changes will not, however, be made without prompting.[80] Although the Register is inaccurate in showing as rights of lease burdened by certain encumbrances what are now rights of ownership burdened by different encumbrances, RoS have no plans for reviewing the title sheets in question. It would, of course, be open to the former

---

70 LL(S)A 2012 s 6(3), (4).
71 LL(S)A 2012 s 6(2).
72 LL(S)A 2012 s 5(1).
73 LL(S)A 2012 ss 29 and 31. Mention might also be made of s 30 (conversion to manager burdens) and s 32 (conversion where conditions expressly enforceable by a third party).
74 LL(S)A 2012 ss 14–28. There were three notices under s 14 (conversion by nomination of a benefited property) and two under s 23 (conversion into personal pre-emption or personal redemption burdens). We are grateful to Registers of Scotland for supplying these figures.
75 LL(S)A 2012 s 7.
76 See para 8.25 above.
77 For 'tell me don't show me', see para 8.11 above.
78 *Registration Manual* (n 25) Topics: Leases – conversion of long leases, Long Leases (Scotland) Act 2012.
79 See para 20.6 above.
80 Registers of Scotland, *Update 45: Long Leases (Scotland) Act 2012* (2015); Registers of Scotland, *General Guidance: Long Leases (Scotland) Act 2012* (v.01, 2015).

tenant, now owner, to apply to the Keeper for rectification.[81] But in practice the correction of the title sheet is likely to have to wait until the next time that the property is transferred.

As the property is now owned rather than leased, the appropriate deed for transfer is a disposition and not an assignation. In the case of registered property the disposition should describe the subjects by reference to the title number of the lease title sheet, if there is one, and otherwise by the title number of the plot title sheet.[82]

---

81 LR(S)A 2012 s 80: see paras 11.13 ff above.
82 *Update 45* (n 80) 2.

Appendix I

Land Registration etc (Scotland) Act 2012 (asp 5)

PART 1

THE LAND REGISTER

The Land Register of Scotland

1 The Land Register of Scotland

(1) There is to continue to be a public register of rights in land in Scotland (which is to continue to be known as the 'Land Register of Scotland').
(2) The register is to continue to be under the management and control of the Keeper of the Registers of Scotland.
(3) The register is to continue to have a seal.
(4) Subject to the provisions of this Act, the register is to be in such form (which may be, or be in part, an electronic form) as the Keeper considers appropriate.
(5) The Keeper must take such steps as appear reasonable to the Keeper to protect the register from—
   (a) interference,
   (b) unauthorised access, and
   (c) damage.

Structure and contents of the register

2 The parts of the register

The Keeper must make up and maintain, as parts of the register—
   (a) the title sheet record,
   (b) the cadastral map,
   (c) the archive record, and
   (d) the application record.

Title sheets and the title sheet record

3 Title sheets and the title sheet record

(1) The Keeper must make up and maintain a title sheet for each registered plot of land.
(2) The Keeper may make up and maintain a title sheet for a registered lease.
(3) The title sheet record is the totality of all such title sheets.
(4) A plot of land is an area or areas of land all of which are owned by one person, or one set of persons.
(5) A separate tenement constitutes a plot of land for the purposes of this Act.
(6) Subject to subsections (2) and (7), there is to be only one title sheet for each plot of land.
(7) The Keeper need not make up and maintain a title sheet for a plot of land which is a pertinent of another plot of land (or of two or more other plots of land) but may instead include it in the title sheet of the other plot or plots of land of which it is a pertinent.

4 Title and lease title numbers

(1) The Keeper must assign a title number to—
   (a) the title sheet of each registered plot of land, and

(b) where a registered lease has a title sheet, to that title sheet.
(2) A title number is an unique identifier consisting of numerals or of letters and numerals.

5 Structure of title sheets
(1) A title sheet is to comprise—
    (a) a property section,
    (b) a proprietorship section,
    (c) a securities section, and
    (d) a burdens section.
(2) A section of a title sheet may be sub-divided if and as the Keeper considers appropriate.

6 The property section of the title sheet
(1) The Keeper must enter in the property section of the title sheet—
    (a) a description—
        (i) of the plot of land (being a description by reference to the cadastral map),
        (ii) of the nature of the proprietor's right in the plot of land, and
        (iii) if the plot is a separate tenement, of the nature of the tenement,
    (b) the particulars of any incorporeal pertinents (including, if there is a burdened property, the particulars of that property in so far as known),
    (c) any agreement registered under section 66(2),
    (d) any entry required under section 18(2)(a) or paragraph 7(a) of schedule 1,
    (e) if the title sheet is a lease title sheet, the particulars of the lease, and
    (f) where there is for the area of land another title sheet (as for example for a plot which is a separate tenement), the title number of that other title sheet.
(2) Paragraph (f) of subsection (1) does not apply where the other title sheet is the title sheet of a flat in a flatted building.

7 The proprietorship section of the title sheet
(1) The Keeper must enter in the proprietorship section of the title sheet—
    (a) the name and designation of the proprietor, and
    (b) in the case of ownership in common, the respective shares of the proprietors.
(2) Paragraph (a) of subsection (1) is subject to section 18(1)(b) and to paragraph 6(b) of schedule 1; and paragraph (b) of that subsection is subject to sections 16(2)(b) and 18(2)(b), to paragraph 7(b) of schedule 1 and to paragraphs 8(b) and 10 of schedule 4.

8 The securities section of the title sheet
(1) The Keeper must enter in the securities section of the title sheet particulars of any heritable security over the right in land to which the title sheet relates (including the name and designation of the creditor in the security).
(2) This section is subject to section 18(3)(b) and to paragraph 8(b) of schedule 1.

9 The burdens section of the title sheet
(1) The Keeper must enter in the burdens section of the title sheet—
    (a) where the right in land to which the title sheet relates is encumbered with a title condition—
        (i) the terms of the title condition,
        (ii) a description of any benefited property (in so far as known to the Keeper), and
        (iii) if the title condition is a personal real burden, the name and designation of the person who has title to enforce it,
    (b) where there is a long lease (other than a long sub-lease) which has real effect, that fact,
    (c) in a case where the title sheet is a lease title sheet, where there is a long sub-lease (other than a long sub-sub-lease) which has real effect, that fact,
    (d) in so far as known to the Keeper, any public right of way (by whatever means) over or through the land,

Part 1: The Land Register 349

(e) particulars of any path order made under section 22 of the Land Reform (Scotland) Act 2003 (asp 2) (compulsory powers to delineate paths in land in respect of which access rights are exercisable), and

(f) any other encumbrance the inclusion of which in the register is permitted or required, expressly or impliedly, by an enactment and the name and designation of the person who has title to enforce that encumbrance.

(2) In subsection (1)—
'encumbrance' does not include a heritable security,
'long lease' means—
 (a) a lease exceeding 20 years, or
 (b) a lease which includes provision (however expressed) requiring the landlord to renew the lease at the tenant's request as a result of which (and without any subsequent agreement express or implied between the landlord and tenant) the total duration could exceed 20 years.

(3) This section is subject to section 18(4) and to paragraph 9 of schedule 1.

10 What is entered or incorporated by reference in a title sheet

(1) The Keeper must, in addition to what is to be entered under sections 6 to 9, enter the matters mentioned in subsection (2) in a title sheet.

(2) The matters are—
 (a) any statement made by virtue of any of subsections (3) and (4)(b) of section 75 or subsection (5)(a) of section 76,
 (b) particulars of any special destination,
 (c) a reference to an entry in the Register of Inhibitions made under section 32(2),
 (d) the terms of any caveat, warrant for which is granted under section 67(3), and
 (e) such other information (if any) as the Keeper considers appropriate.

(3) The Keeper may incorporate by reference in a title sheet—
 (a) a document in the archive record, or
 (b) a deed in any other register under the management and control of the Keeper or of the Keeper of the Records of Scotland.

(4) The Keeper must not enter or incorporate by reference in a title sheet any rights or obligations except in so far as their entry is authorised by an enactment.

(5) The entry or incorporation by reference in a title sheet of any right or obligation, in so far as not so authorised—
 (a) does not constitute notice of that right or obligation, and
 (b) is without any other effect.

(6) Subsection (2)(b) is subject to section 18(3)(c) and to paragraph 8(c) of schedule 1.

The cadastral map

11 The cadastral map

(1) The cadastral map is a map—
 (a) showing the totality of registered geospatial data (other than supplementary data in individual title sheets),
 (b) showing for each cadastral unit—
  (i) the cadastral unit number,
  (ii) the boundaries of the unit, and
  (iii) the title number of any registered lease relating to the unit, and
 (c) otherwise depicting registered rights in such manner as the Keeper considers appropriate.

(2) A cadastral unit which represents a separate tenement must be shown on the map in such a way as will distinguish it as a cadastral unit from other units.

(3) The cadastral map may (but need not) show the boundaries of cadastral units on the vertical plane.

(4) The cadastral map may contain such other information as the Keeper considers appropriate.
(5) The cadastral map must be based upon the base map.
(6) The base map is—
 (a) the Ordnance Map,
 (b) another system of mapping, being a system which accords with such requirements as the Scottish Ministers may, by order, prescribe, or
 (c) a combination of the Ordnance map and such other system.
(7) On the base map being updated, the Keeper must make any changes to the register which are necessary in consequence of the updating.
(8) For the purposes of subsection (1)(a), the Keeper may determine what data is supplementary data.
(9) This section and sections 12 and 13 are without prejudice to section 16.

12 Cadastral units
(1) A cadastral unit is a unit which represents a single registered plot of land.
(2) Subject to subsection (3), the same area of land cannot be represented by more than one cadastral unit.
(3) The Keeper need not represent a plot of land such as is mentioned in section 3(7) as a separate cadastral unit but may instead include it in the cadastral unit representing the plot or plots of land of which it is a pertinent.
(4) The Keeper must assign a cadastral unit number to each cadastral unit.
(5) The cadastral unit number is to be the title number of the plot of land which that unit represents.

13 The cadastral map: further provision
(1) Where a plot of land—
 (a) lies wholly outwith the base map, or
 (b) extends partly outwith the base map,
 the Keeper may adopt such means of representing the boundaries on the cadastral map as the Keeper considers appropriate.
(2) The Keeper may—
 (a) combine cadastral units,
 (b) remove a cadastral unit from the map, or
 (c) divide a cadastral unit.
(3) On dividing a cadastral unit under subsection (2)(c), the Keeper may combine any of the resultant parts with a different cadastral unit.
(4) The Keeper must make such changes to the register as are necessary in consequence of anything done under subsections (2) and (3).

The archive record

14 The archive record
(1) The archive record is to consist of—
 (a) copies of all documents submitted to the Keeper,
 (b) copies of all documents which the Keeper is required to include under land register rules, and
 (c) copies of such other documents as the Keeper considers appropriate.
(2) The Keeper must also include in the archive record such information as is required for the purposes of section 104.
(3) But the Keeper need not include in the archive record a copy of—
 (a) any enactment, or
 (b) any document comprised in any other register under the management and control of the Keeper or of the Keeper of the Records of Scotland.

Part 1: The Land Register   351

(4) A fact which can be discovered from the archive record is not, by reason only of that circumstance, a fact which a person ought to know.

The application record

15 The application record

The application record is to consist of all—
- (a) applications for registration as are for the time being pending, and
- (b) advance notices as are for the time being extant.

Tenements etc

16 Tenements and other flatted buildings

(1) Where the Keeper considers it appropriate in relation to a flatted building to do so, the Keeper may, instead of representing each registered flat in the building as a separate cadastral unit, represent the building and all the registered flats in it as a single cadastral unit.

(2) Where a flatted building and the registered flats in it are represented as a single cadastral unit—
- (a) the cadastral map must show, for that cadastral unit, the title numbers of each registered flat, and
- (b) the respective pro indiviso shares in the pertinents of the registered flats need not be entered in the proprietorship section of the title sheet of any of those flats.

(3) But subsections (1) and (2) do not apply in relation to land pertaining to the flatted building which—
- (a) extends more than 25 metres from the building in so far as it so extends, or
- (b) is further than 25 metres from the building (measuring along a horizontal plane from whatever point of that building is nearest to the land).

(4) In this Act a 'flatted building' means—
- (a) a tenement, or
- (b) any other subdivided building.

(5) A 'subdivided building'—
- (a) means a building or part of a building, not being a tenement, which comprises two or more related flats, at least two of which—
  - (i) are, or are designed to be, in separate ownership, and
  - (ii) are divided from each other vertically, and
- (b) includes the solum and any other land pertaining to the building or part of the building.

(6) In determining whether flats comprised in a subdivided building are related, the Keeper must have regard, among other things, to—
- (a) the title to the building, and
- (b) any real burdens.

(7) In subsection (6), 'title to the building' means—
- (a) any conveyance, or reservation, of property which affects the subdivided building, any flat in the building or any pertinent of the building or of any such flat, and
- (b) the relevant title sheet of the building, any flat in it or any pertinent of the building or of any such flat.

(8) Expressions used in this section and in sections 26 and 29 of the Tenements (Scotland) Act 2004 (asp 11) have the meanings given in that Act.

Shared plots

17 Shared plots

(1) This section applies where a plot of land—
- (a) is owned in common by the proprietors of two or more other plots of land by virtue of their ownership of those other plots,
- (b) is not owned in common by anyone else.

(2) The Keeper may, if the Keeper considers it appropriate, designate the title sheet of the plot of land to be a 'shared plot title sheet'.

(3) In this section and in sections 18 and 19—
   (a) references to a 'shared plot' are to a plot of land the title sheet of which is designated under subsection (2),
   (b) references to the 'sharing plots' are to the other plots of land the proprietors of which own the shared plot in common.

(4) Unless the context otherwise requires, any reference in a document to a sharing plot is to be taken to include a reference to the share in the shared plot which pertains to the sharing plot.

(5) Registration has the same effect in relation to a share in a shared plot which pertains to a sharing plot as it has in relation to the sharing plot (except in so far as may otherwise be provided in the deed registered).

18 Shared plot and sharing plot title sheets

(1) The Keeper must enter—
   (a) in the property section of the title sheet of each of the sharing plots, the title number of the shared plot title sheet,
   (b) in the proprietorship section of the shared plot title sheet, the title numbers of the title sheets of each of the sharing plots.

(2) The Keeper must also enter—
   (a) in the property section of the title sheet of each sharing plot, the quantum of the share which the proprietor of that sharing plot has in the shared plot,
   (b) in the proprietorship section of the shared plot title sheet, in relation to the information required by section 7(1)(b), the respective share each sharing plot has in the shared plot,
   (c) in the securities section of that title sheet, a statement to the effect that the shared plot may be subject to a heritable security registered against a sharing plot,
   (d) in the burdens section of that title sheet, a statement to the effect that the shared plot may be subject to some other encumbrance so registered.

(3) The Keeper must not enter in or, if entered, must omit from—
   (a) the proprietorship section of the shared plot title sheet, the information that would otherwise be required under section 7(1)(a),
   (b) the securities section of that title sheet, the information that would otherwise be required under section 8(1) unless the security is over the shared plot only,
   (c) that title sheet, any matter that would otherwise be required under section 10(2)(b).

(4) The Keeper may, if the condition mentioned in subsection (5) is satisfied and the Keeper considers it appropriate, omit from the burdens section of the shared plot title sheet any entry which would otherwise be required under section 9(1).

(5) The condition is that the encumbrance to which the entry would relate is (or falls to be) registered against each of the sharing plots.

19 Conversion of shared plot title sheet to ordinary title sheet

(1) The Keeper may at any time revoke a designation under section 17(2) of a title sheet as a shared plot title sheet.

(2) Where the Keeper revokes a designation, the Keeper must make such changes to the title sheets of the plots of land that were, in relation to the shared plot title sheet, the shared plot and the sharing plots as are consequential upon the revocation.

20 Shared plot title sheets in relation to registered leases

Schedule 1 makes provision for registered leases tenanted in common similar to that made by sections 17 to 19 for plots of land owned in common.

PART 2
REGISTRATION

Applications for registration

21 Application for registration of deed
(1) A person may apply to the Keeper for registration of a registrable deed.
(2) The Keeper must accept an application under subsection (1) to the extent the applicant satisfies the Keeper that, as at the date of application, the general application conditions are met and—
   (a) where the application is made in respect of a disposition of, or a notice of title to, an unregistered plot, the conditions set out in section 23 are met,
   (b) where section 25 applies, the conditions set out in that section are met,
   (c) in any other case, the conditions set out in section 26 are met.
(3) To the extent the applicant does not so satisfy the Keeper, the Keeper must reject the application.
(4) Subsection (2) is subject to section 45(5).

22 General application conditions
(1) The general application conditions are—
   (a) the application is such that the Keeper is able to comply, in respect of it, with such duties as the Keeper has under Part 1,
   (b) the application does not relate to a souvenir plot,
   (c) the application does not fall to be rejected by virtue of section 6 or 9G of the Requirements of Writing (Scotland) Act 1995 (c 7) (registration of document) or of a prohibition in an enactment,
   (d) the application is in the form (if any) prescribed by land register rules, and
   (e) either—
      (i) such fee as is payable for registration is paid, or
      (ii) arrangements satisfactory to the Keeper are made for payment of that fee.
(2) In subsection (1)(b), 'souvenir plot' means a plot of land which—
   (a) is of inconsiderable size and of no practical utility, and
   (b) is neither—
      (i) a registered plot, nor
      (ii) a plot the ownership of which has, at any time, separately been constituted or transferred by a document recorded in the Register of Sasines.

23 Conditions of registration: transfer of unregistered plot
(1) The conditions are that—
   (a) the application is made by the grantee of the disposition or as the case may be the person in whose favour is the notice of title,
   (b) the deed is valid,
   (c) the deed so describes the plot as to enable the Keeper to delineate its boundaries on the cadastral map,
   (d) where within the plot there is a lesser area in respect of which a registrable encumbrance is constituted there is included in, or submitted with, the application a plan or description sufficient to enable the Keeper to delineate the boundaries of the lesser area on the cadastral map,
   (e) there is included in the application a description of every public right of way (by whatever means) over or through the plot in so far as known to the applicant.
(2) Subsection (1)(c) and (d) do not apply—
   (a) if the plot to which the application relates is a flat in a flatted building, and
   (b) either—
      (i) the flatted building is, by virtue of section 16, represented as a single cadastral unit on the cadastral map, or

(ii) the Keeper has indicated that the flatted building is, by virtue of that section, to be so represented.
(3) Despite subsection (2), subsection (1)(c) and (d) apply in so far as the plot includes a pertinent outwith the flatted building, being a pertinent only of the plot.
(4) Subsection (1)(d) does not apply in relation to an encumbrance which consists of—
   (a) a right to lead a pipe, cable, wire or other such enclosed unit over or under land,
   (b) a servitude created other than by registration.
(5) In this section, 'the deed' means the disposition or as the case may be the notice of title.

24 Circumstances in which section 25 applies

(1) Section 25 applies where any of subsections (2) to (7) apply.
(2) This subsection applies where—
   (a) the application is in respect of a grant of a lease, and
   (b) the subjects of the lease consist of or form part of an unregistered plot of land.
(3) This subsection applies where—
   (a) the application is in respect of an assignation of an unregistered lease, and
   (b) the subjects of the lease consist of or form part of an unregistered plot of land.
(4) This subsection applies where—
   (a) the application is in respect of a sublease granted by a tenant, and
   (b) the subjects of the tenant's lease consist of or form part of an unregistered plot of land.
(5) This subsection applies where—
   (a) the application is in respect of a deed registrable by virtue of section 48(4), and
   (b) the land to which the deed relates consists of or forms part of an unregistered plot of land.
(6) This subsection applies where—
   (a) the application is in respect of a notice of title to a subordinate real right,
   (b) the notice of title is registrable by virtue of section 4A (as inserted by section 53(3)) of the Conveyancing (Scotland) Act 1924 (c 27),
   (c) the last completed title to the subordinate real right is recorded in the Register of Sasines, and
   (d) the land in respect of which the subordinate real right is constituted consists of or forms part of an unregistered plot of land.
(7) This subsection applies where—
   (a) the application is in respect of a standard security granted over an unregistered subordinate real right, and
   (b) the land in respect of which the subordinate real right is constituted consists of or forms part of an unregistered plot of land.

25 Conditions of registration: certain deeds relating to unregistered plots

(1) The conditions are that—
   (a) the deed is valid,
   (b) the deed so describes the plot as to enable the Keeper to delineate its boundaries on the cadastral map,
   (c) where within the plot there is a lesser area in respect of which a registrable encumbrance is constituted there is included in, or submitted with, the application a plan or description sufficient to enable the Keeper to delineate the boundaries of the lesser area on the cadastral map,
   (d) there is included in the application a description of every public right of way (by whatever means) over or through the plot in so far as known to the applicant.
(2) Subsection (1)(b) and (c) do not apply—
   (a) if the plot to which the deed relates is a flat in a flatted building, and
   (b) either—

(i) the flatted building is, by virtue of section 16, represented as a single cadastral unit in the cadastral map, or
(ii) the Keeper has indicated that the flatted building is, by virtue of that section, to be so represented.
(3) Despite subsection (2), subsection (1)(b) and (c) apply in so far as the plot includes a pertinent outwith the flatted building, being a pertinent only of the plot.
(4) Subsection (1)(c) does not apply in relation to an encumbrance which consists of—
  (a) a right to lead a pipe, cable, wire or other such enclosed unit over or under land,
  (b) a servitude created other than by registration.
(5) In this section and sections 30 and 41 in so far as they apply by virtue of this section, references to the plot are to be read as references to—
  (a) where this section applies by virtue of section 24(2), (3) or (4), the area of land which forms the subjects of the lease,
  (b) where this section applies by virtue of section 24(5), the area of land to which the deed relates,
  (c) where this section applies by virtue of section 24(6) or (7), the area of land in respect of which the subordinate real right is constituted.

26 Conditions of registration: deeds relating to registered plots

(1) The conditions are that—
  (a) the deed is valid,
  (b) the deed relates to a registered plot of land,
  (c) the deed narrates the title number of each title sheet to which the application relates, and
  (d) the deed, in so far as it relates to part only of a plot of land or of the subjects of a lease, so describes the part as to enable the Keeper to delineate on the cadastral map the boundaries of the part.
(2) Where the title number of the title sheet of a sharing plot is narrated in the deed, subsection (1)(c) does not require the narration of the title number of the title sheet of the shared plot.
(3) Subsection (1)(d) does not apply if—
  (a) the part to which the deed relates is a flat in a flatted building, and
  (b) either—
    (i) the flatted building is, by virtue of section 16, represented as a single cadastral unit in the cadastral map, or
    (ii) the Keeper has indicated that the flatted building is, by virtue of that section, to be so depicted.
(4) Despite subsection (3), subsection (1)(d) applies in so far as the part includes a pertinent outwith the flatted building, being a pertinent only of the part.
(5) Subsection (1)(d) does not apply in the case of an application which relates to registration to create as a servitude a right to lead a pipe, cable, wire or other such enclosed unit over or under land.

Registration without deed

27 Application for voluntary registration

(1) A person mentioned in subsection (2) may apply for registration of an unregistered plot of land or any part of that plot.
(2) The person is the owner (or, in the case of ownership in common, any of the owners) of the plot.
(3) The Keeper must accept an application under subsection (1) to the extent—
  (a) the applicant satisfies the Keeper that, as at the date of the application, the following are met—

(i) the general application conditions, and
(ii) the conditions mentioned in section 28
[…]
(4) To the extent the applicant does not so satisfy the Keeper, the Keeper must reject the application.
(5) Where the application is in respect of a part of a plot of land, references to the plot in section 28 and section 30 in so far as it applies by virtue of this section are to be read as references to the part.
(6) The Scottish Ministers may by order repeal subsection (3)(b).
(7) Before making such an order, the Scottish Ministers must consult the Keeper.
(8) An order under subsection (6) may make different provision for different areas.

NOTE
Subs (3)(b) repealed by Registers of Scotland (Voluntary Registration, Amendment of Fees etc) Order 2015, SSI 2015/265.

28 Conditions of registration: voluntary registration

(1) The conditions are that—
   (a) there is submitted with the application a plan or description of the plot sufficient to enable the Keeper to delineate the plot's boundaries in the cadastral map,
   (b) where within the plot there is a lesser area in respect of which a registrable encumbrance is constituted there is included in, or submitted with, the application a plan or description sufficient to enable the Keeper to delineate the boundaries of the lesser area in the cadastral map.
(2) Subsection (1)(a) and (b) does not apply—
   (a) if the plot to which the application relates is a flat in a flatted building, and
   (b) either—
      (i) the flatted building is, by virtue of section 16, represented as a single cadastral unit on the cadastral map, or
      (ii) the Keeper has indicated that the flatted building is, by virtue of that section, to be so depicted.
(3) Despite subsection (2), subsection (1)(a) and (b) applies in so far as the plot includes a pertinent outwith the flatted building, being a pertinent only of the plot.
(4) Subsection (1)(b) does not apply in relation to an encumbrance which consists of—
   (a) a right to lead a pipe, cable, wire or other such enclosed unit over or under land, or
   (b) a servitude created other than by registration.

29 Keeper-induced registration

(1) Other than on application and irrespective of whether the proprietor or any other person consents, the Keeper may register an unregistered plot of land or part of that plot.
(2) Where the Keeper decides under this section to register a part of a plot, references to the plot in section 30 are to be read as references to the part.

Completion of registration

30 Completion of registration of plot

(1) This section applies where—
   (a) the Keeper accepts—
      (i) an application under section 21 in respect of a disposition of, or a notice of title to, an unregistered plot of land,
      (ii) an application under section 21 by virtue of it meeting the conditions in section 25, or

   (iii) an application under section 27 in respect of a plot of land or a part of a plot, or
 (b) the Keeper decides to register a plot of land or a part of a plot under section 29.
(2) The Keeper must—
 (a) make up a title sheet for the plot,
 (b) make such other changes to the title sheet record as are necessary or expedient,
 (c) create a cadastral unit for the plot,
 (d) make such other changes to the cadastral map as are necessary or expedient, and
 (e) copy into the archive record any document which—
  (i) has been submitted to the Keeper or, where this section applies by virtue of subsection (1)(a)(ii) or (1)(b), is reasonably available to the Keeper, and
  (ii) is relevant to the accuracy of the register.
(3) Subsection (2)(e) is subject to section 14(3).
(4) Changes under paragraph (b) or (d) of subsection (2) may include—
 (a) cancelling a title sheet and cadastral unit, or
 (b) making up a new title sheet and creating a new cadastral unit.
(5) In a case where—
 (a) this section applies by virtue of subsection (1)(a)(ii) or (1)(b), and
 (b) any name or designation to be entered in the new title sheet to be made up cannot, or cannot with reasonable certainty, be determined by the Keeper,

the Keeper may, in place of or as part of that entry, enter a statement that the name or designation is not known or as the case may be is not known with reasonable certainty.

31 Completion of registration of deed

(1) This section applies where the Keeper accepts an application under section 21 other than an application to which section 30 applies.
(2) The Keeper must as soon as reasonably practicable after accepting the application—
 (a) make such changes to the title sheet, or each of the title sheets, to which the application relates as are necessary to give effect to the deed,
 (b) make such other changes (if any) to the title sheet record as are necessary or expedient,
 (c) make such changes (if any) to the cadastral map as are necessary or expedient, and
 (d) copy into the archive record—
  (i) the deed being given effect to by registration, and
  (ii) any other document which has been submitted to the Keeper and is relevant to the accuracy of the register.
(3) Subsection (2)(d)(ii) is subject to section 14(3).
(4) Changes under paragraphs (a) to (c) of subsection (2) may include—
 (a) cancelling a title sheet and cadastral unit, or
 (b) making up a new title sheet and creating a new cadastral unit.

32 References to certain entries in Register of Inhibitions

(1) Subsection (2) applies where—
 (a) the Keeper accepts an application for registration under section 21, and
 (b) the validity of the deed to which the application relates might be affected by an entry in the Register of Inhibitions.
(2) The Keeper must, as soon as reasonably practicable after accepting the application, enter a reference to the entry in the title sheet.
(3) Subsection (2) does not apply where the entry mentioned in subsection (1)(b) is—
 (a) a notice of land attachment (within the meaning of section 83(1) of the Bankruptcy and Diligence etc (Scotland) Act 2007 (asp 3)), or
 (b) a notice of a signeted summons in an action of reduction of a deed granted in breach of inhibition.

General provision about applications

33 Recording in application record

(1) On receipt of an application for registration, the Keeper must—
    (a) as soon as reasonably practicable, or
    (b) if the application record is not open for the making of entries, as soon as reasonably practicable on the application record next opening for that purpose,
    enter in the application record details of the application (including the date the entry under this subsection is made).
(2) No such entry need be made however if, on receipt of the application, it is immediately apparent to the Keeper that the application falls to be rejected.
(3) On an application being—
    (a) withdrawn,
    (b) accepted by the Keeper, or
    (c) rejected by the Keeper,
    the Keeper must remove the entry relating to it from the application record.

34 Withdrawal and amendments etc of application

(1) While an application for registration is pending, the applicant—
    (a) may withdraw it, but
    (b) except with the consent of the Keeper, may not substitute it or amend it.
(2) Land register rules may specify circumstances in which consent under subsection (1)(b) must be given.

35 Period within which decision must be made

(1) The Keeper's decision as to whether to accept or reject an application for registration must be made within such period as may be prescribed in land register rules.
(2) Different periods may be so prescribed for different kinds of application.
(3) The Keeper must deal with an application without unreasonable delay.

Date of application and registration etc

36 Date of application

Any reference in this Act, however expressed, to the date of an application for registration is a reference to the date an entry in respect of the application is made in the application record under subsection (1) of section 33 (or, but for subsection (2) of that section, would fall to be made).

37 Date and time of registration

(1) Where the Keeper accepts an application for registration, the date of registration is the date of the application.
(2) The time of registration is deemed to be the moment at which, following the application being received by the Keeper, the application record next closes.
(3) The Scottish Ministers may by order—
    (a) amend subsection (2) so as to make different provision as regards time of registration, and
    (b) make such other amendments to this Act as are consequential upon that amendment.
(4) Before making such an order, the Scottish Ministers must consult the Keeper.

38 Power to amend section 6 of the Land Registers (Scotland) Act 1868

If, under section 37(3)(a), the Scottish Ministers amend this Act, they may, in that order, correspondingly amend section 6 of the Land Registers (Scotland) Act 1868 (c 64) (which provides for registration in the General Register of Sasines) and make such other amendments to that Act as are consequential upon that amendment to that section.

Applications in relation to the same land

39 Order in which applications are to be dealt with

(1) The Keeper must deal with two or more applications for registration in relation to the same land in order of receipt.
(2) In the absence of evidence to the contrary, the order of receipt is to be taken to be the order in which the details of the applications were entered in the application record.
(3) Subsection (1) is subject to subsections (4) to (8).
(4) Subsection (5) applies where—
   (a) two applications ('application A' and 'application B') are received on the same date in relation to the same land,
   (b) to accept one of the applications would require the Keeper to reject the other,
   (c) the deed to which application A purports to give effect is a deed in relation to which a protected period is running, and
   (d) the deed to which application B purports to give effect either—
      (i) is not such a deed, or
      (ii) is such a deed but the protected period relating to the deed to which application A purports to give effect began before the protected period relating to the deed to which application B purports to give effect.
(5) The Keeper must deal with application A before application B.
(6) Subsection (8) applies where—
   (a) two applications ('application C' and 'application D') are received on the same date in relation to the same land,
   (b) the deed to which one of them (application C) purports to give effect is a deed in favour of a person ('X'), and
   (c) the deed to which the other (application D) purports to give effect is a deed granted by X.
(7) Subsection (8) also applies where—
   (a) two applications ('application C' and 'application D') are received on the same date in relation to the same land,
   (b) one application (application C) is an application under section 27, and
   (c) the other (application D) is an application under section 21.
(8) The Keeper must deal with application C before application D.

Notification

40 Notification of acceptance, rejection or withdrawal of application

(1) On an application for registration being accepted or rejected, the Keeper must notify—
   (a) the applicant,
   (b) the granter of the deed sought to be registered (if any),
   (c) if notification of receipt of the application was given under section 45(1), those to whom it was given, and
   (d) any other person the Keeper considers appropriate.
(2) On an application for registration being withdrawn, the Keeper must notify—
   (a) the granter of the deed which had been sought to be registered (if any),
   (b) if such notification as is mentioned in subsection (1)(c) was given, those to whom it was given, and
   (c) any other person the Keeper considers appropriate.
(3) The Keeper's duty to notify persons under subsections (1) and (2) only applies in so far as the Keeper considers it reasonably practicable to notify them.
(4) Notification is to be by such means as the Keeper considers appropriate.
(5) Land register rules may make further provision about notification under subsections (1) and (2).

(6) A failure to comply with subsections (1) and (2) or with any rules so made does not affect the competence or validity of the acceptance, rejection or withdrawal in question.

41 Notification to proprietor

(1) This section applies where—
    (a) the Keeper accepts an application under section 21 by virtue of it meeting the conditions in section 25, or
    (b) the Keeper registers a plot of land under section 29.
(2) The Keeper is to notify—
    (a) the proprietor of the plot, and
    (b) any other person the Keeper considers appropriate.
(3) The Keeper's duty to notify persons under subsection (2) only applies in so far as the Keeper considers it reasonably practicable to notify them.
(4) Notification is to be by such means as the Keeper considers appropriate.
(5) Land register rules may make further provision about notification under subsection (2).
(6) A failure to comply with subsection (2) or with any rules so made does not affect the competence or validity—
    (a) of the acceptance of the application in question, or
    (b) of the registration of the plot of land in question.

42 Notification to Scottish Ministers of certain applications

(1) This section applies where an application under section 21 is rejected on the ground that (or on grounds which include the ground that) the Keeper is not satisfied that the application does not relate to a transfer prohibited—
    (a) by section 40(1) of the Land Reform (Scotland) Act 2003 (asp 2) (effect of registration of community interest in land), or
    (b) under section 37(5)(e) of that Act (prohibition pending determination as to whether a community interest in land is to be registered).
(2) However, this section does not apply where the only reason for the Keeper not being satisfied as mentioned in subsection (1) is that the application is not accompanied by a declaration required under section 43(2) of that Act (incorporation of certain declarations into deed giving effect to transfer).
(3) The Keeper must—
    (a) notify the Scottish Ministers, and
    (b) provide them with a copy of the application.

Prescriptive claimants etc

43 Prescriptive claimants

(1) For the purposes of sections 23(1)(b), and 26(1)(a), a disposition is to be treated as being valid despite not being so if the conditions mentioned in subsections (2) to (4) are met.
(2) It appears to the Keeper that the disposition is not valid (or, as regards part of the land to which the application relates, is not valid) for the reason only that the person who granted it had no title to do so.
(3) The applicant satisfies the Keeper that the land to which the application relates (or as the case may be the part in question) has been possessed openly, peaceably and without judicial interruption—
    (a) by the disponer or the applicant for a continuous period of 1 year immediately preceding the date of application, or

Part 2: Registration 361

    (b) first by the disponer and then by the applicant for periods which together constitute such a period.
(4) The applicant satisfies the Keeper that the following person has been notified of the application—
    (a) the proprietor,
    (b) if there is no proprietor (or none can be identified), any person who appears to be able to take steps to complete title as proprietor, or
    (c) if there is no proprietor and no such person (or, in either case, none can be identified), the Crown.
(5) For the purposes of section 26(1)(a), a deed is to be treated as being valid despite not being so if—
    (a) the deed is granted by or is directed against a prescriptive claimant, and
    (b) the application would be accepted were the prescriptive claimant's title valid.
(6) In subsection (5), a 'prescriptive claimant' is—
    (a) a person whose name is entered as proprietor in the proprietorship section of a title sheet, on an application being accepted by virtue of subsection (1),
    (b) a person whose name is entered as holder of a right, in the appropriate section of a title sheet, the entry in relation to the right being one marked provisional under section 81(3)(a)(i),
    (c) any person in right of a person mentioned in paragraph (a) or (b).
(7) Land register rules may make further provision about notification under subsection (4).
(8) The Scottish Ministers may, by order, amend subsection (3) so as to substitute for the period for the time being mentioned there a different period.
(9) Before making such an order, the Scottish Ministers must consult the Keeper.

44 Provisional entries on title sheet

(1) Where the Keeper accepts an application under section 21 by virtue of section 43(1) or (5), the Keeper is to mark any resulting entry in the title sheet as provisional.
(2) The Keeper is to remove the provisional marking from an entry if and when the real right to which the entry relates becomes, under section 1 of the Prescription and Limitation (Scotland) Act 1973 (c 52) (validity of right), exempt from challenge.
(3) While an entry remains provisional—
    (a) it does not affect any right held by any person in the land to which the entry relates, and
    (b) rights set out in the register are not to be altered or deleted by virtue only of the entry.

45 Notification of prescriptive applications

(1) Before accepting an application under section 21 which is received by virtue of section 43(1), the Keeper must notify—
    (a) the proprietor,
    (b) if there is no proprietor (or none can be identified), any person who appears to the Keeper able to take steps to complete title as proprietor, or
    (c) if there is no proprietor and no such person (or, in either case, none can be identified), the Crown.
(2) The Keeper's duty to notify persons under subsection (1) only applies in so far as the Keeper considers it reasonably practicable to notify them.
(3) Notification is to be by such means as the Keeper considers appropriate.
(4) A person to whom notice is given under subsection (1) may object in writing to the application being accepted.
(5) If the Keeper receives such an objection within 60 days of the notice, the Keeper must reject the application.

(6) Land register rules may make further provision about notification under subsection (1).
(7) The Scottish Ministers may, by order, amend subsection (5) so as to substitute for the number of days for the time being mentioned there a different number of days.
(8) Before making such an order, the Scottish Ministers must consult the Keeper.

Further provision

46 Applications relating to compulsory acquisition

In the application of sections 21, 23, 30 and 48 to a case in which transfer of ownership is by virtue of compulsory acquisition, any reference in those sections to a 'disposition' includes a reference to—
(a) a conveyance the form of which is provided for by an enactment,
(b) a notarial instrument, or
(c) a general vesting declaration.

47 Effect of death or dissolution

(1) The Keeper must reject an application if the applicant dies, or as the case may be is dissolved, before the date of the application.
(2) An application is not incompetent by reason only that the person who granted the deed sought to be registered dies, or as the case may be is dissolved, after the delivery of the deed.

Closure of Register of Sasines etc

48 Closure of Register of Sasines etc

(1) The recording of any of the following in the Register of Sasines has no effect—
   (a) a disposition,
   (b) a lease,
   (c) an assignation of a lease,
   (d) any other deed in so far as it relates to a registered plot of land or to a registered lease.
(2) The recording, on or after such day as is prescribed, of a standard security in the Register of Sasines has no effect.
(3) The recording, on or after such day as is prescribed, of a deed other than one mentioned in subsection (1) or (2) in the Register of Sasines has no effect.
(4) On and after the day prescribed under subsection (3), any deed the recording of which would, by virtue of that subsection, have no effect is (subject to the provisions of this Act) registrable in the Land Register.
(5) Where by virtue of this section the recording of a deed, disposition, lease, assignation or standard security in the Register of Sasines would have no effect, the Keeper is to reject any application to record it.
(6) Subsection (1)(a) is without prejudice to sections 4 (creation of real burden) and 75 (creation of positive servitude by writing: deed to be registered) of the Title Conditions (Scotland) Act 2003 (asp 9).
(7) Any day prescribed under subsection (2) or (3) is to be a day no earlier than the day subsection (3)(b) of section 27 is repealed by virtue of subsection (6) of that section.
(8) In subsections (2) and (3), 'prescribed' means prescribed by the Scottish Ministers by order.
(9) An order under subsection (2) or (3) may make different provision for different areas.
(10) Before making an order under subsection (2) or (3), the Scottish Ministers must consult—
   (a) the Keeper, and

(b) such other persons appearing to have an interest in the closure of the Register of Sasines to the recording of deeds as the Scottish Ministers consider appropriate.

Entry of information relating to categories of owners and tenants in the register

48A Power to request or require information relating to categories of owners and tenants

(1) The Scottish Ministers may, by regulations, make provision enabling the Keeper to request or, as the case may be, require information relating to the category of person or body into which a person mentioned in subsection (2) falls.
(2) The persons referred to in subsection (1) ('relevant persons') are—
    (a) owners of plots of land,
    (b) proprietors of registered plots of land and registered leases, and
    (c) tenants of leases which are registered or registrable.
(3) Regulations under subsection (1) may, in particular, make provision—
    (a) about the persons who are owners, proprietors and tenants for the purposes of subsection (2),
    (b) about the information, relating to the category of person or body into which a relevant person falls, provision of which may be requested or required,
    (c) about the form in which the information is to be provided, which may consist of (or include) declarations by, or on behalf of, relevant persons about the category of person or body into which a relevant person falls,
    (d) about the circumstances in which information may be requested,
    (e) about the circumstances in which information requires, and does not require, to be provided,
    (f) about the effect (if any) of providing (or not providing) information,
    (g) about the entry of the information in the register,
    (h) about whether the Keeper's warranty under Part 7 is to apply in relation to information obtained under the regulations,
    (i) about the circumstances in which information obtained under the regulations may be corrected or updated,
    (j) about the circumstances in which information obtained under the regulations may be provided to other persons,
    (k) about the circumstances in which information obtained under the regulations may be published,
    (l) for fees relating to the provision, correction or updating of information under the regulations.
(4) Regulations under subsection (1) which make provision enabling the Keeper to require information may include provision relating to offences for failure to comply with requirements imposed by the regulations.
(5) Where regulations under subsection (1) include provision creating offences—
    (a) they must provide for those offences to be triable summarily only, and
    (b) they must provide for the maximum penalty for those offences to be a fine, which must not exceed level 3 on the standard scale.
(6) The Scottish Ministers must consult the Keeper before laying a draft of regulations under subsection (1) before the Scottish Parliament.
(7) Regulations under subsection (1) may include such incidental, supplementary or consequential provision as the Scottish Ministers consider appropriate for the purposes of, or in connection with, the regulations.
(8) Regulations under subsection (1) may modify any enactment (including this Act).

NOTE

Cross-heading and s 48A inserted by Land Reform (Scotland) Act 2016 (c 18) s 43(2). At the date of going to press, this provision was not in force.

48B Power to enter information relating to categories of owners and tenants in the register

(1) The Scottish Ministers may, by regulations, make provision enabling the Keeper to enter, in the register, information relating to the category of person or body into which a person mentioned in subsection (2) falls.
(2) The persons referred to in subsection (1) ('relevant persons') are—
   (a) owners of plots of land,
   (b) proprietors of registered plots of land and registered leases, and
   (c) tenants of leases which are registered or registrable.
(3) Regulations under subsection (1) may, in particular, make provision—
   (a) about the persons who are owners, proprietors and tenants for the purposes of subsection (2),
   (b) about notification by the Keeper of the intention to enter the information,
   (c) about the circumstances in which the Keeper may enter the information,
   (d) for the information that may be entered and the form in which it is to be entered,
   (e) about the effect (if any) of entering the information,
   (f) about whether the Keeper's warranty under Part 7 is to apply in relation to information entered under the regulations,
   (g) about the circumstances in which information entered under the regulations may be corrected or updated,
   (h) about the circumstances in which information entered under the regulations may be provided to other persons,
   (i) about the circumstances in which information entered under the regulations may be published,
   (j) for fees relating to the correction or updating of information under the regulations.
(4) The Scottish Ministers must consult the Keeper before laying a draft of regulations under subsection (1) before the Scottish Parliament.
(5) Regulations under subsection (1) may include such incidental, supplementary or consequential provision as the Scottish Ministers consider appropriate for the purposes of, or in connection with, the regulations.
(6) Regulations under subsection (1) may modify any enactment (including this Act).

NOTE

Section 48B inserted by Land Reform (Scotland) Act 2016 (c 18) s 43(2). At the date of going to press, this provision was not in force.

PART 3
COMPETENCE AND EFFECT OF REGISTRATION

Registrable deeds

49 Registrable deeds

(1) A deed is registrable only if and in so far as its registration is authorised (whether expressly or not) by—
   (a) this Act,
   (b) an enactment mentioned in subsection (3), or
   (c) any other enactment.

Part 3: Competence and Effect of Registration   365

(2) Registration of such a deed has the effect provided for (whether expressly or not) by—
    (a) this Act,
    (b) an enactment mentioned in subsection (3),
    (c) any other enactment, or
    (d) any rule of law.
(3) The enactments referred to in subsections (1) and (2) are—
    (a) the Registration of Leases (Scotland) Act 1857 (c 26),
    (b) the Conveyancing (Scotland) Act 1924 (c 27),
    (c) the Conveyancing and Feudal Reform (Scotland) Act 1970 (c 35),
    (d) the Law Reform (Miscellaneous Provisions) (Scotland) Act 1985 (c 73).
(4) Registration of an invalid deed confers real effect only to the extent that an enactment so provides.

Specific provisions on competence and effect of registration

50 Transfer by disposition
(1) A disposition of land may be registered.
(2) Registration of a valid disposition transfers ownership.
(3) An unregistered disposition does not transfer ownership.
(4) Subsections (1) to (3) are subject to—
    (a) sections 43 and 86, and
    (b) any other enactment or rule of law by or under which ownership of land may pass.
(5) In subsection (1), 'land' includes land held on udal title.

51 Proper liferents
(1) A deed creating a proper liferent over land may be—
    (a) registered, or
    (b) recorded in the Register of Sasines.
(2) The proper liferent is not created before the deed is so registered or recorded.
(3) Subsections (1) and (2) are subject to any other enactment or any rule of law by or under which a proper liferent over land may be created.
(4) References in this section to the recording of a deed include references to the recording of a notice of title deducing title through a deed.

52 Registration of, and of transactions and events affecting, leases
(1) The Registration of Leases (Scotland) Act 1857 (c 26) is amended as follows.
(2) After section 20 insert—

'**20A Certain transactions or events registrable in the Land Register of Scotland**
(1) A deed mentioned in subsection (2) which affects a lease registered in the Land Register of Scotland is registrable in that register.
(2) The deed is one—
    (a) terminating the lease,
    (b) extending the duration of the lease,
    (c) otherwise altering the terms of the lease.

20B Effect of registration in the Land Register of Scotland
(1) Registration in the Land Register of Scotland has the effect of—
    (a) vesting in the person registered as entitled to the lease a real right in and to the lease and in and to any right or pertinent, express or implied, forming part of the lease, subject only to the effect of any matter entered in that register so far as adverse to the entitlement,
    (b) making any registered right or obligation relating to the registered lease a real right or obligation, and

(c) affecting any registered real right or obligation relating to the registered lease, in so far as the right or obligation is capable, under any enactment or rule of law, of being vested as a real right, of being made real or (as the case may be) of being affected as a real right.

(2) Registration in the Land Register of Scotland is the only means—
   (a) whereby rights or obligations relating to a registered lease become real rights or obligations, or
   (b) of affecting such real rights or obligations.

(3) Subject to Part 9 of the Land Registration etc (Scotland) Act 2012 (asp 5) (rights to persons acquiring etc in good faith), registration of an invalid deed confers no real effect.'.

(3) Schedule 2, which contains minor and consequential modifications of the 1857 Act in consequence on this Act, has effect.

53 Completion of title

(1) The Conveyancing (Scotland) Act 1924 (c 27) is amended as follows.

(2) In section 4 (completion of title)—
   (a) for 'by a title which has not been completed by being recorded in the appropriate Register of Sasines, may' substitute 'may, if the last recorded title to the right is recorded in the General Register of Sasines,',
   (b) the title of the section becomes 'Completion of title: General Register of Sasines'.

(3) After section 4 insert—

'4A Completion of title: Land Register

Any person having right either to land or to a heritable security may complete title by registration in the Land Register of a notice of title in or as nearly as may be in the terms of the form in schedule BA to this Act.

4B Further provision as regards completion of title

(1) If it is competent to register a disposition or assignation in the Land Register, it is not competent for the disponee or assignee to complete title in the manner provided for in section 4 of this Act.

(2) In this section and in section 4A of this Act, 'Land Register' means the Land Register of Scotland.'.

(4) After section 49 insert—

'49A Power of the Scottish Ministers to prescribe forms

(1) The Scottish Ministers may, by order, modify any schedule to this Act.

(2) Such an order may, in particular, substitute for any form, notice, clause, warrant or other deed for the time being set out in such a schedule another such form, notice, clause, warrant or other deed.

(3) An order under this section is subject to the affirmative procedure.'.

(5) After schedule B insert—

'SCHEDULE BA

Form of notice of title: Land Register'

Be it known that *A.B.* (*designation*) has right as proprietor to all and whole (*description*) conform to the last completed title and subsequent writ (*or* writs), which title and writ (*or* writs) have been examined by me, *Y.Z.* (*designation*), Notary Public (*or* Law Agent).

[*Testing clause*]
Y.Z.

NOTES TO SCHEDULE BA

Note 1: Where the notice is in respect of a subordinate real right, other than a registered lease having its own title sheet, for 'proprietor to' substitute 'holder of liferent (*or other right, as the case may be*) over'.

Note 2: Where the notice is in respect of a registered lease having its own title sheet, for 'proprietor to' substitute 'tenant of'.

Note 3: If any writ by which A.B. acquired right contains a new title condition, whether burdening or benefiting the property, the condition is to be inserted in full after the description of the property.

Note 4: in the case of a traditional document, subscription of it by the notary public (or law agent) on behalf of the granter will suffice for the document to be formally valid, but witnessing of it may be necessary or desirable for other purposes: see the Requirements of Writing (Scotland) Act 1995 (c 7) (which also makes provision as regards the authentication of an electronic document).'

54 Registration of decree of reduction

After section 46 of the Conveyancing (Scotland) Act 1924 (c 27) insert—

'46A Further provision as regards decree of reduction

(1) Where a deed mentioned in subsection (2) is reduced, the decree of reduction—
   (a) may be registered in the Land Register of Scotland, and
   (b) does not have real effect until so registered.
(2) The deed is one which—
   (a) is voidable, and
   (b) relates to a plot of land or lease registered in the Land Register of Scotland.
(3) Subsection (1) applies to an arbitral award which—
   (a) orders the reduction of a deed mentioned in subsection (2), and
   (b) may be enforced in accordance with section 12 of the Arbitration (Scotland) Act 2010 (asp 1),
   as it applies to a decree of reduction.'.

55 Registration of order for rectification of document etc

(1) The Law Reform (Miscellaneous Provisions) (Scotland) Act 1985 (c 73) is amended as follows.
(2) In section 8 (rectification of defectively expressed documents)—
   (a) in subsection (3), after 'made to it' insert 'and in either case after calling all parties who appear to it to have an interest',
   (b) after that subsection insert—

   '(3A) If a document is registered in the Land Register of Scotland in favour of a person acting in good faith then, unless the person consents to rectification of the document, it is not competent to order its rectification under subsection (3) above.',

   (c) in subsection (4), for 'section 9(4)' substitute 'sections 8A and 9(4)'.
(3) After section 8 insert—

'8A Registration of order for rectification

An order for rectification made under section 8 of this Act in respect of a document which has been registered in the Land Register of Scotland—
   (a) may be registered in that register, and
   (b) does not have real effect until so registered.'.

(4) In section 9 (provisions supplementary to section 8: protection of other interest)—
   (a) in subsection (2)—
      (i) for 'subsection (3)' substitute 'subsections (2A) and (3)',
      (ii) repeal 'or on the title sheet of an interest in land registered in the Land Register of Scotland being an interest to which the document relates',
   (b) after that subsection insert—

'(2A) This section does not apply where the document to be rectified is a deed registered in the Land Register of Scotland.',
  (c) in subsection (3)—
    (i) in paragraph (a), repeal 'or (as the case may be) the title sheet',
    (ii) in paragraph (b), repeal 'or on the title sheet',
  (d) subsection (6) is repealed.

PART 4
ADVANCE NOTICES

56 Advance notices

(1) An advance notice is a notice—
  (a) stating that a person intends to grant a deed to another person,
  (b) stating the name and designation of both persons,
  (c) describing the nature of the intended deed (as for example whether it is to be a disposition),
  (d) where the intended deed relates to a registered lease or a registered plot of land—
    (i) stating the title number of the title sheet to which the deed is to relate,
    (ii) where the deed is to relate to a registered lease which does not have a lease title sheet, stating the particulars of the lease, and
    (iii) where the deed is to relate to part only of the subjects of the lease, or to part only of the plot, describing the part so as to enable the Keeper to delineate on the cadastral map the boundaries of the part, and
  (e) where the intended deed relates to an unregistered lease or unregistered plot of land, describing the lease or, as the case may be, plot.
(2) Subsection (1)(d)(iii) does not apply if—
  (a) the part to which the deed relates is a flat in a flatted building, and
  (b) either—
    (i) the flatted building is, by virtue of section 16, represented as a single cadastral unit on the cadastral map, or
    (ii) the Keeper has indicated that the flatted building is, by virtue of that section, to be so depicted.
(3) Despite subsection (2), subsection (1)(d)(iii) applies in so far as the part includes a pertinent outwith the flatted building, being a pertinent only of the part.
(4) The Scottish Ministers may by regulations make provision about the description to be contained in an advance notice by virtue of subsection (1)(e).

57 Application for advance notice

(1) A person falling within subsection (2) may apply to the Keeper for an advance notice in relation to a registrable deed which the person intends to grant.
(2) A person falls within this subsection if—
  (a) the person may validly grant the intended deed, or
  (b) the person has the consent of such a person to apply.
(3) The Keeper may accept an application under subsection (1) only if—
  (a) such fee as is payable in respect of the application is paid, or
  (b) arrangements satisfactory to the Keeper are made for payment of that fee.
(4) If the Keeper accepts an application under subsection (1), the Keeper must—
  (a) where the intended deed relates to a registered lease or a registered plot of land—
    (i) as soon as reasonably practicable or, if the application record is not open for the making of entries, as soon as reasonably practicable on the application record next opening for that purpose, enter an advance notice in the application record, and

(ii) where (and to the extent that) section 56(1)(d)(iii) applies in relation to the notice, delineate the boundaries of the part on the cadastral map,
(b) in any other case, record an advance notice in the Register of Sasines.

NOTE
Section 57(4)(a) amended by Land Registration etc (Scotland) Act 2012 (Incidental, Consequential and Transitional) Order 2014, SSI 2014/190, art 4.

58 Period of effect of advance notice

(1) An advance notice has effect for the period of 35 days beginning with the day after the notice is entered in the application record or, as the case may be, recorded in the Register of Sasines.
(2) Subsection (1) is subject to section 63.
(3) The period during which an advance notice has effect is referred to in this Act as the 'protected period'.
(4) Subsection (5) applies where two advance notices in relation to the same plot of land or lease are entered into the application record or recorded in the Register of Sasines on the same date.
(5) The protected period in relation to the advance notice which is first to be entered in the application record, or as the case may be recorded in the Register of Sasines, is deemed to begin before the protected period in relation to the other advance notice.
(6) The Scottish Ministers may, by order amend subsection (1) so as to substitute for the period for the time being mentioned there a different period.
(7) Before making such an order, the Scottish Ministers must consult the Keeper.

59 Effect of advance notice: registered deeds

(1) Subsections (2) and (3) apply in relation to any two deeds ('deed Y' and 'deed Z') relating to the same plot of land where—
  (a) during a protected period relating to deed Y—
    (i) an application is made for registration of deed Z, and
    (ii) on or after the date of that application, an application is made for registration of deed Y, and
  (b) deed Z either—
    (i) is not a deed in relation to which a protected period is running, or
    (ii) is such a deed, but the protected period relating to deed Y began before the protected period relating to deed Z.
(2) If deed Z is registered before the Keeper comes to make any decision as to whether or not to accept the application for registration of deed Y, that decision is to be taken as if deed Z had not been registered.
(3) If the decision mentioned in subsection (2) is to accept the application—
  (a) deed Y has on registration the same effect as if deed Z had not been registered, and
  (b) the Keeper must amend the register so that it gives effect (if any) to deed Z as if it were registered after deed Y.

60 Effect of advance notice: recorded deeds

(1) Subsections (2) and (3) apply in relation to any two deeds ('deed Y' and 'deed Z') relating to the same plot of land where, during a protected period relating to deed Y—
  (a) deed Z is recorded in the Register of Sasines, and
  (b) on or after the date of recording, an application is made for registration of deed Y.
(2) The decision as to whether or not to accept the application for registration of deed Y is to be taken as if deed Z had not been recorded.
(3) If the decision mentioned in subsection (2) is to accept the application—

(a) deed Y has on registration the same effect as if deed Z had not been recorded, and
(b) in making up the title sheet for the plot, the Keeper must give effect (if any) to deed Z as if it were not recorded but registered after deed Y.

61 Effect of advance notice: further provision

(1) A deed to which an advance notice relates, if registered on a date which falls within the protected period, is not subject to—
   (a) an inhibition registered in the Register of Inhibitions against the granter and taking effect before that date but during that period, or
   (b) anything registered or recorded in that register and taking effect, before that date but during that period, as if an inhibition registered against the granter.
(2) Sections 59 and 60 apply irrespective of whether a deed is voluntary or involuntary.
(3) Sections 59 and 60 do not apply in relation to—
   (a) a notice registered, or intended or sought to be registered, under—
       (i) section 10(2A) of the Title Conditions (Scotland) Act 2003 (asp 9), or
       (ii) section 12(3) of the Tenements (Scotland) Act 2004 (asp 11), and
   (b) such other deeds as the Scottish Ministers may by order specify.
(4) Before making an order under subsection (3)(b), the Scottish Ministers must consult the Keeper.

62 Removal of advance notice etc

(1) After the protected period in relation to an advance notice has elapsed, the Keeper must, if the notice was entered in the application record—
   (a) remove it from there, and
   (b) if the notice has not already been entered in the archive record, enter it in that record.
(2) After such period in relation to an advance notice as may be prescribed in land register rules the Keeper must, if the intended deed has not been registered, remove from the cadastral map any delineation effected under section 57(4)(a)(ii).

63 Discharge of advance notice

(1) A person who applied for an advance notice may apply to the Keeper for the discharge of that notice.
(2) An application under subsection (1) may be made only during the protected period.
(3) The Keeper may accept an application under subsection (1) only if—
   (a) the person to whom the intended deed would be granted consents, and
   (b) either—
       (i) such fee as is payable in respect of the application is paid, or
       (ii) arrangements satisfactory to the Keeper are made for payment of that fee.
(4) If the Keeper accepts the application, the Keeper must—
   (a) if the advance notice was entered in the application record—
       (i) remove it from there, and
       (ii) if the notice has not already been entered in the archive record, enter it in that record,
   (b) if the advance notice was recorded in the Register of Sasines, record a notice of discharge in relation to the advance notice.
(5) On the advance notice being removed from the application record or, as the case may be, a notice of discharge being recorded, the advance notice ceases to have effect.

64 Application of Part to specific deeds

(1) The Scottish Ministers may by order modify the application of this Part in relation to any deed of a kind specified in the order.
(2) Before making such an order, the Scottish Ministers must consult the Keeper.

PART 5
INACCURACIES IN THE REGISTER

65 Meaning of 'inaccuracy'

(1) A title sheet is inaccurate in so far as it—
  (a) misstates what the position is in law or in fact,
  (b) omits anything required, by or under an enactment, to be included in it, or
  (c) includes anything the inclusion of which is not expressly or impliedly permitted by or under an enactment.
(2) The cadastral map is inaccurate in so far as it—
  (a) wrongly depicts or shows what the position is in law or in fact,
  (b) omits anything required, by or under an enactment, to be depicted or shown on it, or
  (c) depicts or shows anything the depiction or showing of which is not expressly or impliedly permitted by or under an enactment.
(3) The cadastral map is not inaccurate in so far as it does not depict something correctly by reason only of an inexactness in the base map which is within the published accuracy tolerances relevant to the scale of map involved.
(4) Neither a title sheet nor the cadastral map is inaccurate by reason only that a deed which gave rise to the acquisition, variation or discharge of a real right—
  (a) was voidable and has been reduced, or
  (b) has been rectified under section 8 of the Law Reform (Miscellaneous Provisions) (Scotland) Act 1985 (c 73) (rectification of defectively expressed documents).
(5) This section is subject to section 66(3).

66 Shifting boundaries

(1) This section applies where the proprietors of adjacent plots of land affected by alluvion agree that their common boundary (or part of it) is not to be so affected.
(2) Such an agreement may, on the joint application of both proprietors, be registered in the title sheets of both plots of land.
(3) Where such an agreement is registered, the cadastral map and the title sheets of the plots do not become inaccurate as a result of alluvion affecting the boundary (or part of it) occurring after registration.

PART 6
CAVEATS

67 Warrant to place a caveat

(1) This section applies to civil proceedings—
  (a) for the reduction of a registered deed on the ground that it is voidable,
  (b) which could result in a judicial determination that the register is inaccurate, or
  (c) for an order which, if granted, would be registrable under section 8A of the Law Reform (Miscellaneous Provisions) (Scotland) Act 1985 (c 73) (registration of order for rectification).
(2) A party to the proceedings may, at any time while the proceedings are in dependence, apply to the court for warrant to place a caveat on the title sheet of a plot of land to which the proceedings relate.
(3) The court may, if satisfied as to the matters mentioned in subsection (4), make an order granting the warrant applied for.
(4) The matters are that—
  (a) the applicant has a prima facie case on the merits of the proceedings,
  (b) were warrant for placing the caveat not granted, there is a real and substantial risk that enforcement of any decree or order in the proceedings granted in favour of the

applicant would be defeated or prejudiced by reason of the other party being likely to deal with the plot of land, and
  (c) in all the circumstances, including the effect which granting the warrant may have on any person having an interest, it is reasonable to make the order granting it.
(5) The onus is on the applicant to satisfy the court that the order granting the warrant should be made.

68 Duration of caveat

(1) A caveat, warrant for which is granted under section 67(3), expires 12 months after it is placed on the title sheet unless renewed, recalled or discharged before the expiry of that period.
(2) Subsection (1) applies to a caveat renewed under section 69(2) as it applies to a caveat, warrant for which is granted under section 67(3).
(3) The Scottish Ministers may, by order, amend subsection (1) so as to substitute for the period for the time being mentioned in the subsection a different period.
(4) Before making such an order, the Scottish Ministers must consult the Keeper.

69 Renewal of caveat

(1) The applicant may apply to the court which granted the warrant to place the caveat for warrant to renew it.
(2) The court may, if satisfied as to the matters mentioned in subsection (3), make an order granting warrant to renew the caveat.
(3) The matters are that—
  (a) the applicant has a prima facie case on the merits of the proceedings,
  (b) were warrant to renew the caveat not granted, there is a real and substantial risk that enforcement of any decree or order in the proceedings granted in favour of the applicant would be defeated or prejudiced by reason of the other party being likely to deal with the plot of land, and
  (c) in all the circumstances, including the effect which renewing the caveat may have on any person having an interest, it is reasonable to make the order renewing it.
(4) The onus is on the applicant to satisfy the court that the order renewing the caveat should be made.
(5) The court may renew a caveat on more than one occasion.
(6) In this section and in sections 70 and 71, 'the applicant' means the person who has placed a caveat on the title sheet.

70 Restriction of caveat

(1) Any person with an interest, other than the applicant, may at any time apply to the court which granted the warrant to place the caveat for an order restricting the caveat.
(2) The court may, if satisfied—
  (a) as to the matters mentioned in subsection (3), and
  (b) that it is reasonable in all the circumstances to do so,
  make an order restricting the caveat.
(3) The matters are that—
  (a) the applicant has a prima facie case on the merits of the proceedings,
  (b) there is a real and substantial risk that enforcement of any decree or order in the proceedings granted in favour of the applicant would be defeated or prejudiced by reason of the other party being likely to deal with the plot of land, and
  (c) in all the circumstances, including the effect which granting the warrant to place the caveat may have on any person having an interest, it is reasonable for the caveat to continue to have effect.
(4) The onus is on the applicant to satisfy the court that the order restricting the caveat should not be made.

71 Recall of caveat

(1) Any person with an interest, other than the applicant, may at any time apply to the court which granted the warrant to place the caveat for the caveat to be recalled.
(2) The court must, if no longer satisfied as to the matters mentioned in subsection (3), make an order recalling the caveat.
(3) The matters are that—
    (a) the applicant has a prima facie case on the merits of the proceedings,
    (b) there is a real and substantial risk that enforcement of any decree or order in the proceedings granted in favour of the applicant would be defeated or prejudiced by reason of the other party being likely to deal with the plot of land, and
    (c) in all the circumstances, including the effect which granting the warrant to place the caveat may have on any person having an interest, it is reasonable for the caveat to continue to have effect.
(4) The onus is on the applicant to satisfy the court that the order recalling the caveat should not be made.

72 Discharge of caveat

A person—
    (a) in whose favour warrant to place a caveat has been granted, or
    (b) who has renewed a caveat under section 69(2),
may at any time discharge the caveat.

PART 7
KEEPER'S WARRANTY

Keeper's warranty

73 Keeper's warranty

(1) The Keeper, in accepting an application for registration, warrants to the applicant that, as at the time of registration, the title sheet to which the application relates—
    (a) is accurate—
        (i) in so far as it shows an acquisition, variation or discharge in favour of the applicant, or
        (ii) in the case of an application under section 27, in so far as it shows the applicant to be the proprietor or proprietor in common, and
    (b) is not inaccurate in so far as there is omitted from it any encumbrance the inclusion of which is permitted or required by or under an enactment.
(2) But the Keeper does not warrant that—
    (a) the plot of land to which the application relates is unencumbered by any public right of way,
    (b) the land is unencumbered by a path delineated in an order under section 22 of the Land Reform (Scotland) Act 2003 (asp 2) (compulsory powers to delineate paths in land in respect of which access rights are exercisable),
    (c) the land is unencumbered by a servitude created other than by registration in accordance with section 75(1) of the Title Conditions (Scotland) Act 2003 (asp 9) (creation of positive servitude by writing: deed to be registered),
    (d) a right appearing on the title sheet as a pertinent is of a kind capable of being a valid pertinent,
    (e) a pertinent appearing on the title sheet and of a kind extinguishable or variable without registration against the title of the benefited property has not been extinguished, or varied, without registration,
    (f) the applicant has by registration acquired a right to mines or minerals,
    (g) a registered lease has not been varied or terminated without the variation or termination having been registered,

(h) the title sheet to which the application relates is accurate—
- (i) in so far as it shows an acquisition, variation or discharge more extensive than the deed registered bore to effect, or
- (ii) in the case of an application under section 27, in so far as it shows the applicant to be the proprietor or proprietor in common of a plot of land more extensive than the plot registration of which the application bore to effect, or

(i) alluvion has not had an effect on a boundary.

(3) The benefit of warranty extends to persons to whom the benefit of warrandice by the granter of a deed would extend.

(4) In relation to an application for registration of a deed relating to a title condition, references in subsections (1) and (2) and in section 78 to the applicant are to be read as references to the person benefiting from the deed given effect to.

(5) The Keeper does not warrant as provided for in subsections (1) and (2) where the application for registration is accepted by virtue of section 43.

(6) This section is subject to sections 75 and 76.

74 Keeper's warranty on registration under sections 25 and 29

(1) The Keeper, on registering a plot of land by virtue of section 25 or under section 29, warrants to the owner that, as at the time of registration, the title sheet of the plot—
- (a) is accurate in so far as it shows the owner to be the proprietor or proprietor in common, and
- (b) is not inaccurate in so far as there is omitted from it any encumbrance the inclusion of which is permitted or required by or under an enactment.

(2) Subsections (2), (3) and (5) of section 73 apply to warranty under this section as they apply to warranty under that section.

(3) Subsection (2) of section 73 is subject to the following modifications—
- (a) for paragraph (h) substitute—
  - '(h) in the case of registration by virtue of section 25, the title sheet is accurate in so far as it shows the owner to be the proprietor or proprietor in common of a plot of land more extensive than the area of land which forms the subjects of the lease, to which the deed relates or, as the case may be, in respect of which the subordinate real right is constituted,
  - (ha) in the case of registration under section 29, the title sheet is accurate in so far as it shows the owner to be the proprietor or proprietor in common of a plot of land more extensive than the plot the Keeper sought to register, or',
- (b) references in that subsection to—
  - (i) the application are to be read as references to the registration by virtue of section 25 or under section 29,
  - (ii) to the applicant are to be construed as references to the owner.

(4) This section is subject to sections 75 and 76.

75 Extension, limitation or exclusion of warranty

(1) The Keeper may—
- (a) if satisfied (having regard to sufficiency of evidence as to title) that it is appropriate to do so, grant more extensive warranty than is provided for in section 73 or 74, or
- (b) if not satisfied as to the validity of the acquisition, variation or discharge mentioned in section 73(1)(a)(i) or that the applicant or owner is the proprietor as mentioned in section 73(1)(a)(ii) or 74(1)(a)—
  - (i) grant less extensive warranty than is so provided for, or
  - (ii) exclude warranty.

Part 7: Keeper's Warranty   375

(2) For the purposes of subsection (1), the Keeper must have regard to any relevant caveat placed on the title sheet by virtue of section 67.
(3) Where warranty is granted or excluded under subsection (1), the Keeper must give effect to the grant or exclusion by entering a statement describing it in the title sheet.
(4) If an entry made in the title sheet on an application being accepted by virtue of section 43 ceases to be provisional, the Keeper may—
    (a) grant such warranty as the Keeper (having regard to sufficiency of evidence as to title) considers appropriate, and
    (b) give effect to the grant by entering a statement describing it in the title sheet.

76 Variation of warranty

(1) This section applies where warranty is—
    (a) as provided for in section 73 or 74,
    (b) granted under section 75(1)(a), (b)(i) or (4)(a), or
    (c) excluded under section 75(1)(b)(ii).
(2) The Keeper may, if the Keeper comes to be satisfied (having regard to sufficiency of evidence as to title) that it is appropriate to do so, grant—
    (a) warranty as provided for in section 73,
    (b) less extensive warranty than as so provided, or
    (c) more extensive warranty than as so provided.
(3) The Keeper may not, under subsection (2), grant warranty that is less extensive than the warranty which was originally provided for or granted as mentioned in subsection (1)(a) or (b).
(4) For the purposes of subsection (2), the Keeper must have regard to any relevant caveat placed on the title sheet by virtue of section 67.
(5) Where the Keeper grants warranty or more extensive warranty under subsection (2), the Keeper must—
    (a) unless the warranty granted is warranty only as provided for in section 73, give effect to the grant by entering a statement describing it on the title sheet, and
    (b) remove any statement previously entered under section 75(3) or (4)(b).

Claims under warranty

77 Claims under Keeper's warranty

(1) The Keeper must pay compensation for loss incurred as a result of a breach of the Keeper's warranty.
(2) Liability to pay such compensation arises only if and when the inaccuracy giving rise to the claim for compensation is rectified.
(3) A claimant is not required to exhaust other remedies before making a claim to such compensation.
(4) Payment by the Keeper under this section does not extinguish any rights which the claimant may have against another person in respect of the loss compensated.
(5) But it is a condition of any such payment that the claimant assign any such rights to the Keeper.

78 Claims under warranty: circumstances where liability excluded

The Keeper has no liability to pay compensation by virtue of section 77(1)—
    (a) if the inaccuracy is consequent upon an error in the cadastral map and that error was made in reasonable reliance upon the base map,
    (b) if the existence of the inaccuracy was, or ought to have been, known to—
        (i) the applicant, or
        (ii) any person acting as solicitor or other legal adviser to the applicant, at the time of registration,

(c) in so far as the inaccuracy is attributable to a failure of—
  (i) the applicant, or
  (ii) any person acting as solicitor or other legal adviser to the applicant,
to comply with the duty owed to the Keeper under section 111,
(d) in so far as the claimant's loss could have been avoided by the applicant, owner or claimant taking certain measures which it would have been reasonable for the applicant, owner or claimant to take,
(e) in so far as the connection between the claimant's loss and the inaccuracy is too remote, or
(f) for non-patrimonial loss.

79 Claims under warranty: quantification of compensation

(1) Compensation payable by virtue of section 77(1)—
  (a) is, in so far as it is not compensation mentioned in paragraph (b), to be quantified as at the date on which the inaccuracy giving rise to the claim is rectified, and
  (b) is to include—
    (i) reimbursement of reasonable extra-judicial legal expenses, and
    (ii) compensation for any other consequential loss.
(2) Interest on a sum so payable runs from the date mentioned in subsection (3) until the sum in question is paid.
(3) The date is—
  (a) where the sum is payable other than by virtue of subsection (1)(b), the date mentioned in subsection (1)(a),
  (b) where the sum is payable by virtue of subsection (1)(b)(i), the date on which the claimant paid the sum in question, and
  (c) where the sum is payable by virtue of subsection (1)(b)(ii), the date on which the loss was sustained.
(4) The Scottish Ministers may by regulations make provision as to the rate of interest payable by virtue of subsection (2).

PART 8
RECTIFICATION OF THE REGISTER

Rectification

80 Rectification of the register

(1) This section applies where the Keeper becomes aware of a manifest inaccuracy in a title sheet or in the cadastral map.
(2) The Keeper must rectify the inaccuracy if what is needed to do so is manifest.
(3) Where what is so needed is not manifest, the Keeper must enter a note identifying the inaccuracy in the title sheet or, as the case may be, in the cadastral map.
(4) Where the Keeper rectifies an inaccuracy, the Keeper must—
  (a) include in the archive record a copy of any document which discloses, or contributes to disclosing, the inaccuracy, and
  (b) give notice of the rectification to any person who appears to the Keeper to be affected by it materially.
(5) Land register rules may make provision about—
  (a) the persons to be notified by the Keeper, and
  (b) the method by which such notice is to be given.
(6) A failure to comply with subsection (4) or with any rules so made does not affect the validity of a rectification under subsection (2).

Part 8: Rectification of the Register

81 Rectification where registration provisional etc

(1) This section applies where it appears to the Keeper that rectification of an inaccuracy would interrupt a period of possession—
   (a) which is current, and
   (b) which, if uninterrupted, would, under section 1(1) or 2(1) of the Prescription and Limitation (Scotland) Act 1973 (c 52) (sections which provide for positive prescription), affect a real right.
(2) If the inaccuracy is in an entry marked provisional by virtue of section 44, the Keeper—
   (a) may rectify the register if all those affected consent,
   (b) where there is no such consent, must not rectify the register before the existence of the inaccuracy is judicially determined.
(3) In any other case, the Keeper—
   (a) must—
      (i) mark the relevant entry in the title sheet provisional,
      (ii) enter in the appropriate section of the title sheet the name and designation of the true holder of the right affected by the inaccuracy (if any such person can be identified),
   (b) may rectify the register if all those affected consent,
   (c) where there is no such consent, must not rectify the register before the existence of the inaccuracy is judicially determined.

Referral of questions to Lands Tribunal

82 Referral to the Lands Tribunal for Scotland

(1) A person with an interest may refer a question relating to—
   (a) the accuracy of the register, or
   (b) what is needed to rectify an inaccuracy in the register,
to the Lands Tribunal for Scotland.
(2) The Lands Tribunal must, on determining the question, give notice to—
   (a) the applicant,
   (b) any other person appearing to them to have an interest, and
   (c) the Keeper.
(3) This section is without prejudice to any other right of recourse, whether under an enactment or under a rule of law.

Keeper's right to be heard in proceedings

83 Proceedings involving the accuracy of the register

The Keeper is entitled to appear and be heard in any civil proceedings, whether before a court or tribunal, in which—
   (a) the accuracy of the register, or
   (b) what is needed to rectify an inaccuracy in the register,
is put in question.

Compensation in consequence of rectification

84 Rectification: compensation for certain expenses and losses

(1) The Keeper must pay compensation for—
   (a) reimbursement of reasonable extra-judicial legal expenses incurred by a person in securing rectification of the register, and
   (b) any loss sustained by the person in consequence of the inaccuracy rectified.
(2) A claimant is not required to exhaust other remedies before making a claim to such compensation.
(3) Payment by the Keeper under this section does not extinguish any rights which the claimant may have against another person in respect of the loss compensated.

(4) But it is a condition of any such payment that the claimant assigns any such rights to the Keeper.
(5) Interest on a sum payable under this section runs from the date mentioned in subsection (6) until the sum in question is paid.
(6) The date is—
    (a) where the sum is payable by virtue of subsection (1)(a), the date on which the claimant paid the sum in question,
    (b) where the sum is payable by virtue of subsection (1)(b), the date on which the loss was sustained.
(7) The Scottish Ministers may by regulations make provision as to the rate of interest payable by virtue of subsection (5).

85 Rectification: circumstances where liability excluded

The Keeper has no liability to pay compensation under section 84—
    (a) if the inaccuracy is caused other than by a change made by the Keeper to a title sheet or the cadastral map,
    (b) if the inaccuracy is consequent on an error in the cadastral map and that error was made in reasonable reliance on the base map,
    (c) in so far as the inaccuracy is in an entry made on an application being accepted by virtue of section 43(1) or under section 43(5),
    (d) in so far as the inaccuracy is caused by some act or omission on the part of the claimant,
    (e) in so far as the claimant's loss could have been avoided by the claimant taking certain measures which it would have been reasonable for the claimant to take,
    (f) in so far as the connection between the claimant's loss and the inaccuracy is too remote, or
    (g) for non-patrimonial loss.

PART 9
RIGHT OF PERSONS ACQUIRING ETC IN GOOD FAITH

Ownership

86 Acquisition from disponer without valid title

(1) This section applies where a person ('A'), who is not the proprietor of a registered plot of land but—
    (a) is entered in the proprietorship section of the title sheet as proprietor, and
    (b) is in possession of the land,
    purports to dispone the land.
(2) The disponee ('B') acquires ownership of the land provided that the conditions in subsection (3) are met.
(3) The conditions are that—
    (a) the land has been in the possession, openly, peaceably and without judicial interruption—
        (i) of A for a continuous period of at least 1 year, or
        (ii) of A and then of B for periods which together constitute such a period,
    (b) at no time during that period did the Keeper become aware that the register was inaccurate as a result of A (or B) not being the proprietor,
    (c) B is in good faith,
    (d) the disposition would have conferred ownership on B had A been proprietor when the land was disponed,
    (e) at no time during the period mentioned in paragraph (a)—
        (i) was the title sheet subject, by virtue of section 67, to a caveat relevant to the acquisition by B,

(ii) did the title sheet contain a statement under section 30(5), and
   (f) the Keeper warrants (or is to be taken to warrant) A's title.
(4) The date on which ownership is acquired by virtue of subsection (2) is—
   (a) where subsection (5) applies, the date on which the disposition is registered,
   (b) where subsection (6) applies, the date on which the period of possession mentioned in that subsection expires.
(5) This subsection applies where, as at the date of registration, the land has been in the possession, openly, peaceably and without judicial interruption—
   (a) of A for a continuous period of at least 1 year, or
   (b) of A and then of B for periods which together constitute such a period.
(6) This subsection applies where there is a continuous period of possession such as is mentioned in subsection (5) but that period, though it commences before registration on the application of B, does not expire until a date later than the date of registration.

87 Acquisition from representative of disponer without valid title

(1) Section 86 also applies where a person ('P'), who is not entered in the proprietorship section of the title sheet as proprietor but who would have power to dispone the land—
   (a) were A the proprietor, or
   (b) (where A has died) had A been the proprietor,
   purports to dispone it.
(2) For the purposes of section 86, possession of the plot of land by P is to be treated as if it were possession of the land by A.

Leases

88 Acquisition from assigner without valid title

(1) This section applies where a person ('A'), who is not the tenant under a registered lease but—
   (a) is shown in the title sheet as tenant, and
   (b) is in possession of the subjects of the lease,
   purports to assign the lease.
(2) The assignee ('B') acquires the lease provided that the conditions in subsection (3) are met.
(3) The conditions are that—
   (a) the subjects of the lease have been in the possession, openly, peaceably and without judicial interruption—
      (i) of A for a continuous period of at least 1 year, or
      (ii) of A and then of B for periods which together constitute such a period,
   (b) at no time during that period did the Keeper become aware that the register was inaccurate as a result of A (or B) not being the tenant,
   (c) B is in good faith,
   (d) the lease is extant,
   (e) B would have acquired the lease had A been tenant when the lease was assigned,
   (f) at no time during the period mentioned in paragraph (a) was the title sheet subject, by virtue of section 67, to a caveat relevant to the acquisition by B, and
   (g) the Keeper warrants (or is to be taken to warrant) A's title.
(4) The date on which the lease is acquired by virtue of subsection (2) is—
   (a) where subsection (5) applies, the date on which the deed of assignation is registered,
   (b) where subsection (6) applies, the date on which the period of possession mentioned in that subsection expires.
(5) This subsection applies where, as at the date of registration, the subjects of the lease have been in the possession, openly, peaceably and without judicial interruption—
   (a) of A for a continuous period of at least 1 year, or

(b) of A and then of B for periods which together constitute such a period.
(6) This subsection applies where there is a continuous period of possession such as is mentioned in subsection (5) but that period, though it commences before registration on the application of B, does not expire until a date later than the date of registration.

89 Acquisition from representative of assigner without valid title

(1) Section 88 also applies where a person ('P'), who is not entered in the title sheet as tenant but who would have power to assign the lease—
    (a) were A the tenant, or
    (b) (where A has died) had A been the tenant,
    purports to assign it.
(2) For the purposes of section 88, possession of the subjects of the lease by P is to be treated as if it were possession of the subjects by A.

Servitudes

90 Grant of servitude by person not proprietor

(1) This section applies where a person ('A'), who is not the proprietor of a registered plot of land but—
    (a) is entered in the proprietorship section of the title sheet as proprietor, and
    (b) is in possession of the land,
    purports to create a servitude, with the land as the burdened property.
(2) The servitude is created provided that the conditions mentioned in subsection (3) are met.
(3) The conditions are that—
    (a) the land has been in the possession of A, openly, peaceably and without judicial interruption, for a continuous period of at least 1 year,
    (b) at no time during that period did the Keeper become aware that the register was inaccurate as a result of A not being the proprietor,
    (c) the proprietor of what is to be the benefited property is in good faith,
    (d) at no time during the period mentioned in paragraph (a) was the title sheet subject, by virtue of section 67, to a caveat relevant to the creation of the servitude, and
    (e) the Keeper warrants (or is to be taken to warrant) A's title.
(4) The date on which the servitude is created by virtue of subsection (2) is—
    (a) where subsection (5) applies, the date of registration,
    (b) where subsection (6) applies, the date on which the period mentioned in that subsection expires.
(5) This subsection applies where, as at the date of registration, the land has been in the possession of A, openly, peaceably and without judicial interruption, for a continuous period of at least 1 year.
(6) This subsection applies where there is a continuous period of possession such as is mentioned in subsection (5) but that period, though it commences before registration, does not expire until a date later than the date of registration.
(7) This section is subject to section 75 of the Title Conditions (Scotland) Act 2003 (asp 9) (creation of positive servitude by writing: deed to be registered).

Extinction of encumbrances etc

91 Extinction of encumbrance when land disponed

(1) Where the conditions mentioned in subsection (2) are met, a person ('A') who acquires ownership of land on registration or on a later date by virtue of section 86(4)(b)—
    (a) takes the land free of an encumbrance which is not entered in the title sheet as at the date on which A acquires ownership of the land, and

(b) any such encumbrance is extinguished.
(2) The conditions are that, as at the date on which ownership is acquired—
    (a) A is in good faith, and
    (b) the title sheet is not, by virtue of section 67, subject to a caveat relevant to such acquisition by A.
(3) Subsection (1) does not apply to an heritable security which is not entered in the securities section of a shared plot title sheet by virtue of section 18(3)(b).
(4) 'Encumbrance' in subsection (1) does not include—
    (a) a public right of way,
    (b) a path delineated in an order under section 22 of the Land Reform (Scotland) Act 2003 (asp 2) (compulsory powers to delineate paths in land in respect of which access rights are exercisable),
    (c) a servitude created other than under section 75(1) of the Title Conditions (Scotland) Act 2003 (asp 9),
    (d) a lease, or
    (e) an encumbrance the creation of which does not require registration of the constitutive deed.

92 Extinction of encumbrance when lease assigned

(1) Where the conditions mentioned in subsection (2) are met, a person ('A') who acquires a registered lease on registration or on a later date by virtue of section 88(4)(b)—
    (a) takes that lease free of an encumbrance—
        (i) of a kind mentioned in subsection (4), and
        (ii) which is not entered in the title sheet as at the date on which A acquires the registered lease, and
    (b) any such encumbrance is extinguished.
(2) The conditions are that, as at the date on which the lease is acquired—
    (a) A is in good faith, and
    (b) the title sheet is not, by virtue of section 67, subject to a caveat relevant to such acquisition by A.
(3) Subsection (1) does not apply to an heritable security which is not entered in the securities section of a shared lease title sheet by virtue of paragraph 8(b) of schedule 1.
(4) The encumbrances are—
    (a) a heritable security over the lease,
    (b) a title condition such as is mentioned in paragraph (d) or (e) of the definition of 'title condition' in section 122(1) of the Title Conditions (Scotland) Act 2003 (asp 9).

93 Extinction of floating charge when land disponed

A person who, in good faith, acquires ownership of land from another person ('A'), takes the land free of any floating charge which was granted by a predecessor in title of A.

Compensation in consequence of this Part

94 Compensation for loss incurred in consequence of this Part

(1) The Keeper must pay compensation for loss incurred by a person mentioned in subsection (2).
(2) The person is one who—
    (a) is deprived of a right by virtue of this Part, or
    (b) is the proprietor of a property burdened by a servitude created by virtue of section 90.
(3) A claimant is not required to exhaust other remedies before making a claim to such compensation.

(4) Payment by the Keeper under this section does not extinguish any rights which the claimant may have against another person in respect of the loss compensated.
(5) But it is a condition of any such payment that the claimant assigns any such rights to the Keeper.
(6) The Keeper has no liability to pay compensation—
   (a) in so far as the claimant's loss could have been avoided by the claimant taking certain measures which it would have been reasonable for the claimant to take,
   (b) in so far as the claimant's loss is too remote, or
   (c) for non-patrimonial loss.

95 Quantification of compensation

(1) Compensation payable by virtue of section 94(1)—
   (a) is, in so far as it is not compensation mentioned in paragraph (b), to be quantified as at the date on which the claimant lost the right or, as the case may be, on which the servitude was created, and
   (b) is to include—
      (i) reimbursement of reasonable extra-judicial legal expenses, and
      (ii) compensation for any other consequential loss.
(2) Interest on a sum so payable runs from the date mentioned in subsection (3) until the sum in question is paid.
(3) The date is—
   (a) where the sum is payable other than by virtue of subsection (1)(b), the date mentioned in subsection (1)(a),
   (b) where the sum is payable by virtue of subsection (1)(b)(i), the date on which the claimant paid the sum in question, and
   (c) where the sum is payable by virtue of subsection (1)(b)(ii), the date on which the loss was sustained.
(4) The Scottish Ministers may by regulations make provision as to the rate of interest payable by virtue of subsection (2).

PART 10
ELECTRONIC DOCUMENTS, ELECTRONIC CONVEYANCING AND ELECTRONIC REGISTRATION

Electronic documents

96 Where requirement for writing satisfied by electronic document

(1) The Requirements of Writing (Scotland) Act 1995 (c 7) (the '1995 Act') is amended as follows.
(2) In section 1 (writing required for certain contracts, obligations, trusts, conveyances and wills)—
   (a) in subsection (2)—
      (i) for 'subsections (2A) and' substitute 'subsection',
      (ii) after 'written document' insert 'which is a traditional document',
      (iii) after 'section 2' insert 'or an electronic document complying with section 9B',
      (iv) after paragraph (b) insert—
         '(ba) the constitution of an agreement under section 66(1) of the Land Registration etc (Scotland) Act 2012 (asp 5),',
   (b) in subsection (3)—
      (i) for 'subsections (2)(a) or (2A)' substitute 'subsection (2)(a)',
      (ii) repeal 'written',
      (iii) for 'an electronic document complying with section 2A,' substitute 'section 9B',

Part 10: Electronic Documents etc   383

(c) in subsection (5), for 'subsections (2)(a) or (2A)' substitute 'subsection (2)(a)'.
(3) The provisions of section 1 as amended by subsection (2) become Part 1 of the Act.
(4) The title of Part 1 is 'When writing is required'.

97 Electronic documents

(1) The 1995 Act is further amended as follows.
(2) After section 9 insert—

'PART 3

ELECTRONIC DOCUMENTS

9A Application of Part 3

This Part applies to documents which, rather than being written on paper, parchment or some similar tangible surface are created in electronic form ('electronic documents').

9B Validity of electronic documents

(1) No electronic document required by section 1(2) is valid in respect of the formalities of execution unless—
   (a) it is authenticated by the granter, or if there is more than one granter by each granter, in accordance with subsection (2), and
   (b) it meets such other requirements (if any) as may be prescribed by the Scottish Ministers in regulations.
(2) An electronic document is authenticated by a person if the electronic signature of that person—
   (a) is incorporated into, or logically associated with, the electronic document,
   (b) was created by the person by whom it purports to have been created, and
   (c) is of such type, and satisfies such requirements (if any), as may be prescribed by the Scottish Ministers in regulations.
(3) A contract mentioned in section 1(2)(a) may be regarded as constituted or varied (as the case may be) if—
   (a) the offer is contained in one or more electronic documents,
   (b) the acceptance is contained in another electronic document or in other such documents, and
   (c) each of the documents is authenticated by its granter or granters.
(4) Where a person grants an electronic document in more than one capacity, authentication by the person of the document, in accordance with subsection (3), is sufficient to bind the person in all such capacities.
(5) Nothing in this section prevents an electronic document which has not been authenticated by the granter or granters of it from being used as evidence in relation to any right or obligation to which the document relates.
(6) Regulations under subsection (1)(b) or (2)(c) are subject to the negative procedure.

9C Presumption as to authentication of electronic documents

(1) Where—
   (a) an electronic document bears to have been authenticated by the granter,
   (b) nothing in the document or in the authentication indicates that it was not so authenticated, and
   (c) the conditions set out in subsection (2) are satisfied,
   the document is to be presumed to have been authenticated by the granter.
(2) The conditions are that the electronic signature incorporated into, or logically associated with, the document—
   (a) is of such type and satisfies such requirements as may be prescribed by the Scottish Ministers in regulations, and
   (b) (either or both)—

(i) is used in such circumstances as may be so prescribed,
(ii) bears to be certified,
and that if the electronic signature bears to be certified (and does not conform with paragraph (b)(i)) the certification is of such type and satisfies such requirements as may be so prescribed.

(3) Regulations under subsection (2) are subject to the negative procedure.

9D Presumptions as to granter's authentication etc when established in court proceedings

(1) Where—
   (a) an electronic document bears to have been authenticated by a granter of it, and
   (b) there is no presumption under section 9C that the document has been authenticated by that granter,
   the court must, on an application being made to it by any person who has an interest in the document, if satisfied that the document was authenticated by that granter, grant decree to that effect.

(2) Where—
   (a) an electronic document bears to have been authenticated by a granter of it, and
   (b) there is no presumption by virtue of section 9E(1) as to the time, date or place of authentication,
   the court must, on an application being made to it by any person who has an interest in the document, if satisfied as to that time, date or place, grant decree to that effect.

(3) On an application under subsection (1) or (2), evidence is, unless the court otherwise directs, to be given by affidavit.

(4) An application under subsection (1) or (2) may be made either as a summary application or as incidental to, and in the course of, other proceedings.

(5) The effect of a decree—
   (a) under subsection (1), is to establish a presumption that the document has been authenticated by the granter concerned, or
   (b) under subsection (2), is to establish a presumption that the statement in the decree as to time, date or place is correct.

(6) In this section, 'the court' means—
   (a) in the case of a summary application—
      (i) the sheriff in whose sheriffdom the applicant resides, or
      (ii) if the applicant does not reside in Scotland, the sheriff at Edinburgh, or
   (b) in the case of an application made in the course of other proceedings, the court before which those proceedings are pending.

9E Further provision by Scottish Ministers about electronic documents

(1) The Scottish Ministers may, in regulations, make provision as to the effectiveness or formal validity of, or presumptions to be made with regard to—
   (a) any alteration made, whether before or after authentication, to an electronic document,
   (b) the authentication, by or on behalf of the granter, of such a document,
   (c) the authentication, by or on behalf of a person with a disability, of such a document, or
   (d) any annexation to such a document,
   (including, without prejudice to the generality of this subsection, presumptions to be made with regard to the time, date and place of authentication of such a document).

(2) Regulations under subsection (1) may make such incidental, supplemental, consequential, transitional, transitory or saving provision as the Scottish Ministers consider necessary or expedient for the purposes of, or in consequence of the regulations.
(3) Subject to subsection (4), regulations under subsection (1) are subject to the negative procedure.
(4) Regulations which—
   (a) make provision of the kind mentioned in subsection (1)(b), or
   (b) add to, replace or omit any part of an Act (including this Act),
   are subject to the affirmative procedure.

9F Delivery of electronic documents

(1) An electronic document may be delivered electronically or by such other means as are reasonably practicable.
(2) But such a document must be in a form, and such delivery must be by a means—
   (a) the intended recipient has agreed to accept, or
   (b) which it is reasonable in all the circumstances for the intended recipient to accept.

9G Registration and recording of electronic documents

(1) Subject to subsection (6), it is not competent—
   (a) to record an electronic document in the Register of Sasines,
   (b) to register such a document in the Land Register of Scotland,
   (c) to register such a document for execution or preservation in the Books of Council and Session, or
   (d) to record or register such a document in any other register under the management and control of the Keeper of the Registers of Scotland,
   unless both subsection (2) and subsection (3) apply in relation to the document.
(2) This subsection applies where—
   (a) the document is presumed under section 9C or 9D or by virtue of section 9E(1) to have been authenticated by the granter, or
   (b) if there is more than one granter, the document is presumed by virtue of any of those provisions to have been authenticated by at least one of the granters.
(3) This subsection applies where—
   (a) the document,
   (b) the electronic signature authenticating it, and
   (c) if the document bears to be certified, the certification,
   are in such form and of such type as are prescribed by the Scottish Ministers in regulations.
(4) Before making regulations under subsection (3), the Scottish Ministers must consult with—
   (a) the Keeper of the Registers of Scotland,
   (b) the Keeper of the Records of Scotland, and
   (c) the Lord President of the Court of Session.
(5) Regulations under subsection (3)—
   (a) may make different provision for different cases or classes of case, and
   (b) are subject to the negative procedure.
(6) Subsection (1) above does not apply in relation to—
   (a) a document's—
      (i) being recorded in the Register of Sasines,
      (ii) being registered in the Land Register of Scotland or in the Books of Council and Session, or

(iii) being recorded or registered in any other register under the management and control of the Keeper of the Registers of Scotland,
if an enactment requires or expressly permits such recording or registration notwithstanding that the document is not presumed to have been authenticated by the granter or by at least one of the granters,
(b) the recording of a court decree in the Register of Sasines or the registering of such a decree in the Land Register of Scotland,
(c) the registering in the Books of Council and Session of—
(i) a document registration of which is directed by the Court of Session,
(ii) a document the formal validity of which is governed by a law other than Scots law, provided that the Keeper of the Registers of Scotland is satisfied that the document is formally valid according to that other law,
(iii) a court decree granted under section 9D, or by virtue of section 9E(1), of this Act in relation to a document already registered in the Books of Council and Session, or
(d) the registration of a court decree in a separate register maintained for that purpose.
(7) An electronic document may be registered for preservation in the Books of Council and Session without a clause of consent to registration.'.

98 Amendment of Requirements of Writing (Scotland) Act 1995

Schedule 3, which contains modifications of the 1995 Act consequential on sections 96 and 97, has effect.

Electronic conveyancing

99 Automated registration

(1) The Keeper may, by means of a computer system under the Keeper's management and control, enable—
   (a) the creation of electronic documents,
   (b) the electronic generation and communication of applications for registration in the register, and
   (c) automated registration in the register.
(2) Only a person authorised by the Keeper, whether directly or indirectly, may use the system mentioned in subsection (1) to make applications for registration.
(3) The Scottish Ministers may, by regulations, make provision about the system mentioned in subsection (1) including—
   (a) the kinds of deeds which may be authorised for use in the system,
   (b) the persons who may be authorised to use the system,
   (c) the suspension or revocation of a person's authorisation under subsection (2),
   (d) the method of appeal against any such suspension or revocation,
   (e) the imposition of obligations on persons using the system, and
   (f) the creation of deemed warranties (whether in favour of the Keeper or of other users) by persons using the system.
(4) Before making such regulations, the Scottish Ministers must consult the Keeper.

Electronic recording and registration

100 Power to enable electronic registration

(1) The Scottish Ministers may, by regulations, make provision to enable the recording or registration of electronic documents in any register under the management and control of the Keeper.
(2) Regulations under subsection (1) may, in particular, make provision—
   (a) regulating the making up and keeping of any such register,

(b) regulating the procedure to be followed by any person applying for recording or registration in any such register,
(c) regulating the procedure to be followed by the Keeper in relation to—
   (i) any such application, and
   (ii) the recording or registration of electronic documents to which such an application relates,
(d) that the Scottish Ministers consider necessary or expedient to enable recording or registration of electronic documents in any such register.
(3) Regulations under subsection (1) may modify any enactment.
(4) Before making regulations under subsection (1), the Scottish Ministers must consult—
   (a) the Keeper,
   (b) the Keeper of the Records of Scotland, and
   (c) the Lord President of the Court of Session.

PART 11
MISCELLANEOUS AND GENERAL

Deduction of title

101 Deduction of title
(1) Where a person applies to register a deed mentioned in subsection (2), the deed need not deduce title.
(2) The deed is one validly granted by the unregistered holder of—
   (a) land, or
   (b) a real right in land, to which the deed relates.

Notes on register

102 Note of date on which entry in register is made
When an entry is made in the register there is to be included in that entry the date on which it is made.

Appeals

103 Appeals
(1) An appeal may be made to the Lands Tribunal for Scotland, on a question of fact or on a point of law, against any decision of the Keeper under this Act.
(2) Subsection (1) is without prejudice to any other right of recourse, whether under an enactment or under a rule of law.
(3) Where a person successfully appeals against a decision of the Keeper to reject an application for registration, the application is not revived.

Extracts and certified copies

104 Extracts and certified copies: general
(1) A person may apply to the Keeper for an extract—
   (a) of, or of any part of, a title sheet,
   (b) of any part of the cadastral map, or
   (c) of, or of any part of, a document in the archive record.
(2) A person may apply to the Keeper for a certified copy—
   (a) of an application or advance notice in the application record,
   (b) of, or of any part of, any other document in that record.
(3) The Keeper must issue the extract or, as the case may be the certified copy, if—
   (a) such fee as is payable for issuing it is paid, or
   (b) arrangements satisfactory to the Keeper are made for payment of that fee.

(4) If, on application under subsection (1)(a) or (b), the applicant requests an extract in relation to a title sheet or the cadastral map as at a specific date, the Keeper need comply with the request only to the extent that it is reasonably practicable to do so.

(5) An extract of a part of the cadastral map issued under subsection (3)—
   (a) must include the base map so far as relating to that part either—
      (i) as at the date on which the extract is issued, or
      (ii) if the Keeper considers it appropriate to do so, as at some earlier date, and
   (b) must specify the base map date opted for under paragraph (a).

(6) The Keeper may authenticate the extract or, as the case may be the certified copy, as the Keeper considers appropriate.

(7) The Keeper may issue the extract, or as the case may be the certified copy, as an electronic document if (and only if) the applicant requests that it be issued in that form.

105 Evidential status of extract or certified copy

(1) An extract or certified copy issued under subsection (3) of section 104 in relation to an application under subsection (1)(a) or (b) or (2)(a) of that section is to be accepted for all purposes as sufficient evidence of the contents—
   (a) of the original, and
   (b) of any matter relating to the original which appears on the extract or copy.

(2) An extract or certified copy issued under subsection (3) of that section in relation to an application under subsection (1)(c) or (2)(b) of that section is to be accepted for all purposes as sufficient evidence of the contents—
   (a) of the document as submitted to the Keeper, and
   (b) of any matter relating to the document as so submitted which appears on the extract or copy.

106 Liability of Keeper in respect of extracts, information and lost documents etc

(1) A person is entitled to be compensated by the Keeper in respect of loss suffered as a consequence of—
   (a) the issue of an extract or certified copy under section 104 that is not a true extract, or as the case may be a true copy,
   (b) the provision (in writing or in such other manner as provision is made for in an order under section 107(1)(a)) of other information as to the contents of the register that is incorrect,
   (c) a document being lost, damaged or destroyed while lodged with the Keeper.

(2) The Keeper has no liability under subsection (1)—
   (a) in so far as the claimant's loss could have been avoided by the applicant or claimant taking certain measures which it would have been reasonable for the applicant or claimant to take,
   (b) in so far as a claimant's loss is too remote, or
   (c) for non-patrimonial loss.

Information and access

107 Information and access

(1) The Scottish Ministers may, by order, make further provision as regards—
   (a) information to be made available by the Keeper and the manner in which it is to be made available,
   (b) access to any register under the management and control of the Keeper.

(2) In subsection (1)(a), 'information' includes information in the form of extracts and certified copies.

Part 11: Miscellaneous and General

Keeper's functions

108 Provision of services by the Keeper
(1) The Keeper may provide consultancy, advisory or other commercial services.
(2) Those services need not relate to the law and practice of registration.
(3) The terms on which those services are provided (including the fees charged for provision of them) are to be such as may be agreed between the Keeper and those provided with them.
(4) If the Keeper considers it expedient to do so in connection with the provision of any of those services, the Keeper may (either or both)—
    (a) form, or participate in the forming of, a body corporate or other entity,
    (b) purchase, or invest in, a body corporate or other entity.
(5) This section does not affect any other power or duty of the Keeper.

109 Performance of Keeper's functions during vacancy in office etc
(1) This section applies where—
    (a) there is a vacancy in the office of the Keeper or the Keeper is incapable by reason of ill health of performing the Keeper's functions, and
    (b) no person has been authorised by the Scottish Ministers, under section 1(6) of the Public Registers and Records (Scotland) Act 1948 (c 57), to perform the functions of the Keeper.
(2) A member of the Keeper's staff may perform the Keeper's functions.
(3) Any function performed by a member of the Keeper's staff by virtue of subsection (2) is to be treated as if it had been performed by the Keeper.

Fees

110 Fees
(1) The Scottish Ministers may, by order—
    (a) provide for the fees payable in relation to—
        (i) registering, recording or entering in any register under the management and control of the Keeper,
        (ii) access to such a register,
        (iii) information made available by the Keeper,
    (b) provide for the method of paying any such fees, and
    (c) authorise the Keeper to determine, in such circumstances and subject to such limitations and conditions as may be specified in the order, any such fees.
(2) An order under this section may make different provision for different cases or for different classes of case.
(3) Before making an order under this section, the Scottish Ministers must consult the Keeper about, among other things—
    (a) the expenses incurred by the Keeper in relation to administering and improving the systems of—
        (i) registering, recording or entering in any register under the management and control of the Keeper,
        (ii) providing access to any such register, and
        (iii) making information available,
    (b) in the case of the register, the expenses incurred by the Keeper in bringing all titles to land into it,
    (c) the desirability of encouraging registering, recording and entering in any register under the management and control of the Keeper.
(4) In subsections (1)(a)(iii) and (3)(a)(iii), 'information'—
    (a) includes information in the form of extracts and certified copies,
    (b) does not include information provided by virtue of section 108.

Duty to take reasonable care

111 Duties of certain persons

(1) A person mentioned in subsection (2) must take reasonable care to ensure that the Keeper does not inadvertently make the register inaccurate as a result of a change made in consequence of the grant mentioned in that subsection.

(2) The persons are—
  (a) a person granting a deed intended to be registered,
  (b) a person who, in connection with the grant, acts as a solicitor or other legal adviser to the granter.

(3) A person mentioned in subsection (4) must take reasonable care to ensure that the Keeper does not inadvertently make the register inaccurate as a result of a change made in consequence of the application mentioned in that subsection.

(4) The persons are—
  (a) a person making an application for registration,
  (b) a person who, in connection with the application, acts as a solicitor or other legal adviser to the applicant.

(5) The Keeper is entitled to be compensated by a person in breach of the duty under subsection (1) or (3) for any loss suffered as a consequence of that breach.

(6) But a person has no liability under subsection (5) in so far as—
  (a) the Keeper's loss could have been avoided by the Keeper taking certain measures which it would have been reasonable for the Keeper to take, or
  (b) the Keeper's loss is too remote.

Offence

112 Offence relating to applications for registration

(1) A person mentioned in subsection (2) commits an offence if the person—
  (a) makes a materially false or misleading statement in relation to an application for registration knowing that, or being reckless as to whether, the statement is false or misleading, or
  (b) intentionally fails to disclose material information in relation to such an application or is reckless as to whether all material information is disclosed.

(2) The persons are—
  (a) a person making an application for registration, or
  (b) a person who, in connection with such an application, acts as solicitor or other legal adviser to the applicant.

(3) It is a defence for a person charged with an offence under subsection (1) (the 'accused') that the accused took all reasonable precautions and exercised all due diligence to avoid the commission of the offence.

(4) The defence is established if the accused—
  (a) acted in reliance on information supplied by another person, and
  (b) did not know and had no reason to suppose that—
    (i) the information was false or misleading, or
    (ii) all material information had not been disclosed.

(5) Subsection (4) does not exclude other ways of establishing the defence mentioned in subsection (3).

(6) An accused may not rely on a defence involving the allegation that the commission of the offence was due to reliance on information supplied by another person unless—
  (a) the accused has complied with subsection (7), or
  (b) the court grants leave.

(7) The accused must serve on the prosecutor a notice giving such information identifying or assisting in the identification of the other person as is in the accused's possession—

(a) in proceedings on indictment, at least 14 clear days before the preliminary hearing (where the case is to be tried in the High Court) or the first diet (where the case is to be tried in the sheriff court),

(b) in summary proceedings—

   (i) where an intermediate diet is held, at or before that diet,

   (ii) where no such diet is held, at least 10 clear days before the trial diet.

(8) Subsection (6) does not apply where—

(a) the accused lodges a defence statement—

   (i) under section 70A of the Criminal Procedure (Scotland) Act 1995 (c 46), or

   (ii) under section 125 of the Criminal Justice and Licensing (Scotland) Act 2010 (asp 13) in accordance with the time limits mentioned in subsection (7)(b), and

(b) the accused's defence involves an allegation that the commission of the offence was due to reliance on information supplied by another person.

(9) A person guilty of an offence under subsection (1) is liable—

(a) on summary conviction, to imprisonment for a period not exceeding 12 months, to a fine not exceeding the statutory maximum, or to both,

(b) on conviction on indictment, to imprisonment for a period not exceeding 2 years, to a fine, or to both.

General provisions

113 Interpretation

(1) In this Act, unless the context otherwise requires—

'1995 Act' means the Requirements of Writing (Scotland) Act 1995 (c 7),

'advance notice' has the meaning given by section 56(1),

'application for registration' means an application under section 21 or 27,

'application record' has the meaning given by section 15,

'archive record' has the meaning given by section 14(1),

'the base map' has the meaning given by section 11(6),

'benefited property' has the meaning given by section 122(1) of the Title Conditions (Scotland) Act 2003 (asp 9),

'burdened property' has the meaning given by section 122(1) of the Title Conditions (Scotland) Act 2003 (asp 9),

'cadastral map' has the meaning given by section 11(1),

'cadastral unit' has the meaning given by section 12,

'date of application' (in relation to an application for registration) has the meaning given by section 36,

'date of registration' has the meaning given by 37(1),

'deed' means a document (and includes a decree which is registrable under an enactment),

'designation' includes—

(a) where the person designated is not a natural person—
  (i) the legal system under which the person is incorporated or otherwise established,
  (ii) if a number has been allocated to the person under section 1066 of the Companies Act 2006 (c 46), that number, and
  (iii) any other identifier (whether or not a number) peculiar to the person, and
(b) if the person designated has a right in land in a special capacity, a description of that capacity,

'the designated day' has the meaning given by section 122,

'enactment' includes—
(a) an enactment comprised in, or in an instrument made under, this Act, and
(b) a local and personal or private Act,

'existing title sheet' means a title sheet which is in existence immediately before the commencement of the designated day,

'flat' has the meaning given by section 29(1) of the Tenements (Scotland) Act 2004 (asp 11),

'flatted building' has the meaning given by section 16(4),

'heritable creditor' means the holder of a heritable security,

'heritable security' means—
(a) a standard security, or
(b) any other right in security over heritable property provided that it is not a right in security created as a floating charge,

'the Keeper' means the Keeper of the Registers of Scotland,

'land' includes—
(a) buildings and other structures,
(b) the seabed of the territorial sea of the United Kingdom adjacent to Scotland (including land within the ebb and flow of the tide at ordinary spring tides), and
(c) other land covered with water,

'land register rules' means rules made under section 115(1),

'lease' includes sub-lease,

'lease title sheet' means a title sheet for a registered lease,

'personal real burden' has the meaning given by section 122(1) of the Title Conditions (Scotland) Act 2003 (asp 9),

'plot of land' has the meaning given by section 3(4) and (5),

'possession' includes civil possession (analogous expressions being construed accordingly),

'proprietor' means a person who has a valid completed title as proprietor to a plot of land,

'protected period' has the meaning given by section 58(3),

'the register' means the Land Register of Scotland,

'registrable deed' is to be construed in accordance with section 49,

'sharing plot' and 'shared plot' are to be construed in accordance with section 17(3),

'tenement' has the meaning given by section 26 of the Tenements (Scotland) Act 2004 (asp 11), 'title condition' has the meaning given by section 122(1) of the Title Conditions (Scotland) Act 2003 (asp 9),

'title sheet record' has the meaning given by section 3(3).

(2) A deed on which an application under section 21 is based is 'valid' for the purposes of this Act if—
   (a) by the registration applied for, a right would be acquired, varied or extinguished, or
   (b) the deed is certificatory of an acquisition, variation or extinction which has taken place.
(3) In relation to a lease title sheet, any reference in this Act—
   (a) to a proprietor is (except in section 66) to be read as a reference to the tenant,
   (b) to a proprietorship section is to be construed as a reference to a tenancy section, and
   (c) to ownership in common is to be construed as a reference to tenancy in common.
(4) The Scottish Ministers may, by order, amend paragraph (b) of the definition of 'designation' in subsection (1).
(5) Before making such an order, the Scottish Ministers must consult the Keeper.

114 References to 'registering' etc in the Land Register of Scotland

(1) In this Act (other than subsection (2)), unless the context otherwise requires—
   (a) any reference to 'registration' is to registration in the register, and
   (b) analogous expressions are to be construed accordingly.
(2) Unless the context otherwise requires—
   (a) any reference, however expressed, in any enactment to 'registering' a document in the register, is to be construed as including a reference to giving effect to that document in accordance either with section 30 or with section 31, and
   (b) analogous expressions are to be construed accordingly.

115 Land register rules

(1) The Scottish Ministers may, by regulations, make land register rules—
   (a) regulating the making up and keeping of the register,
   (b) regulating the procedure in relation to applications for registration,
   (c) prescribing forms to be used in relation to the register,
   (d) as to when the application record is open for the making of entries,
   (e) requiring the Keeper to enter in the title sheet record such information as may be specified in the rules or authorising or requiring the Keeper to enter in that record such rights or obligations as may be so specified,
   (f) relating to any other matter which this Act provides may or must be provided for by land register rules, or
   (g) concerning other matters and seeming to them to be necessary or expedient in order to give full effect to the purposes of this Act.
(2) Before making land register rules, the Scottish Ministers must consult the Keeper.

116 Subordinate legislation

(1) Any power conferred by this Act on the Scottish Ministers to make orders or regulations may be exercised to make different provision for different cases or descriptions of case or for different purposes.
(2) Orders and regulations under the following sections are subject to the negative procedure—
   (a) section 11(6)(b),
   (b) section 27(6),
   (c) section 45(7),
   (d) section 48(2) or (3),

- (e) section 56(4),
- (f) subject to subsection (4)(a), section 100(1),
- (g) section 115(1),
- (h) subject to subsection (4)(b), section 117(1).

(3) Orders and regulations under the following provisions are subject to the affirmative procedure—
- (a) section 37(3),
- (b) section 43(8),
- (ba) section 48A(1),
- (bb) section 48B(1),
- (c) section 58(6),
- (d) section 61(3)(b),
- (e) section 64(1),
- (f) section 68(3),
- (g) section 79(4),
- (h) section 84(7),
- (i) section 95(4),
- (j) section 99(3),
- (k) section 107(1),
- (l) section 110(1),
- (m) section 113(4).

(4) Orders and regulations under the following sections which add to, replace or omit the text of any Act are subject to the affirmative procedure—
- (a) section 100(1),
- (b) section 117(1).

NOTE

Subs (3)(ba), (bb) inserted by Land Reform (Scotland) Act 2016 (c 18) s 43(3). At the time of going to press, this provision was not in force.

---

117 Ancillary provision

(1) The Scottish Ministers may, by order, make such incidental, supplementary, consequential, transitory, transitional or saving provision as they consider appropriate for the purposes of, in consequence of, or for giving full effect to, any provision made by or under this Act.

(2) An order under subsection (1) may modify any enactment (including this Act).

118 Transitional provisions

Schedule 4, which contains transitional provisions, has effect.

119 Minor and consequential modifications

Schedule 5, which contains minor amendments and repeals, and amendments and repeals consequential upon the provisions of this Act, has effect.

120 Saving provisions

(1) The amendments to the Prescription and Limitation (Scotland) Act 1973 (c 52) made by paragraph 18(2) and (4) of schedule 5 do not apply in relation to a continuous period which has expired before the designated day.

(2) Despite the repeal, by paragraph 19(5) of schedule 5, of section 28(1) of the Land Registration (Scotland) Act 1979 (c 33), that section continues to have effect for the purposes of sections 15(4), 16, 20 to 22A and 29 of and schedules 1 and 3 to the 1979 Act.

121 Crown application

(1) No contravention by the Crown of a requirement imposed by regulations under section 48A or of section 112 makes the Crown criminally liable.
(2) But the Court of Session may, on the application of the Keeper or any person authorised by the Keeper, declare unlawful any act or omission of the Crown which constitutes such a contravention.
(3) Despite subsection (1), regulations under section 48A and section 112 apply to persons in the public service of the Crown as they apply to other persons.

NOTE

Section 121(1), (3) amended by Land Reform (Scotland) Act 2016 (c 18) s 43(4). At the time of going to press, this provision was not in force.

122 The designated day

The Scottish Ministers may, for the purposes of this Act, by order, designate a day ('the designated day'), being a day which falls not less than 6 months after the order is made.

123 Commencement

(1) The following sections come into force on the day after Royal Assent—
   (a) section 113,
   (b) section 114(1),
   (c) section 116,
   (d) section 117,
   (e) section 122,
   (f) this section, and
   (g) section 124.
(2) The following provisions of this Act come into force on the designated day—
   (a) Parts 1 to 9 (other than sections 53(4) and 64) and schedules 1 and 2,
   (b) sections 101 to 106,
   (c) section 111,
   (d) section 112,
   (e) section 114(2),
   (f) section 115,
   (g) section 118 and schedule 4,
   (h) section 119 and schedule 5,
   (i) section 120, and
   (j) section 121.
(3) The other provisions of this Act come into force on such day as the Scottish Ministers may, by order, appoint.

124 Short title

The short title of this Act is the Land Registration etc (Scotland) Act 2012.

SCHEDULE 1
(introduced by section 20)

REGISTERED LEASES TENANTED IN COMMON

Shared leases

1 This schedule applies where—
   (a) an area of land—
      (i) is tenanted in common by the tenants of two or more registered leases by virtue of their tenancy under those leases,
      (ii) is not tenanted in common by anyone else,

(b) those registered leases have lease title sheets.
2 The Keeper may, if the Keeper considers it appropriate—
   (a) where the area tenanted in common does not have a lease title sheet, make up such a title sheet and designate it as a 'shared lease title sheet',
   (b) where that area is the subjects of a registered lease, make up (if necessary) a lease title sheet and designate it as a shared lease title sheet.
3 In the following provisions of this schedule—
   (a) references to a 'shared lease' are to a lease the title sheet of which is designated under paragraph 2,
   (b) references to the 'sharing leases' are to the other leases the tenants of which are tenants in common of the shared lease.
4 Unless the context otherwise requires, any reference in a document to a sharing lease is to be taken to include a reference to the share in the shared lease which pertains to the sharing lease.
5 Registration has the same effect in relation to a share in a shared lease which pertains to a sharing lease as it has in relation to the sharing lease (except in so far as may otherwise be provided in the deed registered).

Shared lease and sharing lease title sheets

6 The Keeper must enter—
   (a) in the property section of the title sheet of each of the sharing leases the title number of the shared lease title sheet,
   (b) in the proprietorship section of the shared lease title sheet, the title numbers of the title sheets of each sharing lease.
7 The Keeper must also enter—
   (a) in the property section of the title sheet of each sharing lease, the quantum of the share which the tenant of that sharing lease has in the shared lease,
   (b) in the proprietorship section of the shared lease title sheet, in relation to the information required by section 7(1)(b), the respective share each sharing lease has in the shared lease,
   (c) in the securities section of that title sheet, a statement to the effect that the shared lease may be subject to a heritable security registered against a sharing lease,
   (d) in the burdens section of that title sheet, a statement to the effect that the shared lease may be subject to some other encumbrance so registered.

NOTE
Paragraph 7(b), (c) – words substituted by Land Registration etc (Scotland) Act 2012 (Incidental, Consequential and Transitional) Order 2014, SSI 2014/190, art 5.

8 The Keeper must not enter in or, if entered, must omit from—
   (a) the proprietorship section of the shared lease title sheet, the information that would otherwise be required under section 7(1)(a),
   (b) the securities section of that title sheet, the information that would otherwise be required under section 8(1) unless the security is over the shared lease only,
   (c) that title sheet, any matter that would otherwise be required under section 10(2)(b).
9 The Keeper may, if the condition mentioned in paragraph 10 is satisfied and the Keeper considers it appropriate, omit from the burdens section of the shared lease title sheet any entry which would otherwise be required under section 9(1).
10 The condition is that the encumbrance to which the entry would relate is (or falls to be) registered against each of the sharing leases.

Conversion of shared lease title sheet to ordinary lease title sheet

11 The Keeper may at any time revoke a designation under paragraph 2 of a lease title sheet as a shared lease title sheet.

12 Where the Keeper revokes a designation, the Keeper must make such changes to the title sheets of the leases that were, in relation to the shared lease title sheet, the shared lease and the sharing leases as are consequential upon the revocation.

SCHEDULE 2
(introduced by section 52(3))

AMENDMENT OF REGISTRATION OF LEASES (SCOTLAND) ACT 1857

1 The Registration of Leases (Scotland) Act 1857 (c 26) is amended as follows.
2 In section 1 (long leases, and assignations thereof, registrable in Register of Sasines)—
   (a) before first 'record' insert 'register in the Land Register of Scotland or as the case may be',
   (b) for second 'record' to 'thereof' substitute 'register or record assignations and translations of such leases',
   (c) the existing provisions as so amended become subsection (1),
   (d) after that subsection insert—

   '(2) In subsection (1) above, the expression 'lands and heritages in Scotland' is, without prejudice to its generality, to be construed as including the seabed of the territorial sea of the United Kingdom adjacent to Scotland.'.

3 In the title of section 1 as so amended, for 'registerable' substitute 'registrable in Land Register of Scotland or Register of Sasines'.
4 In section 2 (recorded leases effectual against singular successors in the lands let)—
   (a) after 'duly' insert 'registered or',
   (b) in the proviso, after first 'of' insert ', and subject to section 20C of,'.
5 In the title of section 2 as so amended, for 'Recorded' substitute 'Registered and recorded'.
6 In section 3 (assignations of recorded leases)—
   (a) in subsection (1)—
      (i) after first 'been' insert 'registered or',
      (ii) before second 'recorded' insert 'registered or',
      (iii) after 'Schedule' insert '(ZA.) or, as the case may be,',
      (iv) before 'recording' insert 'registering or',
   (b) in subsection (2)—
      (i) repeal 'recording of such assignation or the',
      (ii) after first 'interest' insert 'or the registration of such assignation under the Land Registration etc (Scotland) Act 2012 (asp 5) or the recording of such assignation',
      (iii) for 'and it' to the end substitute 'and, as the case may be, the grantee's interest or the lease had been so registered or the lease had been duly recorded.',
   (c) in subsection (2C), repeal—
      (i) ', notwithstanding section 3(4) of the Land Registration (Scotland) Act 1979 (c 33) (creation of real right or obligation on date of registration etc),',
      (ii) 'of an interest in land under'.
7 In the title of section 3 as so amended, before 'recorded' insert 'registered or'.
8 In section 10 (adjudgers to complete right by recording abbreviate)—
   (a) after first 'lease' insert 'registered or recorded',
   (b) before 'recording' insert 'registering or',

(c) before second 'recorded' insert 'registered or'.
9 In section 12 (preferences regulated by date of recording transfer)—
   (a) after first 'assignations' insert 'of any such lease registered or recorded as aforesaid',
   (b) before second 'recorded' insert 'registered or',
   (c) before 'recording' insert 'registering or'.
10 In the title of section 12 as so amended, before 'recording' insert 'registering or'.
11 In section 13 (renunciations and discharges to be recorded)—
   (a) after first 'aforesaid' insert 'registered or',
   (b) for '(G.)' substitute '(ZG.) (or (G.))',
   (c) after 'duly' insert 'register or'.
12 In the title of section 13 as so amended, before 'recorded' insert 'registered or'.
13 In section 14 (entry of decree of reduction)—
   (a) after 'renunciation' insert 'registered or as the case may be',
   (b) after 'duly' insert 'register or'.
14 In section 15 (mode of registering etc)—
   (a) the existing provisions become subsection (1),
   (b) after that subsection insert—
      '(2) References in subsection (1) above to registration are not to be construed as including references to registration in the Land Register of Scotland.'.
15 In section 16 (registration equivalent to possession), after subsection (2) insert—
      '(3) References in subsections (1) and (2) above to registration are not to be construed as including references to registration in the Land Register of Scotland.'.
16 After section 20B (as inserted by section 52) insert—

'20C Disapplication of Leases Act 1449
The Leases Act 1449 (c 6) does not apply to a lease registrable under this Act and granted on or after the date on which—
   (a) the land to which the lease relates, or any part of that land, became land within an operational area (that is to say within an area in respect of which the provisions of the Land Registration (Scotland) Act 1979 (c 33) had come into operation), or
   (b) section 52 of the Land Registration etc (Scotland) Act 2012 (asp 5) (amendment of Registration of Leases (Scotland) Act 1857 (c 26)) comes into force.

20D Long fishing leases
This Act applies to a contract within the meaning of section 66 of the Salmon and Freshwater Fisheries (Consolidation) (Scotland) Act 2003 (asp 15) (application of Leases Act 1449) as it does to a lease described in section 1 of this Act provided that the contract in question—
   (a) is for a period exceeding 20 years, or
   (b) includes an obligation such as is described in section 17 of this Act.

20E The expression 'the register'
Except where the context otherwise requires, in this Act—
   (a) the expression 'the register' is to be construed as including a reference to the Land Register of Scotland, and
   (b) analogous expressions are to be construed accordingly.'.

17 Before schedule (A) insert—

'SCHEDULE (ZA)

FORM OF ASSIGNATION OF LEASE REGISTERED IN THE LAND REGISTER OF SCOTLAND'.

I, *A.B.* [*designation*] in consideration of the sum now paid to me, [*or otherwise, as the case may be,*] assign to *C.D.* [*designation*] a lease registered in the Land Register of Scotland under title number [*number*] [but (*where the lease is assigned in part only*) in so far only as regards the following portion of the subjects leased, viz (*specify particularly the portion*),] with entry as at (*term of entry*). And [*where sub-lease*] I assign the rents from [*term*]; and I grant warrandice, and I bind myself to free and relieve the said *C.D.* of all rents and burdens due to the landlord or others at and prior to the term of entry in respect of said lease, and I consent to registration for preservation and execution.

[*Testing clause.*†]

† Note—In the case of a traditional document, subscription of it by the granter will be sufficient for the document to be formally valid, but witnessing of it may be necessary or desirable for other purposes; see the Requirements of Writing (Scotland) Act 1995 (c 7) (which also makes provision as regards the authentication of an electronic document).'

18 In each of schedules (A) (form of assignation of lease), (G) (renunciation of lease) and (H) (form of discharge of bond and assignation in security), in the note relating to subscription of the document in question—
   (a) for 'Subscription of the document by the granter of it' substitute 'In the case of a traditional document, subscription of it by the granter',
   (b) after '1995' insert ', which also makes provision as regards the authentication of an electronic document'.
19 In the title of schedule (A), at the end insert 'recorded in Register of Sasines'.
20 Schedule (B) (form of bond and assignation in security) and the note to that schedule are repealed.
21 Schedule (D) (form of translation of assignation in security) and the note to that schedule are repealed.
22 Before schedule (G) insert—

'SCHEDULE (ZG.)

RENUNCIATION OF LEASE REGISTERED IN THE LAND REGISTER OF SCOTLAND'.

I, *A.B.* [*designation*] renounce as from the term of [*term*] in favour of *C.D.* [*or as the case may be*] a lease granted by the said *C.D.* [*or as the case may be*] and registered in the Land Register of Scotland under title number [*number*].

[*Testing clause.*†]

† Note—In the case of a traditional document, subscription of it by the granter will be sufficient for the document to be formally valid, but witnessing of it may be necessary or desirable for other purposes: see the Requirements of Writing (Scotland) Act 1995 (c 7) (which also makes provision as regards the authentication of an electronic document).'

23 In the title of schedule (G), at the end insert 'recorded in the Register of Sasines'.

Schedule 3 (which amends the Requirements of Writing (Scotland) Act 1995) is omitted.

...

SCHEDULE 4
(*introduced by section 118*)

TRANSITIONAL PROVISIONS

Existing title sheets

1. On the designated day an existing title sheet becomes part of the title sheet record.
2. An existing title sheet which becomes, under paragraph 1, part of the title sheet record, may be amended by the Keeper so as—
   (a) to conform with a requirement of, or imposed by virtue of, this Act, or
   (b) to reflect something permitted by, or by virtue of, this Act.
3. An amendment under paragraph 2 may be made on the designated day or at such later date as the Keeper considers appropriate.
4. An existing title sheet as respects an interest of ownership becomes under paragraph 1 a title sheet as respects a plot of land; and the Keeper, on or as soon as practicable after the designated day, must create a cadastral unit for that plot.
5. An existing title sheet as respects an interest of tenancy becomes under paragraph 1 a lease title sheet.
6. Section 12(2) does not apply to a cadastral unit created under paragraph 4.

Common areas: general

7. If, by reason of being owned in common, the selfsame area of land is, immediately before the designated day, included in two or more existing title sheets the Keeper may, if the Keeper considers it appropriate, make up a title sheet for that area and create a cadastral unit for it.
8. Where a title sheet is created by virtue of paragraph 7—
   (a) the Keeper is to make such changes to the other title sheets mentioned in that paragraph and to the cadastral map as are consequential upon its being so constituted, and
   (b) the respective shares of the proprietors of the area of land need only be entered in the title sheet if they were entered in the existing title sheets.

Common areas: developments begun before designated day

9. If, by reason of being owned in common, the selfsame area of land (in this paragraph and in paragraph 11 referred to as 'area A') is, immediately before the designated day, included in two or more existing title sheets and on or after that day title sheets (in this paragraph and in paragraph 10 referred to as the 'new title sheets') are to be constituted for plots of land the proprietors of which will (qua proprietors of those plots) be comprised within those who own area A in common, area A may, by reason of being owned in common, be included in the new title sheets.
10. Where the respective shares of the proprietors were not entered in the existing title sheets they need not be entered in the new title sheets.
11. The Keeper may at any time create a separate title sheet for area A.

Common areas: Sasine arrangements

11A For the period beginning with the designated day and ending with the day before the date prescribed by an order under section 48(3)—
   (a) section 7(1)(b) applies only to shares of proprietors whose right is registered,
   (b) in the case of ownership in common, section 8(1) applies only to heritable securities granted by a proprietor whose right is registered,
   (c) section 17(3)(b) applies to such of the plots of land mentioned in section 17(1)(a) as are registered,

(d) section 27(2) applies also to a person whose right in the plot is registered only as proprietor of a share in the plot, and
(e) section 48(1)(d) applies as if a registered plot of land means a registered share of a plot of land owned in common.

NOTE
Paragraph 11A inserted by Land Registration etc (Scotland) Act 2012 (Incidental, Consequential and Transitional) Order 2014, SSI 2014/190, art 6.

Certain deeds relating to registered leases: Sasine arrangements
11B For the period beginning with the designated day and ending with the day before the date prescribed by an order under section 48(3), for an application under section 21(1) to register a deed (except a sublease or a notice of title) which affects a lease title sheet where the subjects of the lease consist of or form part of an unregistered plot of land, the conditions in section 26 apply with the effect that—
(a) in subsection (1)(b), 'plot of land' is to be read as 'lease',
(b) in subsection (1)(c), 'title sheet' is to be read as 'lease title sheet',
(c) subsections (1)(d), (3), (4) and (5) do not apply, and
(d) in subsection (2), 'plot' in both places it occurs is to be read as 'lease'.

NOTES
Paragraph heading substituted by Land Registration etc (Scotland) Act 2012 (Amendment and Transitional) Order 2014, SSI 2014/346, art 4(2).
Paragraph 11B inserted by Land Registration etc (Scotland) Act 2012 (Incidental, Consequential and Transitional) Order 2014, SSI 2014/190, art 6. Words substituted by Land Registration etc (Scotland) Act 2012 (Amendment and Transitional) Order 2014, SSI 2014/346, art 4(1).

Archive record
12 The Keeper must include in the archive record—
(a) all copies of documents upon which the terms of the existing title sheets are founded,
(b) all copies of documents which relate to past states of title sheets and title plans, and
(c) such other information, in whatever form, as so relates,
in so far as those copy documents, and as the case may be that other information, is held by the Keeper immediately before the designated day.

Pending applications
13 Nothing in this Act, other than provision made by or by virtue of section 35, affects an application under section 4 (applications for registration) of the Land Registration (Scotland) Act 1979 (c 33) (the '1979 Act') provided that the date of receipt of the application is before the designated day.
14 An application by virtue of section 9(1) of the 1979 Act (rectification of the register) falls if it has not been determined by the Keeper as at the designated day.

Claims under the 1979 Act
15 Where, immediately before the designated day, a person has an entitlement to claim indemnity under section 12(1) of the 1979 Act (indemnity in respect of loss) but either—
(a) no such claim has been made, or
(b) any such claim as has been made is as yet undetermined,
nothing in this Act affects the entitlement or claim.

16 Nothing in this Act affects any entitlement to reimbursement under subsection (1) of section 13 of the 1979 Act (reimbursement of certain expenditure) or any claim made by virtue of that subsection.

Bijural inaccuracies

17 If there is in the register, immediately before the designated day, an inaccuracy which the Keeper has power to rectify under section 9 of the 1979 Act (rectification of the register) then, as from that day—
   (a) any person whose rights in land would have been affected by such rectification has such rights (if any) in the land as that person would have if the power had been exercised, and
   (b) the register is inaccurate in so far as it does not show those rights as so affected.

18 For the purpose of determining whether the Keeper has the power mentioned in paragraphs 17 and 22, the person registered as proprietor of the land is to be presumed to be in possession unless the contrary is shown.

19 Where, by virtue of paragraph 17—
   (a) a right is lost, compensation is payable under Part 7 as if warranty had been granted under section 73 in accepting an application by the person in whom the right was vested, or
   (b) an encumbrance is revived, compensation is so payable as if such warranty had been granted in respect of an omission of the encumbrance.

20 Except that—
   (a) compensation is not so payable in so far as, had the Keeper rectified the inaccuracy before the designated day, either a right to indemnity under section 12 of the 1979 Act (indemnity in respect of loss) was excluded by virtue of subsection (2) of that section or there would, by virtue of subsection (3) of that section, have been no entitlement to such indemnity,
   (b) any compensation so payable is to be reduced to the extent that, had the Keeper rectified the inaccuracy before the designated day, the amount of any indemnity would have been reduced by virtue of section 13(4) of that Act (reduction proportionate to the extent to which a claimant has contributed, by fraudulent or careless act or omission, to loss), and
   (c) in construing Part 7 for the purposes of paragraph 19, paragraphs (b) and (c) of section 78 are to be disregarded.

21 Section 77(4) and (5) applies in relation to a payment made by virtue of paragraph 19(a) as that section applies in relation to any other payment under Part 7.

22 If there is in the register, immediately before the designated day, an inaccuracy which the Keeper does not have power to rectify under section 9 of the 1979 Act, then on that day it ceases to be an inaccuracy.

23 Where, by virtue of paragraph 22, a person suffers loss which, had it been suffered by virtue of paragraph (b) of section 12(1) of the 1979 Act, would (after allowing for the effect of subsections (2) and (3) of that section) have given rise before the designated day to an entitlement under that section, the person is entitled to claim compensation, by virtue of this paragraph, from the Keeper in respect of that loss.

24 Sections 94(3) to (6) and 95 apply in respect of a claim by virtue of paragraph 23 as they apply in respect of a claim by virtue of section 94(1), but with the modification that, for paragraph (a) of section 95(1), there is substituted—

   '(a) is, in so far as it is not compensation mentioned in paragraph (b), to be quantified as at the date on which the register became inaccurate,'.

Depiction of tenement etc

25 Section 16(3) does not apply if any of the flats comprised in the flatted building mentioned in that subsection—

(a) is recorded in the Register of Sasines, or
(b) is registered by virtue of an application accepted under section 4 of the 1979 Act.

SCHEDULE 5
(introduced by section 119)

MINOR AND CONSEQUENTIAL MODIFICATIONS

Lands Clauses Consolidation (Scotland) Act 1845 (c 19)

1 In the Lands Clauses Consolidation (Scotland) Act 1845, in the note to schedule (A.) (form of conveyance)—
  (a) for 'Subscription of the document by the granter of it' substitute 'In the case of a traditional document, subscription of it by the granter',
  (b) after '1995' insert ', which also makes provision as regards the authentication of an electronic document'.

Commissioners Clauses Act 1847 (c 16)

2 (1) The Commissioners Clauses Act 1847 is amended as follows.
  (2) In section 59(2) (conveyance of lands by commissioners)—
    (a) in paragraph (a)—
      (i) for 'in accordance with section 7 of, and paragraph 5 of Schedule 2 to,' substitute 'or authenticated in accordance with',
      (ii) for 'subscribed in accordance with the said section 7' substitute 'so subscribed or authenticated',
      (iii) for ', followed by infeftment duly recorded' substitute 'or authenticated, duly registered in the Land Register of Scotland',
    (b) in paragraph (b), for 'word "subscribed"' substitute 'the words "subscribed or authenticated"'.
  (3) In section 75(2)(c) (form of mortgage)—
    (a) in sub-paragraph (i), repeal 'section 7 of, and paragraph 5 of Schedule 2 to,',
    (b) in sub-paragraph (ii), for 'section 7' substitute 'Act'.

Ordnance Board Transfer Act 1855 (c 117)

3 In section 5(2) of the Ordnance Board Transfer Act 1855 (description in conveyances etc), after 'subscribing' insert ', or as the case may be authenticating,'.

Transmission of Moveable Property (Scotland) Act 1862 (c 85)

4 In the Transmission of Moveable Property (Scotland) Act 1862, in the note to each of schedules A (form for assignation of bond or conveyance) and B (form of bond or conveyance)—
  (a) for 'Subscription of the document by the granter of it' substitute 'In the case of a traditional document, subscription of it by the granter',
  (b) after '1995' insert ', which also makes provision as regards the authentication of an electronic document'.

Land Registers (Scotland) Act 1868 (c 64)

5 (1) The Land Registers (Scotland) Act 1868 is amended as follows.
  (2) Sections 13, 19 and 25 are repealed.

Titles to Land Consolidation (Scotland) Act 1868 (c 101)

6 (1) The Titles to Land Consolidation (Scotland) Act 1868 is amended as follows.

(2) In section 159 (litigiosity not to begin before date of registration of notice of summons)—
   (a) the existing provisions become subsection (1),
   (b) after that subsection insert—

   '(2) A notice registered under subsection (1) on or after the date on which section 67 of the Land Registration etc (Scotland) Act 2012 (asp 5) (warrant to place a caveat) comes into force shall not have any effect in rendering litigious any land a title sheet for which is comprised in the Land Register of Scotland or in placing in bad faith any person acquiring such land.'.

(3) In section 159A (registration of notice of summons of action of reduction)—
   (a) in each of subsections (2)(b) and (3)(b), repeal 'register in the Land Register of Scotland or, as the case may be,',
   (b) after subsection (3) insert—

   '(4) This section does not apply in relation to lands for which there is a title sheet in the Land Register of Scotland.'.

(4) In schedule B, in form No 1 (formal clauses of a disposition of land etc), in the note relating to subscription of the document in question—
   (a) for 'Subscription of the document by the granter of it' substitute 'In the case of a traditional document, subscription of it by the granter',
   (b) after '1995' insert ', which also makes provision as regards the authentication of an electronic document'.

Conveyancing (Scotland) Act 1874 (c 94)

7 (1) The Conveyancing (Scotland) Act 1874 is amended as follows.
   (2) In schedule M (form of assignation of right of relief etc), in the note—
      (a) for 'Subscription of the document by the granter of it' substitute 'In the case of a traditional document, subscription of it by the granter',
      (b) after '1995' insert ', which also makes provision as regards the authentication of an electronic document'.

Trusts (Scotland) Act 1921 (c 58)

8 (1) The Trusts (Scotland) Act 1921 is amended as follows.
   (2) In schedule A (form of minute of resignation), in the note—
      (a) for 'Subscription of the document by the granter of it' substitute 'In the case of a traditional document, subscription of it by the granter',
      (b) after '1995' insert ', which also makes provision as regards the authentication of an electronic document'.
   (3) In schedule B (form of deed of assumption), in the note—
      (a) for 'Subscription of the document by the granter or granters of it' substitute 'In the case of a traditional document, subscription of it by the granter or granters',
      (b) after '1995' insert ', which also makes provision as regards the authentication of an electronic document'.

Conveyancing (Scotland) Act 1924 (c 27)

9 (1) The Conveyancing (Scotland) Act 1924 is amended as follows.
   (2) In section 2(5) (interpretation), after 'registrable' insert 'in the Land Register of Scotland or'.
   (3) In section 3 (disposition etc), for 'manner' substitute 'such manner as was (immediately before the repeal of the note)'.
   (4) In section 44 (General Register of Inhibitions and Register of Adjudications to be combined; limitation of effect of entries therein), after subsection (2) insert—

'(2A) A notice registered under subsection (2)(a)(i) of this section on or after the date on which section 67 of the Land Registration etc. (Scotland) Act 2012 (asp 5) (warrant to place a caveat) comes into force shall not have any effect in rendering—
(a) any land or lease for which there is a title sheet in the Land Register of Scotland, or
(b) any heritable security the particulars of which are entered in a title sheet in that register,
litigious or in placing in bad faith any person acquiring such land, lease or heritable security.'.
(5) In schedule B (notice of title), in note 8—
(a) for 'Subscription of the document' substitute 'In the case of a traditional document, subscription of it',
(b) after '1995' insert ', which also makes provision as regards the authentication of an electronic document'.
(6) The title of schedule B becomes 'Forms of notice of title: Register of Sasines'.

Burgh Registers (Scotland) Act 1926 (c 50)

10 The Burgh Registers (Scotland) Act 1926 is repealed.

Public Registers and Records (Scotland) Act 1948 (c 57)

11 Section 4 of the Public Registers and Records (Scotland) Act 1948 is repealed.

Land Drainage (Scotland) Act 1958 (c 24)

12 In section 18(1) of the Land Drainage (Scotland) Act 1958 (interpretation), in the definition of 'long lease', after 'being,' insert 'registered in the Land Register of Scotland or'.

Harbours Act 1964 (c 40)

13 In section 57(1) of the Harbours Act 1964 (interpretation), in the definition of 'long lease', after 'being,' insert 'registered in the Land Register of Scotland or'.

Succession (Scotland) Act 1964 (c 41)

14 In section 21A(a) of the Succession (Scotland) Act 1964 (evidence as to testamentary documents in commissary proceedings), after 'subscribed' insert 'or under section 9C or 9D (or by virtue of section 9E(1) of that Act to have been authenticated'.

NOTE
Paragraph 14 amended by Land Registration etc (Scotland) Act 2012 (Amendment and Transitional) Order 2014, SSI 2014/346, art 3.

NOTE
Paragraph 15 repealed by Co-operative and Community Benefit Societies Act 2014 (c 14) Sch 7.

Gas Act 1965 (c 36)

16 In section 28(1) of the Gas Act 1965 (interpretation of Part 2 of the Act), in the definition of 'long lease' for the purposes of the definition of 'owner', after 'being,' insert 'registered in the Land Register of Scotland or'.

Conveyancing and Feudal Reform (Scotland) Act 1970 (c 35)

17 (1) The Conveyancing and Feudal Reform (Scotland) Act 1970 is amended as follows.
    (2) In section 9 (the standard security)—
        (a) in subsection (2), after first 'to' insert 'grant and register in the Land Register of Scotland or to',
        (b) in subsection (4)—
            (i) after 'duly' insert 'registered or',
            (ii) after 'clear' insert 'the Land Register of Scotland or',
        (c) in subsection (8), both—
            (i) in paragraph (a), after second 'being' insert 'registered in the Land Register of Scotland or',
            (ii) in paragraph (b), after 'be' insert 'registered in the Land Register of Scotland or'.
    (3) In section 10(4) (import of forms of, and certain clauses in, standard security), after 'duly' insert 'registered or'.
    (4) In section 11(1) (effect of recorded standard security, and incorporation of standard security), after 'duly' insert 'registered or'.
    (5) In the title of section 11 as so amended, after first 'of' insert 'registered or'.
    (6) In section 12 (standard security may be granted by person uninfeft)—
        (a) for subsection (1) substitute—
            '(1) Notwithstanding any rule of law, a standard security may be granted over land or a real right in land by a person whose title thereto has not been completed by being duly registered or recorded.
            (1A) If the deed expressing the security is to be recorded in the Register of Sasines, the grantor must, in that deed, deduce his title to the land or real right from the person who appears in the Register of Sasines as having the last recorded title thereto.',
        (b) in subsection (2)—
            (i) for 'such a deed being' substitute 'a deed expressing the security being registered or',
            (ii) repeal 'to which he has deduced title therein',
            (iii) after 'last' insert 'registered or'.
    (7) In section 13 (ranking of standard securities)—
        (a) in subsection (1)—
            (i) after 'duly' insert 'registered or',
            (ii) after 'so' insert 'registered or',
        (b) in subsection (2)(a)—
            (i) after 'duly' insert 'registered or',
            (ii) after 'subsequent' insert 'registration or',
            (iii) after third 'the' insert 'Land Register of Scotland or',
        (c) after subsection (3) insert—
            '(4) An agreement as to the ranking among themselves of two or more standard securities which are granted over the same land or the same real right in land may be registered in the Land Register of Scotland.'.
    (8) In section 14(1) (assignation of standard security), after 'duly', in both places, insert 'registered or'.
    (9) In section 15 (restriction of standard security)—
        (a) in subsection (1), after 'duly', in both places, insert 'registered or',
        (b) in subsection (2), after 'duly' insert 'registered or'.
    (10) In section 16 (variation of standard security)—
        (a) in subsection (1), after 'duly', in both places, insert 'registered or',
        (b) in subsection (2)—

(i) after 'duly' insert 'registered or',
(ii) after 'so' insert 'registered or',
(iii) after 'be' insert 'registered in the Land Register of Scotland or',
(c) in subsection (4)—
(i) after first 'is' insert 'registered or',
(ii) after 'an' insert 'unregistered or'.
(11) In section 17 (discharge of standard security), after 'duly', in both places, insert 'registered or'.
(12) In section 18(3) (redemption of standard security), after 'duly' insert 'registered or'.
(13) In section 19 (calling-up of standard security)—
(a) in subsection (2)—
(i) after 'last', in both places, insert 'registered or',
(ii) after first 'appearing' insert 'in the Land Register of Scotland or',
(iii) after 'record' insert 'of the Register of Sasines',
(iv) before 'Register' insert 'Land Register of Scotland or',
(b) in subsection (3), after the word 'last', in both places, insert 'registered or'.
(14) In section 26 (disposition by creditor on sale)—
(a) in subsection (1), after 'duly' insert 'registered or',
(b) in subsection (2), after second 'the' insert 'registration or'.
(15) In section 27(1)(c) (application of proceeds of sale), after 'duly' inser 'registered or'.
(16) In section 28 (foreclosure)—
(a) in subsection (5)—
(i) after 'duly' insert 'registered or',
(ii) for 'section 15 of the Land Registration (Scotland) Act 1979' substitute 'the Land Registration etc (Scotland) Act 2012 (asp 5)',
(iii) after 'warrant' insert 'for registering the extract of the decree in the Land Register of Scotland or',
(b) in subsection (6)—
(i) after 'duly', in both places, insert 'registered or',
(ii) in paragraph (a), after 'date' insert 'of the registration or',
(c) in subsection (7), after 'due' insert 'registration or'.
(17) In section 30(1) (interpretation of Part 2)—
(a) for the definition of 'duly recorded' substitute—
' "duly registered or recorded" means registered in the Land Register of Scotland or recorded in the Register of Sasines;',
(b) after the definition of 'real right in land' insert—
' "recorded" means recorded in the Register of Sasines,',
(c) after the definition of 'Register of Sasines' insert—
' "registered" means registered in the Land Register of Scotland;'.
(18) In section 53(4) (interpretation of Act other than Part 2), for the definition of 'duly recorded' substitute—
' "duly registered or recorded" means registered in the Land Register of Scotland or recorded in the Register of Sasines;'.
(19) In the notes to schedule 2 (forms of standard security)—
(a) in note 2, after first 'subjects' insert 'and the deed is to be recorded in the Register of Sasines',
(b) in note 3, after first 'security' insert 'to be recorded in the Register of Sasines',
(c) in note 4, after second 'be' insert 'registered in the Land Register of Scotland or',
(d) in note 8—
(i) for 'Subscription of the document by the granter of it' substitute 'In the case of a traditional document, subscription of it by the granter',

(ii) after '1995' insert ', which also makes provision as regards the authentication of an electronic document'.
(20) In paragraph 12 of schedule 3 (the standard conditions)—
  (a) before 'recorded' insert 'registered or',
  (b) before 'recording' insert 'registration or'.
(21) In schedule 4 (forms of deeds of assignation, restriction etc) in each of forms A, C, D, E and F, for 'recorded in the register for......on.....' substitute 'registered in the Land Register of Scotland on.....over title number.....(or recorded in the Register for......on.......)'.
(22) In the notes to schedule 4—
  (a) in note 1—
    (i) after first 'title' insert 'and the deed is to be recorded in the Register of Sasines',
    (ii) before fourth 'recorded' insert 'registered or',
  (b) in note 3—
    (i) after first 'by' insert 'registration of the security in the Land Register of Scotland or',
    (ii) for 'recorded' substitute 'registered (or recorded)',
  (c) in note 5—
    (i) before 'recorded', in the first two places, insert 'registered or',
    (ii) before third 'recorded' insert 'registered in the Land Register of Scotland or',
  (d) in note 6, after first 'subjects' insert 'and the deed is to be recorded in the Register of Sasines',
  (e) in note 7—
    (i) for 'Subscription of the document by the granter of it' substitute 'In the case of a traditional document, subscription of it by the granter',
    (ii) after '1995' insert ', which also makes provision as regards the authentication of an electronic document'.
(23) In schedule 5 (procedures as to redemption)—
  (a) in form A, for 'recorded in the register for......on.....' substitute 'registered in the Land Register of Scotland on.....over title number.....(or recorded in the Register for......on.......)',
  (b) in form D (nos. 1 and 2), for 'recorded in the register for......on.....' substitute 'registered in the Land Register of Scotland on.....over title number.....(or recorded in the Register for......on.......)',
  (c) in each of the notes to form D—
    (i) for 'Subscription of the document by the granter of it' substitute 'In the case of a traditional document, subscription of it by the granter',
    (ii) after '1995' insert ', which also makes provision as regards the authentication of an electronic document'.
(24) In schedule 6 (procedures as to calling-up and default), in each of forms A and B for 'recorded in the register for......on.....' substitute 'registered in the Land Register of Scotland on.....over title number.....(or recorded in the Register for......on.......)'.
(25) In schedule 9 (discharge of heritable security constituted by ex facie absolute conveyance), in note 4—
  (a) for 'Subscription of the document by the granter of it' substitute 'In the case of a traditional document, subscription of it by the granter',
  (b) after '1995' insert ', which also makes provision as regards the authentication of an electronic document'.

Prescription and Limitation (Scotland) Act 1973 (c 52)

18 (1) The Prescription and Limitation (Scotland) Act 1973 is amended as follows.

(2) In section 1 of the Prescription and Limitation (Scotland) Act 1973 (c 52) (validity of right), for subsection (1)(b) substitute—

'(b) the registration of a deed which is sufficient in respect of its terms to constitute in favour of that person a real right in—

(i) that land; or

(ii) land of a description habile to include that land,'.

(3) In section 2 (special cases)—

(a) in subsection (1)(b), for 'recorded or not' substitute 'or not registered or recorded',

(b) in subsection (2)(b), after 'been' insert 'registered or',

(c) in subsection (3), for 'section 3(3) of the Land Registration (Scotland) Act 1979 (c 33)' substitute 'section 20B or 20C of the Registration of Leases (Scotland) Act 1857 (c 26)'.

(4) In section 5 (further provision supplementary to sections 1, 2 and 3 of the Prescription and Limitation (Scotland) Act 1973), after subsection (1) insert—

'(1A) Any reference in those sections to a real right's being exempt from challenge as from the expiration of some continuous period is to be construed, if the real right of the possessor was void immediately before that expiration, as including reference to acquisition of the real right by the possessor.'.

(5) In section 15(1) (interpretation of Part 1 of the Act), at end insert 'and to the registering of a deed are to the registering thereof in the Land Register of Scotland'.

(6) In paragraph 1 of schedule 1 (obligations affected by prescriptive periods of 5 years under section 6 of that Act), after sub-paragraph (aca) insert—

'(ad) to any obligation of the Keeper of the Registers of Scotland to pay compensation by virtue of section 84 of the Land Registration etc (Scotland) Act 2012 (asp 5);

(ae) to any obligation to pay compensation by virtue of section 111 of that Act;'.

(7) In paragraph 2 of that schedule (obligations which, notwithstanding paragraph 1 of the schedule, are not affected by prescriptive periods of 5 years under section 6 of that Act), in sub-paragraph (e)—

...

(b) after 'servitude)' insert 'and any obligation of the Keeper of the Registers of Scotland to pay compensation by virtue of section 77 or 94 of the Land Registration etc (Scotland) Act 2012 (asp 5)'.

(8) In schedule 3 (rights and obligations which are imprescriptible for certain purposes of that Act) after sub-paragraph (h) insert—

'(i) any obligation of the Keeper of the Registers of Scotland to rectify an inaccuracy in the Land Register of Scotland'.

NOTE
Paragraph 18(6) amended by and 18(7)(a) repealed by Land Registration etc (Scotland) Act 2012 (Incidental, Consequential and Transitional) Order 2014, SSI 2014/190, art 2(2).

Land Registration (Scotland) Act 1979 (c 33)

19 (1) The Land Registration (Scotland) Act 1979 is amended as follows.

(2) Sections 1 to 14 are repealed.

(3) In section 15 (simplification of deeds relating to registered interests)—

(a) subsections (1) to (3) are repealed,

(b) in subsection (4)—

(i) for 'registered interest in land' substitute 'plot of land or lease registered in the Land Register of Scotland',
(ii) for 'that interest' substitute 'the plot or lease'.
(4) Section 19 is repealed.
(5) Sections 23 to 28 are repealed.
(6) In section 29(3) (references to recording to include references to registering), paragraph (b) is repealed.
(7) Section 30 is repealed.
(8) Schedule 2 is repealed.
(9) In schedule 3 (enactments not affected by section 29(2))—
  (a) paragraphs 3, 4, 10, 12 and 13 are repealed,
  (b) in paragraph 5, for paragraphs (a) to (c) substitute 'The Whole Act.',
  (c) in paragraph 6—
    (i) for paragraph (d) substitute—
      '(d) Section 12
      (da) Section 14',
    (ii) paragraph (e) is repealed,
  (d) in paragraph 7, paragraphs (a), (c) to (f), (i) and (j)) are repealed,
  (e) in paragraph 8, paragraph (b) is repealed,
  (f) in paragraph 11—
    (i) in paragraph (a), repeal 'and note 2 to Schedule K',
    (ii) paragraphs (d) and (e) are repealed,
    (iii) in paragraph (f), for '24(3)' to the end substitute '24(2) and (3) and that part of subsection (5) from the words 'provided that' to the end',
    (iv) for paragraph (g) substitute—
      '(ga) Section 46',
    (v) after paragraph (i) insert—
      '(j) Schedule J',
  (g) in paragraph 16, for paragraphs (a) and (b) substitute 'The Whole Act.'.
(10) Schedule 4 is repealed.

Education (Scotland) Act 1980 (c 44)

20 In section 16(2) of the Education (Scotland) Act 1980 (transference of denominational schools to education authorities)—
  (a) for paragraphs (a) and (b) substitute 'by registration in the Land Register of Scotland of an ordinary disposition or other deed of conveyance by the persons vested with the title',
  (b) for 'the recording of the deed of conveyance or, as the case may be,' substitute 'such'.

Water (Scotland) Act 1980 (c 45)

21 (1) The Water (Scotland) Act 1980 is amended as follows.
(2) In section 58(5) (termination of right to supply of water on special terms), for 'record' to the end substitute '—
  (a) register in the Land Register of Scotland any agreement entered into, or order made, under the foregoing provisions of this section terminating an obligation to which this section applies if the obligation was itself registered in the Land Register, or
  (b) record in the Register of Sasines any such agreement or order if the obligation was itself recorded in the Register of Sasines.'.
(3) In section 68(2) (agreements as to drainage), for 'recorded in the appropriate' substitute 'registered in the Land Register of Scotland or recorded in the'.
(4) Section 109(5) is repealed.

Matrimonial Homes (Family Protection) (Scotland) Act 1981 (c 59)

22 In section 13(8) of the Matrimonial Homes (Family Protection) (Scotland) Act 1981 (transfer of tenancy), in the definition of 'long lease', for 'section 28(1) of the Land Registration (Scotland) Act 1979' substitute 'section 9(2) of the Land Registration etc (Scotland) Act 2012 (asp 5)'.

Civil Aviation Act 1982 (c 16)

23 In section 55 of the Civil Aviation Act 1982 (c 16) (registration of orders etc under Part 2 of the Act)—
  (a) in subsection (2), repeal 'in the Land Register of Scotland',
  (b) in subsection (3), for second 'as' to 'interest' substitute ', and on being registered shall be enforceable against any person having or subsequently acquiring any right',
  (c) for subsection (4) substitute—

  '(4) References in—
  (a) subsection (2) above to registering a grant or agreement, or
  (b) subsection (3) above to registering an instrument,
  are to registering it in the Land Register of Scotland or, as the case may be, to recording it in the Register of Sasines.'.

Litter Act 1983 (c 35)

24 In section 8 of the Litter Act 1983 (provisions supplementary to section 7 of the Act)—
  (a) in subsection (3)—
    (i) repeal 'Subject to subsection (4) below,',
    (ii) for the words from 'be registered' to 'so registered' substitute '—
      (a) if the land is registered in the Land Register of Scotland, be registered in that register, and
      (b) in any other case, be recorded in the Register of Sasines,
      and if the agreement is so registered or recorded it',
  (b) subsection (4) is repealed.

Health and Social Services and Social Security Adjudications Act 1983 (c 41)

25 In section 23(1) of the Health and Social Services and Social Security Adjudications Act 1983 (arrears of contributions secured over interest in land in Scotland), for 'Land Registration (Scotland) Act 1979' substitute 'Land Registration etc (Scotland) Act 2012'.

Telecommunications Act 1984 (c 12)

26 In schedule 4 of the Telecommunications Act 1984 (minor and consequential amendments), paragraph 71 is repealed.

Matrimonial and Family Proceedings Act 1984 (c 42)

27 In schedule 1 of the Matrimonial and Family Proceedings Act 1984 (minor and consequential amendments), paragraph 28 is repealed.

Bankruptcy (Scotland) Act 1985 (c 66)

28 (1) The Bankruptcy (Scotland) Act 1985 is amended as follows.
  (2) In section 5 (sequestration of estate of a living or deceased debtor), in subsection (4AA)(a)(ii), for '28(1) of the Land Registration (Scotland) Act 1979 (c.33)' substitute '9(2) of the Land Registration etc (Scotland) Act 2012 (asp 5))'.
  (3) In schedule 7 (consequential amendments), paragraph 15 is repealed.

Housing Associations Act 1985 (c 69)

29 In section 68(6) of the Housing Associations Act 1985 (loans by Public Works Loan Commissioners: Scotland), after 'lease' insert 'registered or'.

Law Reform (Miscellaneous Provisions)(Scotland) Act 1985 (c 73)

30 In section 8 of the Law Reform (Miscellaneous Provisions)(Scotland) Act 1985 (rectification of defectively expressed documents)—
    (a) in subsection (7), at end insert 'except that this subsection is subject to subsection (8A) below.',
    (b) after subsection (8) insert—
        '(8A) A notice under subsection (7) above registered on or after the date on which section 67 of the Land Registration etc (Scotland) Act 2012 (asp 5) (warrant to place a caveat) comes into force shall not have any effect in rendering litigious any land for which there is a title sheet in the Land Register of Scotland or in placing in bad faith any person acquiring such land.'.

Electricity Act 1989 (c 29)

31 In schedule 16 to the Electricity Act 1989 (minor and consequential amendments), paragraph 23 is repealed.

NOTE
Paragraph 32 repealed by Property Misdescriptions Act 1991 (Repeal) Order 2013, SI 2013/1575, schedule.

Agricultural Holdings (Scotland) Act 1991 (c 55)

33 In section 75(1) of the Agricultural Holdings (Scotland) Act 1991 (power of tenant and landlord to obtain charge on holding), after 'recorded' insert 'or registered'.

Coal Industry Act 1994 (c 21)

34 In the Coal Industry Act 1994, in schedule 9 (minor and consequential amendments), paragraph 20 is repealed.

Land Registers (Scotland) Act 1995 (c 14)

35 In section 1 of the Land Registers (Scotland) Act 1995 (prepayment of recording and registration fees)—
    (a) in subsection (1), for 'payment' to the end substitute '—
        (a) such fee as is payable in that respect by virtue of section 110 of the Land Registration etc (Scotland) Act 2012 (asp 5) is paid, or
        (b) arrangements satisfactory to the Keeper are made for payment of that fee.',
    (b) subsection (3) is repealed.

Petroleum Act 1998 (c 17)

36 In section 5(9) of the Petroleum Act 1998 (existing licences), after 'subscribed' insert 'or authenticated'.

Public Finance and Accountability (Scotland) Act 2000 (asp 1)

37 In section 9(1) of the Public Finance and Accountability (Scotland) Act 2000 (Keeper of the Registers of Scotland: financial arrangements), for 'section 25 of the Land Registers (Scotland) Act 1868 (c 64)' substitute 'section 110 of the Land Registration etc (Scotland) Act 2012 (asp 5)'.

Adults with Incapacity (Scotland) Act 2000 (asp 4)

38 (1) The Adults with Incapacity (Scotland) Act 2000 is amended as follows.
   (2) In section 56(7) (registration of intervention order relating to heritable property, for 'the updated Land Certificate or an office copy thereof' substitute 'an extract of the updated title sheet'.
   (3) In section 61(7) (registration of guardianship order relating to heritable property), for 'the updated Land Certificate or an office copy thereof' substitute 'an extract of the updated title sheet'.

Abolition of Feudal Tenure etc (Scotland) Act 2000 (asp 5)

39 (1) The Abolition of Feudal Tenure etc. (Scotland) Act 2000 is amended as follows.
   (2) Section 4 is repealed.
   (3) In section 18A(8)(b) (personal pre-emption burdens and personal redemption burdens), for '15(3) of the Land Registration (Scotland) Act 1979 (c 33)' substitute '101 of the Land Registration etc (Scotland) Act 2012 (asp 5)'.
   (4) Section 46 is repealed.
   (5) In section 63(2) (baronies and other dignities and offices), for 'an interest in land for the purposes of the Land Registration (Scotland) Act 1979 (c 33) or a right as respects which a deed can be' substitute 'a right as respects which a deed can be registered in the Land Register of Scotland or'.
   (6) Section 65 is repealed.
   (7) In section 65A (sporting rights), subsection (12) is repealed.
   (8) In section 73 (feudal terms in enactments and documents: construction after abolition of feudal system)—
       (a) in subsection (1)—
           (i) repeal 'or' immediately after paragraph (c),
           (ii) after paragraph (d) insert 'or
               (e) in an extract or certified copy issued under section 104 of the Land Registration etc (Scotland) Act 2012 (asp 5),',
       (b) in subsection (2)(b), for 'subsection (1)(d)' substitute 'paragraph (d) of, or extract or certified copy such as is mentioned in paragraph (e) of, subsection (1)'.
   (9) In schedule 11 (form of assignation, discharge or restriction of reserved right to claim compensation), repeal 'section 3 of'.

Standards in Scotland's Schools etc Act 2000 (asp 6)

40 In section 58(1) of the Standards in Scotland's Schools etc Act 2000 (interpretation), in the definition of 'land', for 'interests in land (within the meaning of the Land Registration (Scotland) Act 1979 (c 33)' substitute 'rights registered in the Land Register of Scotland'.

National Parks (Scotland) Act 2000 (asp 10)

41 In section 15 of the National Parks (Scotland) Act 2000 (management agreements)—
   (a) in subsection (1), for 'an interest' substitute 'a right',
   (b) for subsection (5) substitute—
       '(5) A management agreement which affects a right in land which is—
           (a) a right registered in the Land Register of Scotland, may be registered in that register,
           (b) a right registrable (but not registered) in that register, may be recorded in the Register of Sasines.',
   (c) subsection (10) is repealed.

Housing (Scotland) Act 2001 (asp 10)

42 In the Housing (Scotland) Act 2001—
    (a) in section 23(1)(b) (tenant's right to written tenancy agreement and information), after 'subscribed' insert 'or authenticated',
    (b) in section 24(3) (restriction on variation of tenancy), after 'subscribed' insert 'or authenticated'.

Title Conditions (Scotland) Act 2003 (asp 9)

43 (1) The Title Conditions (Scotland) Act 2003 is amended as follows.
    (2) In section 4 (creation of real burdens), in subsection (1), repeal ', notwithstanding section 3(4) of the 1979 Act (creation of real right or obligation on date of registration etc),'.
    (3) In section 41(b) (deed granted by holder of conservation burden without completing title), for '15(3) of the 1979 Act' substitute '101 of the Land Registration etc (Scotland) Act 2012 (asp 5)'.
    (4) Sections 51 and 58 are repealed.
    (5) In section 60 (grant of deed where title not completed: requirements)—
        (a) in subsection (1), for '15(3) of the 1979 Act' substitute '101 of the Land Registration etc (Scotland) Act 2012 (asp 5)',
        (b) in subsection (2), repeal 'or with section 15(3) of the 1979 Act'.
    (6) In section 71 (development management scheme), in subsection (1), repeal ', notwithstanding section 3(4) of the 1979 Act (creation of real right or obligation on date of registration etc)'.
    (7) In section 73 (disapplication of development management schemes), in subsection (1)(b), repeal 'notwithstanding section 3(4) of the 1979 Act (creation of real right or obligation on date of registration etc),'.
    (8) In section 75 (creation of positive servitudes by writing: deed to be registered), in subsection (2), repeal ', notwithstanding section 3(4) of the 1979 Act (creation of real right or obligation on date of registration etc),'.
    (9) In section 84(2) (extinction following offer to sell), after 'section 2' insert 'or 9B'.
    (10) In section 119 (savings and transitional provisions etc), subsection (2) is repealed.
    (11) In section 122 (interpretation)—
        (a) in subsection (1)—
            (i) in the definition of 'constitutive deed', after 'is' insert ', subject to subsection (4) below,',
            (ii) in the definition of 'title condition', in paragraph (e)(i), for 'assignation of' substitute 'assignations of registered or',
        (b) after subsection (3) insert—
            '(4) If title is completed in the manner provided for in section 4 or 4A of the Conveyancing (Scotland) Act 1924 (c 27) (completion of title) and a midcouple relevant to the title sets out the terms of a title condition (or of a prospective title condition), then for the purposes of this Act the midcouple and notice of title are together the constitutive deed of the title condition.'.

Civil Partnership Act 2004 (c 33)

44 In section 112(9) of the Civil Partnership Act 2004 (transfer of tenancy), in the definition of 'long lease', for '28(1) of the Land Registration (Scotland) Act 1979 (c 33)' substitute '9(2) of the Land Registration etc (Scotland) Act 2012 (asp 5)'.

Stirling-Alloa-Kincardine Railway and Linked Improvements Act 2004 (asp 10)

45 In section 16 of the Stirling-Alloa-Kincardine Railway and Linked Improvements Act 2004 (rights in roads or public places), for subsection (3) substitute—
    '(3) The powers conferred by this section constitute a real right.'.

Tenements (Scotland) Act 2004 (asp 11)

46 (1) The Tenements (Scotland) Act 2004 is amended as follows.
   (2) In section 1(2)(b) (determination of boundaries and pertinents)—
      (a) repeal 'an interest in',
      (b) for 'title sheet of that interest' substitute 'relevant title sheet'.
   (3) In paragraph 1(6) of schedule 3 (sale under section 22(3) or 23(1) of the Act), for paragraph (a) substitute—
      '(a) where the flat or former flat has been registered in the Land Register of Scotland, the description refers to the number of the title sheet;'.

Edinburgh Tram (Line Two) Act 2006 (asp 6)

47 In section 25 of the Edinburgh Tram (Line Two) Act 2006 (rights under or over roads), for subsection (5) substitute—
   '(5) The powers conferred by this section constitute a real right.'.

Edinburgh Tram (Line One) Act 2006 (asp 7)

48 In section 25 of the Edinburgh Tram (Line One) Act 2006 (rights under or over roads), for subsection (5) substitute—
   '(5) The powers conferred by this section constitute a real right.'.

Waverley Railway (Scotland) Act 2006 (asp 13)

49 In section 16 of the Waverley Railway (Scotland) Act 2006 (rights in roads or public places), for subsection (3) substitute—
   '(3) The powers conferred by this section constitute a real right.'.

Companies Act 2006 (c 46)

50 (1) The Companies Act 2006 is amended as follows.
   (2) In section 48(3) (execution of documents by companies), after 'subscribed' insert '(or, in the case of an electronic document, authenticated)'.
   (3) In section 49(4)(b), after 'subscribed' insert 'or authenticated'.
   (4) In section 1022(6)(b) (protection of persons holding under a lease), for 'Land Registration (Scotland) Act 1979 (c 33)' substitute 'Land Registration etc (Scotland) Act 2012 (asp 5)'.

Glasgow Airport Rail Link Act 2007 (asp 1)

51 In section 15 of the Glasgow Airport Rail Link Act 2007 (rights in roads), for subsection (3) substitute—
   '(3) The powers conferred by this section constitute a real right.'.

Bankruptcy and Diligence etc (Scotland) Act 2007 (asp 3)

52 (1) The Bankruptcy and Diligence etc (Scotland) Act 2007 is amended as follows.
   (2) In section 85 (restriction on priority of ranking of certain securities), in new section 13A (to be inserted in the Conveyancing and Feudal Reform (Scotland) Act 1970 (c 35)), in subsection (1)(a), after 'duly' insert 'registered or'.
   (3) In section 128(1) (interpretation of chapter 2 of Part 4), in the definition of 'long lease', for '28(1) of the Land Registration (Scotland) Act 1979 (c 33)' substitute '9(2) of the Land Registration etc (Scotland) Act 2012 (asp 5)'.

Edinburgh Airport Rail Link Act 2007 (asp 16)

53 (1) The Edinburgh Airport Rail Link Act 2007 is amended as follows.
   (2) In section 9(1) (registration of vested land), for 'section 4 of the Land Registration (Scotland) Act 1979 (c 33)' substitute 'Part 2 of the Land Registration etc (Scotland) Act 2012 (asp 5)'.

(3) In section 20 (rights in roads or public places), for subsection (6) substitute—
'(6) The powers conferred by this section constitute a real right.'.

Airdrie-Bathgate Railway and Linked Improvements Act 2007 (asp 19)

54 (1) The Airdrie-Bathgate Railway and Linked Improvements Act 2007 is amended as follows.
(2) In section 9(1) (registration of vested land), for 'section 4 of the Land Registration (Scotland) Act 1979 (c 33)' substitute 'Part 2 of the Land Registration etc (Scotland) Act 2012 (asp 5)'.
(3) In section 20 (rights in roads or public places), for subsection (6) substitute—
'(6) The powers conferred by this section constitute a real right.'.

Energy Act 2008 (c 32)

55 In section 77(7) of the Energy Act 2008 (model clauses of petroleum licences), after 'subscribed' insert 'or authenticated'.

Appendix II

Land Register Rules etc (Scotland) Regulations 2014 (SSI 2014/150)

PART 1
INTRODUCTORY

1 Citation, commencement and interpretation
(1) These Regulations may be cited as the Land Register Rules etc (Scotland) Regulations 2014 and come into force on 8th December 2014.
(2) In these Regulations—
'the Act' means the Land Registration etc (Scotland) Act 2012; and
'plot of land comprising seabed' means a plot of land entirely covered by water that lies within the territorial sea of the United Kingdom adjacent to Scotland.

PART 2
ADVANCE NOTICES

2 Forms to apply for, or to discharge, an advance notice
An application for—
  (a) an advance notice under section 57(1) of the Act must be made—
    (i) in respect of the whole of a registered plot, using the Form set out in Part 1 of Schedule 1;
    (ii) in respect of part of a registered plot, using the Form set out in Part 2 of Schedule 1;
  (b) discharge of an advance notice under section 63(1) of the Act must be made using the Form set out in Part 3 of Schedule 1.

3 Procedure for application for an advance notice
(1) An application for an advance notice relating to the whole of a registered plot or discharge of an advance notice must be sent to the Keeper electronically using a computer system for advance notices under the management and control of the Keeper, unless—
  (a) the computer system notifies the applicant who attempts to use it that it is unavailable for a period of 48 hours or longer; or
  (b) the applicant—
    (i) has no computer facilities with access to the internet; or
    (ii) is the granter of the deed.
(2) Only a person authorised by the Keeper may use that computer system.
(3) An application for an advance notice relating to part of a registered plot must be completed electronically using that computer system before being printed on paper, signed by the applicant and sent to the Keeper on paper, unless—
  (a) the computer system notifies the applicant who attempts to use it that it is unavailable for a period of 48 hours or longer; or
  (b) the applicant—
    (i) has no computer facilities with access to the internet; or
    (ii) is the granter of the deed.

4 Description of an unregistered plot or unregistered lease in an advance notice

(1) An advance notice by virtue of section 56(1)(e) of the Act must contain a description of the subjects of the lease or plot of land sufficient to enable the Keeper to identify those subjects or that plot.

(2) The description mentioned in paragraph (1) must identify the subjects of the lease or plot of land by reference to the—
   (a) description in a deed recorded in the Register of Sasines; and
   (b) postal address (if any).

(3) Where the subjects of the lease or plot of land form part only of the subjects described in a deed recorded in the Register of Sasines, the description mentioned in paragraph (2) must be accompanied by a plan of that part which satisfies the Keeper that the Keeper can delineate its boundaries on the cadastral map.

5 Notification of acceptance of advance notice

(1) The Keeper must notify the applicant or applicant's agent that the advance notice has been entered in the application record.

(2) A notification given under paragraph (1) must be made by email to the email address contained in the application, except in cases where an application has been made using a paper form under regulation 3(1)(b) or (3)(b).

(3) The notification given under paragraph (1) must contain the—
   (a) granter's name and designation;
   (b) grantee's name and designation;
   (c) application number;
   (d) advance notice number;
   (e) type of intended deed;
   (f) particulars of the—
      (i) plot of land; or
      (ii) subjects of lease;
   (g) where section 57(4)(a)(ii) of the Act applies, a PDF file of the delineation on the cadastral map; and
   (h) date when the advance notice is entered on the application record.

6 Removal of delineation from the cadastral map where intended deed not registered

In respect of an advance notice for a deed which is not registered during the protected period, the period prescribed under section 62(2) of the Act, after which the Keeper must remove the delineation on the cadastral map, is 35 days beginning on the day after the date when the notice is entered in the application record.

PART 3
REGISTRATION

7 Form to apply for registration in the Land Register

An application for registration of—
   (a) a deed under section 21 of the Act; or
   (b) an unregistered plot under section 27 of the Act,

must be made using the Form set out in Part 4 of Schedule 1 except where the application for registration is made using the ARTL system as defined in the Electronic Documents (Scotland) Regulations 2014.

NOTE
Reg 7 amended by Land Register of Scotland (Automated Registration) etc Regulations 2014, SSI 2014/347, reg 8(2).

8 Application for registration of plot of land comprising seabed

In respect of an application for registration of a deed in relation to a plot of land comprising seabed, the deed must contain—
  (a) a description of the plot of land based on OSGB36 coordinates; and
  (b) a plan, in a form that the Keeper considers reasonably identifies the location of the plot of land in relation to the coast of Scotland.

9 Affidavits to accompany applications for registration

An affidavit which—
  (a) accompanies an application for registration;
  (b) accompanies an application to vary warranty; or
  (c) provides evidence in respect of rectification of the register,
must be made before a notary public.

10 Application record

(1) Where the Keeper enters an application in the application record, the Keeper must allocate an application number to that application.
(2) An application number is an unique identifier consisting of numerals or of letters and numerals.
(3) Where an application for registration requires the creation of a—
  (a) cadastral unit;
  (b) lease title sheet; or
  (c) title sheet for a flat,
  the Keeper must allocate a provisional title number to that application.
(4) Where additional cadastral units require to be created in respect of an application, the Keeper may allocate additional application numbers and provisional title numbers until registration is completed under section 30 or 31 of the Act.
(5) Where registration is completed under section 30 or 31 of the Act, the provisional title number will become the title number assigned under section 4(1) of the Act.

11 Acknowledgement of application for registration

(1) After an application for registration is entered in the application record, the Keeper must acknowledge receipt of that application if an email address for acknowledgment is contained in the application.
(2) An acknowledgment given under paragraph (1) must contain the—
  (a) type of deed;
  (b) names of the parties;
  (c) date of application;
  (d) application number allocated under regulation 10(1);
  (e) title number or provisional title number allocated under regulation 10(3); and
  (f) particulars of the plot of land or the subjects of lease.

12 Title sheets

(1) In addition to the information required to be entered in the property section by virtue of section 6 of the Act, the property section must contain—
  (a) the date of—
    (i) registration of the plot of land; and
    (ii) the last entry in the title sheet;
  (b) the terms of any caveat;
  (c) in respect of a title sheet created for registration of—
    (i) a deed relating to—
      (aa) an unregistered plot; or
      (bb) part of a registered plot; or
    (ii) an unregistered plot,

particulars of any deed in which servitude rights are constituted;
 (d) a statement where minerals are excepted;
 (e) for a plot of land comprising seabed, the OSGB36 coordinates representing the boundaries of that plot; and
 (f) in respect of a title sheet created for registration of—
   (i) a deed relating to—
     (aa) an unregistered plot; or
     (bb) part of a registered plot; or
   (ii) an unregistered plot,
 the area measurement of the cadastral unit where it is greater than 0.5 hectare.
(2) In addition to the information required to be entered in the property section by virtue of section 7 of the Act, the proprietorship section must contain the—
 (a) consideration; and
 (b) date of entry.

13 Amendments etc of application

Where the Keeper has consented under section 34(1)(b) of the Act to substitution or amendment of an application, the substituted or amended application must be received by the Keeper before the expiry of the period of 42 days beginning on the day after the date of consent.

14 Combination of cadastral units

Where—
 (a) the Keeper combines cadastral units under section 13(2)(a) of the Act; and
 (b) each registered plot of land has a different date of registration,
the earliest date of registration entered in the title sheet of one of those registered plots will be the date of registration of the resultant plot of land.

15 Form to place a caveat on a title sheet

An application to—
 (a) place on a title sheet a caveat granted under section 67(3) of the Act;
 (b) renew a caveat granted under section 69(2) of the Act;
 (c) restrict a caveat granted under section 70(2) of the Act;
 (d) recall a caveat granted under section 71(2) of the Act; or
 (e) discharge a caveat under section 72 of the Act,
must be made using the Form set out in Part 5 of Schedule 1.

16 Form to vary warranty

An application to vary warranty under section 76(2) of the Act must be made using the Form set out in Part 6 of Schedule 1.

17 Corrections

(1) Where the Keeper becomes aware of a typographical error in a title sheet, the Keeper may correct the error.
(2) In paragraph (1), 'typographical error' means an error which is not an inaccuracy (within the meaning of section 65 of the Act).

PART 4
PRESCRIPTIVE CLAIMANTS

18 Notification by prescriptive claimants

(1) An applicant must notify the person mentioned in section 43(4) of the Act by sending the notification—
 (a) at least 60 days prior to submitting to the Keeper the application for registration of a disposition mentioned in section 43(1) of the Act; and

(b) by a postal service which provides for the delivery of the notification to be recorded.
(2) The notification made under section 43(4) of the Act must be in the form set out in Schedule 2.

Regulations 2, 7, 15 and 16   SCHEDULE 1
APPLICATION FORMS TO BE USED IN CONNECTION WITH LAND REGISTRATION

List of forms

Form	Purpose	Relevant provisions of the Rules
PART 1	Application for an Advance Notice relating to Whole of a Registered Plot	Regulation 2(a)(i)
PART 2	Application for an Advance Notice relating to Part of Registered Plot	Regulation 2(a)(ii)
PART 3	Application to Discharge an Advance Notice	Regulation 2(b)
PART 4	Application for Registration	Regulation 7
PART 5	Application relating to a Caveat	Regulation 15
PART 6	Application to Vary Warranty	Regulation 16

Regulation 2(a)(i)   PART 1
LAND REGISTRATION ETC (SCOTLAND) ACT 2012

Application for an Advance Notice relating to Whole of a Registered Plot

In accordance with section 56(1) of the Land Registration etc (Scotland) Act 2012 an advance notice is a notice stating that a person ('the Granter') intends to grant a deed ('Intended Deed Type') to another person (the 'Grantee').

Agent Details

Agent's reference

Agent's telephone number

Agent's email address

Agent's name and address

Payment Details

FAS Number

Payment method

Intended Deed Type
Subjects

Title numbers(s) of registered plot of land or lease affected by this advance notice

Property name

Property number

Street name

Town

Postcode

Description of plot of land with no postal address

Granter Details
Individual
Prefix

Forename

Surname

Property name

Property number

Street name

Town

Postcode

Country

Non-natural person
Prefix

Name

Allocated number (if any, eg company number)

Property name

Property number

Street name

Town

Postcode

Country

Grantee Details
Individual
Prefix

Forename

Surname

Property name

Property number

Street name

Town

Postcode

Country

Non-natural person
Prefix

Name

Allocated number (if any, e.g. company number)

Property name

Property number

Street name

Town

Postcode

Country

Applicant Statement and Declaration

I/We apply for an advance notice in terms of section 57 of the Land Registration etc (Scotland) Act 2012 in respect of a registrable deed which I/we intend to grant. By making such application I/we confirm that (i) I/we may validly grant such a deed (or) (ii) I/we have the consent of a person who may validly do so, in accordance with section 57(2)(a) or (b) respectively, of the Land Registration etc (Scotland) Act 2012.

I/We certify that the information supplied on this Form is complete and correct to the best of my/our knowledge and belief.

Signature(s)

Date

Regulation 2(a)(ii) PART 2
LAND REGISTRATION ETC (SCOTLAND) ACT 2012
Application for an Advance Notice relating to Part of Registered Plot

In accordance with section 56(1) of the Land Registration etc (Scotland) Act 2012 an advance notice is a notice stating that a person ('the Granter') intends to grant a deed ('Intended Deed Type') to another person (the 'Grantee').

Agent Details

Agent's reference

Agent's telephone number

Agent's email address

Agent's name and address

Payment Details

FAS Number

Payment method

Intended Deed Type

Subjects

Title numbers(s) of registered plot of land or lease affected by this advance notice

Are the subjects a flatted building capable of being represented as a single cadastral unit in accordance with section 56(2) of the Land Registration etc (Scotland) Act 2012?

Property name

Property number

Street name

Town

Postcode

Description of plot of land with no postal address

Related Plan

Where application is accepted by the Keeper on paper:

Submit a paper plan

Where application is accepted electronically by the Keeper:

Development Plan Approval Number and Development Plan Approval Plot Number

or

Provide co-ordinates

or

Upload shape file

Granter Details

Individual

Prefix

Forename

Surname

Property name

Property number

Street name

Town

Postcode

Country

Non-natural person

Prefix

Name

Allocated number (if any, eg company number)

Property name

Property number

Street name

Town

Postcode

Country

Grantee Details

Individual

Prefix

Forename
Surname
Property name
Property number
Street name
Town
Postcode
Country

Non-natural person
Prefix
Name
Allocated number (if any, eg company number)
Property name
Property number
Street name
Town
Postcode
Country

Applicant Statement and Declaration

I/We apply for an advance notice in terms of section 57 of the Land Registration etc (Scotland) Act 2012 in respect of a registrable deed which I/we intend to grant. By making such application I/we confirm that (i) I/we may validly grant such a deed (or) (ii) I/we have the consent of a person who may validly do so, in accordance with section 57(2)(a) or (b) respectively, of the Land Registration etc (Scotland) Act 2012.

I/We certify that the information supplied on this Form is complete and correct to the best of my/our knowledge and belief.

Signature(s)

Date

Regulation 2(b)   PART 3
                LAND REGISTRATION ETC (SCOTLAND) ACT 2012
                    Application to Discharge an Advance Notice

Agent Details
Agent's reference
Agent's telephone number
Agent's email address
Agent's name and address

Payment Details
FAS Number

Payment method

Advance Notice Number to be discharged

Intended Deed Type

Subjects

Title numbers(s) of registered plot of land or lease affected by this advance notice

Property name

Property number

Street name

Town

Postcode

Description of plot of land with no postal address

Granter Details

Individual

Prefix

Forename

Surname

Property name

Property number

Street name

Town

Postcode

Country

Non-natural person

Prefix

Name

Allocated number (if any, e.g. company number)

Property name

Property number

Street name

Town

Postcode

Country

Grantee Details

Individual

Prefix

Forename

Surname

Property name

Property number

Street name

Town

Postcode

Country

Non-natural person

Prefix

Name

Allocated number (if any, eg company number)

Property name

Property number

Street name

Town

Postcode

Country

Applicant Statement and Declaration

I/We hereby certify that the person to whom the intended deed would be granted consents to this application to discharge the advance notice relating to that deed in accordance with section 63(3)(a) of the Land Registration etc (Scotland) Act 2012.

I/We certify that the information supplied on this Form is complete and correct to the best of my/our knowledge and belief.

Signature(s)

Date

Regulation 7

PART 4

LAND REGISTRATION ETC (SCOTLAND) ACT 2012

Application for Registration

Unless the context otherwise indicates, any reference in this form to a section of an Act is a reference to a section of the Land Registration etc (Scotland) Act 2012.

PART A

Agent Details

Agent's reference

Agent's telephone number

Agent's email address

Agent's name and address

Notification Details

Email address for applicant's notification

Email address for granter's notification

Payment Details

FAS Number

Monetary consideration

Non-Monetary consideration

Value

Relevant rent (the largest amount of annual rent within the first 10 years of its terms that can be quantified, or estimated where that amount cannot be quantified)

Fee

Payment method

Application Details

Application type

Type of deed

Country

Mark X in the box if more than one title number and insert details in the additional information sheet. ☐

Search Sheet number(s) (if known)

Development Plan Approval number

Date of entry

Property name

Property number

Street name

Town

Postcode

Description of plot of land with no postal address

Mark X in the box if more than one property and insert details in the additional information sheet. ☐

Applicant Details

Individual

Prefix

Forename

Surname

Property name

Property number

Street name

Town

Postcode

Country

Non-natural person

Prefix

Name

Allocated number (if any, eg company number)

Property name

Property number

Street name

Town

Postcode

Country

Mark X in the box if more than one applicant and insert details in the additional information sheet. ☐

Granter Details

Individual

Prefix

Forename

Surname

Property name

Property number

Street name

Town

Postcode

Country

Non-natural person

Prefix

Name

Allocated number (if any, eg company number)

Property name

Property number

Street name

Town

Postcode

Country

Mark X in the box if more than one granter and insert details in the additional information sheet. ☐

NOTE

Under the heading 'Payment Details' 'relevant rent' is substituted for 'annual rent' by Land Registration etc (Scotland) Act 2012 (Amendment and Transitional) Order 2014, SSI 2014/346, art 5.

PART B

Plans Questions – Guidance – *This question is not applicable where the deed being registered affects the whole of a registered plot.*

If a plans pre-registration report has been issued by the Keeper in connection with this application, please quote the report number.

Has all or part of the plot of ground been delineated on the cadastral map?

Yes or No

If yes, please provide the cadastral unit number or title number of which it forms part.

If the extent of the plot has been delineated on the cadastral map as part of an advance notice please provide the advance notice number.

Do the deeds submitted in support of this application include a plan or full bounding description identifying the extent of the plot to be registered?

Yes or No

If yes, please provide the details of the deed or deed inventory number

Common Areas – Guidance – *This question is only applicable where the deed being registered either affects an unregistered plot or transfers part of a registered plot.*

Does the deed being registered transfer any area of ground that is owned in common with another person or other persons?

Yes or No

If yes, has the area of ground been included in any registered title(s)?

Yes or No

Please ensure the deed narrates the title number(s) for the areas of ground and the title number(s) are included in Part A of this form.

RoI Question

Is the validity of the deed to which this application relates capable of being affected by an entry in the Register of Inhibitions and Adjudications ('RoI')?

Yes or No

If yes, has a search of the RoI been carried out on the granter of the deed and any party whose right has vested in the granter by virtue of any unregistered mid-couple or link in title?

Yes or No

If yes, please provide the date to which the search was certified.

Did the search disclose an entry in the RoI which might affect the validity of the deed to which this application relates?

Yes or No

If yes, please provide details.

Land and Buildings Transaction Tax

Is the transaction to which this application relates a notifiable transaction in terms of section 30 of the Land and Buildings Transaction Tax (Scotland) Act 2013?

Yes or No

If yes, has a land transaction return been made, and have arrangements satisfactory to the tax authority been made for the payment of any tax payable in respect of the transaction?

Yes or No

Title examination

Has there been any limitation or restriction on the examination of title?

Yes or No

If yes, please provide details in the further information field.

Certification in relation to links in title

Is the granter of the deed the last recorded/registered proprietor?

Yes or No

By signing this application form you are certifying to the Keeper that appropriate links in title are in place and that the granter has the legal right to grant the deed.

If no, and the deed is a disposition, is the disposition to be treated as valid by virtue of section 43(1) (prescriptive claimants)?

Yes or No

Servitudes – Guidance – *This question is only applicable where the deed being registered affects an unregistered plot.*

Is the plot of ground to which this application relates the benefited subjects in relation to any servitude?

Yes or No

If yes, how was the servitude right created? - ☐ in a deed or ☐ by prescription

Where the plot of ground is the benefited subjects in relation to a servitude right(s) created in a deed(s) please specify the deed(s) (or provide the number of the deed on the inventory of deeds attached to this form) in which the right was constituted.

Where the servitude right has been constituted by prescription under the Prescription and Limitation (Scotland) Act 1973 the application must include the particulars of the servitude and include a plan or a description sufficient to enable the Keeper to delineate the extent of the servitude on the cadastral map.

Heritable Securities – Guidance – *This question is only applicable where the deed being registered affects an unregistered plot.*

Has a search been carried out in the General Register of Sasines to determine if there are any outstanding heritable securities affecting the plot of land?

Yes or No

Is this search certified to the same date as the search of the RoI?

Yes or No

If no, please provide the date to which the last search was certified.

Where the plot of ground is affected by an outstanding heritable security please specify the details of the security or the deed inventory number.

Burdens – Guidance – *This question is only applicable where the deed being registered affects an unregistered plot.*

Is the plot of ground to which this application relates subject to any encumbrance within the meaning of section 9 (eg a long lease, long sub-lease, public right of way, path order, tree preservation order or any other encumbrance the inclusion of which in the register is permitted or required, expressly or impliedly, by an enactment)?

Yes or No

If yes, provide details.

Extension of warranty

Are you applying for an extension of warranty under section 75(1)?

Yes or No

If yes, please indicate the relevant subsection of section 73(2) in respect of which you are applying.

Evidence in line with the Keeper's published guidance must be included with the application or the application will be rejected.

Further Information

If there is any other information material to this application that has not already been disclosed in this application or its accompanying documents, please provide details.

Declaration

Application to register deeds

I/We apply for registration of the deed identified in Part A of this form and certify that this application complies with the general application conditions in section 22, and the particular applicable conditions mentioned in section 21(2).

Where the certification above is made in relation to an application to register a deed, the validity of which is dependent on the registration of a related deed, please provide details of the related deed.

Application for voluntary registration

I/We apply for the registration of an unregistered plot of land.

I/We certify that this application complies with the requirements of sections 27 and 28.

I/We certify that the information given in this form and the answers to the above questions are complete and correct to the best of my/our knowledge and belief.

Name

Signature(s)

Date of Signing

Warning: *In submitting this application you must take reasonable care to ensure that the Keeper does not inadvertently make the register inaccurate as a result of a change made in consequence of it. If you fail to do so you may be liable to pay compensation to the Keeper for any loss suffered as a result (see section 111).*

Land Register Rules etc (Scotland) Regulations 2014

Warning: It is an offence to knowingly or recklessly make a materially false or misleading statement, or to intentionally or recklessly fail to disclose material information, in relation to this application (see section 112).

Supplementary Information

Land Use Question

Please indicate the primary use of the plot of land:

Residential

Commercial

Land Only

Agricultural

Forestry

Other

Inventory of Deeds

Item No.	Deed	Grantee	Date of Recording

Additional Information Sheet(s) – Please use this sheet to provide details of any additional title numbers affected by the registration of the deed to which this application relates and any additional properties, applicants or granters referred to in the deed.

Additional Title Numbers

Additional Properties

Additional Applicants

Additional Granters

Regulation 15

PART 5
LAND REGISTRATION ETC (SCOTLAND) ACT 2012

Application relating to a caveat

Agent Details

Agent's reference

Agent's telephone number

Agent's email address

Agent's name and address

Payment Details

FAS number

Payment method

Subjects affected by caveat

Title number(s)

Property name

Street name

Town

Postcode

Description of plot of land with no postal address

Application type

☐ Noting of a caveat on a title sheet

☐ Renewal of a caveat

☐ Restriction of a caveat

☐ Recall of a caveat

☐ Discharge of a caveat

Existing caveat application number (if affected by this application)

Applicant Details

Individual

Prefix

Forename

Surname

Property name

Property number

Street name

Town

Postcode

Country

Non-natural person

Prefix

Name

Allocated number (if any, eg company number)

Property name

Property number

Street name

Town

Postcode

Country

Registered Proprietor Details

Name

Designation

Signature

Date

Regulation 16

PART 6
LAND REGISTRATION ETC (SCOTLAND) ACT 2012
Application to vary warranty

Agent Details

Agent's reference

Agent's telephone number

Agent's email address

Agent's name and address

Payment Details

FAS Number

Payment method

Subjects

Title number(s)

Property name

Property number

Street name

Town

Postcode

Description of plot of land with no postal address

Applicant Details

Individual

Prefix

Forename

Surname

Property name

Property number

Street name

Town

Postcode

Country

Non-natural person

Prefix

Name

Allocated number (if any, eg company number)

Property name

Property number

Street name

Town

Postcode

Country

Variation of Warranty

In what respect is a variation of warranty sought?

Explain why it is appropriate for the Keeper to vary the warranty currently provided for.

To support this application, I/we enclose the documents/evidence listed below.

Signature

Date

SCHEDULE 2   Regulation 18(2)

FORM OF NOTIFICATION BY PRESCRIPTIVE CLAIMANTS

Name and address of prescriptive claimant
(See note 1 for completion)

Name and address of person notified
(See note 2 for completion)

Description of the land over which a prescriptive claim is sought
(See note 3 for completion)

Applicable paragraph of section 43(4) of the Act
(See note 4 for completion)

Evidence of links in title (required only where person notified under section 43(4)(b) of the Act)
(See note 5 for completion)

Service
(See note 6 for completion)

I swear or affirm that the information contained in this notice is, to the best of my knowledge and belief, true.

Signature of person sending notice

Date

Explanatory Note
(This explanation has no legal effect)

This notice is sent by a person who is seeking to become a prescriptive claimant under section 43 of the Land Registration etc (Scotland) Act 2012 ('the Act') in respect of the land detailed in the notice. This means that the person is seeking to register a disposition in their favour in the Land Register of Scotland which, on certain other criteria relating to possession being met, will result in them becoming the owner of the land in question. You have been notified as a person who (a) appears to be the proprietor of the land or (b) appears to be a person who may be able to become proprietor of the lane or (c) is a representative of the Crown. The notice will specify which of the three categories you have been notified under. If you have been notified as a person who may become owner the links between the last known owner and you will be detailed in the notice.

This notice does not require you to take any action. However, if you consider that you do own or are capable of becoming owner of the land in question and you wish to challenge the prescriptive claim or to negotiate a sale you are advised to contact your solicitor or other adviser.

Please note if the prescriptive claim proceeds to registration you may be notified again by the Keeper of the Registers of Scotland. The Keeper's notification will contain guidance on how to respond to that notification.

Notes for completion of the notification
(These notes have no legal effect)

1. Insert the name and address of the person or persons seeking to take a disposition of the area of land. If there is an additional address for correspondence (such as a solicitor) you may also insert this here and specify it as the address for correspondence.
2. Insert the name and address of the person being notified.
3. Describe the land in a way that is sufficient to identify it. Where the land has been registered in the Land Register the description should refer to the title number(s) of the title sheets for the plot of land or the larger plot of land of which the land forms part. Otherwise it should normally refer to and identify a deed (or deeds) recorded in a specified division of the General Register of Sasines.
4. Insert whether the person is being notified under section 43(4)(a) or 43(b) or (c) of the Act. Where notification is to the Crown in respect of land which has or may have passed to the Crown as bona vacantia or ultimus haeres then notification is to the Queen's and Lord Treasurer's Remembrancer. Where notification is to the Crown in respect of land which is or may be held by the Crown by virtue of the regalia majora, then notification is to the Crown Estate.
5. Where notification is by virtue of s 43(4)(b) list the midcouples or links between the person with the last recorded or registered title and the person being notified.
6. Service – Do not complete until a copy of the notice has been sent to the person being notified. Then insert 'XXX has been sent a copy of this notice by (specify the method of delivery used in compliance with regulation 18(1)(b) of the Land Register Rules etc (Scotland) Regulations 2014 on (date of posting) as (address in notice)'.

NOTE
Para 4 corrected by Correction slip in October 2014.

Index

a non domino disposition
    acceptance and entry on Register, 320–21
    application for registration, 140
    competing applications, 322
    generally, 41, 314n, 315n
    indemnities for loss, 35
    Keeper's duty to notify, 164, 319–20
    notification of proprietor, 317–18, 319–20
    possession for preceding year, 316–17
    prescription and, 314–22
    submitting application, 318–19
    successors and, 321–22
abolition of local registers, 9–10
acceptance of application
    a non domino disposition, 320–21
    degrees of 'satisfaction' of Keeper, 158
    'significant doubt', 159
    wrongful acceptance, 161–62
access to information
    access to past data, 51
    generally, 49
acquirer
    protection of, 37–39
    transfer to a good-faith acquirer, 200
    voidability of acquirer's title, 243–44
advance notices
    adverse deed, 173
    applications for advance notices distinguished, 173–74
    application record, appearance in, 173
    background, 170–72
    competing deeds, 173, 188–91
    deed plans, 88
    deletion on applicant's request, 181–82
    deletion on expiry, 181
    generally, 74, 100
    inhibitions and, 191
    intended deed, 172
    involuntary competing deeds, 188–89
    legal reports compared, 194
    misconceptions, 185
    non-opposability principle, 185–88
    'off-side goals' rule, 193–94
    priority period, 173
    properties still on Register of Sasines, 182–84
    protected deed, 172

advance notices (*cont*)
    protected period, 173, 184–85
    renewal, 182
    Scottish Law Commission proposals, 36–37, 41–42, 172, 185–86
    sequestration and, 192
    terminology, 172–73
    timing, 176
    trusts for behoof of creditors, 192–93
    use of, 174–76
    voluntary competing deeds, 182n, 188–89
    where ineffectual, 193
    see also application for advance notices
advanced electronic signatures, *see* **electronic signatures**
adverse deeds, 170–73
altering the Register, 27, 164–65
    see also rectification
amendment of applications, 160–61
appeals
    authorisation to use ARTL system, 336
    Lands Tribunal, 53–54, 54n
    rectification and, 210
    wrongful rejection, 161
application conditions
    a non domino dispositions, 318–19
    general conditions, 127–29
    deeds in respect of registered land, 130–31
    deeds of servitude, 131
    description of property, 131
    exceptions, 130
    first registration, 131–32
    public rights of way, 132
    registrable encumbrances, 132
    shared plots, 130
    tenements, 130–31
application for advance notices
    advance notices distinguished, 173–74
    application fees, 178
    description of parties, 178–79
    description of property, 179
    development plan approvals and, 180
    eligible applications, 176–77
    format, 177–78
    notification, 180
    part of registered plots, 177
    properties still on Register of Sasines, 177

application for advance notices (*cont*)
  registered plots, 177
  signatures and, 178
  split-off properties, 179–80
application for registration
  applicants, 123–24
  consideration of applications, 157–62
  death and, 124–25
  dissolution of juristic persons, 124–25
  fees, 125–26
  first registrations, 122–23
  forms, 135–45
  generally, 122
  Keeper's duties, 133–35
  registered plots, 122
  types of application, 122–23
  see also application conditions; application forms; application process; first registration
application forms
  adjustments, 144
  ARTL system, 135–36
  common areas, 140–42
  designation of parties, 137–38
  dual registration, 143–44
  individuals, 137
  information regarding fees, 138
  juristic persons, 137–38
  land and buildings transaction tax, 142–43
  limitations or restrictions on examination of title, 138–39
  links in title, 139–40
  mistakes, 149–52
  supplementary information, 144
  see also first registration (application forms)
application process
  amendment of application, 160–61
  consideration of application, 157–62
  delays, 156, 273n
  first registration, 156
  generally, 153–54
  'one-shot' rule, 159–60
  order of dealing with forms, 154–56, 155n
  requisitions by RoS, 160–61
  'state of the legal universe' principle, 157–58
  timescales, 156
  withdrawal of application, 156
  wrongful acceptance, 161–62
  wrongful rejection, 161
  see also notification
application record
  advance notices, 100, 173, 177, 180–81
  date of registration, 168–69

application record (*cont*)
  generally, 25, 45, 55, 74, 153–55, 177
  heritable securities, 147
archive record, 25, 45, 49–50, 55, 73–74, 173
ARTL system
  application fees, 125, 338n
  application forms, 135–36
  applications, 123
  authorisation, 336–37
  date of registration, 168–69
  deeds unsuitable for ARTL system, 331
  electronic deeds, 329, 332–35
  improvement and repair grants, 331
  legislative framework, 330–31
  local registration authority, 336–37
  origins and development, 329–30
  provision of a closed system, 329
  qualifying deeds, 331
  registration process, 337–38
  scope, 337
  signatures, 329
  see also electronic deeds
assignation of registered leases
  1979 Act, 300–01
  2012 Act, 298–300
  ARTL system, 331
  compensation from the Keeper, 235
  first registration, 112–13
  generally, 342
  long leases, 342, 343
  omitted encumbrances, 234–35
  person named as tenant, by, 234
  realignment, 234–35
  registration of, 113, 342, 343
automatic plot registration (APR)
  acceptance of application, 162–63
  applications for registration, 122
  completion of Register, 105–06
  date of registration, 168–69
  first registration, 105, 109, 110–11, 122
  generally, 63, 105, 342
  leases, 339
automated registration of title to land, *see* **ARTL system**

'beneficial ownership', 45
bijural inaccuracies
  generally, 32
  indemnities for loss, 34–36
  rectification, 33–34, 202
  transitional provisions applied regarding inaccuracies, 201–02, 313–14
bijuralism
  Scottish Law Commission proposals, 39–40
  transitional provisions and, 201

Index

boundaries
    base-map and cadastral map boundaries compared, 81–82
    cadastral map and, 81–82, 83–84, 85–86
    disputed boundaries, 211–16
    inaccuracies and rectification of, 211–16
    Keeper-induced registrations, 120
    'occupational' boundaries, 81
    shifting boundary agreements, 83–84
    water features as, 83–84

burdens
    application forms, 147–49
    conservation burdens, 64
    first registration, 147–49
    Keeper's warranty and, 241–42
    real burdens, 64, 92
    transfer of ownership, 292–95

burdens section of title sheets
    conservation burdens, 64
    generally, 58
    KIR title sheets, 119
    leasehold conditions, 64
    long leases, 65
    off-register encumbrances, 65
    paths, 65
    prescriptive servitudes, 65
    public rights of way, 65
    real burdens, 64
    servitudes of way, 65
    servitudes, 64–65

burgh registers, 9n, 14–15

cadastral map
    base map compared, 76, 81–82
    boundaries, 81–82, 83–84, 85–86
    conflicting overlaps, 80
    generally, 45, 72, 75
    mapping conventions, 86
    mineral rights, 80, 86
    'no overlaps' rule, 80
    'no registration without mapping', 79
    Ordnance Map compared, 76
    origins, 77
    salmon fishing rights, 80
    seabed, 82–83
    separate tenements, 80, 85n
    shared ownership overlaps, 79–80
    statutory definition, 78
    supplementary plans, 84–85
    title plans, 79
    water features as boundaries, 83–84
    see also cadastral units

cadastral units
    alterations, 81
    long lease exception, 78
    plots of land and, 56
    souvenir plots, 95

cadastral units *(cont)*
    subordinate real rights, 81
    tenement exception, 78
    tenements, 69–70, 78
    title sheets and, 78

caveats
    definition, 323
    effects of caveats, 325–26
    generally, 62, 100
    giving effect to the decree, 327–28
    lapsed caveats, 326
    obtaining a warrant, 324–25
    purpose, 323
    rejection of applications, 325
    renewal, 327
    restrictions, 326–27
    scope, 323–24
    transfer of ownership, 295

certified copies, 49–50, 173, 269–70

common areas, 58, 79–80, 140–42
    see also shared plots

companies, *see* **corporations and companies**

compensation due from Keeper
    a non domino dispositions, 35
    assignation of registered leases, 235
    basis of compensation due, 256–58
    bijural inaccuracies, 34–36
    conduct defences and, 256
    consequential loss, 257–58
    dispositions, 233–34
    exclusions, 35
    generally, 32
    interest payable, 258
    Keeper's warranty and, 256–59
    liability without limit, 274
    measure of law, 257
    non-patrimonial loss, 258
    quantum and defences, 261–62
    realignment, 233–34, 235
    reasonable foreseeability, 257–58
    rectification, 209, 259, 260–61
    remoteness, 257
    sums involved, 35–36
    transitional provisions, 260–62

competing deeds
    advance notices, 170, 173, 186, 188–91
    generally, 185–86
    involuntary competing deeds, 188–89
    'offside goals' rule, 193
    Scottish Law Commission proposals, 41–42
    voluntary competing deeds, 188–89
    see also adverse deeds

completing the Land Register
    automatic plot registration, 105
    deed-triggered first registration, 105

completing the Land Register (*cont*)
  dispositions, 105
  first registration, 103–04
  Government targets, 106–07
  incomplete Register, effect of, 104–05
  Keeper-induced registration, 105
  mechanisms for completion, 105–06
  no-deed first registration, 105
  PDF confirmation, 51
  Scottish Law Commission proposals, 40–41
  voluntary registration, 105
  see also first registration
conservation burdens, 64
controlling interest, 45
corporations and companies
  advance notices, 178, 186
  controlling interest and, 45
  corporate dissolution, 124
  designation of parties, 137, 151, 178
  floating charges, 233
  generally, 40, 44
  proprietorship section of title sheet, 63
  souvenir plots and, 95
  standard securities granted by companies, 158
  'state of the legal universe' principle, 158
criminal liability, 281–83
Crofting Register, 46
cybercrime, 47

date of registration
  advance notices, 185–86
  corrected applications, 159
  dispositions, 225
  generally, 8–9, 29, 153, 168–69, 286
  good faith and, 228, 254
  heritable securities, 147,
  Keeper's warranty and, 239, 243, 254
  title sheets, 63, 232
decrees of reduction
  generally, 94, 97, 323
  reduction of void deeds, 97–98
  reduction of voidable deeds, 98, 198, 231
  registrable deeds, 97–98, 100
deed plans
  advance notices, 88
  features, 87
  generally, 86
  seabed, 87
  split-off deeds, 87
  steading, 87–88
  voluntary registration, 88
deletion of advance notices, 181–82
designation of natural persons
  joint property, 63
  multiple ownership, 64

designation of natural persons (*cont*)
  occupancy rights of spouse or civil partner, 64
  proper liferents, 64
  proprietorship section of title sheets, 63
development plan approval service
  applications for advance notices and, 180
  generally, 88
digital mapping systems
  generally, 25, 78
  'no registration without mapping', 79, 141n
discrepancies between deed and title sheet, 307–08
dispositions
  ARTL system, 331
  fees, 126
  good faith, 227–28
  person named as proprietor, by, 222–23
  possession and, 224–27
  realignment of rights, 222–34, 246–47
  registration, 94–95, 105
  representatives of person named as proprietor, by, 223
  souvenir plots, 95
  transfers other than by disposition, 223–24
  validity and transfer of ownership, 296
  voidable titles, 231
  see also a non domino dispositions
dual registration, 124, 126, 131n, 143–44, 151, 242–43
duty of care
  Keeper's duty of care, 271–73
  solicitors' duty of care, 277–78

electronic deeds
  advanced electronic signature, 332–33
  ARTL system requirements, 333–35
  authentication, 332–33
  certification of electronic signatures, 333
  digital certificates, 334
  electronic signatures, 334
  format, 334
  generally, 329, 332
  PDF format, 334
  practicalities, 334–35
  technical complexities, 333–34
electronic signatures
  advanced electronic signatures, 332–33
  ARTL system, 329
  digital certificates and, 334
  mandated signatories, 335
  private cryptographic keys, 334
  validity of documents, 335

Index

encumbrances
application conditions, 132
assignations of registered leases, 234–35
burdens section of title sheets, 64n, 65
dispositions, 231–33
first registration, 132
Keeper's warranty, 242–43
omitted encumbrances, 231–33, 234–35
registrable encumbrances, 132
types of encumbrance, 242
see also off-register encumbrances

England and Wales
exceptions to warranty, 241–42
generally, 44
leases, 341
registration of title, 17, 18, 20–21
'search with priority' system, 41–42

examination of title
generally, 29n, 284
long leases, creation of, 296–301
servitudes, creation of, 301–03
standard securities, creation of, 303–04
transfer of ownership, 285–96
exceptions to Keeper's warranty
entries consequent on rectification, 244–45
exceptions to title warranty, 241–42
inaccuracies attributable to subsequent events, 243
voidability of acquirer's title, 243–44
extracts, 49–50

fees
application for advance notices, 178
application for registration, 125–26, 126
ARTL system, 125, 338, 338n
caveats, 325
certified copies, 50
deeds other than dispositions, 126
discounts, 117, 125
dispositions, 126
extracts, 49
Lands Tribunal and rectification, 210
plain copies, 50
plans reports, 89
property value and, 126
table of fees, 126
voluntary registration, 117, 125
withdrawal fee for applications, 156

first registration
application conditions, 131–32
ARTL applications, 123
assignation of long leases, 112–13
automatic plot registration, 110–11, 122
boundary disputes and their rectification, 214–16

first registration (*cont*)
conversion of ultra-long leases into ownership, 113
deeds other than dispositions, 109–16
description of property, 131
dispositions, 107–08, 122
long leases, 111–12
notices of title, 108–09, 114–15
other deeds, 115–16
public rights of way, 132
registrable encumbrances, 132
standard securities generally, 113–14
standard securities over subordinate real rights, 114
standard securities over leases, 114
voluntary registrations, 122

first registration (application forms)
burdens, 147–49
generally, 145
heritable securities, 147
incorporeal pertinents, 147
mistakes, 150
servitudes, 145–47

floating charges, 64, 193, 233, 294

good faith
absence as a defence for Keeper's warranty, 253–56
actual knowledge, 254
carelessness and, 254, 255
constructive knowledge, 253–54
effect on warranty, 255–56
generally, 99, 195, 199, 223n, 236n, 293–95
Keeper's warranty, 252–56
knowledge and, 254–55
positive prescription and, 310–11
section 86 and, 224, 227–28
section 91 and, 232
subjective and objective good faith, 254
transfer of ownership, 285
transfers to a good-faith acquirer, 200
see also realignment of rights

grants of servitude
person named as proprietor, by, 236–37
realignment, 236–38
servitudes by reservation, 237–38
subordinate real rights and, 236
see also servitudes

guarantee by money
Keeper's warranty, 239–40
rectification and, 220–22, 239–62
see also Keeper's warranty

guarantee by mud
assignation of registered leases, 234–35
dispositions, 222–34
generally, 217–20

guarantee by mud (*cont*)
  grants of servitude, 236–38
  realignment and, 220–36
guarantee of title
  determination by type of error, 218–19
  determination by type of right, 219–20
  determination of form, 218–20
  positive and negative aspects, 217
  types of guarantee, 217–18
  see also guarantee by money; guarantee by mud

Henry Committee, 22, 27–28
heritable securities, 64, 147

inaccuracies in the Register
  actual inaccuracies, 31–32
  bijural inaccuracies, 32
  dispositions, 224–33
  disputed boundaries, 211–16
  generally, 60, 195–96
  inaccuracy by commission, 197–99, 224–30
  inaccuracy by omission, 196–97, 231–33
  inaccuracy defined, 196
  transfer to a good-faith acquirer, 200
  transitional provisions, 201–02
  types of error, 31–32, 195
  typographical errors, 31, 195, 199
  see also mistakes; prescription; rectification
inaccuracies by commission, 197–99, 224–30
inaccuracies by omission, 196–97, 231–33
inhibitions
  advance notices and, 191
  entering, 165–66
  Keeper's duties and, 165–66
  Register of Inhibitions, 165, 191
  transfer of ownership, 295
instruments of resignation
  ad remanentiam, 5
instruments of sasine, 5
intended deed
  advance notices, 172, 176, 181, 184

joint and common property
  multiple ownership, 64
  occupancy rights of spouse or civil partner, 64
  proper liferents, 64
  proprietorship section of title sheets, 63
judicial rectification of documents, 99, 203

Keeper of the Registers of Scotland
  administrative nature of role, 13n, 52–53, 53n
  appointment, 52

Keeper of the Registers of Scotland (*cont*)
  compensation attached to rectification, 209
  discretion, 54
  duties regarding application conditions, 133–34
  duty to rectify, 206–07
  legal *vires*, 52
  role, 51–53
  'tell me don't show me', 134–35
  see also Registers of Scotland; Keeper-induced registration; Keeper's warranty; liabilities of the Keeper
Keeper-induced registration (KIR)
  benefit to owners, 121
  completion of Land Register, 105–07, 118–19
  date of registration, 168–69
  form of KIR title sheets, 119
  generally, 41, 135n
  identification of boundaries, 120
  identification of owner, 119–20
  no alterative of substantive rights, 120–21
Keeper's warranty
  beneficiaries of warranty, 245–46
  claims by heritable creditors, 258–59
  compensation, 256–58
  counter-warranty to the Keeper and, 247–48
  defences, 253–56
  downgrades to warranty, 252
  exceptions to warranty, 241–42
  exclusions and limitations: Keeper's practice, 249–50
  exclusions and limitations: statutory provisions, 248–49
  generally, 239–40
  good faith, 253–56
  inaccuracies attributable to applicant or their representatives, 256
  realignment and, 246–47
  rectification and, 252–53
  upgrades to the warranty, 251
  warranty as to encumbrances, 242–43
  warranty as to title, 240–41
  see also exceptions to Keeper's warranty
knowledge
  constructive knowledge, 73, 254–56
  generally, 38–39, 60, 110, 232, 262, 265
  good faith and, 254–55

land and buildings transaction tax (LBTT)
  ARTL system, 338
  generally, 142–43, 151–52
land certificates, 29–30
  see also title sheets

Index 445

Land Register of Scotland
  effects of registration, 30–31
  entry to the register, 27
  establishment, 23
  format, 46
  generally, 56
  inaccuracies, 210
  introduction of, 27–29
  public and private law nature, 46
  public nature of Register, 44–45
  purpose, 46
  Register of Sasines compared, 23–24
  registration process, 29–30
  structure and content, 45, 55–74
Land Registration (Scotland) Act 1979
  application records, 25
  criticisms, 36–42
  generally, 23
  Land Register of Scotland, 23
  long leases, 24
  mirror principle, 24
  overriding interests, 24
  servitudes, 24
  short leases, 24
  title sheets, 24–25
  see also Land Register of Scotland
Land Registration etc (Scotland) Act 2012
  access to information 49
  commencement, 43
  cybercrime, 47
  format of Register, 46
  generally, 36
  implementation, 43
  parliamentary passage, 42
  public nature of Register, 44–45
  registrable deeds, 91–102
  registration areas, 47–48
  seabed, 48
  searchability of data, 49
Lands Tribunal
  appeals, 53–54, 161
  generally, 204–07
  inaccuracy of Land Register and, 210
lease
  duration, 339
  effect of registration, 343–44
  generally, 339
  legislative framework, 339–40
  registrable leases, 342
  registration of real rights, 340–41
  see also long leases
lease title sheets, 56–57, 345–46
leasehold conditions, 64
leasehold conversions, 344–46
legal reports
  advance notices compared, 194

letters of obligation, 171–72, 172n
liabilities of Keeper
  1979 Act, 265–67
  common law liabilities, 270–74
  consequential loss, 264–65
  defences, 264–65
  failure to acquire rights, 267
  generally, 263
  inaccuracies not qualifying for compensation, 269
  information provided and documents lost, 269–70
  Keeper's warranty and, 267
  liability to those securing rectification of Register, 267–69
  loss of chance to rectify, 265–67
  loss of rights generally, 267
  quantum related to realignment, 264–65
  realignment generally, 263–64
  statutory provisions, 263–70
  see also compensation due from Keeper
liabilities of users
  applicants for registration, 280–81
  causation and proof of loss, 278–79
  civil liability, 277–81
  criminal liability, 281–83
  generally, 277
  liability under application forms, 280–81
  parties to the deed, 279–80
  penalties, 283
  solicitors, 277–79
  solicitors' duty of care, 277–78
liferents, 64–65, 97, 132, 168, 200
local/particular registers, 8–10
local registration authorities, 336–37
long leases
  assignation and subletting: 1979 Act, 300–01
  assignation and subletting: 2012 Act, 298–300
  burdens section of title sheets, 65
  cadastral units and, 78
  conversion to ownership, 344
  generally, 24, 97, 111n, 296–97
  lessor's title, 297–98
  realignment, 299–300
  registration of real rights, 340–41
  shared plots, 68
  see also assignation of registered leases

mechanics of registration
  central register, 8
  digitisation, 11
  Land Register of Scotland, 24–25, 29–30
  local/particular registers, 8
  microfiche, advent of, 11
  minute books, 8–9

mechanics of registration (*cont*)
  photocopying, advent of, 11
  Register of Sasines, 8–11
mechanisms for completion of Register
  automatic plot registration, 105–06
  deed-triggered first registration, 105
  dispositions, 105
  generally, 105–06
  Keeper-induced registration, 105
  no-deed first registration, 105
  voluntary registration, 105
Midas touch principle, 39–40, 166–67, 201–02
mineral rights, 55, 62, 80, 86, 295–96
minute books, 8–11
mirror principle, 24, 24n

natural persons, *see* **designation of natural persons**
negative prescription, 199–200
non-opposability principle, 185–88
notices of title, 96–97
notification, 162–64

occupancy rights of spouse or civil partner
  proprietorship section of title sheets, 64
  transfer of ownership, 295
off-register encumbrances
  burdens section of title sheets, 65
  paths, 65
  prescriptive servitudes, 65, 233
  public rights of way, 65, 132n
  real burdens, 64
  servitudes, 64
  servitudes of way, 65
off-register rights, 70–72
'off-side goals' rule, 193–94
'one-shot' rule, 159–60, 249n85
ordinary property law
  effect of registration law, 5–7, 32–33
Ordnance Map
  base map, as, 75–77
  cadastral map compared, 76
  scale, 76
Ordnance Survey
  descriptions of land, 25–27
  see also Ordnance Map
origins of land registration
  generally, 1–2
  Register of Sasines, 2
  registration of deeds, 1–17
  Registration Act 1617, 2–6
  registration of title, 17–22

overlaps
  conflicting overlaps, 58, 80, 80n, 213n
  no overlaps rule, 80

overlaps (*cont*)
  plans reports, 89–90
  shared ownership overlaps, 79–80
over-registration, 120n, 242, 261–62
overriding interests
  assignation of registered leases, 235
  floating charges, 64
  generally, 5, 24, 24n, 27, 30, 294
  off-register rights, 70
ownership
  'beneficial ownership', 45
  conversion of ultra-long leases, 113
  generally, 7, 25n
  multiple ownerships, 64
  shared ownership overlaps, 79–80
  transfer of ownership, 292–95

particular registers, *see* **local/particular registers**
pertinents
  corporeal pertinents, 67n, 68–69, 291–92
  first registration, 147
  incorporeal pertinents, 62n, 68, 147, 241–42, 292–95
  Keeper's warranty and, 241–42
  title sheets, 68–69
  transfer of ownership, 291–93
plain copies, 49–50
plans reports, 89–90
plot title sheets, 56–57
plots of land, 55–56
positive prescription
  2012 Act, 309–10
  discrepancies between deed and title sheet, 307–08
  effect of prescription, 312–13, 321n
  ex facie validity, 310
  generally, 85, 305
  good faith and, 310–11
  inaccuracies by commission and, 199
  invisible titles, 308–09
  migration to Land Register and, 311–12
  requirement as to title, 306–07
  statutory requirements, 305–06
  transitional arrangements, 313–14
prescription
  a non domino dispositions and, 314–22
  curing inaccuracies, 199–200
  successors and, 321–22
  see also positive prescription
prescriptive servitudes, 65, 71–72
presentment book, 11, 11n
primary interests, 25, 28–30, 56n, 103n
priority periods, 173
property section of title sheets
  caveats, 62
  cross-referencing system, 62

Index 447

property section of title sheets (*cont*)
    essential features, 61–62
    generally, 58
    incorporeal pertinents, 61
    KIR title sheets, 119
    section 66 agreements, 62
    seabed properties, 61
    shared plots, 62
    sharing, 62
    tenements, 62
proprietorship section of title sheets
    consideration paid, 63
    corporations, 63
    designation of natural persons, 63
    generally, 58, 63
    joint and common property, 63
    multiple ownership, 64
    occupancy rights of spouse or civil partner, 64
    other juristic persons, 63
    proper liferents, 64
    shared plots, 64
    sharing, 64
    trustees, 63
protected deeds, 173, 185n
protected periods, 173
public nature of land registration, 2–3, 44–45

Queen's and Lord Treasurer's Remembrancer (QLTR), 317–18, 319–20

realignment
    assignations of registered leases, 234–35
    curing inaccuracies, 200
    dispositions, 222–34, 246–47, 305n
    generally, 85
    grants of servitude, 236–38
    guarantee by mud, 220–22
    Keeper's warranty and, 246–47
    long leases, 299–300
rectification
    1979 Act, 33–34
    actual inaccuracies, 32, 32n, 202
    appeals, 210
    bijural inaccuracies, 33n, 33–34, 202, 209n
    compensation from the Keeper, 209
    effect of rectification, 209
    generally, 27, 85
    guarantee by money, 220–22
    implementation of 2012 Act, 210
    Keeper's duty to rectify, 206–07, 259n
    Lands Tribunal and, 210
    'manifest' inaccuracies, 206–07
    possession defined, 204–06

rectification (*cont*)
    pre-8 Dec 2014, 202–03
    proprietor defined, 202–03
    requests for rectification, 208–09
    see also judicial rectification of documents
rectification orders, 99
reductions
    registration of, 343
Register of Applications by Community Bodies to Buy Land, 46
Register of Community Interests in Land, 46
Register of Sasines
    administration, 12–13
    advance notices and properties still on Register of Sasines, 182–84
    burgh registers, 14–15
    closure, 115–16
    effectiveness, 15–17
    entry to the register, 27
    generally, 2
    location, 13
    registration methods, 8–9
    reputation, 15–17
Registers Direct, 11, 11n, 271
Registers of Scotland (RoS), 51–52, 88, 160–61
registrable deeds
    1979 and 2012 Acts compared, 93
    2012 Act, 94–100
    advance notices, 100
    caveats, 100
    decrees of reduction, 97–98
    dispositions, 94–95
    dispositions of souvenir plots, 95
    generally, 6, 9, 91
    judicial rectification of documents, 99
    Keeper's list, 100–02
    language, 93
    leases, 97
    liferents, 97
    notices of title, 96–97
    planning conditions, 92
    ranking agreements, 100
    real burdens, 92
    section 75 agreements, 92
    standard securities, 92
    statute and, 91–92
    unregistrable conveyances, 95–96
Registration Act 1617
    effect on property law, 5–6
    limitations, 5
    protection of third parties, 3–4
    public nature of land registration, 2–3
    registrable deeds, 6
registration counties, 47–48

registration of deeds
  effect on property law, 5–6
  origins of land registration, 1–2
  protection of third parties, 4–5
  public nature of register, 3
  Registration Act 1617, 2–6
  registration of title compared, 17
registration of title
  arguments against, 19–20
  arguments in favour, 19
  development in England, 18
  Henry Committee, 22
  moves in Scotland, 18–19
  origins, 17–18
  registration of deeds compared, 17
  Reid Committee, 21–22
  transaction costs, 19
Reid Committee, 21–22, 26, 32, 42, 214–15
renunciations, registration of, 343
renunciations of wadsets, 5
representatives, 139, 223, 223n, 225, 237
  see also solicitors
requisitions, 159, 160–61
reversions, 1–2, 5
rights of common property
  transfer of ownership, 291–92
rights of way, 65, 132

Scottish Law Commission, 36
seabed
  cadastral map and, 82–83
  Crown ownership, 48
  deed plans, 87
  mapping issues, 48
  property section of title sheets, 61
search sheets, 10–11
section 66 agreements, 62
sector-specific legislation, 167–68
securities section of title sheets
  floating charges, 64
  generally, 58
  heritable securities, 64
  shared securities, 64
  standard securities, 64
separate tenements, 55, 62, 80
sequestration, trustees in
  advance notices and, 191, 192
  generally, 51, 73, 96, 192, 243–44, 246
  section 88, 299
  transfers of ownership, 287
servitudes
  application form, 145–47
  burdens section of title sheets, 64, 65
  creation and 1979 Act, 302–03
  creation and 2012 Act, 301–02
  dual registration, 242
  first registration, 145–47

servitudes (*cont*)
  generally, 24, 301
  Keeper's warranty and, 241–42, 242–43
  transfer of ownership, 292–95
shared plots
  conveyancing shortcut, 68
  long leases, 68
  modifications to title sheets, 67–68
  title sheets, 67–68
short leases, 24, 57, 71, 174, 198n, 232–33, 340–41
  see also off-register encumbrances
solicitors
  causation and loss, 278–79
  liability under s 111, 277–79
  mandated signatories, 335
  solicitors' duty of care, 277–78
souvenir plots, 95
split-off deeds
  advance notices and, 179–80, 181, 183
  generally, 58, 74, 82, 87–90, 237, 301, 331
steadings, 69–70, 87–88
standard securities
  ARTL system, 331
  creation, 303–04
  examination of title, 303–04
  first registration by deed, 113–14
  generally, 64, 342
  granted by companies, 158
  Keeper's warranty and, 258
  ranking agreements, 100
  standard securities over subordinate real rights, 114
  standard securities over leases, 114
'state of the legal universe' principle, 157–58
structure and content of Land Register
  application record, 55, 74
  archive record, 55, 73–74
  cadastral map, 55, 72
  generally, 45
  title sheet record, 55, 56–72
subordinate real rights
  cadastral units, 81
  generally, 114n, 343
  grants of servitude and, 236
  realignment and, 236

technological advances, 11–12
  see also electronic deeds; electronic signatures
tenements, 69–70, 78
  see also separate tenements
title by registration, 31n, 39
title sheets
  1979 Act sheets, 57–58
  application record and, 25

Index   449

title sheets (cont)
  archive record and, 25
  burdens section, 58, 64–65
  cadastral units and, 78
  converted leases, 345–46
  digital mapping system and, 25
  discrepancies, 307–08
  format, 24
  generally, 45
  KIR title sheets, 119
  mandatory contents, 61–66
  mode of making entries, 60–61
  off-register rights, 70–72
  pertinents, 68–69
  plot title sheets and lease title sheets distinguished, 56–57
  plots of land and, 56
  primary interests in land, 25
  property section, 58, 61–62
  proprietorship section, 58, 63–64
  secondary interests in land, 25
  sections, 24–25, 58
  securities section, 58, 64
  shared plots, 67–68
  tenements, 69–70
  trusts and, 60
  what may be included, 58–59
  what must not be included, 58, 59–60
Torrens system, 17–18, 21, 26, 30, 33, 34–35, 341
transfer of ownership
  1979 Act, 290–91
  2012 Act, 285–90
  caveats, 295

transfer of ownership (cont)
  corporeal pertinents, 291–92
  establishing that seller is owner, 285–86, 290–91
  floating charges, 294
  incorporeal pertinents, 292–95
  inhibitions, 295
  KIR titles, 289–90
  minerals, 295–96
  occupancy rights of spouse or civil partner, 295
  possessory requirements, 286–88, 287n
  titles not covered by s 86, 288–89
  validity of disposition, 296
transfer to a good-faith acquirer, 200
trusts for behoof of creditors, 192–93

unregistrable conveyances, 95–96

variations, registration of, 56, 100–02, 343
voluntary registration
  applications for registration, 116–17, 117n, 122
  completion of Land Register, 105–07
  deed plans, 88
  eligibility, 116
  fees, 117, 125
  generally, 41
  long leases, 112n
  new plans, 117
  standard securities, 113n
wrongful acceptance of applications, 161–62
wrongful rejection of applications, 161